CONSUMER PROBLEMS
and PERSONAL FINANCE

CONSUMER PROBLEMS and PERSONAL FINANCE

Arch W. Troelstrup

Director of Family Economics
Stephens College

Third Edition

McGRAW–HILL BOOK COMPANY

New York St. Louis San Francisco Toronto London Sydney

TO ANN AND OUR FOUR CHILDREN
BILL, GLENN, JOHN, AND SUSAN LEE

PREFACE

For over a quarter of a century, the author has been teaching consumer problems and personal finance to American high school and college students. His last twenty-two years have been devoted exclusively to developing for undergraduates a basic course in consumer problems and personal finance.

This text is the product of continuous evaluation of the immediate and foreseeable future needs of college students as consumers and citizens. Some four hundred college graduates have contributed to the course and to the text by volunteering after marriage to describe in detail their most important consumer problems in actual family situations.

In addition to the contributions of undergraduates and some four hundred married couples who had been out of college from four to fifteen years, the author has had the benefit of the advice of a committee of Stephens College instructors who represent a cross section of related disciplines—child study, clothing, foods and nutrition, health, economics, marriage and family, household economics, personal appearance, consumer economics, and psychology. This committee met in two-hour sessions, twice monthly for one year, to analyze the contents, methods, and working relationships of their special fields in order to enrich the course in consumer problems and personal finance.

The cordial reception which college professors, businessmen, and particularly college students and homemakers have accorded the first and second editions is evidence of the need for such a book. But in a dynamic society such as ours, both a book and its author should grow. It is my hope that this third edition represents growth. Much has happened in the area of consumer problems and personal finance since the second edition was published in 1957.

This book was written for college students and others who desire practical help in doing a better job of managing personal or family consumer and financial problems. *Consumer Problems and Personal Finance* fully covers the content of college courses on the subject. Yet the emphasis is on practical information and applications that will help anyone desiring to improve in the art of planning and spending income.

We have tended to overlook the need for developing institutions and practices which will help to make free choice meaningful. Moreover, we have tended to accept with too little question the rapid, recent growth of pressures designed to influence choice by the promotion of irrational appeals. Freedom of choice in the market place becomes an empty boast when the choice is uninformed and irrational. Irrational choice puts an idiot at the economic helm. And uninformed consumer choice risks the sacrifice of the better for the worse—the vote for shoddy goods may win out in the exercise of blind choice. True, most of us have some basis for choice in the market place. But this storehouse of information and skill is rapidly diminishing as the goods and services we buy become more highly fabricated and complex, and as the market is increasingly dominated by sales promotion and credit selling—the sale of debts as well as of goods and services. The modern market place is replete with opportunities to waste money and endanger health by rewarding the less desirable rather than the better product and service. And the penalty of such waste, and sometimes danger to health, is levied both against the family's standard of living and the effective functioning of a competitive market.

The third edition has been thoroughly revised, and three new chapters have been added to reflect the many changes which have taken place since the second edition in 1957. Chapters 1, 9, and 18 have been deleted. A new chapter, The Consumer in Our Society, emphasizes the importance of the consumer in our society, and the increasingly difficult time even a sophisticated consumer has in getting maximum satisfaction when spending money. The multiple questionable practices in the market call for improvement in the three-way partnership of the prudent consumer, the more ethical producer, and the more effective protection of consumer welfare on the part of government. One might refer to Chapter 1 as challenging the reader to see his consumer role in our economy, to recognize the old and the new multiple problems in making good choices, and, finally, to recognize the need for more consumer sophistication on his part, and the need for more effective protection from business and government.

Chapters 8 and 9 in the second edition have been completely rewritten and combined into one chapter called Family Clothing Management. The increasing role of private and government protection for the consumer is illustrated in devoting three new chapters to private aids, Federal government protection, and consumer protection at the state and local levels. All of the recent consumer developments represented in the form of private consumer associations, new state protective agencies as well as the rapidly growing Federal government consumer agencies, are included in these chapters.

A new chapter, The International Consumer Movement, the first chapter in any textbook to include this material, points up the important and rapidly growing international character of the consumer movement. The author's recent visits with Western Europe and Japanese consumer leaders have been extremely valuable in preparing this chapter.

There has been a great surge of interest in the business of funerals, in the complex problems in selecting automobile insurance, and in the so-called "fair trade" laws, more commonly referred to as "quality stabilization" laws. Chapter 19 was written to help people understand the nature of these consumer problems, and the choices that are possible in our society.

There have been many other changes in the third edition. It is not exaggerating to say that other chapters have, in almost all instances, been completely rewritten. The Questions for Discussion, Activity Problems and Suggested Readings at the end of each chapter are for the most part fresh and up-to-date.

The author is indebted to many people for helpful comments on the first two editions and for material included in this edition. Particular credit is due Dorothy Sherrill Miller, well known to home economists, for her extremely helpful and detailed suggestions. Colleagues in other institutions who have used the second edition have given helpful suggestions. The reactions of the author's students and, in many cases, their parents, to the textbook have been extremely useful. The over-all result has been more than changes in content, emphasis, and insight. The author has become even more firmly convinced that the original idea of writing a textbook for students on individual and family consumer problems and personal finance that deals with *life as a whole rather than in its separate parts* is psychologically sound. Such a book appeals to undergraduates and adults who want to go directly to their problems as consumers.

In preparing the manuscript for publication the author's job has been lightened by the help of his wife, Ann, expert and wise in publication matters, and to Mrs. Evelyn Banigan for excellent editorial assistance.

ARCH W. TROELSTRUP

CONTENTS

tional Home. Disadvantages of Conventional Homeownership. How Much Housing Can You Afford? FHA Housing Expense Chart. Shopping for a New Home. Consulting a Real Estate Broker and an Appraiser. On Finding "The" House. Financing Your House. Accessories to the Mortgage. Kinds of Mortgage Loans. FHA-insured Mortgage. Long-term Mortgages and Interest Costs. Discount Points. Your Mortgage and Equity in Your Home. How Much Can You Borrow? Settlement or Closing Charges. First-year Expenses of Homeownership. Service Record of Professional Moving Companies. The Problem of Quoted Prices when Moving. Liability of Moving Companies. A Few Moving Pointers. Fire Insurance Policies. Fire Insurance Premiums. Comprehensive Personal Liability Insurance. Personal Property Floater Insurance. Theft Insurance. Combination Policy. Don't Plunge into Debt for a Dream House. Questions for Discussion. Activity Problems. Suggested Readings.

What the Tax Cut Means to You. Examination of Returns and
Penalties. Suggestions for Legitimate Savings in Taxes. Questions for
Discussion. Activity Problems. Suggested Readings.

Putting the American Way of Life into Action. What Are Savings?
Why Families Save. Who Are the Savers? Increase in Personal Savings. What to Do with Your Savings.

SAVINGS INSTITUTIONS.

Savings and Loan Associations. Operation of Savings and Loan
Associations. How Safe Are Savings and Loan Associations? Divi-
dends. If You Decide on a Savings and Loan Association. Commercial
Banks. Interest on Savings in Commerical Banks. Mutual Savings
Banks. Safety of Deposits in Mutual Savings Banks. Comparison of
Dividend Return. Credit Unions. Federal and State Supervision of
Credit Unions. Comparison of Dividends and Safety. Postal Savings.

INVESTMENTS.

Caution—Investment Entails Risk. Considerations before Investing
in Securities. Basic Investment Principles. Get the Facts, Know the
Risks. Facts about Bonds. Facts about Stocks. Analyzing Industries
and Securities. Selecting a Company for Investment. Buying and Sell-
ing Securities. Where Securities Are Bought and Sold. How Unlisted
Securities Are Bought and Sold. How to Do Business with a Broker.
Round Lots and Odd Lots. Brokers' Commissions. Monthly Invest-
ment Plans. Investment Clubs. Figuring Profit on a Monthly
Investment Plan. Securities and Exchange Commission Study. Why
Common Stocks? What about Bonds? Why Investment Companies?
Two Kinds of Investment Companies. Major Objectives of Investment
Trusts. Selecting an Investment Trust. Performance of Mutual Funds.
Bonds—Federal, State, and Municipal. Bank Stocks and Real Estate
Mortgages. Taxes Affect Financial Planning. Estate Planning and
Wills. Testamentary Trusts. Life Insurance Trusts. Living, or Volun-
tary, Trusts. Trust Management. Qualifications of a Trust Company.
Administrative Costs. Powers Included in a Trust. Should You Create
a Trust Fund? The Necessity for Making a Will. Legality of Wills.
Formalities of Making a Valid Will. Disposal of an Estate. Duties of
the Executor of a Will. A Common Disaster Clause. Letter of Last
Instruction. Wills Should Be Reviewed. Questions for Discussion.
Activity Problems. Suggested Readings.

Problems of Informing Consumers. Business Discovers Consumers
Want to Know. Consumer Cooperation but Not Alliance with Busi-
ness. Alliance of Government with Consumers. Can Consumers Do It
Themselves? Need for Adequate Standards for Consumer Goods.

National Consumer Organizations. International Consumer Organizations.

1

THE CONSUMER IN OUR SOCIETY

"Consumption is the sole end and purpose of all production; and the interest of the producer ought to be attended to only so far as it may be necessary for promoting that of the consumer." *Adam Smith*

What are the major challenges that face Americans in their role as consumers? First, consumers need to know their part in the economy. They should know what makes our economy "tick." Consumers should understand that fraud, deceit, and other undesirable practices persist in the economy because of their own lack of organized resistance as well as ineffective protection on all government levels. They need to realize the importance of substituting rationality for emotion in the market place.

Second, consumers need to be aware of the increasing efforts of business to deceive and misinform the consumer. The business of making and selling is highly organized and calls to its aid at every step complex and expert skills. The business of buying is conducted by the smallest unit, the individual or the family. The capacity of sales personnel to aid the consumer has deteriorated. Furthermore, the trend toward automatic services, self-service, discount stores, catalogue buying, and persuasive advertising has increased the chances of buying uninformedly. The manufacturer and distributor speak with a well-organized and powerful voice in national affairs. The interest of the consumer is often overlooked because he is voiceless.

Third, consumers need to understand their function in the economy. Is their job to spend in order to keep the economy going? Is it to do the bidding of profit-seeking persuaders? Or is their job that of guiding and controlling the production of goods and services with which to satisfy their wants? In other words, what is the function of the consumer?

The Purpose of an Economy. The purpose of an economy is to produce goods and services, large in quantity, high in quality, reasonable in price for maximum satisfaction in consumer use. Every economic system, be it capitalist, communist, or socialist, faces three questions: What shall we produce? How much shall we produce? For whom shall we produce?

Different economic systems solve these problems differently. Today, most economic systems are "mixed" in the way they set up their goals and manage their resources. They are neither purely private enterprise nor purely socialist. And most economic systems are changing constantly.

Business enterprise in the United States is largely private, and its rationale is that consumer demands determine what is produced. Business tries to produce the goods and services that consumers want. And business tries to do so at the lowest possible cost. In most cases, business also seeks to influence consumer demands through advertising and other selling devices. Business will use labor, land, and machinery to produce the goods and services consumers demand. Businesses, in turn, pay out income to workers, landowners, and other suppliers of productive services. These incomes make it possible for consumers, in turn, to buy the goods and services in the market place.

Markets are the places where prices rise and fall in response to changing demands and supplies, and they provide the links that mesh together consumers and businesses. Individuals and businesses save part of their income and invest those savings in new productive facilities.

The rationale of our economy also assumes that individual freedom of choice is central to our economic way of life. But individual freedom of choice is limited by laws and by social and moral pressures, for the protection of the individual and society. Thus, markets and prices are the chief regulator of the allocation of scarce resources. But the government sets the ground rules under which competition takes place, and sometimes participates actively in the processes of production and distribution. And thus we have a "mixed" economy.

Who Is the Consumer? Anyone who spends money buying goods and services is a consumer. We all spend money for goods and services. Therefore, we are all consumers.

At the end of 1963, there were over 190 million consumers in the United States. This number will increase at the annual rate of about 3 million. By 1970, we may have 208 million consumers. In 1941, for contrast, the figure was 133 million.

In 1963, the labor force numbered over 73 million, not counting 50 million housewives, compared with 54 million in 1941. In 1963, over one-third of the married women worked for pay outside the home. Another figure that continues to rise is the number of consumers over 65 years of age—more than 17 million in 1963, compared with only 9 million in 1941. By 1970, we may have over 25 million senior citizens.

Teen-agers are capturing an ever-growing share of the nation's market, both through their own discretionary spending and through effective dic-

tation to parents. Sylvia Porter, in her financial column, in 1961, estimated 20 million teen-agers spending directly 10 billion dollars annually.
By 1970, the number of teen-agers will increase by almost 63 per cent.

Importance of the Consumer in the Economy. Textbooks on economics state
that the purpose of all production is consumption. Yet during the last
half century, economists have consigned the consumer to a minor role in
the economy. Of the three major sectors of the economy, "business" and
"government" are recognized as having contributed most to the growth of
our economy. The third sector, that of the "consumer," has generally been
given a minor role. This assumption is now being questioned. Dr. George
Katona, Director of the Survey Research Center at the University of
Michigan, stated in his book *The Powerful Consumer* that the "consumers
themselves, by understanding what is happening and what they are doing,
provide the best hope for a continuous growth of the economy, not interrupted by severe recessions." [1]

A careful study of the accompanying table, Selected Comparative
Statistics, reveals how economists measure in dollars the performance of
an economy. They measure production, income, and consumption figures.
For example, the "gross national product" (the total output of goods and
services) in 1961 was $521 billion compared to $126 billion in 1941 ($276
billion in 1961 prices).

To get a figure for "net national product" (which is not shown in the
table), depreciation is figured. The resulting figure was $476 billion in
1961 compared to $117 billion in 1941 ($256 billion in 1961 prices). The
"national income" figures were derived by deducting indirect business
taxes from the net national product.

SELECTED COMPARATIVE STATISTICS, 1962–1941
(Billions of Dollars)

	1962	1961	1941	1941 (in 1961 prices)
Gross national product	563	521	126	276
National income	460	430	105	230
Personal income *	450	417	96	210
Consumer disposable income †	389	365	93	185
Consumer expenditures	363	339	82	171
Consumer saving	26	26	11	24
Consumer credit	63	57	9	20

* Wages, interest, rent, dividends, transfer payments, and unincorporated net income.

† The sum left after deducting personal taxes.

[1] Published by McGraw-Hill Book Company, New York, 1960, p. 246.

The amount consumers had in 1961 for spending and saving was $365 billion compared to $93 billion in 1941 ($195 billion in 1961 prices).

The per capita disposable income (not shown in the table) for 1961 was $1,987 compared to $697 in 1941 ($1,458 at 1961 prices).

In 1961, consumer disposable income of $365 billion had become a powerful factor in the stability of the economy. In fact, after many years of obscurity, the consumer is becoming the star of the economic show. He is emerging from the wings and stepping into the spotlight.

The Potentially Powerful Consumer. At the upper end of the purchasing spectrum, there is a remarkably alert contingent of buyers. They insist on quality, they seek facts; they take time to testify before congressional and legislative committees and to write letters. But they are a small minority of what could be potentially powerful consumer groups in the United States.

What all consumers have in common, however, is disposable income— money to spend. Historically, the distribution of national income among families has been unequal, but there has been a decline in this inequality. The accompanying table, Distribution of Consumer Units by Real Income Levels, shows the percentages of families receiving certain incomes in 1960 and in 1941. In 1960, the average income of 56 million families was $6,900. The median income, the middle number, was $5,600. Four million families, however, had incomes under $1,500 a year. In 1961, the Department of Commerce reported that the average family income had increased to $7,020.

DISTRIBUTION OF CONSUMER UNITS BY REAL INCOME LEVELS, 1961 AND 1941

Family personal income in 1960 dollars (before income taxes)	Number of families and unattached individuals (millions)			Per cent distribution		
	1961	1960	1941	1961	1960	1941
Under $2,000	6.8	7.2	11.5	12	13	28
$2,000–3,999	10.7	11.0	12.0	19	20	29
$4,000–5,999	12.4	12.2	9.2	22	22	22
$6,000–7,999	10.4	9.8	4.6	19	17	11
$8,000–9,999	6.4	6.0	1.8	11	11	4
$10,000–14,999	6.2	6.3	2.3	11	11	6
$15,000 and over	3.7	3.4		6	6	
Total	56.6	41.4	55.9	100	100	100

SOURCE: *Survey of Current Business,* May, 1961, and April, 1962.

This table shows that wealth is more evenly distributed now than 20 years ago. There is also a noticeable increase in the number of families in and around the median income group. But there is a trend toward greater inequality in the extreme ends of income distribution. In 1961, according to a study by Robert J. Lampman, the richest 1 per cent of the population owned about 28 per cent of the wealth owned by individuals. A typical adult was worth $4,200 in 1961; but there were 3 million persons worth $60,000 or more. There were 100,000 millionaires, and 10,000 with wealth of $5 million or more.[2]

A close examination of the data in the table reveals a mass purchasing power perhaps unequaled in the world today. Perhaps never have so many people had so many goods and services. This abundance of "things" creates the impression in other countries that we are essentially a materialistic society.

Married Women in the Nation's Work Force. The married woman is playing an increasingly important role as an earning and spending member of the family. A 1962 report by the National Industrial Conference Board states that there were 13,200,000 married women employed in that year. This was about one-fifth of the nation's work force. Working married women were outnumbered by 35 million full-time housewives. Nevertheless, the working wife may well be the mainstay of our present affluent society. The NICB report shows that, in 40 per cent of the 6,500,000 American families with incomes of $10,000 or more a year, the wife brings home a pay check to supplement the income of the husband.

In fact, the higher-bracket incomes are the result of wives moving into the labor force and creating a "highly volatile economic upper class," as well as "a vast and continuous new market for luxury goods and services," according to the 1962 NICB report. Furthermore, three-quarters of these double-income families own their own homes. The possession rate of household appliances is also high; the rate for air conditioners is twice that of all households. Three out of five of these homes are equipped with two or more radios, and one in four has more than one television set. Half of them own two or more cars.

The multi-earner family is here to stay, apparently, and will increase in numbers. The Department of Labor estimated that nine out of ten women will be gainfully employed a large part of their lives. This is, indeed, a new and growing force in our society.

Consumer Expenditures. In 1963, consumers spent $373 billion. Most of this expenditure is family directed. A family having a $6,000 income will spend at least $270,000 in its lifetime. As a purchasing agent, a family would expend its annual income as follows in a given year.

Note that the first 10 items account for 92 per cent of the family expenditure. The figure for food includes all items, not merely food, pur-

[2] *The Share of the Top Wealth Holders in National Wealth.* Princeton, N.J.: Princeton University Press, 1962.

	Per cent of income		Per cent of income
Food	28.0	Recreation	3.7
Housing	12.4	House furnishings	3.6
Income taxes	10.5	Alcohol, reading, school	
Transportation	9.4	supplies	2.0
Medical-dental care	8.4	Personal care	1.8
Clothing	7.8	Gifts and contributions	1.5
Personal insurance	4.3	Tobacco	1.0
Household operation	3.8	Union dues	1.0

chased in food stores. The average American family spends approximately 20 per cent of its income for food. The most notable changes in the foregoing figures in the last decade are increases in expenditure for taxes, transportation, and services.

There is no formal saving figure in this $6,000 family budget, except as concealed in insurance and possibly housing. On a national basis, consumers saved $29 billion in 1963. This saving figure for all consumers represents about 7.3 per cent of disposable personal income. Incidentally, in 1941, personal savings amounted to 12 per cent of disposable income.

Consumers make increasing use of consumer credit (short-term credit). In 1963, the outstanding consumer credit amounted to $70 billion, of which $54 billion was installment credit.

Currently, business is spending over $13 billion annually in advertising to persuade consumers to purchase goods and services. This compares with about $2 billion in 1941. As a percentage of national income, advertising expenditures were about 2.8 per cent in 1962, compared with only 1.8 per cent in 1941.

Consumer Sovereignty. The concept of consumer sovereignty—the consumer is king—still persists after nearly a century of experience. According to this theory, the role of the consumer is to guide the economy to the production of goods and services that he wants. The economist passes no value judgments on the validity of consumer decisions. The only thing that counts is that each consumer is free and competent to make his own decision. In short, the consumer expresses his wishes by casting dollar votes. In this way, the consumer is supposed to determine what shall be produced.

Playing umpire is not a new role for the consumer. In theory, consumer sovereignty, consumer freedom of choice, is indeed the keystone of our economic system. It is from this assumption that the free competition, private enterprise system derives social justification for its division of rewards for effort. Withdraw consumer sovereignty from this concept, and free competition resembles a kind of economic jungle warfare. We are now fairly far along in the process of withdrawing true consumer sovereignty from the market place. The question is: Can we bring back into the market place a rational umpire—the consumer?

Is the Consumer King? Reflection and observation indicate that too many consumers are unprepared for the role of sovereignty in our present complex economy. They are easily manipulated and ignorant concerning the ways of the ever-changing market place. For example, how many consumers ever consider these questions?

1. Are present-day prices competitive?
2. Does present-day competition resemble competition fifty years ago?
3. To what extent are the prices of consumer goods a measure of the actual cost of producing and distributing them?
4. Do consumers know what goods and services are best in terms of their welfare?
5. Do consumers buy only the goods and services that are beneficial?
6. Are consumers able to judge quality?
7. To what extent can consumers check quantity measurements of their purchases?

Economists assume that consumers are rational. Psychologists and sociologists, however, insist that we are social men rather than economic men. Our motivations include a desire for status, for conformity, for prestige, for power, to mention only a few.

Economists also assume that consumers buy only for individual or family consumption, whereas there is much institutional buying today. There is also considerable public buying by the military, by schools, parks, highways, and many other public bodies.

Another serious defect in the assumption that the consumer is king lies in the fact that income is unevenly distributed. Consumers with many dollars can cast many votes. Others have to be satisfied with casting fewer dollar votes. Obviously, such a system gives some consumers more influence than others.

The Inarticulate Consumer versus Pressure Groups. Another reason the consumer is not king in our mid-twentieth-century economy is that consumption is a function common to all and peculiar to none. We are all consumers, but we are first a worker, a manager, a producer, a government clerk, a teacher, a doctor, a farmer, a lawyer. In such roles, each person's interest is direct, and he is willing to promote his direct interest through group action, through organized effort, or through political appeals to governing bodies. In his role as a consumer, his interests are indirect and consequently neglected. Nobody is willing to organize effort, to obtain political support, to rally his fellow consumers solely in behalf of consumer interests. It becomes apparent, then, that in our present-day democratic society, where government responds to pressure groups, inarticulate consumers are largely at the mercy of more effectively organized groups.

Interest groups are organized primarily to improve the relative position of their members. They are never organized to improve the position of all the members in society. While groups attempt to present their own special interests as being identical with the interests of the general public, it frequently results that their behavior indicates a pathetic ignorance of the general welfare. Everybody is for the consumer until more direct interests conflict. Then nobody is for the consumer, and consumer interests are neglected.

As long as the market place was an adequate regulator and coordinator of economic activity, admittedly in the distant past, there was less need for government to act as protector of consumer interests against exploitation by producer interests. But as industrialization developed with its urbanization, consumer dependence on sources of supplies beyond their own control has continued to increase rapidly. This increasing consumer dependence, in turn, has been responsible for partial public realization that the material health of each individual is becoming inseparably bound to the economic health of the entire community.

Other significant economic changes that require revision of the consumer sovereignty assumption have taken place in the economy in the last 25 years. One important change has been the growth of giant corporations to a dominant position in our economy. In 1958, 107 of these giants did a business of $149 billion compared to a volume of $137 billion for nearly 10 million small enterprises.

Another significant change has been the tremendous expenditures by the military for national security—expenditures of such magnitude that a sudden drastic curtailment would most likely cause a recession.

Corporate farming and labor unions have had increasing influence in our economy. Corporation farming is encroaching on family-type farming. Consumers pay an annual multi-billion dollar subsidy for farming. When big business and giant unions reach an impasse, as in the 1959–1960 steel strike, the economy suffers, and consumers usually pay higher prices.

Another change has been the tremendous power of radio and television in stimulating sales. Actually, the price competition of a simpler economy has been replaced by the non-price competition of giant corporations monopolizing the choice listening hours on radio and TV.

These changes can be in the consumer interest. In England, for example, the BBC television reports the results of independent testing of consumer goods, giving brand names and comparative prices. Consumers, however, must recognize the disadvantages as well as the blessings of these changes in our culture.

The Revised Consumer Price Index. The January, 1964, Consumer Price

Index introduces an updated and improved series. Periodic revision of the index is necessary as living patterns of city workers change. For information about living patterns, the Bureau of Labor Statistics (BLS) depends largely on nationwide studies of consumer expenditures. The newly revised index incorporates findings from the most recent of these studies, which describes spending of city consumers in 1960 and 1961. This was the first nationwide urban expenditure study in a decade.

The updating of the index included selection of a new list of goods and services to be priced. Some items previously priced were dropped and many new ones were added. Some of the changes reflect the higher level of living of urban workers and the presence of new consumer goods and services on the market. The weights given to expenditures for the various goods and services have been revised in line with changes in spending patterns. Pricing is done in a new sample of retail stores and service establishments in a new sample of cities, to take account of changes in merchandising practices, shifts in population, and the addition of Alaska and Hawaii as states.

The revised Consumer Price Index also gives recognition to the importance of the single person in the urban-wage-earner and clerical-worker population. It covers single workers living alone as well as families of two or more, while the old index covered families only. Indexes based on the new broader coverage will be published for the United States and for individual cities (17 cities through June, 1965; 23 cities thereafter). In addition, a revised index for families of two or more will be published for the United States, but not for individual cities. The BLS also continues the old index through June, 1964, designating it the "old series" to differentiate it from the revised or "new series" indexes as can be seen in the accompanying table, Consumer Price Index (New Series). The new indexes were linked to the old as of December, 1963, to form a continuous series, so they are the same for that month.

The updated index introduces several changes in the group and subgroup indexes published. Italicized words in the table mentioned above show which indexes were not published previously and footnotes explain some of the changes.

The Consumer in Our Abundant Society. There is almost a frightening abundance of material things in the United States. In contrast, two-thirds of the people of the world still go to bed every night hungry. But here we have almost achieved the eighteenth-century dream—all the material goods we need. The United States, with 6 per cent of the world's population, and less than 7 per cent of its land area, produces and consumes over one-third of the world's goods and services, and receives two-fifths of its income. But the following economic and social facts are already causing changes in our culture.

CONSUMER PRICE INDEX (NEW SERIES) (1957–1959 = 100)

Group	Urban wage earners and clerical workers (including single workers)		Urban-wage-earner and clerical-worker families	
	Dec., 1963	Jan., 1964	Dec., 1963	Jan.,1964
All items	107.6	107.7	107.6	107.7
Food	105.4	105.8	105.4	105.8
Food at home	103.7	104.2	103.7	104.2
Food away from home	114.3	114.3	114.3	114.3
Housing	106.9	106.9	106.9	106.9
Shelter *a*	108.0	108.1	108.0	108.1
Rent	107.3	107.3	107.3	107.3
Homeownership *b*	108.4	108.5	108.4	108.5
Fuel and utilities *c*	107.6	107.7	107.6	107.7
Fuel oil and coal	105.8	106.6	105.8	106.6
Gas and electricity	108.1	108.1	108.1	108.1
Household furnishings and operations *d*	102.9	102.7	102.9	102.7
Apparel and upkeep *e*	106.1	105.0	106.1	105.0
Men's and boys'	106.2	105.2	106.2	105.2
Women's and girls'	103.3	101.4	103.3	101.4
Footwear	111.2	110.9	111.2	110.9
Transportation	108.9	109.4	108.9	109.4
Private	107.5	108.0	107.5	108.0
Public	118.3	118.3	118.3	118.3
Health and recreation *f*	112.7	112.7	112.7	112.7
Medical care	117.9	118.2	117.9	118.2
Personal care	108.8	108.5	108.8	108.5
Reading and recreation	113.1	113.1	113.1	113.1
Other goods and services	108.3	108.3	108.3	108.3

a Includes hotel and motel rates, not shown separately.

b Includes home purchase, mortgage interest, taxes, insurance, and maintenance and repairs.

c Includes telephone, water and sewerage service, not shown separately.

d Formerly separate indexes were given for house furnishings and household operation.

e Includes "other" apparel, not shown separately (formerly a separate subgroup). Includes laundering and dry cleaning of apparel, formerly included in household operation.

f Formerly no combined index for the four subgroups was given.

SOURCE: Bureau of Labor Statistics, U.S. Department of Labor.

1. A rich, materialistic society is emerging from our dynamic economy, creating many new problems, and challenging our whole system of values —our economic values, our social values, and even our moral values.

2. By 1970, a majority of workers will be in the white-collar or blue-

collar highly skilled occupations. This upgrading of jobs means a big change in the personal income pattern. By 1970, there will be 25 million families with over $7,500 a year income (after taxes), comprising two-fifths of all consumer spending income. This means a large increase in the middle-income and upper-middle-income classes. This larger, new mass market will want better food and status food, a fling at the stock market, more travel, longer and more expensive vacations. Many more consumer choices will have to be faced.

3. The two-income family is increasing and will continue to increase. In other words, there are and will be more working wives. Already there are more married women working than single women. Over one-third of the married women work for pay outside the home.

4. After 130 years as a rural nation, and a half century of becoming an urban nation, 1964 found the United States a country of suburban dwellers. Now 50 per cent of our people live in suburbs, and less than 10 per cent of the population are on farms and ranches.

5. With an increasing percentage of families having $7,500 income (after taxes) in the 1960s, this abundance will affect taste and excellence. Will advertising and the present mass media create the taste patterns of these consumers? Can they be educated to want quality as well as variety in their purchases?

6. Demand for new foods will keep increasing in the 1960s, and with it there will be an upgrading of taste and diets. Status foods and more convenience foods will be consumed, but may cost more.

7. In the 1960s, 25 million people will be making a living without work-ing—retired people. How will they prepare for this new way of living?

8. More and more Americans believe in debt as a way of life. This easy system of "buy now, pay later" reduces the future standard of living by 12 to 18 per cent, but does give the immediate use of almost undreamed-of gadgets, housing, and cars. This is a package deal—having everything you need from the first year of marriage. Sadly, all available evidence indicates that few borrowers know or care how much they pay for credit.

9. More and more persons marry today and at an earlier age, have children earlier, and have more children. More children mean more younger consumers. This means a child-oriented society. We may be fac-ing what some sociologists call a "tyranny of children" period. David Riesman writes that the twentieth century may well be known as the century of the child. A generation ago, children were considered a "pro-ducer durable"—meaning the net cost of raising them was less than the net income they produced for the family. Children are now a "consumer durable"—meaning the net cost of raising them is more than the net income they produce for the family—meaning their cost clearly outweighs their income.

Our abundance of material things is frightening because such an abundance carries with it either the seeds of destruction and decay *or* an opportunity to develop a good society with a moral base that could shine as a beacon light to less privileged peoples. Yet, in the midst of this material abundance, there are many new problems facing American consumers.

Questionable Practices in the Market Place. The last twenty-five years have been difficult ones for most consumers in this country. There are several reasons for these difficulties. In the first place, as real incomes have improved, the ability to translate more dollars into goods and services with confidence has diminished. Rational choice has become increasingly difficult. Waste and fraud have siphoned off a part of what higher incomes might have added to living standards.

If we take a serious look at some archaic and questionable practices in the market place, we must admit that there are too many businessmen who prefer the comfort of security from competition. Phony retail list prices are common; planned product obsolescence is general; deceit and fraud prevail in prepackaged foods. There is a $73 billion "buy now, pay later" binge; big labor and big business say to the public, "keep your nose out of our bargaining business"; little businesses want to have their cake and eat it too; there is false and misleading advertising and labeling, even advertising that creates value for otherwise worthless products. During the last two recessions, many retail prices were increased. One weights-and-measures official was even asked to permit the use of a 26-ounce milk bottle that was designed to look as big as the 32-ounce bottle. An oil company requested a larger gallon so that they could advertise "more gas to the gallon." In other words, questionable means to business ends—profits.

Since the economy produces or can produce more things than can be sold (or are needed), business not only has to persuade consumers to spend more money, but at the same time must try to remove the guilt feelings aroused by their advice.

To sell this generous productivity, business has to manufacture wants. In fact, about $13 billion was spent in 1963 to manufacture wants. The result of some of this expenditure is informative, accurate, and in good taste; but much of it is noninformative, in questionable taste, and at best stimulates only a change from one brand to another brand.

Elimination of the Quality Factor. Even more serious is the trend toward eliminating the quality factor in standards for consumer goods. Standards were established to provide an acceptable common language of specifications that functions in the same way that mathematics does in the language of the sciences. When standards are not set up, or if the standards are not enforced, the public is cheated to the advantage of the seller.

13

The general public seems to have no concern over fair dealing between consumer and producer, and does not realize the existence of new and alarming merchandising principles. In less than two decades, in the change-over from an economy of scarcity to an economy of abundance, product integrity has tragically fallen victim. Millions of dollars are spent on promoting the "square look" in kitchen appliances, wafer-thin watches, free-form furniture, sculptured-look irons, and wrap-around chrome on cars. Most of these changes in design might be accepted if it were not true that producers are almost silent on the quality and durability of their goods.

In the market, there is unfolding an array of evidence that makes it impossible for even the sophisticated consumer to make intelligent choices. This is especially true in food supermarkets. In these wonderful palaces of neon lights, there is housed on the average 7,000 different food items. Over 85 per cent of these food items are prepackaged. In a single market area, there are 104 brands of cold breakfast food, 147 brands of hand lotion—all claiming to be the best. To add to the confusion, there is "package-size" madness—giant size that has no accurate meaning; hidden price increases (weight reduced without public notice and price remaining the same); almost elimination of standard weights (half pound, pound, and so on). How can the consumer choose rationally?

Variable Prices and Planned Obsolescence. There are continuous changes in merchandising methods. The consumer is presold on many items. He no longer seeks advice of the retailer nor depends on him for guarantees. Instead he goes to a discount store, buys his appliance by model number, and looks to the manufacturer for a guarantee. Many of these guarantees are meaningless.

There is no longer one price for a commodity in one market at one time as assumed by classical economists. There are many prices. When merchants offer trading stamps, door prizes, coupons, credit premiums, and many other "rewards," the consumer cannot possibly compare prices of a given commodity. Instead of premiums or prizes, why does business not offer, say, 18 per cent more washing powder at the old price?

Many products, especially durable goods such as appliances and cars, are so designed that certain parts wear out after limited use. This has become standard practice, according to independent testing laboratories. It is called "planned obsolescence." This point of view was expressed by the board chairman of a large appliance company in 1960 when he said: "An engineer's principal purpose is to create obsolescence." The effects of "planned obsolescence" on consumers are disguised price increases, shorter period of product life, and often heavier repair bills.

To help sell the abundance of productivity, manufacturers resort to the art of psychological obsolescence. This is the application of the old

Detroit practice of annual model change. The consumer, for example, is enticed by charcoal gray, Mayfair pink, Stratford yellow, and Sherwood green in appliances. Why? Said another executive of an appliance manufacturing company: "It is my belief that color will enable us to reduce significantly the trade-in span from eleven years to perhaps seven or even less."

Deceit and Fraud in Content and Prices. Evidence of shortweighting in foods is common, according to state weights and measures officials and the Federal Food and Drug Administration. Overweight is so rare that it has no statistical significance.

There is considerable deceit and fraud in the drug and prescription business, according to an investigation by a Senate subcommittee. Consumers should be vitally interested in this problem because drugs and prescriptions account for an increasing percentage of disposable income, and, of course, it concerns personal health. There is evidence of lower standards for filling doctor's prescriptions and evidence of unjustified high prices. There are lower standards because most of the prescription business is in multiple brand names. Formerly, doctors used generic or scientific terms when writing prescriptions. To further confuse the doctor and the consumer, some brands are identical in content but different in brand name and in price.

Another type of deceit is the common use of fictitious list prices on many consumer goods in retail stores. This kind of dishonesty, a common practice according to Better Business Bureaus and the Federal Trade Commission, is involved when there is deceptive pricing and savings claims, such as "Formerly sold for $55.95—now $42.95." Such claims can be honest. It is, of course, difficult for a retailer to be honest when many of his competitors are dishonest. One thing is sure. This system makes it difficult for a consumer to make rational decisions in the market.

This is a pretty discouraging picture from the consumer's point of view. It is discouraging enough to witness the decline in the use of standards, in the common use of phony list prices in retail stores, in the fraud and cheating commonly practiced in prepackaged foods, in replacing reliable prescriptions with high-cost brand-name drugs, in the high and hidden cost of consumer credit, in false advertising claims, in planned product deterioration and built-in weaknesses in many products. But all this deceit, fraud, dishonesty, and cleverness is frightening because the public appears to have accepted it as inevitable. So why fight it? And business, too, seems to have reluctantly accepted this attitude. This attitude was brought out clearly in an article by a responsible marketing economist in the *Harvard Business Review:* "If what is offered can be sold at a profit, then it's legitimate. The cultural, spiritual, social consequences of his actions are none of the businessman's business."

Consumer Responsibility. How do you react to these methods and devices for selling the nation's abundant productivity? Are deceit, fraud, dishonesty, illusions, planned obsolescence, and plain cheating the only ways to utilize this abundant productivity? Is there no place for good standards, fairness, and honesty when exchanging dollars for goods and services? And, finally, do you agree with some marketing experts who say that the best way to utilize our abundant production is to "make consumption our way of life, that we should convert buying and use of goods into rituals, that we seek our spiritual satisfactions, or ego-satisfactions in consumption"? In short, these marketing experts say "the way to end glut is to produce gluttons." What do *you* think?

Faced with these multiple issues, what can consumers do about it? In the first place, a consumer can become an alert, informed, and responsible person. Anyone can spend money. A responsible person, however, should know his role and function in the economy. In this way he can influence what is to be produced.

A second consumer responsibility is to exercise independence of judgment and action. Then he is not likely to yield to commercial selling pressures, to conspicuous consumption, to group pressures, and to the lure of excessive credit. This suggests that the mature consumer has a continuing need for consumer information and education.

A third consumer responsibility is to recognize the dangers inherent in needless waste of limited natural and human resources. Many of these resources are irreplaceable.

The consumer also has a responsibility to buy products and services that are produced most efficiently. Such efficiency, however, ought not to be at the expense of exploitation of people on the basis of sex, age, color, or national origin.

The responsible consumer should be honest in his dealings, just as he expects industry, merchants, and repairmen to be honest. He has the responsibility, for example, not to abuse the privilege of trying out merchandise.

He should also take the time to write protest letters to irresponsible industries, merchants, and repairmen. How else will irresponsible businessmen and servicemen know that you are aware of their deceitful and dishonest dealings? Lacking support of informed and responsible consumers, the fair-minded businessmen find it difficult to withstand dishonest and unethical competitors. Consumer awareness of deceit and fraud will help industry help itself. The consumer who knows how he is being filched by dishonest merchants can exercise his sovereignty (his buying decision) by rewarding the honest and more efficient producer with his business.

Sometimes the collective effort of consumers brings about a change.

The consumers who protested against car design in the late 1950s showed their preference for smaller automobiles by purchasing such cars made in other countries. Likewise, consumer protest has led to the creation of new and different ways of distribution of goods and services—for example, discount stores, consumer cooperatives, and credit unions. It is well to remember, however, that people are not prone to organize as consumers. We cannot expect much help through consumer organizations. Why is this so?

Consumer Protection through Education and Representation. A major business witness, when testifying in 1961 before the Senate Subcommittee on Antitrust and Monopoly, on packaging and labeling practices, stated that "the consumer is too smart to be fooled—at least more than once." The reaction of Senator Phillip H. Hart to this statement got to the heart of the problem when he said: "Consumer intelligence is not at stake in this inquiry. The right to information is."

The real question, then, is whether or not consumers are capable of self-protection in the increasingly complex market place. The consumer is not likely to organize effectively for group action in the foreseeable future, because most people are interested first in their occupation, their source of income. Furthermore, even the most sophisticated and effective consumers are incapable of intelligent choices. Evidence of this is shown in the 500 or more annual "this happened to me" letters written by subscribers to *Consumer Reports,* a monthly magazine that reports on performance testing of consumer goods. The actual number of different commodities and services mentioned in these letters is over one hundred. In short, these well-informed consumers, most of them with college degrees, are growing more angry because they find it increasingly difficult to get satisfaction when spending money on goods and services.

Business has not been capable of self-discipline. Better Business Bureaus in the larger cities have had success in correcting some of the dishonest and unethical practices but frankly confess to many important failures. It is obvious that business, through self-discipline, does not have the will or the opportunity to return to reasonably honest and informative transactions in the market place. It may well be that honest businessmen find it impossible to compete with their dishonest competitors. Bad business tends to drive out good business.

As merchandising and marketing practices grow progressively more complex, as business increasingly is incapable of self-discipline, the unassisted consumer becomes progressively more defenseless. Consumer education is as yet not even in the race with technological and marketing techniques and advancement. In fact, it appears that the average consumer is presently becoming more confused and illiterate as a buyer and user of services in an increased ratio with modern business and marketing advancement.

All this is distressing. Is there no hope for the consumer in the foreseeable future? Of course there is hope for improving the consumer position. Looking ahead, there is a fairly good chance that the next quarter of this century will see the consumer, through more effective legislation, assume his rightful role as sovereign in the market place, as originally contemplated in our society. But this right of sovereignty is not likely to occur unless the consumer point of view is adequately represented in government and in agencies of government. More effective consumer education—yes—but with more emphasis that such education may give impetus to the development of an effective consumer point of view in government. We now have "labor" represented in the Department of Labor, "farmers" represented in the Department of Agriculture, and "business" represented in the Department of Commerce. But the consumer remains the forgotten man in the governmental structure.

Consumer Advisory Council. President John F. Kennedy must have had the need for consumer representation in mind when he sent his historic message to Congress, March 15, 1961, on legislation for protection of the consumer. This was the first time a President of the United States had sent a special message on protection of consumers. The President said in part:

Consumers, by definition, include us all. They are the largest economic group in the economy, affecting and affected by almost every public and private economic decision. Two-thirds of all spending in the economy is by consumers. But they are the only important group in the economy who are not effectively organized, whose views are often not heard.

The Federal government, by nature the highest spokesman for all the people, has a special obligation to be alert to the consumer's needs and to advance the consumer's interests. . . .

Speculation about the steps that the President would take to carry out that promise continued during his first year in office. In March, 1962, he announced his intention to appoint an advisory committee. In August, 1962, the twelve consumer appointees of the Consumer Advisory Council (advisory to the Council of Economic Advisers) were welcomed by the President in Washington, D.C. Dr. Helen G. Canoyer, Dean of the School of Home Economics, Cornell University, was appointed the first chairman of the council. Her hope, she said, was that through the Consumer Advisory Council a broader concern for the consumer would be integrated into government planning and action at the highest level.

This may prove to be a difficult job because the council has no power to act; it is advisory. Furthermore, it is advisory, not to the president nor any cabinet member, but to another advisory body, the Council of Economic Advisers. Moreover, business has made it clear that any group designated as spokesman for the consumer in Washington, D.C., is unwelcome.

President Kennedy told the council that he expected it to be "functional, not ornamental," and indicated that a basic function was to alert each and every department of the government to consumer needs.

Indeed, the need for function is pressing. The consumer interest is the interest of the general public. When the consumer's interest is ignored, is ill-defined or misinterpreted, the public welfare suffers. The existence of the Consumer Advisory Council is long-overdue recognition of that fact, and it can be a step toward remedial action. The assassination of President Kennedy and the succession of Vice President Johnson as President led to some important changes.

The President's Committee on Consumer Interests and the Consumer Advisory Committee. The late President Kennedy appointed a Consumer Advisory Committee with a part-time chairman which got some publicity but made no real impact.

On January 3, 1964, President Johnson decided to appoint a consumer voice in the White House. He established a Committee on Consumer Interests and appointed Mrs. Esther Peterson as chairman. Mrs. Peterson is the first special Presidential assistant for consumer affairs as well as chairman of the new Committee on Consumer Interests.

The new Presidential committee will be composed of representatives of the Departments of Justice; Interior; Agriculture; Commerce; Labor; and Health, Education, and Welfare; the Housing and Home Finance Agency; the Federal Trade Commission; and the President's Council of Economic Advisers, together with other government officials designated by the President, and private citizens especially qualified to represent consumer interests.

The citizen members of the committee are the existing Consumer Advisory Council which will continue to function, but as a part of the new committee.

The appointment of Mrs. Esther Peterson means that the 1960 pledge of the late President Kennedy has been fulfilled by President Johnson. For the first time, American consumers will have a top-level representative in the executive branch, with White House status and access to national news media that this carries.

The Function of the Consumer.[3] It should be clear by now that the major

[3] Leland J. Gordon, *The Function of the Consumer in a Free Society*. Westport, Conn.: The Kazanjian Foundation Lectures, 1957.

function of the consumer is to guide and control the production of goods and services which are to satisfy consumer wants. And the purpose of an economy is to produce goods and services in the right quantity, quality, and price for maximum satisfaction in consumer use. It is obvious that, to carry out this function of guiding and controlling, consumers must be better informed and made aware of the need for developing themselves as wise consumers.

One major problem here is the notion that the only way to achieve wise buying decisions is to increase individual or family income. This must be challenged. Furthermore, consumers cannot do their job of spending income efficiently, unless they can exercise intelligent choice among the goods and services on the market. For intelligent choice, they must be better informed not only about goods and services but also about the terms and conditions under which goods and services are promoted and made available.

The task of informing the consumer so he can make more intelligent choices in the market is tremendous and complex. Much more must be done through the schools and mass media and by business itself. And this foundation must be strengthened by a system of law and regulation that sets and enforces rules of proper economic conduct in the public interest.

Another important task is to see that reasonably good standards of quality for consumer goods and services are developed, tested, and publicized in a meaningful way, so that more efficient use can be made of the nation's economic resources. The achievement of good-quality standards that are known by consumers and producers will help protect responsible businessmen as well as the public from misleading and deceptive practices in the market.

Consumers should also remove restraints and rigidities that continue to exist in our economic and legal systems, because they impose an improper burden on useful economic activity. These restraints vary from the price fixing imposed by public law to restrictive tariffs and other obstacles to the necessary research and initiative in attaining consumer goals.

The primary functions of the consumer in our modern, complex economy are these: (1) Consumers need to know their part in the economy. (2) Consumers should be made aware of their need for developing themselves as wise consumers. (3) Consumers should be convinced of the necessity for organization and support of groups that work for the consumer interest. (4) Consumers should insist on effective government and private protection against deceit, fraud, misrepresentation, and dangers to personal health.

All this adds up to what President Kennedy so aptly called the recognition of a "declaration of rights" for consumers in a free society. These rights as consumers are: [4]

1. The right to safety—to be protected against the marketing of goods that are hazardous to health or life.
2. The right to be informed—to be protected against fraudulent, deceitful, or grossly misleading information, advertising, labeling, and other practices, and to be given the facts needed to make informed choices.
3. The right to choose—to be assured, wherever possible, access to a variety of products and services at competitive prices. And in those industries in which competition is not workable and government regulation is substituted, there should be assurance of satisfactory quality and service at fair prices.
4. The right to be heard—to be assured that consumer interests will receive full and sympathetic consideration in the formulation of government policy, and fair and expeditious treatment in its administrative tribunals.

Summary. The essence of this chapter may be condensed into one sentence: The function of consumers in our society is to use their freedom of choice in ways that will maximize consumer satisfactions and minimize the waste of natural and human resources.

If consumers are to perform their role effectively they must be informed and responsible. They must accept the unofficial role of inspectors in the market place. They should support businesses that provide quality merchandise and services at fair prices. On a national basis, they should support private and public agencies that improve standards of business conduct and quality of consumer goods. Finally, the consumer interest is best served when the top-level officials in public agencies, such as the Food and Drug Administration, Federal Trade Commission, and many others are consumer-minded. Public agencies created to protect the consumer interest have been ineffective when managed by people who tend to favor business interests over consumer interests.

As you study the remaining chapters, you will realize that one generalization is paramount: The art of becoming a satisfied consumer is increasingly difficult to achieve in the rapidly changing economic and social conditions in the United States.

[4] Message from the President of the United States relative to Consumer's Protective and Interest Program. Washington, D.C.: House of Representatives Document no. 364, 87th Congress, 2d Session.

2
MONEY MANAGEMENT

Money Management and Budgeting for College Students

Adequate family income depends greatly on the education of the head of the family. In 1961, about half of the families headed by persons with four or more years of college had incomes of $10,000 or more; but only one family in ten of those whose head had only eight years of elementary education had an income this size.

The median income of families headed by persons with four or more years of college was $9,264, or 47 per cent more than the median income of $6,302 of families headed by a person with only a high school education. The conclusions are clear. The more formal education a person has, the higher will be his income. This is demonstrated by the U.S. Bureau of Census in its annual reports on money income received by individuals and families.[1]

Men 14 years of age and older in 1961 and having less than eight years of elementary education received a median income of $2,090; eight years of elementary school boosted the median income to $3,452; four years of high school added over $2,000, to a total of $5,052; and four years of college added over $2,000, to a total of $7,261. Men with five years of college received a median income of $7,691, more than 3½ times that of the median income of a man with less than eight years of schooling.

Education increases the income of women, too. The median income of women 14 years of age and older in 1961 was less than the median income of the men at all levels of schooling. Women with less than eight years of education received a median income of $791; eight years of elementary schooling boosted the median income to $950; four years of high school

---

[1] See *Income of Families and Persons in the United States: 1961,* Current Population Reports, Consumer Income, Series P-60, no. 39. Washington, D.C.: Bureau of the Census, Feb. 28, 1963, p. 44.

increased it to $1,938; and four years of college increased it to $3,179. Women with five years or more of college received a median income of $4,694 a year, or more than six times as much as women with less than eight years of education.

The proportional differences between the income of men and women lessen as the comparison extends to each successive level of education. Women with only eight years of schooling had a median income only 27.5 per cent as large as the median income of the comparable group of men; women with five or more years of college had 61 per cent of that of a comparable group of men.

Analyzing College Expenses. Once it is recognized that future family income is greatly dependent on the education of the head of the family, which in many cases also includes the working wife, the increasing costs of college education must be considered. The average annual expenses for tuition, fees, books, board, and room for an individual college student, which were about $1,500 a decade ago, were $2,000 or more in 1962. At some colleges the costs were over $3,000. The Office of Education in Washington, D.C., estimates that by 1970 college costs will increase 35 per cent.

A University of Michigan study, *How People Pay for College,* found that average college expenses for an unmarried student totaled $1,550 a year in 1959–1960. Of this sum, $950 came from the student's parents, $360 was earned by the student, $130 was scholarship money, and $110 came from other sources. Four families in ten said they found it difficult to meet college expenses; two in ten said not only that they found financing difficult but that their financial aid was inadequate. Some families managed to set aside money in advance, a few reduced other expenses, some borrowed money, and in some cases a mother took a job to help pay for the student's college education.

The typical American family with a median income of $5,600 in 1960 had difficulty in financing a college education of $1,500 a year. Education for one child in a typical state university required more than one-fourth of all the family income.

On the assumption that prices and wages remain the same over an eight-year period, a family would have to spend approximately $12,000 to send two children to a state university. What family of four can afford it?

How to Pay for a College Education. Comparison of college costs and standards of living reveal that simple living prevails on most campuses. Some colleges, however, have higher tuition fees and more expensive social life. Transportation costs may also be one of the deciding factors in selecting a college. If funds are low, the opportunities to work for pay are important. You will also need to estimate the number of years before your formal education is completed. Then compare the total cost of your planned education with available funds, plus a conservative estimate of what you can earn during the college year and during vacation periods.

There is no need to be unduly discouraged if funds are low. If your general health is good and your learning ability average or better, all you need is careful planning. Many college students are getting an education against difficult financial odds. All other things being equal, your success under such conditions depends on the strength of your desire to sacrifice a little now in order to improve your standard of living later.

If work for pay is necessary, investigate the opportunities for earning money or the equivalent in rent, food, or tuition. If a job is uncertain, it is wise to start with enough money to carry you through the first semester or quarter period. Most students who really want jobs manage to find them before the first term ends.

Loans and scholarships are usually available to students with exceptional academic or athletic abilities. Both of these grants are highly prized because their purpose is to help industrious students who might otherwise have to discontinue their education. Many scholarships are continued provided the student achieves a certain minimum grade average.

Loans from Various Sources. Some students obtain financial aid in the form of short-term and long-term loans from various sources. Some colleges offer installment plans. Banks and other types of commercial lending agencies are offering loan plans. Just about anyone with normal credit rating can now obtain an unsecured installment loan for college education purposes.

If you cannot get a loan from a local bank, you may be able to make arrangements with such agencies as Education Funds, Inc., Providence, Rhode Island, The Tuition Plan, Inc., in New York City, and similar agencies. Charges vary widely. The best advice is to shop around and compare interest charges and dollar costs. For example, *Changing Times*, in March, 1962, reported variations from $579.20 to $911 in total costs on a loan of $4,000 over four years of college ($1,000 a year) to be repaid in 72 months.

Unfortunately, these commercial loans for education are buried under a flood of selling clichés. They are like commercial transactions based on profit. Shop for one carefully, comparing interest charges, dollar costs, insurance coverage, repayment periods, and cancellation privileges.

One of the lowest-cost sources, if you qualify and funds are still available, is available under the National Defense Student Loan Act. Qualified students may borrow up to about $1,000 a year for five years of college. This Federal loan, administered by the college, does not require repayment to start until one year after you cease to be a full-time college student. If you teach in an elementary or secondary school on completion of your college work, the present law permits 10 per cent forgiveness a year up to 50 per cent of the sum borrowed. The simple interest rate is a low 3 per cent per year. See the financial aid officer of your college for details.

Before you seek a commercial loan, inquire about financial aid at these sources.

College: Many institutions have their own loan programs, and a few offer installment plans.

State: Find out whether there is a bank guarantee program for long-term, low-interest educational loans in your state.

Federal government: Long-term, low-interest Federal loans are administered through colleges.

Other sources: Long-term, low-interest loans are also available from some religious, labor, and service organizations, and to employees of many corporations.

A student who accepts a loan takes on a responsible financial obligation. He usually signs a note, at a low interest rate or none, until he has a full-time job. Then regular payments are expected. If the responsibility for repayment seems too great, or there is a possibility of endangering health during the first year on a job, it may be unwise to accept a loan. If you are not in actual need of money, do not apply for a loan, because you may prevent someone who needs such help from continuing his education.

Money Management for College Students. As a college student, you have the same reasons as other individuals and families have for planning expenditures wisely. An intelligently planned budget will not deprive you of pleasure. On the contrary, it will help you to decide what to eliminate in order to have the things you need and really want.

If you are an unmarried college student, your family or guardian expects you—more or less—to manage your own expenditures during the college year. If you are a married college student, your budgeting problems will have to be centered around both family needs and college needs. Chapter 3 will be helpful in such a case. The married college student has, in fact, a double problem. He has to take care of all or most of the regular family budgeting problems in addition to his central purpose for the time being—education.

A good reason for devoting some serious attention to money management now is that you are setting habits that will stay with you during your entire lifetime. Good money management habits established now will pay dividends many times during your life. Some will say, "I'll wait until I'm married to set up a good money management program." Others will wait until the car is paid for or until the next raise comes along, or until . . . *ad infinitum.* Somehow they never get around to doing the job because they are always waiting for the right time. The best way to become an expert at managing money is to begin practicing *now.*

You may be one of that group of college students who is spending money not directly earned by you. Perhaps there has been little opportunity for you to learn to manage money well. You may be, however, among the few who are good consumers. If you are a good consumer, you insist on receiving value for your money. If you stick to that principle, you will probably be successful in managing all your resources—time, money, and energy.

You may be facing, for the first time, the full responsibility of deciding for yourself how to plan and spend your money. If so, you belong to the large group of college students who need counseling in the management of personal finances.

"How," you ask, "do I know whether I'm successful in handling my personal finances?"

The answer to that question is not an easy one. It is possible to make ends meet and yet not be successful in money management. It is likewise possible to be a careful buyer of consumer goods and services and not be a successful money manager. The person who is successful in money management is one who plans, buys, and uses goods and services in such a manner that he gets what he most desires from those goods and services.

Money Management IQ. The accompanying questionnaire, Money Management IQ, will help you discover your "dollar sense"—help you evaluate your skill in money management.

If you are below a score of 55, you really need to develop your skills in handling money. If your score embarrasses you, don't be discouraged. Remember the first time you drove a car or tried to hit a little ball with a golf club? Everything went wrong at first. Then, almost without knowing when, you began making the right moves without consciously thinking of them. The same results will happen in learning to handle your money in a planned way. You may think it time-consuming and unrewarding at first. Soon you will be making your money achieve the major goals that you set up.

Define Your Goals. There are two fundamentals of money management for college students. The first is to plan your own budget. It is your money. Establish your own spending pattern, and be sure that your money is going where you want it to go. The second fundamental is to set up your own goals. Knowing what you are aiming for will give a positive approach to budgeting. When you define your goals, you have taken the first step toward reaching them.

As a college student, you have certain financial obligations that can be classified as fixed expenses, such as tuition, board, and room, possibly

MONEY MANAGEMENT IQ

A self-test questionnaire on personal spending habits

This questionnaire, if filled out as accurately as your memory permits, will help you to discover your weaknesses in personal money management. Each "yes" answer rates 5 points. Add the points to find your money management IQ. If your score is:

Over 75, consider yourself a *good* money manager.

Between 75 and 55, consider yourself *average*.

Between 55 and 35, you are *below average*.

Below 35, you are *very poor*.

1. Have you made a rough plan for your large expenses for the year?

2. Have you kept a written record of your expenditures for at least one month?

3. Have you examined your record of expenditures and made necessary changes?

4. Are you seldom "broke" before your next allowance or income is received?

5. When "broke," do you generally get along as best you can until your allowance is received?

6. Do you avoid making yourself miserable and unhappy by fretting about something you want but cannot afford?

7. Are you in the habit of spending moderately on personal grooming?

8. Can you generally be entertained without spending money?

9. Do you usually resist the spending pressures of friends?

10. Do you resist the spending of money according to your whim without regard to what you really need?

11. When 'broke," do you tend to avoid getting an extra sum from your parents or guardian?

12. If you saw a clothing item in a store where you have a charge account, would you be likely to think about how to pay for it before you bought it?

13. Are you careful about not leaving cash in your room or carrying fairly large sums of money on your person?

14. Do you usually avoid buying clothes that you may wear only a few times?

15. Do you spend a moderate amount of money for food between meals?

16. Do you usually save ahead for something you want very much, such as a new dress or suit, a gift, a prom?

17. Do you make it a habit to go to more than one store to compare price and quality before deciding on a big purchase?

18. Would you say that about half your purchases are planned in advance and are not merely "impulse" buying?

19. Do you know whether your family carries personal belongings insurance, protecting such items as your luggage, clothes, jewelry, golf and tennis equipment?

20. Can you resist buying bargains just because they are advertised as bargains?

Your score: The number of checks ( ) × 5 = ( ).

transportation. As a rule you must meet these fixed expenses at a particular time. Then there are many flexible expenses, such as supplies, books, snacks, clothes, grooming items, recreation. The important thing is to be clear about your goals—aims, obligations, immediate and remote wants. Then make a definite plan for spending your dollars to meet your personal needs and wants. Use your spending plan to reach your goals.

A Budgeted Spending Plan. The first step in preparing a college budget is to get a true picture of your expenses by keeping a record of spending for two to four weeks. At the end of each week, total the amount spent for "fixed" or necessary expenses. These always must be paid. Other expenses are "flexible," that is, they can be cut out or cut down, depending

on your needs and income. You are the one to decide which of your expenses are fixed and which are flexible. An accurate spending record and
classification of expenses into fixed and flexible items will help you set up
a spending plan that works.

The accompanying table, A Budgeted Spending Plan, will help you
differentiate between fixed and flexible expenses. Of course, you can add
items or subtract any that you do not need to allow for in your own
spending plan.

You will be one in a thousand if you can actually "balance the budget."
But, like golf and tennis, even money management is a skill to be learned
and practiced, and the attitude toward money management must be
acquired. You can become quite efficient if you learn good management
of your income while in college, and then continue using this skill in
family income planning.

Money Management and Budgeting for the Family

The marriage service is usually full of emotional and spiritual significance. Materialistically it is a contract. Although there is no mention of
financial considerations in the ceremony, they are really implied in the
terms of the contract.

It might be said that the contract establishes an economic enterprise
called the family. In one way, at least, this union is like a private business. It sets out to operate at a profit. If it does not break even or begin
to show a profit, if expenses exceed income for too long a period, the
family enterprise goes into bankruptcy.

There is a big difference, however, when a family goes broke and when
a private enterprise business goes under. When the latter fails, only a
legal entity dies. When a family goes under, human beings suffer. Economic failure of a family can end a marriage or place it under a terrific
strain.

What will be the economic future for your family? It depends on many
things, but basically, there are two important considerations: the size of
the family income, and how you use it. How much income are you likely
to have the first year of marriage? Is it enough to support a family of
two? If you are disturbed because your income may be a modest one,
say $5,000, you are better off than you think. The median income (half
below, half above) of families in 1962, according to Bureau of the Census,
was $7,140. Most of the families below $7,140 managed to make ends
meet. It is well to remember that this figure is based on the entire population and includes families that have been established for years. And
you are only a beginner.

A more accurate measure is to compare the husband's income with that
of others his own age. Assuming that the man is 22, the most common

A BUDGETED SPENDING PLAN

Income	Estimated income	Actual income
Balance on hand (including amounts owed to you)	$_____	$_____
Regular weekly income	_____	_____
Additions to allowance	_____	_____
Earnings	_____	_____
Gifts	_____	_____
Total	$_____	$_____

Fixed expenses	Estimated fixed expense	Actual amount spent
Food	$_____	$_____
Room	_____	_____
Tuition	_____	_____
Transportation	_____	_____
Organization dues	_____	_____
Fees (laboratory, health, etc.)	_____	_____
Other	_____	_____
Total fixed expenditures	$_____	$_____

Flexible expenses	Estimated expense	Actual amount spent
Recreation	$_____	$_____
School supplies	_____	_____
Books	_____	_____
Clothing	_____	_____
Contributions	_____	_____
Grooming	_____	_____
Snacks	_____	_____
Repairs (radio, watch, shoes, etc.)	_____	_____
Gifts	_____	_____
Laundry, dry cleaning	_____	_____
Cultural events	_____	_____
Health	_____	_____
Cigarettes	_____	_____
Beverages	_____	_____
Other	_____	_____
Total flexible expenditures	$_____	$_____
Grand total	$_____	$_____

Actual income $_____
Actual amount spent $_____
Balance left $_____

age for marrying among young men, according to the last Census Bureau findings, the median annual income for men in the 20 to 24 age bracket is $2,514. The census figures show that:

20.2% make less than $1,000	86.3% make less than $5,000
39.8% make less than $2,000	93.7% make less than $6,000
57.6% make less than $3,000	97.5% make less than $7,000
75.3% make less than $4,000	99.8% make less than $10,000

The same census figures show that in the next older age bracket, 25 to 34, the median income of men nearly doubles to $4,904, and 48.4 per cent of them make $5,000 or more.

For a college graduate, the chances are good that the first year's salary will be at least $5,000. Graduates in the sciences often have a beginning annual salary of $8,000 to $9,000.

Perhaps the wife-to-be has a job and will work after marriage. In early marriage, it is safer to include most of the second income in the regular budget; don't be too optimistic about how much of it to include. There are extra expenses attached to any job—perhaps as much as 40 per cent. Then, too, the wife may become pregnant.

What about aid from parents? Attitudes and conditions vary so much that no general rule is possible. One caution is in order—assistance is one thing, dependency another. If a young couple depend on a parental financial prop too long, there will be trouble when the subsidy ends.

Most parents want to help their youngsters financially if such aid will strengthen the young family. Such help can be gracefully accepted and given. There are, however, many young families that never learn to live without financial aid from their in-laws.

Financial Planning before Marriage. After marriage there are at least two persons to consider in using income. The spending patterns used when single cannot be followed successfully after marriage. There are different responsibilities, new motivations, a different kind of household. Before you establish a home, it is essential to have some idea of how far your money will go, where it will go, and who will spend it. As you contemplate marriage, you will probably think, "Other people need to budget, but we understand each other so well that we have no need to bother." Don't believe it! It's surprising how a financial quarrel can turn into a domestic crisis, and it's a shame not to take simple steps to avoid this *before* marriage.

The three most important areas in family finance are budgeting, buymanship, and credit. It's a good thing, therefore, to be sensible about money. It's a good idea to have a plan for spending and saving, and to try to follow it. And this is true not just because good money management makes money do what you want it to do, but because a plan can

mean more happiness, less preoccupation with money, and a better attitude toward life. It is helpful when young couples agree on the answers
to the following questions.

Is the wife going to have a housekeeping allowance?
Exactly what is that going to cover?
Will the wife work for pay outside the home?
Who will keep the necessary income and spending records?
Who will pay what bills?
How much can be set aside for emergencies and savings?
How much can be saved for vacations? Baby expenses?
How much can be allowed for personal spending?

There will be other questions concerned with the particular way you
are going to live, your job or jobs, transportation, insurance, and so on,
which each couple can add to this list. But do settle these questions well
in advance of setting up housekeeping.

Money Management after Marriage. Money management generally is
mentioned as the most common cause, directly or indirectly, for marital
discord. Family finance is often given as the most difficult problem in
homemaking. It is one that causes much worry. The tendency of a young
couple, very much in love, seems to be that they will meet the financial
problems *when they arise.* Such persons say, "When all is well, why
plan?"

The tragedy among some families with this "meet it when it comes up"
philosophy is that they refuse to meet or see the facts when the situation
occurs. Other families, however, do meet the situation, but only by sal-
vaging the results of their lack of planning beforehand. Such persons
would not think of selecting a man to head a business or a surgeon to
perform an operation unless he had had adequate training. Yet so many
couples, deeply in love, are willing to go into marriage without knowing
how to be wise managers of money.

People who cannot live within their income are, in general, poor managers. Money, like time and talent, can be wasted. Money has to be
managed intelligently, or you will be on the losing side. And being on the
losing side in money management is a serious matter, because you are
playing a game for family happiness—for keeps.

How then do you prepare yourself for winning such an important
game? The answer is training. Back of training, however, is attitude.
The first prerequisite to wise management of money is attitude.

So much attention has been given to personality maladjustments as a
cause of marital discord that we are likely to forget that normal people
can achieve creative adjustments. A normal couple discover the facts,
face them honestly, and seek an insight into their own pattern of be-

havior. We know from studies that happily married people are successful homemakers, not because they have no problems but because they face their problems and arrive at a working solution. An important attitude toward handling family finances successfully is the desire for joint planning, joint earning, and joint spending to the end that every member of the family gets the utmost satisfaction from the money spent.

Importance of Values and Goals. The first step to successful money planning is to discuss the values you believe in and what you want out of life. This is a big order. It is important for family members to know, in general, what the family is working toward. Once you know the values you believe in, you will find a way of fitting them into your way of living.

Values determine the goals that give direction to living. Some values are ideals, such as loyalty, courage, and honesty. Religious values generally influence the moral tone of an individual. Other values, such as smartness, sophistication, popularity, cleanliness, comfort, and security, may not be dignified by the term *ideals,* but they influence behavior in an important way.

We learn our values at home, in school, in church, and in countless other places. Certainly one inescapable function of the home is to pass values on to the child, who in turn may accept or reject some of them. These values generally direct his actions without the necessity of making a new decision every time he is confronted with a new situation or problem. These values will change when some new value has greater appeal or worth for the individual or family.

Values, like democracy and authoritarianism, carry over to family behavior. In some families, the father is a "benevolent despot," a "dictator," or perhaps a senior member of a "democratic" family. Mass media —movies, radio, television, newspapers, and magazines—provide additional ways for people to share values. At times, these media lead people to accept values that in turn lead to conflict in the home. Romantic love stories portrayed on television and movie screens may lead to unrealistic concepts that make marital adjustments more difficult. On the other hand, these media have helped to improve parent-child relationships. Literature and art, scientific studies, and lectures have had direct influence in creating new values for many people. On the whole, values come from our family, our religious beliefs, our own peer group, our educational experiences, and our culture.

Values do change. Few of us escape the initial conflicts that generally accompany changing values. This conflict should be accepted as a part of growing up—maturing—which is characterized by the ability to acquire meaningful relationships from changing values. Until there is clarity and meaning in your value system, your individual and family goals are out of reach.

Goals Depend on Your Values. Established personal or family goals will help you to realize the beliefs or values you hold. Long-term goals are related to your philosophy of living. Your beliefs or values, which determine your philosophy, are given priority in planning your life, depending on the importance you attach to them. It is the order of this priority, which may change, that determines the goals you set. If financial security is placed high in your value system, then financial security becomes a long-term goal. Saving a little each week or month and investing it immediately becomes a short-term goal whose basic value is financial security. Values are the "criteria against which goals are chosen."[2]

The value you hope to realize in attaining a certain goal becomes the goal value you will plan for and work toward. For example, parents who prize financial security for the family include this objective in such specific activities as planning a savings program; putting money in the bank; providing for various types of insurance; budgeting; securing information on good investments, annuities, and mutual funds; and investigating the reliability of the companies that offer such services. The goal values are the specific ones that are important to the objective—in this case, financial security.

A goal value must be clearly understood before it can be achieved. For example, you might say that the goal of the family is to achieve maximum happiness for all its members. This is too general. It is important to know how you intend to achieve your goal. One family may believe that happiness can be achieved by acquiring expensive clothes and cars. Another may believe that it is better to control expenditures at present and save money for education of the children. A third family may think of happiness in terms of good music, art, and literature. Each family must decide its own value goals, decide what things it wants to achieve with its time, energy, and financial resources.

In general, individuals and families are more successful in achieving their goal values when they take these steps:

1. Make a plan based on the goal values sought.
2. Put the plan into action.
3. Evaluate the action periodically in terms of the goal values realized.
4. Make a new plan, if necessary, based on the evaluation of the old plan.

Long-term Planning Gives Goals for Happiness. The length of each stage will vary from family to family. If a family chooses, it can make long-term plans to meet the needs of these stages. Such planning should not be considered final. Perhaps the best that a long-term plan can provide is direction. One can see the inevitable financial problems that must be

[2] Talcott Parsons and Edward A. Shils, *Toward a General Theory of Action.* Cambridge, Mass.: Harvard University Press, 1952, p. 429.

met in the various stages of the family life span. By long-term planning, most families can get the greatest satisfaction from the spending of their income for the entire family.

What a young couple wants out of life is of major importance. These goals or mental standards create pictures of the kind of life one prefers to see develop in the family. Knowing what we want, even in the face of defeat, is an essential step toward achieving happiness. It certainly is a prerequisite to intelligent money management, because eventually goals must be translated into dollars-and-cents terms. Family goals can be achieved best through efficient financial planning.

Joint Planning to Eliminate Irritants. It is particularly important for a couple to learn how to plan together when they are first married. No bride from one family and a husband from another family can expect to have the same views on spending money. But they can learn to understand each other's views and to compromise. It is wise to remember that men and women do not always spend money in the same way. Men cannot understand why women say they have "nothing to wear," when the closet seems to be bulging with clothes. On the other hand, women do not understand why men appear to spend money as no woman ever would. So, understanding and compromise are necessary.

Needless irritants should be reduced or eliminated. For example, no member of the family should be placed in the embarrassing position of continuously asking someone for money. Children are a part of the family, and as such are entitled to a fair share of everything because of this relationship.

A husband should not expect his wife to do the impossible in stretching the dollar. A practical, workable plan for handling family money should be worked out jointly. The details of the plan should fit the particular family. Such a plan should provide for major family expenses and for individual responsibility in spending. It should take care of personal allowances, education, and cultural growth of all members of the family. It should provide for savings, for retirement, and for financial crises.

When a member of the family continuously demands this and that only for himself, conflict is inevitable. Cheerful compromise, although not ideal, is often the best way to settle some of these demands.

Time was when dad controlled the purse strings and doled out the money. It is almost impossible for such a father to avoid becoming a financial dictator or a benevolent despot. As a benevolent despot, children often come to feel that the father is the important cog in the family wheel.

We all know that the mother contributes just as much toward the family income by being a wise manager of the home. As a final spender of around 55 per cent of the family income, the purchasing power of the dollar depends to a great extent on her. She can add dollars to the monthly check by careful planning, buying, and using. This is in addition to her orderly managing of the household.

All in all, husband and wife are inseparable partners who, when functioning as a family team, can work wonders with the use of income. Such a family is building a foundation for happiness. Good attitudes toward the wise use of money are not enough. There must also be efficient planning.

Bedeviled by Undisciplined Dollars. Said a young wife after her first year of married life, "I had no idea there were so many things to be paid for." Exactly true. And for so many it seems that there never is enough money. Many families are constantly worried about meeting their bills. But even if they manage to pay the bills, the family may not have a satisfactory spending plan.

Most families are worried from payday to payday. Many of them go through life forever bedeviled by undisciplined dollars. Such financial bedevilment may be due to one or more of the following reasons:

1. Overestimating family income
2. Underestimating expenditures
3. No long-term plans
4. Irregular or uncertain income
5. Too many fixed expenses
6. Not enough family participation in management
7. Arguing over who should be the manager
8. Divergent attitudes about money management
9. Differences in attitudes toward values
10. Poor buymanship
11. Paying high interest on debts

Many of these practices can be avoided or modified. Financial advisers at banks, insurance companies, and social agencies believe that in many instances people shy away from doing anything about their money mismanagement because they have so many misconceptions about family spending plans. Let's take a look at a few of these misconceptions.

Misconceptions about Budgets. Madelyn Wood interviewed a number of family financial counselors who had helped thousands of persons plan budgets. According to these experts, there are four major misconceptions about budgeting.

1. *A budget is not bookkeeping.* Mrs. Jones came to the bank, proudly bearing a bookkeeper's ledger representing a year's expenditures. "I've kept a record of every penny," she told the budget adviser. Entered in neat script were such items as "postage, 3 cents, phone call, 5 cents." "And still we can't save money," wailed Mrs. Jones. Tactfully the expert told her the truth: she had been wasting her

time. She had made herself and her family miserable with the mistaken notion that budgeting means keeping a record of everything you spend. . . . Budgeting isn't bookkeeping. You can have a workable budget—without any bookkeeping.

2. *A budget is not a system of fixed percentages.* An earnest Chicago housewife told a budget expert that she had calculated everything scientifically. She knew the formula which said you were supposed to spend "x" per cent on clothing, "y" per cent on housing, and so on. This had called for changing the family's living habits, because they had been spending too much on housing. They had moved, and now their rent was lower. But they were no longer happy. The expert explained that nobody could say how much you "ought" to spend on housing. The fixed percentage formula is a fallacy. There is only what you have to spend and what you want to spend. Every expenditure involves a choice—buy one thing and you can't buy another.

3. *A budget is not pinching pennies.* Mrs. Green was on the verge of a nervous breakdown when she came to an adviser. "When we worked out our budget," she explained, "we figured all kinds of ways to save money. John agreed to cut out two packages of cigarettes a week. Tom, our 15-year-old boy, said he could get along on half his usual allowance." She followed with a long list of deprivations, totaling five dollars a week. But she admitted that everyone in the household was unhappy. She had the wrong idea. Budgeting is not nursing nickels and mortifying the flesh with painful forms of thrift.

4. *A budget is not only for people with small incomes.* A successful Washington physician asked his bank for a loan. The facts he laid before a financial adviser were shocking. His income was $24,000 a year, yet he "owed everybody." Extravagance? He didn't think so. He and his family had felt unable to afford a winter vacation trip. His teen-age daughters complained that they weren't as well dressed as other girls at school. The doctor was keenly aware that something was wrong, but he honestly didn't know what. "Just a case of careless spending," the adviser said. "What you need is a budget."

What Is a Good Budget? Let us begin with what a budget is not. It does not, will not, and cannot tell how to spend money. Furthermore, it is not designed to keep us away from the things we want. It is not an end in itself. It is not even a plan to restrict spending. What *is* it, then?

A budget is a plan for distributing income in order to give every member of the family the utmost satisfaction from the money spent. There are no restrictions except the ones the family makes. The plan will do for a family just what the members want. It is custom-tailored to fit individual family needs and desires. In the last analysis, a budget is actually a guide to acceptable choices.

Henry Bowman, in *Marriage for Moderns,* correctly compared a budget to a dam. He said the dam "holds back the undirected flow of the river in order to turn the waters into channels that supply power generators, so that electric current may be provided now here, now there, as needs arise."

Since a good family budget can do what a family wants it to do, there is no valid reason for not having one. The next question, then, is this: "How does one go about making a family budget?"

Family Lifetime Income Is Big Business. A typical American family with an income of $6,000 will spend at least $270,000 in the earning lifetime of 45 years from age 20 to age 65 for the head of the family. This is big business! And it will be bigger. Because family income is usually divided into weekly or monthly payments, and is so obligated in paying bills, it is easy to lose sight of how big the total is. What an important and worthwhile job it can be to manage the family income well!

As you shop for groceries, for example, you may think it of little value to save a few cents here and there. But in terms of the total amount of money spent for food in a month, year, or lifetime, the prospect of saving 5 or 10 cents on a dollar can begin to take on real meaning. This is indeed a good return on the investment of learning to be a good consumer. And the place to begin managing personal income is in sensible budgeting.

Making a Family Budget. There are many ways for newlyweds to budget. One way is to see how other people spend their money, then allocate the family income more or less accordingly. Here is the national estimate of how personal spending is divided.

	Per cent		Per cent
Food, beverages, tobacco	26.6	Personal business	6.3
Clothing, accessories	10.3	Transportation	12.4
Personal care	1.6	Recreation	5.9
Housing	12.8	Education	1.4
Household operation	13.9	Contributions	1.4
Medical care	6.5		

The trouble with the above percentages is that they include all kinds of people in all sorts of situations. No family is a national average family. Therefore, these percentages will not necessarily apply to your case. In fact, no family should try to operate on a national average or on another family budget. A family budget should be an individual affair. It must be geared to your goals and your personal needs. But it does help to know how other people live and how they divide their income to try to make ends meet.

The two budgets devised by the Heller Committee for Research in Social Economics at the University of California reproduced in the accompanying table, Master Budgets, reflect the actual living costs of two families at two income levels in the San Francisco Bay area in 1961. The blank column is for your use in estimating the distribution of your own income. Every household would not require the same data or use the same percentages. But those given in the first two columns of the table can help you to decide what items to include in your own budget.

MASTER BUDGETS

	Salaried man		Wage Earner		You	
	$	%	$	%	$	%
Total income	9,742.41	100.0	6,777.59	100.0		
Income taxes	1,256.07	12.9	755.66	11.1		
Total take-home pay	8,486.34	100.0	6,021.93	100.0		
Food	2,407.85	28.4	1,831.41	30.4		
At home	1,915.49	22.6	1,791.89	29.8		
Away	492.36	5.8	39.52	0.6		
Beverages	80.55	1.0	57.98	1.0		
Housing	1,378.07	16.2	978.00	16.2		
Household operation	461.99	5.5	282.93	4.7		
House furnishings	330.51	3.9	216.86	3.6		
Clothing	756.33	8.9	503.54	8.4		
Man	248.10	2.9	136.21	2.3		
Woman	245.72	2.9	143.90	2.4		
Boy, 13	140.17	1.7	120.37	2.0		
Girl, 8	122.34	1.4	103.06	1.7		
Transportation	1,003.98	11.8	587.70	9.8		
Auto	850.33	10.0	570.08	9.5		
Carfare	153.65	1.8	17.62	0.3		
Medical, dental care	671.28	7.9	575.89	9.6		
Insurance	375.30	4.4	290.68	4.8		
Personal care	152.97	1.8	115.15	1.9		
Recreation	435.07	5.1	235.69	3.9		
Tobacco	119.08	1.4	119.08	2.0		
Reading	57.51	0.7	39.26	0.7		
Education	69.79	0.8	8.77	0.1		
Union dues	...	...	68.09	1.1		
Gifts, contributions	155.06	1.8	93.40	1.5		
Miscellaneous	31.00	0.4	17.50	0.3		

The Monthly Ledger. The division of your income according to the Master Budget, after many revisions, will testify to the care that went into preparing it. Once the final version is completed, you are ready to draw up a monthly ledger that will make your master budget work. This is the real workhorse of financial management. You may use an ordinary sheet of ruled paper or buy a ledger book for the purpose.

The Monthly Ledger shown here is easy to follow. To find the amount for column 5, End of Month Balance, compare total spending in column 4 with the total available in column 3. If you spend less than allocated, enter the sum left over in column 5 as a plus balance. And, of course, enter any increased spending as a minus balance.

Then, for the following month, copy the month-end balances from column 4 to column 1 for the new month as Balance Brought Forward.

There is nothing sacred about this system. Modify it to fit your family. One important merit is that the monthly ledger brings to light immediately both surpluses and deficits. It is, therefore, possible to make timely corrections in next month's spending.

Persistent surpluses or deficits in any one item will alert you to the defects in your budget estimates. Corrections can be made easily and accurately from year to year and thus provide for sensible flexibility in planning.

In any event, you don't have to be an accountant to manage your money as here described. All it takes is some skill in adding and subtracting, some ruled paper, and a desire. Budgeting cannot add dollars to your pay check, but it can make you richer in peace of mind and in real satisfaction.

The chances are that you will not have a definitive budget until after the first year. Some kinds of expenditures vary according to seasons, and some expenses, like mortgage payments and taxes, may occur only once a year. But once you complete a full year, you will know how your income should be distributed.

How to Cut Expenses. When you have kept track of your family spending for a few months, you may discover that you need to reduce expenditures. Here are some possibilities for savings.

1. *Reducing food bills.* Select the least expensive but adequate food substitutes. Produce some food on your land. Cook and bake more at home. Eat more meals at home. Buy food according to use.

2. *Reducing clothing bills.* Plan your wardrobe at least one year in advance. Select color schemes that are economical to fulfill. Shop around. Pay cash and compare values. Buy at regular sales.

3. *Reducing fuel bills.* Insulate and put on window stripping. Learn to control the heating system. Teach the family how to use the lights and hot water without excessive waste.

4. *Reducing rent.* If you have an extra room, rent it. Accept a less convenient location for lower rent. Find an older house that you can fix up.

5. *Reducing servicing bills.* Do more of your own personal grooming. Cut down on the use of your checking account. Repair more of your own clothes.

6. *Reducing medical bills.* Take better care of the family. Investigate low-cost hospital and medical plans. Eat nutritious meals.

7. *Reducing amount spent on impulse buying.* Buy according to plan.

8. *Reducing recreational cost.* Use public facilities for swimming, fishing, picnics, free lectures, and concerts; organize your own entertainment. Serve simple and inexpensive refreshments. Well-chosen gifts need not be expensive.

9. *Reexamining your long-term expenditures.* Perhaps you are spending too much for a house, for insurance, for investments, or for a car.

10. *Refinancing your debts.* Installment buying is expensive. Your bank may be able to refinance debts at a considerably lower cost.

MONTHLY LEDGER

Estimate of Monthly Cash Income

Annual income	$_____
Interest, dividends	_____
Other income	_____
Total	$_____
Deductions	_____
Spendable income	$_____

Monthly Working Details

	(1) Balance brought forward	(2) This month's allocation	(3) Total avail- able	(4) Month's spend- ing	(5) End-of-month balance (+ or −)
Fixed expenses					
Mortgage or rent	$0.00	$110	$110	$110	$ 0.00
Life insurance					
Savings					
Taxes					
Personal allowances					
Church, charities					
Variable expenses					
Food:					
At home	6.00	90.00	96.00	82.00	+14.00
Away					
Household operation					
Clothing					
Medical, dental					
Car upkeep, repair					
Fuel					
Light					
Water					
Recreation, entertainment					
Investments					
Christmas savings					
Vacation savings					
New furniture savings					

In attempting to cut these day-to-day expenses, do not scrimp too much on the little items. Don't deny yourselves comfortable allowances. Go after the more important economies.

How to Waste Money. During the first months of married life, you will discover that there is "too much month and not enough money." So consider the following common ways of wasting money before they can get a hold on the family income. Much of the material in this book will discuss the following wasteful habits and show how to prevent them.

1. Buying what you don't need—impulse buying, keeping up with others, compulsive buying, neurotic need
2. Buying worthless things, such as most gadgets, advertised medical concoctions, etc.
3. Being a victim of "something for nothing"—gimmicks like coupons, premiums, frauds, gyps, bait advertising
4. Wasting money when buying food
5. Wasting food in the home
6. Paying more for all types of purchases than you need to pay
7. Buying only the top-priced merchandise
8. Using household equipment, car, and clothing carelessly
9. Gambling—track, lotteries, games
10. Using installment credit unwisely
11. Selecting the wrong kind of life insurance
12. Buying a home before financially able

Fitting Large Expenditures into a Long-range Plan. Most families cannot afford more than one or two large extra expenditures in any one year. It may be for a down payment on a house, for a baby, for an expensive piece of furniture, or for a college education fund.

Under such circumstances, it may be wise to stagger these items over a period of years. Obviously, a fund for a college education must be started early by most families. A television set may have to wait until next year because a refrigerator is needed this year. Saving a certain amount each year for specific purposes is the safest way for people on modest incomes to get what they want and can afford. A few items might be kept on that "nice to have but do not need now" list. When the family can afford it, these wants can be effectively met.

Families that can agree on these matters are not likely to be in the unhappy and embarrassing position of the family that has a $4,000 annual income but attempts to keep up with families in the $10,000 income bracket. In such a situation, the pressures, direct and indirect, are so great that a family with no financial plan is likely to spend far beyond its income. Such a family cannot escape certain inevitabilities.

The day comes when the unhappy financial condition must be faced. Family discord is almost automatic. The discovery is made too late of what should have been an accepted principle from the beginning of the family life—make spending fit income.

Effective plans for retirement are almost always made to fit into long-range planning. Unless a retirement program is planned carefully along with all other needs, a family may become "retirement poor." In other words, it is possible to put so much current income into a retirement fund, especially before the children have completed their education, that other essential needs are neglected. There are certain times in a family life cycle when additional money can be allowed for retirement without affecting the family's present standard of living.

Planning for Emergencies. Some families get into a financial jam because they failed to prepare in advance to meet the emergency "blockbusters." These are the expenditures that, as a rule, cannot be timed. They may be expensive surgery, a long siege of illness, or an unfortunate lawsuit.

Savings should be made for emergencies whenever possible. Savings may also take the form of paying off debts when income is more favorable. In this manner, loans are more easily available in times of need. Savings may take many forms, such as government bonds, insurance—especially covering death, illness, surgery, accident, and fire—real estate and homeownership, commercial stocks and bonds, and cash savings. Making a legal will can also help to reduce financial hazards for the family.

The Family Inventory. At the end of each year, it is wise to take inventory of the family's assets and debts as shown in the accompanying Family Financial Statement. This is a good way to see what economic progress, if any, the family has made. Such data are also useful in discussion of possible changes in the distribution of the family income, and they are helpful, even necessary, in applying for a loan for a large outlay of money—to build or buy a house, for example.

The net worth of the family may not be much during the first years of marriage. The important thing is to face whatever the condition is and decide how to increase the net worth. Note that the first three items in the assets column of the Family Financial Statement are liquid assets. Is enough money being put into certain kinds of investments? Are the assets adequately insured? Discussion of the specific items in such a financial statement will eventually lead to changes that will increase the net worth of the family.

Methods of Handling Money. The method of handling money is not, perhaps, so much a question of who is the manager as it is a question of how the money is managed and to what end. Nor are all the methods of equal merit.

Some families have a financial dictator who makes all the decisions and doles out money for specific purposes. Then there is the kind of family that divides management responsibilities. The mother is respon-

FAMILY FINANCIAL STATEMENT

January 1 to December 31, 19____

Assets		Debts	
Cash on deposit	$_____	Mortgages	$_____
Market value of bonds	_____	Borrowed from life insurance	
Market value of stocks	_____	companies	_____
Market value of house	_____	Borrowed from banks	_____
Market value of real estate	_____	Accounts at stores	_____
Resale value of car	_____	Other debts	_____
Social security assets	_____		
Cash surrender value of insurance	_____		
Notes	_____		
Resale value of household goods .	_____		
Other assets	_____		
Total assets	$_____	Total debts	$_____
Net worth (total assets minus total debts) $_____			

sible for managing food and clothes, and the father makes decisions in regard to investments, taxes, and insurance.

Some families have joint checking accounts, and others have separate accounts. Some rely on the envelope system—placing in envelopes money earmarked for specific purposes, such as rent, insurance, clothes. Since there is a chance of losing money kept in envelopes, some families write postdated checks. In this way, the check stubs are filled, and the records show that such money has been used.

There are other schemes. The important thing to remember is that the method decided on should accomplish what is intended.

Make Your Plan a Family Team Job. It is easier to get cooperation on a family spending plan if the whole family helps to make it. There was a time when father thought that taxes, insurance, and investments were his own private headache. Mother worried about food and clothing prices all by herself. And too often the only thing the children heard about family expenses was the terse parental "We can't afford it now."

This is not true in many families today. Everyone except the tiny members has some part in planning the distribution of the family income. Parents have found that children are surprisingly cooperative, even eager, about giving up this and that demand on the pocketbook when they understand where the money goes. A plan made by and for the whole family has an excellent chance of succeeding. It is doomed to failure if any one member of the family makes a plan alone and tries to carry it out in the face of opposition or indifference. Therefore, make a family plan. But how?

The first step is to arouse the interest of the family in the plan. All the members should agree finally that a plan is needed, even if they have to

be sold on the idea. When the plan has been explained and all questions
have been answered, every member of the family should be willing to try
it out. More than that, every member should have a responsibility, because responsibility, even if small at first, and a voice in the plan go hand
in hand.

Common sense should be used in such a family council. Not all financial
details can be entrusted to all children. Neither should they be exposed
to worrisome debts. At least, not until problems arise that necessitate
revealing such information. Many families have discovered that even
small children can be entrusted successfully with important family data.
If such information creates worry and emotional distress, it may do
more harm than good. Much depends on the approach taken by the
parents and on the respect that children have for their parents.

When family financial planning becomes a reality, there is almost no
resentment, no argument, no nagging. The results, in terms of improved
human relations in the family, are so positive and good that one wonders
why more families do not try it.

Joint planning, joint spending, and joint responsibility are an exciting
idea. For those who join in the idea, there is understanding, friendliness,
and cooperation. Such a family has the necessary financial foundation
for a successful and happy life together.

Who Should Be the Manager? A family, like a business enterprise, needs
a manager with skill or one who is willing to learn. Managing successfully on a small or a large income is a real achievement. This takes planning, insight, and cooperation on the part of husband and wife. They must
decide how the income will be distributed and who will be responsible for
its distribution. Then they must cooperate fully in carrying out the plan.

Certain divisions of money distribution between husband and wife
seem natural. In most American families, the plan as it relates to food for
home consumption, clothes for the family, and household operation and
equipment tends to give responsibility to the wife. On the other hand, in
many families the husband takes care of insurance, investments, house
payments, and the car. The wife's responsibility is usually great in paying the bills, in buying, and in keeping necessary financial records.

Ideally, the husband and wife share all financial plans together from
the beginning. If both know all the financial facts and make joint decisions in regard to all important spending policies, much resentment and
unhappiness is prevented. This method also enables the wife to be prepared to carry on alone in the event that it becomes necessary.

Newlyweds can expect to make changes from their first plans. Gradually, however, they will develop a pattern of joint planning and responsibilities that will fit their needs.

There are some men who still feel that they should handle all the family financial business. They prefer to write the checks, keep the records, and perhaps make all important spending decisions. If necessary, let them try it for a few months. Some men, after trying to handle the household exchequer, have gone to the other extreme. They have thrown the job into the wife's lap with the remark: "Here it is. You can have it, I don't want it." This, too, is unfortunate, unless they decide to be sensible and make it a cooperative affair.

There are a few men who, gallantly, feel that they should shield the little woman from the big, cruel business world. This is an old-fashioned idea. It has no place in modern life. Young people today discuss everything from sex to family finances. Moreover, many women have had considerable financial experience before marriage. In fact, a strong case can be made in favor of the argument that "money is a wife's business."

When Financial Crises Come. You may wonder why an account of family financial crises is included here. The most important reason is that no family can escape financial crises. Virtually all families, at one time or another, face one or more of the following family crises: loss of a child, orphanhood, hospitalization, widowhood, nonsupport, infidelity, illegitimacy, desertion, suicide, imprisonment, homicide, divorce, loss of job, sudden increase in income, and so forth. To the price paid in emotional stress is added always dollars-and-cents charges.

Death, the crisis perhaps least talked about, will normally come to the average family several times. Sudden impoverishment hovers constantly over all families except perhaps the wealthiest. Sudden and appreciable increases in income are difficult for many families to meet and too often become the focal point in family quarrels.

Many of these crises are blows when they come, but they are a part of living and cannot be escaped. The sensible conclusion is to be prepared, as much as possible, to regard them as challenges. The main question, then, is not "How can family crises be avoided?" but rather "How can family crises be met?"

Would More Money Solve Your Problems? The fact remains that for many families, wants seem to be one jump ahead of income no matter how high the income. Some years ago a Gallup poll asked this question: "What do you want most for your family?" The answer, in overwhelming numbers, was "Ten per cent more income."

That was in 1947. Apparently our economy rubbed Aladdin's lamp, and the responding genie worked overtime. The real income of the average American family rose not a mere 10 per cent but over four times that much. Measured in 1962 dollars, the average family that earned $100 a week in 1947 earned over $150 in 1962.

We are a lot better off financially. Most families have upgraded their standard of living. There is more money for homes, cars, appliances, color TV sets, new furniture, vacations, clothing, stereo, and motorboats. On the surface all is well. But probe a little deeper and you can see both boon and blight. Along with many material comforts have come financial woes of which our thrift-minded grandfathers never dreamed.

The astonishing contradiction of our time is the failure of a disturbingly large number of families to avoid financial stress in the face of continuously increasing real incomes. Money troubles beset many older families but especially younger people just getting started.

At least half of our families owe money on possessions (not including homes). The nation's installment debt was over $50 billion in 1963— about one-tenth of the total wealth produced in the country in one year. Add to this over $150 billion of home mortgage debts that still have to be paid off, and the outlines of the financial burden begin to become clear. All this affluence is by no stretch of the imagination bought and paid for.

A good part of the take-home pay is tagged for the bill collector even before it is received. Nationally, about $13 out of every $100 in take-home pay has a lien on it to pay installments due. Ten years ago, the figure was about $7. But creditors must be paid. If they are not, then a catastrophe like bankruptcy may come.

Bankruptcy and Foreclosure. There has been a big jump in family or consumer-type bankruptcy filings (at least 160,000 in 1961).[3] This is over 400 per cent increase in the last decade, a decade, incidentally, in which real income zoomed 37 per cent. Were these bankruptcies caused mainly by unemployment, costly illness, or substandard income? The American Bar Association found that wage seizures are a primary cause of consumer bankruptcy.[4] A study by a national insurance company found that "the dominant reason why most debt-ridden families are that way is simply incompetent management. . . . [they are] living up the salary check and mortgaging it to the hilt, with no margins for emergencies."

Mortgage foreclosures are on the upswing. Thousands of families who took the bait on low or no down payments but with large monthly payments have been reaping the bitter fruits of incompetent financial planning. In 1961, 72,000 families lost their homes through foreclosures. The FHA foreclosure rate doubled between 1959 and 1963. At the end of 1962, 1.6 per cent of all FHA-insured home loans were foreclosed.

If we are going to live successfully with affluence, more families must bridge the gap between acquisition and good sense about spending, saving, and budgeting. Coping with money management in a family is as

[3] For an excellent review, see Charles Neal, Jr., *A Guide for Family Financial Counseling*. Greeley, Colo.: Council on Consumer Information, 1962.

[4] *Ibid.*, p. 28.

important as good financial management of a business. There are principles that must be observed, certain records to be kept, and careful
planning for both short-term and long-term expenditures.

The thoughtful consumer is introspective about his values and goals.
He determines that, when it comes to money, he will be the master, and
the dollar his servant. When these roles become reversed, financial distress or disaster may follow—even among the affluent.

The Debt-adjustment Business. Technically, a debt-adjusting firm is a
prorating company or a prorater. Popularly, they go by such names as
debt poolers, debt counselors, or budgeting services. They work something like this. The prorater makes an analysis of the debtor's income
and expenses and, after a counseling session on the family budget, has
his client sign a contract naming the prorater as his agent to manage the
debts. The client agrees to pay a fee running from 10 per cent of the listed
debts in some states to 15 per cent in others. In some states, where regulation is nonexistent or unenforced, his fee may be 17 per cent of the
listed debts ($25 minimum), plus 17 cents per month per creditor, plus 6
cents per check written. This could come to $500 total. Reputable serv-
ices charge a straight 12 per cent of the listed debts.

The prorater talks to the creditors and persuades them to accept
scaled-down but regular payments until all the debts are paid. A good
prorater is supposed to pay off all the client's debts in full. He is not
supposed to buy the accounts from creditors at a discount. He is not
supposed to function as a bill collector.

There are prorater crooks. The Better Business Bureaus have been
deluged with inquiries and complaints. An out-and-out crook can set up
a business, collect a few payments, and skip town. Most complaints stem
not from larceny or embezzlement but from practices that are within
the law or so close to the legal line that it takes a court to determine
the case. In some cities, like St. Louis, in a survey conducted by the
Better Business Bureau, 70 per cent of the merchants queried said they
refused prorating arrangements.

Are there good proraters? Charles Neal, Jr., an authority in this field,
says that among the three hundred proraters, about fifty or sixty belong
to the American Association of Credit Counselors, a professional group
trying to effect ethical professional practices and an upgrading of the
business. They conduct classes, issue bulletins, write books, and actively
participate in consumer education in their community. A member usually
will not accept a debt case unless he feels that it can be successfully
worked out.

A typical case comes to about $2,500 (not including the home mort-
gage) owed to 12 different creditors and has $150 a month pledged to
creditors. It may take two years to clean up the debts. Over 60 per cent

of the cases handled avoid bankruptcy, partly because ethical adjusters work so hard to prove themselves. Great care, however, must be used when selecting a prorater.

There have been recent developments in debt-adjusting counseling. The National Foundation for Consumer Credit, supported by commercial credit firms, has clinics in most major cities. The National Retail Credit Association with headquarters in St. Louis, Missouri, is also sponsoring counseling services. This service works through local credit bureaus in one way or another. A few credit bureaus, like that in St. Paul, have set up their own debt-adjustment clinics. The Family Service Agencies in some cities operate a debt-adjustment service for their clients. If in doubt, get advice from the Legal Aid Society, if available, or from any county bar association.

Sudden Loss in Family Income. During economic depressions, more families experience serious income losses than at any other period. A major depression creates a crisis in family life, through loss of work and income, for which the family has no accustomed responses. The family may have to abandon certain plans, such as buying a home. It may not be able to continue membership in certain social clubs and thus no longer conform to its social standards. It may not be able to pay bills on time, a standard in which it has always taken pride. It may experience the shifting of a dominant role from father to mother or to an older child. Not only is the entire family disorganized, but each member of the family may be personally disorganized over the loss of accustomed activities, over failure to meet financial responsibility, or over a feeling of lowered status.

The realization that the family cannot continue its past habits of social life usually causes severe emotional reactions. This period of acute emotional stress is terminated either by an adjustment to the situation or by the development of pathological reactions. If a family completely breaks or fails to adjust, the family life may disintegrate, or one member may be led to escape through mental illness, suicide, or running away.[5]

How can a family effectively meet a financial crisis? There are, say the experts, no pat answers. The following actions have aided some families.[6]

1. Face the facts as a family.
2. Agree on a temporary plan or procedure.
3. Clear the air of accusations with reference to "fixing the blame."
4. Cooperate in reducing expenses sufficiently.

[5] Ruth S. Cavan and Katherine H. Ranck, *The Family and the Depression*. Chicago: The University of Chicago Press, 1938, pp. 6–7.

[6] Howard Becker and Reuben Hill (eds.), *Marriage and the Family*. Boston: D. C. Heath and Company, 1942, pp. 531–533.

5. Cooperate in pooling all family income for family use.
6. Discover together new cultural and psychological resources.
7. Look forward to reestablishing the business or profession.

Sudden Increase in Family Income. There are no adequate studies of the effect of sudden prosperity on families and their members. But most of us know families that have had such an experience. Perhaps we also know, in a general way, that disintegration often takes place among such families. Apparently, family happiness is not automatically achieved by a sudden increase in family income.

It is not a simple case of saying, "Now we can get what we have always wanted and do the things we have always wanted to do." Foster and Wilson, in reporting on the case study of 78 married women, concluded that "even when the income was increased, further obligations, a little exceeding the increase, were incurred." [7]

While we do not have sufficient accurate information on the effects of sudden prosperity, it may be that well-organized families remain organized, and disorganized families may tend to disintegrate further. Whether we agree with the above assumption or not, most of us will agree that any experience holds the potential of being either a destructive crisis experience or a constructive learning experience.

In the interest of reducing the chances of family unhappiness, we need to learn how to meet family crises. Crises involving decreases or sudden increases in family income can disintegrate family life on the one hand or serve as the means of discovering or rediscovering a new and pleasant family relationship. Financial crises cannot be separated from other aspects of life. No problem is met in an isolated group of circumstances, but in relation to the total life of an individual.

The High Cost of Divorce. We are concerned here only with the dollar cost of divorce. This is not to suggest that the psychological, emotional, and personality costs are not as important as the financial price. Since all these aspects are interrelated, no single factor can be recognized as most important.

To the price paid in emotional stress in divorce must be added the dollar cost. Today, when 1 out of every 3.5 marriages ends in divorce, we need to know about some of the lesser known facts of the economic costs of divorce.

Some wit has called desertion a "poor man's divorce." The high dollar cost of divorce works in the other direction at times. Rather than desert, and unable to pay for a divorce, the couple may decide to remain married.

We might as well try to answer: "How high is up?" as to attempt to

[7] Robert G. Foster and Pauline Park Wilson, *Women after College*. New York: Columbia University Press, 1942, p. 52.

give actual money costs of divorce. Every state has different divorce
laws, and lawyers' fees are not standard. There are cut-rate divorces, but
there are dangers involved in these. Sometimes cases are handled dis-
honestly. Consequently, it is difficult to know whether one is legally
divorced. Whatever the costs are, the final money arrangements will
depend on the financial condition of the husband. If considerable money
is spent seeking a divorce, less money is available afterward for the
divorced couple.

Alimony plus support. The heaviest expenses in any divorce are alimony and the sum decreed for the support of children. In 1962 in the
United States, there were nearly 3 million divorcees who received almost
$4 billion in alimony. The following figures give a general picture of how
much a divorce costs in alimony and support of children.

Income per week	Alimony (no children)	Alimony and support (children)
$100	$ 40	$ 55– 60
200	75	100–120
311	105	140–165

The amounts of alimony and support are usually based on the financial
condition of the husband and wife; their earning capacity and property;
the inheritance of either of them; the manner of living to which they are
accustomed; the duration of their marriage; their age, health, and social
position; and which of them is the guilty party and to what extent.

The real crux of how much a husband must pay, at least for the average salaried person, is the time-honored phrase, "the manner of living to
which they are accustomed." The courts generally will not let a wife
improve her standard of living by getting a divorce. Most divorce lawyers
have a form that provides them with fairly concrete proof of the standard of living to which a wife has been accustomed and of the money
needed to support the children.

The ease of divorce in many states is an economic delusion to men
of modest means. Some divorces are necessary, marriage experts say, no
matter what the resultant hardships may be. But the impulsive divorce
is not only a moral mistake but a financial one. Every available possibility for reconciliation should be thoroughly explored.

Emotional cost of divorce. Divorce is never a clean break if children
are involved. Every year, more than 225,000 children are affected by
divorce in this country. If the mother and father fight for custody of the
children, difficulty is inevitable in visiting arrangements.

The dollar costs, as well as emotional upsets, seldom end with the divorce. Young couples should be aware of these facts. It is unwise to assume that your case may be different. There is no such thing as an easy divorce. It costs more than emotional and psychological pain to all concerned and especially to the children. It also costs more money than most people think. There is no such thing as a "bargain divorce."

Spend for What You Really Want. A good budget should be your servant, never your master. The essence of successful money management is to get all the ideas you can from reliable sources but work out your own plan.

The important thing about your spending is the kind of life you are buying with your money and your savings. If you are buying family happiness and long-term security, your money management plan is a good one. If this is not the case, all the members of your family need to sit down together and work out another plan for spending the family income—a plan to fit your family and its income.

Some people spend their lives looking for the ideal place to invest money—where they can earn 5 to 10 per cent or more. Few people realize that wise management of money in their day-to-day living and in their day-to-day purchasing decisions can net some of the best returns available. Each time the family spends nickels, dimes, and dollars, it is investing in a little piece of a way of living. Some find they have made a good investment, while others find they made their investment in such a haphazard, uninformed way that they have really made no gains in their way of life. The biggest investment that a person will ever make is in the way of life he purchases for his family.

QUESTIONS FOR DISCUSSION

1. Why is the spending of money considered an art as well as a science?

2. What importance would you attach to parental attitudes toward money management?

3. What should be the relationship of family goals to money management?

4. What are some of the most difficult problems that many families experience in the handling of money?

5. Jot down your previous conceptions about a family spending plan or budgeting. How do they compare with Madelyn Wood's list given in this chapter?

6. If you were contemplating marriage, how would you go about making a spending plan for the first year of married life?

7. Under what conditions might it be necessary to keep expenditure records for the family?

8. Can you see any dangers for a family with a $5,000 annual income being constantly with a family having a $10,000 income?

9. After considering various methods for handling family spending, which one appeals to you?

10. Do women, as a rule, manage family spending better than men?

11. What are the implications of the remark that a family cannot escape financial crises?

12. How can a family be prepared to meet financial crises?

13. How does a divorce affect the family standard of living?

14. What value is there in studying so-called "model family spending patterns"?

ACTIVITY PROBLEMS

1. Ask several married persons these questions: "Do you have a family budget?" "What is the purpose of a family budget?" Record the answers. How many felt that the purpose of a family budget is to help the family get the greatest satisfaction from the use of its income?

2. Consider what the expressions "good living" and "high standard of living" mean to you. Make a list of the characteristics or ingredients of these two expressions.

3. What goals do you want for your family? Arrange these goals in the order of their importance to you. Which of the goals are short-term and which are long-term? (For ideas, read two short articles in the January, 1950, *Journal of Home Economics*, by Ruth L. Bonde and Howard F. Bigelow, under the general title "Financial Plans in the Family Cycle.")

4. Should housewives be paid a salary? It may sound ridiculous, but ask some of your married friends, male and female. Would a wife be happier washing dishes if she received a salary for doing it? Do men think that "creating a home for the family" is compensation enough?

5. What kind of money manager would you prefer in your own home? A financial dictator? A benevolent despot? A compromiser? A dual manager?

6. Do you agree with the statement: "A carefully planned budget does not ensure a marriage free from money worries"? (See Banning, *Enough to Live on*.)

7. In some of the larger cities, budgeting service is sold for a fee. Try to evaluate these services. What fees do they charge? Who seeks this kind of help? What are some of the techniques for helping a person in financial distress? How successful are they?

8. When financial crises hit a family, there is generally no accustomed response. If possible, check this assumption with people who have had financial crises. How did these families meet the problem? Do you think that these families met their problem successfully? (Read Cavan and Ranck, *The Family and the Depression*.)

9. Observe several families you know who are at various stages of the family life cycle. What do their needs seem to be? How do they seem to spend their money?

10. Read the two articles in the September, 1959, *Ladies' Home Journal*, entitled, "We Have No Children, a Split-level Home and Overspend on $18,000 a Year," and "We Have Five Children, an Old Mansion and Save on $18,000 a Year." What kind of philosophies do these two families have about money? What

were their goals and values? What goals and values does your family have? How are these likely to affect your spending now? How much income will you need before you can save? Is the amount of income the most important factor in whether a family can save?

SUGGESTED READINGS

Angell, Robert C. *The Family Encounters a Depression.* New York: Charles Scribner's Sons, 1936.

Banning, Margaret Culkin. *Enough to Live on.* New York: Harper & Row, Publishers, Incorporated, 1940.

Bonde, Ruth L. *Management in Daily Living.* New York: The Macmillan Company, 1946, pp. 53–74.

Butterfield, Oliver M. *Planning for Marriage.* New York: D. Van Nostrand Company, Inc., 1956, chaps. 2, 8.

Cavan, Ruth S., and Ranck, Katherine H. *The Family and the Depression.* Chicago: The University of Chicago Press, 1938, pp. 6–7, 147–149.

Changing Times. "Money Talk for Newlyweds," June, 1963, pp. 6–17; "Family Budget: Make It New for '63," January, 1963, pp. 7–13; "12 Ways to Wreck a Budget," November, 1960, pp. 23–24; "How Living Costs Vary by Cities," May, 1963, pp. 21–23; "Loans for College," May, 1963, p. 24.

Cohen, Jerome B., and Hanson, Arthur W. *Personal Finance.* Homewood, Ill.: Richard D. Irwin, Inc., 1963, chaps. 1, 2.

Donaldson, Elvin F., and Pfahl, John. *Personal Finance.* New York: The Ronald Press Company, 1961, chap. 2.

Fortune. "Budgeting: Opiate of the Middle Class," May, 1956, p. 133.

Gilbreth, Lillian M., Thomas, Orpha Mae, and Clymer, Eleanor. *Management in the Home.* New York: Dodd, Mead & Company, Inc., 1954, pp. 7–41.

Glick, Paul C., and Miller, Herman P. "Educational Level and Potential Income," *American Sociological Review,* June, 1956, pp. 307–312.

Goodyear, Margaret R., and Klohr, Mildred Chapin. *Managing for Effective Living.* New York: John Wiley & Sons, Inc., 1954, pp. 3–16.

Gordon, Leland J. *Economics for Consumers.* New York: American Book Company, 1961, pp. 305–320.

Hamilton, David. *The Consumer in Our Economy.* Boston: Houghton Mifflin Company, 1962, pp. 103–116.

The Heller Committee for Research in Social Economics. *Quantity and Cost: Budgets for Two Income Levels.* Berkeley, Calif.: University of California Press, 1962.

Hillis, Marjorie. *Orchids on Your Budget.* Indianapolis: The Bobbs-Merrill Company, Inc., 1937.

Household Finance Corporation. *Your Budget,* Chicago, 1962; *Money Management for Young Moderns,* 1963.

Hoyt, Elizabeth E., Reid, Margaret G., McConnell, Joseph L., and Hooks, Janet. *American Income and Its Use.* New York: Harper & Row, Publishers, Incorporated, 1954, pp. 65–77, 178–198.

Institute of Life Insurance. "Young Couples Make Money Work," 1961.

Kidd, Bj. *Women Never Go Broke.* Philadelphia: J. B. Lippincott Company, 1948, pp. 49–62.

Komarovsky, Mirra. *The Unemployed Man and His Family: The Effect of Unemployment upon the Status of the Man in Fifty-nine Families.* New York: The Dryden Press, Inc., 1940, p. 163.

Koos, Earl L. *Families in Trouble.* New York: King's Crown Press, 1946, p. 139.

Lasser, J. K., and Porter, Sylvia F. *Managing Your Money.* New York: Holt, Rinehart and Winston, Inc., 1961, pp. 3–54.

Morgan, James, Martin, H. David, Cohen, Wilber J., and Brazer, Harvey E. *Income and Welfare in the United States.* New York: McGraw-Hill Book Company, 1962, chap. 23.

National Consumer Finance Association. *Slide Rule: Divided Responsibility Family Budget Plan,* Washington, D.C., 1961.

Phillips, E. Bryant. *Consumer Economic Problems.* New York: Holt, Rinehart and Winston, Inc., 1957, pp. 39–54.

This Week Magazine. "You Can't Afford a Divorce," Oct. 17, 1954, p. 7.

U.S. Department of Agriculture. *Farm and Home Financial Planning: Guiding Family Spending,* Miscellaneous publication 661.

Weeks, H. A. *Family Spending Patterns and Health Care.* Cambridge, Mass.: Harvard University Press, 1961.

3

MONEY AND MARITAL HAPPINESS

Spending money may be America's favorite sport, but marriage is our favorite institution. Ninety per cent of our population marries. Why do so many marry? Ask the average married couple, and they will probably answer, "We love each other." Just as simple as that.

Most of these couples believed that they could have a happy and successful marriage. But love alone is not enough, apparently. More and more marriages end in divorce. Prior to World War II, there was 1 divorce to every 5 marriages in this country. In 1963, there was about 1 divorce to every 3.5 marriages. And we ask, "Why?" What happens to all these marriages that begin with such high hope?

Changing Times and Customs. Customs are changing so fast that each generation lives in a world of its own, known only in part to the one that precedes it or the one that follows. Home as grandmother knew it does not exist. It can never return. We have a kind of family life that is quite different from grandmother's family. Of course, we cannot and should not cut ourselves off from our roots. There are certain basic family needs that can be served well by the application of grandmother's philosophy. But the differences between the generations are great. We need, desperately, to understand these differences and then do something about them to help young couples to "live happily ever after."

In 1890, about 65 per cent of American families lived in the rural areas. In 1961, 92 per cent were living in cities.[1] Grandmother never went far from home. She was almost constantly under neighborly surveillance. City young people are free from external and neighborly controls within 10 minutes from the time they leave the house or apartment. They are on their own. Their standards, on the whole, come from within them-

[1] *Agricultural Chartbook Outlook,* Agricultural Research Service, U.S. Department of Agriculture, 1963, p. 23.

selves. At first, these standards are usually set by the home. Soon they find that many of the home standards are in conflict with other standards. What was "right" at one time becomes relative to the time, the place, and the people. And this experience is likely to be confusing.

Challenging Choices. In 1870, there were only about 338 vocations. Today, as a result of industrialization, there are from 30,000 to 35,000 vocations. A son no longer has to follow in his father's footsteps. A daughter can have a career in the business and professional world. She can work or not, as she pleases. She does not need to marry for her "board and keep."

The automobile, too, has changed our recreational experiences tremendously. Cars and good roads have revolutionized personal activities. The choices are numerous and confusing. The problems of wise choice about where to go, what to do, how much to spend, and what to be are always present. From this array of new experiences, and many not mentioned here, you must select those that are to be your way of life. The choices made now will be, in large measure, the blueprint for marriage later.

We use money and spend it as our parents and grandparents probably never dreamed of using and spending it. We live in a money world. We depend on money for food, clothing, shelter, recreation, and education. We even depend on money alone to take care of us when we are old, rather than the family farm or a family business.

We run much of our lives on a cash basis, and therefore feel the pressures of money. And money troubles may be a cause of worry. Money can set up a host of problems. Sometimes there are tragic disagreements in a family about how money is to be used. And at times money may become a symbol of other disagreements and problems. If a member of a family hungers for an argument, he can always argue about money. Can it be that we are confused about the right values and goals for a happy family life?

The Confused American Family. Why are American families the richest in the world and yet so often in debt and unhappy? First, we should be careful to avoid false and antisocial answers to the question of why American families are increasingly getting into debt. We need to consider the possibility that the real answer may be that many families are very confused about what standard of living they ought to have. Second, we should recognize that this confusion is not only the fault of the borrower. The confusion is probably the result of tremendous changes taking place in our society. The third idea is that American society is certainly going to keep on changing. And with change, we are likely to witness the rise of new standards and morals about borrowing and saving money. And some of us are going to disagree with the new standards.

It may be alarming to read about the $66 billion short-term consumer credit debt in 1963. Some people believe that most consumers are so deeply in debt that they cannot possibly get out. In fact, they have been saying that for decades. Yet somehow most debtors manage to liquidate their debts.

There must be a limit to debts, but the basic problem may not be whether or not the debts will be liquidated. They continue to be liquidated right along. The real problem is: "Why has it become so common for families to have such worries and guilt feelings about their debts?" The answers to this question are important because they are related to money and marital conflicts.

Many of us are familiar with the guilty suspicion that our neighbors are having less difficulty in paying their bills than we are having. Actually, this may not be true. In a study A. D. Spectorsky made of residents in the wealthier suburbs of New York City, where men were earning from $12,000 to $30,000 a year, he found that the average family was spending about 40 per cent more than its annual income. He also found that every Tom or Harry in the community believed that he was the only man who had to borrow $500 to buy a hi-fi set, while his neighbor, Dick, could afford to go to Bermuda. Dick felt guilty about owing $500 for his "fly now, pay later" Bermuda vacation, when his neighbor, Tom, could afford an expensive hi-fi set.

Tom and Dick illustrate a lot of boring statistics. Most families know that it has become quite common among American families, except the poorest and the richest, to owe enough money to feel anxious and guilty.

Individual worries are not the only problems resulting from the high consumer debt. Some economists mention it as a factor in the instability of our economy. And some sociologists have mentioned it as a factor in social disorganization. Psychiatrists mention it as a factor in the climbing rate of mental illness.

Willingness to Incur Debts. So the fact that relatively well-off families are becoming more and more willing to incur debts is an important change in our society. One of the consequences of this change, especially for "young marrieds" and "growing families," is that this system is promoting debt as a way of life. In other words, more families want more immediate possessions than they can afford on a cash basis, and consumer credit is made to order for them.

Why has an increasingly large number of families changed from paying cash to assuming debts? There are many answers, but most of them appear to be unsatisfactory.

The first theory is found in most consumer-economics textbooks and in the Federal Reserve Board's excellent six-volume study of consumer credit. This answer says that people always have wanted more things than they could afford at a given time and that consumer credit was a natural evolution of merchandising methods to satisfy these wants. People used to buy laundry service from a man who owned a laundry, and transportation from a man who owned a livery stable, but nowadays they buy their own washer-dryer, their own automobile, and their own TV set. They can do this because they can get credit to buy these and many other expensive possessions immediately.

All this is true, but it is not the complete answer. People have always wanted more than they had, but Noah could not have paid for the Ark on the installment plan because such plans did not exist then. Credit is so much a natural evolution of distribution methods that you cannot help but wonder why it almost never existed until the twentieth century.

Part of the answer is simple. Throughout most of history, borrowing and lending at interest had been considered immoral and had been strictly taboo. The lender was usually considered a parasite and often a criminal. The borrower was usually considered improvident and even a sinner.

What Happened to Traditional Morals? What changed such morals? Can it be that more people use more credit nowadays because they are economically more rational? The danger of this answer or theory is that it assumes the borrower is not confused by moral traditions and is acting by some kind of new, sensible standard. But the credit manager who assumes that every loan applicant knows what he is doing is asking for trouble.

The other two kinds of inadequate theory offer an answer to what happened to traditional morals, which is that people are becoming more immoral. There are the "naïve moralists" who blame high debt levels on immoral individuals, and the "sophisticated moralists" who blame it on a bad system that forces people into debt. The naïve moralists are people like John Keats, who says that immoral people are imitating the government's philosophy of deficit spending, and that we are becoming a nation of immature people who like to open Christmas presents the week before Thanksgiving. Or they are men like William Whyte, the sociologist, who says borrowers are immoral because of a contagious social-psychological neurosis called "budgetism"; or Eugene Barnes, a psychologist who believes that people have no "credit conscience."

But how can these explanations explain enough, especially when we consider that year after year the same percentage of different income classes have personal debts. About one-third of factory-worker families are in debt; about one-half of white-collar workers are in debt even though their average income is higher than the self-employed. It seems a strange thing when the same percentage of individuals decides to be "immoral" as concerns debt year after year in the different groups of our society. It is a little like criminals. Criminals have been considered immoral, and society has generally worked on them as individuals to mend their ways. But when society realized that slums turn out high percentages of criminals, a study of the effects of their environment began. We still don't know all that causes criminals, but at least society no longer believes that they are merely immoral individuals.

Involvement of the Social System. In much the same way that slums help produce criminals, white-collar jobs help produce debtors. More white-collar workers have debts than self-employed people, whether the income of the self-employed is higher, lower, or the same. It would seem, therefore, that the social system is involved in some way.

The sophisticated moralists recognize this fact. The naïve moralists still insist that borrowers are basically immoral, but they blame the system for making them that way. John McPartland, the novelist, blames the "easy credit system" for tempting him. A. C. Spectorsky, the sociologist who conducted the study in the wealthy New York City suburbs, blames the "status" system. John Galbraith, the economist, blames the whole economic system for just plain overselling of consumer goods.

All these suggestions are part of an adequate explanation. Perhaps they explain too much. The systems they mention do exert constant pressure. But they do not explain why, year after year, one-third of blue-collar workers do not have debts, nor do two-thirds of the self-employed, nor one-half of the white-collar workers.

Besides, history shows that it is best to be suspicious of every generation that says that the younger generation is becoming more and more immoral. As often as not it has turned out that the morals were changing, and that often the new morals were better for their times.

We have to remember that before social morals were established, it was all right for a man to knock any other man over the head and drag away his property and his woman. Most husbands are grateful for the change in morals since that time.

Basic personal morals like the Ten Commandments remain generally unchanged. But specific little morals, in areas like economic and political behavior, change with the times. Economic behavior that produced the Robber Barons of two generations ago and was admired or at least accepted at the time would now be immoral and illegal.

Are Credit Users Immoral? It seems that when a set of morals becomes obsolete, and when there is no workable set of standards to replace the old ones, people become confused and begin experimenting until a suitable set of new morals is developed and accepted. Perhaps the rapid expansion of consumer credit represents that kind of experimenting, caused by that kind of confusion.

Let's consider the confusion that might make the former morals regarding thrift and debt become obsolete. In our early economy, capital had to be created largely by thrifty acts of individuals. Therefore, the virtue attributed to thrift, along with the moral taboo on using credit for consumer goods, was essential in causing a rapid rate of economic growth.

Thrift also had important motives for the individual. Before 1900, success came along usually with the "expansible possession"—that is, a little farm or a little shop or business that required only constant thrift to gain enough capital to become a big estate or a big factory or business.

But things have changed for the economic system and the individual. It appears at present that the economic system can form capital more easily than it can maintain purchasing power. And the individual does not as often find success with the expansible possession. Instead, he pins his hopes on the forward-looking job. To make the most of a job or position, thrift is not of much help. What is needed is a standard of living that will show that the family appreciate and want better things—even if they have to borrow to buy them.

So it seems that for both the economic system and the individual times have changed, and it makes more sense to attach moral virtue to spending than to thrift.

This is by no means a full explanation of the eagerness for credit. Perhaps social change could have removed the moral restrictions on credit without its resulting in a $58.5 billion consumer debt if American families were not so eager to borrow. Perhaps this eagerness may be the result, not of confusion about changing morals, but confusion about standards of living.

Desire for Change in Standard of Living. Your *level* of living is based on the amount of money you spend. Your *standard* of living is the way you want to live. One man's standard may require a shack by the seashore, one good suit, and regular meals. Another man's standard may require a trilevel home, two cars, and a yardman.

Where do these standards come from? Through most of human history, they simply became a part of a people during the process of their growing up in families. Chances are that most of us came from a middle-class family. Chances are that a majority had grandfathers or even fathers who were farmers, immigrants, or factory workers with less education than their children. The point is that each generation could not live according to the standards of the preceding generation because each grew up in a different environment. And millions of American families have been experiencing this environmental change.

In a situation where every generation is living in a different kind of world from the preceding one, of what use are many of the living standards of grandfathers or even fathers? Each generation has to experiment with new standards. We are generally guided by our own ambitions and by the standards of friends—the Joneses who have debts we don't know about. Or maybe we are guided by the mass media—TV, motion pictures, magazines. If, under these circumstances, the average American family were not confused about an approximate standard of living, you would have something really difficult to explain.

The growth of consumer credit, then, may not be so much a matter of immorality as a consequence of confusion, and this confusion may be rooted in actual moral social change, not in bad psychology.

Near the beginning of this century, credit institutions and others helped make it respectable for people to admit that they needed to borrow in emergencies. At midcentury, it was standard practice for young married couples to place heavy mortgages on their future earnings in order to start out with a standard packet of durable goods when they needed them most. This packet might now include a stove, refrigerator, washing machine, dishwasher, a car, a television set, and a record player. By the end of the century, who knows? A family-size airplane, clothes that you toss into the ashcan after a few weeks' use—well, you guess!

The trend will likely be more use of "buy now, pay later," until we move out of the form of credit that has induced ownership, and move into a system of less ownership, but more continuous renting of needed goods and services. If this happens, credit will have a different meaning. In the future, it is not unlikely that various social insurances will reduce the frequency of emergency loans, that expensive revolving credit plans and credit-card schemes will be outgrown, and there may be enough mature voting citizens to insist that consumer credit contracts reveal *all* the costs of credit in a common language easily understandable by all people.

And perhaps we ought to do our part to eliminate the obsolete feelings of worry and guilt that keep people from talking about their use of credit. Too many people are like the man who went to the psychiatrist because he worried all the time. The doctor asked how he lived, and he listed numerous expensive habits. The doctor said, "This is wonderful, why worry?" The client said he was making only $5,000 a year. The psychiatrist answered, "My friend, you're not sick. You're simply overextended and overconfused."

Education Neglects Our Needs. Most families perform their functions well when they have learned how. Grandmother's family, for example, taught children the kind of responsibilities they needed in their time. It was really an apprenticeship. And apparently they did a pretty good job as long as the family functions remained the same. But when the family functions changed, this system broke down. Something else was obviously needed.

The modern family has a real job in building personalities capable of adequately meeting the complexities of modern life. Understanding a child today is quite different and considerably more complicated or involved than it was years ago. Apprenticeship will no longer do the trick. Customs change too rapidly. We need families that can grow in their ability to live together happily and successfully. Divorce and separation statistics and other evidence of marital discord indicate that something is out of gear somewhere. What are the causes for modern marital unhappiness?

Conflict in Marriage. Marriage experts, in general, agree that some conflict is inevitable. Some conflict is open quarreling. Then there may be what William Graham Sumner termed "antagonistic cooperation." This kind of conflict may be more subtle. Some couples learn to live with such problems. It would seem, then, that the attitude taken toward a disagreement is significant in working out a satisfactory solution.

What causes marital conflict? Marriage counselors are not absolutely certain about the basic causes for conflict. As tensions develop in a family, any incident may spark the disagreement. The incident may not actually be the real cause for the conflict. Thus what seems to be the cause may not be so at all. An analysis of the major causes of conflict as reported by married couples may give us some tips for successful marriage.

The *Ladies' Home Journal* asked representative American women the question: "What things have you noticed husbands and wives quarrel about most frequently?" The reasons were given in this order: money, jealousy, rearing of children, little things, drinking, and in-laws.

Clifford Adams, Penn State psychologist, reported the testimony from one thousand married couples.[2] He selected the replies from one hundred of the most unhappy marriages. The following reasons for marriage conflict are in the order of their frequency: lack of companionship, lack of money, sex, in-laws, housework, children, social life, personal traits, lack of affection, and religious differences.

Judson T. Landis, professor of sociology at the University of California, received information from 409 couples, married an average of 20 years, who were parents or friends of students taking the marriage course at Michigan State College.[3] This group was above average in income and education. Most of the husbands and wives agreed that it had

[2] *Ladies' Home Journal,* January, 1949, p. 26. Reprinted with special permission. Copyright 1949. The Curtis Publishing Company.

[3] Associated Press report, May 29, 1948.

taken longer to achieve sex adjustment than adjustment in any other area. The second most difficult adjustment was in reaching an agreement on how to spend the family income. For some of them, it took an average of seven years to end disagreement. About 10 per cent were still quarreling over money problems. Other causes for conflict included quarreling over social and recreational activities, in-laws, religion, and mutual friends.

Effectiveness of College Education on Marital Conflict. C. Robert Pace reported on a study of 951 former University of Minnesota students between the ages of 25 and 34. Half were men, half were women; half had graduated, and half had left college after one to three years. The questionnaire aimed to probe the effectiveness of a modern college education. The results, shown in the accompanying table, Effectiveness of College Education, throw light on the inadequacy of family relations education.

EFFECTIVENESS OF COLLEGE EDUCATION

	Percentage of husbands who frequently disagreed	Percentage of wives who frequently disagreed
Management of income	17	19
Religion	10	7
Politics	11	14
Relatives	16	20
Entertainment of relatives	7	9
Choice of friends	10	9
Ideals of conduct	9	10
Philosophy of life	12	12
Recreations	16	14
Entertainment of friends	7	9

SOURCE: C. Robert Pace, *They Went to College*. Minneapolis: The University of Minnesota Press, 1941, p. 82. Reprinted with permission.

Disagreements occurred most frequently over the management of money. This is an interesting sidelight, because money management is the most frequent cause of conflict among couples in the upper third or fourth of the nation's families according to economic status. Pace says that "bringing together evidence from all parts of the study relating to income management leads to the generalization that, although many of the young adults expressed a desire for more information about ways to economize, many were also engaging in uneconomical practices."

A brief analysis of the discrepancies and inconsistencies between attitudes and practices among this group is most revealing. In spite of relatively high incomes, most of them were dissatisfied with their incomes. While they said that they had good food, were well dressed, comfortable, and happy on their present incomes, nevertheless 35 per cent of them found it difficult to keep out of debt. Over 40 per cent expressed the need for money management information, yet less than half had a family spending plan. Furthermore, their marketing habits were needlessly expensive. About one-fourth had medical indebtedness, yet less than one-fifth of these took advantage of health insurance plans. With such discrepancies between feelings and practices, it is not difficult to understand why income mismanagement was a frequent source of conflict between these husbands and wives.

The case studies of about 100 college graduates from coast to coast (78 of whom were married) by the Merrill-Palmer School in Detroit throws further light on the nature of marital conflicts. The accompanying table, Percentage of Problems of 78 Married Women, shows that the chief cause for marital difficulties was the conflict over finances. More specifically, these conflicts were over (1) how the money was to be spent, and (2) who was to make the decision. Most of the women had taken a course in economics in college. Yet there seemed to be little or no carry-over from such a course into the everyday problems of money management. When the counselors mentioned budgeting, nearly all the women resisted the idea as a device of Satan designed to restrict their spending habits. Nor did the size of income alter the general complaint that they could not make ends meet.

PERCENTAGE OF PROBLEMS OF 78 MARRIED WOMEN

Type of problem	Per cent of cases
Personality	98
Financial	97
Health	96
Husband-wife	89
Relations with associates	88
Recreational	84
Housekeeping	82
Relations with relatives	80
Parent-child	78
Crisis	74
In-law	60
Sex	56
Religion	52
Vocation	34
Education	20

SOURCE: Reproduced from Robert G. Foster and Pauline Park Wilson, *Women after College.* Copyright 1942 by Columbia University Press, p. 27.

These women had almost entirely ignored the evident need to be prepared to meet certain inevitabilities in their lives—to be intelligent, effective, conscientious consumers. Most of them had prepared for a job, but neither college nor home had prepared them for the time when they would give up a job and manage a home.

It is strange that, although many college women expect to marry and have a home and children, few really prepare for this important function. Fewer yet do any mature thinking on combining homemaking and a career. Too many do not look on homemaking as a career for which they have to fit themselves. This fact goes a long way toward solving many of the problems that puzzle social economists and moralists. For it is at the bottom of much of the discontent that permeates many homes.

Problem of Human Relations. Money management may be the primary cause for marital discord. Behind the problems of money management, however, and all the other so-called "big" causes are the hard-to-analyze human behavior relationships. Whether the area of conflict concerns money or sex, characteristic and basic behavior patterns are revealed in subtle and, at times, unconscious ways. Along with each outward act go certain feelings and attitudes that are impossible or difficult to see.

In some cases, two persons will react differently to the same general problem. For example, a certain husband battled continuously with his wife over her "extravagant spending." Another husband's reaction to his wife's extravagant spending was: "I'll just prove to her that I can make more money than she can spend." The attitude toward the same general situation was quite different. Open conflict resulted in the one case, and an acceptance of the situation in the other.

It would seem logical to conclude that we need to discover the personality traits that lead married people to quarrel over money, sex, or any of the other "big" causes for family disagreements.

Psychologists tell us that the relationship between husband and wife is loaded with disguised impulses. And sometimes the least important part is what we see. Yet what we see and hear are extremely important, because they may be the advance signs—a symptom of what cannot be seen. A timely recognition of the symptom may give the clue that will lead to the solving of the difficulty.

Income versus Success and Happiness. In New York, a well-dressed woman called on a personal finance adviser at her bank. She said that, despite her husband's income of $18,000 a year, they had no money for fun. A Hollywood actor with an income of $100,000 a year went bankrupt. He had only $3,000 in assets to meet liabilities of $50,000.

The assumption of certain economists that most personal problems would be solved if the income of each couple could be raised sufficiently is not borne out by some studies of marital adjustment. In the case studies of 78 married women, the Merrill-Palmer School clinicians found that regardless of their incomes—whether they had $3,000, $5,000, or $10,000 —they felt that it was insufficient.[4] In fact, as income increased in arithmetical ratio, personal problems seemed to increase in geometric ratio.

Somewhat in contrast, Cottrell's study of 526 couples found that families on moderate income seemed to have made better adjustments than when incomes were either high or low.[5] Hamilton, in studying 200 persons —50 husbands with incomes over $5,000, and another 50 husbands whose incomes were less—found happiness approximately equally distributed.[6] Terman found little relationship between happiness and income.[7]

Robert C. Williamson reported that economic variables are more important in marital adjustment than has been generally observed in previous investigations.[8] A total of 210 couples, representing a cross section of the Los Angeles white population, were interviewed in their homes by two interviewers. The husband and the wife were interviewed separately with a questionnaire that contained personal background and social and economic items, as well as a marital-adjustment test. On the scores secured in the adjustment test, the sample was divided into happily and unhappily married groups. The happy group totaled 86 men and 85 women; the unhappy group, 66 men and 62 women. There was an intermediate small group that could be considered neither happy nor unhappy. Some of the important economic variables in marital adjustment were these:

1. Lower incomes (below $436 a month) prevailed among the unhappy group. Conversely, higher incomes were found among happy husbands and wives.
2. Both the men and the women in the poor residential area were maritally less happy than those in the better areas.
3. It was found that for both partners there was a higher percentage of happy marriages among those having savings of at least $600.
4. The husbands who had no debts, or less than $300 in debts, were significantly happier than those who had $300 or more in debts.
5. The highest proportion of happy husbands and a still higher proportion of

[4] Robert G. Foster and Pauline Park Wilson, *Women after College*. New York: Columbia University Press, 1942, p. 51.

[5] Ernest W. Burgess and Leonard S. Cottrell, *Predicting Success or Failure in Marriage*. Englewood Cliffs, N.J.: Prentice-Hall, Inc., 1939, pp. 152–153.

[6] G. V. Hamilton, *A Research in Marriage*. New York: Albert & Charles Boni, Inc., 1929, p. 97.

[7] Lewis M. Terman, *Psychological Factors in Marital Happiness*. New York: McGraw-Hill Book Company, 1938, pp. 169–171.

[8] Robert C. Williamson, "Economic Factors in Marital Adjustment," *Marriage and Family Living*, November, 1952.

happy wives were among the highest security ratings (insurance, savings, debts, and type and regularity of employment).

6. There was no significant difference between the happy and unhappy groups in the matter of keeping budgeting records.

7. There was a significant difference favoring successful adjustment among those who did not overspend more than two months per year.

8. There was a significantly higher percentage of maladjustment among those who admitted having to borrow three or more times during the past 5 years than among those who borrowed less or not at all.

Economic Factors in Marital Adjustment. Frances Lomas Feldman, who directed the research of the Money Management Project of the Welfare Planning Council of the Los Angeles Region, made these interesting observations of the feelings of people about money.

The world we live in is characterized by continual change. There are technological advances, increasing population with shifting urbanization and explosive suburbanization movements, economic depressions and recessions, wars, and changing fashions and standards of living. One pivotal factor, however, remains constantly important: money. But never before in the history of western civilization has the word "money" meant so much to so many. Money is the medium of exchange, a means for distributing the vast and increasing outpouring of the goods and services of our economic system. Money is a symbol of status and achievement, often the measure for human values and dignity. This is truly the age of the economic man.

Economists have tended to view money as having an objective reality, a life of its own, isolated from the emotional and intellectual life of the human beings whom it was designed to serve. They have applied complicated mechanistic concepts, frequently expressed in elaborate mathematical formulas, to describe objectively the flow and use of money. Recently, however, there has been a mounting awareness and emphasis on the importance of the so-called subjective aspects of money, on the unique significance of psychosocial influences. There is increasing cognizance that an essential ingredient in skillful working with people is the understanding of the objective and subjective influences which affect, and are the effect of, money—the understanding of the dynamics of the interactions in the socioeconomic and cultural climate in which the individual grows and develops.

The universality of money as a causative or symptomatic component in a strikingly high proportion of the problems and preoccupations of human beings in our culture is evidenced almost daily in the headlined stories in the public press. One reads about the distraught husband who kills his wife because of "arguments over finances," about the parent who solves his inability to provide for his children by ending their lives or by armed robbery. One reads about the divorce suit in which "stinginess" is offered as one justification for the action, or about the divorced wife petitioning for increased child support from the ex-spouse who has remarried and has another family to support.

The ironic humor of the many current cartoons with a money theme provides another barometer of the feelings of people in our society about money.[9]

Financial columnist Sylvia Porter in 1962 quoted top jurists as saying: "Quarreling about money is a major reason for America's unprecedented divorce rate. It is difficult to overestimate the vicious part financial trouble is playing in destroying the American home."

There are other, unexpected areas where failure to manage money properly can produce dire results. More and more personnel officers are asking applicants direct questions about how they handle their family income.

Couples seeking to adopt children through reputable agencies also must account for the disposition of their income. One adoptive case worker said: "Young couples—both employed and with joint incomes of from $12,000 to $14,000—come in here and tell us they have assets of no more than $200 or $300. Before we will even consider their application, we ask them to demonstrate to us that they can change their values. We give them a year to do it."

From these studies and surveys it is evident that economic variables are more important in marital adjustment than has been generally recognized. The chain of cause and effect, however, is very complex in marital adjustment. The relationship that exists, for example, between savings and a happy marriage may be due in part to education or high intelligence. Or the negative relationship of loss of income to marital happiness may be a reflection of some other factor, such as illness. All this adds up to the fact that economic factors have never received sufficient attention in the studies of marital relations.

Attitudes toward Spending Money. Happy working partnerships of husband and wife are not common. They are difficult to achieve, largely because of the complicated attitudes of both husband and wife toward money and work. Contemporary society is regrettably money-conscious. Too often, a husband is judged, not by how fine a father he is, but by how good a provider he is.

If money stands for success and perhaps authority, the manipulation of the family income and spending takes on emotional relationships. These relations may be handled satisfactorily or disastrously, depending on the attitudes of husband and wife. A husband might ask his wife to come to him for every little expenditure. He may be led to feel that he is not a good provider. This feeling can easily creep into ordinary discussions. Can we afford a new car? Can we go away for the summer? Each of these questions may be interpreted as an attack on the husband's ability to provide adequate income. On the other hand, such things need

[9] *Journal of Home Economics,* December, 1957, p. 267.

not be turned in the direction of conflict if the attitude itself is proper.

Money matters, however, cannot always be handled rationally. Psychological attitudes toward spending money are as real as the money itself. One family may agree, for example, to spend one-fourth of their income on clothes. "And why not?" they say. "We get more fun out of planning and wearing new clothes than we do in seeing a dozen shows. We live within our income, and we like it this way." This attitude apparently is right for them. On the other hand, such disproportionate spending of money on clothes could be a focal point for a serious quarrel in another family.

"Living Up to the Joneses." Spending more money than your neighbors is not necessarily dangerous to family happiness. But "living up to the Joneses" is potential dynamite, because such a mental attitude leads to the strain of living beyond one's means. When John found that his promising insurance business could not provide for everything that Jane and he wanted, he gave it up to enter his father-in-law's business. Soon John became so resentful over his lack of vocational independence and his wife's extravagance that divorce was the result. John returned to his first love, insurance, and later married a girl whose charge accounts were in harmony with their income.

Helen, a society girl, married Dick, whose wholesale vinegar business went bankrupt two years after their marriage. Helen's friends were sure she was headed for divorce. Instead, Helen mastered typing and shorthand, and pitched in as her husband's secretary. Several years later, their business was flourishing. A woman who marries with the expectation of mink is likely to prove an unhappy partner if she finds herself wrapped in rabbit—unless she does something about her attitude.

Foster and Wilson, in reporting on the case studies at the Merrill-Palmer School, concluded that the economic position of her associates may accentuate many of the individual's attitudes about her own position.[10] They report that among a few of the women of the study who belonged to the same sorority there were wide differences in income. One woman, who had the lowest family income and was unable to dress and entertain as elaborately as the others, accepted the situation, participated actively in the group, and took life in her stride. In this same set was a woman whose income was several times as great. But she constantly complained about her clothes, her home, and so on. She felt that her income was insufficient.

Attitudes toward housekeeping problems are important, too. Dislike for household tasks, lack of skill, and difficulties with household help are

[10] Foster and Wilson, *op. cit.*, p. 51.

usually the foremost problems in this area.[11] These dislikes and diffi-culties are important because they are related to family happiness and success. Some women manage these tasks well and are able to use artistic and creative ability in many of the household duties. The new household aids might help to solve some of these problems. But modern appliances will not of themselves alter attitudes toward household duties.

Too High a Financial Goal. There is the danger, too, of setting the money goal too high. The young husband who is determined to make a million dollars before he reaches the ripe old age of 35 years is a menace to himself and his family. Edward was such a person.[12] Most of his friends and business associates thought he was a hard worker and never knew a day of worry in his life. He worked long and hard and seemed to thrive on it. Soon he had the highest salary in his office. Still he was not satisfied. A little success spurred him on to greater effort. He began to spend money lavishly, bought a large house, and put money in risky investments. He became so excited that he neither slept nor ate well.

Then Edward began to change. He lost his feeling of self-confidence. He was no longer so sure of his business judgment. He often stayed away from his office. He told his wife that he would soon lose his job and began to blame himself for ruining his family.

Most psychologists would call Edward's difficulty a "manic-depressive" illness. Manic-depressives become so when they are not attaining the goals they have set for themselves. Most of them are ambitious. They are overly anxious to achieve financial and social success. When they fall short, conflict results. Psychologists say that this kind of worry or moodi-ness is dangerous. Many of these people are potential suicides. Too high a financial goal is no solution to family happiness and success.

Money Isn't Everything. Money is not only dollars and cents. It is a sym-bol of personal attitudes toward marriage and life. The first essential is to acquire financial attitudes that will harmonize with what you and your family want out of life. It is not the amount of money but the way it is spent that counts.

Some families have a savings complex. The attitude of excessive sav-ings in proportion to income can lead to unhappiness. Generally, each blames the other for spending too much money. These people usually do not realize that they are living so completely in the future that they cannot find happiness in their day-to-day living. Perhaps this spending complex is related to what some psychologists refer to as "compulsive spending," which is merely an attempt to answer some other need.

[11] *Ibid.,* pp. 48–50.
[12] George Thorman, *Toward Mental Health.* New York: Public Affairs Committee, 1946, pp. 7–9.

Women in the Labor Force. You are probably mulling over the question of job plus home and family. This question deserves your attention. For the fact is that about three-fifths of the women in the nation's labor force are married. An increasing proportion of married women augment the family income by employment; in 1961, 61 per cent of the women in the labor force were married, compared with 52 per cent in 1950, as shown in the accompanying chart. Although employed wives contribute substantially to the income of their families, by no means all of the wife's gross earnings are available for family living.

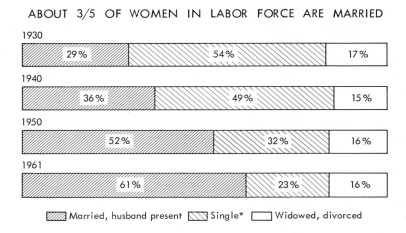

ABOUT 3/5 OF WOMEN IN LABOR FORCE ARE MARRIED

1930

| 29% | 54% | 17% |

1940

| 36% | 49% | 15% |

1950

| 52% | 32% | 16% |

1961

| 61% | 23% | 16% |

▨ Married, husband present   ◫ Single*   ☐ Widowed, divorced

* 1930 data include unknown marital status.   Census and Bls. data.

U. S. Department of Agriculture   Neg. 62 (8)–5703 Agriculture Research Service

SOURCE: *Agricultural Chartbook Outlook,* **Agricultural Research Service, U.S. Depart-ment of Agriculture, 1963, p. 90.**

Studies by the U.S. Department of Agriculture indicate that about 40 per cent of the average employed wife's gross earnings are required for job-related expenditures, including higher family income taxes occasioned by her earnings. Job-related expenses are closely associated with family income and family type. For employed women with children under 6 years of age, payments for child care frequently are an important job-related expenditure. In March, 1961, 46 per cent of the wives under 35 years of age had children under 6 years of age, as shown in the accompanying chart, Many Working Wives Have Young Children.

Does the Family Need a Second Income? Many articles on the contemporary woman's choice of roles oppose homemaking to job holding, implying that women must choose between the two. Other articles suggest a series of roles, employment immediately after marriage, followed by childbearing and rearing, and a return to employment after the children reach the age of remaining in school all day. In the latter role, it is conceivable that a woman may work at a job for 30 to 35 years after marriage.

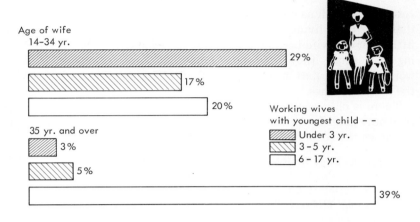

MANY WORKING WIVES HAVE YOUNG CHILDREN

Age of wife
14-34 yr.

29%

17%

20%

Working wives
with youngest child - -

35 yr. and over

3%

Under 3 yr.
3 - 5 yr.
6 - 17 yr.

5%

39%

Bls. data   *Wives (husband present) in the labor force, March 1961.

U. S. Department of Agriculture   Neg. 62 (8)-5702 Agricultural Research Service

SOURCE: *Agricultural Chartbook Outlook,* Agricultural Research Service, U.S. Department of Agriculture, 1963, p. 90.

Dr. Mary Bunting, president of Radcliffe College, said, "I am convinced the road that lies ahead for women is a dual one of motherhood and career. It will not only be possible but almost mandatory to do both if you want to do either well." [13]

Most authorities agree that before a family decides that financial problems can be solved by a working wife, the following questions should be discussed.

1. Will the wife's salary add enough extra dollars to the family income?
2. Can a suitable schedule be arranged?
3. Is the wife qualified for the job she seeks?
4. Will the family suffer emotionally?
5. Will a second income really solve the family problems?

[13] *Life,* Jan. 13, 1961.

Clothes and related items that cost money are likely to consume a greater share of the family income since the wife must appear well dressed on a job. Furthermore, a working wife cannot devote sufficient time to effect economies in buying and in preparing food. More meals are eaten away from home. The more expensive prepared foods are purchased.

A young couple should estimate how much could be saved if the wife did the marketing, cooked the meals, and managed the home personally, possibly decreasing family costs by one-third, and health and recreation costs by as much as one-half. One couple, keeping cost records, discovered that the "total living expenses (exclusive of savings) decreased by one-fifth after the wife became a full-time homemaker." [14] If the wife's earnings are small, they may not compensate for the added expense of working. There may also be psychological compensations that outweigh the economic ones.

There is only one sure way to get your own answer to the question of economic gain. Keep a record of expenses for at least one normal month. Jot down the costs for:

1. Lunches away from home. (Noon lunches need not be costly.)
2. Extra cost of food. (More evening meals will be eaten at restaurants.)
3. Transportation costs to and from work.
4. Clothing. (Upkeep costs are higher; larger supply is necessary; more expensive, perhaps.)
5. Additional beauty parlor care.
6. Increased laundry costs.
7. Full-time or part-time maid service.

Other Reasons Wives Work for Pay. It is more difficult to evaluate the noneconomic motivations for wives and mothers to work. According to the National Manpower Council report, desire for more income may symbolize independence, power, defense against financial tyranny of the husband, neurotic needs, boredom, distaste for housework, uncongenial neighbors, loneliness, unrewarding community activities, desire for more conveniences or luxuries, better use of leisure time, self-fulfillment of talents, meeting new people, being accepted, real interest in a job, or real ability to organize home life while working outside the home.

This does not mean that most of the women in the labor force no longer find significant satisfaction in their homemaking activities and in the rearing of children. The major point is that married women can have vastly more free time than was possible a generation ago, and those who have time are increasingly motivated to put it to constructive use.[15]

[14] *Money Management for Newlyweds.* Chicago: Household Finance Corporation, p. 9.

[15] See *Womanpower,* by the National Manpower Council. New York: Columbia University Press, 1957, pp. 5–16; *Work in the Lives of Married Women,* by the National Manpower Council. New York: Columbia University Press, 1958, pp. 111–114.

What has happened is that a whole complex of developments has produced new options for married women that were not present previously. It is useless to deplore the revolution in the role of women since it cannot be reversed in the foreseeable future. What we can do is to attempt to rectify the undesirable results and learn to benefit from the good that it has produced.

Some alarm has been sounded about the high correlation between delinquent children and mothers who work. Of course, negligence of children is always possible, but based on some of the research of family life, there is considerable evidence that working mothers are better mothers.[16]

There is no doubt that many families pay a penalty if the wife works. Many children, for manifold reasons, need their own mothers full time. They not only need their mothers at home when they are there, but they need also the security of knowing their mothers are in the home even when they are at school or just outdoors. Much more research needs to be done to determine the effect on the child of the mother's working, especially in the middle-class family where the father is the primary provider.

Regardless of the reason for the mother's working, and regardless of whether she works full time or part time, regularly or occasionally, the consequences for her children will be on the positive side only if she derives some satisfaction out of working and if her relations with her children are consistently affectionate, warm, and understanding. These positive consequences assume that adequate supervision is available for children when needed, that the husband is at least tolerant of his wife's employment, and that her reasons for working are not neurotic but realistic.

Good Effects of Wife's Working. Certain advantages, of course, come to some families where wives are gainfully employed.

1. It gives a woman a choice of a career. Not all women are interested in housekeeping or gifted as homemakers.

2. Marital companionship is promoted through similar interests in business.

3. Personal growth in tolerance, understanding of work conditions, and broadmindedness sometimes brings about better understanding between husband and wife.

4. Increase of family income makes life more comfortable for the entire family.

5. A husband may become more interested in his wife because outside employment makes a wife keep up her appearance.

6. The ambition of a man may increase because he does not like to be outdistanced by his wife in money-making.

7. The home becomes a cooperative proposition.

8. Additional income makes possible college education for the children.

[16] See *Work in the Lives of Married Women,* Part V; also Sheldon Glueck and Eleanor Glueck, "Working Mothers and Delinquency," *Mental Hygiene,* no. 3, 1957, p. 327.

9. An outlet for energy and talent is provided.

10. Young people can marry earlier.

11. Modern homemaking does not always keep a woman occupied. This is especially true in some cases before children are born and after the last child leaves the home.

12. A wife will know how to adjust herself financially in the event that the husband dies or is incapacitated.

13. A mother does not become too dependent on her young adult children for interest or become completely lost as a person when the children leave the home permanently.

Bad Effects of Wife's Working. Although the good effects generally outnumber the bad effects, some of the bad effects are just as important to the morale of the husband and to the happiness of the family. Some of the bad effects may not be due entirely to the wife's gainful employment. The most often mentioned bad effects that come to families with working wives are these:

1. Disappointment and frustration may come to the husband because of a feeling of inability to make an adequate living for his family.

2. A sense of inferiority comes to some husbands if they do not make as much money as their wives.

3. Some men are disappointed because their wives do not assume a more active part in the management of the home.

4. Husbands may lose their fine sense of responsibility if they do not feel that they have to hold their jobs.

5. The health of some wives is broken as a consequence of holding two jobs.

6. Quarrels are more frequent because of irritation over minor things when tired.

7. Husbands feel neglected because wives have interests outside the home.

8. Some jobs do not keep women alert and alive, consequently they receive little satisfaction from outside work except the pay check.

9. The children may be seriously neglected.

10. There may be too much dependence on the joint income.

11. The young couple may lose the desire to have a family.

These advantages and disadvantages of gainfully employed wives are so entangled that extrication looks hopeless. Perhaps the best that can be said is that each couple must carefully square the possible good and bad effects with their own economic condition and personality traits. What may be considered a bad effect by one couple may be turned into an advantage by another couple.

Minimizing the Risk to Family Happiness. Since such a high percentage of married women work for pay outside the home, a practical question is: "How can a wife who wants to work after marriage minimize the risk to family happiness?" The risk can often be reduced by:

1. Selecting a vocation that can be successfully combined with homemaking.
2. Selecting a husband who possesses cooperative characteristics.
3. Knowing whether her family will benefit from a full-time mother, a part-time mother, or a full-time career mother.

Some vocations can be more successfully combined with homemaking than others because of certain characteristics. It is advantageous, for example:

1. If the employer has a sympathetic attitude toward the working married woman.
2. If the job pays enough so that help can be hired for some of the housework.
3. If the job is such that the mother can leave work early or report late when necessary.
4. If the hours of work allow enough time to be with the children.
5. If a minimum amount of overtime is required.
6. If transportation costs in terms of money, time, and energy are reasonable.
7. If advancement is possible.
8. If the job provides congenial and cultural experiences.
9. If maternity leaves are permitted.
10. If vacations coincide with those of the husband.
11. If the pay is more than enough to offset the increased expenses connected with the job.

Personality Traits Must Be Analyzed. It goes without saying that a woman cannot always select a husband who has the traits that best fit the needs of a working wife. Nevertheless, it is desirable that the husband be:

1. Willing to do his share of the housework and care of children.
2. Willing to help in managing household assistants.
3. Willing and able to do for himself many things usually left to a wife.
4. Capable of intelligent discussion of family problems.
5. Appreciative of the contribution that the wife is making to the welfare of the family.
6. Capable of resisting the temptation to become lazy on his own job.
7. Understanding when the wife seems more concerned with her job than with her homemaking.
8. Capable of not feeling inferior if the wife's income exceeds his own.
9. Capable of divorcing himself from parental influence if it interferes with the welfare of his own family.

High qualifications these, but important in realizing maximum family happiness when both husband and wife work for pay outside the home.

Family happiness does not automatically come merely because a wife or mother spends all her time in the home. Under some circumstances, it may be better for the wife to work for pay outside the home or to continue a career. For example:

1. If she is so temperamentally built that she is likely to blow up if home duties do not keep her busy.
2. If she has a particular talent—author, artist, teacher.
3. If the family is in need of more income.
4. If the children are adequately cared for while she is away from home.
5. If she intensely dislikes home duties.
6. If a career outside the home makes her a more interesting mate.

These suggestions may oversimplify the entire relationship. The fact remains that if the wife works away from home, the happiness and success of the marriage are dependent on many tangible and intangible factors.

Hints for the Working Wife. Some of the more tangible matters that may help to make a successful marriage when both husband and wife work can be directed by the wife.

1. Make every possible effort to assure the husband that his happiness comes first.
2. Do not make a butler of the husband. He may begin to feel like the "little man who wasn't there"—and that is what he may sooner or later wish to be.
3. Be fair about using wardrobe space.
4. If you have a professional name, be known socially by the husband's name and endeavor to have it used when he is present.
5. Invite the husband to social functions in the line of your business duty, but do not insist that he attend all such functions.
6. Do not socialize with business associates to the extent that the husband seeks companionship elsewhere.
7. Agree on the division of home and family responsibilities. This arrangement is no longer considered "sissy."
8. Relax with the husband in an interesting and attractive way.
9. Show interest in the husband's job and problems.
10. Yet do not be the "clucking" type who does too much for the husband. He may not appreciate it after a while.

The problems of human relations in marriage are so intricate and so much is unknown that it may seem presumptuous to discuss the matter of when to be a full-time wife and mother. Yet studies of many marriages in which the wife worked point to many little things that end in serious marital conflict. We can identify some of the principles that have helped many couples. For example, the following tips may be useful for deciding when a wife ought to return to homemaking on a full-time basis.

1. When it is necessary for the happiness and morale of the husband.

2. When the children need her. Watch for, anticipate if possible, the symptoms of emotional troubles. Most small children coming home from school want to be greeted by mother.

3. When the wife's job forces her to tear away from the children in the morning without giving them the help and guidance necessary for cleanliness, neat dressing, and nutritious eating, and for the sense of security felt by the child who can say, "Good-by, Mom, see you after school."

4. When she finds that she is returning from work too tired to be civil, and before long is snapping at husband and children.

5. When she begins to feel guilty about neglecting the family and is developing the habit of lavishing too much affection on a child, of forgiving him for matters that require sensible discipline, and perhaps undermining the household assistant who cares for the child during the day. Junior may become confused and rebellious and may play one off against the other.

6. When the job does not permit sufficient fun and recreation with the entire family together.

Much planning is required for the working wife and mother to do things with and for her family. The wife who remains at home can do such things more easily, but it is true that she does not always take advantage of this.

The Wife's Personal Income. What share of the family expense does an average working wife pay? This was one of the questions investigated by the National Association of Business and Professional Women's Clubs in a study of its membership's economic and employment status. The association asked: "Aside from your personal needs, how much of the family's expenses are paid by your income?" The results, tabulated according to family income, are given in the accompanying table.

AMONG WIVES WHOSE FAMILIES HAD THIS TOTAL INCOME	HERE IS HOW MANY PAID VARIOUS SHARES OF FAMILY EXPENSES				
	All	About three-fourths	About one-half	About one-fourth	None
Under $4,000	16%	12%	39%	19%	14%
$4,000 to $6,000	5	11	43	25	16
$6,000 to $8,000	4	7	42	28	19
$8,000 to $10,000	4	6	44	27	19
$10,000 and over	5	5	34	28	28

SOURCE: *Changing Times,* March, 1955, p. 45.

Should a wife use her own income regardless of the source—an inheritance, royalties, or personal earnings from a regular job—for general family use? Most young married couples may not realize the marital conflicts that can result from a wife's additional income. If they are sensible in discussing the problem, an acceptable solution is generally possible. But there are people who do not consider all the known good principles of solving this problem in family money management. The result—unhappiness.

There was a time when the laws in most states deprived a married woman of virtually every right to her personal property, whether earnings, an inheritance, wearing apparel, or jewelry. All such things, on a girl's marriage, immediately came under the control of the husband. He could give them away, sell them, or lose them through claims of his creditors. Most states have now changed such laws, particularly those relating to ownership, control, and use of real property and other possessions.

Joint Control of Income. In comparing happy and unhappy marriages, we can identify some of the problem areas when personal income of the family is not controlled and used jointly. There is, for example, the danger of either the husband or wife acting as though he or she owns most of the family wealth. There is the further danger of creating one person as the High Priest and Distributor of Money. The children are likely to feel that the distributor is the more successful parent. Disintegration of character of husband or wife may result because of a feeling of failure and unworthiness. After a while, the injured parent may seek to create escapes and build emotional defenses.

Some men, under such emotional pressures, have made money-making the major goal of their lives, the main objective being competition and status. With as much money as his wife has available for use, or more, such husbands feel they can compete on even terms for status. Money-making, under such conditions, becomes a vicious game, and everybody loses, including the children.

At this point, it is important to recognize that snap judgments are more common than opinion based on facts. Let us face the facts. Not every working wife is endangering her family's happiness. Reuben Hill, research professor of family life at the University of Minnesota, says:

Consensus of the research to date is that gainful employment of the wife is not a significant factor either in marriage success or in marriage failure. It is a peg on which conflict can be hung, a socially approved area in which to disagree, as are religion, child-rearing practices, money matters, in-laws, and other areas of conflict.

How can this problem be handled for the best interests of all the family? Generalizing is dangerous, but the following principles have worked successfully for some families.

1. Discuss, but do not debate, all sides of the family income thoroughly before making decisions about its use.

2. Work out a practical plan for the distribution of the total income of the family. In early marriage, do not use both incomes for day-to-day living expenses.

3. Set up a plan that makes children feel that their material wants are satisfied by the use of money from a common source, the joint family bank account or the equivalent.

4. When there are children over 10 years of age, set up a family money management council to carry out the plan for distribution of the family income.

Earning or getting an income is only half the story. Spending it wisely for family happiness is the other half. Some arrangement agreeable to both parents must be worked out if conflict is to be prevented.

Sharing a Home with Others. Should a young couple marry when there is the economic necessity of sharing a home with others? Usually such sharing is with "in-laws" or with friends. Few married couples choose to make their home with in-laws or friends, but housing shortages and high rents often create an emergency situation for thousands of young couples who want to get married. Consequently, couples faced with the alternative of living more or less doubled up with other families or postponing marriage might profit by close examination of living conditions of families that have lived "doubled up."

What is it like, living double? "It's murder," a young lieutenant said, and continued, "we've lived doubled up all over this country. It just doesn't work. Either you have to give up everything you want, or you have to keep battling for it all the time. They want to play the radio; you want quiet. You like your steak rare; they want it well done. I'll never forget that steak when we were living with in-laws. One day she had a big juicy steak, and she was going to *fry* it, of all things! I persuaded her to broil it, and it was fairly rare. Then the teen-age daughter said at the table, 'Oh, I can't bear it. It's all bloody.' So her father scolded her, and it started a family row. And it was all supposed to be my fault. No matter what you do, you're in the wrong."

An ex-Wave said, "I certainly would not say that living double is any picnic; but it can be made to work. My husband and I are sharing a two-room apartment with a friend and his wife and baby, and we get along."

Though sharing a home may not be desirable, does it actually reduce the chances of married happiness? A study of couples living with in-laws, reported by Clifford R. Adams, sheds light on this question.[17] The study, based on the evidence of a thousand couples, revealed that, of the couples

[17] Clifford R. Adams, "Making Marriage Work," *Ladies' Home Journal,* November, 1949, p. 26. Reprinted with special permission. Copyright 1949. The Curtis Publishing Company.

who consider their marriage happy, 28 per cent had lived with in-laws at some time. But among the couples who rated their marriage unhappy, the proportion was 57 per cent—more than twice as many. Apparently, living with the in-laws is more than an inconvenience; it can be a real threat to happiness.

"It Can Be Done." The 28 per cent of the couples who had lived with in-laws and felt that the arrangement worked satisfactorily leads one to believe that "it can be done." What, then, are the most favorable circumstances for successful living with in-laws? The following suggestions are based on the experience of the couples who felt they lived successfully under such an arrangement.

1. The couple should pay a fair rent and board or its agreed-on equivalent in work.

2. The husband's work should be approved by the in-laws with whom the couple lives.

3. The husband should not be in business with the in-law with whom the couple lives.

4. The in-laws should be happily married, really want the couple to live with them, and be reasonably free from financial worries.

5. The house should be large enough to assure some measure of privacy for all persons.

6. Both husband and wife should agree definitely that living with in-laws can be a satisfactory arrangement.

7. If the couple has a child, success is unlikely.

8. Living arrangements, financial arrangements, and obligations of each family to the other should be defined and fully accepted by both families when they begin to live together.

When these conditions are met, there remains one essential. In this, as in most problems of marriage, one of the most important factors is the determination to make it work. The cards, however, are stacked against the couple that decides to live with in-laws.

How Much Money Is Needed for Marriage? The amount of money needed for marriage depends on the couple contemplating matrimony. Cost of living can be reduced by sharing a home, by using personal income, if available. Both husband and wife can work. The wife can add to the family income by planning and spending wisely. Strictly speaking, this is not adding to the number of dollars of family income, but by intelligent purchasing the wife actually extends the use of the family dollar.

There are, of course, many other ways of beginning a marriage on a minimum income. Whether a couple can have a happy marriage on a minimum income depends on the will to make it successful, if it is coupled with sufficient consumer information and skills. Obviously, there is no single answer to the question.

Money has value only when translated into satisfying wants. Since wants are unlimited, a young couple contemplating marriage needs to compare the number of their wants (standard of living) with the money cost of satisfying those wants. For example:

How much income is each accustomed to?
How low a standard of living is each willing to accept?
Has either partner other financial responsibilities?
How much is it costing for each to live before marriage? (Remember, two can live as cheaply as *two*.)
How much, if any, will each lose by way of support coming from his own family?
Is each willing to start on an income below that of his parents at the present time?

These questions have to be answered by both the prospective bride and the groom. Comparatively little help can be offered in the form of studies on the dollar cost required to maintain a family of two on a modest but adequate standard of living. But some help was given in Chapter 2 as to the income that college graduates may expect to have as a result of higher education.

When you marry, Uncle Sam extends to you the privilege of filing a joint income tax return. This tax-saving privilege, in addition to allowing an extra $600 personal exemption, can mean a big annual saving, as shown in the accompanying table.

JOINT INCOME TAX SAVINGS

Income	Married person's tax	Single person's tax	Tax saving
$ 4,000	$ 800	$ 840	$ 40
8,000	1,680	1,960	280
12,000	2,720	3,400	680
16,000	3,920	5,200	1,280

1962 Federal income tax rates.

Premarriage Savings. There is no pat answer to the question: "How much should we have in a savings fund before marriage?" The amount of reliable information on this question is limited. Some family experts suggest a cash reserve fund of at least twice the monthly income. However, the amount of money that a young couple should have on hand when starting married life depends on several factors.

Potential earning power, probable expenditures, gainful employment of the wife, condition of health, and possession of property are among the more important factors to consider. Other assets like bonds, stocks, cars, land, insurance with loan value, and sharing in parental estates should be considered when discussing premarriage economic assets. Some of these assets cannot be used immediately, and certain assets that can be currently used may sustain a loss if used immediately.

Since the most common purpose of savings is to provide some protection in the event of emergency, the savings should be in the form of available cash or assets that can be made liquid without suffering a loss, within a short period of time. Most couples, for example, need cash to buy furniture and household equipment.

If the beginning income is so modest that it will be impossible to save during the first year, premarriage savings become even more important. Just a small reserve fund may make the difference between feeling free to grasp a new opportunity and the fear of letting go of present security.

Some couples enter marriage with no cash or its equivalent in reserve. A few have the handicap of debts or the responsibility of contributing to someone's support. It takes courage, faith, or some other sustaining force to enter marriage without a cash reserve. While such a fund does not automatically ensure happiness, its absence may cause much unhappiness later. This may be the case if Junior arrives before a young couple is prepared to meet at least the major financial costs of a birth in the family.

How Much Does a Baby Cost? Most parents do not think of the baby in terms of dollar cost. Many parents have discovered, however, that their baby has been far from inexpensive. The recently married couple is likely to be a little vague about the time when they can afford to have a baby. When young married couples know approximately how much a baby costs and are financially, as well as physically and emotionally, prepared to greet that million-dollar bundle when it arrives, there is less family tension. The child, too, has a better chance of growing up free from any feeling of insecurity.

Every mother-to-be (except those on public assistance) faces approximately the same expenditures—doctor's fees, hospital charges, the layette, care at home, and other miscellaneous costs. The size of the family income and savings will largely determine how these costs are to be met. A baby can be budgeted down to the last dollar, in most cases, if a careful investigation is made of the costs in the particular community beforehand.

It is a known fact that the expenses of having a baby vary, depending on the size of the community, type of maternity care and service expected, equipment needed, general health of the mother and child, and on whether there is hospital and medical insurance. Because costs vary according to the above factors, the best we can do here is to present the average costs in small and large communities. Let's begin, however, by investigating the fees of doctors.

Selecting the Doctor. There is usually a capable doctor within one's price range. There should be no hesitation in asking a doctor his total fee. It is well to keep in mind that the doctors who charge the highest fees are not necessarily the best.

Generally, doctors who have a diploma from the American Board of Obstetrics and Gynecology are regarded as first class. Their fees, of course, are higher—probably around $375 for a patient having a private room and $300 for a semiprivate room. There are, at present, probably less than two thousand of these specialists in the United States. They do their own surgery.

Then, there is the doctor who limits his practice to obstetrics and gynecology, but who has not taken the Board's examination for the classification listed above. His fees, as a rule, are lower. The average fee ranges from $150 to $300 for a family in moderate financial circumstances. These specialists handle all aspects of a case, normal or otherwise.

Some doctors have a general practice but give special attention to obstetrical cases. Such a doctor is likely to plan for more prenatal care than does the general practitioner. Fees average approximately $100 to $150.

The general practitioner, sometimes called the family doctor, delivers many babies in this country. His fee per delivery may average from $50 to $100. If there are complications, a good general practitioner advises consulting a specialist. Sometimes it is cheaper to have a specialist from the beginning.

This discussion of doctors' fees assumes normal births, which are the case in over 90 per cent of the births in this country. When surgery is necessary, such as a Caesarean, the specialist may charge more. These fees, as a rule, cover prenatal care, birth, and six weeks' care after the baby is born.

Hospital Charges. Almost 80 per cent of American babies are born in hospitals. How much do hospitals charge for room and board and for necessary medical supplies, services, and the like? Again, there is no set answer. Each baby runs up an average bill of $271, according to a study reported in *Changing Times*, June, 1961.

Doctor and hospital costs can be reduced considerably if hospital and medical insurance is taken out in time. Chapter 11 shows how Blue Cross Hospital Insurance, Blue Shield, and other group and individual insurance polices can reduce costs materially. Of course, the premium rates continue each month, but the cost is distributed over a period of years, and thereby easily budgeted by families of moderate income.

THE COST OF HAVING A BABY

Items	Expenditure per baby		Per cent of total cost	
	1952–1953	1957–1958	1952–1953	1957–1958
Hospital bills	$ 82	$128	42	47
Doctor's fees	91	118	47	44
Drugs and medicines	10	17	5	6
Laboratory fees	3	2	2	1
Other expenses	7	6	4	2
Total costs	$193	$271	100	100
Insurance payments	129	187	67	69
Family payment	$ 64	$ 84	33	31

Two Can Live as Cheaply as *Two*. The persistent question that this chapter raises and attempts to settle is: "Will our pocketbook be ready when our hearts are ready for marriage?" The answer must depend largely on the young couple who are thinking of marriage. Some couples achieve a successful and happy marriage on a surprisingly low income during the first years. Such couples have an abundance of courage and faith, and perhaps other sustaining forces.

This is no argument for a premature marriage. A couple very much in love is in the disquieting position of thinking via the heart. It is so easy to conclude that two can live as cheaply as one. It is wiser to figure that two can live as cheaply as *two*. We have pointed out that studies show that financial conflicts are the most-mentioned cause or symptom of marital unhappiness. While money in itself does not bring happiness, the absence of money can bring much unhappiness.

QUESTIONS FOR DISCUSSION

1. In what ways are the present choices of young people and corresponding challenges different from those of a generation or so ago?

2. How would you explain the statement that "education neglects our needs"?

3. What are some of the limitations to be kept in mind when discussing causes of marital unhappiness?

4. With your answer to question 3 in mind, what part does money sometimes play in marriage?

5. How can one overcome the discrepancy and inconsistency between attitudes and practices in money management?

6. Would an increase in income solve the problems of marital discontent for a family that constantly quarrels over money management?

7. Is it possible to be a success in making money but a dismal failure in spending it?

8. How do you account for the increasing tendency of wives to work outside

the home? What problems may arise when both parents **work** full time outside the home?

9. Can two persons live as cheaply as one?

10. After examining the good and bad effects that may result from both parents' working full time outside the home, how do you believe it would be possible to reduce the risks of family unhappiness?

11. Can you conceive of the problems that may arise when a wife earns more money than her husband?

12. How can you know when a wife should be a part-time or a full-time working woman outside the home?

13. Is living with in-laws during periods of financial distress a real threat to a happy marriage? Are there ways to reduce this risk?

14. What are some of the important factors to consider when raising the question: "How much income do we need to marry?"

15. How much does it cost to have a baby?

ACTIVITY PROBLEMS

1. Many studies show that management of family income is often a major reason for disagreement and marital discord. Perhaps you know two or three families who feel that disagreements over family financing are largely responsible for unpleasant family relations. Further investigations may reveal discrepancies and inconsistencies between attitudes and practices. For example, you might check on uneconomical practices such as (a) use of charge accounts, (b) meals at restaurants, (c) poor buying habits, (d) expensive recreation, and so on. If serious uneconomical practices seem to prevail among these families, what could be done to lessen such tensions?

2. Make a survey of the attitudes of 25 or more college students with regard to whether their education is meeting their needs. Questions such as: "Why are you in college?" may be included in the questionnaire, along with a prepared list of questions on possible benefits of a college education: (a) occupational training, (b) greater appreciation of the culture of people, (c) better opportunity to get ahead, (d) preparation for marriage, (e) opportunity to make valuable contacts, and so on. Make an analysis of the answers.

3. Using the ideas in this chapter with regard to marital problems when both husband and wife work outside the home, prepare appropriate questions for interviewing married couples who have had or are now having this experience. A summary of these experiences could be the basis for a lively class discussion.

4. Should marriage be subsidized by parents? Invite married couples who have had such experience to discuss this issue with the class.

5. Why is it so difficult to identify the causes for marital unhappiness? Interview a marriage counselor or a psychologist to get his point of view on this question. On the basis of what you learned in the interview, how would you react to the following statement: "Money management is generally the most common cause for marital discord."

6. Ask ten students: "How much money do you need to get married?" Summarize the answers. What are your reactions to their answers?

7. How much does it cost to have a baby in your community? Make a survey of local hospital charges and doctors' fees.

8. Make up a complete list, day by day, of important time-consuming activities or jobs to do in the home for a typical week. Give estimated time needed for each job, availability and cost of equipment, and the like. Then answer the questions: "Will the wife be able to work full time outside the home?" "How much would it cost to hire some of these jobs done?"

9. What are lifetime income prospects for a boy or girl who does not finish high school? How many high school graduates go to college? How many complete college? What do we know about employment opportunities of the future based on current trends in employment and technology? What kinds of education and training will be needed in the future? Is a person's education ever finished?

10. Dr. Mary Bunting, president of Radcliffe College, said, "I am convinced the road that lies ahead for women is a dual one of motherhood and career. It will not only be possible but almost mandatory to do both if you want to do either well." *Life,* Jan. 13, 1961.

Do you agree? If this is true, what does this mean to you in the selection of your courses? How far in the future can you make intelligent plans? Can you plan for your first job? Can you plan beyond your first job? Can you prepare for each of these roles? If you can plan, how and when should the preparation take place?

SUGGESTED READINGS

Adams, Clifford R. "Making Marriage Work," *Ladies' Home Journal,* November, 1949.

American Council on Education. *The Education of Women: Signs for the Future,* Washington, D.C., 1959, pp. 51.

Atwood, William, Leonard, George B., and Moskin, Robert J. *The Decline of the American Male.* New York: Random House, Inc., 1958.

Bell, Daniel. "The Great Back-to-work Movement," *Fortune,* July, 1956.

Bergler, Edmund. *Money and Emotional Conflicts.* New York: Pageant Books, Inc., 1959.

Bernays, Doris F. *A Wife Is Many Women.* New York: Crown Publishers, Inc., 1956.

Blaisdell, Richard S. "More Women Are Working," *Journal of Home Economics,* April, 1958.

Burgess, Ernest W., and Cottrell, Leonard S. *Predicting Success or Failure in Marriage.* Englewood Cliffs, N.J.: Prentice-Hall, Inc., 1939, pp. 152–153.

——— and Locke, Harvey J. *The Family.* New York: American Book Company, 1953, pp. 462–464.

Changing Times. "Should Mother Take a Job or Stay at Home with the Kids?" September, 1953, pp. 22–24; "Should the Wife Work?" January, 1957, p. 33.

Davis, Alice M. "Young Women: Look before You Weep," *College Placement Annual,* 1959, pp. 27–29.

Ellzey, W. Clark. *How to Keep Romance in Your Marriage*. New York: Association Press, 1954, chap. 5.

Family Economics Review. "Clothing Expenditures of Employed Wife," September, 1962.

Gruenberg, Sidonie M., and Krech, Hilda Sidney. *The Many Lives of Modern Woman*. Garden City, N.Y.: Doubleday & Co., Inc., 1952.

Hamilton, G. V. *A Research in Marriage*. New York: Albert & Charles Boni, Inc., 1929, pp. 6–77.

Harper's Magazine. "The Two-income Family," December, 1951.

Household Finance Corporation. *For Young Moderns*, Chicago.

Komarovsky, Mirra. *Women in the Modern World*. Boston: Little, Brown and Company, 1953.

La Follette, Cecile T. *A Study of the Problems of 652 Gainfully Employed Married Women Homemakers*. New York: Columbia University Press, 1934, pp. 93–110.

Life. "My Wife Works and I Like It," December, 1956.

Locke, Harvey J. *Predicting Happiness or Divorce in Marriage*. New York: Holt, Rinehart and Winston, Inc., 1951.

Marriage and Family Living. "Marital Disagreement in Working Wife Marriages as a Factor of Husband's Attitude toward Wife's Employment," November, 1957, pp. 373–378.

Muller, Leo C., and Muller, Ouida G. (eds.). *New Horizons for College Women*. Washington, D.C.: Public Affairs Press, 1960, chap. 8, "The Myth of the Marriage-Career Conflict."

Myrdal, Alva, and Klein, Viola. *Women's Two Roles, Home and Work*. London: Routledge & Kegan Paul, Ltd., 1956.

National Manpower Council. *Womanpower*. New York: Columbia University Press, 1957.

———. *Work in the Lives of Married Women*. New York: Columbia University Press, 1959.

Nimkoff, Meyer F. *Marriage and the Family*. Boston: Houghton Mifflin Company, 1947, chaps. 4–6.

Pace, Robert C. *They Went to College*. Minneapolis: The University of Minnesota Press, 1941, pp. 82–83, 87–89.

Redbook. "How to Make a Subsidized Marriage Work" and "My Parents Support Us and I Hate It," December, 1955.

Smuts, Robert. *Women and Work in America*. New York: Columbia University Press, 1959.

Terman, Lewis M. *Psychological Factors in Marital Happiness*. New York: McGraw-Hill Book Company, 1938, pp. 85–89, 169–171.

Vincent, Clark E. "Role Clarification for the Contemporary College-educated Woman," *Journal of Home Economics*, October, 1953, pp. 567–570.

Williamson, Robert C. "Economic Factors in Marital Adjustment," *Marriage and Family Living*, November, 1952, pp. 298–301.

Woman's Home Companion. "The Married Woman Goes Back to Work," October, 1956.

4

CONSUMER CREDIT AND BORROWING MONEY

Consumer credit is joked about and glimpsed in ridiculing caricatures. These are some examples: "To make time fly just buy something on the installment plan." Or this one, "The people that economists used to say were underprivileged are now described as overfinanced." And *Life* magazine editorialized on "Is Thrift Un-American?" Said the multimillionaire Texan, Sid Richardson, "Out here in Texas, we judge a man's wealth by how much he owes." And Vance Packard calls us a "credit-card society." One magazine writer chose for his article the title, "Are You a Credit Drunk?" A symbolic case is that of the clerk earning $73 a week who went on a $10,000 binge with his credit card. After he was caught by the "credit detectives," he wrote, "All of a sudden the credit card was just like an Aladdin's lamp, and you didn't even have to rub it."

Charles Dickens gave the world one of its most famous harried consumers, Mr. Micawber, David Copperfield's friend. Micawber always had a terrible time making ends meet. But despite his inability, he knew where the trouble lay: "Annual income twenty pounds, annual expenditure nineteen pounds six, result happiness. Annual income twenty pounds, annual expenditure twenty pounds ought and six, result misery."

But there are two sides to modern consumer credit—good and bad. Wisely used, it can lead to a higher standard of living. Unwisely used, it can lead to misery. Not too many decades ago we used to boast, "Pay as you go or stay home." Of course, few Americans can make such a boast today. Charge plates, revolving charge accounts, installment credit, credit cards, and loan applications in hand, American consumers pay around $15 billion each year in pure interest to buy on credit goods and services that, in 1963, were worth over $69 billion.

What Is Consumer Credit? The terms "consumer credit," "consumer debt," "short-term credit," "installment credit," and "mortgage credit" have been bandied about so much that some clarification of their meaning is needed. Essentially, of course, credit is the asset side of the ledger, and debt the liability side. Thus, "consumer credit" is money or purchasing power extended by the lending agencies to consumers, and "consumer debt" is money owed the lending agencies by consumers.

Indebtedness of individuals can be broadly broken into two classes: mortgage debt (or real estate debt) and shorter-term debt, which includes a number of types of commitments, usually payable within a period of 1 to 36 months. In many publications, the term "consumer credit" is confined to a consideration of the shorter-term obligations. It is in this sense that consumer credit is used here.

Short-term or intermediate-term consumer credit may be further divided into two large groups: installment credit, and noninstallment credit. Credit to be repaid in a series of installments is of various types, for example, automobile paper, other consumer-goods paper—such as loans on refrigerators or furniture—home repair and modernization loans, personal installment loans. The term "paper" used in connection with consumer credit means installment sales notes held by banks, other financial institutions, or retail outlets. Personal installment loans, frequently made by banks, are for unspecified purposes, as distinguished from installment notes for the purchase of automobiles and the like. They are frequently used for emergency medical care and other personal expenses, but they also may be used for the purchase of a car, modernization of a house, or the purchase of household equipment. They are also used for refinancing previous commitments, particularly in cases where a number of loans are being consolidated.

Noninstallment consumer credit consists of charge accounts, service credit—such as that extended by doctors, dentists, utility companies, and dry cleaners—and single payment loans that are repaid in a single lump sum at the end of a specified time period.

Arguments for and against Consumer Credit. Because of its tremendous growth, consumer credit has become a subject of considerable concern to economists, public administrators, and those who counsel families. Some economists argue that the growth of debt obligations for goods and services actually improves the position of the consumer. Increased purchases of goods stimulate production and, since production requires a labor input, results in greater income for consumers. Others argue that a large amount of consumer credit outstanding imperils the stability of the economic system and therefore the financial security of the families who are a part of it.

Family counselors can also argue pro and con on the subject of consumer credit. Consumer credit permits families to enjoy higher levels of living because they can purchase in advance of earned income such consumer durables as automobiles and large household appliances. However, consumer credit is costly, and many families get into financial difficulties by taking on too large a total obligation.

Concept of Collateral Has Evaporated. Many people are unaware of the changes that have taken place in the practices of debt financing of consumer goods and services in the last decade or so. Dr. Colston Warne, professor of economics at Amherst College, pointed this out to the Senate Banking and Currency Committee when he said, "The most significant change has been the transmutation of this financial device into a merchandising tool."

In the first place, according to Dr. Warne, the concept of collateral has evaporated. Even in automobiles, 36-month terms, together with rapid new car obsolescence, have rendered the goods small surety for the loan. The resale value of other durables (white goods, TV sets, furniture, and the like) is so low in today's market that no lender considers them as collateral. Their repossession on delinquency is almost universally accompanied by a deficiency balance charge that becomes, of course, a lien on any income or property of the debtor. Hence, credit contracts for these goods constitute at bottom little more than a disguised wage, chattels, or mortgage lien—often unrecognized by the borrower. Finally, the great increase in the use of credit to finance the purchase of soft goods and services is incontrovertible evidence of the divorcement of consumer credit from any concept of the goods financed serving as collateral for the debt.

In short, consumer credit extensions are made singly and solely against the lender's expectations of (1) the consumer's ability to maintain current income, or (2) the lender's ability to exercise command over the borrower's assets via the courts. To put it another way, in their extensions of credit for consumption, lenders are looking first to the Federal government's ability to maintain nearly full employment for surety, and second, are depending on the police power at their command to tap existing equities in homes and cars. Thus, the theorizing of the past about the functions of consumer credit, which was based on the concept of pacing time units of consumption with payments over the period of use of the durables that secured the debt, fails to fit reality.

Retailers Acting as Agents for Lenders. A second concept of consumer credit that has evaporated, except in the case of a few of the largest retailers, says Dr. Warne, is the seller's responsibility for the loans disguised as sales. Although the courts and a good many state legislatures make a distinction between "carrying charges" and "interest," the practice that gave rise to that distinction is all but extinct. The retailer generally acts as an agent for a lender. Typically, the forms filled out by the consumer for the installment purchase of goods have been furnished the retailer by a lender. All conditions attending the loan, including a commission (kickback) for the retailer from a dealer reserve held out by the lender have been set by a financing institution.

No longer does a retailer "carry the consumer" over a period of time, as the general store once carried the farmer between seeding and harvesting. As soon as the paper is signed, it is turned over to the lending agency. Only the old-style 30-day charge account offered by department stores can in any sense be called a retailer-carrying service, and this is the only form of consumer credit that has failed to increase.

The New Term—Credit Selling. The retail trade press has been using a term for a number of years that best expresses the present meaning of consumer credit. They speak repeatedly of "credit selling." Credit selling means two things: selling goods on credit, and selling credit as well as goods.

Credit selling is generally recognized as the core of present-day profitable retailing operations for four reasons. (1) The consumer buying on credit tends to buy higher-priced merchandise (he is easy to "trade up"), to buy more in volume, and to buy more frequently than the cash customer. (2) The credit customer does not shop around, he "marries" his seller-lender. (3) The amount of purchase per credit sale is typically enough larger than the cash sale to more than compensate for the extra overhead of credit selling. (4) Earnings on credit extensions frequently equal or better the net return from markups on merchandise. The National Automobile Dealers Association, for example, reported one year that the net profit from most dealers' operations was exactly equal to the small percentage return as a financing rebate to the dealers from the lending agencies to whom they transferred their consumer paper.

Throughout retailing, therefore, there is a heavy and continuing pressure to sell debt. Salesmen in automobile showrooms and appliance stores are given larger commissions for credit sales. Department store employees are paid "spiffs" from $1 to $2 for each new credit customer signed up. Bank personnel are "spiffed" to bring in check credit, bank credit card, or personal loan customers. And, as one after another seller-lender has placed increasing promotional emphasis on loans disguised as sales, as new lending schemes tied to sales have multiplied (credit cards and bank schemes), the traditional lender to consumers—the small loan company—has accordingly been forced to greater promotional efforts. Thus, the advertising of debt as a way of life has expanded into a national propaganda effort of phenomenal proportions.

Growth of Consumer Credit. In light of the many-faceted, continuous, and mounting sales pressures on consumers to use credit, the rapid expansion of consumer debt from $20 billion in 1950 to $44.9 billion in 1957, steadily climbing to $69.8 billion in 1963, is not surprising. Installment credit amounted to $53.7 billion, consisting of $22.1 billion in automobile paper. Noninstallment credit totaled $16.1 billion. These figures are shown in the accompanying table, Consumer Debt, prepared by the Federal Reserve Board.

CONSUMER DEBT
Short-term Intermediate-term Consumer Credit Outstanding
(In Millions of Dollars)

Type of credit	1963	1960
Installment credit, total	$53,745	$42,832
Automobile paper	22,199	17,688
Other consumer goods paper	13,766	11,525
Repair and modernization loans	3,389	3,139
Personal loans	14,391	10,480
Noninstallment credit, total	16,145	13,196
Single-payment loans	5,959	4,507
Charge accounts	5,871	5,329
Service credit	4,315	3,360
Total consumer credit	$69,890	$56,028

Although consumer credit has increased markedly, as shown in the accompanying chart, Growth of Consumer Credit, consumer assets have increased also. It is significant to note that, among the various types of credit extended, the greatest increase has taken place in automobile installment paper.

Is Installment Debt a New Way of Life? It is among the younger households that the really dramatic consumer debt growth occurs. The number of family units headed by someone under age 25 will rise 89 per cent between 1963 and 1970. These young people will exercise great influence on markets because they are lavish users of installment credit. The annual surveys of consumer finances by the University of Michigan show that roughly 60 per cent of the spending units in the 18 to 24 age bracket owe on installment contracts, with indebtedness averaging $450. Households in the 25 to 34 age bracket are growing relatively slowly. This group is considerably more important than younger households in the over-all spending pattern. In 1961, for example, 65 per cent of this age group used installment credit with an average outstanding indebtedness of $680.

All types of people buy on time. According to the University of Michigan Institute for Social Research, the most frequent credit users have incomes from $7,500 to $10,000, are 25 to 34 years old, and live in smaller, urban communities. The families in the $7,500 to $10,000 income class are making annual debt payments to less than **20** per cent of their income after taxes. Installment debt has become a way of life for the groups that the sociologists call the "young marrieds" and the "growing families."

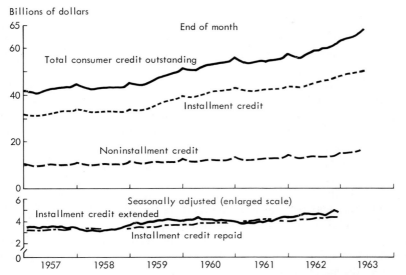

GROWTH OF CONSUMER CREDIT

Billions of dollars

Source: Board of Governors of the Federal Reserve System   Council of Economic Advisers

SOURCE: *Finance Facts Yearbook,* **National Consumer Finance Association, Washington, D.C., 1964, p. 39. (Taken from Federal Reserve Board data.)**

One of the unfortunate aspects of the use of consumer credit is that most people don't know what interest rate they pay when they buy on credit. Research surveys found that 2 out of 5 people questioned had no idea of what it cost them to buy cars via installments, and the others guessed from 6 to 13 per cent. The research center also reported that college graduates were as misinformed as the rest of the public. This is not as bad as it sounds because the deceptive way in which the total finance charges are stated is astounding, as we shall see shortly.

There are many reasons why the young to middle-age families have most of the consumer debt in the United States. Younger families want to upgrade their status and to enjoy the good materialistic things now. The scramble to lend more money and to move more goods produced a general loosening of credit requirements. Many retailers use credit as a "merchandising tool" or selling device with all the evils long associated with the promoter's activity. Retailers and credit men claim that installment credit is a system of "enforced savings" that puts a debtor on a regular monthly budget. It also has an opposite effect.

The easy availability of credit works constantly to lessen a buyer's resolve and breaks down self-discipline. Said the Rev. John Driscoll, S.J., dean of the Boston College School of Social Work, "We're all taught to live up to the height of our income." Debt is, indeed, our way of life.

Since consumer credit has become easier to obtain, the consumer's problem is more how to resist it than how to get it. Merchants have found that credit buyers increase their sales. If a customer is tied to a store by an old-fashioned charge account or a revolving account, he will tend to return to that store because the initial red tape in opening an account need not be repeated.

Consumer Credit Is Expensive. Consumer or short-term credit is more expensive than any other kind of credit. Why? Most of the money used for this kind of credit is obtained from bond issues and from large banks and is distributed by the large wholesale lenders to the smaller retail outlets and lenders. The unit costs of extending credit are large when the retail unit is small. The retailer has about the same expense-credit department and legal fees for a $100 credit as for one of $10,000. The cost markup on small loans is therefore heavy.

The price of credit is called interest, but is not to be confused with the general meaning of interest. The charges for the use of money are arrived at through complex cost accounting that takes into consideration many separate costs, such as overhead, wages, cost of money, repayment periods, and so on. Unfortunately for the consumer, the costs that go into the price of credit are stated in different ways so that it is impossible, under present conditions, to make comparative credit pricing. In fact, the cost of credit is deliberately concealed from the borrower.

Until a generation or so ago, the vast majority of the urban population had only limited experience with loans disguised as sales. For the most part, their familiarity with short-term indebtedness was limited to automobile financing and perhaps personal loans. Furthermore there was, and there still is, a stubbornly held folk myth about 6 per cent as a legal limit on interest rates. And the Federal government contributes to this myth by limiting income tax deductions for payments of interest to a true annual interest rate of 6 per cent on the debt.

Sellers of debt are well aware of the existence of this popular delusion about our usury laws. In their statements of finance charges for consumer loans, lenders almost always keep their percentage figures below 6 per cent. They describe their loan in such terms as 1½, 2, or 3 per cent a month, or simply (and meaninglessly) as "low bank rates," or "pennies a week," or "$1 a month for each $50," and so on. Then to make matters even more difficult, the time extensions on contracts are running increasingly to odd limits, such as 5, 8, 17, or 29 months, and so on.

Add to these complexities the well-known and confusing factors of insurance fees, investigation fees, and other special charges, and you have a system that leaves the buyer in the dark about the annual rate of his total loan. This lack of essential information prevents him from obtaining the best buy in the field of credit. As a matter of fact, George Katona, director of the Consumer Research Center at the University of Michigan, discovered that even college graduates were approximately as ill-informed as the average consumer about the terms of credit now in use.[1] In the Hearings on S. 2755, William McChesney Martin, Jr., chairman of the Board of Governors, Federal Reserve System, confessed difficulty in figuring out the total rate cost of credit as advertised. Since it is frequently impossible to figure out the actual charge, it is, of course, impossible to compare costs. And when you cannot compare competitive costs in the market place, how can you make an intelligent choice?

What You Pay for Consumer Credit. Surveys tell us that most people do not shop around for credit money. This is the big mistake, all other things being equal. The National Bureau of Economic Research, in its study of the average annual charges per $100 of credit, found that they varied from $9 to $24 among four types of institutions—consumer finance companies, sales finance companies, commercial banks, and federal credit unions.[2] A glance at the accompanying table, Typical Terms by Lenders on Various Types of Loans, reveals the sharp variations in the approximate true annual rate of interest.

There are two major types of consumer installment credit loans: (1) the per cent in advance method, sometimes called the "discount" method, and (2) the unpaid balance method, the simple interest method used by loan companies. If the per cent of interest is added in advance to the purchase price, and the total is repaid in 12 monthly installments, here is the true annual interest rate you pay, as compared with the rate stated by the lender.

When the lender says:	You pay in true annual interest:
4% per year	7.3%
6% per year	10.9%
8% per year	14.5%
10% per year	18.0%
1% per month	21.5%

In the above cases, you pay interest in advance, which ties up money you could be using otherwise. You pay back in installments, so you are

[1] Hearings on S. 2755, "Consumer Credit Labeling Bill," p. 285.
[2] *Cost of Providing Consumer Credit*, New York, 1962, p. 5.

TYPICAL TERMS BY LENDERS ON VARIOUS TYPES OF LOANS

Purpose and type of loan	Plan offered by	Price of merchandise or amount of loan	Down payment or discount	Number of months to pay	Approximate true interest rate (annual)
Home-modernization loan	Bank	$1,500	—	30	7.8%
Home-modernization materials	Mail-order house	350	—	36	12.6
Furniture or major appliance	Mail-order house	360	$ 10	24	14.6
Unsecured personal loan	Consumer finance company	100	—	20	35.6
Unsecured personal loan	Consumer finance company	500	—	20	16.9
Unsecured personal loan	Consumer finance company	1,000	—	20	15.0
Unsecured personal loan	Bank	1,500	131	15	14.0
Holiday tour	Airline	291	30	20	21.6
Holiday tour	Airline	909	91	20	18.9
Holiday tour	Airline	2,763	277	20	16.1
Auto loan	Bank	1,500	—	30	7.5
Auto loan	Bank	2,000	—	12	7.5
Auto loan	Bank	2,000	—	36	10.0
Auto loan	Bank	3,126	1,042	30	6.6
Auto loan	Sales finance company	3,126	1,042	30	11.1

SOURCE: Institute of Home Economics, U.S. Department of Agriculture.

using only part of the money you borrowed. Your real cost, in addition to the true interest rate, may be more if you have to pay fees for investigation, insurance, and so on.

If simple interest is charged on the unpaid balance, the rates compare as follows:

Quoted interest rate:	You pay in true annual interest:
¾% per month	9%
⅝% per month	10%
1% per month	12%
1¼% per month	15%
1½% per month	18%
2½% per month	30%

According to the National Bureau of Economic Research study, here is what it cost the borrower to have the use of $100 for one year from the following lenders:

9 consumer finance companies	$24.04
10 sales finance companies	16.59
9 commercial banks	10.04
all Federal credit unions	9.13

Federally chartered credit unions charged the least for the use of $100 for one year. Most of the variations in the finance charges were traced to differences in operating expenses. Operating expenses related to finance charges ranged from $3.30 to $14.25 per $100 of outstanding credit. Credit unions had the lowest operating costs—$3.30—and the consumer finance companies had the highest operating costs—$14.25. It does pay to shop around for credit.

Your Credit Rating. Is your credit "slip" showing? One way to find out is when you open your first credit account in a store. The store may open an account for you in less than an hour; sometimes it takes a day or longer. Behind the scenes of establishing credit is an elaborate national and international credit system. Your local credit bureau is at the center of the network. There are over 2,200 local credit bureaus in the United States. These bureaus are amassing data on everyone who uses credit. The facts come from many sources—banks, court and police records, press stories, directories, employers, other credit bureaus, personal references, other merchants, your neighbors and landlord, lending agencies, school and medical records, and legal records like judgments, bankruptcies, Federal tax liens, and collections. In fact, you name it, and the bureau has it.

All this information is made available to all other credit bureaus through membership in the Associated Credit Bureaus of America. This means that your credit follows you wherever you go. You can't clear your record, if it is not a good one, by moving to another town or state.

Are you a better credit risk when you make $10,000 rather than $8,000 a year? Not always. The right to credit must be earned. Stability of income counts for you. The accompanying table, How Your Credit Is Rated, shows the standards recommended for the use of bankers in a manual prepared by the American Bankers Association.

How Your Credit Is Rated

	Favorable	Unfavorable
Employment	With good firm two years or more. Job involves skill, education.	Shifts jobs frequently. Employed in seasonal industry such as construction work. Unskilled labor.
Income	Steady, meets all normal needs.	Earnings fluctuate, depend on commissions, tips, one-shot deals. Amount barely covers requirements.
Residence	Owns own home or rents for long periods in good neighborhoods.	Lives in furnished rooms in poor neighborhoods. Changes address frequently.
Financial structure	Has savings account and checking account that requires minimum balance. Owns property, investments, life insurance.	No bank accounts. Few, if any, assets.
Debt record	Pays bills promptly. Usually makes large down payment. Borrows infrequently and for constructive purpose.	Slow payer. Tries to put as much on credit as possible. Frequent loans for increasing amounts.
Litigation	No suits by creditors.	Record of suits and other legal action for nonpayment. Bankruptcy.
Personal characteristics	Family man. Not many dependents relative to income. Mature.	Large number of dependents. Marital difficulties. Young, impulsive.
Application behavior	Seeks loan from bank with which he regularly deals. Answers all questions fully and truthfully.	Applies for loan at banking office far removed from his residence or place of business. Makes misstatements on application. In great hurry to obtain cash.

Which Charge Account Is Best for You? Charging purchases has become so much a part of the new way of managing family income that three out of five persons now say, "Charge it," when buying clothing and household necessities, as well as food in the small markets. What exactly do these words mean to these customers? They can mean: "Just put it on my account," or "I'll pay in 90 days," or "I'll take the installment plan," or "Put it on my revolving credit account."

Which of these and other types of store credit are best for family purposes? What does this kind of credit cost the consumer? The answer depends on the kind of purchase, the family income, and the money management habits of the family.

Most of us are familiar with the *monthly charge account*. Normally, such an account must be paid in 30 to 60 days from the date you buy the goods. Its chief advantage is convenience. You can shop in a hurry. You do not have to wait for change. There are no papers to fill out. And you do not need to carry a large sum of cash on your person. A charge account is advantageous for busy people who like to order by telephone. It is a boon to those who prefer to balance their accounts at the end of each month and want a record of family purchases. This kind of credit is satisfactory if you are sure you can pay every month and if you can control the family spending. Do not use it if you have trouble making ends meet, if you are going to make heavy purchases, if you are in debt, or if you are an easy spender.

Many stores now offer a *budget account* that is given various names, such as "monthly installment plan," "merchandise certificate," "scrip plan," "extended credit plan," "payment plan," "optional charge account," and so on. Use such a plan if you want to avoid a large bill at the end of the month because these plans allow 3 to 12 months to pay, usually at no extra cost. Another advantage of a budget account is that bills are easier to pay if you save enough each month prior to payment. You can also take advantage of sales, even though you do not have cash in hand at the time of a sale.

There are some disadvantages. You may pay a service charge if you take more than 90 days to pay, and you may have to make a down payment. Some service charges are deceptive. A service charge may be $3 per $100 of purchased goods. If this is repaid in six monthly installments, the discount rate is 12 per cent because you have the use of only half the money during the life of the loan. Another disadvantage is that it is easy to overbuy.

Revolving credit is the fastest-growing form of paying on time. It combines the convenience of the simple 30-day charge account with installment buying. Originally, each customer had a maximum limit on how much he could buy on credit—$75, $200, $1,000, etc. These limits were determined by his monthly payments. Any time the balance fell below the maximum limit, the customer could continue to buy more goods until he again reached his limit. These revolving accounts now include some new types.

The *option account* is a combination charge account and revolving account. You can either pay your bill within the charge account limit (30 to 90 days usually) or extend the payment to a year or longer. When you extend the credit, there is a service charge.

The *continued secured account* is a combination revolving account and installment account. You sign a revolving account agreement for major purchases, such as a washing machine or a fur coat, and there is no need to sign an installment contract every time you purchase a large item. There is, of course, an upper limit on your credit.

The *chart plan* is flexible since there is no preset limit to the amount you may owe. Monthly payments, however, have to conform to a prescribed schedule attached to the bill.

You Always Pay for Credit. You always pay for credit, even in ordinary charge accounts. Charge accounts are a business cost for the merchant, and he has to add such costs to the prices of merchandise or reduce his net profit. He is not likely to reduce his profit. How much does he add to the price of goods? Macy's large department store in New York City claims that it can sell for 6 per cent less by not offering the ordinary charge account. Many of the large department stores and some mail-order houses have two prices: the basic cash price, and a higher price if purchased on credit.

A few large mail-order houses are discouraging the use of the ordinary charge account and promoting—in some cases, requiring—a revolving charge account for credit. The revolving account is generally expensive, 1 to 1½ per cent per month on the balance, or 12 to 18 per cent true annual interest. There is little doubt that some stores make more net profit on revolving charge accounts than on much of the merchandise sold. When this occurs, merchants' interests turn to banking rather than to merchandising.

Teen-age Credit. "Charge it" is a magic phrase to most adults. This magic phrase in the mouths of teen-agers is now an explosive buying weapon that adds to the already staggering problems of American families. Sharp warnings are being voiced in banking circles and in Washington.

Witnesses at hearings of a Senate banking subcommittee in 1961 reported that retail chains and some department stores are encouraging youngsters to sign up for revolving charge accounts. Junior charge accounts have been encouraged for several years by A. L. Trotta, manager of the Credit Managers Division of the National Retail Merchants

Association. Mr. Trotta recommends the teen-age market as "a made-to-order opportunity for the sales-minded credit executive." In 1960, Sears Roebuck announced the opening of teen-age credit accounts in several of its stores.

The teen-age market is burgeoning at an astonishing rate. By 1970, when the teen-age population expands from the present 18 million to an expected 28 million, youngsters may be spending $20 billion annually—twice as much as in 1962. Many retailers, to get their share or more of this business, represent their juvenile charge accounts as "community services" and "living educational programs in money management." Senator Paul H. Douglas, on the contrary, brands teen-age charge accounts as "one of the unfortunate developments in consumer credit." The president of the Bowery Savings Bank, in New York City, says such credit is "something like teaching the young to use narcotics."

In 1961, *Consumer Reports* expressed some doubts about teen-age charge accounts on the grounds that state laws allow 33 to 80 per cent interest on junior credit accounts. Interest rates are quoted by some department stores at 1½ per cent on the balance, or 18 per cent in true annual interest. But when the legally established rate of 1½ per cent per month yields less than the minimum amount stipulated by some state laws, as would occur when a teen-age account is limited to a maximum of $25, higher minimum rates apply. In New York State, for example, the legal minimum interest on a $25 charge account would be 33.6 per cent in true annual interest. In Montana, the minimum would be 80 per cent, or a $20 interest charge on a $25 credit.

Some credit plans do not require the signatures of parents. A few stores test teen-age credit cards. And one bank plan has three high school students acting as a teen-age loan board, passing on loan applications from youngsters, and issuing loans without collateral or parental co-signers at 2½ per cent interest.[3] Mrs. Helen Ewing Nelson, California Consumer Counsel, has stated that easy credit terms to teen-agers is creating a serious problem in California because "it is legal to charge at least $1 a month." Mrs. Nelson said, "The youngster may be paying interest which actually is greater than 30 per cent."

Teen-age charge accounts can be good experience if the youngsters understand the high costs of credit attached to them. Parents, however, should think twice before they permit their teen-agers to open a charge account without proper understanding of the costs of credit and their responsibility in using such an account.

Installment Accounts. Installment accounts are used for buying expensive items like cars, washing machines, furniture, television sets, and even for clothing and travel. Installment accounts are contractual obligations for

[3] Reported in Lawrence Galton's column in the *St. Louis Post-Dispatch*.

equal monthly payments, after a down payment, for a specific item or purchase. The buyer signs the equivalent of a promissory note, which requires him to pay off the note over a specified period for a considerable amount of service charges or interest.

Protection for the seller. There is no doubt that the seller protects himself in installment contracts. He can offer any one of three written contracts. (1) The conditional sale, where title remains with the seller until final payment. In case of repossessing the item for failure to make payments, the money already paid is retained as rent, unless state laws prevent this. (2) The chattel mortgage, where a promissory note is secured by a mortgage on the item purchased, which usually permits repossession in case of nonpayment, and resale of the item at a public auction with the sale money applied to the promissory note. The buyer is also liable for the deficiency. (3) The bailment lease—seldom used except in Pennsylvania—where title remains with the seller until the final payment. If the buyer fails to meet his payments, the seller takes back his goods and retains all previous payments.

All these contracts have one purpose—to protect the seller. In fact, the installment contract is so one-sided that the losses to sellers are less than $\frac{1}{2}$ per cent of total installment sales.

Protection for the buyer. The buyer's best protection is to buy for cash. Next to this unrealistic advice is the realistic suggestion that he read and understand the installment contract. Some parts of a contract need special attention, particularly any "add-on clause." Such an open-ended contract can be used for other purchases, but failure to make a final payment could end in losing all the goods purchased on this contract. A "wage assignment clause" gives the right to attach, or garnishee, wages from the employer in case of default in payments. An "acceleration clause" makes all other payments immediately due and payable after a default in one payment. "Balloon" contracts, sometimes used in selling cars on installment, may allow easy payments on a 12-month contract for the first 11 months, and then hit the buyer with a blockbuster, say, $400.

There may be other hidden clauses. The only sensible thing to do is to read and understand all the contract. If you do not like it, do not deal.

True Interest Rates on Installment Contracts. The true rate of interest on an installment contract is not the percentage figure that is given. The actual interest rate can be found by computing the *annual cost rate* of the credit, or by finding the *dollar cost.*

For example, a used-car dealer may offer an automobile for $705 with a down payment of $235 and an insurance charge of $30. The unpaid balance of $470 is to be paid in 12 monthly installments at 6 per cent interest. What does this mean?

You can figure the true rate of interest by using the "constant ratio" formula, which is given here.

$$\text{Rate per year} = \frac{2MI}{P(N+1)}$$

$R =$ true interest rate (see p. 102)

$M =$ number of payment periods a year (for monthly payments M is 12; for weekly payments, 52)

$I =$ interest charge in dollars

$P =$ unpaid balance (cash price less down payment)

$N =$ number of payments to be made after down payment

In the example given above, the $30 insurance charge is added to the unpaid balance of $470, which gives P, the principal on which the interest is figured. The interest charge in dollars is found by multiplying the principal, $500, by 6 per cent, which gives $30. Substituting these figures for their corresponding letters in the formula, we have

$$\frac{2 \times 12 \times \$30}{500 \times 13} = \frac{720}{6500} = 0.1107, \text{ or an annual cost rate of 11 per cent a year}$$

If the interest rate is expressed at a certain rate per month, 3½ per cent, for instance, the true interest rate is 42 per cent for 12 months.

On a $100 loan, repayable in 12 monthly installments, the borrower will not pay $42 interest, however. He will pay $22.75, because the interest is figured on the balance of the loan as each installment is paid. To calculate this roughly, figure the use of the total sum of money for one-half the total time, or $100 × 21 per cent = $21.

A more accurate way of finding the dollar cost of this loan, when the rate of interest a month is on the decreasing balance of the principal, is to apply the following formula.

$$I = \frac{RP(N+1)}{2M}$$

$$R = 0.035 \times 13 = 0.455$$

$$I = \frac{0.455 \times \$100 \times 12}{2 \times 12} = \frac{546000}{24} = \$22.75, \text{ the dollar cost}$$

It is always wise to learn the cost of credit in dollars, in addition to the cost at true annual interest rates.

Extremes in Carrying Charges. On installment buying and automobile finance plans, the differences in carrying charges can be extreme. Dr. Allen J. Jung, of the University of Chicago Graduate School of Business, discovered this in an investigation of credit costs in 123 Ford and Chevrolet dealers and 104 department stores, discount stores, and other appliance dealers located in 9 large cities from coast to coast.[4] From car dealers and local banks, he sought the cost of financing $1,500 toward a new car over a period of 36 months. From retail stores, he sought the finance costs for paying a $200 balance on a washing machine over a period of 12 months. His conclusions were these:

1. There were no standard financing charges for cars or appliances. The average charge on the appliance ranged from 16.7 to 19.3 per cent in true annual interest rates. The lowest rate was 9.2 per cent and the highest was 27.7 per cent. For car financing, the average cost ranged from 11.7 to 13.3 per cent. The lowest rate was 8.8 per cent and the highest was 15.8 per cent. Bank rates ranged from 0.3 to 3.3 per cent under the dealer rates.

2. Financing costs for appliances tended to be lowest in department stores and highest in discount houses. For cars, they were lowest in commercial banks, highest from dealers.

Shopping for the lowest price of a product is therefore only half the battle. The other half is locating the lowest cost on financing and carrying costs. Remember that banks vary, too, in their rates. One good source for credit, not mentioned in the above study, is a credit union if you are a member. Charges are about 1 per cent on the balance, or about 12 per cent for 12 months. So if you qualify for a cash loan, go to a commercial bank or to your credit union.

When You Need a Cash Loan. It has been estimated that nearly half of all consumer credit in this country is in the form of cash loans. Rare is the consumer who does not need to borrow at some time or other. Cash borrowing is generally made because of such hard-to-budget emergencies as operations, hospital and nursing bills, funeral expenses, a daughter's wedding, and a host of other expenses that can be financed only by careful planning and saving.

Most families have some savings. But savings are not easily accumulated, and are usually modest sums. One serious illness, and the family savings are wiped out.

According to many surveys, the chief reason for getting a small loan is to consolidate debts previously contracted and to refinance them with a single loan. Then, and usually in this order, come loans for doctor, dentist, and hospital bills, followed closely by clothing, fuel, food, and rent. Automobiles, furniture, and taxes are some of the other reasons.

Most consumer borrowers are not prepared to cope with the various sources for cash loans. They are usually emotionally upset and are not armed with sufficient comparative facts about sources, rates, obligations, and budgeting. Consequently, the typical consumer looking for a cash

[4] Reported in *Changing Times,* March, 1963. (Original article in *The Journal of Business.*)

loan is a rank amateur competing with a professional. Most of the un- happy endings to borrowing could have been prevented if the consumer had had a little basic knowledge about this business. It is important to be forearmed so that if the time comes to borrow a sum of money, you can go about the business in an efficient, knowing manner.

Before seeking a cash loan, analyze your situation. Compute how much money you need and what payment burden you can carry. Set up a plan to refinance yourself out of debt. Next come the general considerations.

1. Shop for cash just as you would shop for clothing or household equipment.

2. Do not shop with the attitude that you are in a bad spot, and that the "loan sharks" have the advantage.

3. Offer the best security possible because the best lenders give the lowest rate on good security.

4. Borrow the smallest amount of cash that will cover your need.

5. Be alert to compare the costs of borrowing money.

6. Avoid unlicensed agents.

7. If you are uncertain about a lending agency, consult the personal loan de- partment of a commercial bank.

8. Listen to the agents who take time to discover the facts about your debts, your income, ability to repay, and your budgeting plans.

9. Know the exact borrowing terms.

10. Figure the true interest rate yourself, and ask for the financing cost in dollars. Interest rates can be confusing and misleading.

Where to Borrow Money. Every community has people who would like to lend money. Therefore, the secret of borrowing is to go shopping for money as you would for any other important commodity. It is all in knowing where to look and what to look for.

Let us assume that you are seeking a justifiable, moderate-size loan from a reputable lender. There are six major sources: a commercial bank, a life insurance policy, a credit union, an industrial bank or loan com- pany, a small loan company, and a pawnbroker. Before selecting the lender, examine the many points on which each differs from the others. Personal loans have many variations and are subject to state and local laws and conditions. Now for an inspection tour through each of the six major personal loan sources.

Commercial Banks. Suppose you need a few hundred dollars. The first place to go is your bank, if you do not belong to a credit union. There are three kinds of loans. An *unsecured loan* is one on which you give your personal note. If you borrow $200 for 90 days, the interest may be about 6 per cent, or a total of $3. The principal falls due at the end of 90 days.

A second type of unsecured loan is an *unsecured installment loan*. The bank takes out the interest in advance—that is, it discounts the loan.

You pay off the total in monthly installments. Thus, a $200 discount loan at 6 per cent costs you nearly $24 a year net. The true rate of interest amounts to twice the discount rate or about 12 per cent a year. Many banks charge a fee also.

Another type of loan is a *secured loan*. It is possible to get a loan up to 60 per cent of the value of stocks, the "blue book" value of your car if fairly new, or the cash value of life insurance policies. It generally takes a few days to complete such a loan. Interest rates on secured loans are lower than rates charged on unsecured installment loans, usually 6 per cent true interest rate per year. This is less than installment sales carrying charges for one year.

Commercial banks are the largest single source of consumer credit, as shown in the accompanying table, Distribution of Installment Loans by Holder. The average personal loan comes to about $575.

DISTRIBUTION OF INSTALLMENT LOANS BY HOLDER, 1962

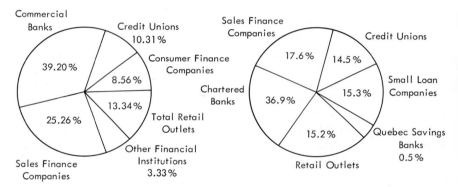

SOURCE: *International Credit Union Yearbook*, CUNA, Madison, Wis., 1963.

Credit Unions. Credit unions lend only to members. They are cooperative associations chartered by the state or Federal government. The members may be employees of a firm or institution, or they may be from church or other community groups. Each member deposits savings in the credit union, receives interest in dividends, and may borrow from the union. There were more than 21,032 credit unions with over 13½ million members in the United States in 1962.

The true rate of interest is 1 per cent a month on the unpaid balance. The dollar cost is a maximum of $6.50 for $100 for a year. A few credit unions have rates as low as ½ per cent a month on the unpaid balance. Loans usually range from $25 to $750. About one-half of the loans are unsecured. The Federal maximum is $750 for an unsecured loan. Larger amounts are permitted for secured loans. The Federal law limits loans to a maximum of 5 years. State laws are usually more liberal.

The highest rate permitted, 12 per cent, is usually well under the rates charged by appliance dealers and stores. The rates are likely to be cheaper than for car-dealer loans, and compare favorably with commercial banks, when you include credit life insurance and fees in a bank's over-all finance charges.

Consumer Finance Companies. There are more than 2,000 consumer finance companies in the United States, with over 13,000 offices. These small-loan companies operate in most states under a special small-loan law that licenses lenders and fixes the amount they may lend and the interest rate they may charge. The loans range from $10 to $500 and occasionally up to $5,000.

Small-loan companies quote true interest rates—so much a month on the unpaid balance. The rates vary from less than 2 per cent a month on large loans to 3½ per cent. This adds up to between 30 and 42 per cent annually. Dollar costs on a $100, 12-month loan are $16 to $23. Large loans cost less. A $500 loan in one state costs 2½ per cent a month on the first $300 and ½ per cent on the rest, or about $11 per $100.

Almost half of all these loans are unsecured. Most of the rest are secured by furniture mortgages. The companies are especially geared for persons without established credit. The better small-loan companies give personal budgeting counseling service. You apply for loans much as you do at a commercial or industrial bank. Your application, however, may go through faster. You sign a note for the amount you get. Each month you make a payment on the principal, plus interest for the preceding month. As a rule, there are no other fees. Some may try to sell you life insurance. If you want it and need it, good. If you do not, go to another lending agency.

Small-loan Laws. All but two states (Arkansas and Texas) and the District of Columbia have laws setting the maximum rates that small-loan firms can charge and the amounts they may lend. The rates are generally fixed by "steps." You pay one rate of interest for loans up to a certain amount, and then a lower rate for any amount over that limit up to the top-sized loan the law permits.

The accompanying tables, Legal Rates for Small-size Loans, and Legal Rates for Larger Loans, in 15 states, were prepared by the National Consumer Finance Association. Rates were computed on the basis of a 12-month personal installment loan, and the dollar finance charges are given in terms of a $100 loan. To get the dollar cost of, say, a $300 loan, multiply the $100 cost by 3. For example, a $300 loan in Virginia costs $51.72, 3 times $17.24.

LEGAL RATES FOR SMALL-SIZE LOANS IN 15 STATES

	Legal limit of loan	Rate per month on declining balance	Dollar charges per $100 for year
California	$200	2.5%	$16.88
Connecticut	100	3.0	20.60
Delaware	100	1.3	8.70
Illinois	150	3.0	20.48
Kansas	300	3.0	20.48
Massachusetts	200	2.5	16.88
Michigan	50	3.0	20.84
Missouri	500	2.2	14.98
Nevada	100	3.1	21.00
New Jersey	300	2.5	17.00
North Carolina	100	2.9	20.00
Ohio	500	2.4	16.00
Rhode Island	300	3.0	20.84
Virginia	300	2.5	17.24
Wyoming	150	3.5	24.20

LEGAL RATES FOR LARGER LOANS IN 15 STATES

	Legal limit of loan	Rate per month on declining balance of top segment of loan	Approximate average rate per month on declining balance of total loan	Dollar charges per $100 on total loan for year
California	$5,000	⅚%	1.1%	$ 7.00
Connecticut	600	¾	1.9	12.96
Delaware	5,000	1.3	1.3	8.70
Illinois	800	1.0	1.9	12.68
Kansas	2,100	⅚	1.4	9.10
Massachusetts	1,500	¾	1.9	12.60
Michigan	500	¾	2.3	15.42
Missouri	5,000	⅔	1.0	6.23
Nevada	2,500	1.2	1.5	9.84
New Jersey	500	½	2.1	14.29
North Carolina	600	9⁄10	1.8	11.83
Ohio	2,000	1.1	1.5	9.75
Rhode Island	300	3.0	3.0	20.84
Virginia	600	1½	2.2	15.16
Wyoming	1,000	1.0	2.0	13.24

If you think the maximum interest rates are high for these small-loan companies (as indicated in the table), you are right when comparison is made with bank or credit union rates. Actually, small-loan companies developed in the early 1900s because banks hesitated to lend to consumers with no collateral. These people had to go to loan sharks or illegal lenders. States, therefore, permitted small-loan companies to serve borrowers in exchange for strict regulation of their activities.

Industrial Banks and Loan Companies. There are about 250 industrial banks and loan companies in some 40 states. They carry out two basic bank functions: they accept savings accounts and they make loans. Some states permit them to do other kinds of banking business, and some have become regular commercial banks—among them many Morris Plan banks, the oldest industrial banks. They lend $50 and up, with an average loan size of about $500. Industrial banks have about the same type of credit standards as commercial banks, although some are less strict.

Industrial bank charges are discounts, although they are usually given as a dollar sum rather than as a percentage. This dollar cost ranges between $5 and $15 a year per $100 borrowed. The ordinary charge would be $7 or $8, including fees. The true interest rates run from 12 to 24 per cent, with an average of about 12 per cent.

Industrial loan companies are usually permitted larger and longer loans than most industrial banks. Rates vary considerably. Florida allows $10 add-on per $100, plus other charges. Minnesota permits 8 per cent discount, plus a fee of $1 for each $50 up to $500, and 1 per cent of any sum over $500. Fees are limited to a maximum of $15.

Life Insurance Loans. You can borrow directly from your life insurance company up to the full cash value of the policy. Rates range from 5 to 6 per cent simple interest. Each permanent insurance policy has the exact terms spelled out. The loan can be arranged by your local insurance agent or by writing to the home office.

Veterans having permanent life insurance can borrow directly from the Federal government at only 4 per cent simple interest. There is a drawback to borrowing on your life insurance via the company. It is easy not to repay the loan in regular payments, because the company adds the amount due to the debt (if there is enough cash value left). For some people it might be better, therefore, to use the policy as collateral and get a regular loan at a commercial bank or, if you are a member, at a credit union.

Remedial Loan Associations. There are only about 17 remedial loan associations in existence today, and these are located in the large cities. The major purpose of these associations, set up by social-minded leaders in a community, is to permit a loan on the basis of a pledged asset to persons who otherwise might go to a pawnbroker or loan shark. The personal finance companies have been replacing these associations in some parts of the country.

The interest rates vary, usually from 2 per cent a month for chattel loans and less for pledged loans. The true rate on these small loans ($100 limit) ranges from 6 to 36 per cent a year. The asset—usually jewelry—must be given up until the loan is repaid. In the case of chattel mortgages on household goods and automobiles, the asset may be retained. In general, these associations are considerably better places to do business than pawnshops and loan sharks.

Illegal Lenders. There are lenders in every community who are not regulated by law. You may know of such persons, who are not necessarily loan sharks. On the other hand, persons who are in the lending business without benefit of the law are there for a reason, usually wrapped up in one word—profit. In other words, they are selling their cash in the form of loans at more favorable rates to themselves than they would receive by working through legitimate and regulated lending channels.

The loan shark is definitely on the dangerous and shady side of the lending business. He is out to keep his victims in debt. The longer he can keep them in debt, the higher the rate of interest (up to 1,200 per cent or more), and the more he can bleed them.

This breed of lenders flourishes in states that do not permit legal small-loan agencies. In such states, the legal rates of interest are too low for small-loan companies to function. When these companies leave the state, the unlicensed lenders enter and reap a bountiful harvest. The best advice to give to a person who contemplates business with a loan shark is not to enter his door. Anyone who is caught by a loan shark should get advice from the Better Business Bureau, the Legal Aid Society, the district attorney, or an accredited lawyer.

Pawnbrokers. The establishments of pawnbrokers range from dingy stores to plush emporiums that generally lend only on jewelry. Charges range widely from 2 to 10 per cent a month true interest rate. Perhaps a common rate is about 3 per cent a month. These loans represent exact dollar costs since the loans are not repayable monthly: an average of 30 cents a month for each $10 owed.

A pawnbroker makes his loan on the personal property left with him for security. Ordinarily, he lends from 60 to 90 per cent of the sale value of the pledge. When the loan is paid back, plus interest, the property is redeemed. If it is not paid, the pawnbroker has the right to sell the pledge. The interesting fact is that there is nothing to sign. Therefore, the borrower cannot be forced to pay back the loan or the interest, but the pledge is forfeit. In all fairness to pawnbrokers, there are not many lenders who will hand out $5 for a few days or lend $150 on 10 minutes' notice.

Passbook Loans. If you have a savings account at a bank or a savings and loan association, you can borrow against your own rates up to about 5½ per cent simple interest. The rate should be low because you are pledging your own cash. The institution takes possession of the passbook, and you can withdraw funds only with its approval.

Why should you borrow your own money and pay the institution interest? It is a form of discipline for persons who have a difficult time replacing money withdrawn from a savings account. They know the withdrawal, when in the form of a loan, has to be repaid.

How Much Consumer Debt Can You Carry? There is no easy answer to the question of how much debt you can carry. There is constant controversy on this question. Families with the same income may differ as to number of dependents, age, future plans, and the way they earn their money. Statistics show that the national consumer debt keeps increasing.

Year	Total outstanding	Average per adult
1956	$42.3 billion	$406
1958	45.0 billion	425
1960	55.8 billion	513
1962	58.5 billion	527
1963	69.9 billion	569

But personal incomes are also increasing, and the debt burden is not growing quite so fast.

Year	Income after taxes	Consumer credit (per cent of income)
1956	$292.9 billion	14.4
1958	317.9 billion	14.2
1960	349.4 billion	16.0
1962	381.8 billion	15.03

Though the consumer debt as a percentage of personal income appears favorable, many individuals are carrying too much debt, and bankruptcies are increasing.

Year	Personal bankruptcies per 100,000 adults
1956	48
1958	60
1960	82
1962	107

The administrative courts of the United States Courts report the following figures for personal bankruptcies.

Year	Personal bankruptcies
1945	11,051
1960	94,750
1963	139,191

In most cases these personal bankruptcies were due to carrying debts beyond their financial ability to make satisfactory payments. Quite typical of the bankrupt person or family was the case of a family with a monthly take-home pay of $214 but fixed monthly payments to nine creditors amounting to $216.

How Much Credit Is Enough? Credit men generally feel that the total amount you owe should not exceed 20 per cent of the take-home income for the family for any one year. This excludes mortgage on a house. If the take-home income is $4,800, the debt limit would be about $1,000. Actually, hard-and-fast rules cannot be applied to all families. Obviously, a man with five children to support on an average family income might have to keep his outstanding debt around 10 per cent of his yearly take-home income. A young married couple with no children may stretch their outstanding debt to 25 per cent or more of their joint income.

Another yardstick would set the limit at about 10 per cent of take-home income over an 18-month average. Thus, on $4,800 take-home income, the debt limit would be around $720.

A third yardstick suggests limiting total debts to about a third of discretionary income for the year. *Discretionary income* is that part of family income that is *not* spent for food, clothing, and housing (including utilities). To apply this test, let us assume that the above items in a budget come to $3,000 for the year. Discretionary income, the balance, is $1,800 for a family with take-home income of $4,800 annually. One-third of $1,800 is $600, the debt limit according to this yardstick.

These yardsticks indicate that the maximum family debt, exclusive of mortgage on the home, for a family having take-home income of $4,800, should be between $600 and $1,000.

Lenders will usually help you determine your debt limit. They are likely to subtract expenses and savings from monthly take-home income and set the amount left over as the sum you can safely afford to pay in monthly installments on your total debt.

Lenders usually follow certain standards when granting credit. Here are a few illustrations.

Charge accounts. Most retail merchants will obtain a credit bureau report on you. They may limit you to credit equivalent to two weeks' or a month's pay on a 30-day charge account.

Installment accounts. The limits of your monthly payments are figured as a percentage of your monthly income. A credit manager does not like to grant installment credit of more than 10 per cent of monthly income. He will scan most carefully that part of the credit report that shows steady employment and ability to keep up payments on past long-term accounts.

Car loans. This is an easy loan to negotiate because the loan is secured by the value of the car. The loan balance is seldom more than the cash value of the car. The loan is paid off faster than the car normally depreciates. The borrower has to carry insurance, which further protects the lender against loss. Many credit people believe that car loan payments can safely run from 15 to possibly 30 per cent of the monthly take-home income.

Personal loans. Personal loans are usually less than $1,000. One general rule used by small-loan companies is that the amount of the monthly repayment should be no more than about 6 per cent of monthly income. They figure that the total amount of the loan should not be more than 10 to 20 per cent of annual income.

Avoiding Intricate and Deceptive Consumer Credit. As you understand by now, consumer credit is intricate and deceptive. A few conclusions may be helpful.

1. Use credit only when necessary or where benefits justify the cost and risk involved.

2. Assume no more debt than you can safely repay out of current income.

3. Shop for the best credit bargain. None of the credit terms are easy.

4. Go to a bank or your credit union first to investigate loan possibilities.

5. Know your lender or dealer.

6. Do not expect too much from creditors. After all, their main concern is to collect your debt.

7. Use 30-day charge accounts intelligently. Do not use them to spend next month's income, or charge accounts will become real debts.

8. Do not let an installment debt run so long that the psychological enjoyment of "having it now" wears off before the debt is paid.

9. When buying major items, such as a car and expensive appliances, it is not wise to sign up for terms that will have you owing more than the resale value of the article you bought. In some car deals, the buyer's debt exceeds the value of the car for 15 or more months in the case of a small down payment and 36 months to pay.

10. In general, make the down payment as large as possible and the repayment period as short as possible. The lower the down payment, the greater the percentage of cars that have had to be repossessed.

11. Avoid *balloon notes,* in which the installments pay off only a part of the debt, and after the last installment is paid the balance is due in one payment. When you cannot handle the lump-sum payment, you are in difficulty.

12. Finally, let yourself be "sold down." The merchant or lender "sells down" when he believes that you are assuming too big a debt risk and suggests that

you make a larger down payment, postpone the purchase, or use a layaway plan instead. The chances are such businessmen know what they are talking about.

It is well to remember that "credit is a good servant but a bad master."

The Need for Truth in Lending. By now it should be clear that most people do not understand the cost of credit. And some prefer not to know these costs. Even college graduates are as ignorant about the cost of credit as other consumers. But before we condemn ignorance, we should remind ourselves that the system of arriving at total credit cost is complex.

There is seldom full disclosure of true interest rates. And there are other credit costs than interest. So long as interest rates on consumer credit are concealed by misleading representations, such as $1\frac{1}{2}$ or $3\frac{1}{2}$ per cent a month, $1 a week for the loan, 10 per cent fee, $5 carrying charge for $50 worth of merchandise for 6 months, service charge of 2 per cent a month, carrying charge $10 per $100, 1 per cent a month on the declining balance, and so on, it is difficult for even the sophisticated borrower to know the total credit costs in a language that can be used effectively in the market place.

In no case, except for the single payment loan, will the buyer-borrower for consumption goods be made aware of the true interest rate he is paying for the loan. And figuring out the true interest rate for competing offers is not a simple task. A buyer-borrower should not have to perform complicated figuring to determine the comparative costs of competing sellers of credit. Consumer sovereignty cannot be exercised when a meaningful final price is concealed.

It is generally accepted that there are several methods for calculating, in terms of true annual interest, the carrying charges made for goods and services bought on time. The Federal Reserve Bank of Philadelphia offered in its *Monthly Bulletin,* April, 1960, a formula for making such calculations. The Bowery Savings Bank of New York published a full-page advertisement in local newspapers in which the cost of subway tokens was calculated as though they were sold on various ride-now-pay-later credit terms. The Board of Governors of the Federal Reserve System also chose a particular formula to use in its monumental study, *Consumer Installment Credit,* published in 1957.

Since there are several possible formulas available, the problem is one of selection—which formula. So far as the buyer-borrower is concerned, the all-important issue is not so much which formula is finally chosen as that some formula be accepted as standard. Without a standardized statement of total costs, consumers cannot shop for credit as they do for goods, and they must venture unprotected into a credit market where the price for this service, concealed by misleading statements of cost, varies from a low of 8 to 10 per cent in true annual interest terms up to highs above the 129.5 per cent calculated by one of Senator Wallace F. Bennett's panel of experts.

It does not appear to be unreasonable or illogical to request full disclosure of credit costs by use of an acceptable standardized formula. In both the courts and the market place, the principle of the truth, the whole truth, the principle of full disclosure, has been accepted as the *only* basis on which exchange and trade can be carried on. Society has succeeded in standardizing weights and measures, fabric identification, most agricultural products, medical supplies and drugs, and many other services and products. Why not credit costs?

This is not a commitment of belief that sellers who use goods to induce debt would become fully moral if they abided by the principle of full disclosure but it certainly would be a step in the right direction. It would be the first evidence that there has been an influence of moral and social responsibility exercised on the sellers of credit. But the first attempt that has ever been made in this country to require this long-established principle of truth and full disclosure in this field was the so-called Douglas bill, and almost all seller-lenders have rejected the proposal. These rejections based on the fears that full disclosure or an honest labeling of credit sales would depress the economy are, themselves, one of the compelling evidences of the need for acceptance of a uniform or standard formula for calculating total buyer-credit costs. These openly expressed fears are a remarkably candid admission that current credit practice is deceptive. It is highly doubtful that responsible economists, business leaders, or government representatives would wish to argue that deception of the consuming public is essential to a healthy functioning of the American economic system.

It therefore seems that a satisfactroy solution to this present complex problem of short-term credit with its concealed costs cannot be found in futile efforts to educate the public. Nor is satisfactory solution to occur through the present system of fifty, more or less, different state laws. A satisfactory solution for full disclosure of all the costs in using short-term credit is more likely to occur if *all* the costs of credit are reduced to a common language—a language that means the same to all the people in all the states. Surely, a culture that has produced complex computing machines has the ability to create a formula for disclosing all the costs of credit.

The obstacle to full disclosure of credit costs is not our inability to construct an acceptable, standardized formula. The major obstacle lies in the short-run selfishness of man. The major problem, then, centers on the desire of business and society to sell short-term credit with meaningful and full disclosure of the total costs. And the solution will, in part, depend on the businessman's conception of his moral and social responsibilities and, in part, on the information, attitude, and action of the public.[5]

QUESTIONS FOR DISCUSSION

1. What are the various purposes for which consumers use credit?
2. What sources of credit are available in most communities?
3. What would you include in a list of "do's and don"t's" for users of consumer credit?
4. When families use credit or borrow cash, does it mean that they are poor money managers?
5. Why is it difficult to get facts on the cost of charge accounts to retail stores?
6. How sound is the assumption that installment selling is necessary for a healthy, prosperous economy?
7. How do some automobile dealers continue to gouge the buyers who finance the purchase of their cars through those dealers?
8. Why is it important to get the total dollar cost for financing a purchase?
9. If the maximum true rate of interest permitted for small loans in a state is 12 per cent, can legitimate small-loan companies afford to do business in that state?
10. How do you account for the increased interest of commercial banks in the consumer credit field?
11. How would you figure the cost of various types of consumer credit?
12. What is a credit-rating bureau?
13. What did Dr. Warne mean when he said that many retailers use credit as a "merchandising tool"?
14. Why do younger families have most of the consumer debt?
15. Is it true that you can never escape from your personal credit record?

ACTIVITY PROBLEMS

1. Make an analysis of the sources of consumer credit in your community. For each credit source, find out (a) how to apply for credit, (b) amount of money you can borrow, (c) time limit on the credit, (d) method of repayment, (e) true annual interest rate charged, and (f) any conditions, penalties, or special privileges attached to the loan.
2. When analyzing the various purposes for which consumers use credit, name specific cases under each classification that you would rate wise for using credit, and name other cases where it would be wiser to pay cash.
3. There are several methods for computing the cost of credit. Using different types of consumer credit, work out accurate methods for comparing their costs.

[5] See Arch W. Troelstrup, "The Influence of Moral and Social Responsibility on Selling Consumer Credit," *The American Economic Review*, May, 1961.

4. The payment on a small home was as follows:

Appraised value	$5,500
Down payment	$600
FHA-insured mortgage	$4,900
Term of loan	25 years
Average monthly payments	$30

What is the dollar cost of this credit? What is the annual rate?

5. Obtain sample installment contracts for cars, furniture, or jewelry. Then find in each case the cash price, the dollar cost of credit, and the annual cost rate. Are the advertised rates accurate?

6. Introduce yourself at a bank as one who would like to know how the commercial bank serves small borrowers. Ask such questions as: "What questions are asked?" "What are the terms and the cost of small loans?" "Is the interest rate deducted in advance? If so, how does this affect the cost of the loan?"

7. Visit a local General Motors or Ford dealer and obtain information on the cost of financing a new car, assuming your trade-in allowance of $550 on the old car as the down payment on the new car. Compare total credit costs with those offered at a commercial bank or a credit union.

SUGGESTED READINGS

American Bankers Association. *A Bank Manual on Personal Loans*, New York, latest edition.

AFL-CIO Industrial Union. *In Your Interest: The Need for the Truth in Lending Bill;* and *Consumer Beware*, Washington, D.C., 1962.

Barack, Arnold B. (ed.). *Kiplinger's Family Buying Guide*. Englewood Cliffs, N.J.: Prentice-Hall, Inc., 1959, chaps. 17–19.

Black, Hillel. *Buy Now, Pay Later*. New York: William Morrow and Company, Inc., 1961.

Board of Governors of the Federal Reserve System. *Consumer Installment Credit*, Washington, D.C.: Government Printing Office, 6 vols., 1957.

Bowery Savings Bank. *Quick Credit Cost Computer*, New York. (Free slide rule)

Changing Times. "All about Credit," March, 1963; "Credit Unions: Do-it-yourself Financing," June, 1961; "Do You Owe Too Much?" May, 1960; "Easy Credit for Teenagers," December, 1960; "Watch that Easy Credit," June, 1959; "Why It Pays to Shop for Credit," January, 1962.

Cohen, Jerome B., and Hanson, Arthur W. *Personal Finance: Principles and Case Problems*. Homewood, Ill.: Richard D. Irwin, Inc., 1964, chaps. 3, 4.

Congressional Record. "Truth in Lending Bill," speech by Senator Paul H. Douglas, Feb. 7, 1963.

Consumer Reports. "Before You Finance Your Car," April, 1960; "Built-in Cost of Credit Cards," March, 1959; "The Tangle of True Annual Interest," August, 1960; "The Teenage Market," May, 1960.

Council on Consumer Information. *A Guide for Family Financial Counseling*, Greeley, Colo., 1962.

CUNA. *International Credit Union Yearbook*, Madison, Wis., 1963.

Duscha, Julius. "Your Friendly Finance Company and Its Friends on Capitol Hill," *Harper's Magazine*, October, 1962.

Federal Reserve Bulletin. "Consumer Spending and Incomes," June, 1963.

Hearings before a Subcommittee of the Committee on Banking and Currency. "Consumer Credit Labeling Bill," U.S. Senate, 86th Congress, 2d Session, S. 2755. Washington, D.C.: Government Printing Office, 1960.

Household Finance Corporation. *Consumer Credit Cost Calculator*, Chicago. (Free); "The Course of Consumer Credit in the Middle Sixties," May 18, 1962; Dauer, Ernest A. "The Role of the Consumer and of Consumer Credit in the American Economy," 1960.

International Consumer Credit Association. *How to Use Consumer Credit Wisely*, St. Louis, 1962.

Margolius, Sidney. "A Guide to Consumer Credit," Public Affairs Pamphlet no. 348, 1963.

Michigan Credit Union League. *Workshop on Bankruptcy*, Detroit, 1961. (Mimeographed)

National Better Business Bureau. *Facts You Should Know about Borrowing*, New York, latest edition.

National Consumer Finance Association. *Finance Facts*, Washington, D.C., published quarterly. (Free)

National Foundation for Consumer Credit. *Consumer Credit Counseling Service*, Washington, D.C., 1962.

Neifeld, Morris R. *Neifeld's Manual on Consumer Credit*. Easton, Pa.: Mack Publishing Company, 1961.

Newsweek. "The American Debtor—He Gets the Credit," Jan. 8, 1962.

Packard, Vance. "Our Credit Card Society," *National Education Association Journal*, January, 1961.

Phelps, Clyde W. *Using Installment Credit*, Studies in Consumer Credit no. 4. Baltimore: Commercial Credit Company, 1955.

Smith, Paul. *Cost of Providing Consumer Credit*. New York: National Bureau of Economic Research, Inc., 1962.

Troelstrup, Arch W. "The Influence of Moral and Social Responsibility on Selling Consumer Credit," *The American Economic Review*, May, 1961.

U.S. Department of Agriculture, Institute of Home Economics. *Family Economics Review*, "Calculating Installment Credit Risks," March, 1960.

The Wall Street Journal. "Installment Debt," June 5, 1963.

Whyte, William H., Jr. "Budgetism: Opiate of the Middle Class," *Fortune*, May, 1956.

5

MONEY AND DEMOCRACY IN HOME MANAGEMENT

Money Neuroses: Distorted Attitudes toward Money

Money does more than buy the goods and services that we use every day. We live in a money world. Money influences us in our relationships with members of our family as well as with others around us. It affects our standard of living, our goals, and our emotions. It takes considerable experience to establish sound money values and to develop desirable relationships with all members of the family. In fact, close students of family relationships are beginning to see a correlation between distorted parental attitudes toward money and family unhappiness. Indulgent parents often deprive their children of the knowledge and experience that will help them to have the proper attitude toward money throughout their lives.

No one is born with ability to handle money intelligently. If children are to grow up as happy, independent, economically competent adults, they must learn to use money wisely, just as they learn to read, write, spell, and figure.

Normal and Neurotic Attitudes toward Money. Psychologists and psychiatrists say that almost everyone has some form of money neurosis. A surprisingly large number of people act peculiarly in matters concerning money. Dr. Edmund Bergler, a psychiatrist, in his book *Money and Emotional Conflicts* presents a behavior chart that helps the layman understand normal and abnormal attitudes toward money.

A case in point is that of a young husband with a wife and three small children who patronized the merchandisers of debt until he found himself in a psychologist's office. After considerable discussion of his attitudes toward money, he snorted: "Nonsense! There's nothing emotional about my money worries. I'm trying to pay off a mortgage, a washing machine, an automobile, and a fur coat. I'm not neurotic—I'm just broke!"

ATTITUDES TOWARD MONEY

Normally, money is a means to an end, that end the acquiring of things one desires.

Neurotically, money is an end per se.

Normally, one does not allow himself to be taken advantage of in money matters and will do his best to avoid it.

Neurotically, the fear of being taken advantage of in money matters is greatly out of proportion to the threat itself.

Normally, one tries to make money as best he can and as much as he can, but in the process will not sacrifice either health, love, hobbies, recreation, or contentment to this end.

Neurotically, money becomes the center of life; everything else—love, health, hobbies, recreation, and contentment—is subordinated to the urge to possess it.

Normally, money has no infantile strings attached to it.

Neurotically, money is a blind for existing and repressed infantile conflicts.

Normally, the spending of money is taken for granted; it needs no surgical operation to put a dollar into circulation.

Neurotically, the possession and hoarding of money becomes the predominant motif.

Normally, unjustified demands for money are warded off (out of necessity) in a matter-of-fact way.

Neurotically, demands or requests for money generate fury, excitement, and indignation.

Normally, the phrase "I cannot afford it" is a simple statement of an objective fact.

Neurotically, the phrase, "I cannot afford it" represents a defensive triumph.

Under questioning, however, he revealed that he bought the expensive house to "knock the eyes out" of his patronizing in-laws, the mink coat so his wife could go to parties with his boss's wife, and the car, a European sports model, "just for fun." Clearly this highly emotional mixture of childish self-indulgence, antagonism, and snobbery (all common symptoms of a neurotic) was responsible for his agonizing money problems.

It is human to want to live a cut or two above one's means. It is probably all right to attempt it, especially during those years when family needs seem to grow faster than pay checks. We know the future can stand some mortgaging, but we may certainly question the emotional stability of the many thousands of irresponsible borrowers and spenders who have an adequate income but are outraged at the idea of being forced to live within it. Their homes are crammed with new furnishings and gadgets, yet they are not satisfied. Once the new acquisitions have been exhibited to admiring or envious neighbors, the proud owners lose much of their interest. It is the spending itself that gives these people a thrill.

At the other end of the scale are the people who find a miserable kind of happiness by living—and usually insisting that their families live—far below their real means. These people go in for endless shopping for bargains. They haggle over prices. They boast that they never buy anything on time. Every penny is accounted for. In such a family, the child who mislays a quarter is in for real trouble. In such a family, the money neurotic usually wears the pants.

It is obvious that both types, the penny pincher and his more wildly spending counterpart who cannot meet his bills are tortured by inner anxiety. Both unfairly blight the lives of their mates and children.

The Emotional Power of Money. Marriage counselors have taken a new look at money problems in marriage. They have found that it is no more possible to be objective about money than about love. If a husband and wife are constantly arguing about their spending, the source of the problem lies in their attitudes, not in their arithmetic. Dollars are important, but studies tend to show that marital happiness is less likely to be affected by the size of the weekly check than by the difference in opinions on how to spend it. Strangely enough, many married couples know little about each other's point of view when it comes to money, and are often confused about their own attitudes. If you doubt this, ask a wife or a husband to guess how much the family spent on clothing in the last six months! Ask what each of them would do with a $500 legacy?

Almost invariably there is a breakdown in communications in a family because of the tremendous emotional power that money exercises over people's lives. To one person, money means love; to another, power; to another, a weapon to fight with; to yet another, protection from life's cruelties; and to others, comforts.

Emotional money disorders, like so many other disorders, grow out of the experiences of early childhood. When a little child is given a toy, which has cost money, he recognizes this as a gesture of love. Is it any wonder, then, that after several such experiences a child reasons that money (the receiving of things that cost money) means love? The child very early translates money and material things into symbols of love. Some parents try to get rid of their guilt feelings toward a child by material overindulgence. This is especially true in many white-collar and middle-income families where both parents work, particularly where the mother is working to buy nice things for the home. Feelings that the child is somehow being deprived often cause overgiving, even to a very young child.

Because of their personality structures, parents sometimes are unable to meet a child's emotional needs or to handle child-training problems constructively. Money then may become a substitute for love or an instrument for manipulation and control or a weapon for punishment. The use of money as a bargaining agent to secure a child's cooperation in doing his fair share of the family tasks is a poor substitute for helping him to achieve a sense of his importance, both as a contributing and as a receiving member of the family.

Bribing a child with money to put forth more effort in his schoolwork or to practice his music lesson sets up a false stimulus for achievement. It emphasizes the reward rather than the personal development and the increased satisfaction that come from accomplishment. Likewise, depriving a child of money to force him to atone for a misdeed or for an injury to another is also unwise, since the payment of money cannot in fact compensate for such actions and may actually lead him to believe that any kind of conduct is acceptable as long as he can pay his way out of consequences.

The Real Relation of Money to Life. The inappropriate use of money or its substitution for the basic elements in the parent-child relationship obscures the child's view of the value of money. The real relationship of money to life becomes clouded, and this creates a handicap for him when he grows up. And all of us know grownups whose money attitudes are still those of a child of five. A woman who clings to the notion of equating love and money cannot tolerate a budget that threatens to deprive her of things— clothes and accessories—that to her mean love. Unfortunately, such a person has no idea that this belief—money or things equals love—and not her limited income, may be the real cause of her budget trouble. If necessary, she will manufacture a dozen other reasons for her money difficulty.

Not long ago Dr. William Kaufman, a Boston psychiatrist, told the American Association for the Advancement of Science that "money sickness is the most common psychosomatic illness of our times." He said that the trouble does not necessarily come from how much money you have or don't have. It comes from the particular "meaning" you have come to place on money, and how you spend it. And he said it could come from the feeling that you need more money when actually you do not need it. He, too, believes that the attitude toward money you have as an adult begins in childhood. Most of us have experienced childhood disappointments when our parents were unable to provide all the things we desired. Dr. Kaufman said the manner in which a child resolves his early conflicts about money will determine some of his basic personality and behavior patterns. Parental bribing, he goes on to say, substitution of handouts for real love, or overcriticism of a child's use of money may establish habits that, if uncorrected, may set the stage for a money-sickness candidate in later life.

Analyzing Attitudes toward Money. Actually, how many ordinary people do you know who are well balanced in their attitude toward money? Do you know an embarrassingly stingy tipper? A couple always in debt? People who insist on telling how much they paid for everything? A family trying to keep up with other families in the neighborhood? People trying to live up to the standard of living of their neighbors and friends? Persons who find peace of mind through entrapment? People who are using installment credit without figuring total costs? Friends who unknowingly are paying 18 per cent a year on the unpaid balance of a department store revolving credit plan? You will probably discover that the percentage of level heads and the amount of good judgment based on known family goal values is frighteningly low!

Reports of many psychiatrists show that about 75 per cent of their patients are suffering from some degree of abnormality in their attitudes toward money. This does not mean that you need to consult a psychiatrist about your attitude. Why not determine for yourself whether your attitude toward money is healthy and useful or damaging and potentially dangerous to a happy family life?

Democracy in Home Management

Fiction writers, sociologists, anthropologists, educational philosophers, psychologists, and others have recognized the importance of the home in promoting the democratic way of life. Jan Struther, for example, has written:

Democracy begins at home, and it begins very early in the morning—not at breakfast, but when the first reluctant eye is opened by the first devilish trill of the alarm clock and when everybody thinks that everybody else takes much too long in the bath. The home, and not a college of political science, is the place to learn democracy—but it's no good for us grownups to try to teach it to our children unless we teach it to ourselves as well—and oh my! we've certainly got a lot to learn. . . .[1]

Sait and Nimkoff, sociologists, expressed themselves as follows:

Consideration for others and willingness to cooperate are fundamental social attitudes. They are best secured through an orderly home routine, designed in such a way that, as early as possible, the child begins to help himself and to engage in communal tasks. . . .[2]

Science has established two facts meaningful for human welfare; first, the foundation of the structure of human personality is laid down in early childhood; and second, the chief engineer in charge of this construction is The Family.[3]

Margaret Mead, the well-known anthropologist, recognized the importance of the democratic family when she wrote: "Unless we democratize family life it is idle to talk of democracy." [4]

[1] "Democracy Begins at Home," *Adult Education Journal,* vol. 1, no. 3 (July, 1942), p. 118.

[2] Una B. Sait, *New Horizons for the Family.* New York: The Macmillan Company, 1938, p. 687.

[3] M. F. Nimkoff, *The Family.* Boston: Houghton Mifflin Company, 1934, p. ix.

[4] "The Comparative Study of Culture and the Purposive Cultivation of Democratic Values," *Science, Philosophy and Religion.* New York: Conference on Science, Philosophy and Religion and Their Relation to the Democratic Way of Life, 1942, p. 63.

An educator, H. Gordon Hullfish, said: "The family is probably the first place in which to begin the growth of democratic understanding." [5]

Democracy Begins at Home. What is democratic living? To answer this question is not easy. Definitions are tricky and inadequate, especially when they deal with an idea or a way of life. Fundamentally, democratic living means sharing—sharing of rights and responsibilities, duties and decisions based on beliefs. This definition is almost meaningless unless considered in relation to ordinary daily family experiences.

When turning the spotlight on daily family experiences, keep in mind that there is no one "right" way, no simple pattern. Democracy as a way of life may be expressed quite differently in different families. What is important is that the spirit of democracy—of cooperative sharing, of consideration for the rights of each in the family—is expressed through whatever is done. The following family rules, although incomplete and no doubt debatable, will help your family to lead a democratic life.

1. Assign well-defined chores to each person.
2. Talk over with the children decisions that affect the entire family.
3. Give the children a reasonable amount of privacy.
4. Avoid favoritism.
5. Encourage the children to invite their friends into the home.
6. Encourage the children to help select their own clothing.
7. Have fun with your children.
8. Consider the family tastes when planning meals.
9. Allow the children freedom to be themselves.
10. Give fixed allowances to the children to cover ordinary expenses.

The child who learns democracy in his family circle will be better able to practice it as a member of his gang, as a student, and as a citizen. University of Chicago social scientists found that children from democratic homes were better equipped for the give-and-take of daily life. They seemed to get along better with their playmates and with teachers, church workers, and scout leaders. They also rated higher in such traits as loyalty, honesty, moral courage, friendliness, and responsibility.

They were preferred by adults as after-school employees. They even tended to earn higher grades in school—perhaps because they were able to work to the full extent of their abilities.

There seems to be little doubt that the foundations of democracy are laid in the home. There, better than anywhere else, children can learn to do their share of the work and to make their share of the decisions, to respect each other's differences, to sacrifice together, and to have fun

[5] "Education and Post War Economics," *Educational Research Bulletin,* vol. 21 (Jan. 14, 1942), p. 4.

together. There they can learn to recognize the rights of others and to reject the idea of special privilege—even for themselves.

Evidence of Sharing in Homes. There are insufficient data on the evidence of the democratic way of life in the homes of this country. It seems probable, by the definitions given above, that only a modest percentage of American homes practice democracy as a way of life. Mary S. Lyle, in her study of 120 homes in a small town and surrounding area in Iowa, came to the following conclusions.[6]

1. In 75 per cent of the homes the husband shared the financial management with his wife, but children had a voice in management in only about 17 per cent of the families.

2. Planning for the use of the total family income by all the family members mature enough to understand the situation was rather rare.

3. Slightly over 40 per cent of the 147 high school students reported that they "had no choice in the duties they did or how they were to be done." Only slightly over 18 per cent of the students "exercised some volition in what they did."

4. Over 53 per cent of the students claimed "home duties as a subject of some disagreement."

5. Recreational activities were shared by several family members in the majority of these homes but 30 per cent of these families did not share recreation.

6. Some families seemed to plan together for family projects and seemed to have a common understanding of the family goals, but the evidence was too meager to proclaim this as characteristic of the group.

7. The pattern of these families tended toward autocracy rather than democracy.

This picture, if general among American families, is serious in terms of maximum development of all the members of the family. This is especially true if we agree that first among the values looked for in home life is the quality of family relationships that permits full development of the personalities that make up the family.

Achieving Personality Fulfillment. Studies show that families in which psychological relationships are sound can absorb severe strains in crises. These same studies reveal that the kind of personality each individual has is chiefly determined by the kind of family in which he grew up. When children are young, they need secure environment. They need to be loved generously and spontaneously. Children who experience rigid controls usually build up resentments that often are carried into adult life. Children need parents who can help them to build confidence in themselves and to feel that they have an important role to play in the family.

[6] Mary S. Lyle, *Adult Education for Democracy in Family Life.* Ames, Iowa: The Iowa State University Press, 1944, pp. 65–69. Reprinted with permission.

Children learn to be considerate of others and willing to cooperate for the family good when they are given increasing responsibility in family affairs. Even young children can help plan (1) how some of the family income is to be spent, (2) how leisure time is to be used, and (3) how, when, and by whom family chores are to be done. They, too, can contribute to discussions on how grievances and difficulties can best be handled.

This does not mean that parents should abdicate. Children cannot always have their way. But the chance to express themselves fully, to weigh ideas of others in the family, is important in development of personality. Procedures need to be planned for giving children more and more responsible independence, because eventually they must assume complete responsibility for their own actions. Many children have never had to think about the problems a family has to face. Someone else did all their thinking.

If family problems are shared according to age and ability, all members become aware of the realities of living. Thus they discover that family life consists of more than sweetness and love.

Division of Work in the Family. No one can prescribe exactly how work should be divided for every family. The family chores differ according to the financial status of the family and according to whether they live in the city or country, in a house or in an apartment. These differences must be recognized in family conferences about sharing activities and work.

The woman's role in homemaking activities might be characterized as manager of the household. This is generally more true for the full-time mother in the home. Farm women work about nine hours a day in the home in contrast to homemakers in the larger cities, who work about seven hours. This does not include time for eating and personal care. These long hours mean that the woman carries the main burden in the home.

Children's contributions to household tasks can be of considerable importance. In the pioneer family, the children were expected to assist with the homework as early as age and ability permitted. There never was a question about this matter in those days. Today, there is much the same situation on the farms, according to Mary Lyle's study of democracy in family life. Her study of rural and small-town families in Iowa revealed that "in the majority of the farm families who had children, the children were cooperating in the daily tasks." [7]

The situation was different in the town families, for in "only 38.6 per cent of the homes with children were these children participating in the common tasks." This was not because the children of town families were too young to participate, for there were only three town families whose children were under the age of six, as compared to seventeen farm families with children younger than six. On the farms, nearly "100 per

[7] *Ibid.,* p. 63.

cent of the children over six years of age shared the everyday tasks while in the town less than 50 per cent of the children over six years had this privilege."

Furthermore, many of them participated unwillingly in home tasks. Home duties expected of the children ranked fourth among sixteen subjects of possible disagreement with their parents. Mary Lyle concluded that "it may well be that the autocratic procedure followed by the parents was in a measure responsible for some of the conflict." [8]

Life in city apartments presents some problems when it comes to work in and around the home. There, almost all activities must relate of necessity to the household. Outside jobs are not available as a rule. The distinctions between the sexes in regard to household work become less marked than on farms or in small towns. Still, here as in rural homes, there are floors to be waxed, windows to be cleaned, some painting that can be done, and perhaps furniture to be repaired. These tasks are in addition to cleaning, preparing meals, bedmaking, dishwashing, and caring for babies and pets.

It is easier today, in contrast to pioneer days, for the family to neglect to plan work experience for their children. With fewer children per family, parents become more child-conscious and perhaps overprotective. It is so easy to decide: "I had to work too hard in my home when I was a child. I'm going to see that my child does not have to work so hard." While some parents, no doubt, had to work too hard at home, that fact does not justify taking the extreme opposite point of view. In a home dominated by that kind of philosophy, how are the children going to become mature and responsible persons? One cannot suddenly become mature through intellectualizing about the problem. Work experience is needed in the home, in an atmosphere where parents and children live, plan, and work cooperatively.

The chief reasons for having children work in and around the home are to give them a feeling of usefulness and importance in relation to their family and to society and to develop worthy attitudes and skills that will build family solidarity and happiness. Their help also reduces the time and energy spent by father and mother in home tasks.

Democratic Conception of the Family. There was a time when many families lived under the rule of a parent dictator or tyrant. In such homes, the parents were the source of all wisdom and control. In some of these homes, this control was stern and serious; in others, it took the form of benevolent despotism. In the latter type of family life, the parent may be a kindly person who believes that he is doing everything possible for the welfare of his family. He may, in fact, be completely self-sacrificing.

This kind of patriarchal or matriarchal family is gradually being re-

[8] *Ibid.,* p. 68.

placed by the democratic family, which emphasizes the importance of the dignity and responsibility of the individual.

The democratic family (1) recognizes that human relations should be characterized by respect for each person in the family, (2) recognizes sharing according to age and ability in policy making as well as in the effort to achieve jointly determined goals, and (3) believes in intelligent discussion as to the means of successfully solving conflicts and settling family problems.

Both children and adults can assist in deciding (1) how to divide work, (2) who is to do it, (3) how to use family income for the maximum happiness of all, (4) how to participate in community activities, (5) how to use the vacation period, and (6) how to solve many problems of family life. Through sharing in the planning, all can feel the responsibility for carrying the plans through successfully.

The democratic process of sharing does not mean that there is no control and no direction. On the contrary, there are regulations; there is direction. The basic change is in the means to the end—the process. The rules and regulations are developed by those whom they directly affect.

Children, and everyone else, resent controls if they cannot see sense and purpose in them. Rules discussed and made by the group are more easily adhered to by the individuals who discussed and made them. If the regulations do not work out as planned or wished, each member of the group knows that they can be restudied and changed. Uncooperative action becomes the concern of all the members. As a result, disapproval of the group is often more effective than discipline by one member of the family.

There are always times in a family when adult control must swing into action. Safety of a child, for example, demands mature control when the child is too young to understand the consequences of dangerous actions. Gradually, as the child matures, he can take on more and more personal responsibility for his own and the family's safety.

The Family Council. The so-called "family council" is one effective way in which to carry out the democratic idea in family life. Each family will have to decide on the kind of council suited to its members.

Whether a family session is formal or informal is of no great importance. There are times when informal sessions may be more appropriate— such decisions as to holiday outings, preferred foods, clothes, play equipment, hours, and so on.

With added experience, an older child can have a part in the more difficult decisions. In time, the area of choice may be expanded until each child is able to make or help make major decisions.

When there is joint planning, suggestions made by the children should be accepted with an open mind. Even an impossible idea needs to be handled so that the child will continue to feel free to say what he thinks and know that his idea will be heard and treated fairly. He must be taught, however, to accept other points of view and in the end, possibly, negative group voting.

Discipline should not be handled in a family meeting. Cross-examinations of such matters as who daubed paint on the neighbor's garage or why the lawn wasn't mowed are best handled outside the family council. In fact, family councils often help to prevent such problems.

What are some of the ways of making a family council work successfully?

1. At first, plan a meeting to take care of something simple and perhaps pleasurable, in which all can have a part—a picnic.
2. Select a time for the session when the whole family is naturally together.
3. Listen to each person's ideas respectfully—even silly ideas.
4. See that everyone has a chance to air his opinions.
5. Get all the important facts.
6. Compromise when necessary.
7. Try different solutions in dividing the common family chores until satisfactory agreements are worked out.
8. Be sure that the entire group makes the decisions.
9. Praise growth in responsibility and cooperation with others.

The Role of the Expert. The democratic family accepts the principle of the "role of the expert." There are certain decisions that the expert, usually mother or dad, must make without benefit of the children's advice. The distinction between sharing policy making and heeding expert advice should be clarified with the children as soon as they can grasp the idea. A family vote on a policy-making matter is one thing, and the advice of the expert to carry it out is another thing.[9]

Parents should not use the false technique of allowing the family a voice in certain matters and then arranging a final outcome different from the family decision. Likewise, parents should not stack the cards so that in reality no choice is possible. Other tricks are used by some parents in family conferences, but such actions are deceitful. They will affect the children's attitudes toward their parents and will lead to distrust and misunderstanding of the democratic process as a means of developing a successful and happy family.

Children and Money

The younger generation is "going to the dogs." A great philosopher said: "Our youth now love luxury. They have bad manners, contempt for

[9] See James S. Plant, "Democracy Turns to the Family," *Journal of Home Economics,* January, 1942, p. 4.

authority. They show disrespect for elders and love chatter in place of
exercise. Children are now tyrants, not the servants of their households.
They no longer rise when elders enter the room. They contradict their
parents, chatter before company, gobble up their food, and tyrannize
their teachers."

If Socrates had not written this statement in the fifth century B.C., it
would be considered a present-day comment. There are, of course, some
differences in the 1960s. Most children are urbanites. Nearly half of them
live in suburbs surrounding a large city. There are fewer opportunities
for parents to teach their children certain kinds of responsibilities. Homes
are filled with laborsaving devices. As the children grow older, many
mothers are reluctant to trouble them with the few chores that remain
around the house. Instead, the drive is all for the children being "successful," and it is difficult for some parents to recognize how proficiency
in bedmaking will contribute to their children's success in life. Many
children won't mow the lawn or wash the car without pay.

The affluent child—and there are many of them—hears a good deal of
talk at home about shortages of money, but usually these conversations
make little sense to him. If parents are short of money, how come they
have a second or third car? How come parents can go to Florida for two
weeks to escape winter? Why talk about saving money when there is
always more where the last supply came from? Can money really be short
when a child can usually squeeze more cash or more presents out of his
parents through tricks of the trade?

Money Training for Children. Money affects everybody. In our homes,
money determines our standard of living. More than that, money determines our outlook on life. Money also determines the relations of members of the family and, to a large extent, our relations to the community.

Said a regretful parent: "I wish somebody had given me the chance
to have some sound and happy first impressions of money. I must have
thought that money grew on trees by all the trouble I've had making it
behave in my grown-up years." The regret of this parent could have been
prevented if his parents had realized that we learn how to handle money
just as any other skill is mastered.

We are not born with "money sense." It takes time and experience on
the part of parents to help children learn how to handle money for maximum use and happiness. The attitude of parents toward money, therefore,
is of primary importance.

Children generally become conscious of money very early in life. Their
attitudes toward money are shaped by much the same forces as their
attitudes toward anything else—family, friends, school, hobbies, and
many other forces. Advertising on radio and television and in newspapers, magazines, and movies leaves impressions of considerable weight.

Then, too, children face some of the same problems that adults must face when managing money. Their wants are greater than their ability to purchase. They are tempted to buy things because friends have done so. Children, too, can become selfish or generous, conservative or impulsive, about spending money. They can easily mistake money as a "goal" in itself rather than as a means to good living.

In a certain sense, money training cannot be set apart from a child's general upbringing. Child-guidance and family-finance experts generally agree that money problems really stem from the more basic emotional and social problems of growing up. The two are easily confused. For example, a child needing social acceptance within his group may place the blame for his frustration on the lack of money. Therefore, parents need to be aware of the needs and drives, the pains and pangs, of their growing children. By identifying the underlying difficulties, much needless bickering is eliminated, and money training can be relatively free of emotional entanglements.

The Teen-age Consumer. Not all children follow the pattern just described. In a well-documented book, *Teen-age Tyranny*, Fred and Grace Hechinger compiled a list of facts to prove what modern parents had already suspected: willy-nilly adolescents are taking over large portions of American society. The authors fear that society is opening up "vast opportunities for commercial exploitation and thereby sets off a chain reaction which constantly strengthens teen-age tyranny."

Time was when a boy's chief possessions were his bike and baseball glove and bat, and a girl's party wardrobe consisted of a fancy dress with costume jewelry. What parents once considered luxury items, children now regard as necessities. Teen-agers are surrounded with a great array of expensive items—13 million cameras, 10 million phonographs and hi-fi sets, 1 million TV sets, plus cars and sports equipment. No one knows accurately how much parents spend on them nor to what extent the youngsters act as hidden persuaders.

Another development, charged with dynamite, is the trend toward charge accounts for teen-agers. For good or bad, credit cards for youngsters are a reality added to the educational responsibilities of parents. This should be disquieting to some parents, because credit plans frequently do not require the signature of parents.

Income and Savings of Teen-agers. The average income of junior and senior high school students in spring, 1962, was $6.77 a week, according to a nationwide survey. Senior high school boys averaged $11.67 a week and girls $7.24, while junior high school boys averaged $4.29 and girls $3.88 a week.

Over half the students reported at least two sources of income. Some 49 per cent received a regular allowance, 48 per cent earned money from part-time jobs away from home, 33 per cent received odd amounts from parents, and 18 per cent earned funds by doing special tasks at home.

The average amount saved was $4.78. Of those who had received money during the week before the survey, 72 per cent had saved some part, according to the study. Over two-thirds mentioned that they kept saved money at home; about two-thirds saved in a bank or savings and loan association; 15 per cent bought United States savings bonds; 8 per

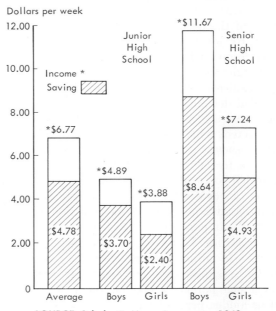

AVERAGE INCOME AND SAVING
OF JUNIOR AND SENIOR
HIGH SCHOOL STUDENTS

SOURCE: Scholastic Magazine survey, 1962.

cent belonged to a Christmas or vacation club plan; 7 per cent bought insurance.

But are young people wise consumers? Are they good managers of money? What are their values and goals? Do they know their legal rights as consumers? And, finally, who is largely responsible for teaching them the basic beginnings of good money management, wise consumership, and responsibility to the family? This all leads us to the all-important responsibility of bringing up our children in an ever-changing money world.

Money Adulthood for the Teen-ager. Many teen-agers are not prepared to shoulder, in later years, their own important personal or family financial responsibilities because their parents neglected this part of their education. This neglect is understandable, because nothing that concerns a teen-ager is easy, and money training is no exception.

There is, however, one important fact that parents can use to good advantage. The world of money and finance is an adult world. A teen-ager longs for adulthood. And learning how to handle money is one of the steps that carries him into that proud estate. But how can this objective be achieved?

Because family beliefs and goals as well as family situations vary greatly, it is difficult to give tips on how to teach money management to a teen-ager in ten easy lessons. Nevertheless, the following suggestions, coming from experienced child-guidance experts and from parents who have experimented with their adolescent children, should be of considerable help to other parents.

1. The example the parents set will be as influential as any specific training. If the family makes no attempt to plan its spending, the youngsters can hardly be expected to do so.

2. Teen-agers should know the approximate family income and the major expenses.

3. In the light of the family income and major expenditures, children's allowances should be discussed in relation to expected responsibilities. Family income is not pocket money, but each member shares in the family funds. A child's share should include as much of the money spent on him as is known. It certainly should include most or all of the money normally used for his clothing expenses.

4. Let each child be responsible for his own money matters. Mistakes will be made. Let him learn from these mistakes. Almost overnight most youngsters will turn into thrifty shoppers. Advice, formerly unwanted and often viewed as nagging, will not only be accepted but sought.

5. When the occasion arises, help each child to understand the legal rights of the retailer and the legal rights of the consumer. Sometimes guarantees of goods are confusing to the uninitiated. He will need and want help in these matters and in many other intricacies of the business world.

6. Encourage children to use the services of a bank. Show them how to write a check, how to use charge accounts. Let them see how the family invests its money and how insurance is used to protect the family.

7. Encourage teen-agers to earn money outside the home. They should not be paid for doing their share of routine work in and around the house.

8. Do not discipline a child by withholding his regular share of the family income. Rather, investigate the real causes for the misbehavior or action.

9. Encourage each child to become an "expert" on certain expenditures for the whole family. This helps to build confidence as well as to give a child the feeling of contributing to the well-being of the family.

10. Do not treat matters that stem from more basic emotional and social

problems of adolescence as money management problems. The two are easily confused.

Parental Attitudes in Money Training. Unfortunately, many parents show extreme immaturity when it comes to helping their children learn how to manage money. Mary S. Lyle, in her study of families in a rural-town community in Iowa, made the following conclusions.[10]

1. One hundred fifty-eight high school students, checking problems that troubled them most, mentioned "learning how to spend money wisely," "having to ask parents for money," and "having no regular allowance or regular income" more often than any other human relations problem. There were 330 problems listed in the check list.

2. Nearly half of these boys and girls were "very sure they were not getting (intellectual) stimulation in money management."

3. Less than one-third of their parents were providing stimulation for the children to learn to plan for and select most of their clothes within a given amount of money.

4. "Planning for the use of the total family income by all the family members mature enough to understand the situation was rather rare."

It was quite obvious that the parents of these 120 families were not helping their children to learn to handle money in the best way.

Why don't parents give their children a chance to handle the money that will be spent on them? Parents object to giving their children allowances for many reasons, such as:

"Money is a sordid business. I don't want my children to have to worry about it until they have to."

"I earned my own spending money when I was a boy."

"I'll give them money when they need it."

"My children spend enough money without giving them allowances, too."

All such arguments reveal poor insight with regard to the real purpose of children's allowances, and back of them are bits of family history, custom, folklore, inertia, and certainly lack of understanding.

Just how do most children get spending money? There are many schools of thought, each with its champions, on this question.

Whim of the parent. "He who pays the piper may call the tune" sums up one point of view. What the children are given depends on the whim of the giver. Some parents use this to show their "power." Others use it to purchase love. Such a parent tries to purchase the affection of his children, substituting material things for understanding. He has little to offer his family in the way of human understanding, capacity for play,

---

[10] Lyle, *op. cit.,* pp. 61, 66, 158. Reprinted with permission.

imagination, humor, or simple sociability. He has one major virtue—a source for money. This virtue is made to work overtime. Consequently, his children's attitude toward money often tends to succumb to parental standards or to rebel against them, and become warped in either case.

Money revealed to children only as a symbol of power and success may lead to feelings of inferiority, bitterness, and unhappiness in the parents. This same unhappiness and maladjustment tend to spread to the children. In such an atmosphere, money can easily seem to be the one good that has the power to dispel sorrow, or quite as falsely, become the root of some, if not all, evil.

Wheedling and collusion. A second approach is the one of wheedling father or mother into buying things that previously have been refused by the other parent. Sometimes there may be collusion between parent and child. Mother, for example, may say to her child, "I'd try asking your father for money after he has had his second cup of coffee."

At times, wheedling takes on a "cute" manner. In this case, children master certain tricks that net the biggest returns. Parents of such children may be educating them unknowingly for future trickery in business.

Money as whip or reward. A third approach is to use money as a whip or a means of enforcing discipline. "If you are a good boy, I'll give you a nickel." Should a child grow up believing that virtue always is rewarded by cash? Sometimes business deals are made for music practice, for getting good or even passing marks in school, or for household chores. Or a child is fined for poor schoolwork or for lying.

When John comes home late from baseball practice two nights in a row, mother suddenly announces that she will deduct 15 cents from next week's allowance. In such a case, the mother reduces the responsibilities of her child to a cash basis. John will have to decide, when challenged again, between 15 cents less cash or more fun playing baseball.

The real issue, personal responsibility with regard to other members of the family, is completely disregarded. In the second place, John is entitled to a part of the family income because he is a member of the family. Money should not be used as a club to discipline a member of the family. Using money to discipline a child confuses his thinking with regard to his family responsibilities, the value of money, and its proper uses.

Adults frequently are confused over how to settle accidents caused by a child's carelessness. Bill broke a neighbor's window. His father decided that the cost of the new window must come out of Bill's allowance, so much each week. Is placing a mortgage on a child's allowance because of a careless act a wise policy? In a clear case of an act of carelessness resulting in a material loss, the parents might preferably decide to pay for replacement of the glass.

The important issue concerns the attitude of the child. Most children are sorry when they destroy someone's property. With a child, the problem is to ease his conscience and to help him make his peace with all parties concerned. Help him without reducing the issue to monetary discipline, which may only confuse the problem of wrongdoing. For Bill, the important thing is forgiveness, that no one will hold anything against him, and that he will want to be more careful in the future.

Reward a Child after Accomplishment. When parents "purchase" better grades and honors, they confuse buying and bribery. Most parents know that there is no relationship between scholastic attainment and cash. It seems to be the path of least resistance. But are there not better ways of showing parental appreciation and for giving praise and approval? To pay cash for success in school, for accomplishment that is for the good of the child, is to give the child a false scale of values and relationships. For example, is an "A" in history worth the same as an "A" in grammar or arithmetic?

Why not celebrate after something has been done unusually well? Everyone loves a celebration. A gift or money in appreciation *after* the accomplishment might be a nice gesture. The important thing is that the child understands the difference between a spontaneous gift and a calculated contract, such as "If you get a 'B' in geography, I'll give you two dollars." It is preferable, after a child has accomplished a certain objective, for a parent to say, "Because you worked so hard to succeed, we are going to buy you that bicycle."

The problem is one of sharing, not making a deal. Those who have studied children have found that the way a child acts is not so important as *why* he acts a certain way. A child who usually carries out responsibilities within his ability range does so because he feels cooperative and because he gets parental approval. "We try to please those we love" is a more satisfactory approach to life than "We please those who pay us."

Should a Child Earn His Allowance? A fourth point of view of some parents is that children should not be given money unless they earn it. Such a parent says, "When a child needs money, make him earn it. He won't be handed money for nothing when he grows up." With as poor logic, you would refuse to button the dress of a two-year-old because she will not be likely to have a maid when she grows up. After all, a small child is helped to do things until he can manage unaided. A healthy youngster wants to learn to do things alone. Children want to master buttons, to walk instead of being carried, because independence is an intriguing goal.

If a boy is taught that only earners can be spenders, is he likely to turn over most of his income to a wife for the family food, clothes, and rent? Grown up, he may feel that a full-time homemaker is not actually earning money and therefore is not entitled to a voice in how the family income is to be spent. A girl so taught may feel that as a housewife she is thwarted and be content only if she is actually receiving money earned outside the home.

If earning is to be the only source of a child's allowance, parents will find that they are paying for all home chores, since outside jobs available to children are strictly controlled by state labor laws. The family must decide which household jobs are to be done as a family team working together for the happiness of each member and which jobs can properly be paid for.

This is not a simple problem, because what is an outside hired job in one family may be just a family chore in another. Each family should discuss and come to an agreement on this matter. Usually it boils down to this proposition: "Here are some jobs we have to hire someone to do. If you want to do them, we'll pay you instead. How about it?"

Sharing Family Chores—Pay or No Pay. This leads to the fifth point of view, the most sound, with regard to children's allowances and work— making a child feel that all the family should share in the family work, pay or no pay. It should not be hard to impress all members of the family that they must share the family work just as they share the total family income.

It is easy to point out that there is really no way of paying mother for the thousands of dishes she is washing for the entire family. Likewise, there is no way of paying father for making a living for the family. And there is no way of paying for the love and care that both parents give to a child, especially in sickness. These things are taken for granted because parents want to do them.

When the family income and work are shared by every member of the family, it is not unreasonable to conclude that:

1. Every member of the family is entitled to a fair share of the family income, including an allowance, because he is a part of the family.
2. Every member of the family should do certain chores in and around the home to keep family life happy and successful.
3. Jobs around the home that ordinarily involve hired help can be assumed by the children, according to their abilities and strength, for mutually agreed-on money payment.
4. Jobs for pay, outside the family, can be undertaken if such work is beneficial for all the family.

Reactions Caused by Parental Attitudes. Inseparable from the children's allowance system is the way the parents manage the total family income. The spending pattern and the methods used by the parents are significant in terms of child development. First, it determines the kind of living the child will experience for many years. Second, it influences his attitudes and feelings toward other people. Third, it sets before him a way of life in which relative values are revealed.

Most parents do not discover until a serious argument occurs that their attitude toward money is influencing all their relations with their children. In a study of 7,000 high school students, it was found that two-fifths of the quarrels between adolescents and their parents were over money matters.[11] In homes where money matters are permitted to become a focal point for argument, the children grow up with immature money concepts, which may continue for still another generation.

Here are some of the techniques resorted to by children in families with immature money management concepts.

1. Having to beg for every cent of spending money is not foreign to some homes. The variations of method depend on the degree of resistance on the part of the parents and often on the skill of playing one parent against the other. Such a child knows that it is especially hard to resist appeals for money if a visitor is within hearing distance or if mother is very busy.

2. Some children take advantage of parents when on a shopping expedition. "Won't you buy me this?" pleads little Tommy. If mother refuses, Tommy says, "I'll lie down and scream unless you buy it." What should the mother do? Call his bluff in a crowded store? Give him a sound spanking right there? Lack of money education on the part of Tommy's parents, or possibly always giving in to the child's way of handling a situation, invited such a public display. It is a human relations problem, not a mere matter of money management, though money is the focal point of the dispute.

3. In an effort to break through parental defenses, older children sometimes misuse the family charge account. This can be prevented by the parents, but too often the remedy comes after one or more bad experiences. For example, when a mother refused to give her daughter money for a birthday gift for a friend, the girl charged an expensive gift to the family account.

4. Children sometimes resort to pilfering in stores. It may be candy, gum, small toys at first, later perhaps a baseball, a doll, or even a clothing item. Usually, they are personal items that could be purchased by an adequate allowance. A variation of pilfering is shaking coins from the child's bank, "borrowing" cash from mother's purse, or shortchanging the parents when making a family purchase.

5. In some homes, the lack of an allowance system leads to seeking an outside job. This is not too bad if it is not forced on a child by parents who do not invite the child's confidence in money matters.

Today, youngsters spend more money than their parents spent in their day. Movies, soft drinks, milk shakes, and entertainment cost as much

[11] Evelyn Millis Duvall, *Keeping Up with Teen Agers*. New York: Public Affairs Committee, 1947, p. 77.

as the necessities of life may have cost a generation ago. But parents should remember that they helped to bring into existence these miracles of production and distribution. The problem cannot be solved simply by limiting a child's spending money or restricting it entirely. It must be met by helping a child to assume responsibility for spending his money intelligently—that is, teaching him to have money sense.

The Allowance System. Children learn how to swim and to play baseball, hockey, and other games by experience in each of these sports. Likewise, they can learn how to use money by experiencing the spending of money. The best way to distribute family money to normal children is via the allowance system.

An allowance gives a child a chance to handle some of the money that will be spent on him anyway. A child consumes food, clothes, and many other items from the time he is born. And he keeps this up on an ascending scale for many years.

Since youngsters must have certain essentials without actually earning them, why should money be an exception? Children should receive some money, then, just as they receive food and clothes. They can use such money to buy their own notebooks, paper, pencils, books, paints, and other personal items. This helps them to become acquainted with money, its limitations, potentialities, and value. They will learn money sense best by handling and spending money.

Even a preschool child can learn the use and value of money if he is permitted to hand the conductor the bus fare or to pay for things that mother buys in a store. In marketing, a child has the opportunity to see that mother has to make choices and decisions in buying.

Alice may say, "Mother! see the nice strawberries. May we have some for lunch?" Mother explains that those strawberries are expensive because they are out of season and she must plan to buy another fruit. Alice may be convinced after returning home if mother prepares another attractive dessert and compares its cost with the out-of-season strawberries. Add to these experiences, and soon even a preschool child begins to weigh the pros and cons of decisions in buying. Thus, when a child is put on an allowance and is confronted with the necessity for a decision, he will be more likely to weigh one desire against another.

What Is an Allowance? An allowance is a specified sum of money given to a child at regular intervals, which is his to spend, save, give away, or even lose. It is cash received over and above any family income allotted for the child's normal care and necessities. As such, it should be set aside as a regular part of the family expenditures, like those for clothes, food, rent, and the car.

The allowance should not be treated as something earned or deserved; it should be distinct and separate from any form of discipline or parental desire. Also, it is desirable to avoid giving a child the feeling that his allowance is a gift from his parents. An allowance, no matter how small, should have no restrictions. Education, yes; but the child should have complete and exclusive control of the use of his allowance.

Restrictions, in place of information and education, reduce the experience to a point where the child is merely acting as a disbursing agent. This might rightly be called an allowance under false pretenses.

Guiding Principles for Allowances. Planning an allowance is not unlike any other educational venture. Certain fundamental principles are important. In addition to those given above, educational experts generally agree on the following.[12]

1. Start a child on an allowance when he begins to make fairly regular requests for money for personal needs or desires. A child under 6 might need or desire such items as paints, crayons, ice cream cones, candy and chewing gum, Sunday school money, gifts for others, children's books, and playthings. A child between the ages of 6 and 9 might begin to request money for magazines, movies, carfare, school lunches, box-top offers, and records, in addition to the items just listed.

2. The allowance should be matched with the child's ability to handle new responsibilities. Each child, even within the same family, is different. Usually you cannot handle two cases in the same way at the same age. A common mistake is to make the child assume too much responsibility or too little. Each year, additional responsibilities should be added, and corresponding increases in the allowance should be provided. By the time the child is of high school age, the allowance should cover most of his needs, including clothes.

3. The amount of the allowance should be determined after needs and costs have been listed by the child and discussed with the parents. Any cutting by the parents should be explained to the child and be fully understood and accepted by him. The amount will have to be based on the financial circumstances of the family. If possible, the sum should include a fair amount above and beyond such necessities as carfare and school lunch money; otherwise, the child has no opportunity to decide how to spend his own money for his desires as well as needs. He must get sufficient experience in making decisions.

4. The age and experience of a child will determine the length of time over which his money management has to stretch. If the family income is based on weekly payments, the allowance may have to fit into weekly spacing. Ordinarily, a young child, just beginning to have an allowance,

---

[12] For more details, see especially Sidonie M. Gruenberg and Benjamin C. Gruenberg, *Parents, Children, and Money*. New York: The Viking Press, Inc., 1933; Household Finance Corporation, *Money Management: Children's Spending,* Chicago, rev. ed., 1955.

might be paid twice a week; later, weekly or twice a month; and finally, monthly.

5. It is important that full payment be made on the day agreed on. All the rules must be known and agreed on in advance. Then stick to this agreement until changes are mutually made. This is a good time to invite a child to participate in an informal family discussion of the total income and spending setup. As years go by, more and more of such information can be revealed, until by the time he is about ready for college, he will know the total financial situation. The sooner this is done, other things being equal, the easier it is to get cooperation without unpleasant bickering.

6. After an allowance has been set up, the child should understand that part of it must be used for necessities and perhaps for savings, and the rest is his to spend as he chooses. Here is where parents need the patience of Job and the wisdom of Solomon. They must not expect too much. This might be illustrated by a remark that a student made in a money management conference: "When I was about twelve years old, my parents expected me to handle money as if I were thirty years old." It is usually unwise for parents to take over until they are invited. How else is the child to learn how to spend wisely? He should have the experience of indulging in whims, even in splurging for one big desire in order to learn the lesson of choices, of delaying certain purchases, and of using money as a means to a desired end. This is what Gruenberg refers to as "arithmetic, forbearance, thrift, hope deferred, projected imagination with delight of anticipation, all in one: it is sound educationally, economically, morally." [13] Children must be trusted to learn for themselves. It is much better for them to make some mistakes in planning and judgment when they are young. It is generally good insurance for their future.

7. An allowance should not be tied to jobs done at home. The allowance should be distributed because the child is a member of the family and is entitled to it as such. Work at home should be divided according to age and abilities. This is a separate responsibility, and each child should be expected to do his part.

8. If a child requests more money, even though he understands the agreement, it is usually a good idea not to give him more money before his next allowance is due. While there are exceptions to all good rules in human relations, the exception can too easily become the rule. It might be wiser to say: "If your needs are more than your allowance, make a new list of them, and we'll talk it over again." Most children will consider that this is a fair attitude. At the same time, the parents are not placing themselves in the position of putting the child through a third degree.

[13] Gruenberg and Gruenberg, *ibid.*, p. 40.

He, then, will have time to do a little adjusting for himself. This is sound psychology and good economics.

9. If a child loses his allowance, it is important to take time to learn all the facts in a calm discussion of the matter. If money is needed for necessities, replace it to that extent. The extra amount should be deferred until the next allowance is due. This may seem to be a little rough, but it is conditioning the child for similar experiences that he will have later.

10. If a child begins to hoard his money, observe whether it is a passing stage or whether it reflects maladjustment to living. Some children are influenced by their parents' attitude or by pressures and demands on them during their growing-up years. It may also be a symptom of personal insecurity.

11. When a child is eager to contribute money to an organization or a school or community group, it is important that he understand its purpose. He should not give money to inflate his ego or just to hold his status among his friends. He should not derive satisfaction out of proportion to his allowance.

12. Saving ought to be active and meaningful, not a routine stuffing of the child's bank. Saving can be encouraged if the objective is specific— for personal use or for a gift for someone the child loves—and the spending should not be delayed too long. A young child may save for a doll displayed in a window. A high school student may save for the annual dance. Saving for a rainy day—just putting away money—has no significance for a child.

A 4-year-old is not a saver. He must start with spending. In time, he may save to spend later. But the only way to learn this is by experience. When a child is 9 to 12 years old, he can begin to understand the principle of saving for future spending, but he must first discover the meaning of the future.

13. If a loan is made to a child, repayment should be arranged within a reasonable time, but without too much sacrifice. Borrowing and lending are constantly going on in our society. A child needs sympathetic guidance if requesting a loan that is out of proportion to his ability to pay. Disappointment can be accepted gracefully if parents use tact and display friendly counsel in such matters. It is not easy for parents to judge the value of the things for which children want money. A seemingly small want can produce intense emotional stress. Many parents still carry such emotional scars from their own childhood.

14. When a child is concerned because his friends have more money than he has to spend, two things are necessary. Discover what the allowances of the friends have to cover. Reexamine the child's needs and allowance. If the old agreement, or a new one, is consistent with the family income or with the needs of the child, he usually accepts it. Some-

times it is necessary to give him a clearer sense of values. Above all, a child must know why.

15. If a child has experience in handling money, by the time he enters high school, he is ready to assume more responsibility. The urge for independence is strong when a child is of high school age. He begins to resent any attempt to keep him young and dependent. He insists on making his own decisions. His money needs are greater, too. The allowance should grow, but so should the responsibilities. The child now should learn how to handle a checking account, how to order merchandise and pay bills, how to decide on tips, how to buy his own clothing and care for it.

16. Record keeping for a child is useless unless he can be made to feel a specific gain from the effort. A teen-ager may discover for himself that some records are necessary. This is especially true if he is granted increases in his allowance only on the basis of reasonably proved needs. Often this must take the form of evidence of where his money went.

Democratic Ways to Promote Happy Families. There is no substitute for happy, understanding family relationships. The best preparation for such relationships is for parents to teach their children to share the family chores, to cooperate in family discussions, and to handle money wisely. Children having such experience learn to face situations objectively, to analyze and solve difficulties and problems in later life.

This does not mean that children should be weighed down with family responsibilities before they are old enough to understand them. On the other hand, they should not be shielded or overprotected from the realities of family life. They should be allowed to join in family discussions and in final decisions as soon as they are old enough to understand what is involved.

QUESTIONS FOR DISCUSSION

1. What are your reactions to the following statements since studying this chapter?

   a. "If you are a good boy, I'll give you a dime."

   b. "I'm going to take fifty cents out of your allowance if you are late for supper again."

   c. "I had to earn my own spending money when I was a boy."

   d. "I'll give them money when they need it."

2. Do you agree that most of us are "born with money sense"?

3. When money is considered by parents as a symbol of power and success, what may be the effect on children in such a family?

4. When parents pay for better grades and honors in school, have they the best interests of their children in mind?

5. How can a child be made to understand that everybody in the family

should share in the family work, not for pay, but because he is a member of the family team?

6. From your observation and perhaps from your own experience, what percentage of quarrels between parents and children are over money matters?

7. Is pilfering in stores and at home related in part to parental neglect in teaching children good money management?

8. Does application of the democratic process in the home mean that all controls are off?

9. How do you account for the fact that some people who have made considerable money have not learned to live happily with their wealth?

10. Can a child be spoiled by giving him money whenever he wants it?

ACTIVITY PROBLEMS

1. Plan a class discussion or a recording of a discussion based on the topic "Parents and the Child's Pocketbook." Ask a father, a mother, a boy and a girl, ages 10 and 17, from different families, to participate in this project. See that illustrations of important principles in children's allowances, work in the home, human relations, school grades, and activities are brought into this discussion.

2. Ask several college students how they obtained things they wanted when they were living at home. Make a list of the techniques they employed. Discuss and evaluate these methods.

3. The question is often asked: "When should you start a child on an allowance?" An interesting way to gather evidence is to interview children in various age brackets. Ask them to name their regular personal money needs. Make a list of these needs, and classify them according to age groups, such as Under 6, Age 6 to 9, Age 9 to 12, Age 12 to 18.

4. How would you teach a child to save money? Begin by asking friends and classmates how they learned to save money. Perhaps they failed to learn how to save money. Analyze good and bad techniques.

5. Recall all the major experiences that you have had with the use of money. Keep in mind the principles involved in these experiences. Check these principles against a list of children's allowance principles that you consider sound. What changes would you make for your own children?

6. Conduct a panel on "Are Mothers Necessary?" The answer may be affirmative, but you may argue about the process of growing up and breaking away from the family apron strings.

SUGGESTED READINGS

Barton, Mary N. "The Older Child," *Parents' Magazine,* January, 1952, p. 41.

Baruch, Dorothy. *How to Live with Your Teen-ager.* New York: McGraw-Hill Book Company, 1953.

Beasley, Christine. *Democracy in the Home.* New York: Association Press, 1954.

Butterfield, Oliver M. *Planning for Marriage.* Princeton, N.J.: D. Van Nostrand Company, Inc., 1956, chap. 14.

Cavan, Ruth S. "The Family in the Suburb," *Marriage and Family in the Modern World.* New York: Thomas Y. Crowell Company, 1960, pp. 63–65.

Changing Times. "Do Your Kids Spend Too Much?" August, 1956, p. 19; "99 Ideas on Your Money Job," "Will Your Child Know the Value of a Dollar?" "Teach Money to Your Teen-ager," July, 1954.

Child Study. "Cooperation in the Family: Dream or Possibility?"; "Family Finances and Your Child"; "Questions about Family Income"; "Parents Speaking"; "The Facts of Money"; Fall, 1955.

Forbes, Kathryn. *Mama's Bank Account.* New York: Harcourt, Brace & World, Inc., 1943.

Goodyear, Margaret R., and Klohr, Mildred Chapin. *Managing for Effective Living.* New York: John Wiley & Sons, Inc., 1954, chap. 4, "Work Simplification"; chap. 11, "Time and Energy Management in the Family."

Gruenberg, Sidonie M. "The Growing Child's Budget," *National Parent-Teacher,* March, 1944.

———. "Test Yourself: Do You Exploit Your Husband?" *Woman's Home Companion,* February, 1956, p. 36.

——— and Gruenberg, Benjamin C. *Parents, Children, and Money.* New York: The Viking Press, Inc., 1933, p. 219.

Household Finance Corporation. *Money Management: Children's Spending,* Chicago, rev. ed.

Journal of Home Economics. "The Family in Our Democratic Society," September, 1952, pp. 498–501.

Landis, Paul H. *Understanding Teen-agers.* New York: Appleton-Century-Crofts, Inc., 1955, chaps. 7, 10.

Lyle, Mary S. *Adult Education for Democracy in Family Life.* Ames, Iowa: The Iowa State University Press, 1944.

Morrison, Joan. "Democracy Begins at Home," *Better Homes and Gardens,* November, 1954.

Overstreet, Harry A. *The Mature Mind.* New York: W. W. Norton & Company, Inc., 1949, chap. 10.

Parade. "We Take a Vote," Apr. 3, 1955, p. 2.

Plant, James S. "Democracy Turns to the Family," *Journal of Home Economics,* January, 1942, p. 4.

Pounds, Eleanore T. "Teaching a Child the Value of Money," *Parents' Magazine,* January, 1952, p. 40.

Prevey, Esther E. "Developing Good Habits in Use of Money," *Journal of Home Economics,* February, 1946, p. 79.

Public Affairs Committee. *Democracy Begins in the Home,* February, 1953.

Sister M. Paul Clare. "Teen-age Attitudes toward Money Management," *Journal of Home Economics,* February, 1963, p. 124.

Strecker, Edward A. *Their Mothers' Sons.* Philadelphia: J. B. Lippincott Company, 1948.

——— and Lathbury, V. T. *Their Mothers' Daughters.* Philadelphia: J. B. Lippincott Company, 1956.

This Week Magazine. "What's Wrong at Home?" Dec. 4, 1955, p. 7.

6

INTELLIGENT CONSUMER CHOICE

The real challenge of this chapter on intelligent consumer choice rests on the consumer's desire, ability, and willingness to get the maximum satisfactions from the spending of his money, time, and energy.

Choice is a fundamental problem for all human beings, and it is also a complex problem—complex because we are living in an "embarrassment-of-riches" age. There are new products, new kinds of entertainment, new services coming along constantly. Shop windows, newspapers, magazines, radio, television, movies, and travel influence us to want more and more. Consumers are literally overwhelmed by a variety of goods and services. Choice making is therefore more difficult than in the make-what-you-need economy of pioneer times.

The choices we make, consciously and subconsciously, determine to a large extent the character of our lives. In other words, our choices determine what we get out of life. It goes without saying, however, that setting up goals of family spending is not enough. We need the ability to work them out. Nevertheless, if we can decide on major goals, we are doing something that many people seem unable to accomplish. The biggest determinant of what we *get* out of life is what we *want* out of life. It follows then that intelligent choice is the first important step in wise consumption.

One of the major aims of consumer education should be to teach consumers how to spend their money, time, and energy to bring expressed wants into harmony with considered needs. And all this should be done within the limits of the income of each family.

The average person needs little food, shelter, clothing, and recreation. But many are not satisfied with supplying only these needs. They want a great many things they do not need, often more intensely than what is needed. A man may commit suicide if he is jilted by the lady he loves. Some parents risk all they have for the sake of sending a son or daughter to a university. So often, the things prized the most are the things needed the least. Why? Perhaps it is because people do not consciously and deeply consider what they want most out of life and how best to get it.

If consumers will probe through the surface reasons for wanting certain things, they may get down to the real reasons and thus make more intelligent choices so as to get the fullest satisfaction out of supplying their important wants.

The Growing Power of Advertising. According to Dr. George Katona, professor of psychology and economics at the University of Michigan, it takes two things to make a consumer buy: ability to buy and willingness to buy. The ability to buy is simple enough. You either pay cash or use credit. But willingness is something else.

According to Donald B. Armstrong of McCann-Erickson, an advertising agency, "The biggest salesroom in the world is the human mind." In support of this idea, there are some 3,300 advertising agencies in the United States. The growth of their power can be seen in the increase in advertising costs from $2 billion in 1940 to about $12 billion in 1963. Approximately $65 is spent each year on each person in the United States solely to coax him into a "willingness to buy."

The growing power of advertising is related to the ever-increasing role that selling plays in our economy. This emphasis on selling, in contrast to production, is explained in the tremendous growth in the gross national product—from slightly over $250 billion in 1950 to nearly $600 billion in 1963. To absorb this fantastic amount of goods, more must be sold. The big problem for the producer is to cut down the time lag in buying something. Even when consumer needs are satisfied, advertising is out to create new, unrealized wants and needs in the minds of consumers.

To move more goods into homes, advertisers are making consumers discontented with what has just been bought. They try to persuade consumers that their cars, refrigerators, TVs are hopelessly dated. Advertisers call this "creating psychological obsolescence."

Another factor in the growing power of advertising is the increased standardization of competing products. Consumers can no longer detect important differences in competing brands of gasoline, most cigarettes, tires, cake mixes, and a host of other consumer products. Often it is the advertising man's genius that makes many products appear to be different.

A third reason for the increasing influence of advertising is the trend toward self-service selling at supermarkets and discount stores and through vending machines. Manufacturers and retailers know that modern consumer goods must be presold through advertising as they no longer can depend on a salesclerk. Some of the advertising techniques used to create the product's image are of questionable taste.

How Low Is Consumer IQ? In pictorial presentations, men sell whisky while seated sideways on a white horse; men with beards sell tonic water; shaggy dogs sell rum; kangaroos sell airline tickets. We begin to wonder whether a pound of coffee is still 16 ounces after seeing some coffee roasters offer a surplus of cups per pound. Why is one cigarette "every inch a man's," and what will happen if a woman smokes this brand? And now we learn a boy falls in love because the girl likes the boy's cigarette. Why do advertisers speak in terms of half quarts instead of pints? Could it be that it sounds like more? As for soaps, detergents, and cleaners, the viewer is totally baffled. Each product is supposed to do a better job than the others.

It is truly a moronic sound that greets the ears and meets the eyes. Is this the best that advertising can do toward informing the consumer? Perhaps a better day is coming. A top Madison Avenue advertising man urged all admen to "grow up." He said, "I wish we'd grow up and realize our audience has grown up. . . . The people we want most are the people we are interesting the least. They're bored with what we have to say and bored with the way we say it. . . ." Today's consumer wants "facts, not fancy; straight talk, not double talk; news, not nonsense." [1]

Some types of advertising are doing good work in informing consumers of new products on the market, and they perform a legitimate service in the world of business and industry. But what kind of society will be created where consumers are led to believe that their feelings and self-fulfillment and worthwhileness depend in large part on the kind of cars they drive, the clothes they wear, the cosmetics and gadgets they buy, and not on their individual quality and character as human beings?

Motivation Research: "Engineering Consumer Consent." The greatest commotion in advertising circles has centered on a probing technique called "motivation research." This "depth approach" to consumers involves the use of psychiatry and the social sciences to get inside the consumer's subconscious to discover the "psychological hook" that will stimulate him to buy a certain product.

Interestingly enough, the man who is quoted more frequently than any other on consumer motivation is Thorstein Veblen, whose basic concept in *The Theory of the Leisure Class* is the desire of people for *conspicuous consumption.* Conspicuous consumption has its roots in man's desire to conform outwardly to the consumption practices of his neighbors, or to surpass them. Veblen gives most attention to pecuniary emulation, the desire to equal or excel one's neighbors in relatively costly ways by showing that one can afford expensive things.

Veblen's basic motivation is still used by some consumers, but according to marketing experts, there are at least 600 different motives for being willing to buy. Therefore, motivation as practiced in advertising and

[1] Reported in the *Chicago Sun-Times,* Oct. 11, 1958, p. 45.

selling today is exceedingly complex and has advanced far beyond the conspicuous consumption stage.

Decline in Conspicuous Consumption. One retreat from conspicuous consumption is discussed by William H. Whyte, Jr., giving the results of a *Fortune* magazine analysis in Park Forest, Illinois, a Chicago suburb.[2] Mr. Whyte calls it "The Consumer in the New Suburbia." In this suburb, most of the families had moderate incomes, and all the families were more or less in the same social and economic class. Everyone was supposed to live up to a certain minimum standard, but to go beyond this standard was bad form and antisocial. This is called "inconspicuous consumption." What was found in this Chicago suburb could no doubt be supplemented in other suburbs. It is especially true in college and university housing for young married couples.

A second retreat from Veblen's theory is what David Riesman and Howard Roseborough call the "package."[3] Though all families have some of the same things, each family combines them in a pattern of its own, and in addition selects some objects because of individual interests, or experience. For example, one family may spend more money on antiques or art objects, another may have a lovely Japanese garden. Though these special interests, and the packages of which they are a part, may resemble conspicuous consumption, this kind of consumption is more subtle than that emphasized by Veblen. These packages represent more variation in individual taste than would have been found one or two generations ago.

Another retreat from Veblen's idea is pointed out in Dr. Riesman's *Individualism Reconsidered*.[4] He points out that American society has a rising birth rate. Married couples formerly said, and some still say, that they cannot afford a child because they must pay for this or that expensive gadget or service; but now to many couples, "children are a kind of unequivocal good in a world of changing values."

Perhaps the reasons for a decline in conspicuous consumption as a motivation for buying are partly economic and partly social. Conspicuous consumption seems to flourish most when people feel a need to impress others. It is a feeling of insecurity. But during the last 25 years, there has been a trend toward more equal distribution of income in the United States. This has been augmented by more equal taxation and by such government provisions as social security. Therefore, conspicuous consumption could be expected to decline.

More important, however, is the fact that real purchasing power has increased greatly, as has the range of goals and services. Conspicuous

---

[2] L. H. Clark (ed.), *Consumer Behavior*, vol. I. New York: New York University Press, 1954, pp. 1–14.

[3] *Ibid.*, vol. II, 1955, pp. 1–18.

[4] New York: The Free Press of Glencoe, 1954, p. 277.

consumption is likely to be strongest where selections and innovations are limited and imaginations are weak. In the latter situation, people tend to copy one another. With wide variation in brands, personal choice can be exercised to a greater extent. If conspicuous consumption is not the major motivation in purchasing, what is the motivation?

Probing Present-day Consumer Motives. With over 600 identifiable motives for being willing to buy, admen have had a field day in exploring the possibilities for influencing and learning more about the behavior of the consumer. Batten, Barton, Durstine & Osborn, Inc., set up a division called the National Panel of Consumer Opinion. Several thousand housewives on this panel can earn merchandise premiums by answering questions about products and about their daily buying habits. Dr. George Gallup, long a researcher for advertisers, set up a "sample bank" of people that he called "Mirror of America" and began probing the consumer to discover what triggers the sale of a product.

Most of the leading advertising agencies now have psychologists and psychiatrists on their pay rolls. Meanwhile, several dozen motivation research firms have sprung up. The most famous is the Institute for Motivational Research, Inc., at Croton-on-Hudson, New York. Several hundred people in the area constitute Dr. Ernest Dichter's "psycho-panel." They have been depth-probed and card-indexed as to their hidden anxieties, hostilities, and so on. If he wants to know how much impact a sales message has on hypochondriacs, for example, he has a group of bona fide hypochondriacs on call. Rival corporations are raiding each other's customers with selling campaigns mapped out by these doctors of psychology.

Among the more common techniques used to lure consumers are playing on anxiety feelings; selling sexual reassurance; creating a personal image in the product (playful gasoline for playful people); encouraging impulse buying; reminding consumers that a product can fill hidden needs (security, self-esteem); selling a status symbol; offering ways, via the product, to channel aggressive feelings; conditioning the young; making consumers style-conscious and then switching styles.

Questionable Probing Techniques. A few of the techniques used to probe consumer motives are largely borrowed from psychiatric clinics and sociological laboratories: social-layer analysis, lie detectors, projective picture and word-association tests, psychoanalysis (minus the couch), and hypnosis. When other motives are discovered, the mind experts bait the hooks that hopefully will lure the consumer.

Motivational researchers have performed constructive services for good products. The successful job that Dr. Dichter performed on prunes is a case in point. The lowly prune just wasn't selling. Why? Dr. Dichter's probers discovered that the prune, in our society, had a host of unfortunate connotations—"dried-up old maids," "witches," "constipation," "boardinghouses." So the fruit has been "rediscovered" as the "California wonder fruit," and advertising pictures the prune in colorful, gay, zestful settings. The prune industry has shown a healthy revival of a good product.

The probers, however, are also using techniques that give cause for concern. These techniques are planned to catch the consumer when his conscious guard is down. An example is the inserting of "flash" sales messages in TV and movie film. The film flash is so fast that bits of film are not "seen" by the conscious eye. In 1956, the London *Sunday Times* stated that advertisers had produced a notable increase in ice cream consumption at a cinema in New Jersey during experiments in this subliminal advertising. The use of this technique raises an ethical question, especially if hidden appeals are used for political purposes.

A large advertising agency explored the subconscious minds of sample humans to find out how to prepare messages that would have a great impact on people of high anxiety, hostility, passiveness, and body consciousness.

To learn how to sell cake mixes more effectively, another agency has experimented with a psychiatric study of women's menstrual cycle and the emotional states that go with each stage.

Efforts are made to manipulate children. One agency made a study of the psyche of straight-haired little girls to discover how to persuade them and their mothers that little girls might feel doomed to ugliness and unhappiness if they did not have lovely, curly hair. The agency, of course, was promoting the sale of home permanents.

A final example of questionable appropriateness in the use of motivational research is the effort to exploit the consumer's deepest sexual sensitivities. The Institute for Motivational Research counseled motorboat builders that men could be appealed to on the basis that power boats express the feeling of power in "almost a sexual way."

Responsibility for Constructive Advertising Techniques. Advertising, in general, is constructive and indispensable in the economy. But some of the agencies are becoming too powerful, and some need to be more responsible in the use of the newer techniques. Many thoughtful people are raising questions like these:

1. Should advertising invade the privacy of the mind?
2. Should advertising provoke anxieties in people, since some are especially sensitive?

3. Should advertising promote waste in the areas of limited resources?
4. Should advertising push consumers toward conformity and passivity?
5. Should advertising encourage consumers to be irrational in their buying?

Motivational research in promoting the selling of consumer goods and services is here to stay. It can perform a useful service to consumers, but quackery and irresponsibility in the field needs control. Said Dr. Wallace H. W. Wulfeck of the Advertising Research Foundation's committee on motivational research: "Not more than twenty of the 120 firms offering this kind of service are really qualified to do it." [5]

A significant point of view on the scientific engineering of consent was expressed by the editor of *Printer's Ink,* an advertising trade journal. He said in part:

Are scientists getting ahead of advertising's ability to use their findings wisely? . . . As few and tentative as are the studies in the field of psychological research, they point the way to a more skillful manipulation of the human mind. The results can be as dangerous as they are significant. . . . The very real possibility that the techniques of social research and psychology will be used by those ill-fitted to use them presents to advertising one of the greatest challenges in its long history.[6]

How Families Buy. Let us examine some of the evidence on how consumers—particularly women—buy. Women not only purchase most of the goods consumed by American families but have a large voice in determining what is bought.

Someone has said, "Never underestimate the power of a woman." At any rate, that seems to be the moral of a marketing survey by Paul D. Converse and Merle Crawford of the University of Illinois, which is depicted in the accompanying chart, Family Buying: Who Does It? Who Influences It? The study shows that women buy about 55 per cent of all the consumer goods for the family; men buy 30 per cent; husbands and wives shopping together buy 11 per cent; and children buy 4 per cent. These percentages represent actual purchases.

Women are even more important when it comes to determining what is to be purchased. Women, according to the same survey, have 57 per cent of the influence in determining what is to be bought; men have about 35 per cent, and children, 8 per cent.

The influences within families were marked. Converse found that women buy 88 per cent of their own clothing, but that men have 16 per cent and children 3 per cent of the influence on its purchase. Women buy only about 4 per cent of men's suits and overcoats, but they influence

[5] Harry Henderson, "Why You Buy," *Pageant,* January, 1956, p. 9.
[6] Reported in *Consumer Reports,* June, 1957, p. 301.

27 per cent of the purchases. Wives also have about **27** per cent influence in buying the family car, although they actually purchase only **6** per cent of the cars sold.

The following changes in family purchasing habits were brought out in the same survey.

FAMILY BUYING: WHO DOES IT? WHO INFLUENCES IT?

WHAT TO BUY?
Mom, Pop, and the Kids exert this much
influence on buying decisions, but......

WHO BUYS IT?
Here's who actually makes the purchases
across the retail store counter

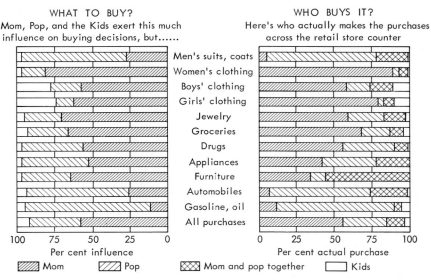

SOURCE: By permission of *Business Week*, Jan. 7, 1950, p. 30; data from *Current Economic Comment*, Bureau of Economic and Business Research, University of Illinois, November, 1949, pp. 38–50.

1. Men are apparently making more of the family purchases, women some-what less, children slightly more, and there seemed to be more shopping together of husband and wife.

2. Men nowadays are doing more of the shopping for women's clothes, women's toilet articles, draperies, and kitchenware, although women still make most of their own purchases.

3. Men are buying more of the furniture than ever before.

4. There has been an increase in joint shopping, especially for groceries, women's clothing, kitchenware, draperies, hardware, gas and oil, and drugs.

While the old contention that women did about **80** to **85** per cent of the family purchasing may not stand up against present-day marketing surveys, the fact remains that they still play the major role in family purchases, as well as in influencing what is purchased. This being true, any progress made in teaching women how to get greater satisfaction and results from the spending of the family income will no doubt be appreciated by them as well as by their families.

The University of Oregon, in 1957, reported a study by Theodore B. Johannis, Jr., of 1,027 high school students and their parents in Tampa, Florida. The significant findings are shown in the accompanying table.

PER CENT OF FATHERS, MOTHERS, AND TEEN-AGE SONS AND DAUGHTERS
PARTICIPATING IN SELECTED FAMILY ECONOMIC ACTIVITY
(N = 1,027 Nonbroken White Families)

Activity	A shared activity	Father	Mother	Teen-age son	Teen-age daughter
1. Selects large household equipment	61.9	68.7	90.2	5.0	6.8
2. Shops for furniture and furnishings	61.3	62.3	93.5	4.6	13.7
3. Shops for groceries	55.1	42.5	84.1	32.0	37.4
4. Plans family's savings	47.2	68.8	73.2	3.0	2.1
5. Shops for family's clothes	46.4	29.3	95.6	30.1	44.3
6. Shops for family's new car	46.4	91.3	46.5	10.8	15.0
7. Provides children's spending money	45.7	77.3	56.1	21.4	4.6
8. Pays bills	39.7	76.8	58.2	7.4	7.6
9. Earns money for family	38.3	97.9	32.8	15.7	2.2
Range					
High	61.9	97.9	95.6	32.0	44.3
Low	38.3	29.3	32.8	3.0	2.1

SOURCE: *The Coordinator,* September, 1957, pp. 15–16.

The fathers were found to be playing their traditional role of family provider in 98 per cent of the homes. Two mothers out of five had jobs outside the home. Mothers were the central figures in family purchasing agent roles in all but one of the five items studied. This one exception was the car, for which nearly twice as many fathers as mothers shopped.

Shopping for furniture, household furnishings, and large household equipment was shared actively in six out of ten families. The central figure in the financial operation is the mother. Shopping for food was a shared activity with mother playing the central role. About an equal proportion of fathers and mothers planned the savings program.

In general, the participation by members of the family in economic activities followed along fairly recent traditional lines. Teen-agers, on the whole, were not given a real chance to learn to be intelligent consumers. The data indicate that the sharing process in the family economic field has not moved as far along as had been believed.

Consumer Buying Habits. A habit is any activity repeatedly performed in the same manner without much conscious attention to how it will be done each time. If habits are long-established, they tend to become customs. Many daily actions, such as dressing and eating, tend to become habits. While there are several kinds of habits, here we are primarily concerned with the buying habits of modern Americans.

People are creatures of habit. More human activity is habitual than deliberate. This may be due to the fact that change requires work. Of course, there are people, probably a minority, who enjoy tackling new problems and modifying habits. However, firmly established habits are not easy to change. Custom, too, tends to impose barriers to progress that are difficult to modify.

Buying, spending, and using habits are receiving a great deal of attention because of producers' efforts to meet consumer demands. The Consumer Testing Institute estimates that seven out of ten customers are habit buyers. The following summary of various studies reveals some consumer buying habits.

1. 69.8 per cent of bakery-goods purchases were bought on impulse.
2. 57.2 per cent of supermarket shoppers shopped only one supermarket; 36.2 per cent shopped in two or more; and 15.5 per cent shopped at an independent market also.
3. 42.4 per cent of the families studied made only one shopping trip a week to supermarkets; 19.9 per cent made two trips a week; and 13.7 per cent marketed six times a week.
4. Approximately 50 per cent of supermarket customers do not use a shopping list, compared to only about 15 per cent in the early years of the supermarkets. Over one-third of all purchases were impulse purchases. Eight out of ten customers do some impulse buying.
5. There is a steady trend toward the more convenient one-stop, self-service retail units.
6. Buying at department stores has increased less rapidly than total retail sales. A larger percentage of upstairs customers are shopping the basement departments. Many department stores stage special campaigns for male customers, since they are taking a more active role in the purchasing activities of their families.
7. Within a few days after receiving the pay check, most of the money is spent. People tend to pay the first bills that come and let the others wait.
8. Charge account customers purchase three times as much as cash customers.
9. There is a tendency to buy on "easy terms" (installment buying) without considering the total cost of the merchandise.
10. People tend to spend five dimes more readily than 50 cents. This accounts

for listing the price of an article on the basis of several small prices for each of the parts of a single piece of merchandise.

11. There are a large number of consumers who do their shopping after buying. Customer abuse of the return goods privilege is a buying habit acquired only by a small percentage of customers. These irresponsible consumers, however, account for millions of dollars of loss to retail merchants. This loss, as a rule, is added to the cost of goods.

12. Goods well bought are often used improperly to the disadvantage of the consumers. For example, failure to read and follow instructions for mechanical goods is said to account for about 40 per cent of all service calls.

Thus, habits dominate large areas of consumer conduct. It should be remembered, however, that habits are not necessarily associated with poor consumership. A good habit can economize on time and energy. Good habits can actually raise one's standard of living just as poor habits can lower it. The challenge to consumers is in the direction of desiring to learn good buying habits.

Characteristics of Male and Female Shoppers. Generalizations about the characteristics of male and female shoppers are a little dangerous. However, considerable evidence of a fairly reliable nature has appeared with regard to shopping characteristics of men and women. Here are a few observations of women as shoppers.

1. Women, more than men, are influenced by their senses. A faint but pleasant smell, for example, is likely to help them make a decision in favor of certain merchandise.

2. Women are sensitive to appearance and to failure to cater to their comfort and convenience.

3. Women are inclined to believe that "high price means high quality."

4. Women tend to be submissive, especially if the sales technique shows a delicate touch of erotic dominance, usually in the form of male admiration of her choice of goods or her personality.

5. Women prefer to be led into decision making.

6. Women want "good living" now.

7. Women like to have things that are different from those of their friends and neighbors.

8. Women tend to follow closely the buying habits of the social group above them.

9. Women find it hard to resist a "bargain."

10. Women are better than men in comparing store prices and qualities.

The following are characteristics of men shoppers.

1. Men are less strongly influenced by brand names and personal emotional reactions to store salespersons.

2. Men tend to avoid store sales. They cannot or will not stand the rush and the crowds.

3. Men are likely to be satisfied by shopping one store.

4. Men are more influenced by friendships and fair dealings.

5. Men tend to make quicker decisions and to return far less merchandise.

6. Men make larger individual purchases and they expect fewer special concessions.

7. Men customers are more loyal to a store but also are likely to be more quickly alienated by "sharp" practices.

What is the significance of such a list of characteristics of men and women as shoppers? It matters not so much whether you agree or disagree with the above generalizations. What does matter, however, if you want to get better satisfactions as a shopper, is that you analyze your own personality in terms of what makes you buy something. Such an analysis is a complex process. Yet business is spending huge sums of money on motivational research in the hope of learning more about consumer behavior.

Motivational research has reached a stage in growth that has forced economists to take a new and critical look at it. As a matter of fact, these broader studies in consumer behavior add to the theories of the conventional economist the facts offered by sociologists, psychologists, psychiatrists, and anthropologists. These studies are of importance because they are greatly influencing consumers on what to buy. Since the retailer wants to sell more goods and services, it is largely up to the consumer to learn how to plan and buy as rationally as possible.

Basic Advertising Drives. What have these motivational researchers turned up by way of the basic drives in people?

1. Sex and sex-connected feelings probably head the list. One lingerie company's campaign, for example, was based on a picture of a woman looking at herself in a mirror with a slogan: "See yourself in ———."

2. Exhibitionism rivals sex as a basic drive, as witness the advertisements featuring undergarments on partly undressed models.

3. Security is also used to influence buying. The Wrigley Company, for example, discovered through depth interviews that people chew gum to relieve boredom and tension and to work off hostility. A test area was used where living standards and literacy were low, frustrations high. The objective was to convince them that they could relieve their tensions, which they refused to admit they had, by chewing gum. A series of comic strips was used in which people of all ages faced with daily tensions overcame their difficulties by chewing Wrigley's gum. Sales boomed.

4. Longing for social ease and equality is another basic human drive. A series of depth interviews on beer drinking showed that many people enjoy beer most when it makes some social event more relaxed and friendly. Thus, ads show

family and friends in informal gatherings in contrast to pictures of groups of "men of distinction."

5. People generally do not like persons with pretensions of expertness or superior status. In one TV commercial test, a chef was shown pulling pastry out of an oven. In another TV commercial test, a little girl was shown proudly pulling the pastry out of the oven. The little girl "out-pulled" the chef, four to one.

6. Many consumers react to reassurance of virility. Researchers, for example, discovered that among Americans tea drinking carried with it a stigma of effeminacy. The pale-color ads of the Tea Council of the United States used to read: "Tired? Nervous? Try tea." On advice of the researchers, the colors were changed to bright red with a slogan: "Make it hefty, hot and hearty, take tea and see." Tea sales rose 13 per cent in two years.

Results from motivational research indicate that it is here to stay. At least it will stay as long as consumers do not develop new defenses against the attack. Will consumers develop a subconscious defense to use as a sort of psychological storm cellar? Instead, why not make a conscious effort to buy as rational human beings regardless of the stimuli?

What Is a Good Shopper? In reviewing the studies of how consumers benave as buyers and of their future intentions, one is struck by the feeling that much, if not most, buying is routine. Only when a major purchase is contemplated—a TV set or a house—do consumers indulge in serious, conscious decision making before the actual purchase.

In routine buying, habit appears to dominate. But the question of how habit develops is as yet too elusive for the research analysts to risk answering. The experts are also careful about their generalizations on how habit is changed. However, it is apparent that some consumers are "good" routine shoppers and some are "bad." A good routine shopper plans with care, is more discriminating, brings more information into use, shops around intelligently, and reads labels more carefully than a bad shopper. The buying skills of good shoppers must have been learned sometime, somewhere, however habitual these skills may have become.

Perhaps one may correctly assume that many, if not most, good shoppers received their earliest consumer education from their parents. If questioned, many women—the most active shoppers—will say that they received their early shopping skills from their mothers and later improved by themselves. It may be surprising how many women buy "new" products and rate them, generally using rule-of-thumb criteria but with fair results. Among criteria for fabrics, for example, they commonly ask whether a garment will retain its color, how it washes in an automatic washer, how it feels on the body, how long it will wear, whether it will shrink, and so on.

It would seem that, even though researchers have not had much luck as yet in isolating consumer decision-making behavior, considerable decision making does go on. True, much sounder decision making could be encouraged if more parents taught good shopping principles to their children, or if effective consumer education were taught in schools and colleges.

Rational decision making is more obviously at work when major purchases are contemplated. Researchers like George Katona and others have made a beginning at isolating and describing some of the motives in decision making. They have apparently learned that "patterns of motives" are more common than single motives. But where do they go from here? Thus far, they have had to be satisfied to record the end decision—whether one will buy a new house or a new car—without getting satisfactory answers to the "whys." In other words, they have not been able to tell much about consumers as people.

Consumer Choice in Our Economy. Consumer choice is a complex process in a complex world. Most mature persons realize this fact. Even so, many statements appear today that repeat the standard simplicities of classical economists. For example, "The free market system permits determination by the consumer of the amounts, types and qualities of products he wants at prices he is willing to pay."

In actual practice, consumers rarely feel that they are the final arbiters when they spend their money. Intelligent consumers are not unaware of the efforts of business, agriculture, and labor to escape the conditions of a free market. They know that, under the farm programs, food prices are not determined by the consumers; they also know that many manufactured products are priced by the producer before the consumer has any chance to exercise sovereignty.

Consumers are also aware that in many instances their ability to judge the quality of their purchases is limited considerably. They know, for example, that they cannot always express their own aesthetic views but are at the mercy of mass fashions and fads.[7] Typical of the efforts made by producers to force fashions on consumers is the following one by Earl Puckett, of Allied Stores Corporation, in a speech to a group of fashion experts.

We must accelerate obsolescence. . . . It is our job to make women unhappy with what they have. . . . You might call us "merchants of unhappiness." . . .

[7] See Leland J. Gordon, *Economics for Consumers.* New York: American Book Company, 1961, chap. 8.

We must make these women so unhappy that their husbands can find no happiness or peace in their excessive savings.[8]

Consumers also know that a price they pay for the benefits of a broad or national market is the rather effective enforcement of mass standards by advertising that generally aims to bring conformity. It is true, of course, that successful national advertising quickly and cheaply spreads the benefits of mass-produced goods in all fields that have learned how to use it. For the most part, then, consumers are at a relative disadvantage compared with producers. They are unorganized and, on the whole, untrained as consumers; they operate largely as individuals or at best as a family unit; and many are unable to judge quality and price relationships. Some cannot determine their needs because they are not able to analyze them and interpret their needs in terms of goods and services. Commonly, people place consumption in a secondary role to fun, social life, and relaxation. Of considerable importance is the fact that consumers lack reliable, measurable standards by which to judge products and services, despite the sincere and useful effects of such organizations as Consumers Union and Consumers' Research to help consumers improve their standards of buying. Accordingly, the consumer might be forgiven if he believes that he is not sovereign in the market place.

This is not to say that the role of the consumer is hopeless, that the producer is an absolute monarch. Most of the remaining chapters in this book will suggest specific ways for consumers to improve their position and their standard of living. At this point, however, it is well to reexamine, first, consumer responsibilities and, second, shopping principles that will help consumers get more satisfaction from spending their money.

Consumer Responsibilities. An intelligent modern consumer has certain general responsibilities that are important to his welfare.

1. To know what makes our economy tick.
2. To cooperate with government, labor, and business in finding better solutions to common problems.
3. To praise and patronize businessmen who introduce better goods and services at reasonable or lower prices.
4. To report instances of poor merchandise and unsatisfactory service to management.[9]
5. To inform businessmen of wants that are not serviced as yet and to suggest improvements in present goods and services.
6. To recognize that in the American economy, with its ability to vary

[8] *The Nation*, Nov. 24, 1951, p. 440.

[9] See Jules La Barth, "Current Developments and a Look Ahead in Clothing and Textiles," *Journal of Home Economics*, September, 1959.

quality in goods, price comparisons are valuable mainly between the same qualities and services.

7. To recognize that in a dynamic, competitive economy, rivalry among producers for consumer patronage will lead to innovation and improvement of consumer goods and services. Intelligent advertising and sales promotion are necessary to achieve this objective.

8. To use customer services and privileges offered by business without abusing them.

9. To inform the proper agency by reporting immediately all cases of dishonesty, fraud, and violation of the law.

10. To give salespersons essential information of needs and requirements when buying goods and services.

11. To make intelligent use of consumer buying guides and information on the use and care of merchandise.

This list of the responsibilities of consumers does not pretend to be complete. It does suggest, however, a few of the more obvious responsibilities of consumers, which, if carried out, would help to improve consumer interest as well as business interest.

Tested Shopping Techniques. Besides having responsibilities that are related more directly to the better functioning of our economy, consumers have responsibilities that will help them attain a higher standard of living. These shopping principles, difficult to execute in our complex society, are nevertheless attainable to a considerable degree by the consumer who is willing to give time and thought to increase his efficiency as a shopper.

1. Know what to buy, where to buy, and when to buy.

2. Compare values. Shop around. But don't make the mistake of using an hour or more of time and energy, and perhaps gasoline for your car, shopping around to save 25 cents on a $3 purchase. Therefore, select stores for certain kinds of merchandise and services, and thus minimize shopping around.

3. Use good buying guides, such as *Consumer Reports* and *Consumers' Research Bulletin* before shopping. Often, good salespersons and advertising will help you to overcome apathy and prejudice against new products in particular. Do not succumb to high-pressure selling or unwise buying.

4. Select basic styles. Basic styles do not become "dated," and a larger proportion of the cost has gone into materials and construction.

5. Generally, stick to the medium-priced lines. Be sure a lower-priced item has the basic qualities you want. Likewise, be sure that expensive items are worth the additional cost.

6. Buy on the basis of intended use. Fresh fluid milk may be desired for table use, but powdered milk can be used for most cooking purposes at more than a 50 per cent reduction in cost and no loss in nutritional value.

7. Whenever possible, buy on the basis of standard grade labels and reliable

standards or seals, such as "USP" on drugs and U.S. Department of Agriculture grades on processed food products.

8. Shop the private brands. The retailer's own brands will generally give you more for your money. This suggestion is complex in its application because it assumes that you will ask for and receive correct information about such brands. Many nationally advertised brands are manufactured and sold to large retail outlets that are permitted to sell the merchandise under another brand name and at a lower price than the nationally advertised product.

9. Buy staples in bulk quantities and in larger sizes. Be sure that such goods will not deteriorate, or you may lose more than you gain.

10. Plan your needs in advance, particularly the more expensive items, to take full advantage of regular sales.

11. Pool your buying. Pooled buying is increasing in this country. Several families can often pool purchases and save money. Many large city banks and other businesses have buying clubs for their employees. Retailers and wholesalers can afford to sell more cheaply to groups than to individuals because their costs of doing business with groups are lower.

12. Pay cash. Avoid installment buying unless the pleasure you gain compensates for the increase in the cost of the article. Even then, you can do better by using your own savings or by making a loan at a commercial bank or your credit union.

13. Avoid buying on impulse.

Intelligent application of these shopping techniques, developed in detail in the remaining chapters of this book, will help you attain greater satisfaction from the spending of money. In our highly specialized economy, there is an ever-increasing informational gap between producers and consumers. This gap can be closed considerably if more consumers will (1) give some thought to what they want most out of life—that is, to their goals; (2) put first things first; and (3) continuously learn how, when, and where to select the commodities and services that will give them maximum satisfaction. Most consumers want more things than they can afford. It is only by following these three guides that, as an intelligent consumer, you can keep your money from disappearing with unsatisfactory results.

Intelligent consumer choice is a fundamental problem for all human beings. Choice, in our modern economy, is not a simple process. This study of consumer problems is dedicated to helping you to learn how to obtain more of what you want out of life. Intelligent consumer choice, more than any other single factor, is the basis for improving the quality of living for each member of the family. To achieve a high quality of living, consumers have certain responsibilities, and this goal can only be achieved when these responsibilities are carried out intelligently.

QUESTIONS FOR DISCUSSION

1. While the wife apparently still does most of the purchasing for the family and makes even more of the decisions on what should be bought, how do you account for the increase in husband and wife shopping together?

2. Comment on the following statements.

a. "High price means high quality."

b. "Women prefer to be led into decisions."

c. "Women make more impulsive purchases than men."

d. "Men are generally satisfied at shopping one store."

3. In what ways are our choices determined by what we want out of life?

4. What are the ingredients of an adequate standard of living according to your desires?

5. What part does consumer choice play in our daily living?

6. How is consumer choice restricted?

7. Is intelligent choice making always based on reasoned judgment?

8. Perhaps you have recently purchased a hat, sweater, suit, dress, radio, or something else of sufficient value and price to require careful consideration. Why did you buy it? Make a serious effort to get down to your basic motives. Be honest. Avoid rationalization except as it may have been a factor in the purchase.

9. Why is it difficult to analyze motives for choices and purchases?

10. Is it necessarily wrong to spend money to win social recognition and to feel more adequate or superior?

11. "People are creatures of habit." In what respect do you regard yourself as a habit buyer?

12. Are consumer buying habits good or bad?

13. In what respect do you agree or disagree with the foregoing analyses of men and women as shoppers?

14. Business is spending millions of dollars on motivational research to influence you to buy more goods and services. As a consumer, should you try to build a defense against this psychological barrage? If so, what can you do?

15. Why do consumers feel that they are not the "final arbiters" when they spend their money?

16. Explain the statement: "There is an ever-increasing informational gap between producers and consumers."

17. Are there any dangers in the ways that the human mind is influenced by some advertisers?

ACTIVITY PROBLEMS

1. Make a study of the real underlying motives that determined your purchase of certain merchandise, services, or pleasures. For each purchase, give the reasons that come to mind first. Then consider possible hidden or subconscious motives. Would you spend your money again for the same item, service, or fun?

2. Examine several advertisements in popular magazines. Identify and classify the kinds of sales appeal in the advertisements. How effective are these appeals?

3. After reading Thorstein Veblen's theory about "conspicuous display" in *The Theory of the Leisure Class*, can you find illustrations in present-day consumption? Are there new motives for consumption today?

4. Trace the history of a particular fashion. Who created this fashion? Were consumers ready for it? Did it need sales promotion? Was there any noticeable consumer resistance? How long did the fashion last? Who was most satisfied with this particular fashion article? Was there an economic waste?

5. William James said that "man is a bundle of habits." Some of these habits may be good and others bad. How would you try to change a bad habit? How would you strengthen a good habit? Reflect on the habits that influence choices in the market.

6. Is your behavior as a consumer consistent with your philosophy? This is really a tough question. It involves probing questions like these: "What do you want out of life?" "Have your choices been consistent with your goals?" "Are your goals consistent with your moral principles?"

7. What is meant by "the good life"? What is meant by "plain living" and by "high thinking"?

8. How have beliefs changed through the years (early man, Greeks, Romans, Ascetics, Epicureans, Puritans, and so on)?

SUGGESTED READINGS

Baker, Stephen. *Visual Persuasion*. New York: McGraw-Hill Book Company, 1961.

Britt, Steuart Henderson. *The Spenders*. New York: McGraw-Hill Book Company, 1960.

Business Week. "Ads You'll Never See: Invisible Commercials," Sept. 21, 1957, pp. 30–31.

Changing Times. "Do You Buy on Impulse?" March, 1956; "TV Commercials: Wonderful World of Make Believe," May, 1962.

Cheskin, Louis. *Why People Buy*. New York: Liveright Publishing Corporation, 1959.

————. *Business without Gambling*. Chicago: Quadrangle Books, Inc., 1963.

Cone, Fairfax M. "Advertising Is Not a Plot," *The Atlantic Monthly*, January, 1958, pp. 71–73.

Consumer Behavior, vol. I. New York: New York University Press, 1954; Foote, Nelson N. "The Autonomy of the Consumer"; Whyte, William H. "The Consumer in the New Suburbia."

Consumer Reports. "Consumer Motivation," June, 1957; "The Little Ad That Isn't There," January, 1958, pp. 7–10.

Editors of *Fortune*. "Markets of the Sixties." New York: Harper & Row, Publishers, Incorporated, 1958.

————. "Why Do People Buy?" New York: McGraw-Hill Book Company, 1953.

Fortune. "Motivational Research," June, 1956.

Gilbert, Eugene. *Advertising and Marketing to Young People*. New York: Printer's Ink Book, 1957.

Gordon, Leland J. *Economics for Consumers*. New York: American Book Company, 1961, chaps. 1–4, 7–10, 14, 24, 25.

Hamilton, David. *The Consumer in Our Economy*. Boston: Houghton Mifflin Company, 1962, chaps. 5, 6, 9, 10.

Hanan, Mack. *The Pacifiers*. Boston: Little, Brown and Company, 1960.

Hess, Max, Jr. *Every Dollar Counts*. New York: Fairchild Publications, Inc., 1952, chaps. 1–5, 12.

Katona, George. *The Powerful Consumer*. New York: McGraw-Hill Book Company, 1960, chap. 9.

Martineau, Pierre. *Motivation in Advertising*. New York: McGraw-Hill Book Company, 1957.

Mayer, Martin. *Madison Avenue U.S.A.* New York: Harper & Row, Publishers, Incorporated, 1958.

Minnesota University Center for Continuation Study, *Proceedings of an Institute on Consumer Problems*, 1956: Evans, Herbert. "People as Consumers"; Whyte, William H. "Advertising and the Consumer"; Whyte, William H. "The Consumer in Modern Society."

Newman, Joseph W. *Motivation Research and Marketing Management*. Cambridge, Mass.: Harvard University Press, 1957.

Packard, Vance. *The Hidden Persuaders*. New York: David McKay Company, Inc., 1958; Packard, Vance. *The Status Seekers*. New York: David McKay Company, Inc., 1959; Packard, Vance. *The Waste Makers*. New York: David McKay Company, Inc., 1960.

Pei, Mario. *The Consumer's Manifesto*. New York: Crown Publishers, Inc., 1960.

Reck, Dickson. *National Standards in a Modern Economy*. New York: Harper & Row, Publishers, Incorporated, 1956, chaps. 28, 30.

The Reporter. "Ain't Nobody Here but Us Commercials," Oct. 17, 1957, pp. 35–37.

Samstag, Nicholas. *Persuasion for Profit*. Norman, Okla.: University of Oklahoma Press, 1957.

Seeley, John P., Sin, R. Alexander, and Loosley, Elizabeth W. *Crestwood Heights*. New York: Basic Books, Inc., Publishers, 1956.

Veblen, Thorstein. *The Theory of the Leisure Class*. New York: The Viking Press, Inc., 1912.

Voorhis, Jerry. *American Cooperatives*. New York: Harper & Row, Publishers, Incorporated, 1961.

Walgast, Elizabeth H. "Do Husbands or Wives Make the Purchasing Decisions?" *Journal of Marketing*, October, 1958, pp. 151–158.

Whyte, William H., Jr. *The Organization Man*. New York: Simon & Schuster, Inc., 1956, chap. 24.

Wolff, Janet L. *What Makes Women Buy*. New York: McGraw-Hill Book Company, 1958, chap. 10.

7

FOOD SHOPPING BEGINS AT HOME

Food problems exist in almost every family regardless of income and home production. And food problems arise even in connection with the pleasant things in family life. In fact, the busier and happier a family becomes, the greater the increase of food problems. Home, husband, children, friends, and social and business contacts are all dependent on the strength and vitality that are on a direct line with the kitchen and the market place. And no matter where or how a food problem originates, a woman faces it in the kitchen and to a large extent in the market.

Food management is therefore one of the most important jobs in the home. The health and happiness of the family are directly dependent on the skill and information used in the kitchen and in the market place. The family pocketbook is affected, too, because food is the largest single expense most families have in their budgets.

Getting along on poor diets takes its toll in chronic fatigue, shifting aches and pains, and digestive disturbances. These discomforts may not keep a person in bed. They do, however, cut down on efficiency. Inadequate diets also lower natural resistance to infection. They destroy the sense of well-being, the joy of being actively alive and able to work and play hard.

Buying Nutritional Food. American families spend about one-fifth of their income for food. Of course, they can spend much more, but they can be well-nourished by spending much less than this amount. To get the most food value for your dollar, you must have knowledge about foods and stores, you must plan and buy carefully the food your family needs and likes. Everyone needs the same basic foods. How much each person needs depends largely on age, sex, occupation, and general health.

The first step toward buying nourishing foods is to learn the type of nutrients that are essential to the family's health and well-being. The second step is to learn which foods are good sources of these nutrients.

166

Nutritionists generally divide foods into groups to show how to select the right foods for good health. The U.S. Department of Agriculture Leaflet no. 424, *Food for Fitness*, suggests these four groups:

1. *Milk group.* Includes milk and dairy products like cheese and ice cream. This group gives calcium, protein, vitamin A, and riboflavin. These nutrients are so important that they should be supplied daily as follows:

Adults	2 or more cups
Teen-agers	1 quart at least
Children	3 to 4 cups
Pregnant and nursing mothers	1½ quarts at least

The alternatives and equivalents to milk on the basis of calcium furnished are:

1-inch cube cheese equals ⅔ cup milk
½ cup cottage cheese equals ⅓ cup milk
½ cup ice cream equals ¼ cup milk

2. *Meat group.* Includes meat, eggs, dry beans; provides protein, iron, and B vitamins. Two or more servings of beef, veal, pork, lamb, poultry, fish, or eggs should be provided daily. Alternates are cooked dry beans, peas or lentils, nuts, peanuts or peanut butter, soya flour, grits, and soybeans. The amount of one serving is two or three ounces of lean meat, poultry, fish, or lentils, four tablespoons of peanut butter, or two eggs.

3. *Vegetable and fruit group.* Provides chiefly vitamin A and vitamin C plus calcium, iron, and some of the B vitamins. Four or more servings should be provided daily for everyone. Serve at least every other day a citrus fruit or some other fruit or vegetable with lots of vitamin C and a dark green or deep yellow vegetable for vitamin A. But don't ignore potatoes and many other good vegetables and fruits.

4. *Bread and cereal group.* Four or more servings in any form that is either whole grain, enriched, or restored provide other B vitamins, iron, calories, and roughage. One serving equals one slice of bread, or a like amount in the form of crackers or baked goods, one ounce of dry cereal, or one-half to three-fourths cup of cooked cereal, corn meal, grits, macaroni, noodles, rice, or spaghetti.

Fats and sugars, added in cooking and at meals, provide calories for energy.

Good Nutrition Is Not Expensive. With nutrition as the basis for decision, a well-balanced diet can be planned at comparatively low cost. The accompanying table, Basic Nutrients at Variant Costs, shows how the average adult can get a whole day's supply of vitamins C and A from different quantities of vegetables and fruits. Compare the costs per serving.

The second part of the table shows that eggs, cheese, dry beans, and peanut butter are all good substitutes for the higher-priced protein foods. Dry beans and peas are especially good bargains, but should be used in combination with a small amount of meat to best satisfy nutritional needs.

BASIC NUTRIENTS AT VARIANT COSTS

The average adult can get a whole day's supply of . . .

Vitamin C		Vitamin A	
By eating or drinking . . .	At this cost	By eating or drinking . . .	At this cost
1½ c raw cabbage	4¢	¼ c carrots	2¢
I orange	4¢	½ c kale	3¢
¾ c canned or frozen orange or grapefruit juice	4¢–5¢	¼ c spinach	3¢
⅔ c broccoli	7¢	1 c broccoli	9¢
1⅓ c kale	7¢	⅓ cantaloupe	12¢
2¼ c cooked cabbage	11¢	2 c canned tomato juice	15¢
2 c canned tomato juice	15¢	3 tomatoes	26¢
¾ c frozen strawberries	20¢	5 c green snap beans	36¢
2½ tomatoes	20¢	3–4 c canned peas	36¢
⅔ cantaloupe	21¢	2 lb (2 compact heads) lettuce	40¢
5 c mashed potatoes	22¢	4 c canned peaches	44¢
3¼ c canned pineapple juice	27¢	2½ c fresh asparagus	48¢

Calcium		Protein (⅓ of a day's supply)	
By eating or drinking . . .	At this cost	By eating or drinking . . .	At this cost
2½ c nonfat dry milks	5¢	1½ c cooked dry beans	4¢
2½ c evaporated milk	10¢	½ c cottage cheese	7¢
2½ c skimmed milk	12½¢	5⅓ T peanut butter	11¢
3 c buttermilk	15¢	3 oz Cheddar cheese	12¢
3 oz Swiss cheese	15¢	3 large eggs	15¢
4 oz Cheddar cheese	16¢	2⅔ c milk	16¢
3 c whole milk	18¢	3⅓ oz beef liver	17¢
3½ c cottage cheese	49¢	3⅓ oz chuck roast	18¢
5 c ice cream	70¢	3 oz halibut	18¢
		11 strips bacon	28¢
		3½ oz rib roast	29¢
		3½ oz pork chops	29¢
		3½ oz ham	33¢

SOURCES: *Changing Times*, June, 1960; *Family Economic Review*, June, 1963, p. 5.

Prices are nationwide averages prepared by the U.S. Department of Agriculture, and the amounts for one day's supply are based on recommendations of the National Research Council's Food and Nutrition Board.

Menus can be planned that will provide well-balanced meals from a large variety of foods, as shown in the accompanying table, Menu Patterns with Examples of Light and Heavy Meals, prepared by the Institute of Home Economics, U.S. Department of Agriculture.

MENU PATTERNS WITH EXAMPLES OF LIGHT AND HEAVY MEALS

Menu Pattern	Light Meal	Food Group	Heavy Meal	Food Group
BREAKFAST				
fruit	orange juice	(3)	half grapefruit	(3)
cereal, milk	cereal, milk	(4, 1)		
egg or meat			bacon, eggs	(2)
bread, butter	cinnamon toast	(4)	toast, butter	(4)
milk (children)	hot chocolate	(1)	hot chocolate	(1)
coffee or tea	coffee		coffee	
LUNCH				
soup ⎫ Choose	chicken salad			
main dish ⎬ 1 or 2	sandwich	(2, 4)	broiled ground beef	(2)
salad ⎭	carrot sticks	(3)	green salad	(3)
fruit	apple	(3)	peach halves	
bread, butter			(canned)	(3)
			muffins, bread	(4)
beverage	milk	(1)	milk	(1)
DINNER				
main dish	meat loaf	(2)	pork chops, gravy	(2, 1)
potato			baked potato	(3)
vegetable	broccoli, cheese			
	sauce	(3, 1)	spinach	(3)
salad	chef's salad,			
	French dressing	(3)	cabbage slaw	(3)
bread, butter	bread, butter	(4)	bread, butter	(4)
dessert	oatmeal cooky	(4)	frozen lemon	
			custard	(1)
beverage	milk (children)	(1)	milk (children)	(1)
	coffee		coffee	

Tasty Tips for Meal Planning. Feeding the family is first a mental process, beginning with the planning of meals and menus and extending through the selection of the right markets on to the actual buying of the food items. It also includes proper storage of food supplies, daily preparation of meals, appetizing service to the family, proper restorage of food, and even changes in plans for the next meal or two.

Daily meals should be appropriate, attractive, satisfying, and nutritious, and should fit the family pocketbook. This is a big order. Let us begin with a few practical suggestions in planning the menu.

1. Choose methods of food preparation suitable to the persons being served.
2. Plan menus that can be prepared in the time available for each meal.
3. Include some foods that do not require last-minute preparation.
4. Plan baked foods that require the same oven temperature as others that must be prepared at the same time.
5. Use only one or two foods that are difficult to digest in the same meal.
6. Plan for a contrast in texture, such as crisp and soft foods.
7. Balance the different types of food in each meal.
8. Serve the same food only once in the same meal.
9. Serve no more than one strong-flavored or highly seasoned food at one meal.
10. Plan pleasing combinations of acid, bland, and sweet foods.
11. Plan colorful meals in which the colors harmonize.
12. Use natural shapes.
13. Do not introduce two new foods at the same meal.

How Food Money Is Wasted. There are many ways to waste your food money. In fact, food marketing techniques are usually a step or two ahead of buyer knowledge and skill. It is becoming increasingly difficult to be sophisticated in the buying of food. Sometimes there is too little planning at home before marketing. Frequently, consumers fall for "specials" that are not real specials, or for premiums, or for expensive convenience foods.

Nutritional quackery costs Americans about $500 million annually. A Post Office survey revealed that food fads represent the most popular fraud in the United States, taking some $300 million from consumers annually.[1] Many of the costly abuses are traced back to the manufacturer or processor and the retail stores. Let's take a look at a few of the major ways in which the food dollar is wasted.

The Food and Drug Administration has been increasingly concerned about food fallacies and nutritional quackery. FDA Commissioner George Larrick in his talk to the National Congress on Medical Quackery in 1962 said:

The most widespread and expensive type of quackery in the United States today is the promotion of vitamin products, special dietary foods, and food supplements. Millions of consumers are being misled concerning their need for such products. Complicating this problem is a vast and growing "folklore" or "mythology" of nutrition which is being built up by pseudo-scientific literature in

[1] *Medicine at Work,* Pharmaceutical Manufacturers Association, October, 1961, p. 3.

books, pamphlets, and periodicals. . . . Food quackery today can only be compared to the patent medicine craze which reached its height in the last century. Especially disturbing is the tendency shown by some big and hitherto respected food concerns to use quackery in their sales material.[2]

Nutrition authorities agree that the best and cheapest way to buy minerals and vitamins is in the packages provided by nature—vegetables, fruits, milk, eggs, meats, fish, whole grain bread and cereals. Suggestions in these pages include such a variety of foods that most persons can hardly fail to have an ample supply of essential good nutrients.

Poor Food-buying Habits. Here are conclusions concerning the food-buying habits of the average consumer, as gathered in a comprehensive study by the Du Pont Corporation Film Department.[3]

1. The average shopper does little detailed planning at home. Only 4 out of 1[4] purchases made at the supermarket were planned beforehand. Of the other ten, seven are things the shopper never dreamed of buying.

2. The shopper is open to suggestions "through point-of-sales influences in today's supermarket." The decisions made in the store are more likely to favor items on which the grocer makes the highest profit margin—gourmet goods.

3. The modern shopper is "taking more time to buy more merchandise." Here is the opportunity for the seller to influence the shopper to buy more expensive foods.

There also appears to be a tendency to buy more expensive foods, not always better quality, because more families have higher real incomes. This is a condition made-to-order for merchandisers who desire to promote the sale of higher-profit foods.

Convenience Foods: Economy or Extravagance? How good are you at measuring cost and timesaving advantages of convenience foods compared to home-prepared foods? The Marketing Economics Division of the U.S. Department of Agriculture made a study of this question, which was reported in September, 1962.[4] They found that 42 of the 158 convenience foods were less expensive than if prepared at home. The greatest savings in convenience foods are realized in frozen and canned orange juice, instant coffee, chicken chow mein, and beef stew. The greatest extravagances in convenience foods are frozen chicken and turkey dinners, fresh ready-to-serve yeast rolls, mashed potatoes, precooked rice, and frozen broccoli—all much more expensive in convenience form.

[2] Quoted in a talk by Carla S. Williams, Director of Consumer Programming, FDA, Oct. 4, 1962.

[3] Du Pont Corporation, Film Department, Wilmington, Del., *The Shopper and the Supermarket.*

[4] *Convenience Foods in the Grocery Basket,* Marketing Bulletin no. 22, U.S. Department of Agriculture, September, 1962.

HIGHLIGHTS FROM TODAY'S BUYING DECISIONS

The "Buying Decisions" portion of the Study was based on *63,795 items* purchased by 4,661 shoppers in 225 supermarkets. Broadly, those "decisions to buy" were made as follows:

30.5% were specifically planned and purchased	"HOME" DECISIONS **30.5%**
15.9% were planned in a general way and purchased	
2.7% were purchased as a substitute	"STORE" DECISIONS **69.5%**
50.9% were purchased without previous plan	

IN OTHER WORDS, TODAY'S AVERAGE SHOPPER... who bought 13.7 items

Specifically planned and purchased	**4.2 items**	"HOME" DECISIONS **4.2 items**
Generally planned and purchased	**2.2 items**	
Substituted for some planned purchase	**.4 items**	"STORE" DECISIONS **9.5 items**
Purchased without previous plan	**6.9 items**	

A SIGNIFICANT TREND!

COMPLETELY UNPLANNED PURCHASES REPRESENT A GROWING PERCENTAGE OF BUYING DECISIONS MADE IN THE STORE . . .

STORE DECISIONS (generally planned, substituted, and unplanned) account for about 7 out of 10 buying decisions. Of these *store decisions*, unplanned purchases have grown from 57.6% in 1949 to 73.3% in 1959.

1949	1954	TODAY
57.6%	**67.6%**	**73.3%**

SOURCE: *Today's Buying Decisions,* E. I. Du Pont De Nemours & Co., Inc., Wilmington, Del., p. 7.

In June, 1960, *Changing Times* magazine reported a study by the *Food Field Reporter,* a trade newspaper, showing that, for 11 relatively new convenience foods, consumers were paying 51.2 per cent over regular prices for built-in service features. Here are examples of this study.

Product	Price in cents per ounce	Per cent extra cost
Heavy sweet cream	0.04	
Reddi-Whip	0.11	175.0
Ritz crackers in jumble pack	2.19	
Ritz crackers in wax packets	2.58	17.8
Pillsbury flour	0.76	
Pillsbury shaker	1.64	115.8

Another U.S. Department of Agriculture pamphlet, *The Food We Eat,* July, 1961, states that:

Three "ready-to-serve" meals costing $6.70 for a family of four for one day could be prepared in the home kitchen for $4.90, or $1.80 less. But the "ready-to-serve" meals cost the homemaker only 1½ hours of her time, compared with about 5½ hours for the three home-cooked meals.

The same government publication claims that consumers now pay $7½ billion a year more than in 1948 for the convenience of having some of the food preparation transferred from the kitchen to the processor, and for additional transportation and packaging costs.

Most of these studies are, no doubt, reasonably accurate. However, consumers need to be aware of certain factors: (1) the time consumed in preparing food in the family kitchen may be more important to a career wife with a job than to some full-time housewives; (2) food prices vary considerably from year to year; and (3) home recipes may contain more meat or more edible solid food. This last fact is not always considered in some studies. The housewife should compare the information on labels to spot the amount of liquid versus solid food. Then compare the price of the ingredients, if put together in the kitchen, with the price of convenience food.

Self-liquidating Premiums and Other Deals. There has been a flood of premiums to lure the consumer into buying particular brands. Some of these practices tend to mislead or to cause overpricing. The fact is that many premium deals are based on the premise that the average shopper is easily fooled. There are deals, for example, that offer "5 cans for x cents, plus the premium coupon." Some, no doubt, represent real value, but many are no saving at all. The manufacturer is banking on the consumer's inability to perform rapid arithmetic.

Another scheme usually not profitable to the consumer is the multi-million dollar business of "a box top and $1.98." *Consumer Reports*, November, 1959, studied 1,500 premium offers, half of them costing the consumer a dollar or more, and found that the declared value of all of them exceeded the actual market value.

SOURCE: *Supermarket News*, Fairchild Publications, New York.

Deceptive Packaging Practices. Under the investigation of Senator Philip H. Hart, a disturbing array of evidence has shown how difficult, if not impossible, it is for even a sophisticated shopper to make intelligent choices in typical supermarkets. In these palaces of neon lights, there are on the average about 7,000 different food items. Of the food in these markets, 85 per cent is prepackaged.

Prepackaged food practices are such that it is almost impossible to compare prices and thus make prudent choices. It has become frustratingly difficult to know the basic price per pound or pint of what is bought. Odd-size packages are the rule. Here are some examples brought to light by graduate students at the University of Missouri in the summer of 1961.

Supermarket C displays four brands of instant mashed potatoes, all selling at 33 cents a package, and all claiming in large letters to serve 8 people. Apparently, manufacturers have varying ideas of how much potatoes 8 people will eat, for the net contents of the packages (printed in very small letters) are as follows: brand A, 7¼ ounces; B, 7⅕ ounces; C, 7 ounces; and D, 5½ ounces. Strangely enough, the less potatoes in the package, the larger the package. The brand D package, which contains only three-quarters as much as the A package, has a cubic capacity three times larger.

Dr. Helen Nelson, Consumer Counsel to Governor Edmund G. Brown of California, reported a survey made in 1962. She found in one supermarket 14 different packages of rice, and not one was a pound package. There were 20 choices of peanut butter, and only 4 were pound packages. Among 26 choices of hot cereal, only 4 were pound packages.

Time was when the consumer could buy food in standard, easy-to-figure weights—half-pound, one pound, one pint, one quart, and so on—and weight and price comparisons were relatively simple to figure. Try figuring the cost of 7¼ ounces in packages marked 3 for 59 cents. Apparently, processors are more interested in packaging to display, packaging to meet the competition, not in packaging to aid the confused consumer.

Package-size and Hidden-price-increase Deceits. Consumers are all acquainted with the package-size craze—"king size," "large size," "big size." Are bigger sizes actually larger? Senator Hart's committee reported that "regular" size packages of some brands contained as much net contents as the "large" packages.

Then there is the common hidden-price-increase deceit. A popular brand of rolls was reduced in weight from its "Multi-Pak," containing 9 ounces, to 8¼ ounces, but the price remained the same. In this instance, the wrappers also remained the same for a short time with the old net weight printed on them. Most companies indulging in this form of hidden-price-increase deceit simply reduce the net weight and retain the same size package.

Sometimes net weight changes are used to indicate a false amount for an advertised price reduction. One 14-ounce jar sold for 83 cents. One day the label carried the pleasant news that the "price had been reduced to 67 cents, a price cut of 25 per cent." Actually, the new jar held 12 ounces instead of 14 ounces. Had the company lived up to its claim of 25 per cent price cut, the cost should have been 53 cents rather than 67 cents.

"Truth-in-packaging" Bill. Consumers spend approximately $70 billion a year on food purchased in stores, representing almost one-fifth of the average family's budget. Because of the common abuses in the food marketing area mentioned above, and many not mentioned, a bill popularly called "Truth in Packaging" was introduced in Congress in 1962 and

This exhibit was prepared and shown by the Grand Street Consumers Cooperative in their supermarket located in the lower East Side of New York.

SOURCE: Consumers Union of U.S., Inc., Mount Vernon, N.Y.

again in 1964. The proposed legislation directs the Food and Drug Administration (for foods, drugs, and cosmetics), and the Federal Trade Commission (for other consumer commodities) to promulgate regulations that will require packages to give essential product information accurately and clearly and to represent the contents fairly.

The aim of the bill is threefold: (1) to extend antitrust laws to the relatively new forms of nonprice competition represented by modern packaging, (2) to make it possible for ethical processors to compete, and (3) to give consumers exact information about the size, quality, and price of the goods they consider purchasing.

There appears to be only one answer to the problem of unannounced shifts in can sizes—standardized can sizes, and only one answer to the other kinds of deceptive packaging—standardized package sizes. Some years ago the National Conference on Weights and Measures adopted a resolution in favor of Federal legislation to establish standards for all package sizes. The need for standards is obvious. A Gresham's law is operating in packaging: deceptive packaging driving out honest packaging, just as bad money drives out good money. The problem can be solved.

Short Weights in Foods. Short weights are common in many prepackaged foods. Before the days of prepackaged foods (now 85 per cent of family food), the consumer had to watch the "butcher's thumb" or worry about inaccurate store scales. That old problem is still with us, but supermarkets need to weigh only about 15 per cent of their food products.

In the spring of 1959, the Food and Drug Administration made a survey of 107,000 packages of 35 commonly purchased prepackaged foods.[5] The most significant shortages were in corn meal, butter, margarine, oatmeal products, rice, coffee, sugar, macaroni products, liquid salad dressings, and vegetable shortening. About the only products not significantly short weighted were frozen fruit juice concentrates and fruit and vegetable baby food preparations. Losses in butter for the consumer are estimated at about $25 million annually. In 10 of the 35 most commonly purchased foods, short weight occurred in 32 to 54 per cent of the commodities checked. In all, 39 per cent of the 32,225 packages of the 10 foods mentioned were short in weight.

Also in the spring of 1959, the Wisconsin Weights and Measures Division checked 318 food stores in 114 cities, involving 16,181 prepackaged fresh meat, poultry, and potatoes, and found that 44 per cent of the fresh meat, 48 per cent of the fresh poultry, and 37 per cent of the potatoes were short weighted below the tolerance level permitted by law. Instances of overweight were so uncommon that they had no statistical significance.

[5] Reported in the *Industrial Union Department Digest,* Washington, D.C.: AFL-CIO, fall, 1960.

There is no doubt that packaging has joined the primrose path of promotion. A *Printers' Ink* package panel of experts concluded that "the package designer will more than ever have to concentrate on reaching the consumer through her emotions." Said a large food advertiser, "We're not selling products these days as much as we're selling packaging." A package designer said, "Thousands of packages that silently scream for the customer's attention do the selling in today's supermarkets."

Consumer Precautions for Self-protection. Self-protection is limited to those who have the time and skill to use a slide rule. Even such rare persons could not detect nonmathematical deceit, as in the case of slack-fill (oversize packages), misleading artwork on the package face, concealing fat or bone waste in prepackaged bacon and steaks, box-top premium offers, and misleading nutritional information.

The consumer is not, however, entirely without resources for self-protection. Here are a few precautions:

1. Always read the label, especially the net contents.
2. Don't buy a brand that hides the net weight in small print.
3. Purchase the brand whose net contents are in standard weights and measures—8 ounces, half-pound, pound, pound and a half, one pint, one quart, one gallon.
4. Compare the unit prices (price per ounce or pound or price per fluid ounce, pint, or quart) of competing brands.
5. Look for excessive slack-fill in packages and bottles.
6. Inform the store manager about a package or bottle that you believe is deceptively labeled, filled, or priced. Write a letter to the manufacturer, to the local or state weights and measures official, or to the Food and Drug Administration, Washington, D.C.

The Controversial Trading Stamps. In the controversial trading-stamp business, the consumer is interested primarily in this question: "Do stamps really save money?" There is no doubt about the fact that consumers are participating in a trading-stamp craze. For seventy years trading stamps have been offered in the United States, and there are now about three hundred different kinds. Close to 90 per cent of the 375 billion stamps that are issued each year are from eight of the three hundred or more stamp companies.

In 1961, the retail value of the goods moved off redemption-center shelves approximated $800 million on the basis of nondiscount-store prices. Stamp premium outlets accounted for 14 per cent of all the heating pads sold in 1961, 8 per cent of the toasters, and 4 per cent of the coffee makers. According to *Changing Times* magazine, August, 1956, "between 25 and 30 billion dollars' worth of retail goods and services" are sold via trading stamps, or about 7 to 8 per cent of the nation's gross annual product.

The trading-stamp business is big business. This is how it works. A stamp company sells stamps to the participating store. Prices range from $2 to $3 a thousand stamps, or two-tenths to three-tenths of a cent per stamp. The store usually gives one stamp for every 10 cents spent there, which is around a 2 per cent rebate. The shopper fills a book with the stamps, about 1,200 per book, and therefore spends about $120 to fill one book. The stamp company redeems the stamps for merchandise or cash. Each book is valued at between $2 and $3 at retail prices.

Does the Consumer Gain Financially? Whether the consumer gains financially may never be forthcoming in absolute terms. One of the complicating factors is that the stamp craze has tended to stifle price competition. A careful study made by Consumers Union (*Consumer Reports,* October, 1962, p. 512) found that, except for a scattered handful of specials that were easily recognized, the weekly advertisements were selling trading stamps, not food. This is most unfortunate because price competition in food stores is one way for alert shoppers to decide where to buy what.

Another factor that must be weighed carefully is the difference in the value of the premiums when exchanged for stamps. So how much do you have to spend to fill one book? It depends (1) on whether a book requires 1,000, 1,200, or 1,500 stamps; (2) on extra-stamp offers; (3) on the price of the stamps when redeemed and the quality of the goods at the redemption center; and (4) most important, the price of the goods elsewhere for which the stamps were issued.

But figuring the value of the premium is not simple. For example, in a current stamp catalogue, one model of an electric shaver cost 10½ stamp books. Figuring from the list price of $32.50 for that shaver, each stamp book was worth $3.09. But at a discount store, it might be possible to get that same shaver for $17.49, making the value of each book only $1.67 for that particular purchase. So, item by item, the book versus cash prices must be calculated as retail and discount prices fluctuate.

The St. Louis Better Business Bureau, in their April, 1962, bulletin, reported investigation of the various claims of the large stamp companies as to the value of a book of 1,200 stamps. They found that the superior claims of the companies are not warranted. Sometimes the books have a retail value of $1.50, and sometimes on up to $2.50.

Stores must price their merchandise to cover the cost of the stamps. In 1962, over 50 per cent of retail grocery sales were being made by stamp-issuing stores in contrast to about 30 per cent in 1956. In Los Angeles, perhaps as much as 90 per cent of grocery sales are made at stamp-issuing stores. No one has been able to figure accurately how much more stores have to charge to cover the value of stamps.

The A & P chain, last of the big chains to join the stamp parade, admitted at a stockholders meeting, as quoted in *The Wall Street Journal,* that they had to "raise some prices to cover the cost." Roughly, retailers pay between 1½ and 2½ per cent of their sales for the stamps they give. If such an expenditure increases sales income by enough to cut the unit cost of rent, light, heat, labor, insurance, and other expenses, the cost of the stamps is compensated for by the cut in unit cost.

Buying Rationally in a Stamp-happy Market. When all the stores have stamps, what then? If most of the stamp plans are approximately equal in exchange value, the competing merchants are back where they were before stamps became icons. They have to go back to price and quality competition and to become better merchants again.

How, then, can homemakers buy rationally in a stamp-happy marketing area? Ignore stamp offers, and try to buy on the basis of price and quality. Take the stamps, if offered. If food is selected on a price and quality basis first, chances are that the stamps will cost the thoughtful homemaker less and offer more in the long run than they do to people who buy to satisfy "inner satisfactions" that have nothing to do with competitive price and quality analysis. Compare food and quality prices at cooperative and discount food stores, if such stores are available in your marketing area. Cooperative patronage dividends average around 3 per cent on total purchases today.

Use the Food Ads. Food shopping begins at home. Studying the food ads in the local papers and listening to local radio food programs will often suggest the best daily or weekly buys. Comparing food costs *before* marketing is both economical and timesaving.

Place all the desired ads before you, with your grocery list handy. When comparing the price of veal shoulder roast, for example, circle the best buy and double-circle the next-best buy. Jot down the name of the retail store opposite the particular food on your list.

After an experience or two in comparing prices and knowing what you want before you leave home to shop for food, you will find that you have saved as much as half an hour or more in the market place—and been much easier on your pocketbook.

Weekend Food Shopping: Does It Pay? Generally, it pays to market for food on weekends. In national food chain stores, most price reductions occur on Thursday, Friday, and Saturday. On Monday, prices frequently increase. In one survey of retail national food chain stores, about 86 per cent of the fresh fruits and vegetables were reduced on Thursday, Friday, and Saturday. Spot surveys also indicate that some food prices are increased in the latter part of the week.

Independent food stores seem to have a more flexible price policy than many national food chain stores. There is evidence to support the conclusion that food prices are also reduced in many independent stores during the weekend. Like the national chain food stores, independent stores tend to increase some prices on Monday. One may conclude, therefore, that shoppers can make their best buys in the latter part of the week.

One result of weekend price reductions is the heavy concentration of shoppers and consequent crowding, particularly in afternoons and evenings. Some competent marketing observers have concluded that marketing costs could be reduced if sales were more evenly distributed throughout the week. In view of the pressure of retail competition and force of habit on the part of the retailers themselves, any corrective measure is likely to make slow progress.

The Stanford University Food Research Institute, a few years ago, in Palo Alto, California, compared 1,546 price observations of 225 food items advertised as specials. They found that in 96 food items (1) the consumer could have saved over 20 per cent if he had purchased all the specials; (2) most of the specials offered were standard foods commonly purchased weekly; (3) the stores with the lowest-priced specials generally maintained higher prices on other food products than their competitors.

"How to Save $200 a Year in a Supermarket." In February, 1961, *Consumer Reports* published the results of food shopping in New York City supermarkets. The conclusion was: "By intelligent supermarket shopping today, it is quite possible for a great many families to save at least $200 a year, and probably more." Any alert shopper could save from 10 to 20 per cent by seeking bargains widely available at most competitive supermarkets. How?

Unfortunately, there can be no precise "buy this brand" directives because the price picture changes daily or weekly. But the consumer who becomes aware of the strategy that characterizes the "brand battle" for shelf space and price advantage is in the best position to spot real bargains.

There are, in the grocery business, "private or store brands" and "nationally advertised manufacturer brands." Both kinds of brands are nationally advertised, but the private or store brand is found only in a given retailer's stores. Manufacturer brands are found in most retail food stores. When Consumers Union checked Safeway's Piedmont and A & P's Ann Page store brands with manufacturer brands of mayonnaise of comparable quality and quantity, they found that the store brands cost 33 per cent and 49 per cent less than the manufacturer brands. Checks made on a couple of dozen other commonly purchased food items showed store brands to be 10 to 12 per cent less.

One of the devices to promote manufacturer brands is to offer the retailer an "advertising allowance," a form of price cut not passed on to the consumer but usually spent on local advertising. This would seem to indicate that manufacturers have placed emphasis on promotional strategy rather than on price competition. Interestingly, the retailer generally receives a larger markup on his own brands than from the sale of higher-price manufacturer brands, according to a study made by *Supemarket News,* a trade paper, in 1959, as reported in *Consumer Reports,* February, 1961.

Unfortunately, the job is not as easy as just picking up the store's own brand when marketing. This is especially true in regard to canned goods. The price spread between the store's own brands is as great as the spread between store brands and manufacturer brands. Usually, price is not a good guide to quality as tests have shown for years. The University of Illinois, taking 18 samples of 59 brands of six different vegetables and fruits from six different Illinois towns, compared prices and tested for quality, with findings similar to the Consumers Union testing results cited above. In other words, "You don't get what you pay for" in many canned fruits and vegetables.

According to a number of trade surveys, retailer or store brands are likely to be featured in the following foods: canned fruits and vegetables, coffee, frozen food, candy, canned meat and fish, salad dressings, peanut butter, cake mixes, dairy products, bread, cooking oils, ice cream, margarine, tea, fruit juices. Changes do occur, so make your own comparison from time to time.

How Much to Spend for Food. Though the average family in the United States spends about one-fifth of its income for food, about three-fourths of this expenditure is for food consumed at home and the remainder for food consumed outside the home.

The expenditure for food goes up as the income increases, but the proportion spent for food goes down. Families with annual incomes of $5,000 to $20,000 spend about 11 per cent for food, but those with incomes under $1,000 must spend over 50 per cent for food.

Statistics tell what the average family in a certain city or region, or in the country as a whole, spends for food. Data are also available on how much is spent on food at different ages and for various needs. The principal value in looking at data of this kind is to use the figures as a guide to judge, examine, and compare your food spending with that of others. The *Family Economics Review,* published quarterly, gives the cost of one week's food at home in each issue. For example, the accompanying table. Cost of One Week's Food at Home, is from the March, 1963, issue.[6]

[6] Good sources are free from the Office of Information, U.S. Department of Agriculture, Washington, D.C.: *Family Economics Review,* "Family Food Plans and Food Costs"; also Bureau of Labor Statistics, "Retail Food Prices by Cities."

Cost of One Week's Food at Home

Estimated for Food Plans at Three Cost Levels, January, 1963—U.S.A. Average

Sex-age groups	Low-cost plan	Moderate-cost plan	Liberal plan
Families			
Family of two, 20–34 years	$14.10	$19.40	$21.80
Family of two, 55–74 years	12.60	17.40	19.60
Family of four, preschool children	21.10	28.10	32.10
Family of four, school children	24.30	32.80	37.30
Individuals *			
Children, under 1 year	3.10	3.90	4.20
1–3 years	3.80	4.70	5.40
4–6 years	4.50	5.80	6.90
7–9 years	5.30	6.90	7.90
10–12 years	6.20	8.30	9.60
Girls, 13–15 years	6.50	8.90	10.20
16–19 years	6.60	8.80	10.10
Boys, 13–15 years	7.10	9.80	11.20
16–19 years	8.40	11.40	12.90
Women, 20–24 years	5.50	7.70	8.90
35–54 years	5.40	7.50	8.50
55–74 years	5.10	7.00	8.00
75 years and over	4.90	6.60	7.50
Pregnant	6.90	9.00	10.00
Nursing	8.70	11.10	12.30
Men, 20–34 years	7.30	9.90	11.10
35–54 years	6.80	9.20	10.30
55–74 years	6.40	8.80	9.80
75 years and over	6.20	8.40	9.30

* The costs given are for individuals in 4-person families. For individuals in other size families, the following adjustments are suggested: 1 person, add 20 per cent; 2 persons, add 10 per cent; 3 persons, add 5 per cent; 5 persons, subtract 5 per cent; 6 or more persons, subtract 10 per cent.

Food Costs Vary for Different Ages. Average spending data are one comparative yardstick to use in figuring food costs. Eventually a family is likely to have children of both sexes and of different ages, each with food requirements of his own. As a rule, food costs increase with age until a person reaches around 20 years. Then costs begin to decrease. Until age 12, girls are likely to eat as much as boys. After that the male eats more food. As a rule, teen-agers cost more to feed.

If there are less than four in the family, add to the sum of the expenses for the individuals 35 per cent for one, 20 per cent for two, and 10 per cent for three. The U.S. Department of Agriculture estimates are based on grocery lists and menus that meet basic nutritional standards. They reflect average eating habits. Use them as a guide.

Nutritious Food Habits Still a Major Family Problem. Feeding the family nutritious and interesting food remains, as yet, one of the major family problems. Our food habits are not ruled by the desire for health. Dietary surveys and other evidence reveal the embarrassing fact that one-third of American families are eating below the optimum level for proper nutrition.

We know now, thanks to the science of nutrition, what foods will maintain good health for the entire family. It remains to put this information to use. Eating habits of Americans have improved somewhat in terms of consumption of fruits, vegetables, and dairy products, but unfortunately the eating of grain products and potatoes has decreased.

The first important job for the homemaker is menu planning before going to market. But good planning at home must be followed by intelligent marketing. This, in turn, must be followed by proper preparing of food for the table and its conservation for use throughout the week, as well as adequate storage.

The next chapter will introduce you to the fascinating but complex world of supermarkets.

QUESTIONS FOR DISCUSSION

1. Keep a record of the kind, quality, and quantity of all the food you eat during one week. Then evaluate your diet according to the data in this chapter. What foods should be added or changed and in what quantity to give you an adequate diet?

2. What are some of the important factors that determine the proportion of the family income that is spent for food?

3. What evidence indicates that Americans are not as well fed as they should be on present family income?

4. Can food habits be changed? Is it hard to give up poor food habits? Why?

5. Do the national trends in eating habits indicate that American families are improving their diets?

6. What proof is there that better diets improve health?

7. How would you go about comparing food costs and marketing for any weekly period?

8. Does spending more money for food automatically improve the diet?

9. In many countries, the major food problem is a shortage of food. In the United States, it is a matter of poor selection of foods in most families. What are the implications of these two statements?

10. Do you believe that Congress should pass effective legislation on packaging abuses?

11. Discuss this issue: "Is it possible for supermarkets to give trading stamps

and have effective competition in the price of food? Is one strategy superior to the other for the retailer? For the consumer?"

ACTIVITY PROBLEMS

1. A famous physiologist told a House committee investigating the use of chemicals in foods: "We feed our best grains to hogs and cattle—we eat the poorest part." What are the implications of this statement?

2. Keep a record of the food you eat for about one week. Evaluate your diet. Make a list of the deficiencies and the foods that should be added to improve your diet.

3. Using *Consumer Reports* and *Consumers' Research Bulletin*, compare the price and quality of various brands of the same kind of food. Are the best buys always the most expensive?

4. Some nutritionists claim that the day can be started with a breakfast that will improve efficiency and well-being but not necessarily add pounds. Investigate this claim, and report to the class.

5. It is generally difficult to get people to buy the foods that are most plentiful at certain times. Some food experts claim that if you "eat by the calendar" you can cut food costs by as much as 20 per cent. Investigate this statement, using local markets as the chief source for information.

6. Make a study of the food habits of several persons you know. Are they eating well-balanced meals? List their poor and good food habits.

7. Compare the costs of eating similar meals at home and in various public eating places.

8. Study the food advertisements in a newspaper. Make a list of what you consider the best buys. How certain are you that they are the best buys? What, then, are the advantages and the limitations in searching newspaper food advertisements for the best food buys?

9. With a typical weekly shopping list visit a supermarket. Study the location of the various departments in the store. Then arrange the list so that you need not backtrack for items. Keep this in mind when making such shopping lists hereafter.

10. Make a survey of food bargains as featured in the local ads. Are these items bargains? How do you know?

SUGGESTED READINGS

AFL-CIO. *It's What's Inside That Counts*, Publication no. 52, Washington, D.C.
Bogert, Jean. *Diet and Personality*. New York: Garden City Books.
———. *Nutrition and Physical Fitness*. Philadelphia: W. B. Saunders Company, 1960.
Changing Times. "Why Don't They Cut the Price?" April, 1962; "Trading Stamp Craze," August, 1957; "Nutrition: Fad vs. Fact," July, 1963.
Consumer Reports. "Deceptive Packaging," September, 1960, p. 448; "Glue on Our Tongues," October, 1962.

Family Economic Review. "Dollar Values in Nutrition" and "Trading Stamps," June, 1957, pp. 9–12.

Federal Trade Commission. *Economic Inquiry into Food Marketing.* Washington, D.C.: Government Printing Office, 1960, chaps. 1, 2.

Fitzsimmons, Cleo. *Consumer Buying for Better Living.* New York: John Wiley & Sons, Inc., 1961, chap. 10.

Gordon, Leland J. *Watch Your Weights and Measures.* Greeley, Colo.: Council on Consumer Information, 1957.

Hearings before the Subcommittee on Antitrust and Monopoly of the Committee on the Judiciary. "Packaging and Labeling Practices," U.S. Senate, 1st Session, S. Res. 52, part 1, Washington, D.C.: Government Printing Office, 1961.

Household Finance Corporation. *Your Shopping Dollar.*

House Government Operations Committee Report. "Activities for the Prevention of Fraudulent and Deceptive Sales Practices," part 3, Washington, D.C.: Government Printing Office, 1963.

Journal of Home Economics. "It's What's Inside That Counts," April, 1961, p. 281.

Lipsyte, Robert M. "Trading Stamps," *Esquire,* April, 1963, p. 90.

Senate Bill 387. "Unfair and Deceptive Methods of Packaging or Labeling . . . ," 88th Congress, 1st Session. Washington, D.C.: Government Printing Office, Jan. 21, 1963.

U.S. Department of Agriculture, Superintendent of Documents. *Do Trading Stamps Affect Food Costs?* Report no. 147; *Food, the 1959 Yearbook of Agriculture.*

The Wall Street Journal. "Games Offering Cash Join Trading Stamps as Supermarket Lure," Mar. 27, 1963, p. 1; "The Great Trading Stamp War," Apr. 26, 1962, p. 32.

8

FOOD SHOPPING IN THE MARKET

Shopping for food is a complex problem. All the information that is valuable to consumers cannot be condensed into one chapter. It is necessary to select what experienced home economists have found to be the most useful advice for a typical family. When consumers have done a good job of mental food planning at home, they will not want to lose that benefit by poor buying in the market. To have tasty, nutritious food at all times at an economical price, food costs demand constant attention to win the "battle of the budget."

The right quality and quantity of food for the family depend mainly on the buying practices of the homemaker, on her information and skill in choice making, on her willingness to shop at the stores where the best buys are available, and on her actual selection of the food. She must decide:

1. What to buy.
2. Where to buy.
3. When to buy.
4. How much to buy.
5. Whether to buy bulk or package, canned or fresh, frozen or dehydrated foods.
6. How to pay.
7. What quality or grade to use for specific purposes.
8. Who will buy.

This sounds like a full-time career in itself.

Management of Time for Family Food Shopping. The management of time for family food shopping has become increasingly important. Experienced shoppers have their time for marketing well organized. A study of food-shopping activities, made by Deanne Suneson at Cornell University in

1961, may still be useful to experienced shoppers, and young housewives can surely profit by this study.[1]

To study the management of time for family food shopping, a random sampling procedure was used to select 100 families in the Ithaca, New York, area. The major food shopper in each family was interviewed between February and April, 1961, with questions pertaining to the food shopping done by the family during the week prior to the interview. Information was obtained about the time used for all the activities connected with family food shopping: planning and preparation, shopping in the markets, transportation to and from the markets, and storage of foods purchased.

Almost one-half of the major shoppers felt that food shopping was a pleasure; only eleven major shoppers felt it to be a chore. The remainder said that shopping was just a routine that could not be avoided.

Planning for the major shopping was done by a written list in over three-fourths of the families. One-half of the families used the newspaper in planning for food shopping, mainly to look over specials and bargains.

Eighty-six per cent of the families made a major food shopping trip once a week. Two-thirds of the families did their major shopping on Thursday or Friday, mainly because time was available or the pay check came then. The hours during which the major shopping was done showed a fairly even distribution as to morning, afternoon, and evening.

Families made an average of about three shopping trips per week; on an average, one of these three shopping trips was unscheduled or unexpected. Forty-three families made no unscheduled trips, however. There was a significant difference in the total number of shopping trips made by employed homemakers and full-time homemakers, with the latter making slightly fewer trips.

Most of the families went to the market by car for the major food shopping; only six families walked to the market from home. Most of the families lived within three miles of the most distant food market they had shopped in during the week. Almost one-half of the families combined the major shopping trip with another errand or activity, while the other half went on the major trip with food shopping as their sole purpose.

All the households in the study had mechanical refrigerators; one-fourth of the households had separate freezers for food storage. In over three-fourths of the households, between 6 and 20 linear feet of cupboard space were available for storage of dry groceries.

Sixty per cent of the families received no home deliveries of food. More full-time homemakers than employed homemakers had home deliveries

[1] Deanne Suneson, "Use of Time for Family Food Shopping Activities," unpublished master's thesis. Ithaca, N.Y.: Cornell University, 1961.

of food. Three-fifths of the families had done no home production of food of any type during the previous year, and over two-thirds of the families had not purchased food in quantity during the previous year.

The total time used for all shopping activities by the two groups, employed homemakers and full-time homemakers, was nearly the same.

An increase in the time used for all food-shopping activities was noted in families that reported the following:

1. More persons eating in the home regularly
2. More meals prepared in a week
3. More shopping trips made in a week
4. Greater complexity of meals
5. Greater household work loads for tasks done daily and for tasks not necessarily done daily
6. More family members participating in food shopping
7. More money spent for food in a week
8. Negative attitude of the major shopper toward food shopping
9. Age of the major shopper being over 60 years

Five Factors in Selecting Food Stores. Several economic factors are involved in the intelligent selection of food stores, such as quality of food, price, convenience, and service.

A *range of quality foods* at various prices is usually desirable. Some stores deliberately cater to one class of consumer. The quality factors also include cleanliness of the store and personnel and a rapid turnover, particularly of perishable foods.

It is smart to be conscious of *price and values* when selecting food stores. It is one thing, however, to be conscious of paying higher prices for elaborate service and atmosphere and quite another to be unconscious of the extra dollars it takes to trade in such retail stores. It is wise to shop around until you discover which stores give good value at reasonable prices. The price range should match your pocketbook.

Almost always it is necessary to shop from three to five food stores to get quality, price, and value when buying food. The stores that sell at higher prices are not necessarily handling the better foods. Likewise, the store with low prices is not necessarily selling lower-quality goods. You must learn by intelligent appraisal, by being objective and not too easily taken in by persuasive salesmanship, conspicuous display, and catering to your ego.

Convenience to markets is also a consideration in selecting food stores. Sometimes the distance to the best food marts, or the parking problem, is so great that one must shop the more expensive small neighborhood stores. Usually, however, when shopping is done on a basis of once a week or so, it pays to go farther to the large supermarkets.

The *services* rendered by salespeople and by store policy constitute another important factor. Some stores cut down expenses by having a small "consumer-aid" staff and lower the prices of their products. Other stores reduce personnel costs but do not pass on the savings to the consumer. It is smart to discover these things and to identify the store accordingly.

Some stores have elaborate service for customers. As a rule, such stores subordinate price appeal to pleasing service. They usually take telephone orders, deliver food to the home, and extend credit. This service costs money. Consumers buying in these stores must expect to pay more.

There is still another factor that wise buyers should consider—honesty and fair business ethics. An honest merchant can be judged by the following business ethics.

1. He gives consumers accurate information about his products—in his advertising, in the reliability of the labels on the containers and packages of food that he features, and in the guidance of his salespeople.

2. He makes fair adjustments. Most merchants try to be fair in this matter. If he is evasive or tends to argue about his rights, perhaps it is time for a change of market.

3. He provides good working conditions and fair wages for his employees.

Supermarketing—the Retailing Revolution. With the factors in selecting food stores in mind, we can consider the development of food supermarkets. It is well to keep in mind, also, that the average family spends between 21 and 30 per cent of its income for food. It is therefore vitally important to learn how best to spend those dollars. And not too much information has been given to consumers on the marketing of foods— that is, on how to make the food store give the most in desired quality and quantity with reasonable convenience and satisfaction at the lowest price.

A food supermarket has generally been regarded as a store that does more than a million dollars worth of sales annually and is almost or entirely self-service. It generally carries complete grocery, meat, delicatessen, frozen-food, and fresh produce departments, and often housewares and drug and cosmetic departments. A typical supermarket may carry as many as 8,000 different items. Because sales are high, it can generally afford to operate on a low margin—from a low of 15 per cent to about an average of 22 per cent.

National food chains work on low net profits of 1 to 2 per cent, according to *Business Week* magazine, June 4, 1960. The same magazine says that in 1960 there were 33,000 food supermarkets in the country, in contrast to only 40 per cent as many in the early 1950s. Currently, about 5 per cent of a supermarket's sales is in nonfoods. Usually, the profit margin on nonfood items is higher. Most supermarkets are cash stores.

Seventy-five per cent of the business is done on Thursday, Friday, and Saturday, despite efforts to get more shoppers into the stores on Monday, Tuesday, and Wednesday. Food is checked and paid for at check-out counters.

So well has the food supermarketing revolution succeeded that supermarkets have hardly anyone left to fight except each other—and the more recent food-discount store that will be discussed later.

Some authorities are of the opinion that supermarkets may increase their share of grocery sales another 3 or 4 per cent in the 1970s. Their dwindling competitors—the delicatessens, the "Mom and Pop" stores— may succeed in retaining about 25 per cent of the grocery store business. These smaller competitors can fill in the chinks between the large stores, offering greater convenience of location, longer selling hours, and more services, such as credit, delivery, and Sunday sales.

Supermarkets have total annual grocery store sales of about $54 billion, according to the industry magazine *Progressive Grocer*. By 1970 they might be close to $90 billion. Future competition may be largely a matter of super versus super. And trading areas have been shrinking. The Super Market Institute reported in 1960 that the potential number of people served by each new supermarket had dropped from 13,300 to 7,300 in just two years. If this trend goes on, there may be more superettes.

A more recent phenomenon in retailing centers has been the development of one-stop shopping centers. Multimillion-dollar shopping centers are merely an extension of conventional retailing out of the central business districts, part of the migration to suburbia. At the end of 1961, there were 5,500 shopping centers; another 1,000 were opened in 1963. Each of these centers has one or more food supermarkets.

National Food Chain Supermarkets. In 1960, the Federal Trade Commission released its 338-page report on concentration and integration in retailing. It shows how well the food supermarket has furthered the expansion of the chains. Between 1948 and 1959, the chains—defined as companies owning 11 or more stores—increased their share of grocery store sales from 34.5 to 43 per cent. Their dollar sales went from $7.8 billion to $19.1 billion. The bigger chains (operating 101 to 500 stores) showed the greatest sales gain, 114 per cent, from 1953 to 1958. All food chains reported only a 56 per cent gain. Sales averaged about $425,000 annually at each of the 18,300 food chain stores in 1948, and in 1958 average sales increased to $1,100,000. The Big Four food chains—the Great Atlantic & Pacific, Safeway, Kroger, and American Stores—maintained the same rank during the 11-year period from 1948 to 1959. At the end of this period, these four chains accounted for 19 per cent of total food sales, according to the FTC report.

The national food chains have thousands of stores from coast to coast, all of which are owned, controlled, and operated by the parent corporation. Such full-scale retail food organization makes it possible to reduce prices on food for several reasons.

1. Decrease or elimination of costly services
2. Large-scale buying, cash payments, and preferential allowances
3. Streamlined low-cost distribution from the source to the cash register
4. Rapid turnover of stock
5. Scientific selection of store locations
6. Training schools for personnel
7. Development of store brands
8. Cash and carry
9. Self-service

The economic advantages to the consumer of national food chains depend largely on food information and skill in buying. The specific advantages in shopping the national food chains are as follows.

1. Shop the supermarket of a chain in preference to a smaller store of the chain because the prices are usually a little lower in the former. This is often true for meat prices.

2. Watch for the weekend leaders of a chain. Do not have the wrong idea that all its food prices are lower than competitors' prices during that week. Commonly advertised leaders are packaged cereals, evaporated milk, nationally advertised canned soups, and sugar. Sometimes, prices of the chain's own brands are cut.

3. Generally, the best buys are the average qualities rather than the fancy grades. This is due largely to a lower profit on the former.

4. Some chains have a policy of meeting their competitors' prices on the same grade or quality and quantity of food.

5. Most of the large national chains grade their own products, notably canned goods. Private grades are generally considered less reliable than the U.S. Department of Agriculture grades, but they are a step in the right direction.

6. Meats and fresh fruits and vegetables in the chain stores are worth checking every week.

7. Usually, store brands are more economical buys than manufacturer brands.

Independent, or Voluntary, Food Chains. The competition of the national food chains has induced some independent stores to form "voluntary associations" that sponsor their own brands. In some instances, the initiative in setting up these associations came not from the retailers but from wholesalers whose sales were jeopardized by the direct buying of large retailers. This form of voluntary, or cooperative, chain has been defined as "an association of independent retailers acting cooperatively in buying, advertising, or in the performance of other merchandising functions or activities." [2]

In both kinds of voluntary chains, wholesale or retail controlled, the retail store is independently owned. The owner pays a fee to the association and agrees to certain things. For example, greater efficiency is gained through:

1. Centralized buying
2. Group advertising
3. Promotion of leaders
4. Private brands
5. Efficient methods of stock control, accounting, display, and selling

The rapid rise of the national food chains has forced the independent store operators and the wholesalers to band together. These counter movements have taken two forms: retailer-owned cooperatives and wholesaler-sponsored voluntary groups. Growth rates of these associations of supermarkets—IGA, Red & White, Clover Farm, and others—have been impressive. In 1948–1958, their shares of grocery store sales increased from 10 to 17 per cent for the wholesale cooperative group, and from 16 to 20 per cent for the voluntary chains, according to the Federal Trade Commission report in 1960. In 1958, 146 retailer-owned cooperative wholesalers served more than 34,000 stores, with more than 1,500 of them doing an annual business over $1 million.

Voluntary independent chains sponsored by wholesalers, numbering 330 in 1958, serviced nearly 36,000 stores, most of them small, but more than 1,000 had annual sales over $1 million. Total sales of voluntary wholesalers increased 119 per cent between 1948 and 1958, or about as much as retail sales of national chain stores. Total retail sales of the voluntary group stores was $9 billion in 1958 or about 18 per cent of the national food chain sales that year.

Over the years, these food supermarkets have competed quite successfully with the national chains. Generally, these stores offer competitive values, especially in their advertised leaders and in store brands.

Consumer Cooperative Food Stores. The consumer cooperative store is wholly owned by its patrons, who buy dividend-paying co-op stock. It is run by a manager appointed and supervised by an elected board of directors. A co-op member patron thus:

1. Buys his food at competitive prices at a store in which he has a financial interest.

[2] Paul W. Stewart and J. F. Dewhurst, *Does Distribution Cost Too Much?* New York: The Twentieth Century Fund, 1939, pp. 333–367.

2. Receives a patronage refund. (National average is about 2 per cent; high is Berkeley, California, 4.04 per cent in 1961.)

3. Collects dividends on his stock.

4. Has an interest in the organization as stock ownership gives him one vote—regardless of the amount of stock he may own.

There are only about 1,000 cooperative food stores in the United States. They did less than 1 per cent of the food retail business in 1958.[3] Only about 50 of these stores are in the $1 million a year or more class. Few

SOURCE: Cooperative League of the U.S.A., Chicago.

wholly new stores have been organized in the past two decades. The largest clusters of stores are in the San Francisco Bay area, around Washington, D.C., in New England, and in the towns and small cities in northern Wisconsin and upper Michigan. A Chicago co-op operates the largest food store in that city. The few large volume stores operate with efficiency comparable to the national food chains.

The co-op in Ithaca, New York, does $2.1 million a year in 12,000 square feet of space, and achieved in 1961 a 2.2 per cent net as per cent of sales. The Shattuck Avenue store in Berkeley, California, more than twice as big, did $4.7 million in 1961, helping the five-store Berkeley

[3] *The Marketing and Transportation Situation,* February, 1962, p. 32.

Co-op to achieve a high 5.99 per cent net. The Greenbelt Co-op in and around Washington, D.C., with almost 24,000 members, paid a 5 per cent dividend on $2 million in outstanding stock in 1961. The Hyde Park Co-op in Chicago had sales of nearly $4 million in 1961.

Stressing co-op private labels—a line comparable in variety of items to those of A & P and Safeway, and quality-controlled right down the line—and stressing operating efficiency, co-ops achieve a high-volume, high-net operation, besides being about the only food stores in the United States that retain many of the U.S. Department of Agriculture graded foods. These stores cater to the needs and interests of their members not only for food but for protection against sharp practices, such as deceptive packaging and labeling.

The problem for most consumers is that few cities and communities have a co-op food store. Also, many American consumers are not aware of certain buying advantages at cooperative food stores. They are inclined to think that consumer cooperatives are only a social crusade and may have overlooked the following advantages.

1. Members have the advantage of a patronage refund at the end of the fiscal year if a profit exists.

2. Generally, there are more quality foods, properly graded and carrying descriptive information, than in other food stores. There is no point in taking advantage of the customer because the profits are returned to buying members.

3. Most cooperatives carry many or all of the U.S. Department of Agriculture grade labels. In addition, they carry cooperative graded foods developed in their own testing kitchens.

4. Some of the best buys are the cooperative brands. Grade A is identified by a red label; grade B by a blue label; and grade C by a green label.

5. In the better-quality foods, the cooperative may have better buys than similarly priced foods in the national chains. (In the lower-quality foods, the national chains usually have lower prices.)

6. Because the members own the store, they have a direct line of communication to their elected board of directors.

It is difficult for some cooperatives to compete successfully with the largest national chains on fresh meat and fresh fruits and vegetables because, as yet, the cooperatives are largely dependent on noncooperative sources for most of their supplies. There have been monopolistic practices by the big food chains.

Food Retailing by Discount Houses.[4] There has been a new development in food retailing. Food is being sold by discount houses and by a few large national food chains in departments in some carefully selected

[4] U.S. Department of Agriculture, Economic Research Service, *The Marketing and Transportation Situation,* February, 1962, pp. 38–41.

discount stores. The number of these stores or departments has been increasing rapidly. The Marketing Economic Research Service of the U.S. Department of Agriculture estimated that annual food sales by discount houses in 1962 amounted to about $2 billion (about 4 per cent of total retail food sales).

Many of the major national food chains have entered the discount field by acquiring discount outlets or securing food concessions in existing discount houses. Kroger converted one of its regular stores in Detroit into a discount operative; so have National Tea, Food Giant of Texas, David & Goliath stores (owned by Dilbert Quality Supermarkets).

By dispensing with some or most of the frills, the food chains hoped to regain business they had been losing to big general discounters like GEM, International (26 food departments), Two Guys (14 East Coast food departments at end of 1962).[5] Richard G. Zimmerman, publisher of *Super Market Merchandising*, said, "There isn't a food merchandiser in America who isn't talking about food discounting, worrying about it, converting to it, competing with it, or planning for it." [6]

An indication of the nature of this competition with conventional supermarkets can be seen by the following facts. Some discount houses carry a greater variety of food items than typical supermarkets carry. A few discount houses limit food items to those that have rapid turnover. Many of the food departments in discount houses do two or three times the dollar volume of regular supermarkets. A large amount of business is done in perishable foods—fresh fruits, vegetables, and meat. Annual sales in the food departments often exceed $2.5 million.

Little information was available in 1963 on how effectively discount food departments were being operated. There was no reliable information on margins and prices. It is likely, however, that discounters have been more efficient than conventional supermarkets for these reasons: (1) less costly interior decor, (2) more food sold to each customer, (3) tray-pack method used for shelf stocking, (4) overhead shared with other occupants in the same building, (5) some slow-moving and high-markup foods and nonfoods not stocked, (6) advertising costs reduced by greater use of hand bulletins.

Discount houses are here to stay. They are a means of mass low-cost distribution. They should show phenomenal growth—possibly to $8 billion in 1966. Discount houses have filled the gap left by supermarkets as the latter moved from low-cost distribution to higher-cost, noncompetitive food practices (trading stamps rather than lower food prices). It is likely that discount houses will go through a similar cycle of increasing costs and will in turn be vulnerable to a new type of low-cost operation. By

[5] *The Wall Street Journal,* Dec. 3, 1962, p. 1.
[6] *Ibid.*

1964, however, consumers located conveniently to discount food departments were likely to have considerable price advantage in food buys.

Shopping the Supermarkets. Supermarkets are advantageous for knowledgeable shoppers, but confusing and expensive for the uninformed and impulsive buyer. The uninformed and disorganized buyer drifts around the place almost in a trance. A noted designer, Gerald Stahl, claims that these types "are in a mild hypnotic trance induced by mass displays, lights, signs, slogans, pictures, and brilliant colors." [7] This may be slightly exaggerated, but have you ever gone into a supermarket for a dozen eggs and come out with a jar of olives, a new anchovy spread, and a gadget can opener?

Bend down at the dairy case for milk, and your eyes come level with jars of fresh fruit salad or imported Swiss cheese—impulse items ready for you even when stooping. Make a turn around the corner, and you nearly collide with red tomato ketchup bottles, so you take one. Red always attracted you. Another stratagem is to place big-profit items in several different places in the store. For the toddlers (heaven help you if you have one with you), the lowest shelves are baited with cereals, cookies, candies, and everything advertised on children's TV programs.

Aisles are arranged to direct you into sections you didn't intend to visit. Steaks are often surrounded with green leaves because they make the meat look redder, more appetizing. Women, say color specialists, are likely to fall for packages that feature turquoise, yellow, or pink. So watch out, the pay-off is at the check-out counter!

How, then, should the wise consumer shop a supermarket? Successful shoppers say:

1. Study the food ads before leaving home.
2. Have a shopping list.
3. Organize the items by departments so that you do not need to retrace your steps.
4. Select stores where prices in relation to quality are lower.
5. Jot down the price of each item on your list.
6. Ask for help when you need it.
7. The best bargains are the foods that are plentiful in the market.
8. Store brands are likely to be a better buy than manufacturer brands.
9. Buy according to use. (In canned goods, half peaches for an attractive salad; sliced peaches for other purposes.)
10. Look for the U.S. Department of Agriculture grade stamp on fresh meat.
11. Read all labels.
12. Check the checker. (They do make mistakes.)
13. Pay cash.

[7] UP news item reported by Robert G. Shortal, June 4, 1956.

What Is Wise Buying? Half the battle in getting the most help from good salespeople lies in being able to ask intelligent questions. You cannot do this unless you have a knowledge of wise buying.

To buy wisely, you must know four things: (1) your needs, (2) your money allotment for food, (3) comparative prices, and (4) quality and grades of food products. It is not difficult to get information about the first three. How can you increase your knowledge about the fourth?

The facts given in the remainder of this chapter will provide a foundation for gaining knowledge of comparative prices, quality, and grades, but you must be alert to use this information and add to it when you become involved in family buying.

Food Standards. Thirty years ago the typical American food store stacked only seven hundred different food items. Today, the typical supermarket offers between six thousand and eight thousand different food items. And about 85 per cent of all food sold in food stores is prepackaged. This means that the consumer must rely on food standards and on important information on the label. The processing and labeling of these foods is subject to Federal, state, and local regulations. To make the best use of the information on packaged foods, you need to understand food laws, standards, and labels.

The food label on a package or can tells the kind of food, its type and quality, all ingredients, added nutrients and seasonings, and often suggestions for use. By studying and comparing these labels, you can select the brand and type that is best for a certain use, with the seasonings your family prefers. Thoughtful selection will give you the best return for your money.

Three kinds of food standards have been established: (1) standards of identity, (2) standards of quality, and (3) standards of fill of container. Specifically exempted by Congress are most fresh and dried fruits and vegetables.

Standards of Identity. The standards of identity were determined by the Food and Drug Administration (FDA) in cooperation with processing and food specialists. The standard for preserves and jellies, for example, requires 45 parts, by weight, of fruit or fruit juices, and 55 parts of sugar ingredients. Standards have been established for about two hundred food products, including such common foods as canned salmon, tuna, sardines; some prepared meat products; dairy products; margarine; salad dressings; tea; chocolate and cocoa products; and wheat, corn, and flour products. You may also find on the label a listing of optional ingredients.

Since the Supreme Court decision (March 26, 1951), substandard low-fruit jams are legal if labeled "imitation." This decision could nullify the identity standards because the FDA does not have the manpower to handle abuses. Fortunately, anticipated abuses apparently have not developed to the extent that was feared. Unfortunately, the net weight on the label does not make a distinction between the weight of the solid and the liquid. This distinction should be incorporated in the law.

Standards of Quality. Standards of quality have been established for a number of leading varieties of canned fruits and vegetables. These are minimum standards for such qualities as tenderness, color, and freedom from defects. They do *not* provide a basis for comparing foods as grades do, but they fix minimums. Canned foods that fall below standard in appearance must be labeled "Substandard" or "Below Standard in Quality," or "Good Food—Not High Grade" with the reason—"excess peeling" or "excessively broken."

Unfortunately for the consumer who wants to cut food expenses, such products seldom appear in retail stores. "Below Standard" foods are wholesome and entirely satisfactory. Where appearance and texture of the food is lost, there is no loss in nutritional value.

Standards of Fill of Container. These standards apply chiefly to canned fruits and vegetables, tomato products, and shellfish. They were set up to prevent deception of consumers. Packers must adhere to regulations on how full containers must be to avoid prosecution for "slack filling." Similar standards have been set up informally for many other foods such as olives, pickles, and spices. Cheating of the consumer still exists, but it is not as common as it used to be.

Standards for Enriched Products and Dietary Regulations. Usually, food standards are thought of as devices for protecting the consumer's pocketbook. For example, Cheddar cheese must contain at least 50 per cent milk fat (moisture-free) and not over 39 per cent moisture. But these standards also insure that a food has the required nutritional value, as in enriched flour, corn meal, farina, macaroni products, oleomargarine, evaporated milk, and rice. However, the purpose of the standard originally was to promote "honesty and fair dealing" among processors.

The law guarantees uniformity of enrichment as well as a substantial amount of enrichment. A regulatory action by the FDA is in order if the "enriched" flour or meal does not contain the specified proportions of thiamine, riboflavin, niacin, and iron or if margarine does not contain the required amount of vitamin A.

Regulations have also been established by the FDA regarding foods for special diets. Such foods include low-calorie and low-sodium products, designed for infant feeding or for persons with an allergy, or to be used for their mineral and vitamin content.

Families who follow Jewish dietary laws can look for authorized symbols on the labels of processed foods. These symbols indicate that the products have been certified as kosher. About 1,000 foods have been identified as kosher by the use of the letter "K" or "U" of the Union of the Orthodox Jewish Congregations.

In addition to the services of the FDA, which sets the rules for labeling foods, drugs, and cosmetics that move interstate, the Meat Inspection Division of the U.S. Department of Agriculture has authority to require that all meat and meat food products intended for interstate commerce be approved before they are sold to consumers. Likewise, the Poultry Division of the Agricultural Marketing Service requires fresh and frozen ready-to-cook poultry and canned poultry and frozen poultry products to be inspected and marked correctly. Standards for certain prepared fish products, including fish sticks and ready-to-cook shrimp, are established by the Bureau of Commercial Fisheries of the Department of the Interior.

Label Reading Is Important. It pays to develop skill in label reading. The brand name is not enough. Learn to compare ingredients, amounts, and costs of various products. Choose the best ones suited to your family needs and your food dollars.

Label reading in the supermarket is difficult. It is better to practice in the kitchen with packages and cans already purchased. You may be surprised to note that of three brands of chicken pie, one brand has five vegetables, another has three, and a third has only one vegetable. One brand of oyster stew may use skim milk, whereas another brand may use whole milk. At any rate, develop the habit and the skill to read the labels. There is a difference in foods as a general rule.

How to Buy Meat. Meat is the largest single item in your food budget, usually taking 25 to 30 per cent of the family food dollar. At times you have to defend your food dollar by looking for better values in meats and by relying on other animal protein foods, such as cheese, milk, eggs, poultry, and fish. It is wise to use these high-protein foods to stretch the food dollar rather than starchy extenders, such as bread, potatoes, and cereals, which do not provide the complete proteins you get from animal foods.

Meat, dairy, and poultry products are the only sources of proteins containing the amino acids that are essential in the diet. In terms of protein count, for example, bacon is usually about 50 per cent more expensive than rib roast. Cheddar cheese is one of the lowest-priced protein yielding foods on the market, while bacon is one of the more expensive protein foods.

A larger cut of meat is frequently an economy. But the larger cut does not have to be cooked all in one piece. One pot roast, for example, with a little help from the meat man, can be easily divided at home into cuts for beef stew, Swiss steak, and pot roast. Likewise ham, pork butt, leg of lamb, pork loin, and rib roast can be divided for different purposes. The accompanying charts, Meat—Thrifty Use of Larger Cuts, show how larger cuts may be divided for cooking and serving as different meat dishes.

An expensive American habit is the preference for only six to eight cuts of meat from each carcass. From each 1,000-pound steer, for example, about 465 pounds reach the retail counter. Only about 75 of the 465 pounds constitute the most purchased, expensive cuts: porterhouse, T-bone, club, and sirloin steaks. Another 45 pounds comprise the popular rib roasts. This leaves 345 pounds of less expensive cuts: round, chuck, blade, rump, hamburger, and stewing meats. These are lower priced but make tasty and nutritious meat dishes. Add to this the nutritious and usually lower-priced variety meats: heart, kidney, liver, tongue, tripe, and oxtail.

Price variations from month to month and season to season also represent possible savings. Round steak, pork chops, bacon, and eggs usually show more than a 10 per cent change in monthly price averages during the year and should be used often during periods of low prices. Rib roast, whole ham, fryers, and chuck roast show a monthly price range from 5 to 10 per cent. Frankfurters, cheese, and hamburger vary slightly in price during the year. In general, beef bargains in September and low-cost pork in December save money for the consumer. Watch for the weekly or monthly reports on meat prices in the food section of your daily newspaper.

Here are tips worth remembering when buying meat.

1. Get on buying terms with the many cheaper cuts of beef, pork, veal, and lamb.

2. Price has nothing to do with the nutritive value of meat. The lower-priced cuts are usually as tasty and rich in vitamins, protein, and other nutrients as the higher-priced cuts.

3. Buy grades and cuts of meat according to intended use.

4. Look for the largest amount of lean meat for your price. Fat and bone are useful, but they can be purchased at a lower price.

5. Buy United States–inspected and graded meats for health and economical reasons, because the grades and inspection marks provide information to assist in selecting cuts for wholesomeness and quality.

6. Buy the cheaper varieties of liver, kidney, and heart.

7. Purchase canned meat for variety. Canned meat packed with vegetables is not an economical buy.

8. The lean meat from cheaper cuts of meat from the same carcass is just as nutritive as the lean meat from the expensive cuts. The higher price paid is for tenderness.

9. Meats showing streaks of fat are more flavorful because fat helps to distribute flavor.

How to get three fresh-cooked meals from one pot roast

With a simple bit of meat cutting in your kitchen you can get three different meals from a thick round-bone pot roast like this.

1. Beef Stew

From the round end of the roast, cut a piece to use for meal number one. Cut this boneless meat into cubes for a beef and vegetable stew.

2. Pot Roast

Cut a piece from the center for a chunky pot roast. It will be thick, for best results in cooking—and easy carving, too.

3. Swiss Steak

With a sharp knife and a saucer under your hand for safety, you can easily split the remaining piece to make two attractive Swiss steaks.

How to make four fresh-cooked meals from half a ham

When ham is on your shopping list, it's a real economy for the average size family to get a full-cut shank half large enough to make 4 meals, as shown here.

1. "Boiled" Dinner

Have your meat-man saw off a generous shank end for lots of flavor in a "boiled" dinner. Simmer it with carrots, onions, potatoes and wedges of cabbage.

2. Baked Ham

You can easily divide the center part of the ham half into two portions as shown here. Bake the piece with the bone. The slices will be small, but no less delicious.

3. Fried Ham Slices

The remaining piece is easily sliced with a sharp knife. Cut fairly thick slices from the larger end to fry or broil.

4. Ham and Scalloped Potatoes.
Cut the smaller end into thinner slices. Use them in alternating layers with sliced potatoes to make a dish of scalloped ham and potatoes.

How to make three fresh-cooked meals from one pork butt

It's a real economy purchase to get a whole fresh pork shoulder butt (5 to 7 pounds) and cut it at home as shown.

1. Pork Roast

A pork shoulder butt has only one bone. It extends only part way through the piece. Cut with a sharp knife, as shown in the diagram, to divide easily into two pieces. The piece with the bone is your smaller, one-meal roast.

2. Pork Steaks

The remaining piece is clear, solid meat. From it you can cut boneless steaks about one-half inch thick.

Braise the pork steaks just as you would pork chops. Make a panful of gravy with the drippings.

3. Chop Suey

As you get to the small end of the boneless piece, cut the remaining meat into small half-inch cubes. Use the diced pork for a meat-stretching dish of chop suey or, if you prefer, a casserole of corn and pork.

SOURCE: American Meat Institute, Chicago

w to get steaks,

oast, a stew from

leg of lamb

hree freshly cooked meals, buy a
t leg of lamb. Ask your meat-man
off a few lamb steaks, and to cut
gh the shank, leaving about a
l of meat on the bone.

1. Lamb Steaks to Broil

Broil the lamb steaks just as you would loin
chops. Serve sizzling hot with broiled pineapple slices.

2. Lamb Roast

Here's your Sunday roast—just the easy-to-
carve center portion of the leg. Make a panful of gravy and serve with potatoes and peas.

Remember, you'll get more juicy slices and
less cooking shrinkage if you roast lamb at a
low oven temperature (no higher than 325° F.).

3. Stew or Casserole

Later in the week, cut the meat from the
shank into cubes for another freshly cooked
meal. Use these tender, boneless cubes of lamb
in an Irish stew—or a more glamorous dish
such as lamb curry or shish kebob (marinated
pieces of lamb grilled on skewers along with
green pepper, onions and tomatoes).

---

w to get three

sh-cooked meals

m a pork loin

st

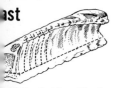

se this method for getting three
different meals—all fresh-cooked
ct the more economical rib cut of
loin. The larger your family, the
the cut you will need.

1. Meaty Barbecued Backbones

Have your meat-man saw through the
ribs high enough to leave an inch-thick
layer of meat on the backbones. Ask
him to chop these "country style" backbones into serving-sized pieces. Cook as
you would spareribs.

2. Pork Chops and Gravy

Later, cut enough chops for another
meal from the remaining piece by slicing between the ribs. You'll find that
this is now easy to do because the backbone has been removed.

3. Easy-to-Serve Pork Roast

You still have a piece left to cook as a pork
roast for your third fresh-cooked meal. Be
sure to cook pork thoroughly. Use an oven
temperature of 325-350° F. and roast about
40 minutes to the pound.

---

w to make a

roast do double

y

s a thrifty trick that lets you get
aly a fine party dinner from that
ome beef rib roast but also another
cooked meal of braised short ribs.
ou can depend on it, that man in
life goes for short ribs.

1. Braised Short Ribs

Here's what you do. Have your
meat-man saw through the bones at
A and B as in the picture. You can
then cut between the ribs to make
individual servings of short ribs.
Braise them slowly with vegetables
to stretch their good meat flavor
further in the meal.

2. Juicy Roast Beef

Now, for your roast, you have
just the tenderest "heart" of
the piece you bought. To
make it juicier—and to get
more servings from it, too—
keep oven heat at 325° F. to
cut shrinkage to a minimum.
One hour before done, put
peeled potatoes in the pan to
brown in the drippings.

10. The percentage of waste, when figuring the cost of lean meat, varies from nothing in flank steak and tenderloin to about 11 per cent in porterhouse, 16 per cent in sirloin, 20 per cent in chuck, and about 27 per cent in rump with the bone left in.

11. Improper cooking of meat can offset gains in wise planning and shopping.

12. Buy roasts large enough to serve for two meals. Small roasts dry out in cooking and do not carve well.

13. The price of meat is generally lowest when the supply is largest.

14. For hamburger, meat loaf, and stews, Standard or Commercial beef may be just as satisfactory as Choice or Good and is usually more economical.

United States Inspection and Grades. All meat shipped interstate has a Federal government inspection stamp on it, a purple circle. This is important because it means that the animal was healthy when slaughtered. The U.S. Department of Agriculture has also established grades for the quality of meat in beef, veal, lamb, and mutton. Pork is usually not graded because all the cuts are tender. Grades are not measures of nutritive value or wholesomeness.

The beef grades used are:

U.S. Choice (highest retail grade)
U.S. Good

SOURCE: U.S. Department of Agriculture.

U.S. Standard (from younger beef)
U.S. Commercial (from mature beef)
U.S. Utility
U.S. Cutter (used in processed meats)
U.S. Canner (used in processed meats)

The grades for veal, lamb, and mutton are:

U.S. Choice
U.S. Good
U.S. Commercial
U.S. Utility
U.S. Cull

The U.S. Department of Agriculture amended the Federal Meat Inspection Regulations in 1962 to require that certain essential information for consumers remain intact on the labels of federally inspected meat and meat food products. The amendment applies to such products after they leave the packing or processing plant and are available to buyers at the point of sale.

Although this label requirement has long been a part of the Meat Inspection Act, the Federal Meat Inspection Regulations have not pinpointed the requirement as it applies to a product *after* it leaves the packing establishment. The new amendment to the regulations does this. (The regulations serve as a detailed guide for processors and inspectors.)

It is also illegal to remove, mask, or tamper with a label so that the information is concealed or the product misrepresented. Allowance is made for unavoidable damage to marks or labeling in the normal cutting, slicing, or other handling of a product.

Variety Meats. It is wise to include variety meats—glands and organs—in the weekly menu because they supply excellent nutrients and, comparatively speaking, are lower priced.[8]

Calf liver is preferred by most families, and therefore costs more than other kinds of liver. Pork liver is richer in iron and as rich in vitamin D as calf liver and beef liver.

Usually, lamb kidneys are the highest in price, then come veal kidneys, with beef and pork kidneys usually the lowest in price.

Brains are very low in price, comparatively. They are sold whole by the pound and sometimes by the pair. Brains should be firm.

Beef, veal, lamb, and pork hearts should be firm and full, with fat surrounding the muscles. Beef heart is the largest, but is less tender than the others.

[8] See *Variety Meat Recipes*. Chicago: National Live Stock and Meat Board.

USDA GRADE MARKS AND THE FOODS ON WHICH THEY ARE USED

The grade names on the various grade marks shown here are merely illustrative. There is a range of grades for each of these products but different grade names are used. For a list of grades see "Grade Names Used in U. S. Standards for Farm Products" (AH–157) and "Shopper's Guide to U. S. Grades for Food" (HG–58).

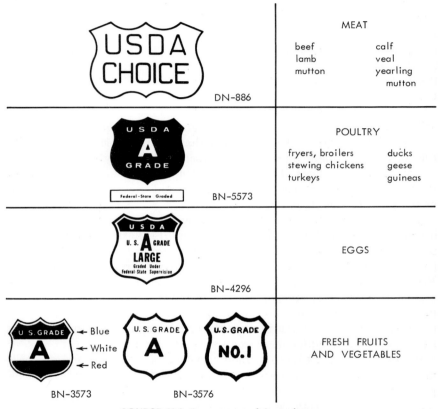

	MEAT	
beef	calf	
lamb	veal	
mutton	yearling mutton	

POULTRY

fryers, broilers, stewing chickens, turkeys, ducks, geese, guineas

EGGS

FRESH FRUITS AND VEGETABLES

DN–886, BN–5573, BN–4296, BN–3573, BN–3576

SOURCE: U.S. Department of Agriculture.

Beef tongue is generally less expensive than the smaller veal, lamb, and pork tongues.

Sweetbreads are the thymus glands of the calf or lamb. These are often purchased by the pair. The part near the heart is preferred.

Comparative Costs of Canned and Fresh Meats. All canning of meat for retail selling is federally inspected. The costs of canned and fresh meat may be compared by keeping in mind that 12 ounces of canned meat equals 15 to 18 ounces of raw boneless meat.

Not all canned meats are better buys than fresh meats. Some are in the luxury class. Those that usually offer good comparative value over fresh meats include canned corned beef, canned hamburgers and beef with gravy, canned luncheon meats, and canned lamb and pork tongue.

Comparisons are based on the cost of meat per pound, taking comparative quality and estimating waste of trimmings and shrinkage of fresh meats during cooking. Some experts estimate that trimmings account for 6 per cent of an average roast; shrinking accounts for 19 per cent more; and in serving, the bones and fat account for 32 per cent more waste.

Getting the Most for Your Meat Dollar. Buy the appropriate grade and the right cut of meat according to its intended use to get more food value from your meat dollar. When buying meat for stew or soup, for example, select shank, plate or brisket, or round cuts in the U.S. Commercial grade.

The table on pages 210–212, Tips When Buying Fresh Meat, gives the various cuts, their use, and the approximate quantity for four persons.

The most economical cuts are those that provide the most nutritive value for the money spent. Lean cuts are highest in protein, while cuts with considerable fat are highest in food energy. A thrifty homemaker buys the cuts that yield the greatest number of servings per dollar. Both nutritive content and yields in servings are influenced by the proportions of lean, fat, and bone, which vary with grade and cut. A careful study of the accompanying charts, Cost of Lean in Retail Beef Cuts, and Cost Per Pound of Lean in Pork Cuts, will pay big family dividends. The price you pay for a pound of lean in different beef and pork cuts at given prices can be easily seen on these charts.

Prepackaged Meat. In most food stores, retail meats are offered in prepackaged form on a self-service basis. They include a variety of fresh cuts, cold cuts, variety meats, frozen meats, smoked and cooked sausage products, and other cuts. The meats are wrapped and sealed in transparent film, and displayed in self-service refrigerated cases.

The labels on fresh meat packaged in plants under United States inspection must meet requirements of Federal inspection. The label should show the name of the cut, price per pound, total weight, and cost of the package of meat.

A survey showed that discoloration is the major retailer's problem with some fresh cuts of meat. Rewrapping packages, especially roasts and steaks, is sometimes necessary because of handling by customers. Prepackaged meat either must be trimmed to remove much of the surplus fat and bone, or must have most of the fat and bone clearly visible. The quality throughout the package should be as high as that of the meat that can be seen.

COST OF LEAN IN RETAIL BEEFCUTS

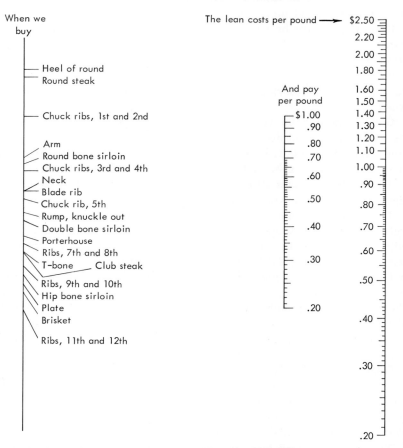

Cost per pound of lean, choice beef. Lay a straightedge at the name of the cut on the left-hand scale and at its price per pound on the center scale. Where the straightedge crosses the right-hand scale is found the cost of a pound of lean. EXAMPLE: arm (chuck), at $0.80 per lb . . . cost of lean (by scale at right) = $1.18 per lb.

To find cost of lean for cuts higher than $1 per lb, use half the price per pound on the center scale and multiply the figure obtained on the right-hand scale by 2. EXAMPLE: porterhouse at $1.20 per lb, $0.60 on the center scale (½ of $1.20) . . . cost of lean = $2.16 per lb (2 times reading on right-hand scale).

SOURCE: *Meat for the Table*, U.S. Department of Agriculture, Bulletin S, 1951.

COST PER POUND OF LEAN IN PORK CUTS

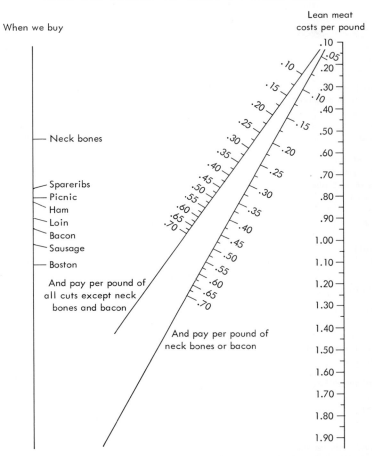

Lay a straightedge at the name of the cut on the left-hand scale and at its price per pound on the proper center scale. Where the straightedge crosses the right-hand scale is found the cost of a pound of lean. EXAMPLES: bacon at $0.65 per lb costs $1.45 (on the scale at the right) per lb of lean; ham at $0.65 per lb costs $1.04 per lb of lean.

For cuts higher than $0.70 per lb, use half the price per pound on the proper center scale and multiply the figure obtained on the right-hand scale by 2. EXAMPLE: bacon at $0.72 per lb, $0.36 on the center scale (½ of $0.72) . . . cost of lean = $1.60 per lb (2 times reading on right-hand scale).

SOURCE: *Meat for the Table*, U.S. Department of Agriculture, Bulletin S, 1951.

TIPS WHEN BUYING FRESH MEAT

Cut	Use	Approximate quantity for four persons *
	BEEF	
Low-cost cuts:		
Shank	Soup, stew	2 to 3 lb
Navel	Stew, boiling meat	3 to 4 lb
Thick plate	Stew, boiling meat	
Corner piece	Pot roast	3 to 4 lb
Brisket, fresh or corned	Boiling meat, stew	3 to 4 lb
Stew meat		1½ lb
Neck	Stew, mincemeat, meat loaf	Boneless, 3 to 4 lb
Ground	Hamburger or meat loaf	1 to 1½ lb
Medium-cost cuts:		
Heel of round	Stew, pot roast	3 to 4 lb
Blade roast, 2 ribs	Roast	3 to 4 lb
Top chuck	Pot roast, stew	3 to 4 lb
Rump	Pot roast, corned	3 to 4 lb
Round	Minute steak, Swiss steak, pot roast, stew	1½ to 2 lb
Top sirloin	Roast	3 to 4 lb
Flank	Braised steak, stew	1 medium
Chuck	Pot roast, stew	Boneless, 3 to 4 lb
Short ribs	Pot roast	2½ to 3 lb
High-cost cuts:		
Sirloin	Broiled steak, roast	2½ lb
Porterhouse	Broiled steak	2½ lb
Prime rib roast, 6 ribs	Roast	3 to 4 lb
Tenderloin	Broiled or roast	1 to 1½ lb
Other edible parts:		
Heart	Stew, stuffed, braised	
Kidney	Stew, meat pie	
Liver	Fried, braised, liver loaf, liver paste	⅔ to 1 lb
Tongue, fresh, corned, pickled, smoked	Boiled	1 lb
Tripe, fresh, pickled	Broiled, fried, creamed	1 to 1½ lb
Oxtail	Stew, braised, soup	4 lb
	VEAL †	
Low-cost cuts:		
Heel	Fricassee, pot roast, ground meat	1½ lbs
Neck	Fricassee, stew, patties	1½ lbs
Breast	Fricassee	2 to 3 lb
Foreshank	Soup, fricassee, ground meat	2 to 3 lb
Stew meat	Stew	1½ lb
Shank	Soup, fricassee, ground meat	4 lb

Cut	Use	Approximate quantity for four persons *
	VEAL † (continued)	
Medium-cost cuts:		
Rump	Pot roast	3 to 4 lb
Rack	Roast	3 to 4 lb
Shoulder	Pot roast, fricassee	3 to 4 lb
High-cost cuts:		
Round	Cutlets, veal birds	1⅓ to 1¾ lb
Loin and rib chops	Braised chops	1½ to 2 lb
Loin	Roast	3 to 4 lb
Other edible parts:		
Heart	Stew, stuffed, braised	2
Kidney	Stew, meat pie, broiled	3
Liver	Broiled, fried, braised	⅔ to 1 lb
Tongue, fresh, corned, pickled, smoked	Boiled	1
Brains	Fried, braised, scrambled	⅔ to 1 lb
Sweetbreads	Broiled, creamed, in salad	⅔ to 1 lb
	LAMB ‡	
Medium-low-cost cuts:		
Cushion shoulder		1
Rolled shoulder		3 to 3½ lb
Neck slices	Stew	4 double slices
Shank	Soup, stew, meat patties	4
Breast and flank	Stew, stuffed roast, meat patties	1
Stew meat	Stew	1½ lb
Ground lamb	Broiled	1 to 1½ lbs
Medium-cost cuts:		
Square chuck	Boned roast, stew, Saratoga chops	3 to 4 lb
Shoulder lamb chops	Broiled or pan-broiled	4
High-cost cuts:		
Leg	Roast	3 to 3½ lb
Loin	Broiled loin chops	4 (1⅓ lb)
Rib or rack	Broiled rib chops	4 (1⅓ lb)
Crown shoulder	Roast	3 to 4 lb
Other edible parts:		
Heart	Stew, braised	4
Kidney	Broiled on toast	8
Liver	Broiled, fried, braised	⅔ to 1 lb
Tongue, fresh, corned, pickled, smoked	Boiled	8
Brains	Fried, braised, scrambled	⅔ to 1 lb

Cut	Use	Approximate quantity for four persons *

PORK

Low-cost cuts:

Feet	Boiled, pickled	4
Spareribs	Baked, boiled	2½ to 3 lb
Neck bones	Cooked like spareribs	3 to 4 lb
Jowl square	Sliced, fried, seasoning for vegetables	1 to 1½ lb
Sausage meat	Broiled	1 to 1½ lb
Salt pork	Pan-fried	1½ lb

Medium-cost cuts:

Brisket (forepart of bacon)	Seasoning for vegetables	1
Cured picnic shoulder	Baked or boiled, fried or braised	1 to 2 lb
New York style shoulder	Cooked like ham	3 to 4 lb
Boston butts	Cooked like ham	1 to 2 lb
Loin butts (end of pork loin)	Roast	2
Cured hams (purchased whole or half)	Baked, boiled, fried, broiled, or braised slices	¼ to ½ ham
Fresh hams	Roast	3 to 4 lb
Fresh hams	Braised steak	1 to 1½ lb
Spareribs	Braised or roasted	2½ to 3 lb

High-cost cuts:

Bacon (without rind)	Broiled, fried	½ lb
Cured ham, center slices	Broiled, fried, braised	1 to 1½ lb
Fresh pork loins	Roast, crown roast	3 to 4 lb
Cured pork loins	Canadian style bacon	½ to ¾ lb
Pork chops, loin or rib	Braised	4
Link sausage	Broiled	1 to 1½ lb

Other edible parts:

Heart	Stew, braised	4
Kidney	Stew, meat pie	3 to 4
Liver	Fried, braised, liver loaf, liver paste	⅔ to 1 lb
Tongue, fresh, corned, pickled	Boiled	1 to 2
Brains	Fried, braised, scrambled	⅔ to 1 lb
Head	Headcheese, scrapple	1

* These amounts are indicative only. Those for roasts and pot roasts furnish enough meat for leftovers.

† Veal from very young calves, 3 to 8 weeks old, is most plentiful from January to July. Veal from calves 3 to 10 months old is most plentiful from June to November.

‡ Lamb is tender at any age. Spring lamb 3 to 5 months old is most plentiful from May to September. Meat from more mature lambs, 6 to 12 months old, is most plentiful from September through April.

SOURCE: *Buying Food for the Family*, Bulletin 526, July, 1942. Cornell University, New York State College for Home Economics, pp. 26–27. Reprinted with permission.

Terms and Grade Labels for Poultry. Poultry is an expensive meat to purchase, as a rule, because there is only a small percentage of meat in a dressed bird. The Department of Agriculture has compiled the percentage of meat in six kinds of dressed bird. To figure cost per pound, divide the price per pound for a dressed bird by the percentage given here.

	Per cent		Per cent
Fattened roasting chickens	63	Unfattened broilers	54
Unfattened roasting chickens	57	Fattened hens	64
Fattened broilers	61	Turkeys	68

POULTRY GRADE LEVELS AND INSPECTION MARKS

Graded Ready-to-Cook

Graded and Inspected
Ready-to-Cook

Inspected for
Wholesomeness
Ready-to-Cook

Graded Dressed

SOURCE: Agricultural Marketing Services, U.S. Department of Agriculture.

If you need only a few pieces of chicken, it may be cheaper to buy just those you want. Breasts from roasters contain about 72 per cent edible meat; drumsticks yield about 75 per cent. If you want a turkey meal without eating turkey all week, buy turkey cuts.

On January 1, 1950, a revised program of the U.S. Department of Agriculture for the grading and inspection of poultry went into effect. Although a voluntary program, the regulations apply to those members of the poultry industry who request the inspection and grading services of the department.

An important part of the program deals with the requirements for the sanitation of dressing plants. Since January 1, 1951, all ready-to-cook poultry prepared in official plants approved by the Department of Agriculture have been processed under the same sanitary standards.

Broiling and frying chickens are now one class and may be termed *broilers* or *fryers.* Stewing chickens may be described as *hens, stewing chickens,* or *fowl.* The term *dressed* is used for birds that have been bled and picked, but not drawn. *Ready-to-cook* describes poultry that has been fully drawn, or eviscerated.

The official grade label, in the form of a shield, states the quality (U.S. Grade A or U.S. Grade B), the style of processing (dressed or ready-to-cook), and the class (stewing chicken). The label also states that the product is government graded.

Ready-to-cook poultry that has been inspected for wholesomeness by a Federal veterinarian but not graded for quality carries an inspection mark in the form of a circle. Ready-to-cook poultry that has been both graded and inspected carries a combination label, a shield within a circle.

How Fish Is Marketed. Fish may be purchased fresh, frozen, or canned. It also pays to know the most common ways fish are marketed.

Whole or round. This term refers to fish just as they come from the water. Before cooking, internal organs must be taken out and scales removed. Remove the head, tail, and fins except on some small fish or fish to be baked. For broiling or frying, the fish may need to be split or cut into serving portions.

Drawn. Internal organs are already removed. Prepare for cooking just as whole or round fish.

Dressed or pan dressed. Internal organs and scales are removed. Most dressed fish also have head, tail, and fins removed.

Steaks. These are cross-sectional slices of the larger dressed fish. Steaks are ready to cook as purchased. A cross section of the backbone is usually the only bone in a fish steak.

Fillets. These are meaty sides of the fish, cut lengthwise away from the backbone. Fillets are practically boneless and require no preparation for cooking. Sometimes the skin, with scales removed, is left on one side of the fillet; other fillets are completely skinned.

Sticks. These are pieces of fish cut from blocks of frozen fillets into portions of uniform dimensions, usually about $\frac{1}{2}$ inch wide, 3 inches long, and $\frac{3}{8}$ inch deep, weighing approximately 1 ounce.

Whole fish may be cheaper than steaks, fillets, or sticks, but include considerable waste. Steaks have little bone or waste, and fillets and sticks have none at all.

Dairy Products. Consumer expenditures for dairy products in 1961, according to the Milk Industry Foundation report of 1963, totaled $11.2 billion. The amount spent for dairy products constituted about 13 per cent of the total family food bill. Next to meat (25 to 30 per cent), dairy products take the biggest share of the consumer food dollar.

More milk is used by consumers in fluid form than any other, as shown in the accompanying chart, How 1961 U.S. Milk Supply Was Used.

Grades and Kinds of Milk. The U.S. Public Health Service Milk Ordinance standards have been adopted by most American cities. This ordinance provides for three grades of fluid milk.

1. Certified milk: Very rigid sanitary requirements; sold only by licensed dealers; expensive.

2. Grade A, pasteurized: Must not contain more than 30,000 bacteria per cubic centimeter; must have hooded caps; must be kept below 50 degrees at all times.

3. Grade B, pasteurized: May contain as many as 50,000 bacteria per cubic centimeter when delivered to the consumer; need not have hooded caps.

4. Grade C, pasteurized: Is below Grade B requirements.

HOW 1961 U.S. MILK SUPPLY WAS USED

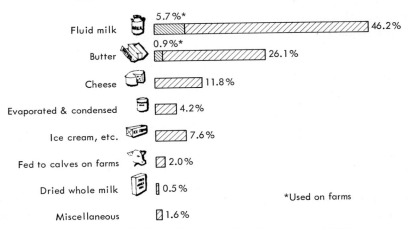

Fluid milk	5.7%* 46.2%
Butter	0.9%* 26.1%
Cheese	11.8%
Evaporated & condensed	4.2%
Ice cream, etc.	7.6%
Fed to calves on farms	2.0%
Dried whole milk	0.5%
Miscellaneous	1.6%

*Used on farms

SOURCE: *Milk Facts*, Milk Industry Foundation report, 1963.

The ordinance also provides for three grades of raw milk, A, B, and C.

Grade A pasteurized milk is the most common form of milk for table use. Milk delivered to the home costs from 2 to 4 cents a quart more than when purchased at milk stores in gallon and half-gallon quantities.

Homogenized milk is processed so that the fat does not separate and rise to the top of the bottle. It is thought to be more digestible, but authorities are still battling over this assumption. Some pediatricians believe that only in the case of infants is there value in homogenization, since it softens the curd of milk. There are no extra food values in homogenized milk, but the consumer pays 1 to 2 cents a quart more for it, though the process costs are very low.

As yet, science has discovered no milk substitute. It is possible, however, to reduce the cost of milk without decreasing the food value. This can be done by using evaporated milk.

Evaporated milk mixed with an equal volume of water is whole milk slightly above the average for the composition of bottled milk. Some evaporated milk is enriched with vitamin D. One pint of evaporated milk (before water is added) is equal in food value to a quart of fresh milk, at a little more than half the price. A 14½-ounce can of evaporated milk selling for 15 cents is a cheaper source of milk than a quart of whole milk that costs 24 cents.

Many homemakers prefer evaporated milk for cooking, and it is recommended for cream sauces, gravies, cream soup, chowder, scalloped vegetables, custards, puddings, dessert sauces, cakes, cookies, breads, frozen desserts, and candy. Undiluted evaporated milk is used by many families in coffee, candy, and frozen desserts, and as an emulsifier in mayonnaise. When thoroughly chilled, it can be whipped like cream.

Dried milk (powdered milk) is used largely for cooking purposes, in the proportion of ¾ cup of dried milk to 1 quart of water.

Skim milk (*nonfat milk*) can also be used for cooking purposes. The cost of this product may be from 15 to 19 cents a quart.

Milk equivalents in the diet. Here are some substitutes for fresh whole milk in mathematical terms, which will help in calculating food values.

> 1 quart of skim milk plus 1½ ounces of butter equals 1 quart of fluid milk.
> 1 pint of undiluted evaporated milk equals 1 quart of fluid milk.
> ⅓ pound of Cheddar cheese equals 1 quart of fluid milk.
> ¼ pound of dried whole milk equals 1 quart of fluid milk.

How to Buy Cheese. The most food value for the money is in *American Cheddar cheese.* About 5 quarts of milk are required to make 1 pound. Thus all the proteins, fats, minerals, and vitamins found in whole milk are found in Cheddar cheese.

There are over four hundred varieties of cheese made in this country. The fancy processed cheese is generally Cheddar, processed with inexpensive fillers and water.

Sharp cheese costs more than mild cheese because it is aged.

Cheese is not a complete substitute for meat or eggs, because it is low in protein, although high in butterfat.

The Federal government has established the following quality grades for American Cheddar cheese, and some manufacturers use them.

	Quality score
U.S. Extra Fancy	95 and above
U.S. Fancy	92–94
U.S. No. 1	89–91
U.S. No. 2	86–88
U.S. No. 3	83–85
Culls	Below 83

Cottage cheese is usually the next best buy in food value. It is made from skim milk, and therefore has no butterfat or vitamin A. It cannot replace whole milk in the diet. No U.S. grades have as yet been produced for cottage cheese, but rigid specifications have been set to cover its manufacture and quality. Cottage cheese may carry a shield stating that it is "Quality Approved" by the U.S. Department of Agriculture.

Grades of Butter. Butter is the dairy product most widely sold on the basis of U.S. grades. The letters "U.S." before the grade mark on the carton or wrapper indicate that the butter has been graded by an authorized grader of the U.S. Department of Agriculture.

The letters AA, A, B, or the numerical score, 93, 92, 90, without the prefix "U.S." on the package indicate that the butter has not been certified by a Federal butter grader.

Some states have enacted a law requiring that butter be grade labeled, and in these localities the letters or grade names on butter cartons denote state standards, applied by state graders. Such state grades do not carry the prefix "U.S.," but may show the state name or seal.

A grade mark on the package without the prefix "U.S." or state identification reflects the manufacturer's or distributor's own standard of quality. This butter may be of good quality, but since it is not federally graded the consumer must necessarily rely on the distributor's statement that it meets the quality designation on the package.

U.S. grades for butter include U.S. Grade AA (U.S. 93 score), U.S. Grade A (U.S. 92 score), and U.S. Grade B (U.S. 90 score). "Score" refers to the total number of points allotted a sample on the basis of the quality of several factors—chiefly flavor, but also including body, texture, color, and salt.

To be rated U.S. Grade AA, butter must have a fine, highly pleasing aroma and a delicate, sweet taste. Americans like butter, though it is comparatively expensive. It takes from 10½ to 11 quarts of milk to produce 1 pound of butter. About 26.1 per cent of the milk supply went into butter in 1961.

Standards for Margarine. Oleomargarine, or margarine, as it is more generally called, when fortified with vitamin A, has as much food value as butter, according to the American Medical Association. In addition, margarine does not become rancid as quickly as butter. Margarine is a genuine food, made from refined food fats, such as cottonseed oil, soybean oil, peanut oil, and meat fats. These oils are blended with pasteurized cultured skim milk and salt for flavor. The retail price of margarine is usually less than half the price for the same weight of 92-score butter.

Many laws, both state and Federal, have been passed in the last 50 years to protect the butter interests. Congress finally repealed the 64-year-old antimargarine taxes and license fees and permitted the sale of yellow margarine in interstate commerce on July 1, 1950.

The quality and purity of margarine that enters interstate commerce is guarded by two Federal agencies. For instance, margarine that contains animal fats is inspected by the Federal Meat Inspection Service. Margarine that contains only vegetable oils comes under the supervision of the Federal Food, Drug, and Cosmetic Act. Margarine must contain 80 per cent fat, which corresponds to the 80 per cent fat requirement for butter.

Know the Eggs You Buy. The alert consumer always considers value in purchases more than price. When prices are high, it is especially important to know where and how to get the most for your egg money. To get the best buy, know quality or grade, know size or weight, know about shell color, and know their food values.

In many places, eggs are sold by grade, and the quality is stated in terms of grade on the label of the egg carton. An egg in one of the top grades, AA or A, should have a large amount of firm white and a round, upstanding yolk. Eggs of such quality are preferred for poaching, frying, and cooking in the shell.

Grade B eggs, just as satisfactory for scrambling and for baking and cooking, have thinner whites and somewhat flatter yolks. They offer the same food values as the top grades. Grade B eggs may cost as much as 10 or 12 cents a dozen less than Grade A eggs of the same weight.

In terms of value on a scale, the size of eggs means the same as weight. A dozen jumbo eggs weigh not less than 30 ounces. A dozen eggs labeled Extra Large must weigh at least 27 ounces, and eggs of the more common size, Large, weigh not less than 24 ounces to the dozen.

Let us stop here a minute: 24 ounces equals 1½ pounds. That is worth remembering when you consider relative prices of eggs, meat, fish, cheese, and other protein foods that are purchased by the pound. It takes only 8 large eggs, two-thirds of a dozen, to make a pound, and they cost two-thirds the price of a dozen. But you buy eggs by the dozen unit, and you get 1½ pounds of a meat-alternate food in 12 large eggs.

If you pay 60 cents for a dozen large eggs (weighing 24 ounces or more), you are actually paying only at the rate of around 40 cents a pound, because the shells, the only waste, weigh very little. This waste is especially small when compared with that of many other protein foods.

Medium eggs run 21 ounces or more per dozen eggs, and small or pullet eggs weigh 18 or more ounces per dozen. The small eggs are seldom on the market except in late summer and fall, when they are usually good buys. Any time of year, it pays to figure the relation between the price of eggs and their weight or size. The accompanying table, Comparative Values in Grade A Eggs Based on Weight, will help you to compare egg weight values.

COMPARATIVE VALUES IN GRADE A EGGS BASED ON WEIGHT

When large Grade A eggs, at least 24 ounces per dozen, cost	Medium-sized Grade A eggs, at least 21 ounces per dozen, are as good a buy or better at	And small Grade A eggs, at least 18 ounces per dozen, are as good a buy or better at
$.46–$.50	$.40–$.44	$.34–$.38
.51– .55	.45– .48	.39– .41
.56– .60	.49– .52	.42– .45
.61– .65	.53– .57	.46– .49
.66– .70	.58– .61	.50– .52
.71– .75	.62– .66	.53– .56
.76– .80	.67– .70	.57– .60
.81– .85	.71– .74	.61– .64
.86– .90	.75– .79	.64– .68
.91– .95	.80– .83	.69– .71

Comparing the price of eggs of the same size (large, for example) but of different qualities (Grades AA, A, B) is also worthwhile. For instance, such a comparison may show that Grade B and Grade C eggs are priced from 10 to 15 cents a dozen lower than higher-quality eggs of the same weight.

Shell color also may affect price. Yet there is no advantage to the consumer in paying a premium for shell color. Sometimes white shell eggs are priced higher than brown eggs or a mixture of brown and white. White eggs may cost from 5 to 10 cents a dozen more in some markets. In other sections, brown eggs are more in demand and bring higher prices. But the "meat" of the eggs, inside the shell, is the same in food value and flavor because the color merely depends on the breed of the hen.

Finally, know the food values that eggs have to offer: high-quality protein, iron, vitamin A, riboflavin, thiamine, and some vitamin D, all stored inside an egg shell. Eggs rate as a protective food along with meat, poultry, fish, dry peas, and beans. And of them all, none of these protein foods is so versatile as eggs. They fill the bill for young and old alike at any meal—as a main dish, in soup and salad, or in the beverage or dessert.

Increase Family Use of Fruits and Vegetables. Nutrition experts figure that about 21 per cent of the family food costs should go into the purchase of fruits and vegetables. This is probably far above typical family expenditures, because most families usually do not have enough of these foods in their diets.

Modern science has discovered that fruits and vegetables are valuable to the diet in many ways. First, leafy vegetables, skins, and fibers provide needed roughage. Second, fruits and vegetables are rich in vitamins that

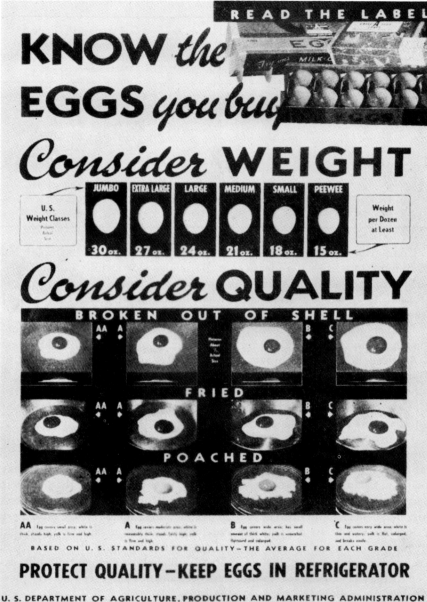

SOURCE: Production and Marketing Administration, U.S. Department of Agriculture.

are essential to good health. Third, some fruits and vegetables are good sources of minerals. And finally, some fruits and vegetables are rich in fuel content.

Generally, green and yellow vegetables, such as green lettuce, sweet potatoes and tomatoes, peaches, and apricots, are rich in vitamin A.

Oranges, lemons, grapefruit, tomatoes, limes, and tangerines are rich in vitamin C. Since vitamin C cannot be stored in the body, we need a fresh supply every day.

The B family of vitamins (thiamine, riboflavin, niacin) are found in apples, apricots, bananas, cabbage, kale, and dried peas. Iron is supplied by the green leafy vegetables, such as broccoli, chard, spinach, lettuce.

How to Buy Fresh Fruits and Vegetables. How can you know what to look for when buying fresh fruits and vegetables? Each fruit and vegetable has different characteristics, so no one set of rules can be exactly applied. It is well to remember that if you order fruits and vegetables by telephone or depend on a clerk, the chances for the best selection are not so good. This job takes personal shopping.

Every family should have the latest edition of *A Fruit and Vegetable Buying Guide for Consumers* (U.S. Department of Agriculture, Miscellaneous Publication 167). The following information about grapefruit and oranges is typical of the facts and advice given by government experts.

When selecting *grapefruit,* for example, the experts claim that russet-colored fruit is generally cheaper than the clear yellow grapefruit and is a better buy. Select a thin-skinned fruit because it contains more juice. If the skin is wrinkled or rough, it is likely to be thick. Prices in the summer months are usually higher.

When selecting *oranges,* the same source recommends, for juice, a thin-skinned, soft, heavy orange like the Valencia from Texas, California, or Florida. The navel orange from California is best for slicing or eating in sections because it is seedless, thick-skinned, and rich-colored. Oranges wrapped in paper are mechanically washed and polished, which improves the appearance and increases the cost but does not improve the flavor. Adding artificial coloring to oranges to satisfy consumers is merely an added expense. Oranges of a green color are, as a rule, fully ripened fruit. Medium-sized oranges (number 150 to 216) are usually the best buy.

There are many ways in which you can get more for your money when purchasing fresh fruits and vegetables. The following suggestions are used by wise shoppers.

1. Select fruit and vegetables the family likes.
2. Select fruit and vegetables that are most plentiful in the market.
3. Use fruit and vegetables that are in season.
4. By using a variety of fruit and vegetables, it is easier to keep costs down.

5. Purchase in as large quantities as use and storage without loss permit.

6. If possible, shop personally and as early in the day as demands on your time permit.

7. When handling fruit (the touch system), be careful, because careless handling increases spoilage and adds to the price that consumers pay.

8. Low price is not necessarily an indication of poor quality. There may be an oversupply of that particular product.

9. The most expensive quality may not be the best buy for a particular use. For example, topless carrots sold by the pound are just as good for stews and soups, or served raw, and they are cheaper than bunch carrots.

10. Blemishes on fruit may affect the looks but not the eating quality. Shriveled, wilted, and discolored vegetables, however, are usually poor buys.

11. Buy by weight rather than measure whenever possible, because numbers, pints, or quarts do not have consistent meaning. Cauliflower heads, for instance, may vary from 25 to 50 ounces.

12. Sometimes packaged fruits have poor-quality specimens in the lower layers, and fruit or vegetables in bags are not always all of the same quality.

13. Carrots, kale, collards, spinach, and green cabbage are often the least expensive vegetables, but they have high food value.

14. Compare prices in the food advertisements and in the stores.

15. Compare the costs of fresh, canned, frozen, and dried fruit and vegetables.

Grading Fresh Fruits and Vegetables. The U.S. Department of Agriculture has established standards at the wholesale level for some 70 fresh fruits and vegetables. There are 12 consumer level standards at retail stores. All Federal inspection is based on these standards, but their use is permissive.

Each fruit and vegetable has its own set of quality grades. The principal United States grades are U.S. Fancy, U.S. No. 1, U.S. No. 2, U.S. Commercial, and U.S. Combination. The quality grade is marked on the container, which speeds the handling of the produce. Some use has been made by homemakers of standard grades in the purchase of apples, grapefruit, oranges, peaches, and potatoes in quantity.

One reason that consumers do not see the grade quality is the fact that by the time the consumer gets the fruit, a lot graded U.S. No. 1 may have deteriorated to U.S. No. 2. This is, of course, no argument in support of keeping the consumer ignorant of grade classifications. It is merely a reason given by many retailers.

Sizes of Apples and Citrus Fruits. Boxes of apples are usually stamped with numbers to represent the count per standard box. Here are the sizes that are found in the market.

48	80	100	125	163	210
56	88	104	138	165	232
64	96	113	150	180	252
72					

Likewise, the size of citrus fruit is indicated by the count of fruit in a box. The size of fruit packed in a California box will be a little smaller than that packed in Florida or Texas. This variation is due to the California box capacity of 1⅖ bushels and the Texas and Florida boxes of 1⅗ bushels capacity. The following sizes are found in the market.

Grapefruit		Lemons		Oranges		Tangerines	
28	80	180	420	64	220	48	150
36	96	210	432	80	226	60	168
46	112	240	442	96	250	76	176
54	126	252	490	100	252	90	192
64	150	270	540	112	288	96	200
70		300	588	126	324	100	210
		360		150	344	120	246
				176	360	144	294
				200	392		
				216	420		

Processed Fruits and Vegetables. Processed foods may be canned, frozen, dehydrated, or dried. Each of these processes has an effect on food values and on the price paid by the consumer. Generally, the most food value in relation to the cost is found in fresh fruits and vegetables in season and properly cared for; then, in the following order: dried and dehydrated foods, canned foods, and frozen foods. This generalization needs to be checked from time to time, because processes improve, and consumer demand is an uncertain factor at best.

Dried and Dehydrated Foods. Dried foods are usually more economical buys, because they are the least expensive to handle and ship. The Food and Drug Administration standard for dried fruits does not permit more than 24 to 26 per cent moisture in fruits that are dried in a dehydrator. When not more than 5 or 6 per cent moisture remains in the fruit, they are called dehydrated foods.

The food value in dehydrated foods varies, but generally the minerals and calories do not vanish in the water. Some vitamins, however, are lost. As yet, dehydrated foods are not very popular because the process needs improvement.

The process of drying fruits changes the food values to a considerable extent. Fuel value is greatly increased, and mineral value is increased to a less extent. In some cases, vitamin value is also increased. Nearly all dried fruits are excellent sources of vitamin A. Dry beans are often used as a substitute for meat, but they need to be supplemented by animal proteins, such as milk, eggs, fish, or cheese.

The Federal standards for dry edible beans and peas are widely used by the trade, but the grades rarely appear on consumer packages.

Grades for beans and peas are based on such factors as color, presence or absence of defects, foreign material, and beans or peas of other classes. Defects may be those caused by weather, disease, insects, or mechanical means.

There are special "handpicked" grades for beans, which are well adapted for consumer sales. The top grade is U.S. Choice Handpicked, followed by U.S. No. 1 Handpicked, U.S. No. 2 Handpicked, and U.S. No. 3 Handpicked. In other than the handpicked grades, grades for beans are simply numerical. Grades for dry peas, both whole and split, are also numerical.

Frozen Fruits, Juices, Vegetables, and Precooked Frozen Foods. Total sales of frozen fruits, juices, and vegetables in 1959 exceeded $762.5 million according to a Federal Trade Commission report released on January 24, 1961. Since that date, total sales have probably risen to over $1 billion annually in the United States, and the use of frozen foods keeps increasing. If consumer prices of frozen foods appear comparatively high, it may be due to high costs in handling this convenience food. The *Food Field Reporter*, December 5, 1960, for example, reported that while "only 4.09 per cent of supermarket dollar volume is derived from frozen foods, an educated guess might put the total cost of handling this frozen merchandise at up to 25 per cent of over-all supermarket operations."

One of the major problems is in the mishandling of frozen foods before they reach the consumer. During the past decade, food and drug officials and the frozen food industry have become increasingly disturbed over the mishandling of frozen foods. There has been little effort to alert consumers to this problem, despite their need to know about damage to the quality of frozen food by temperatures above 0 degrees Fahrenheit. Consumers Union reported (February, 1961) how much demage could be done by mishandling in the case of its test on frozen fish sticks: 10 of the 26 brands tested were down to Grade B because of deficiencies caused by mishandling after the fish sticks were packed.

The *Food Field Reporter* (December 5, 1960) presented a comprehensive study made by Donald Deskey Associates of New York, analyzing the flaws in typical distribution and storage processes of frozen foods. This study reported "deplorable conditions in the handling of frozen foods at every level from shipping point to selling point." As a result, frozen foods deteriorate in quality and taste. Instances were found where certain frozen foods had been inadvertently thawed and refrozen as often as 14 times. Due to the danger of bacterial growth, frozen foods require careful handling. Ideally, they should be maintained at temperatures of 0 degrees Fahrenheit or less; the higher the temperature, the greater the nutritional damage. This study stated that temperature damage, once it occurs, is permanent; that temperature damage is cumulative; that every time a frozen food product rises above the critical temperature, losses of nutritional value, color, and flavor occur. Once this has happened, they can never be restored.

Another problem that concerns the consumer is the report that many plants have failed to maintain adequate sanitary facilities. For example, in 1960, the FDA surveyed 63 such plants and found that certain precooked frozen foods, such as bakery goods, potpies, and similar products, contained a high bacteria count. The tests did not include frozen vegetables and juice concentrates, which make up most of the sales to consumers.

So disturbed was the Association of Food and Drug Officials of the United States (AFDOUS), which includes state and Federal officials, that in June, 1959, they drafted a model frozen food code for states to use in passing their own laws. It called for the maintenance of all frozen frozen foods at 0 degrees Fahrenheit from packer to consumer. The vocal leaders of the frozen food industry supported the model code, but most industry efforts are against mandatory application of it. From the consumer's point of view, one solution to this is mandatory government regulation. But a rather bitter struggle has been going on between government food officials and industry leaders over the nature, extent, and timing of the code.

Freeze-dried Foods. Freeze drying is one of the greatest techniques known for drying foodstuffs, causing far less damage to flavor, texture, and color than conventional heat drying. In freeze drying, food is first frozen; then, in a partial vacuum, the ice crystals thus formed in it are transformed directly into vapor without melting. When processing is done carefully, the cellular structure of the food remains intact, little shrinkage or shriveling results, and nutritive values are fairly well preserved. Because the dried product is nearly full size and is porous, reconstitution is quite easy.

The advantages are obvious. Food does not have to be refrigerated, and weight is reduced. It is claimed that products resume the taste, texture, and appearance of fresh foods when they are reconstituted.

This is a promising new process, but in 1963 it was not quite ready for the mass market. The process worked only on fairly thin pieces of food, half an inch thick or so. Some foods (broccoli) do not freeze-dry well, and others (carrots) are better dried by conventional methods. The process is still quite expensive, and packaging problems are keeping prices up.

The first of such foods to be widely distributed for retail stores was Lipton's chicken-rice soup and meats in some of Campbell's Red Kettle soups and in Armour Star Lite outdoor foods. There are others entering this market, a market that the *Reader's Digest* billed as "the greatest

break-through in food preservation since the invention of the tin can."
Time will tell.

Canned Fruits and Vegetables. Canned fruits and vegetables are very
popular with the homemaker. There are, however, minor losses of minerals
in canning. Water-soluble nutrients are dissolved in the liquid in which
the food is canned. Thus, it is wise to use all the liquid in the can.

Vitamin A is only slightly affected in canning. There is some loss of
thiamine and riboflavin. The retention of vitamin C is higher in citrus
products than in tomato juice and canned vegetables. In some cases,
food analysts have found canned vegetables superior in nutrients to fresh
produce that has been allowed to stand in a market, especially in sunlight
or warmth, or that has been washed.

Brand Identifications and Grade Labeling. Brand identifications do not
give consumers the information needed to make an intelligent selection.
Adequate label information should accompany brand names. The permissive standardized labeling program promoted by the National Canners
Association is an attempt to "describe" the contents in addition to the
statements required by law under the Federal Food, Drug, and Cosmetic
Act.

Descriptive labels do not give information about quality, except in
general terms not based on accepted standards. To select canned foods
wisely, consumers need, in addition to brand names and standard descriptions, standard quality grades. Some canneries and large chain stores
and consumer cooperatives have included standard graded canned fruits
and vegetables.

Grade-labeling Facts for the Wise Shopper. For the wise shopper who
wants to buy by standard grade rather than by guess and by grab, here
are the necessary facts.

Grade A or Fancy stands for "excellent." Use it for special occasions.
Grade B, Choice or Extra Standard, is for "good." Use it for everyday.
Grade C or Standard is for "fair." Use it for thrift.

All grades have the same food value, but each serves a different purpose
and has a different price. Over 40 fruits and vegetables now have standards worked out by the cooperative efforts of the U.S. Department of
Agriculture and private canners.

The U.S. Department of Agriculture inspects and certifies these products as to quality and condition on requests of processors, buyers, Federal
and state purchasing departments, or other interested parties. These
applicants pay the cost of inspection.

Some canners, freezers, and distributors use grade designations on their
labels. Labels may also carry additional information descriptive of the

product, such as the number of halves in canned peaches or pears, the sieve size of peas, strength of syrup in canned fruits, sweeteners in frozen fruits, number of servings, cooking instructions for frozen vegetables, or special statements for dietetic foods.

SOURCE: Production and Marketing Administration, U.S. Department of Agriculture.

Any processor or distributor may use the terms "Grade A," "Grade B," or "Grade C" on labels to describe the quality of his products, whether or not they have been inspected. However, products thus labeled must meet the specifications of the Department's standards for the grade claimed; otherwise, the products may be considered as mislabeled.

Some processing plants operate voluntarily under continuous inspection —a service offered by the U.S. Department of Agriculture at a nominal fee to packers. These plants have been carefully selected and thoroughly inspected to make sure that they meet strict sanitary requirements. Processors who operate their plants under U.S. Department of Agriculture continuous inspection may use the prefix "U.S." before their grade designa-

SOURCE: Production and Marketing Administration, U.S. Department of Agriculture.

SOURCE: Production and Marketing Administration, U.S. Department of Agriculture.

SOURCE: Production and Marketing Administration, U.S. Department of Agriculture.

tion on their label (such as U.S. Grade A), as well as the statement "Packed under continuous inspection of the U.S. Department of Agriculture."

A wise shopper will look for the brand and a reliable standard grade. Grade labels are not common in food stores because they are in the developmental stage. Consumers can cast an economic vote for grading by patronizing the stores that stock graded foods. Let your store know that you appreciate graded foods, because this is the best way of convincing the producers and the food store owners of the importance of graded labels.

Some hints for buying canned fruits and vegetables are:

1. Compare different brand prices for the same grades.
2. Find the brands and the grades best suited to your family uses.
3. Buy the largest size of can that you can economically use.
4. Purchasing in quantity—case lots—saves from 5 to 10 per cent.
5. Look for the special sales, especially just prior to the appearance of the new crop in cans. Last year's crop in the cans is just as nutritious and good as ever.
6. Buy by grades according to intended use of the food.

Your Money's Worth in Food: A Recap. If your family is typical, very likely 40 to 50 per cent of your money for food goes for meat, dairy products, and eggs. About one-fifth of this is spent for vegetables and fruit. The rest is nearly equally divided among the grain products; the fats, oils, sugar, and sweets; and such items as vinegar, spices, leavening agents, coffee, tea, and other beverages.

Question: "Do you wonder if your money for food is spent to the best advantage?" A good way to determine this is to compare foods in each of the groups by their yield in nutrients as well as by their price. A few examples will point this up.

Meat, poultry, fish, and eggs are important for their high quality protein, iron, and the B vitamins. To make worthwhile savings, judge them on a comparative basis. Some meat has bone and gristle. Buying the less expensive cuts of meat can save money with no loss in food value, provided the cuts do not have large amounts of bone, fat, and gristle. Dry beans or peas as a main dish is an economical substitute for meat. Buy lower-grade eggs for scrambling or baking. Small eggs are as economical as large ones when they are at least one-fourth cheaper.

As for the dairy products, everybody needs milk in some form because it is the best source for calcium and an important source of protein and riboflavin. One serving of fluid whole milk, evaporated milk, buttermilk, skim milk, or dry milk furnishes about the same amount of nutrients but at widely different costs. Dry milk generally costs least and fluid milk the most per serving. Cream cheese and ice cream are more expensive for the value received than most other milk products, except butter and cream. Cottage cheese is a bargain for protein and riboflavin. Cheddar cheese is a more economical source of calcium than cottage cheese.

Vegetables and fruits furnish a large share of the vitamin A value and most of the vitamin C. Certain vegetables and fruits, however, are better buys than others, although prices vary with locality, season, and form or processing. Usually, the best buys for vitamin A—dark green or deep yellow vegetables—are carrots, collards, kale, spinach, sweet potatoes, and winter squash. Most other common fruits and vegetables, including light green and pale yellow ones, are usually more expensive sources of vitamin A because they contain only small amounts. It would take about 7 cups of corn to give as much vitamin A value as $\frac{1}{4}$ cup of carrots, and would cost about 10 times more than the carrots.

Oranges, grapefruit, and raw cabbage generally supply the most vitamin C for the money. Some dark green leaves, potatoes, and sweet potatoes—properly cooked—also give vitamin C at moderately low cost. Tomato juice and canned tomatoes usually are cheaper sources for vitamin C, except possibly fresh tomatoes in season. Most other common fruits and vegetables furnish less vitamin C and cost more. Some vegetables and fruits have both vitamins A and C—tomatoes and sweet potatoes—and may be good buys.

Canned, frozen, dried, and fresh fruits and vegetables vary considerably in price per serving. As a rule, these foods in canned and dried form are cheaper. The safest way, however, is to make a comparison of price per serving.

Whole-grain, restored, or enriched cereals and bread can mean extra food value for the money. Natural whole grains are significant sources of iron, thiamine, riboflavin, and niacin. Many breakfast foods have nutrients, lost in milling, "restored." There is no Federal standard for restored cereals. It is, therefore, safer to purchase enriched bread or flour, because the Federal standards require a minimum amount of iron, thiamine, riboflavin, and niacin for enrichment. If breads of various types cost the same or a few cents more per pound of bread, the whole-grain or enriched kinds are the best nutrient buys for the money. The same is true of cereals. Cold cereals are not as good nutrient buys as cereals that have to be cooked.

It is well to remember that many convenience foods are still more expensive, if you discount the time element, than those prepared at home from the ingredients. Canned and frozen fruits and vegetables are often best buys, because they are canned and frozen when supplies are large and prices low. There is also none of the waste that occurs in the handling and storage of perishable produce.

Final Tips on Buying Food. Pay cash for food. Credit costs money, and you will pay for the extra cost. In selecting supermarkets, compare prices for food value. Remember that gimmicks like trading stamps, premiums, and the forms of lottery or games of chance, such as "Split the Dollar," "Hidden Treasure," "Spell C-A-S-H," and "Super Poker," do not necessarily reduce the cost of food. When you spend almost one-fifth of your income for food, it pays to get the most value per dollar for your family. You can be well nourished if you spend considerably less than this amount. These last two chapters were designed to help you plan and select (1) food that keeps your family well fed, (2) food that is economical and nutritionally good, and (3) food that pleases your family.

QUESTIONS FOR DISCUSSION

1. What is the implication of the statement that we "tend to buy where the ego psychology is stressed"? Is this good or bad?

2. What are the advantages and disadvantages in shopping at the national food chain stores? Independent or voluntary food chain stores? Consumer cooperative food stores? Small independent food stores? Discount food stores?

3. Make a careful survey of differences in the retail prices of a dozen commonly used foods. Select half a dozen different kinds of food markets. Which store has the lowest prices for similar grades or quality of the food items you selected?

4. How can you get accurate information on the quality of food products?

5. How can you cut the cost of milk and milk products without reducing quality and nutritive value?

6. Did Congress act in the interest of the consumer as well as in the interest of our free enterprise system when it eliminated the Federal tax on oleomargarine?

7. Why is it better to shop personally rather than by telephone?

8. How can you cooperate with other consumer citizens to establish a standard of values in marketing fresh fruits and vegetables?

9. Are frozen foods economical buys? What can be done about the mishandling of frozen foods?

10. What are the advantages in purchasing U.S. Department of Agriculture graded food products?

11. Most families know from experience that meat costs can easily wreck the food budget. How can you reduce the proportion of money spent for meat and yet serve nutritious and interesting meat dishes?

12. Visit a large food store. What percentage of the poultry in that shop is U.S. Department of Agriculture graded and inspected? Or find out why the store does not handle standard grades and inspected poultry.

13. If you plan to purchase food for your family according to intended use, would it be easier if most foods had standard grades?

14. Are convenience foods economical buys?

ACTIVITY PROBLEMS

1. At current prices, from what cuts of meat does the homemaker get the most protein for the dollar she spends for meat? You might select five cuts each of beef, veal, pork, lamb, and sausage. Get the retail price of each cut at one of the large efficient food stores. The *Protein Values per Pound of Food as Purchased* may be found in U.S. Department of Agriculture Handbook 8, June, 1950. Decide which cuts of meat are the best buys on a particular day.

2. What protein foods can be used in place of meat to cut costs and yet not jeopardize health? Be sure to get scientific facts and make accurate current cost calculations.

3. Keep a record of the kinds and quantity of food that you eat for seven consecutive days. Evaluate the diet. List the deficiencies and indicate the foods that should be added. Remember that health experts say you need balanced food for each meal.

4. Select ten foods that are highly advertised. Compare the facts mentioned in the advertising with the known facts revealed by independent testing agencies. You might use the *Consumer Reports* or the *Consumers' Research Bulletin* for scientific information.

5. Make a comparative study of the types of food stores in your locality according to (a) kinds and varieties of food carried, (b) services, (c) sanitation, (d) convenience in location of food departments, (e) U.S. Department of Agriculture graded goods, (f) prices, and (g) parking space.

6. Select certain foods and make an investigation of the most economical buys in terms of quality, quantity, and price relationship. You might like to compare fresh, canned, dehydrated, and frozen fruit. Be accurate.

7. The claim is made that impulse buying is likely to be common among home-

makers who do not plan their menus and marketing. Perhaps you know of a family where meal planning does not exist beyond the next meal. Ask the home-maker to make a list of foods that were purchased on impulse. Keep this record for seven consecutive days. Then prepare menus for the next seven days. Compare the impulse food buying during these two weekly periods. Would you conclude that it pays to shop with a grocery list?

8. Assume that you are married with no children as yet. Plan menus for all meals at home for seven consecutive days. Prepare a grocery list of the food you need to purchase. List the kinds of food, quantity, brand, and price, and the name of the food store or stores where you might purchase the items. Since you want to have balanced, nutritious meals at the most economical cost in sufficient quantity and food that is liked, check all essential facts. How much will the food cost? Have you used all the tips and information given in the text about selecting food stores, selecting food for specific purposes, quantity buying, prices, and quality?

9. Investigate the statement: "U.S. Department of Agriculture meat grades are designed to serve the best interests of the entire public. . . . Private grades are designed to serve the interests of the private firm originating them."

SUGGESTED READINGS

Agricultural Research Service. *Food for Fitness: A Daily Food Guide,* Washington, D.C., March, 1958.

American Dietetic Association. *Food Facts Talk Back,* Chicago, 1957.

American Meat Institute. *A Lesson on Meat: The Thrifty Use of Larger Cuts,* Chicago.

The Atlantic Monthly. "Giveaways," July, 1960.

Beckman, Theodore N., Maynard, Harold H., and Davidson, William R. *Principles of Marketing.* New York: The Ronald Press Company, 6th ed., 1957.

Changing Times. "Supermarkets of Tomorrow," October, 1956; "How to Buy Meat," March, 1957.

Coles, Jessie V. *Consumers Look at Labels.* Greeley, Colo.: Council on Consumer Information, 1964.

Consumers' Research Bulletin. Washington, N.J.

Consumers Union, Inc. *Consumer Reports,* Mount Vernon, N.Y.

Cooperative League of the U.S.A. *Food Topics,* November, 1962; *Cooperatives U.S.A. 1961–1962.*

Federal Trade Commission. *Economic Inquiry into Food Marketing,* part I. Washington, D.C.: Government Printing Office, 1960.

Household Finance Corporation. *Your Food Dollar,* Chicago.

Journal of Home Economics. "Food Additives—A Many Sided Problem," November, 1960.

National Live Stock and Meat Board. *Meat Manual,* Chicago.

Seebye, Alfred L. (ed.). *Marketing in Transition.* New York: Harper & Row, Publishers, Incorporated, 1958, chaps. 3, 9, 10.

U.S. Department of Agriculture. *Food, The 1959 Yearbook of Agriculture,* 1959; Agriculture Marketing Service, "Federal Grading of Meat: Its Economic Meaning," *The Livestock and Meat Situation,* bimonthly, June, 1959, p. 18;

"A Fruit and Vegetable Buying Guide for Consumers," Home and Garden Bulletin no. 21, April, 1955; "How to Buy Eggs," USDA Grades and Weight Classes, Leaflet no. 442, October, 1958; "Shoppers Guide to U.S. Grades for Food," Home and Garden Bulletin no. 58, September, 1958; "Nutrition Up to Date Up to You," Home and Garden Bulletin no. 58, September, 1958; Economics Research Service, "The Food Marketing Industries: Recent Changes and Future Prospects," *The Marketing and Transportation Situation*, February, 1962, p. 15.

U.S. Department of Health, Education, and Welfare, Food and Drug Administration. *What Consumers Should Know about Food Standards*.

U.S. Department of Labor. *How American Buying Habits Change*, 1959.

The Wall Street Journal. "Group Grocers," June 8, 1959; "Supermarket Chains Cut Frills and Prices in New Discount Units," Dec. 3, 1962.

9

FAMILY CLOTHING MANAGEMENT

There are no norms for choice in clothing as there are in the nutritional needs of the body. Clothing problems in a family must be analyzed in terms of the individual in a group setting. Style, fashion, and fad need to be adapted to individual differences within the financial limits of the family.

In addition, the way we wear our clothes is as important as what we wear. Being well dressed for the occasion, and being aware of it, benefits all members of the family psychologically, physically, and socially. It helps a person to be self-confident, to act and speak more effectively in public. People who are well dressed in the sense of having used good taste in the selection of their clothes are more readily accepted in most social situations.

But the managerial problems of clothing the family so that all members are properly dressed for all occasions are numerous and often difficult. Adequate income does not always solve clothing problems. Even families with luxury incomes are not necessarily style-conscious and may not use good sense and taste in costume coordination.

For moderate-income and low-income families, clothing expenditures are not regular. Seasonal demands and sudden disintegration of garments make it difficult for every member to have an adequate wardrobe at all times. And even the best-planned clothing budget can be ruined by unexpected expenses, such as medical and housing bills.

Right Clothes Are a Mental Stimulant. Whether we like it or not, a girl gets more flattering masculine attention if she is attractive and knows how to wear clothes than if she has a Phi Beta Kappa key. A lady's looks and general grooming are a powerful magnet, and, no doubt, women appraise men in the same way. We hasten to add that attractive dress is not enough in the long run to hold the attention of others, but the right clothes, worn well, give a mental stimulus to the wearer, to the family, and to personal friends, and promote an air of confidence.

If there is truth in the assumption that our innermost life tends to become evident in the choices we make, it might follow that a glance at a family's wardrobe may be more revealing than a composite diary of its members.

Some women, especially mothers devoted to their children, seem to stand still in the matter of dress when the world about them moves forward. Often a wife allows herself to look dowdy, and perhaps, as a result, considerably older than her husband, because she has let household duties absorb all her interest. But the husband's contacts with the business and professional world may have kept him alert and well groomed in keeping with his position and associates. On the other hand, a man who allows himself to slip in his grooming may be slipping in his business and social life.

Other women of a retiring nature are perhaps too conservative in their dress. Still others wear too youthful or extreme clothes or make up in a conspicuous manner. Generally, conspicuous dress emphasizes rather than conceals, age in either sex. If a woman's dress or hat, or a man's suit or tie, dominates the picture, that person is not well dressed in spite of the fact that those items originally may have worn a high price tag.

Family Happiness Is Involved. The family attitudes toward dress, especially on the part of the mother, are important to the good mental health of each member of the family. Good grooming, good taste in dress, active interest in style, fashion, and even fads are assets to family happiness.

The clothing one wears plays an important part in adjusting to the social group. Clothing management, as such, is largely a psychological problem, because it affects the personality development and happiness of each member of the family. No one but the family or close friends may observe our eating manners and food standards, but as soon as we step outside the door, our clothes and how we wear them are appraised by those we meet. Much of this appraisal is unconscious. Perhaps we need to build a consciousness of good dress without creating the value that good dress is everything.

Parents who allow their children to feel unhappy about their methods of dress may be responsible for personality maladjustments later in their lives. The clothing needs of children differ because of individual differences in personality and in physique. A study made by the Bureau of Home Economics on measurements of children shows that many children of like age have entirely different body proportions and dimensions.[1]

[1] Ruth O'Brien and Meyer A. Girshick, *Children's Body Measurements for Size Garments and Patterns.* U.S. Department of Agriculture, Bureau of Home Economics, Miscellaneous publication 365, 1939.

Ignorance of this fact often results in unhappy relationships between mother and children. It is of utmost importance to help a child to feel no different from others, even when the body is developing in a different way.

Considerable unhappiness can be needlessly generated if, for example, a mother insists on dressing a rather tall, early-teen-age daughter in knee-length dresses, with hair in long braids, when the girls in her set are wearing longer skirts, sweaters, and bobs with curled ends. Insistence on "bucking the crowd" usually produces a weepy, irritable, unhappy youngster. At the same time, parents need to help youngsters understand that there is not an unlimited amount of money for clothing.

It is wise to let children gradually assume responsibility in selecting their clothes. By intelligent discussion of their personal assets and liabilities, children can develop skill in self-analysis and in selecting or creating clothes that are acceptable to others and at the same time accentuate their individual personalities.

Training Children to Select and Care for Clothing. Children who are accustomed to an environment of good grooming and common sense in dressing are not likely to fail to acquire these good habits. They may go through certain stages of refusing to wear suitable footwear, for instance, or adequate clothes on the pretext that such things are not "in style." At times, they may wear the most illogical clothes because these happen to be the fad. High school and college-age youngsters are usually the worst offenders in this respect. In time, sense and intelligence in dressing will return, plus an individual style and air—the reverse of the herd instinct.

Even preschool children can be taught how to select, wear, and care for their own clothing. If a young child is going to attend a birthday party, let him select what he will wear. Let him choose from among several around-home garments. Then, let him select from two pairs of shoes that are acceptable for the occasion, but quite different in appearance. At a store, let him select from two or three garments first picked out by the parent.

As the child grows in responsibility, allow him to plan his clothing needs for six months, then perhaps for the next twelve months. Follow this by allowing absolute independent action with parents as permissive consultants only. By this time, the child should have a monthly or annual clothes allowance; so make him responsible for living within his clothing budget and for selecting and caring for his personal clothing.

No one child should be favored above some other member of the family in sharing the family clothing budget. This is almost a certain invitation to family squabbles and possible maladjustments. The manner in which these group problems are handled reveals the kind of spirit that exists in the family. If the family has succeeded in creating individual responsibility in budgeting the family income, the stage is set for continuance of this frank and friendly policy in determining individual clothing expenditures and responsibility for care and upkeep of clothes.

In some homes, proper family attitudes toward sharing space for clothing must also be developed.

Developing Skills in Clothing Management. For a vast majority of families, an adequate wardrobe for every member is possible only by intelligent management. Here is the most practical way to plan and carry out a clothing budget.

1. Know the maximum amount of money available for the family clothing.
2. Analyze the characteristics of each member of the family as applied to clothing needs.
3. Plan, even two and three years in advance, the wardrobe needs of the family.
4. Select the best stores for values, and shop the sales.
5. Select the right garments for specific uses.
6. Use all available information concerning quality, workmanship, shrinkage, colorfastness, suitability, care, and upkeep of clothes.
7. Teach children good clothing habits in terms of care and upkeep.
8. Teach teen-age budgeting for clothes.
9. Discover family resources for home production of clothing items.

All these problems involve information, correct family attitudes, some skills, and time and energy, particularly when the family income is inadequate. But a limited income can be offset by skill in planning (1) how to buy, (2) when to buy, (3) where to buy, (4) care and upkeep, and (5) home production.

How Much to Spend for Family Clothing. Everyone wants to be well dressed, but it is difficult to agree on what it should cost to achieve this objective. This is a good time to turn to the figures compiled by budget experts. It is well to keep in mind, however, that no family is "average" in its expenditures. It depends on the age, sex, and number of persons in the family; on the climate; on personal taste, social needs, and occupations; and, importantly, on the family income.

A second point to keep in mind is that, as income increases, the family tends to spend proportionately more on clothing, although as a nation we are spending a smaller share of total income on clothing than in the past. Out of every dollar spent for all goods and services, only about 8 cents go for clothing in the 1960s against 11 cents in 1948.[2] This declining long-run trend in clothing expenditures has been due to increased competition for other goods and services, changing composition of the population,

[2] "Supplies and Prices of Clothing and Textiles," *Family Economics Review*, December, 1962, p. 10.

casual mode of dressing, and price changes in clothing compared with other expenditures.

As the family makes more money, the members are likely to spend more dollars and a bigger share of the family income on clothing, according to Federal government surveys. A family of four in the $5,000 to $6,000 income range tends to spend 7 per cent more for clothing than a family that makes $4,000 to $5,000. A family in the $6,000 to $7,500 range averages about 16 per cent more; at $7,500 to $10,000, about 24 per cent more; over $10,000 as much as 34 per cent more.[3]

The Heller Committee for Research in Social Economics of the University of California suggests that a family of four (boy age 13, girl age 8) in the San Francisco area would need an income of $6,892 to live there. The committee allocates $501 for family clothing and clothing care such as dry cleaning and shoe repairs. This sum would be divided as follows, the family using about 7.3 per cent of its total income for clothing.

Husband	$135	Boy	$119
Wife	$145	Girl	$102

The committee suggests the following clothing budget for a professional or executive family of four earning $9,815, a total expenditure of $743 to be divided in this way:

Husband	$241	Boy	$137
Wife	$245	Girl	$120

As the children grow older, the family spends more dollars on clothing. The Community Council of Greater New York estimates the following clothing costs as minimum.

	Age	Annual cost
Child:	infant	$ 36.40
	1–3	70.20
	4–6	83.20
	7–9	109.20
Girl:	10–12	114.40
	13–15	130.00
	16–20	145.60
Boy:	10–12	119.60
	13–15	137.80
	16–20	158.60

[3] Quoted in *Changing Times*, March, 1962, p. 31.

One of the reasons for rising clothing costs is the rise in living standards. Perhaps more important is the exodus of more wives from the home to places of employment. Women, like men, need more clothes and clothing service when they work outside the home. For example, the *Family Economics Review*, September, 1962, presents a study of job-related wives in four Georgia cities, with incomes from under $3,000 to about $9,000. The average expenditure of employed wives for clothing for general wear plus extra because of working exceeded that of unemployed wives by $88 in the families with husbands earning less than $3,000, by $117 in families with medium incomes, and by $155 with high incomes.

These figures do not presume to tell what each family should spend for clothing. They merely try to determine what clothing may cost under certain income standards.

Pay Cash for Clothing. When buying clothing, you have the choice of paying cash or using credit. Generally, it is best to pay cash. The best method, however, depends in part on your situation. Families with irregular incomes have more of a payment problem than families with regular weekly or monthly income. Regardless of the nature of the income, there is a compelling principle related to the decision of how to pay for clothing. It is this: clothes are consumer goods that do not earn income for the buyer and therefore should be paid for in cash. Credit can be used with some justification, other things being equal, for clothing that outlasts credit payments. Credit costs, however, are high for typical credit plans.

Ideally, a family should allocate some percentage of its income for clothing, thus making cash more readily available for clothing. The percentage of cash set aside for clothing will vary with different families, but 6 to 8 per cent is a reasonable allocation in terms of the most recent studies on clothing expenditures.

The Power of Fashion. Fashion, style, fad, craze, and good taste have various meanings to various people. Paul H. Nystrom, in his classic *Economics of Fashion*,[4] defines these terms as follows:

"Style is a characteristic or distinctive mode or method of expression, presentation or conception in the field of some art."

"Fashion is nothing more or less than the prevailing style at any given time." Whenever a style is accepted or followed it is the fashion.

"A fad is merely a miniature fashion in some unimportant matter or detail."

"A craze is a fad or fashion accompanied by much crowd excitement or emotion."

"Taste . . . is the ability to discern or appreciate what is beautiful or appropriate." Good taste is present when one makes the most artistic use of current fashions.

[4] Paul H. Nystrom, *Economics of Fashion*. Copyright 1928 by The Ronald Press Company, New York, pp. 3–7. Reprinted with permission.

Fashion, says Nystrom, seems to be the result of powerful forces in human nature. We laugh, sometimes, at fashion, but generally we accept it. Strangely enough, the influence of fashion is such as to make a style, when accepted, seem beautiful, no matter how hideous it might have appeared at other times.

Fashion is perhaps the most extravagant force in clothing selection, for imitation and conspicuous consumption play important roles. As fashion changes, garments become socially obsolete. And conformity tends to become so important, if you want that well-dressed appearance, that all other values are rejected. This is especially important during the teen-age period. If necessary, teen-agers will sacrifice health, comfort, economy, and even becomingness to achieve conformity and social acceptance.

The following account of a shopping expedition of a college freshman girl exemplifies the force of fashion.

I have been contemplating the purchase of a brown cardigan sweater for almost a year now (sounds impossible but very true), since that's the general procedure I have to go through before coming through with a major purchase. My indecision came when trying to decide between a cashmere, which was more durable but far more expensive, and a good-quality wool sweater. Before coming to college there would have been no question. I would have simply purchased a wool sweater, since I hadn't come into contact with the cashmere-conscious students. Well, I made the rounds of all the stores comparing the different cashmere and wool sweaters and trying desperately to decide, or rationalize, which would be the more satisfying for the amount of money in the long run.

I couldn't decide! Was a cashmere worth three times more than a wool one? If I got *one* cashmere, would it go well with my wool pull-overs? If I got one, would I ever be satisfied with anything else but cashmere? Yet, I figured—everyone has cashmere and admires it and would comment on mine, if I got one. I could wear it on a casual date and be much more in style and would possibly make a better impression. But would it be a false impression? Could I afford to continue buying sweaters of that quality?

Time was short! I had to decide. My eyes wandered and suddenly landed on a cashmere sweater in a shade of green that I just loved. It was deep and striking. I asked to see the sweater. It happened to be a turtle-neck. I shouldn't wear such high-necked things but, on the other hand, many people did, and it *was* different from anything else I had. Well, I was all keyed up to the point where I *had* to buy something, preferably a sweater, and since I couldn't decide about the brown cardigan, I bought the green one that I had no intention of buying.

The final factor in determining this purchase was the girl's feeling of conformity and of social acceptance by her group.

Wardrobe Planning by Inventory. An adequate wardrobe is not dependent on how much money you spend. It depends as much or more on careful planning and good management of the clothing dollar. The first step in having an adequate wardrobe on a modest income is in knowing what you have and what you need—in short, a common-sense clothing inventory. To dress each family member properly, there must be no last-minute hasty buying and needless mistakes.

There is really no average family. Each individual and each family lives a slightly different life from other families, and their clothing requirements are bound to differ. Income, occupations, social life, climate, vacations, and travel plans must be taken into account. For most families, the clothing dollar needs to be spent for comfort, usefulness, good style, and quality, rather than for quantity. It is necessary to buy with foresight and not fall into temptations of the moment, nor be led astray by whims, purchasing a dress, for instance, because "it looked so lovely in the window."

Each purchase should be backed by reason rather than rationalization, although the latter may be fun for the moment. Everyone enjoys a nonsensical fling once in a while, but it is wise to control such flings by channeling them into the inexpensive and less basic clothing items.

Buying new clothes without first knowing what is in the clothes closet is like buying food without knowing what is in the pantry. For good wardrobe planning, it is necessary to be on spending terms with the six clothing inventory principles given on page 243. Accompanying this list of principles are two clothing replacement inventories, one for the husband and one for the wife. Similar inventory lists can be prepared for each child in the family.

Expected Life-span of Clothing. Wardrobe planning may be a little less frustrating if you have some idea of how long the more expensive clothing items can be expected to wear. A study by the U.S. Department of Agriculture in the accompanying chart, Life-span of Clothing, should be helpful.

Analyzing Flops and Successes. The value of analyzing the flops and successes in your clothes closet depends, to a great extent, on the insight gained from the analysis. One mother, on analyzing the items and cost, found that she had spent five times as much for little-used garments that hung in the closet as for those she used regularly. She decided to spend more of her share of the family clothing money for good suits, versatile dresses, and semiformal or informal dresses, and less on vacation and formal clothes that she seldom wore. With the money saved, she could afford accessories for each costume and a much-needed casual coat.

Another mother, analyzing the clothing inventory of her two grade-school boys, discovered that one child was spending twice as much for clothes as his brother, because he was careless and destructive. This mother had a job outside the home. In checking on her own clothing expenditures, she decided that too large a percentage was being spent on

LIFE SPAN OF CLOTHING
Rural Families in a Low-Income Area

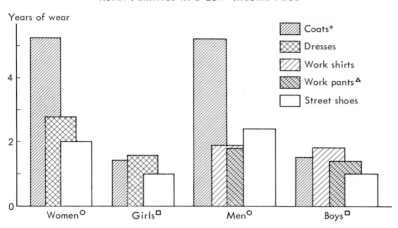

Years of wear

Coats*
Dresses
Work shirts
Work pants▲
Street shoes

In open country, Kentucky, 1956–57

*Women, heavy coats only; men, overcoats, top coats □ 2 to 15 years of age

○16 years of age and older ▲ Includes overalls, jeans, etc.

U. S. Department of Agriculture   Neg. 58 (9)–5574 Agricultural Research Service

SOURCE: *Agricultural Chartbook Outlook,* **Agricultural Research Service, U.S. Department of Agriculture, 1959, p. 30.**

luxury underwear and hose. She switched to simple types of underwear and daytime-sheer hose for general wear, and transferred the difference to good dresses and suits.

A third family had two fashion-conscious girls whose associates had much more money to spend for clothes. When the mother and the girls studied their clothing inventory, they realized that they obtained pleasure and use from a wide variety of garments. They decided to buy jackets, sweaters, skirts, and blouses that could be alternated and changed by scarves, costume jewelry, and similar accessories. They could double the value of their dress allowances by making each garment serve a double duty wherever possible. They learned to use many style-right ideas that took little time and money.

Teen-age Clothing Budget. If there are teen-agers in the family, the mere fact that a family clothing inventory has been made does not necessarily mean that the family has solved its clothing problems. The subject of clothes can be one of the greatest little peace wreckers in any modest-income household. Teen-agers believe that clothes are about the most important things in the world. They are at the age when classmates and rivals are playing the game of trying to outdress each other. This game usually results in tears and much unhappiness for parents and children. When this happens, a family meeting is in order.

CLOTHING REPLACEMENT INVENTORY—HUSBAND

Annual Replacement Cost $_____   Total Cost $_____

Present items	Stock	Annual replacement	Unit price	Annual cost
Hats: felt	_____	1	$10.00	$10.00
sport	_____	_____	_____	_____
straw	_____	_____	_____	_____
Overcoats	_____	⅓	60.00	20.00
Sweaters	_____	_____	_____	_____
Suits: business	_____	_____	_____	_____
tuxedo	_____	_____	_____	_____
Slacks	_____	_____	_____	_____
Shirts: dress	_____	_____	_____	_____
collar attached	_____	_____	_____	_____
Socks	_____	_____	_____	_____
Underwear: shirts	_____	_____	_____	_____
shorts	_____	_____	_____	_____
Bathrobes	_____	_____	_____	_____
Pajamas	_____	_____	_____	_____
Shoes: dress	_____	_____	_____	_____
sport	_____	_____	_____	_____
business	_____	_____	_____	_____
House slippers	_____	_____	_____	_____
Ties: bow	_____	_____	_____	_____
other	_____	_____	_____	_____
Gloves	_____	_____	_____	_____
Bathing trunks	_____	_____	_____	_____
Emergency	_____	_____	_____	_____
Annual upkeep cost:	_____	_____	_____	_____
Cleaning overcoat	_____	_____	_____	_____
Cleaning suits	_____	_____	_____	_____
Pressing suits	_____	_____	_____	_____
Blocking hats	_____	_____	_____	_____
Repairing shoes	_____	_____	_____	_____

1. All usable clothes are listed. Discarded clothes are made wearable. Individual replacement needs are made known, and their approximate costs are listed.

2. The total clothing allotment is subdivided to suit the needs of each individual member of the family.

3. Purchases are made in the order of urgency before desirability.

4. Purchases may be made with a long view for coordination and economy, and may even be based on a three-year plan for the most expensive items, such as a winter overcoat or a fur coat.

5. Plans are made for upkeep and general care of clothing.

6. A flexible balance is left, even if small, for unforeseen emergency requirements.

CLOTHING REPLACEMENT INVENTORY—WIFE

Annual Replacement Cost $_____   Total Cost $_____

Present items	Stock	Annual replacement	Unit price	Annual cost
Hats: winter	_____	_____	$_____	$_____
summer	_____	_____	_____	_____
casual	_____	_____	_____	_____
Coats: fur	_____	_____	_____	_____
winter cloth	_____	_____	_____	_____
casual	_____	_____	_____	_____
Suits: wool	_____	_____	_____	_____
other fibers	_____	_____	_____	_____
Blouses: cotton	_____	_____	_____	_____
other fibers	_____	_____	_____	_____
Sweaters	_____	_____	_____	_____
Dresses: evening	_____	_____	_____	_____
dinner	_____	_____	_____	_____
afternoon	_____	_____	_____	_____
casual	_____	_____	_____	_____
house	_____	_____	_____	_____
Slacks	_____	_____	_____	_____
Lingerie	_____	_____	_____	_____
Foundation garments	_____	_____	_____	_____
Bathrobes	_____	_____	_____	_____
Housecoats	_____	_____	_____	_____
Nightgowns	_____	_____	_____	_____
Stockings: sheer	_____	_____	_____	_____
semisheer	_____	_____	_____	_____
Shoes: evening	_____	_____	_____	_____
dress	_____	_____	_____	_____
sports	_____	_____	_____	_____
Slippers	_____	_____	_____	_____
Rainwear	_____	_____	_____	_____
Bathing suits and beachwear	_____	_____	_____	_____
Gloves: leather	_____	_____	_____	_____
fabric	_____	_____	_____	_____
Handbags: evening	_____	_____	_____	_____
street	_____	_____	_____	_____
Emergency	_____	_____	_____	_____
Annual upkeep cost:	_____	_____	_____	_____
Cleaning and glazing fur coat	_____	_____	_____	_____
Cleaning and pressing garments ...	_____	_____	_____	_____
Repairing shoes	_____	_____	_____	_____

If children have not been brought up on a family budget based on increasing consumer responsibilities as they grow older, it may not be too late to lay the problem wide open and honestly face it. Let them know how much money is available for clothes for each youngster, and why.

If everybody agrees, for example, that each teen-ager may have $150 a year for his clothes, including repairs and cleaning bills, the chances are good that they will jump at the opportunity of making their own decisions. The clothing budget will have a personal meaning because they have a voice in deciding on what they need.

For inexperienced youngsters, it is better to give the clothing allowance in quarterly payments, because they are likely to go wild at first. It is also wise to insist that they (1) buy sturdy shoes for school wear, (2) keep supplied with rainy-weather equipment, (3) do not wear ragged underwear and socks to save money, and (4) do not expect that the next quarterly allowance will be advanced if they have spent their money unwisely.

Many youngsters under such a clothing budget have tracked down bargains like hunting dogs. The girls think twice before buying junk jewelry, a scarf that won't launder, a blouse that might require dry cleaning. They learn that a cheap sweater that will not launder is no economy even if it costs only half as much as a good sweater. Boys are likely to develop amazing caution about buying a sports jacket that does not look well with more than one pair of slacks.

Both boys and girls are more likely to keep their best clothes for dress occasions and to take better care of all their clothing. Shoes are taken to the repair shop before it is too late; girls take better care of blouses and sweaters. The lost-clothing problem will probably end abruptly. And, perhaps best of all, in some families the youngsters will forget to remind parents "what the other kids get." This, indeed, would be welcome in many homes.

Combine Buying Skill with Care of Clothing. There is no satisfactory substitute for the feeling of being properly dressed for the occasion. This, in turn, contributes to personal happiness. It is not necessary to spend a lot of money to have an adequate wardrobe for the family. How well the homemaker plans and how skillfully she buys and oversees the buying of all members of the family are as important as the amount of money spent.

The first requirement for a satisfactory wardrobe is to take stock of what you have and make a list of what you need for the year. Be sure they are necessary items. Extras can follow the essentials. One hundred well-planned dollars can bring more satisfactions than two hundred unplanned dollars.

Your money interest, however, does not cease with a well-planned wardrobe. Proper care of clothes can prolong their life. Managing the care of clothing, however, is more successful and costs less money if skill and all possible information are used in the selection of clothing in the market.

Good Buying Principles. Gains that may come from wise planning of the family wardrobe can be easily lost through careless shopping in the stores. Getting your money's worth depends on intelligent shopping for the wardrobe you planned at the prices you expect to pay.

The following seven shopping principles can help you save money and get lasting satisfaction from the purchases that not only are necessary to clothe the family but actually keep its members happy and contented.

Compare values. Clothing stores vary in price, even on similar items. Some stores change some of their prices daily and weekly. The higher-priced suit, for example, is not always the best buy in terms of value and style. No two stores have identical operating costs; therefore, their margins of profit are different. The more efficient stores often sell goods of equal quality and style at lower prices. Experienced professional comparative shoppers say that it is necessary to shop at least five stores before purchasing expensive clothing items, such as a coat, suit, or good-quality dress.

Select basic or classic styles. Classic styles almost always mean simple styling, which can mean better-quality fabric and finish. Many stores now feature such styles with the suggestion that they do not become dated. In addition, their appearance can be changed by different accessories. Simple lines also mean lower cleaning costs. One manufacturer of women's clothing put a date on his labels so that purchasers could see how long a particular line remained in fashion.

Buy clothes that fit your needs. Do not develop a case of "bargainitis." Do not buy an article merely because you like the color or because the price has been reduced. It is difficult to resist a bargain, but no garment is a bargain unless it fits your needs. The color that you found irresistible in the store will soon cease to delight you if it does not harmonize with your wardrobe.

Purchase middle-price items. Most stores have several price ranges for all types of clothing. Salespersons, especially those on commission, may attempt to "trade up" customers to the highest-priced group, but this group may not have enough additional value and style to offset its high price. The lowest-priced goods usually cut costs by using cheaper-quality raw materials, resulting in unsatisfactory wear. The middle-price lines are usually safest to buy because good-quality materials may be used but costs saved by eliminating nonessentials do not affect good styling and wear.

Shop store brands. It is possible to save up to 25 per cent on many clothing items of the same quality and style as the nationally advertised brands. Some manufacturers make identical clothes that are sold under several brand names at different price levels. Large retailers, such as department stores and mail-order houses, have their own store brands.

They can often sell clothes more cheaply than smaller competitors who handle nationally known brands, because costs of a wholesaler and of national advertising are eliminated. Store brands exist because prices for nationally advertised clothing are seldom reduced after the items have won public acceptance. Moneysaving store or private brands have made considerable headway, especially in the staple clothing, hosiery, and shoe lines.

Shop regular store sales. When you know your clothing needs in advance and plan for cash purchases at reliable sales, it is possible to save up to 50 per cent on some clothing purchases. Get acquainted with the months for such sales in your locality, as suggested later in this chapter.

Pay cash. You get more for your money at stores that have strictly cash terms, unless the customer buys on the installment plan and pays a reasonable interest rate. Installment buying is expensive and should be avoided if possible. Some credit stores mark up clothing prices considerably to pay for the cost of credit and, in some cases, for their delivery costs. Some cash clothing stores can sell an identical dress, for example, for 25 per cent less than a competitor who offers credit.

How to Select Clothing Stores. There are many kinds of clothing stores to serve the variety of tastes of consumers. Since methods of merchandising vary, the problem is to discover the stores that serve your purposes most satisfactorily.[5] The general answer is found in the answers to these five questions.

Does the store stock a fairly wide range of qualities at different prices? Some retail stores cater only to one class of customers. Thus, an exclusive women's apparel store may offer dresses at $50 and up. Or a men's clothing store may offer suits at a top price of $29.50. Neither store is seeking to interest all consumers. In addition, a good store will have a wide variety of styles, colors, and sizes.

Does the store give good value for the money? Intelligent consumers are price-conscious and value-conscious. Some consumers like an expensive atmosphere and settings and are willing to pay more for such a shopping environment. This factor constitutes value for them. Others prefer to have the value in goods rather than in atmosphere. Nevertheless, almost everyone tends to shop around for the stores that give the most value for the money spent.

The store that charges the highest prices does not necessarily offer the best goods. The outlet with low prices may not be sacrificing quality. Some stores have low prices but offer poor-quality merchandise. The

---

[5] For an excellent source for selecting clothing stores, see Sidney Margolius, *The Consumers' Guide to Better Buying.* New York: New American Library of World Literature, Inc., 1963.

consumer needs to develop skill in buying to see through the camouflage of atmosphere or of too persuasive selling.

Is the store conveniently located? Most people are willing to accept some inconvenience in terms of distance and accessibility when shopping for the more expensive clothing items, because this occurs only a few times a year. They are willing to drive to a larger city or to shopping centers where there are branches of large city department stores.

Mail-order houses offer a convenience that appeals to consumers who want good-quality merchandise at medium prices. The catalogues are attractive and, on the whole, carry accurate descriptive information.

What kinds of service are offered by the store? Besides convenience in terms of distance, a store should have enough salespeople to serve customers promptly. Some stores reduce their sales force, but pass on the savings to the consumer. The appeal in such stores is based on price rather than on quick service. Other stores emphasize delivery service, charge accounts, liberal policy on returned goods, comfortable lounges, and even nurseries for the children. These services cost money. But some people are willing and can afford to shop such retail establishments.

When shopping in such stores, remember that you are paying for service in addition to your actual purchases. But also remember that you can save money by shopping around and comparing price and quality values.

These four considerations—quality level, price level, convenience, and service—are the most important economic factors in selecting clothing markets. There remains another quality that may be just as important when selecting a store—fair business ethics.

Does the store practice honesty and fair business ethics? [6] The best merchants are not satisfied unless they can help their customers get their money's worth. Shrewdness and trickery have no place in a good store.

The merchant who serves you best gives expert guidance concerning all important information about clothing items. Examine his advertising. Is it accurate and sufficiently informative? Read the labels. Do they tell you everything you want to know? Observe the salespeople. Are they well informed and competent, and do they show a desire to serve you?

Know the adjustment policy of the store. Are they reasonably fair in making adjustments? If they hide behind every legal right, if they are evasive, give some other store your business and economic vote.

Some consumers are interested in the way stores treat their help and in other personnel policies. Union members, in particular, prefer to buy in stores that sell merchandise produced and sold by union labor.

All other things being equal, an honest, informative merchant is your best bet in the continuous struggle to get the most value for your money.

[6] See your Better Business Bureau, financed by business in most cities of the country, for investigations of sharp and tricky practices.

Outlets	Description	Advantages	Disadvantages
Retail stores: Business establishments engaged in selling merchandise to consumers	Department: Chain or independent store merchandising a large variety of goods, divided into departments for purchasing, promoting and selling	Many services are usually offered. One-stop shopping is possible. A wide selection of goods is provided in every price range. Merchandise may be returned.	The size of the store and location of departments may make it difficult to find what you want. Department stores are often located in areas beyond your neighborhood.
Chain: Member of a group of stores with similar goods and policies	Specialty: Chain or independent store specializing in a limited type of merchandise, such as children's wear, shoes, clothing, books, furnishings, or groceries	There is greater variety within the area of specialty than in general stores. A wide range of prices is available in the specialty items. Salespersons are usually trained and their knowledge of the specialty results in good service and advice.	One-stop shopping is not possible. Prices may be higher than in larger stores.
True chain: Owned and operated by one company			
Voluntary chain: Independent stores associated for common buying and promotional activities	Variety: Chain or independent store selling a variety of consumer goods usually in a low price range and with a high amount of self-service and open counter display	Merchandise is openly displayed. Self-service is speedy. The price range is low. Great variety is available.	Salespeople may not be well trained. Shopping traffic may be heavy. Few services are provided.
Independent: Operated by the owner	Discount: Chain or independent store selling some known lines of merchandise at low prices	Parking is convenient. Self-service is speedy. Prices may be lower than other retailers. Stores are usually open for night shopping.	Usually little effort is made to display merchandise attractively. Service is limited. Return privileges are limited. Little or no home service on appliances or equipment is provided. Location may be

		Advantages	Disadvantages
Nonstore retailers: Businesses established to sell goods to consumers on a nonstore basis	Direct door-to-door: Selling in the consumer's home	Shopping at home is convenient. Often the product is demonstrated for you. Offers the opportunity to see or use items in your home before purchasing them.	There is little opportunity for comparisons of products and prices. Investigating the qualifications of the salesman is up to you. Salesman may come at an inconvenient time. There is limited selection and price range.
	Mail order: Selling through orders received and delivered by mail	Armchair shopping is convenient. Saves time and energy. Return privileges are offered. Prices are usually reasonable. Catalogue descriptions are usually accurate and helpful.	There is no opportunity to see and inspect merchandise before buying. You pay the cost of delivery. The time lapse between ordering and delivery may be inconvenient.
	Vending machines: Providing goods through a coin operated machine on a self-service basis	It is quick and easy. It offers 24-hour service.	There is limited opportunity to inspect products. Machines are impersonal. No returns or services are possible.
Cooperatives: Associations created and jointly owned by their members, operated for their mutual benefit	Consumers' cooperatives: Formed by private consumers to buy products and services jointly at favorable prices for selling to members	Profit is divided among members. Prices compare with and are often lower than in retail stores.	The amount and variety of merchandise may be limited. There may be a lack of professional retailer know-how. Services may be limited. Location may be inconvenient.

SOURCE: Reproduced with permission from Household Finance Corporation, *Money Management: Your Shopping Dollar*, Chicago, 1962, pp. 20–21.

Various Shopping Facilities. The accompanying chart, Shopping Facilities, describes the various kinds of available shopping facilities, comparing their advantages and disadvantages. You have probably noticed also the following trends in retail business.

1. Variety stores, supermarkets, and drugstores carry clothing items, usually the lower-priced goods.
2. Drive-in stores sell shoes and clothing.
3. Some stores are now self-service, and there are self-service departments in regular department stores.
4. Door-to-door selling is used by some department stores.
5. Shopping centers are established within easy distance of residential centers.
6. Discount stores have been established, and there is discount selling in regular department stores to meet this competition.
7. Vending machines are set up in convenient places for quick and easy service and round-the-clock selling.

Typical Margins of Department Stores. You may be a better shopper by knowing approximate markups of important clothing items. The margin or markup percentage varies from store to store and from item to item. For example, *Changing Times* magazine published margins used by department stores with annual sales of $2 million to $5 million.[7] The percentages came from a report of the National Retail Merchants Association.

Item	Amount added on as per cent of wholesale cost
Costume jewelry	81.8
Handbags, small leather goods	70.9
Women's, children's gloves	72.1
Women's shoes	77.6
Children's shoes	70.0
Women's, misses' coats and suits	67.5
Men's clothing	71.8
Boys' clothing	61.0
Men's, boys' shoes	69.2

Only part of this margin is profit because the markup has to cover the expenses of the store. Nevertheless, the margins help you to figure approximate price reductions. For example, a 15 per cent cut on an item with a 25 per cent margin is better than a 15 per cent cut on an item with a 77 per cent margin.

Usually, stores figure markups on a percentage of the retail price rather than on the wholesale cost. An item that costs 40 cents and sells for 60 cents may have a margin of 33⅓ per cent (20 cents divided by 60 cents).

[7] February, 1963, p. 8.

Discount Stores. Legitimate discount stores have forced a change in prices and in merchandising goods. Some large department stores have reduced personnel and expensive services, and have cut prices to meet this new competition. A few department stores have rented space in their own stores to regular discount chains. Others have set up their own discount units or stores.

Do you usually get lower prices for comparable quality in discount stores? Studies indicate that, on the whole, prices in discount houses are lower than prices in standard department stores and independent specialty stores. But in highly competitive areas, the specialty and department stores often meet discount prices. Some discount stores may have a few items marked higher than those in other competing stores. Successful discount stores usually sell fast-moving items and may offer less variety in size, color, style, and quality. A few manufacturers will not sell to a discount house or will sell the same item under a different label. Often, discount stores make a "special purchase" deal with a manufacturer and then offer an exceptional bargain to consumers.

Nondiscount stores are increasing their "private label" brands. These retailers also purchase "distress" goods—surplus stocks of manufacturers, wholesalers, and other stores—and offer them at much lower prices built around a "special purchase." However, some of these "sales" are fictitious.

Textile Fiber Products Identification Act. Consumers have a new shopping aid when buying clothing, rugs, curtains, slip covers, and various household textiles. This Federal law, which became effective March 3, 1960, requires that all textile products carry a label stating the exact percentage of each fiber in the fabric. Furthermore, when trade-marks and trade names are used on labels, the generic name [chemical family category] must also appear "in immediate conjunction therewith and such trademark and generic names must appear in type or lettering of equal size and conspicuousness." If it is a two-sided label, the front side must show clearly the words "fiber content on reverse side."

Consumers must become acquainted with the generic names that are on textile labels. Most consumers know the properties and characteristics of the natural textile fibers—cotton, wool, silk, and linen—but many of the synthetic fibers were known only by their trade-marks or trade names. Now the more than seven hundred trade names for man-made fibers are classified within one or more of the 16 generic groups that have been defined by the Federal Trade Commission. The qualities of these generic groups, when understood, serve as guides to proper washing, drying, pressing temperatures, and to the durability of the fabrics.

To aid consumers in understanding the generic groups of man-made textile fibers, the following list of properties, trade names, and use is presented in the accompanying chart, A Quick Guide to Synthetic Fibers.

A QUICK GUIDE TO SYNTHETIC FIBERS

Chemical generic name	Some trade names	Properties
Acrylics	Acrilan, Vyleran, Orlon, Zefran, Creslan	Soft hand, lightweight, bulk (warmth without weight); resistant to sunlight; wrinkle-resistant; good dimensional stability; dries fast; pleats and creases can be heat-set permanently.
Modacrylics (modified acrylic)	Dynel, Verel	Similar to acrylics but nonflammable; very sensitive to heat; subject to pilling.
Polyesters	Dacron, Kodel, Vycron	Wrinkle-resistant; pleats and creases can be permanently set by heat; dimensionally stable; good body, drape, and hand; little or no ironing necessary, so adds easy-care qualities; favored for its worsted hand.
Nylon	Nylenka, Ban-lon, Chemstrand, Agilon, Du Pont, IRC	Strongest of all fibers even when wet, yet lightweight; resists abrasion; wrinkle-resistant; dries fast; dimensionally stable; resists perspiration damage; good elasticity; wear and tear resistance; easy care; pleat retention in a multiplicity of fabrics.
Olefin	Olane, Prolene, Reevon	Auto seat covers; outdoor furniture; marine rope, belts; handbags. Strong and lightweight; highly resistant to rubbing and stretching; easily cleaned.
Nytril	Darvan	Deep-pile women's coats; soft, resilient quality; used in sweaters.
Saran	Dawbarn, Velon	Excellent resistance to soiling and staining; resistant to acids and alkalies and to attack by bacteria and insects. Principally used in screens, upholstery, fabrics, carpets, and in blends with other fibers for drapery and casement cloth.
Spandex	Tycron, Vyrene	Elasticity; softer than rubber but having many of the same properties; extremely lightweight; used in foundation garments and swimwear.
Vinal	Vinylon	Reported to be useful in a wide variety of textile applications including all forms of wearing apparel, blankets, curtains, sheets, carpets, tire cord, fish nettings, tents, and ropes. High softening temperature; high dry strength.

A QUICK GUIDE TO SYNTHETIC FIBERS (continued)

Chemical generic name	Some trade names	Properties
Vinyon	Vinyon, Rhovyl T	Resistant to moths and mildew; nonflammability (melts but does not flame); low melting point, can be easily molded.
Rayon	Tyrex, rayon, Fortisan, Super L, Corval, Topel	Absorbency; washability; will shrink unless treated for shrinkage; easy ironing with a fairly hot iron. No resistance to wrinkling; special finish required if resistance is desired. Flammability if napped; fabric should be treated for flame resistance.
Acetate	Arnel, Avisco, Celanese, Estron	Little absorbency, so dries rather quickly. Heat sensitivity, so fabric must be pressed with a cool iron to prevent fusing at thick places. Triacetates will stand higher ironing temperatures. Some wrinkle resistance. Poor resistance to fume or gas fading (color change due to atmospheric conditions). Spun or dope dyeing developed to overcome this problem. Tendency to accumulate static electricity.
Azlon		Fabrics made from protein fibers. Following properties are usually contributed by these fibers: softness, elasticity, absorbency, dimensional stability.
Glass	Fiberglas, PPG, Uniformat	Little absorbency, so can be washed easily and dried quickly. Flame-resistant; resistant to fungi, microorganisms, moths, acid, and rot. Little resistance to flexing, having tendency to break along crease lines. Freedom from odor.
Metallic	Lurex, Reymet, Fairtex, Malora, Lame, Metlon	Metallic fibers coated with plastic; widely used as ornamental fibers in clothing and household textiles; do not tarnish with wear or use. Plastic coating has tendency to stick to iron if too high heat is used.
Rubber	Polyisoprene	Core for covered yarns used in a wide variety of fabrics; foundation garments, suspenders, garters, and similar garments. Yarns vary greatly in tensile strength but have great elongation and 100 per cent elastic recovery. Do not absorb moisture and are moderately resistant to heat. Should not be exposed to excessive sunlight or heat, to oils, fats, or greases (lotions or creams).

Acceptance of the Man-made Fibers. The "battle of the fibers" was a cliché when man-made fibers entered the textile field. Now the problem is not a question of survival, but of assimilation, of combining the beauty and comfort of the natural fibers with the utility of the man-made fibers. The dominance of cotton for clothing is not yet seriously threatened. Actually, new finishes to provide better wash-and-wear qualities and the blending of cotton and synthetics have promoted the popularity of cotton. In 1950, 66 per cent of fiber consumption in the United States was cotton. In 1960, it was 62 per cent, but the total amount of cotton consumption has remained stable.

In 1960, man-made textiles represented over 30 per cent of fiber consumption. Despite this rapid growth, the field of completely synthetic fibers is still in the early stages of development. The number of possible chemical constructions is almost unlimited; already there are several hundred, and many more are under study. Blending of different constructions still goes on in research laboratories. Gradually, the best combinations of different fibers will be discovered. We already know that effective blends for apparel are 65 per cent Dacron, with rayon or cotton; 50 per cent Dacron and 50 per cent Orlon; and 50 to 55 per cent Dacron, with wool.

Silk represents only a small fraction of the total fiber consumption, but there is increasing demand because of experiments with washable and stain-resistant finishes. Wool has held at a fairly steady 9 to 12 per cent of consumption since 1920.

Among new product ideas are nylon zippers, drip-dry woolens, a new finish to provide permanent pleating in woolen fabrics, shrink-resistant wool, cottons that are nonwrinkle when tumble-dried, stretch fabrics for women's clothing, synthetics to replace shoe leather. It would seem that there is no end to new discoveries for textiles.

Performance Standards for Textile Fabrics. A publication of the American Standards Association, *American Standard L-22, Performance Requirements for Textile Fabrics,* lists performance standards for nearly all textile fabrics for almost any type of consumer use. The Federal government requires compliance with the Textile Fiber Products Identification Act, but compliance with L-22 is voluntary. Therefore, noncompliance with the latter by manufacturers may cost the consumer many dollars. Even with the protection afforded by the Fiber Identification Act, truth-in-textile labeling remains an unreached goal for the American consumer. A few pennies saved by industry in the dyeing and finishing of a fabric through not complying with the minimum requirements of L-22 may cost the consumer who buys an unsatisfactory garment several dollars.

Consumers must indicate interest in and desire for the industry's compliance with L-22 in labeling all products. The board of directors of the

National Retail Merchants Association has already accepted and approved the L-22 standards. It has also approved the use of standardized symbols on sewn-in labels, to give the consumer permanent information on how to clean the garment. Such symbols would be designated by the American Standards Association and made part of the L-22 standards.

The Low Cost of Quality Value. As far as the family pocketbook is concerned, the higher cost to obtain better wearing qualities is not a big problem. Few persons, when they know the facts, are unwilling to pay a little more to get a better return for their clothing dollar. Often, the difference in the cost of a serviceable dress and one that is unsatisfactory can be measured in pennies. For example, the added cost of a fabric dyed satisfactorily to resist fading from laundering, dry cleaning, or light runs from 1 to 5 cents a yard. Proper preshrinking of a fabric, so that a garment will not shrink out of fit even after repeated washings, adds only a few cents more a yard. Belts, trimmings, and accessories that will resist laundering and cleaning likewise cost only a trifle more.

Not only is good value less costly than you might have assumed, but it can be purchased, in part, by using your mind as well as your dollars. Why not check your clothing knowledge by answering the accompanying questionnaire, What Is My Clothing IQ? It would be a good idea to save your "Yes" and "No" answers to be compared with answers you will give to this questionnaire at a later period.

WHAT IS MY CLOTHING IQ?

1. Have you any costly clothing mistakes hanging in your closet?

2. Do you make an annual or periodical replacement inventory of all your clothing?

3. Do you set aside a certain amount of your income for clothes and keep within that limit?

4. Do you save money in advance and shop the genuine clothing sales?

5. Do you generally buy clothing that fits your needs?

6. Do you shop several stores and compare quality, value, style, and fit?

7. Do you generally compare the store brands and the nationally advertised brands?

8. Do you know what to check when shopping the more expensive clothing items?

9. Do you avoid "bargains" when you have no immediate need for the merchandise?

10. Do you know how to combine friendliness, courtesy, and good buying techniques when consulting a salesperson?

11. Do you always read the clothing tags and labels that are available?

12. Do you take the time to tell a salesperson who is helping you that it would be a good idea to have more informative labels?

13. Do you handle clothing in a store carefully to prevent damage and to minimize waste?

14. Do you realize that credit and delivery add to the cost of clothing purchased in stores that offer these services?

15. Do you always purchase clothing with the intention of keeping it and return goods only if they have material defects?

16. Do you buy clothing when you are bored or when you are angry or upset about something?

17. Do you think about the upkeep cost when buying clothing?

18. Do you build your wardrobe around two or three color schemes or around many colors?

WHAT IS MY CLOTHING IQ? (Cont'd)

19. Can you clearly describe to a salesperson exactly what you want?

20. Do you ask to see more than one quality level for comparison to get the best value for the money or possibly save money?

21. Do you avoid buying clothing in chain stores and department stores?

22. Do you generally buy clothing at the highest price level that your budget can stand?

23. Do you file for later reference valuable information that teaches better buymanship?

24. Do you file for future use any tags and labels that explain how to care for garments that you purchase?

QUESTIONS FOR DISCUSSION

1. How do you rate on What Is My Clothing IQ?

2. Have you ever analyzed your reasons for purchasing a certain item? Try it. Search below the surface for underlying motives.

3. What are the characteristics of good clothing stores?

4. What type of sale is considered best in terms of reliable merchandise?

5. When shopping for clothes, do you generally get all the information necessary to make an intelligent selection? Can you get most of this information from the label attached to the merchandise, or is the salesperson competent in answering your questions?

6. Using the Clothing Replacement Inventory suggested in this chapter, can you determine what minimum annual sum and garments you need to keep your present wardrobe up to a standard that is satisfactory for your way of life?

7. Why is consumer interest important in promoting better information on labels?

8. Make a study in your local clothing stores of any deceptive selling practices. If you discover deceptive practices, what is your responsibility?

9. Check labels on clothing for evidence of the effectiveness of the Textile Fiber Products Identification Act.

10. Do your local discount stores have lower prices for comparable quality clothing?

ACTIVITY PROBLEMS

1. Organize a class project on how to buy clothing. Let each student select a clothing item in which he is interested. Use information prepared by competent persons. Give all the sources used. An editorial committee of three persons might collect all the investigative reports and prepare a mimeographed collection that can be distributed to each person in the class.

2. Report on a recent clothing purchase. Name the garment purchased; considerations given to fashion, style, color, fabric, workmanship, cost, use, brand, and advertising; stores visited; observations; examination of article; decision and reasons for it; and method of payment.

3. Collect several clothing labels and analyze the statements on each label.

a. What is the item made of?

b. What treatment or finishes have been given to the material?

c. What service can be expected from it?

d. What special care will it require?

e. Who makes or sells it?

f. How could each label be more helpful?

4. Outline ten suggestions to help your future wife or husband buy clothes. What? Where? When? Why? How?

5. College women can compare and discuss the cost of making their own clothes with the price they would have to pay in the retail stores. Keep accurate records of all cost, even of the thread used.

6. Make an investigation of how to buy children's clothing. Take into consideration such factors as family income, size of the family, age, growing periods, use, feeling of security, upkeep costs, fabric, fit, and appropriateness.

7. If you live in a large city, compare the price of the same garment in two or more stores owned by the same company. Why would the cost of the same garment differ in stores owned by the same company?

8. Visit several clothing stores to determine which have the best values in particular kinds of clothing. Prepare a report on your findings.

9. Make a study of the advertising of several important clothing stores in your community. Using reports from the Better Business Bureau and other sources, evaluate the advertising in terms of accuracy, ethics, and information given. (Use *A Guide to Retail Advertising and Selling* by the Better Business Bureau as your guide.)

10. Ask a good shoe merchant to demonstrate the characteristics of good and poor shoe construction. He may be willing to take an old shoe apart to identify the following: upper, sole, insole, toe, lining, shank, counter, box, and heel.

11. Stage a fashion show for the class or for a larger audience and include illustrations of poor clothing choices, each followed by a superior choice.

12. Identify and rate the wearing qualities of all the fur clothing items that students will permit to be used in a classroom demonstration. In place of students, you might ask a furrier to make the analysis and report on it to the class.

13. Try to discover from families you know how they distribute the family clothing dollar. Be alert in regard to such matters as (*a*) unfair distribution, (*b*) percentage of family income spent for clothing, (*c*) difference in amount of money spent for a daughter as compared with a son, (*d*) unhappy experiences, and (*e*) happy experiences. On the basis of this investigation, formulate sound principles on how a family should distribute the clothing dollar for maximum contentment for every member.

14. Write an editorial on "The Power of Dame Fashion." During crises and war periods, nations often experience shortages in textile materials and labor. But Dame Fashion marches on—war or no war. What about it?

15. Confess the clothing mistakes hanging in your closet: (*a*) name one or more articles, (*b*) why a mistake, (*c*) lesson learned, and (*d*) advice to others based on your experience.

SUGGESTED READINGS

American Standards Association. *American Standard L-22, Performance Requirements for Textile Fabrics,* New York, 1959.
Association of Better Business Bureaus. Recent pamphlets, New York.

Changing Times. "Shoppers Guide to Bargain Sales," February, 1963; "What Other People Spend on Clothes," March, 1962.

Fairchild's *Dictionary of Textiles.*

Family Economics Review. "Clothing Expenditures of Employed Wives," September, 1962; "Outlook for Clothing and Textiles," December, 1961; "New Developments in Functional Clothing," March, 1962; "Supplies and Prices of Clothing and Textiles," December, 1962.

Federal Trade Commission. *Rules and Regulations under the Textile Fiber Products Identification Act,* Washington, D.C., 1960.

The Heller Committee for Research in Social Economics. *Quantity and Cost Budgets for Two Income Levels.* Berkeley, Calif.: University of California Press, 1962.

Hess, Katharine Paddock. *Textile Fibers and Their Use.* Philadelphia: J. B. Lippincott Company, 1954.

Household Finance Corporation. *Money Management: Your Shopping Dollar,* 1962; *Your Clothing Dollar,* 1959.

Journal of Retailing. Current issues. New York: New York University School of Retailing.

Jungerman, Martha. "Textile Fiber Products Identification," *What's New in Home Economics,* February, 1960, pp. 76–78.

Nystrom, Paul H. *Economics of Fashion.* New York: The Ronald Press Company, 1928, pp. 3–7, 157–159.

Stote, Dorothy. *Men Too Wear Clothes.* Philadelphia: J. B. Lippincott Company, 1950.

U.S. Department of Agriculture. *Clothing Fabrics, Facts for Consumer Education,* Home Economics Research Report no. 1, April, 1957; Agricultural Marketing Service, *Consumer's Concept of Fabric,* Marketing Research Report no. 338, 1959; Agricultural Marketing Service, *Economic Effects of Wash and Wear Cotton,* September, 1959.

U.S. Department of Labor. *How American Buying Habits Change,* 1959, chap. 6.

Women's Wear Daily, New York. (The retailers' daily newspaper.)

10

A HOME FOR YOUR FAMILY

What do young married couples want most after they are married? Their own home. But the shelter problem is not a simple one. There are many complex factors in the economics and sociology of housing. Modern fixtures and hidden costs present technically subtle and expensive options. Schools, neighborhood, and other environmental factors in the urban centers present complicated and future mobile risks for the family that is tied to an owned home.

High carrying charges and unexpected tax assessments for modern municipal developments put a premium on foresight about ability to pay for a house out of regular income. Mortgage companies and other links of the modern corporate housing industry involve technicalities with which few persons are prepared to deal intelligently and safely. Dozens of risks, big and little, are smothered under sales talks. One of the major risks is deciding how much to budget for shelter.

The following questions represent the problems that must be decided and overcome by young couples who wonder whether it is wiser to keep renting the family shelter or to begin planning for ultimate purchase of a home.

Should we buy or rent quarters?
How much can we afford to spend on housing?
If we purchase a house, how can we finance it at the least cost?
What are the legal pitfalls and problems?
How do we go about selecting a good site or location?
How difficult is it to rent if you have small children?
What are the advantages and disadvantages in owning or renting a home?
Is it cheaper to own than to rent?
Where can we get reliable information in settling these problems?
Are there many unexpected expenses when moving into a new home?
How much will hazard insurance cost on a home?

What is involved when working through a real estate broker?

Is the home that is being considered in keeping with future family needs?

There is an almost universal prejudice against children on the part of landlords. Some young married couples postpone having children because they are unwilling to subject themselves to the indignities often encountered in searching for adequate living quarters for a growing family. In the first place, rental charges are too high. And in the second place, even with sufficient income to rent modern quarters in a good neighborhood, landlord prejudice against young children limits the rental possibilities.

Families that are forced to buy or build homes under these two pressures are likely to find it difficult to regain the flexibility of rental status without inconvenience, loss of equity, or both, if they cannot carry the expense of their purchase.

Your Housing Goals. Finding the best place to live is one of the most important decisions an individual or family makes. The values responsible for choices in housing vary from family to family and for one family for different periods in its life cycle. Even though few families can achieve all their housing goals, a more satisfying decision can be made if a family is aware of the goals it desires the most.

Many families want reasonable privacy, comfort, health and safety, facilities for leisure-time activities, convenient and accessible stores and good schools, prestige (good address and the right playmates for the children), congenial neighbors, churches, good playgrounds, and other goals.

When thinking about your housing goals, picture your family's daily needs and activities. Children need play and study space, breadwinners need to relax, and the family needs space and facilities to live together as a unit. The more you plan how you want to live, the more likely are the prospects of knowing what kind of living space to rent, buy, or build.

Housing and the Family Life Cycle. The requirements of a family home change during the life of the family. These changes, moreover, parallel changes in the family life pattern. Also, family members undergo many changes: financial; physical and mental; cultural interests; children growing up, then leaving home for schooling, then getting married. These and other changes affect family life from beginning to end, dividing the family cycle into the (1) beginning family, (2) expanding family, (3) launching family, (4) middle-age family, and (5) old-age family.

The modern home, in whatever form, is usually the center of family life. There have been changes in the functions of the home, but basically most American homes provide space for cooking, eating, sleeping, recreation—play, hobbies, listening—carport or garage, personal hygiene, laundering, and storage. Most people never own a home in which they live out the entire family cycle from early marriage to death. Why? For one reason, we are a "mobile people." The United States Chamber of Commerce has reported that in one year 35 million people, 21 per cent of the population, moved to different homes—23 million to different homes in the same county, 7 million to a different county in the same state, and 5 million to a different state or out of the country. For another reason, American families strive to become more affluent, and their wants and desires include better or more expensive housing when there is increased ability to pay for it. All in all, selecting housing for a family is a highly complex problem that should not be taken lightly.

Basic Concepts in Housing. When considering the various alternatives in family housing, use the following basic concepts as guidelines.

1. The choice of a home is related to family goals.
2. The consumer considers alternative ways of securing shelter.
3. Housing requires large amounts of capital.
4. Homeownership is ordinarily a long-term investment.
5. Housing investment is sensitive to future trends.
6. Fixed charges and operating expenses are significant factors of homeownership.
7. Houses are relatively immobile (3 to 4 million people live in trailers).
8. Housing is beginning to benefit from mass production techniques.
9. Construction materials are shortest when demand is greatest.
10. Restrictive practices sometimes prevent use of new, economical designs, materials, and construction methods.
11. Housing may involve a "do-it-yourself" program.

Is Homeownership a Good Trend? The percentage of total United States housing that is owner occupied has continued to climb with the supply. In the first 40 years of this century, an average of only 45 per cent of housing units were owner occupied, compared to a new high of 62 per cent in 1964.

Faced with the tremendous gain in homeownership is the accompanying foreclosure problem. A study by the Federal Housing Administration on FHA-insured homes disclosed an alarming increase in foreclosures. In the first half of 1962, foreclosures rose to 41,190—1.2 per cent of all the agency's insured mortgages—from 4,828 or .49 per cent in the first six months of 1948. *Business Week* magazine, April 4, 1964, reported nearly 100,000 nonfarm home foreclosures in 1963. The over-all foreclosure rate was about 4 per cent in 1963. The FHA figure was 9 per cent, and the VA figure was 6 per cent. As the accompanying chart shows, foreclosures have shot upward since 1957. The question is whether more families can safely be switched into their own homes.

Most mortgages on homes are "conventional" mortgages, those not insured by the Federal government. The Mortgage Bankers Association, checking 2.8 million mortgages held by its members on December 31, 1961, found that 0.37 per cent of those insured by FHA and 0.32 per cent of those insured by the Veterans Administration were in default, but only 0.07 per cent of conventional mortgages were in foreclosure.[1] Conventional mortgages are in less difficulty possibly because they usually require down payments of one-quarter to one-third of the price of the home.

HOUSING UNITS OWNER-OCCUPIED AND
HOME MORTGAGES IN DEFAULT

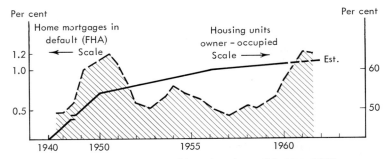

SOURCE: *Impact,* Business News Associates, February, 1963.

The FHA study also disclosed that mortgages with low down payments had a "much higher" incidence of foreclosure than those requiring higher down payments. Low-value homes were more frequently foreclosed than costlier dwellings, and long-term mortgages were more vulnerable than short-term mortgages.

Scarcity of Middle-income Housing. Adequate housing for the low-income groups can be provided only through public subsidy. But what can be done for the middle-income families with incomes from $5,000 to $8,000 annually? Studies show that this is the income group that does not qualify, as a rule, for public housing and constitutes a large section of those who try to own a home. Middle-income housing is scarce and growing scarcer. It threatens to become tomorrow's tragedy.

The natural solution to this problem is in multiple apartments like the East Hills in Pittsburgh, Pennsylvania, sparked by Action, Inc., a national group devoted to better communities. Given proper land and equable tax and monetary policies, middle-income housing can probably

[1] *The Wall Street Journal,* Apr. 2, 1962, p. 1.

be built even by private enterprise. Generally, however, there are few signs of action in middle-income housing.

The other side of the problem may be that the mass of families in the middle-income bracket are unwise in judging what they can really afford in housing. Any way one looks at the problem it is complex. In all probability, too many families attempt to own homes, not realizing the major costs in homeownership or considering the alternatives to living in a single-family house.

For more people who are living in urban and suburban areas, renting or owning an apartment unit or living in a mobile home—a trailer—may be an acceptable choice until adequate income and less costly financing make homeownership possible. A cooperative apartment, a "shell"—a partly built, "do-it-mostly-yourself" home—or a modestly priced pre-fabricated home may be a good alternative for other families.

Apartment Living. There was a time when many families were forced into buying a home because suitable apartments were not available. When this condition eased, more families could make a choice of owning a house or renting an apartment.

Some people are apartment renters by temperament, experience, and desired way of life. Others are by temperament inherently homeowners; it is a way of life for them that is satisfying even if more expensive. There are other factors to consider—family status, job prospects, age. For those who are childless, young, single, widowed, divorced, aging, ill, or subject to frequent moving, an apartment could be a better choice.

Modern apartments are likely to have a good location and outlook or view, air conditioning, wall-to-wall carpeting, elevator service, and possibly a swimming pool and tennis court free to tenants. For many families, especially those who have tried ownership and failed, apartment living may be wise. Owning a good home is still too expensive for most American families.

The chief items that represent the expenses of homeownership, as compared with apartment rental expenses, are shown in the accompanying table, Renting or Owning. All these expenses need to be itemized by the prospective homeowner. There is danger in a too quick comparison because ownership costs keep mounting according to the desires of the homeowner to improve his property and even add rooms to his house. The following additional costs may be a trap for the homeowner, to name only a few: seed, fertilizer, power mower, tools, painting, decorating, repairs, replacement of equipment, and a steady procession of improvements ranging from closet shelves to a flagstone terrace and a barbecue corner and finishing off the attic as the family increases.

Cooperative Apartments. Cooperative housing is at least 50 years old in the United States. The usual procedure is to create a corporation to

RENTING OR OWNING

Ownership expense	Apartment expense
Financing (principal, interest)	Rent
Real estate taxes	Utilities
Insurance	Other
structure	
personal property	
liability	
Maintenance, repairs, improvements	
Heating	
Electricity	
Water	
Garbage, trash	
Interest on down payment at 4 per cent	
Other *	

* Possible depreciation.

hold title to the building. Sometimes it is organized as a trust, but the corporate form is more common.

When the prospective apartment owner purchases an apartment, he receives stock in the corporation, the amount depending on the size of the apartment. He is given proprietary lease, which amounts to outright ownership of the apartment. As a part owner in the building, there is no rent, but there is a monthly charge for a proportional share of the total costs—debt service, taxes, upkeep, reserve fund, and operating expenses. The business of the corporation is handled by an elected board of directors who, in turn, hire a professional manager for the property.

Many of the cooperatives are known as "213's." This means they have been financed under a special FHA plan authorized by section 213 of the National Housing Act. Under this plan, the FHA can make loans at a low interest rate, as low as $3\frac{1}{8}$ per cent in 1961. The cooperative is in the hands of a group of sponsors who act as trustees until all the apartments have been sold.

The Girard Terrace East apartment in Minneapolis is a "213 type." The original down payment was $150, with charges of $85.76 to $108.21 a month, depending on the size of the apartment. This included interest, principal, and taxes. Owners also pay from $18.25 to $22.75 a month for heat, electricity, gas, hot water, decorating, and repairs.[2]

Section 213 cooperatives may also be a management type in contrast to the sales type described above. The management type is organized by people who will live in the building.

There have been over 1,100 FHA cooperatives built since 1950. This

[2] *Midland Cooperator,* Minneapolis, Apr. 30, 1962, p. 9.

is far from being a trend in apartment building in this country. There are certain disadvantages in owning a cooperative apartment.

1. The initial down payment is often as much as a down payment for a house ($400 to $650 a room).
2. The monthly payment is not fixed because costs change.
3. There is less freedom of choice in location.
4. In selling or remodeling, an apartment owner is at the mercy of his fellow owners.
5. There are bound to be some defaulters and delinquents.

There are these advantages, however, in cooperative housing:

1. Almost invariably, total housing costs are less than for comparable quarters.
2. There is no landlord's profit.
3. Each apartment owner's share in the equity is an investment in real estate.
4. The building may appreciate in value. (In a luxury cooperative on Chicago's Gold Coast, apartments bought in 1945 for less than $6,000 sold for an average of $25,000 per apartment.)
5. Each apartment owner has a voice in the care and upkeep of the building and in decisions concerning prospective apartment owners.
6. Monthly charges are about 15 per cent below rents for comparable apartments in the same area.

Mobile Homes. Estimates indicate that over 3½ million Americans live in mobile homes. According to the Mobile Homes Manufacturers Association (MHMA), most of these are classified as young married families and retired people. The others are military personnel and migratory workers.[3]

Modern mobile homes are a far cry from the early type of short trailer. A typical mobile home includes such modern features as a wall oven, countertop range, freezer-refrigerator combination (all in color), mirrored wall over vanity table, indirect lighting, a divided bathroom. Typically, it would be over 50 feet long, 10 to 12 feet wide, and a pull-out room expander might add 70 square feet of space, providing a room 20 to 22 feet wide. Some models have automatic dishwashers, garbage disposals, air conditioners, electric or gas fireplaces, two bedrooms, and a built-in china closet in the dining room.

The average price in 1963, according to the MHMA, was $5,600. The average price per square foot, about $11, is lower than the $14 to $16 of an average house in an urban center. Thus, mobile homes appeal to the economy-minded for easy housekeeping and mobility.

Financing a Mobile Home. Most mobile homes are purchased with a down payment of 25 to 33⅓ per cent, with up to 5 years to complete the payments. Financing is generally more expensive than financing a

[3] *The Wall Street Journal,* June 4, 1963, p. 1.

house because it is easier to "skip" with your home. The banks depreciate a mobile home to zero after 5 years. Therefore, final payments are made within that period. A new $4,800 mobile home is likely to have a $1,200 down payment and a 5-year mortgage plus these expenses:

	Per month
Amortization and insurance	$ 82.00
Registration fee	.84
Trailer site rent	27.50
Electricity and gas	6.00
Total	$116.34

Most young families living in good mobile homes are not anxious to move into conventional homes. They do recognize certain disadvantages, such as lack of good mobile parks, trailer depreciation, no space for children to play on rainy days, being referred to as "gypsies," outside noises in summer, local and state property taxes, window leakage, not enough closet space.

The advantages seem to be overwhelmingly in favor of the good mobile home—lower housing costs, pride of ownership, easy housekeeping, outdoor play space for children, less expense when moving, modern conveniences and attractive furnishings included in the cost of the trailer, friendly environment, easy supervision of children, more time to enjoy hobbies, free of debt in 5 years, good market for selling home, and inexpensive enlargement as wanted.

Advantages of a Conventional Home. Because emotions alone must not be the guide, this most important single financial decision in the life of the average family—buying and owning a home—merits thoughtful, logical analysis. First, let us examine the ten arguments for homeownership.

1. It is said that homeownership stabilizes the annual cost of a family's housing, because you can figure the immediate and future costs, and thus keep housing costs at a set amount. This is an advantage when figuring the annual family budget.

2. It is contended that homeownership is a fairly safe form of investment. It is claimed that rent money is spent money. Why not pour the rent money into your own house? At the end of 15 or 20 years, you have the house and lot as an investment of your rent money. If the value of your home increases, you can sell it at a profit.

3. There are possible income tax advantages in homeownership. You may deduct taxes and interest charges on your loan. For example, you may be paying a loaning agency $800 a year for your house—$130 may represent property taxes, and $310 may represent interest on the mortgage. Both these payments are proper income tax deductions.

4. There is more incentive to save when you own your home. Accord-

ing to this widespread belief, a family puts in a safe place savings that might tide them over hard times. With a home to pay for, the family will even forego other pleasures or needs. Some families might not save a dime if not forced to do so by the fact of homeownership.

5. Homeownership improves the credit status of the family. The equity in the home investment is good collateral for an emergency loan.

6. Homeownership gives the family a sense of increased security, especially for old age. Once a home is owned clear, it may afford cheaper housing than renting, and if a drop in income comes with old age, the family will at least have a roof over its head.

7. The desire to provide a better home environment encourages many families to buy a home. It is believed that the children will have more favorable circumstances for play and work.

8. Closely connected with the preceding argument is that homeownership strengthens the general social and financial prestige of the family. This is regarded by some people to be likely if the house "shows well." Professional people are likely to be house-proud. This value placed on property ownership is based, in part, on middle-class emphasis on property as an index of social and economic status. Many homeowners like the feeling of homeownership.

9. Some people buy homes to free themselves from the authority of landlords. The homeowner is his own master. The rent cannot be raised. He will not be evicted. The owner can make any alterations he can afford. The home can be changed to suit the way of living.

10. Homeownership has also been cloaked with the virtues of good citizenship. Homeowners are supposed to have a greater feeling of civic interest. As a local taxpayer, the homeowner has a protective interest in the management of his town or city.

The above reasons sound convincing. Each of these ten arguments has played a part in the decisions of millions of Americans to own their homes. But prospective homeowners should also investigate the *problems* of homeownership.

Disadvantages of Conventional Homeownership. There are, of course, some disadvantages in homeownership. The upkeep of house and property takes time, and work, and additional money other than the expense involved in the original purchase.

1. There is work and expense in maintaining the house and grounds. Time must be given to cutting grass, trimming shrubs and hedges, gardening, painting and decorating, and other tasks. Some families do not find these tasks burdensome, but rather enjoyable, a refreshing change from normal employment. But other families lose interest in this work in time, and deterioration sets in and lowers the value of the property.

2. There must be constant maintenance of a house, the amount de-

pending on the age and construction. A sum of money should be set aside each month to provide for whatever comes up that needs renewing or repair.

3. As time goes on there will be reasons, perhaps, for wanting extra space—finishing a room or two in the attic, remodeling the basement recreation space, adding new kitchen equipment. Of course, this extra expense is offset by family happiness and contentment because of the increased livability of the home.

4. Besides the mortgage and interest payments and the fees in connection with the original purchase, there will be monthly utility bills and real estate taxes, and hazard insurance must be arranged.

5. There is a strong tendency for families to underestimate their ability to pay for a new home. Too often, costs of maintenance and depreciation are never considered or figured beforehand.

How Much Housing Can You Afford? This is the crucial question once you have made the decision to buy a conventional home. Experts have devised general rules of thumb to guide a family that is planning homeownership. One rule is that a family can afford a home that costs 2½ times their annual income; another rule is one week's pay out of each month's salary.

These are only general rules. They never fit a specific family's way of living, size of family, or income. To find out how much of your income you can afford toward buying a home, first make a list of your expenses and income. (Do not include the wife's income if it is expected to be temporary.) The accompanying table, Your Income for Housing, will give you an idea of what to include in your list.

YOUR INCOME FOR HOUSING

Total monthly income .... $_____

Total monthly wage or salary deductions, such as withholdings for income taxes, retirement, social security benefits, hospitalization insurance (subtract the second figure from the first) ....

    Total take-home pay .... $_____

Expenses:

  Monthly savings budget .... $_____

  Food and clothing .... _____

  Medical care .... _____

  Life insurance .... _____

  Recreation .... _____

  Utilities and fuel .... _____

  Transportation .... _____

All other expenses (membership dues, contributions, charge account and installment payment, etc.) .... _____

  Total expenses (subtract from take-home pay) .... _____

Your income for housing .... $_____

You now have the approximate sum available for your housing on a monthly or yearly basis. Locate your housing income figure in the table, How Much Housing Can You Afford? to find the amount of the loan you can afford. The data in the table include principal and interest charges on a mortgage and allowances for taxes and insurance. Taxes have been estimated at $18 and insurance at $3 annually for every $1,000 loaned. Make adjustments to conform with your situation.

Suppose your income available for housing is $125 a month. According to the table, you can afford a home loan of $14,425, plus your down payment, at 5½ per cent for a 20-year mortgage. This sum does *not* include costs of maintenance, which vary greatly.

How Much Housing Can You Afford?

Income for housing		At 5 per cent			At 5½ per cent		
Monthly	Annual	10 years	15 years	20 years	10 years	15 years	20 years
$ 40	$ 480	$ 3,245	$ 4,140	$ 4,800	$ 3,180	$ 4,035	$ 4,615
50	600	4,055	5,170	6,000	3,975	5,040	5,770
60	720	4,865	6,205	7,200	4,770	6,050	6,920
80	960	6,485	8,275	9,600	6,360	8,070	9,230
100	1,200	8,110	10,345	12,000	7,950	10,085	11,540
125	1,500	10,135	12,930	15,000	9,935	12,605	14,425
150	1,800	12,160	15,520	18,000	11,920	15,125	17,310
175	2,100	14,190	18,105	21,000	13,910	17,650	20,190
200	2,400	16,215	20,690	24,000	15,895	20,170	23,075
225	2,700	18,245	23,275	27,000	17,880	22,690	25,960
250	3,000	20,270	25,860	30,000	19,870	25,210	28,845

Income for housing		At 6 per cent			At 6¼ per cent		
Monthly	Annual	10 years	15 years	20 years	10 years	15 years	20 years
$ 40	$ 480	$ 3,115	$ 3,935	$ 4,485	$ 3,075	$ 3,870	$ 4,405
50	600	3,895	4,920	5,605	3,845	4,840	5,505
60	720	4,675	5,900	6,730	4,615	5,805	6,605
80	960	6,235	7,870	8,970	6,155	7,740	8,805
100	1,200	7,790	9,835	11,215	7,690	9,675	11,010
125	1,500	9,740	12,295	14,020	9,615	12,095	13,760
150	1,800	11,690	14,755	16,820	11,540	14,515	16,515
175	2,100	13,635	17,215	19,625	13,450	16,935	19,265
200	2,400	15,585	19,670	22,430	15,385	19,355	22,020
225	2,700	17,530	22,130	25,235	17,310	21,775	24,770
250	3,000	19,480	24,590	28,035	19,230	24,195	27,525

SOURCE: Courtesy of United States Savings and Loan League, *What You Should Know before You Buy a Home*, p. 8.

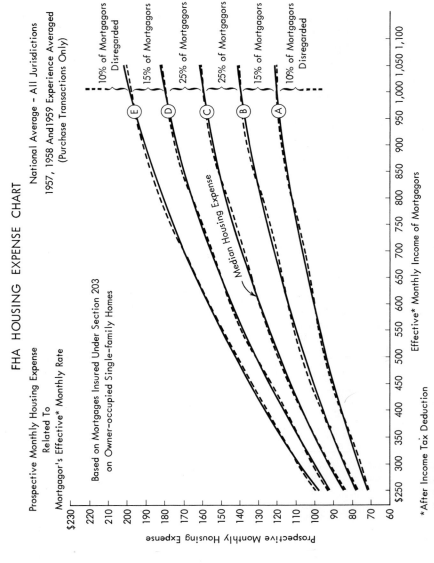

FHA HOUSING EXPENSE CHART

Prospective Monthly Housing Expense
Related To
Mortgagor's Effective* Monthly Rate

National Average – All Jurisdictions
1957, 1958 And 1959 Experience Averaged
(Purchase Transactions Only)

Based on Mortgages Insured Under Section 203
on Owner-occupied Single-family Homes

10% of Mortgagors Disregarded
15% of Mortgagors
25% of Mortgagors
25% of Mortgagors
15% of Mortgagors
10% of Mortgagors Disregarded

E
D
C
B
A

Median Housing Expense

Prospective Monthly Housing Expense

Effective* Monthly Income of Mortgagors

*After Income Tax Deduction

SOURCE: *Estimating Ability to Pay for a Home,* Federal Housing Administration, Washington, D.C., rev. ed., November, 1962.

272

FHA Housing Expense Chart. The FHA Housing Expense Chart shown here sets forth the relationship of dollar amounts of total housing expense to amounts of mortgagor's net effective income for a large sample of cases processed and approved throughout the United States in 1957, 1958, and 1959. To use the chart effectively, it is necessary to understand the terms used.

Mortgagor's effective monthly income is an estimate of the amount of dependable income (after deducting Federal income tax) that is likely to prevail through the first third of the mortgage term. The estimate is made by deducting from current earnings any income that may be temporary, such as overtime, bonuses, and room rent. The income of the wife is included only when it is reasonably certain and is an established characteristic of the family.

Prospective monthly housing expense includes mortgage principal and interest, insurance premium on mortgage, service charges, hazard insurance, taxes, assessments, cost of maintenance and repair, heating, air conditioning, and other utility costs.

The general principle followed is that the relationship of a mortgagor's prospective housing expense to effective income should be kept within those limits found to be favorable through experience in insured mortgage lending.

Generally, prospective housing expense falling above Curve E will indicate too high a risk, especially for the lower income ranges. Each case, however, is handled individually.

For consumers the chart has real value. For example, if income (after taxes) is $500 a month, a reasonably safe median housing expense is about $118 per month. If this family elects to spend over $140 for all housing costs, it may be in financial trouble. In budgeting, such a family may have to cut corners elsewhere to carry the heavy housing cost.

None of these "How much can you afford?" systems are perfect. You can use them only as guides. The trouble is that too many families disregard the realities of homeownership costs. The alarming increase in foreclosures is one consequence of family budget mismanagement.

Shopping for a New Home. If you have made up your mind to buy a house and have figured the maximum sum you can use for total costs of housing, you are prepared to look for a home. It is best to have a fairly good idea of what you want in housing before selecting a real estate broker.

Professional appraisers consider the following factors important in judging the merits of a house and neighborhood.

1. Neighbors who are of the same social, educational, and economic background
2. Physical attractiveness of the neighborhood

3. Proximity to community facilities (schools, buses, playgrounds)
4. Adequate transportation
5. Taxes within your income

In selecting a house, it is well to keep in mind that "no house is perfect." But there are four important things to check in any house that you are considering.

1. Size—at least 1,000 square feet. Check size of all the rooms.
2. Design should be functional and pleasant, provide privacy and save steps.
3. Lot size and orientation. Check distance between houses, drainage, exposure of various rooms, trees, shrubbery.
4. Construction. Check cracks, squeaky floors, trim around doors and windows, insulation, weather stripping, heating and hot water units, electrical outlets, roof and gutters for leakage, air-conditioning system.

As there are other things to check in selecting a house, it is wise to hire a reliable home builder to go over any house you are considering thoroughly.[4] This is good insurance against possible later unlooked-for expense.

Consulting a Real Estate Broker and an Appraiser. It is wise to consult a real estate broker. If you do not know a reliable broker, get at least three A-1 names, perhaps from your bank. Then be candid in telling a broker how much you can afford as well as the type of house you prefer. The more the broker knows about your wants, the better service he can give. This will save time that would be wasted in looking at houses that are beyond your income. The broker's fee is usually 5 to 6 per cent of the selling price, and it is paid by the seller of the house.

If you want to know the present real worth of a house before buying it, the best way to get it is from a professional appraiser. The cost is around $25. The final estimate will be a fair judgment of what the house can be sold for. An appraisal for mortgage loan purposes will estimate its future value over many years. What you get is an opinion only, but it is an informed one, carefully reasoned, based on factual data, and unbiased.

On Finding "The" House. When you have decided on your house you will be asked to sign an "agreement to purchase," in which you agree to buy at a specified price, subject to certain conditions. Usually you have to put up a deposit, or "earnest" money—possibly $1,000. This contract will permit a return of your money if the specified conditions are not met, such as inability to get mortgage money, or a clear title to the property. The agreement should cover sales price, amount of cash payment, manner of financing, date of delivery of property, right to inspect

[4] See *Home Buyer's Check List.* San Antonio, Tex.: Southwest Research Institute.

the property, delivery of clear title, and possibly a survey. It also specifies what goes with the house—perhaps carpeting and draperies—provisions for prorated payment of taxes, and special assessments, if any.

It is a good policy to have an attorney inspect and offer advice *before* signing any instruments of sale. He should pass on the "title" and the "abstract," and should be on hand when "closing the deal." The attorney's fee, usually a modest one ($25 to $35), will pay for itself over and over again.

Financing Your House. To finance your house, you will need a mortgage loan. A *mortgage* is a conditional assignment of the property to the lender, which can be put into effect if the borrower fails in the terms of the contract. Most home loans are made by savings and loan associations, savings banks, commercial banks, insurance companies, and individuals. More than 90 per cent of the families who buy homes do so with a mortgage loan. Of the three types of institutions, only the savings and loan associations specialize in making home loans exclusively. Currently they finance about 40 per cent of all homes in the United States.

If you wish to do business with an insurance company, you will have to deal with a local real estate broker or an insurance agent. A loan may be secured from an individual, but it may cost more than from a financial institution.

An amortized loan requires the borrower to make a fixed monthly payment that not only includes the interest (and possibly taxes and insurance) but also reduces the principal of the mortgage debt after each month's payment. The earlier monthly payments include mostly interest. It is possible, therefore, to make payments for several years with only a small proportion going into your equity in the house.

In a 5 per cent, 20-year amortized loan, more than 63 per cent of the first payment is interest. In the seventh year, payments are split about fifty-fifty between interest and principal. When you think you are paying yourself instead of a landlord in the case of renting, this is not quite true during the first few years of an amortized loan.

Taking over an old mortgage. You may be fortunate enough to qualify for taking over a mortgage that is old enough to be a low-cost mortgage. Sometimes an old mortgage can be taken over for $4\frac{1}{2}$ to 5 per cent instead of $5\frac{3}{4}$ to $6\frac{1}{2}$ per cent or more. Incidentally, but important to the seller, if you assume the old mortgage, the seller is still responsible in case you default.

In some states, a mortgage cannot be assumed without the lender's consent. It is also well to remember that the previous owner has a sizable equity to recover. So you may have to make a bigger down payment than under a new mortgage. Balance a larger down payment against lower interest charges to see if the deal is worthwhile.

Accessories to the Mortgage. Before shopping for a mortgage loan, it is wise to know the terms, or language, of the lending trade.

An *open-end mortgage* allows you to borrow more money in the future without rewriting the mortgage in case you want to repair or enlarge the house.

A *prepayment privilege* grants you the opportunity to prepay the mortgage before maturity without penalty. You may wish to refinance at lower rates or to pay it off completely.

A *packaged mortgage* covers the cost of household equipment as well as the house itself.

A *deed* is the written instrument that transfers the title of property from one party to another. There are two principal kinds of deeds.

A *quitclaim deed* conveys to the grantee whatever title the grantor may have had and throws the risk on the grantee.

A *warranty deed* conveys title, and the grantor warrants that his title to the property and his right to transfer it are not defective. The grantee can go to court to recover from the seller in the event of breach of the warranty.

An *abstract* is one of four methods of checking the safety of a title to property. This involves a history of the ownership of the property. Most or all liens, legal transactions, deeds, mortgages, sales, etc., are recorded in the abstract. It provides reassurance for the buyer.

Title insurance is a guarantee for a fee against any defects. *Certificate of title* is a certification by an attorney that he has examined the records of the property and in his opinion there are no unsettled or prior liens or claims.

The *Torrence certificate,* used largely in big cities, is issued by a governmental unit evidencing and registering title to real property.

Kinds of Mortgage Loans. There are three possible choices for a mortgage loan: conventional loan, VA (Veterans Administration) loan, FHA (Federal Housing Administration) guarantee loan. All three types are available from the same sources—savings and loan associations, commercial banks, savings banks, insurance companies, and mortgage bankers.

In a *conventional loan,* you offer only two kinds of security: the mortgaged property and your own credit and investment worth. There is no third party to back the loan, which explains why such loans are more conservative. Most mortgage loans are conventional loans, which represent the basic forms of wholly private financing. But these loans vary widely in form.

In a *VA loan,* the Federal government guarantees payment of a large portion of the loan. This means extra safety to the lender, so the cost is generally less than for the other kinds of loans. Only qualified veterans can apply for VA loans.

There is an important difference between VA and FHA guarantee loans and conventional loans. The object of the VA loan guarantee is to help veterans buy homes. VA appraisals are usually very strict, because the Federal government does not want a veteran to be overcharged. VA appraisal, therefore, serves as a good guide to a fair price for a home.

FHA-insured Mortgage. The Federal Housing Administration does not actually make loans. It agrees to insure the lender against loss in case of default. It insures mortgage loans made by banks, savings and loan associations, mortgage companies, and other lending institutions approved by the FHA.

The borrower pays ½ per cent premium for this insurance on the unpaid balance of the loan. This added security usually makes it possible for a buyer to finance a home on more liberal terms than would otherwise be available—a larger loan with longer time to pay, probably at a lower interest rate.

You can apply for an FHA-insured mortgage loan to any approved lending institution. The lender will supply the necessary forms, help you to complete them, and, if willing to make the loan, will submit your application to the FHA insuring office.

When your application reaches the FHA office, the staff must process it. FHA processing involves a thorough analysis of the entire transaction—your qualifications as a mortgagor; the property's estimated value and conformance to FHA minimum property standards for location, design, and construction; and the suitability of the mortgage terms for you and for the FHA.

After the lending institution notifies you that the FHA has approved the application, it arranges with you for the closing of the loan. At closing, the FHA endorses the mortgage for insurance. Closing costs consist of such items as the lender's service charge, the cost of title search and insurance, and charges for preparing, recording, and notarizing the deed and mortgage.

The chief requirements for the borrower are a good credit record, the cash required for down payment and closing costs, and a steady income to make the monthly mortgage payments without difficulty.

The FHA has no arbitrary rules with respect to age or income. It does consider these factors, but only in relation to ability to repay the loan over the period of the mortgage. Each application received by the FHA is considered individually on its own merits. There are guidelines, but they are not rigid. No two families have exactly the same circumstances. Family obligations, responsibilities, future prospects, and ideas on spending all differ widely.

Long-term Mortgages and Interest Costs. The availability of long-term mortgages with their lower monthly payments, along with progressively lower down payments, has doubtless been an important factor in the increase in homeownership. In 1940, 44 per cent of all United States families owned the homes they occupied; by 1950, this had increased to 55 per cent, and by 1964 to 62 per cent. The proportion of owner-occupied homes that were mortgaged increased from 44 per cent in 1950 to 57 per cent in 1960.

By using a long-term rather than a short-term mortgage, a family with a specified amount available for shelter each month can buy a more expensive house, or a family buying a house at a specified price can make smaller monthly payments. However, the investment or equity in the house builds up very slowly with a long-term mortgage, and it will cost much more for interest by the time the mortgage is paid off.

For example, the accompanying table, FHA-insured Mortgages—Length of Term, shows that the total amount of interest a family would pay on a $15,000 loan at 5¼ per cent would be $17,823 if it took 35 years to pay, and $9,264 if it took only 20 years—a difference of over $8,500. The monthly payments on these mortgages would be $78.15 and $101.10, respectively. Total interest costs on a 5¼ per cent mortgage exceed the original amount of the loan when it takes more than 30 years and 3 months to pay off the loan.

FHA-INSURED MORTGAGES—LENGTH OF TERM
Monthly Payment and Total Interest Costs on $15,000 Loan
at 5¼ Per Cent Annual Interest

Term of loan (years)	Monthly payment on principal and interest	Approximate total interest costs *	First date payment on principal exceeds payment on interest
20	$101.10	$ 9,264	6 years and 11 months
25	90.00	12,000	11 years and 10 months
30	82.95	14,862	16 years and 9 months
35	78.15	17,823	21 years and 11 months
40	74.85	20,928	26 years and 11 months

* Calculations are based on the assumption that the regular monthly payment will be required for the final month to discharge the obligation. Overpayment each month due to rounding of the monthly payment to the nearest cent may be sufficient to reduce or eliminate the last one or two payments.

SOURCE: Housing and Home Finance Agency, Washington, D.C.

With the 35-year loan for $15,000 at 5¼ per cent, only $12.53 of the first monthly payment of $78.15 is repayment of principal. Moreover, less than half of each payment goes to principal for almost 22 years.

If the 20-year loan is used, $35.40 of the first monthly payment of $101.10 applies to repayment of principal, and less than half of each payment is for principal for almost 7 years.

If the interest rate on a $15,000 loan is 6 per cent instead of 5¼ per cent, the total interest cost would be $20,923 for a 35-year mortgage, and $10,793 for a 20-year period. The effect of even this small increase in the interest rate on the total cost of interest emphasizes how important it is for the prospective purchaser to shop for the best credit terms available.

Interest rates vary from time to time depending on the supply and demand for mortgage money. In July, 1963, FHA regulations limited the rate for any insured home mortgage to not more than 5¼ per cent a year on the loan balance each month, and an insurance premium of ½ per cent a year.

Discount Points. The rate of interest that lenders can charge on mortgages insured by the FHA is lower at times than the yield required by lenders in the market. For this reason, lenders often discount FHA mortgages—that is, they charge a certain number of points (a point is a dollar per hundred dollars of mortgage amount) to make up the difference between the FHA interest rate and the yield that they can get elsewhere in the market.

The number of points charged in different places varies at different times and among different lenders. On a $10,000 mortgage, four points would be $400. Sometimes the additional cost in financing a house is substantially higher because of discount points.

Your Mortgage and Equity in Your Home. Some arguments for long-term mortgages are (1) they enable lower-income families to become home-owners; (2) they enable a family, by smaller, easy monthly payments, to buy a more expensive home; and (3) it may be easier to sell the house, because prospective buyers are often attracted by a long-term mortgage and a small cash settlement.

A family should consider its income, needs, and goals before deciding on the kind of mortgage to assume. A long-term mortgage with smaller monthly payments leaves more family income for attaining other important goals. Also, a long-term mortgage allows a more expensive home, one providing more space and desired special features, perhaps in a better neighborhood. In the latter case, such costs as real estate taxes, utilities, and maintenance are likely to be proportionately higher. In any event, the family should make sure that the mortgage contract permits larger payments if the family income improves later, thus gaining some of the advantage of a short-term mortgage.

If the family expects to keep the house a long time, it may find that the advantages of building up equity faster by using a short-term mortgage outweigh the advantages to be gained from a long-term mortgage.

Assuming that a house has a life expectancy of 45 years (a figure frequently used), a buyer who gets a 35-year, 5¼ per cent loan for the entire purchase price of a new house will owe more than its depreciated value until early in the 21st year, if prices of new houses remain constant. If he gets a 30-year, 5¼ per cent mortgage, he will owe more than its value until the middle of the 13th year.

Because of a general increase in prices of houses since the early 1940s, most owners have experienced a rise in value of their homes rather than a decrease by depreciation. Probably few have had a situation in which their mortgage debt exceeded the sale value of the house. In 1963, however, it was reported that real estate prices had stabilized in many areas. If they continue to level off or decline, many owners with long-term mortgages may find they cannot sell their homes for enough to pay their remaining debt.

How Much Can You Borrow? Lenders must restrict the amount you may borrow and how long they may give to repay it. These limits are a matter of law, enacted to prevent lenders from making unsound loans. Each class of lender is subject to separate legal limits. National banks have one set of rules and state banks another set. Federally chartered savings and loan banks have yet another set of legal limits. All these controls apply to conventional loans.

In the case of FHA and GI mortgage guarantee loans, with Federal government support, lenders can safely lend much more because of the added security. The accompanying table, FHA-guaranteed Mortgage Loans, shows the monthly payments and total cost of interest and mortgage insurance for typical loans at 5¼ per cent interest.

The loan that is best for you will depend on the supply and demand of mortgage money at the time, on the laws, and on your individual needs in relation to your income. If you must have a high-percentage loan, try for an FHA or, if eligible, a VA loan. If your requirements are modest, a conventional mortgage may be better, and it is advisable to shop around for mortgage money.

Settlement or Closing Charges. Settlement day is when the property officially becomes yours. Among the papers you will sign are likely to be the following: *note* (promise to repay the loan); *mortgage* or *deed of trust* (rights of lender to enforce payment); *title insurance policy* (protection against defect in title); copy of *survey* of the land. You should receive five documents: note, mortgage, deed, survey, and the title insurance, plus receipts for all payments you make. Ask for copies of all papers.

Closing costs are likely to be higher than you figured—from $100 to

FHA-GUARANTEED MORTGAGE LOANS

Monthly Payment to Principal and Interest, Mortgage Insurance Premium, and Total Monthly Payment at 5¼ Per Cent

Term of loan	$10,000 loan			$15,000 loan			$20,000 loan		
	Principal and interest	Mortgage insurance premium	Total monthly payment	Principal and interest	Mortgage insurance premium	Total monthly payment	Principal and interest	Mortgage insurance premium	Total monthly payment
20 years	$67.40	$4.11	$71.51	$101.10	$6.17	$107.27	$134.80	$8.22	$143.02
25 years	60.00	4.13	64.13	90.00	6.19	96.19	120.00	8.26	128.26
30 years	55.30	4.14	59.44	82.95	6.21	89.16	110.60	8.28	118.88
35 years	52.10	4.15	56.25	78.15	6.22	84.37	104.20	8.29	112.49
40 years	49.90	4.15	54.05	74.85	6.23	81.08	99.80	8.30	108.10

Total Cost of Interest at 5¼ Per Cent and Total Mortgage Insurance Premiums

Term of loan	$10,000 loan			$15,000 loan			$20,000 loan		
	Interest	Insurance premium	Total	Interest	Insurance premium	Total	Interest	Insurance premium	Total
20 years	$ 6,169	$ 588	$ 6,757	$ 9,254	$ 882	$10,136	$12,339	$1,175	$13,514
25 years	7,954	757	8,711	11,930	1,136	13,066	15,907	1,515	17,422
30 years	9,839	937	10,776	14,758	1,405	16,163	19,678	1,873	21,551
35 years	11,851	1,129	12,980	17,777	1,693	19,470	23,702	2,258	25,960
40 years	13,931	1,327	15,258	20,896	1,990	22,886	27,862	2,653	30,515

SOURCE: Federal Housing Administration. *A Guide for Home Buyers and Owners.* Washington, D.C., April, 1962.

$500. Not all lenders make the same charges. Fairly typical charges might run as follows:

Survey	$ 35.00
FHA processing fee	20.00
Your lawyer	25.00
Title insurance	60.00 (many people omit it)
County recording fee	7.50
Mortgage tax—state	25.00
Total	$172.50

If you deal with a bank, you may have *origination charges* of around $100. This sum covers bank expenses in securing the loan, lawyer's fee, cost of drawing note or bond, mortgage, and so on. Under VA procedures, these costs are limited by law—at present to 1 per cent of the sale price of the house.

First-year Expenses of Homeownership. Outfitting a new house or moving from one home to another costs money. Besides moving expenses, you are likely to need several items for making the home livable. Few people budget enough money for these purposes. The University of Houston surveyed 218 new homeowners and found they spent an average of $1,580 on new furniture and equipment the first year.[5] The main items are shown in the accompanying table, First-year Expenses of Homeownership, in relation to the value of the house.

[5] *Changing Times,* April, 1960.

FIRST-YEAR EXPENSES OF HOMEOWNERSHIP

	Value of house		
Items	$10,000 to $15,000	$15,000 to $20,000	Over $20,000
Power lawn mower	$ 60.00	$ 55.00	$ 93.00
Fencing	207.00	197.00	257.00
Carpets, carpeting	190.00	186.00	1,085.00
Draperies, curtains	72.00	105.00	432.00
Furniture, living room	217.00	173.00	780.00
Furniture, bedrooms	240.00	133.00	579.00
Furniture, dining room	150.00	250.00	—
Furniture, den	92.00	116.00	566.00
Shrubbery	104.00	78.00	266.00
Patio	90.00	—	217.00
Furniture, outdoor	53.00	57.00	83.00

Some of this spending may not be necessary immediately or at all. The fact remains that there will be costly items to buy other than air conditioner, kitchen appliances, and laundry equipment that you normally foresee and plan for. Watch out for these budget busters. If you are moving from a rented apartment, chances are that you will need yard tools, grass seed, fertilizer, and other such items not in your budget. It may, therefore, be wise to provide about 10 per cent of the cost of the house for planned and unplanned expenditures the first year.

Service Record of Professional Moving Companies. At best, moving experiences are a strain on the whole family—a strain undergone by one-fifth of the population of our country annually.

The service record of professional moving companies has been documented by the Interstate Commerce Commission, which regulates van lines operating between states. From a sampling of all household moving jobs in 1960, the ICC came up with these findings.

1. Promises of delivery dates are broken 30 per cent of the time.
2. Price estimates are underestimated 50 per cent of the time.
3. Claims for damage or loss are filed as a result of one in every four moves.

In a study of 2,000 subscribers who had changed addresses in 1962, Consumers Union documented a considerable amount of advice on how to buy moving service.[6]

The van lines serving the whole country are usually systems of local moving companies that act as agents. According to ICC regulations, each local company may operate for itself only in a restricted geographical area. When moving contracts are destined for more distant points, the big "parent van lines" take over.

Acting as an agent, the local company makes the price estimates and directs the packing and loading of the shipment. But between the loading and unloading, the national line takes control. It runs the traffic arrangements on which each shipment is scheduled. The average van holds 16,000 pounds. The typical householder's load weighs 3,000 pounds. Thus, most vans carry three or four different households on a given trip.

The ICC is the Federal regulating agency on interstate hauls. But the ICC is too often dominated by the van lines and promotes the private rather than the public good. This is shown by the fact that most of the broken promises suffered at the hands of movers are condoned by the law and the rules of the ICC. ICC Commissioner William H. Tucker put it this way, talking to the moving industry: "At your basic rates, all you are really offering the customer is to load his goods and eventually deliver them in some undetermined condition."

[6] *Consumer Reports,* July, 1963, pp. 340–346.

The Problem of Quoted Prices when Moving. The local vans make the estimate (prices quoted to the customer), but these estimates are not binding according to ICC rules. Consequently, estimates are always understated. Likewise, the estimate of when the van will arrive at its destination is not binding on the company. This can mean that part of the load may come later. If the van is not fully loaded, the delivery may be delayed several days until another shipment is found to fill it.

How close were the estimates of shipments for the 2,000 subscribers of *Consumer Reports?* Moving costs were understated in 30 to 40 per cent of the cases; the difference in the estimate and the actual bill was as much as 100 per cent, and the average margin of error was around 25 per cent. (You have to pay the bill before the shipment is unloaded—in cash, by money order, or by certified check.) Furthermore, if you are not ready to pay at this time, the van charges "waiting time" at the rate of $10 an hour, starting one hour after they are ready to unload; on moves over 200 miles, the extra charge begins three hours after they are ready to unload. If necessary, the driver can put your goods in storage at your expense.

The householder can demand that the van be reweighed if there is a public scale in the vicinity. If the weight proves to be within 2 per cent of the estimated pounds, you pay the weighing charge of about $10.

Liability of Moving Companies. Packing charges are usually $3 to $3.50 per 100 pounds. Unless you pay extra, the company is liable for only a small percentage of the value of the goods. For example, a $100 radio could disappear, but since it weighed only 10 pounds, the moving company would pay only $3. Van companies set the value of a typical shipment at $1.25 to $1.50 a pound.

Since damaged and lost items are quite common, you should carry more insurance than the minimum stated above. Under present tariffs you can do this in several ways. One way is for the van line to assume full liability for specific valuables at a charge equal to 2 per cent of the amount you say they are worth.

Sometimes a *co-responsibility clause* is in a contract that appears to give full-liability coverage. Thus a full claim of $100 could be settled for about $60. Read the contract carefully.

A Few Moving Pointers. Before contracting for moving, check with your own insurance agent concerning your household insurance. It is likely to give some coverage in case of moving. Then consider the following precautionary measures.

1. Before moving, sell as many goods as possible—especially, heavy, outdated items.
2. Very low bids are likely to be unrealistic.

3. When awarding the job, get a copy of the contract stating the rate to be charged, liability, and dates of pickup and delivery.

4. Choose insurance from other sources than the van company. Insure against major damage or loss. Check your present coverage first.

5. Keep a list of what is in each box or package.

6. Make a complete inventory of all items.

7. When loading, challenge any written statement by the van mover that a piece is already "marred and scarred" if it is not.

8. Count all crates, boxes, and barrels as they leave the house.

9. Get from the local agent the name and address of the destination agent, the file number and van number of your shipment, and the driver's name.

10. Request advance notice of lateness and immediate notice of actual charges. Better have a certified check for 50 per cent more than the estimate of the costs.

11. If the van is overdue, contact the local agent and keep a record of all resultant expenses.

12. After the van arrives, examine the bill of lading carefully. Note weight before paying.

13. When unloading, tell where to put the various items. Insist that all disassembled pieces be put together.

14. When unloading is over, indicate any damaged or lost articles before signing. You may write in: "Accepted subject to concealed loss or damage." Later, when damaged goods or lost articles are identified, file damage and loss claims. State the original value because the company will depreciate the value. If you do not get action, report the matter to the Interstate Commerce Commission, Washington, D.C. As a last resort, a letter from your lawyer to the van line's headquarters may help.

Fire Insurance Policies. Fire insurance pays for the replacement value, less depreciation, of property destroyed. It is important, therefore, to cover the present-day value of your home. But the standard fire insurance policies are no longer adequate.

Fire policies on the structure or house itself may be extended to include losses by hailstorm, tornado, wind, aircraft, motor vehicles, explosion, and rust or smoke damage. This is known as *extended coverage* and costs very little—about 6 to 8 cents per $100 of protection per year.

Some companies also offer *additional extended coverage* to cover losses against water damage from plumbing and heating systems; vandalism and malicious mischief; glass breakage; ice, snow, and freezing; falling trees; and collapse of building. The rate is a very modest 4 cents for $100 of protection for one year.

Coinsurance means that if you fail to carry insurance amounting to 80 per cent of the value of the property, in the event of a loss you share the loss with the insurance company. For example, for property valued at $20,000, you should carry $16,000 worth of fire insurance (80 per cent). If you carry only $8,000 of fire insurance and a fire causes an $8,000 loss, you cannot collect the whole loss. As a coinsurer with the company, carrying only half the insurance that was needed to qualify for the 80 per cent coverage, you collect only one-half of the loss, or $4,000. With 80 per cent of value, or higher coverage, you collect the whole loss.

Fire policies can be voided for several reasons. If you leave the house unoccupied for more than 60 consecutive days, it may void the policy. If a room is added, you need more insurance to cover all your household furnishings. You must keep an inventory of all the contents of your house to prove your loss in event of fire. Most insurance companies have inventory booklets for this purpose.

You should have a 10 per cent *off-premises coverage*—protection of personal property away from home. It also covers a detached garage, renting a room or apartment if forced out of your home, and personal property when traveling.

When you have a fire loss, report it immediately to the company representative. Do the best you can to protect the remaining property. Prepare an inventory of your losses supported as much as possible by canceled checks, vouchers, and bills. A household inventory booklet, filled in and up to date, with the items in each room inventoried—when purchased, original cost, and present cash value—is usually accepted by the company adjuster.

Fire Insurance Premiums. Fire premiums, or rates, vary greatly depending on the fire defenses of the community, construction of the building, and the loss experience of the company.

Fire defenses in larger communities are graded by the National Board of Fire Underwriters.[7] The board considers the water supply, fire department, fire-alarm system, police department, fire-prevention activities, enforcement of building codes, construction and congestion of buildings, and adverse climate. The board grades the towns on a sliding scale of 1 to 10, with 1 being the best.

A frame house is generally considered a poorer risk than one constructed of brick, stone, steel, or masonry. A veneer of brick over the outside of the frame usually does not allow a better fire rating.

An increase in fire losses tends to push rates up. A drop should reduce the rates. The bulk of the work on fire losses is done by the National Board of Fire Underwriters and the Mutual Insurance Advisory Association. Their figures are given to fire insurance rating bureaus in the various states. These bureaus, private but supervised by state agencies, file the rates with the state. Typical rates for a one-family house are shown in the accompanying table.

Fire insurance paid up for a three-year period costs 2½ times the annual premium. A five-year policy costs 4 times the annual premium.

---

[7] *Risks We Face, an Introduction to Property Insurance*, rev. ed. A free copy is available from National Board of Fire Underwriters, New York.

COST PER YEAR FOR $100 OF INSURANCE IN FIRE PROTECTION ZONE

| | High | | Medium | |
	Building	Contents	Building	Contents
Frame house	14¢	21¢	15¢	22¢
Brick house	9¢	17¢	10¢	18¢

Comprehensive Personal Liability Insurance. Comprehensive personal liability insurance protects against many types of liability for bodily injury and property damage to a nonmember of the family on or off your property. These situations illustrate the coverage for damages and resulting medical expense: a guest falls, your dog damages a neighbor's flower bed, your have a hunting accident, a household employee is injured, a neighbor's child is injured on your property, your child injures a playmate off your premises, a passer-by is hurt, fire on your property spreads to a neighbor's property, there is damage to a parked car on your property, a tradesman is injured on your property.

Formerly it took several policies to cover these protections. Now you can buy a comprehensive personal liability policy covering them all for $10 to $15 a year. This premium provides a $10,000 policy that pays damages up to the face value and medical bills up to $250. You can buy larger policies for very little increase in premium cost. The cost can be cut by a deductible clause and by a three- or five-year prepaid premium.

Personal Property Floater Insurance. A personal property floater policy provides all-risk protection against many common hazards, such as damage or loss of furniture, clothing, cameras, sporting equipment, silver, rugs, linen, books, furs, luggage, and many other things, both in the home and away from home. Almost all risks are covered, with exceptions of cars, planes, pets, dampness, vermin, moths, and war risks.

The floater policy provides protection for both town and farm families. Ordinary robbery and theft insurance is generally unavailable to farm families. Loss of cash is usually limited to $100, loss of securities to $500, and loss of unscheduled jewelry, watches, and furs to $250.

Theft Insurance. Theft insurance covers robbery, burglary, and larceny. Residential theft insurance covers stealing of goods from the home and damage to home and property by thieves. *Mysterious disappearance* ("I don't know what happened to it!") should be included in the policy.

A *broad-form theft policy* is very inclusive in its protection. It may cost from $14 to $22 per $1,000 of protection for one year. You save from 15 to 20 per cent by taking out a three-year policy. You can also buy deductible insurance, paying the first $25 or $50 yourself, and reduce costs another 15 to 20 per cent.

One caution: Insurance paid on a loss is based on current value at the time of the loss, which is the replacement value of the item less depreciation.

Combination Policy. Casualty companies have worked out a combination policy of (1) insurance on the residence or structure, (2) insurance on household personal property, (3) comprehensive personal liability protection, and (4) theft insurance. It may pay to buy a combination policy, because it usually costs 20 to 30 per cent less than several separate policies. Besides, you have one transaction, one contract, one premium to pay, plus a lower agent's commission. On the negative side, you might be paying for more coverage than is needed in your area.

It would pay to purchase a prepaid three-year combination policy, because the cost for the same coverage is much lower. For example, a policy including $15,000 fire insurance with all extended coverages on a frame house, $1,500 insurance on such outbuildings as a garage, $6,000 insurance on personal property on the premises plus $1,000 off the premises, $3,000 insurance for additional living expenses, and personal liability insurance up to $10,000 may cost approximately $183 for a three-year premium. The same coverage purchased in separate policies for a three-year period may cost around $297 from the same company. The combination policy would save about $114.

Investigate your own situation, compare coverage and cost, and the chances are good that you can save many dollars by purchasing a combination policy.

Do Not Plunge into Debt for a Dream House. Next to food, housing is the greatest need of every family. Today, families spend from 25 to 35 per cent of their total income on shelter. When such a large percentage of income must be spent for housing, it is wise to give close attention to the problems of securing satisfactory shelter at an economical cost. Every family must decide whether to rent, buy, or build a home.

Since a home is the base of family operations, it deserves high priority in the family spending plan. It is wise to investigate whether renting a house or apartment, or buying or building a house, is the intelligent choice for your family. The maximum amount that can be expended for shelter and still leave adequate income for other aspects of family living must be figured before allowing dreams to plunge the family into debt.

QUESTIONS FOR DISCUSSION

1. Is it cheaper to own a house or to rent?
2. What would you include in a check list to aid a young married couple in selecting a house?
3. What are the advantages and disadvantages in renting a dwelling?

4. Study a house lease and then name some of the legal responsibilities of the lessor and the lessee.

5. How do you obtain title to real estate in your state?

6. What makes a house a home?

7. What reactions do you have to the following statements?

a. "You have to build two houses before you get what you want."

b. "Never build a house before employing an architect."

c. "All contractors must be watched carefully."

8. How can you know how much you can afford to pay for a house?

9. What is the meaning of "discount points"?

10. Why is it difficult to know which loan is best?

11. Why do fire rates on homes vary greatly?

12. Why is it important to carry fire insurance on the structure of a house amounting to at least 80 per cent of the present value of the property?

ACTIVITY PROBLEMS

1. Draw a design of a home, a kitchen, or a summer cottage of your own choice. Does it meet all the essential requirements suggested by authorities?

2. Investigate your house or someone else's and report on whether it is planned well or poorly as regards flexibility of room space, circulation, orientation, storage space, utilities, and furniture placement. (Read *Designing the Home*, University of Illinois, Small Homes Council, Circular ser. C2.1.)

3. Report on the suggestions for better use of land for shelter that are given in the housing report of The Twentieth Century Fund, *American Housing—Problems and Prospects*, New York, 1944.

4. Study a standard lease used in your community when renting a home. Make a report to the class on the legal information necessary for renters.

5. Prepare a check list for a young married couple to aid them in selecting a house for renting and for owning. Are the things to check different if you plan to buy a house rather than rent one? Are the problems different when selecting a rural home? A suburban residence?

6. Consider a possible house site that you have seen. Report on its accessibility, assessments, taxes, insurance or water rates, neighborhood characteristics, public and utility services, zoning restrictions, and schools. (Read *Selecting a Home Site*, University of Illinois, Small Homes Council, Circular ser. B2.1.)

7. Interview a homeowner you know. Ask such questions as: "What were your biggest problems in acquiring a home to fit your family needs?" "How did you solve these problems?" "What advice would you give to others who are contemplating owning a home?" Evaluate the answers to these questions. Ask yourself, for example: "Could these problems have been solved better?" "How?"

8. A family buys a house costing $12,500. A down payment of $4,000 is made. A 5½ per cent mortgage loan is made for the balance of $8,500 over a 15-year period. What monthly payments will have to be made to retire the loan? What will the actual total cost of the house be at the end of the 15-year period? Will income tax deductions of the interest reduce the total cost of this house?

9. Make an investigation of some phase of housing in which you are especially interested. Some suggestions are:

a. Call on a bank, savings and loan company, or other lending agency and obtain information on borrowing money to build or buy a house.

b. Visit the register of deeds at the county courthouse.

c. Interview a builder or contractor of houses.

d. Investigate the zoning laws in your community.

e. If you live in a large city, talk to the manager of a title insurance company.

10. Report to the class the preliminary costs connected with the purchase of a house in your community.

11. Observe a house under construction. From time to time, talk to the architect or general contractor about the important stages in the construction of the house. Try to discover any problems of the owner during the period of construction.

12. If your parents or other relatives or friends are building a house during your absence from home, keep a log of the week-to-week problems that arise. If snapshots are sent to you, include them in the project. What is your reaction to the building of the house as gleaned from letters?

SUGGESTED READINGS

American Institute of Banking, American Bankers Association. *Home Mortgage Lending*, latest edition.

Bryant, Willis R. *Mortgage Lending*. New York: McGraw-Hill Book Company, 2d ed., 1962.

Business Dealings with the Architect and the Contractor. Circular Series A2.0. Urbana, Ill.: Small Homes Council, University of Illinois, 1953.

Changing Times. "Prepay Part of Your Mortgage," June, 1957; "Tips to Help You Sell Your House," May, 1957; "How to Shop for a Mortgage," October, 1955; "How Much House Can You Afford?" October, 1958; "It's a Good Time to Buy a House," April, 1963; "The Price of Fire Insurance," February, 1961; "Know What Your House Is Worth," September, 1962; "Apartments Make Sense, Too," May, 1962; "New Look at Prefab Houses," March, 1958.

Cohen, Jerome B., and Hanson, Arthur W. *Personal Finance*. Homewood, Ill.: Richard D. Irwin, Inc., 1964, chap. 10.

Conklin, Groff. *The Weather Conditioned House*. New York: Reinhold Publishing Corporation, 1958.

Consumer Research Bulletin. *Buying a Mobile Home*, February, 1961.

Extended Payment Tables for Monthly Mortgage Loans. Boston: Financial Publishing Company, 1958.

Federal Housing Administration. "Estimating Ability to Pay for a Home," Washington, D.C., November, 1962; "FHA Home Mortgage Insurance," January, 1963; "Summary Statement on Cooperative Housing," September, 1961.

Fortune. "The Danger in Mortgage Debt," 1956.

Greenwald, William E. *Buy or Rent*. New York: Twayne Publishers, Inc., 1958.

Household Finance Corporation. *Your Shelter Dollar*, Chicago.

Keats, John. *The Crack in the Picture Window.* Boston: Houghton Mifflin Company, 1956.

Levy, Michael H. *Your Insurance and How to Profit by It.* New York: Harcourt, Brace & World, Inc., 1955, chaps. 8–11.

McCall's. "New Look of Mobile Homes," July, 1961.

National Better Business Bureau. *Facts You Should Know about Buying or Building a Home,* New York, latest edition.

U.S. Department of Labor. *How American Buying Habits Change.*

United States Savings and Loan League. *What You Should Know before You Buy a Home,* January, 1961.

The Wall Street Journal. "Rolling Home Rise," June 4, 1963, p. 1; "Home Loan Woes," Apr. 2, 1962, p. 1.

11

BUYING GOOD HEALTH THROUGH MEDICAL SERVICES

Buying good health is not the same as spending money for food, clothing, and shelter. These needs can be budgeted because their cost facts are constant. But health and medical costs are uncertain and unpredictable. It is possible for a young family to budget $20 a week for food expenditures, but who can say that the health and medical expenditures of this family will average $3 or $15 a week? For this reason, the cost of ill health is, for most families, the hardest of all expenditures to face. A large percentage of families live in constant fear of loss of income resulting from disability. Earnings are usually reduced or stopped completely during an extended illness or recuperation from an accident.

Family budget experts have sometimes said that the medical expenditures of the average family should not exceed 6 to 8 per cent of the net income. There are, as yet, no complete reliable statistical data on medical and health needs to aid in constructing accurate premium rates. Meantime, unpredictable medical costs confront families and sometimes lead them to make costly bargains for health by becoming victims of faddists and charlatans, even of superstitions.

Basic Measures in Keeping Well. How, then, can a person provide optimum health at reasonable cost for himself and his family? There is no easy answer because the basic requirement for good health does not depend entirely on doctors and hospitals, important as doctors and hospitals are today. Indeed, there are important health protection virtues in a good standard of living, in adequate housing, in proper nutrition, in exercise and recreation, in education, and in sound personal hygiene. In fact, keeping well depends more on these and other protections than on medical care. Appropriate patterns for healthful living will serve as a guide in reaching maximum health for yourself and your family.

There are several valuable health measures that go far toward preventing acute and chronic disorders: (1) good nutrition, (2) moderate smoking, (3) regular exercise, (4) avoidance, or at least careful use, of proprietary drugs, and (5) periodic health examinations.

The importance of a well-balanced diet of natural foods must not be underestimated. Eating too much leads to obesity, which in turn aggravates vascular and other diseases. It is well to remember that medical authorities on the "battle of the bulge" say that there is no painless road to effective, long-term weight reduction. No dietary aid, no drug, no passive-exercise device can substitute for a supervised program of diet, moderate exercise, and psychological support.

In the light of much research, moderation in smoking is a good rule to follow. Excessive smoking of cigarettes is definitely one of the factors causing cancer of the lung and aggravating coronary artery heart disease and peptic ulcer.[1]

Regular exercise, all year round, has not been appreciated. Long brisk walks, cycling, skating can be practiced the year round.

Avoidance of proprietary drugs and devices is also wise. Intelligent people, as a rule, avoid self-treatment with patent medicines. Beware of medical frauds like "dietless" reducing schemes; "sure cures" for cancer, arthritis, skin troubles, baldness, and lost manhood; and medical quacks who deal in "atomic" medicines and "electronic" claptrap devices with flashing bulbs, ticks, and buzzes. The Food and Drug Administration tries to track down these quacks and their wares. A study of over 500 cases since 1938, however, shows that most of these violations do not come to the attention of the FDA until months or years have elapsed.[2] Unfortunately, the chief witnesses die before the cases reach the courts.

Periodic Health Examinations. Everyone should have a periodic health examination. Disorders detected early are usually easy to treat and reduce sickness and economic loss. Cost, however, is an important barrier against periodic checks by the family physician or an internist. Most people are already struggling with paying for medical care for existing common illnesses and find it difficult to pay the cost of routine comprehensive examinations for the entire family. Life extension examiners charge about $35 for a standard periodic examination.

The typical fee for one visit at the doctor's office may range from $3 to $25. Routine blood and urine tests and chest X-ray tests cost from $10 to $20. Microscopic examinations, blood sugar test, sedimentation

[1] *The Consumers Union Report on Smoking and the Public Interest.* Mount Vernon, N.Y.: Consumers Union of U.S., Inc., Also the Surgeon General's Report on Smoking and Health, Washington, D.C.: Superintendent of Documents, 1963.

[2] *Consumers Can Protect Their Own Health.* Greeley, Colo.: Council on Consumer Information, p. 28.

test, and stool examination add another $10. An electrocardiogram costs about $15. Such an annual outlay of nearly $50 for each member of the family is a serious barrier for a majority of families. When hospitalization is needed, the cost is nearly prohibitive for most families. Twice-a-year dental examinations for each member of the family further add to the serious problem of paying for the needed services to keep healthy.

Unfortunately, even regular medical and dental checkups cannot give absolute health security or prevent vulnerability to major acute or chronic illnesses. But next to keeping the body healthy via proper eating, sleeping, exercise, and other personal health measures, routine physical examinations are valuable preventive medicine.

Budgeting for Health. The big budgetary question is: How can the family pay for adequate medical care for all its members? It means little to the average family to say it should budget about 6 to 8 per cent of take-home pay for health. Rather, a budget for health should include (1) a reserve fund for routine health expenses and minor unexpected expenditures and (2) protection against major medical costs, as serious long-time illnesses can wreck any family budget.

To get the maximum return from your health dollars (1) follow the recommended good health practices, (2) know where and how to get the best professional medical help, and (3) protect the family with health insurance, especially against the cost of major and prolonged illness and disability.

General Physicians and Specialists. The right choice of a family physician is very important. He should be well trained in the science and art of medicine. The possession of a medical degree does not necessarily mean that a doctor is competent. It only means that he has completed the minimum requirements of a medical school.

A good general physician is trained to treat a wide variety of bodily illnesses and is likely to have specialization in general medicine. The American Academy of General Practice requires two years of hospital training as a prerequisite for membership and also requires that a member complete 150 hours of postgraduate work every three years for continuation of membership. Today, the internist is taking the place of the former general practitioner as the family doctor. He is likely to have a certificate from the American Board of Internal Medicine.

A specialist is a physician who has general medical training but, in addition, has concentrated on a special area of the body or a special branch of medical practice. Specialization requires two to five years of postgraduate training. Here are some specialists you may consult for treatment in their fields.

1. Internist—general field of diagnosis and treatment of physical diseases
2. Surgeon—operations for a variety of physical ailments

3. Obstetrician—medical care during pregnancy and birth
4. Pediatrician—medical care of children
5. Ophthalmologist—diseases of the eye
6. Otolaryngologist—ear, nose, and throat diseases
7. Dermatologist—skin diseases
8. Psychiatrist—diseases of the mind
9. Neurologist—diseases of brain, spinal cord, and nervous system

A well-trained doctor can be identified not only by his professional degrees and hospital associations and bedside manner, but also by his office procedure. A good physician, on the first examination of the patient, takes a detailed history of the family. He needs to know the nature of the patient's occupation and personal and family problems. He is then ready for a thorough examination, which includes a pelvic examination for women and a rectal examination for men and women. The urine is tested, and the hemoglobin concentration of the blood is determined, and there are other laboratory tests. The physician then discusses the findings and recommendations with the patient.

Hospitals and Hospital Services. Most patients enter whatever hospital their doctor recommends. It is usually a good recommendation. The ideal time to choose a hospital, however, is when you are searching for a good internist. There are three important questions to ask about a hospital. (1) Is the hospital accredited by the Joint Commission on Accreditation of Hospitals? (This is a minimum safeguard against substandard hospital care.) (2) Is it a "teaching hospital"? (A hospital is more likely to provide good medical care if the level of teaching doctors is high.) (3) Is it a voluntary, nonprofit community hospital or a privately owned, proprietary hospital? Many good doctors prefer the voluntary, nonprofit community hospital because it is dedicated to good medical care on a nonprofit basis.

The basic charge for hospital service is figured on day-to-day use of private, semiprivate, or ward accommodation and includes general nursing care and meals. Charges for the operating room, anesthesia, commonly used drugs and dressings, laboratory tests, X rays, physical therapy, special medicines, and other special services are added to the regular day-rate charge.

Hospital bills may be presented weekly, monthly, or at the time the patient leaves the hospital. When a patient enters the hospital, his credit is likely to be investigated if he does not have an insurance company credit card or a hospital service plan card such as Blue Cross. He may make advance payment or show other evidence of ability to pay. As a rule, credit is investigated after admission to the hospital.

Nursing Homes. Nursing homes or recovery wings of a hospital provide care for patients who are chronically ill or recovering from illness or injury. They do not require the more expensive costs of regular hospitalization. As the costs of regular hospital care have increased (more rapidly than the general cost of living), attention has been given to the construction and operation of nursing or general recovery homes. Your physician can be helpful in selecting a nursing home with good standards.

The Medically Needy. Community and tax-supported health services are available in most communities for medically needy individuals and families. Most of these people are able to finance ordinary expenditures. A variety of health services and clinics are available at little or no cost through local or state health departments, welfare departments, medical schools, large business organizations, and other sources, such as: mental hospitals, armed-forces facilities, child guidance clinics, dental clinics, treatment clinics, employees' health clinics, preventive public devices, eye clinics, prenatal clinics, vocational rehabilitation centers for physically handicapped persons, and privately supported organizations like the Red Cross and Junior League "Homemaker Services."

Solo Practitioners and Fee-for-service System. The "fee-for-service" system, long upheld by the medical fraternity, is under fire. Yet most physicians still cling to this system of payment.

Historically, the physician is presumed to adjust his fee according to his own notion of what the patient can afford. As a method of payment, say competent medical leaders, such fees may have been suited to the era of family doctors and home visits, but it is not satisfactory in these days of specialization, better hospital care, complicated surgery, necessary laboratory tests, and medical teamwork. Dr. James Howard Means, a former president of the American College of Physicians, made this observation:

Doctors by and large tend to work too long and too hard either for their own good or for that of their patients. The competitive nature of their work is largely responsible for this situation. The fee-for-service method of payment, in my opinion, is the chief source of trouble. Under that system of private practice, the more fees he collects the better off the doctor is. Naturally he works hard to get them and charges what the traffic will bear. . . .

Fee-for-service is scientifically indefensible, because it makes little if any provision for preventive medicine, and because it actually makes the patient reluctant to call the doctor even when really ill. For most laymen it makes medical expense unbudgetable. Organized medicine nevertheless clings to it and is willing to fight to the last ditch to retain it.[3]

A prime reason that physicians are able to command fees that often are inordinately high is the shortage of doctors in the United States. In 1900, there was one doctor for every 578 persons; by 1962, there was only one doctor for about 935 persons. Even these figures tend to overstate the

[3] *Doctors, People, and Government.* Boston: Little, Brown and Company, 1953.

actual number of physicians available to patients, because doctors doing research or otherwise not actively practicing medicine are included.

The shortage of physicians has become so acute, and the pressure for government action so great, that the American Medical Association has tried to ward off Federal funds for tuition and subsidization of medical students by developing its own plan which would create about 50 medical school scholarships annually. This modest proposal will not solve the problem of the shortage of doctors in our country.

Medical Group Practice. Medical leaders are of the opinion that group practice or teamwork is the rational approach to the tremendous growth of medical knowledge, the increase of medical specialties and new techniques that are far beyond the ability of a solo practitioner. In group practice, each doctor can turn to his colleagues for consultation. The information of specialists is shared.

Many doctors prefer group medicine. In addition to other great hospitals, such institutions as the Mayo Clinic in Rochester, Minnesota, the Lahey Clinic in Boston, the Ochsner Clinic in New Orleans, and such famous hospitals as Johns Hopkins in Baltimore and Massachusetts General in Boston are evidence that the medical profession has long recognized that group practice is the logical way of making better medical care widely available, of bringing new medical knowledge and techniques to medical practice.

A survey conducted by the American Medical Association shortly after World War II among more than 10,000 doctors leaving military service found that over two-thirds of them preferred to enter some form of group practice. An increasing proportion of physicians is in group practice. A 1956 survey showed that 35 per cent of 1945 medical school graduates was in group practice compared to only 12 per cent of the 1935 graduates.[4]

Many of these group plans provide for advance payment of fees, usually monthly, in return for the services of the medical team. Some groups offer comprehensive plans on a prepaid insurance plan.

In addition, many communities have private group-practice organizations in which several different types of specialists pool their talents but charge patients on the expensive fee-for-service basis. Many such groups provide high-quality medical care, but this kind of service is too costly for most American families.

High Cost of Drugs. No discussion of the cost of medical care would be complete without mention of the shocking revelations of administered prices in the drug industry made by the investigation of the Senate Subcommittee on Antitrust and Monopoly Legislation, which was headed by the late Senator Estes Kefauver.

The high cost of drugs is of immediate interest to everyone, especially

[4] Public Affairs Pamphlet, *Making Medical Care Better,* May, 1959, p. 5.

aged persons. Over a quarter of the $21.1 billion spent on medical care in the United States in 1961 went toward drugs and medical appliances. Nearly as much money was spent in 1961 for drugs as for doctors' services.[5]

The cost of prescriptions has gone up by about one-third in the last decade. Sales of "ethical" pharmaceuticals—those drugs sold only by prescription and advertised only to the medical profession—totaled roughly over $2 billion in 1962.

Pricing Practices of Drug Firms. The Kefauver inquiry turned up startling evidence on the pricing practices of the leading drug firms. Incredible price markups—some ranging up to 10,000 per cent—were brought to light. One example was a markup of 7,079 per cent by the Schering Corporation on estrogen hormone drugs, used in the treatment of female ailments. Merck and Company, another pharmaceutical concern, charged druggists $170 for 1,000 tablets of a steroid hormone drug that cost only $13.61 to produce. Carter Products sold Miltown, a widely used tranquilizer, for 5.1 cents per tablet, although it cost only $\frac{7}{10}$ of a cent to make. Many other examples were put into the record. (See *How to Get Safe Drugs and Cut Their Cost,* by David Cushman Coyle, Public Affairs Institute, 1960.)

The toll taken by these practices in terms of human suffering and deprivation can only be imagined. Testimony was given that many persons were confined to mental hospitals who could remain in the community if they were able to pay the high cost of certain tranquilizer drugs. Many aged sufferers of arthritis are unable to gain relief because the cost of cortisone derivatives is too high. Indications of dismay among older persons about staggering drug prices abound. The Kefauver committee received over 10,000 complaints within a few weeks about the cost of drugs. The American Association of Retired Persons and its affiliate, the National Retired Teachers Association, have set up a mail-order pharmacy to sell drugs to their 640,000 members at discounts. This is only one evidence of growing consumer resistance.

Among the facts brought to light by the subcommittee was that small drug firms often sell the same drugs as large firms at much lower prices. The price to the druggist of 100 five-milligram tablets of prednisone, a drug used for the relief of arthritis, for example, when sold by Schering, a major producer, was $17.90, a markup of 1,863 per cent. At the same time, Nysco Industries, a small firm on Long Island, New York, sold the identical product for $2.70.

It was also revealed that drugs identical to those sold in the United States under trade names sell in other countries for a small portion of the price. However, the major American producers, by expensive advertising campaigns directly to doctors, the use of "detail men" sent to

[5] Health Insurance Institute, *Source Book of Health Insurance Data,* 1962, p. 63.

persuade physicians to prescribe drugs by brand name, and other tactics, are usually able to corner a large portion of the market despite the wide price differentials.

Advertising campaigns do not always maintain the high level that drug manufacturers pretend they do. In a 1959 campaign, Pfizer Laboratories mailed to every physician in the country a release describing a new antibiotic that included the names and addresses of eight doctors using the drug. The *St. Louis Post-Dispatch*, in checking on the doctors listed, uncovered the fact that they did not exist.

Large Profits Defended by Drug Firms. Through monopolistic practices, the drug industry has been able to make large profits at the expense of ailing Americans. A study made by the Federal Trade Commission (FTC) revealed that the drug industry has a higher rate of return on its investment after taxes than any other industry. The return for the drug industry, in the figures given by the FTC, is 21.4 per cent, as compared to such other high-profit industries as automobiles at 15.5 per cent and steel at 12.4 per cent.

The drug industry has attempted to defend its pricing policies on the ground that it spends a great deal of money on research, some of which never leads to a salable product. However, a subcommittee study of 20 major drug firms demonstrated that research accounted for only 6.4 per cent of all revenue. The profit, after taxes, of these companies, on the other hand, is 13.1 per cent of revenue, and sales activities accounted for 24 per cent of revenue.

Testimony before the subcommittee also indicated that much of the "research" being done by large drug makers is directed at finding minor patentable variations of successful drugs already in existence. The major result of research by drug firms is thus a rapid obsolescence of drugs rather than genuine medical progress.

Perhaps the most depressing aspect of the revelations made in the pricing of drugs is the reaction of the industry to the investigation. Industry spokesmen expressed great resentment of the inquiry, as if a topic of such immediate and immense concern to so large a body of citizens was beyond the legitimate role of investigation by Congress. Rather than acknowledging the antisocial results of its policies and seeking to change them, it has stubbornly defended and attempted to justify its actions. Typical of this attitude is a statement made by Dr. Austin Smith, president of the Pharmaceutical Manufacturers Association, in a speech delivered on December 9, 1959, before representatives of leading drug companies: "I am sure that all of us feel the greatest compassion for elderly people who find it difficult to pay for medication. If the pharmaceutical industry is at fault here, it is because it has helped to create a pool of millions too old to work by prolonging their lives."

More Vigorous Enforcement of Drug Laws. Numerous measures to curb drug firms have been suggested. A more vigorous enforcement of existing antitrust and food and drug laws is clearly called for. The amendment that requires the Food and Drug Administration to pass on the efficacy and usefulness as well as the safety of new drugs will serve to discourage the endless introduction of nearly identical drugs under new brand names. A revision of the patent laws in regard to drugs may also be required.

Some critics of the existing practices believe that only actual price control of drugs by a Federal agency will bring the large drug makers into line. Other observers hope that public discussion and exposure will result in the same end. They feel that if the public can be made aware of the situation, and if doctors can be persuaded to prescribe drugs by generic rather than brand names, the large producers will find price-gouging practices difficult to continue.

Rising Costs of Medical Services. Medical care cost the public a record high of $21.1 billion in 1961, almost twice as much as in 1951. This was 6.2 per cent of the amount Americans spent for all their personal needs, as shown in the accompanying table, Personal Consumption Expenditures in the United States. The average American family spent about $406 for medical care in 1961 compared to about $205 in 1955.

PERSONAL CONSUMPTION EXPENDITURES IN THE UNITED STATES, 1961

Type of product	Personal consumption expenditures (billions of dollars)	Per cent of total
Food *	$ 70.9	21.0
Household operation	47.3	14.0
Transportation	40.1	11.8
Housing	43.9	13.0
Clothing, accessories, and jewelry	34.5	10.2
Recreation	20.6	6.1
Personal business	21.6	6.4
Medical care †	21.1	6.2
Alcoholic beverages	10.2	3.0
Tobacco	7.6	2.2
Personal care	5.8	1.7
Religious and welfare activities	5.0	1.5
Foreign travel and remittances	2.9	0.9
Death expenses	1.7	0.5
Total	$338.3	100.0

* Does not include meals outside the home.
† Includes expenses for health insurance.

The Consumer Price Index indicates that costs under the medical care category have shown greater increase than any other type of personal expense. From the base year 1947–1949 to April, 1963, medical care costs rose a staggering 67.8 per cent, as shown in the accompanying table, Increases in Medical Care and Other Major Groups in the Consumer Price Index. In April, 1963, these costs showed an increase of more than 23 per cent over the previous 5-year period.

INCREASES IN MEDICAL CARE AND OTHER MAJOR GROUPS
IN THE CONSUMER PRICE INDEX

Year	All medical care items	General practitioners' fees	Surgeons' fees	Dentists' fees	Optometric examination and eyeglasses	Hospital room rates	Prescriptions and drugs
1947	94.9	96.9	96.2	95.2	96.2	87.4	96.1
1948	100.9	100.6	101.0	100.3	100.2	102.1	101.2
1949	104.1	102.5	102.9	104.4	103.5	110.4	102.7
1950	106.0	104.0	104.5	106.9	104.5	114.6	103.9
1951	111.1	108.0	107.3	110.9	109.2	126.9	106.9
1952	117.2	113.0	111.5	113.3	110.5	139.5	107.9
1953	121.3	116.1	113.9	117.0	109.4	148.2	108.9
1954	125.2	119.9	115.2	120.9	108.0	156.8	110.1
1955	128.0	124.3	116.4	122.0	109.5	164.4	111.2
1956	132.6	128.4	118.2	124.4	111.2	173.3	113.7
1957	138.0	134.5	120.9	127.4	115.5	187.3	116.7
1958	144.4	139.3	122.7	131.4	116.7	198.0	120.7
1959	150.8	144.2	125.8	134.6	118.0	208.9	122.6
1960	156.2	147.8	129.2	137.3	121.0	223.3	122.8
1961	160.9	151.7	131.6	137.9	124.9	240.3	121.3

SOURCE: U.S. Department of Labor, Bureau of Labor Statistics, 1962.

Price index rates for hospital rooms showed the greatest rise—140 per cent from 1947 to 1961. General physicians' fees, with a 52 per cent increase, had the next highest rate of growth. The cost of dentists' fees ranked third with a rise of 38 per cent. Surgeons' fees rose 32 per cent, optometric examinations and eyeglasses showed a 25 per cent increase, while drugs and prescriptions rose 21 per cent.

Charges for medical services vary from city to city, as shown in the accompanying table, Average Cost of Specified Medical Services. The average cost to hospitals (per patient day) to treat a patient in 1961 was $34.98 a day, an increase of 109 per cent over 1951. During the same 10-year period, the average cost to the patient for a hospital stay in-

Average Cost of Specified Medical Services in 20 Large Cities in the United States (1961) *

| City | Hospital daily service charge | | | Physician services | | | | | | Dental services |
| | Men's pay ward | Semi-private room | Private room | Office visit | House visit | Obstetrical case | | Surgical fee | | Tooth filling † |
						Including Wasserman test	Excluding Wasserman test	Appendectomy	Tonsillectomy	
Atlanta	$13.38	$15.38	$18.25	$4.50	$ 7.83	$168.33	$	$166.67	$ 80.83	$4.83
Baltimore	19.12	20.50	24.25	4.41	6.00	......	180.45	145.83	66.67	4.20
Boston	26.62	29.88	33.50	4.85	6.22	200.83	.....	158.33	75.83	5.17
Chicago	21.40	24.40	28.90	5.00	8.83	......	160.00	195.83	92.50	4.50
Cincinnati	12.00	19.00	21.88	4.11	6.28	110.00	159.38	160.42	75.00	4.00
Cleveland ‡	30.10	33.33	38.92	4.78	7.72	155.00	167.86	168.75	73.33	5.17
Detroit	21.75	23.75	28.38	4.56	8.18	148.93	187.50	155.00	67.08	5.25
Houston	11.38	14.25	18.00	4.44	9.65	161.88	185.00	177.08	68.33	5.50
Kansas City	14.86	16.92	20.05	4.28	8.06	186.88	150.00	150.42	72.50	4.58
Los Angeles	26.10	29.00	34.20	6.25	11.11	.....	244.69	240.28	113.33	9.40
Minneapolis	23.15	25.35	28.55	4.22	7.56	130.42	.....	170.83	70.83	4.67
New York §	23.20	26.40	32.60	5.85	8.68	224.07	162.50	206.17	91.88	5.75
Philadelphia	16.00	20.38	24.75	4.28	6.36	187.50	200.83	145.88	75.00	5.17
Pittsburgh	17.80	22.30	26.20	4.50	6.69	......	167.50	145.83	69.17	5.00
Portland, Ore.	23.06	25.56	27.94	4.75	8.88	156.67	171.67	185.42	67.00	6.58
St. Louis	15.88	18.30	21.80	4.28	7.88	156.11	.....	154.17	75.00	5.33
San Francisco	27.88	30.62	34.88	6.17	9.53	......	211.59	217.17	96.67	8.71
Scranton	12.00	15.50	19.67	3.58	5.00	.....	117.50	170.83	59.17	4.00
Seattle	27.00	29.75	33.25	5.22	9.29	173.33	.....	177.08	72.00	6.67
Washington, D.C.	19.12	21.00	26.00	5.21	7.82	225.00	207.27	145.42	70.00	7.50

* Data for the last month available of year. The table is based on data collected primarily for calculation of Consumer Price Index not adjusted for comparability. Cost differences among cities may be due to variation in quality of service priced. Cost differences from time to time for a city may be due to changes in outlet sample, changes in service priced, and corrections.

† Amalgam, one service.

‡ Combination of quotations from hospitals using daily service charge and inclusive rate plans for men's ward, semiprivate and private room.

§ Combination of quotations from hospitals using daily service charge and inclusive rate plans for men's ward rooms only.

source: U.S. Department of Labor, Bureau of Labor Statistics.

creased 91 per cent to reach $265.85 in 1961. The average length of time a patient remained in the hospital decreased from 8.3 to 7.6 days between 1951 and 1961.

Hospital Bills Paid by Health Insurance. According to data released by the United States National Health Survey, 7 out of 10 patients discharged from short stays in hospitals in the United States have a part of their bills paid by health insurance. More than half of them reported that three-fourths or more of their hospital bills were paid by such policies.[6]

This study was based on data collected in household interviews from July, 1958 to June, 1960. The proportion of the bill paid by health insurance was determined by the respondent's own estimate of the part of the total hospital bill paid or expected to be paid by insurance.

Among the total discharged patients, the U.S. National Health Survey reported that 71 per cent of male patients and 66 per cent of female patients had some portion of hospital charges paid by health insurance. It was noted that when deliveries were excluded, the percentage for female patients was also 71 per cent.

For total discharged patients, some 56 per cent of male patients and 49 per cent of female patients had three-quarters or more of the hospital bill paid by health insurance. Of patients for whom health insurance paid some portion of the hospital bill, 79 per cent of the males and 73 per cent of the females had three-quarters or more of the hospital bill paid.

Among discharged patients below age 65, from 70 to almost 80 per cent had some portion of the hospital bill paid by health insurance. The exception was the age group 15 to 24. Some 66 per cent of males and 52 per cent of females in this particular age group had a portion of their bills paid by health insurance. When deliveries are excluded, 60 per cent of females in the 15 to 24 age bracket had part of their bills paid by health insurance.

Surgical Expenses Paid by Health Insurance. Health insurance also has an important role in paying for the cost of surgical care. Surveys conducted by the Health Information Foundation and the National Opinion Research Center of the University of Chicago, conducted during the summers of 1953 and 1958, determined how much families and individuals spent for surgical care and how much of these expenditures was covered by surgical benefits from health insurance.

Estimated nationwide gross expenditures for surgical care were $800 million during the 12-month period 1952–1953. Surgical expenditures reached $1.1 billion during 1957–1958. This accounted for a 37-per cent increase in surgical expenditures over this 5-year period.

[6] Conducted by the U.S. Department of Health, Education, and Welfare and reported in *Health Insurance Data, 1962,* by the Health Insurance Institute, New York, pp. 63–65.

The surveys further indicate that health insurance benefits for surgical care totaled $300 million during 1952–1953 and $500 million during 1957–1958, a 5-year rise of 67 per cent and almost twice the increase in surgical expenditures.

The progress of health insurance in providing more benefits toward the cost of surgical care is illustrated by the surveys. In 1952–1953, for example, 45 per cent of the families with surgical expenses who received benefits had 80 per cent or more of their surgical bills paid by health insurance. In the 1957–1958 survey, 53 per cent of families had this degree of reimbursement.

In addition, the median (the points at which half the families were above and half below the percentages given) increased from 75 per cent in 1952–1953 to 81 per cent in 1957–1958. Furthermore, 90 per cent of the families with surgical expenses who received benefits in 1957–1958 had 40 to 80 per cent or more of their bills paid by health insurance. This compares to only 79 per cent of families with this degree of reimbursement during 1952–1953.

The limitations of the above studies must be taken into consideration when estimating the proportion of medical care costs that is paid by health insurance. The most costly medical care—long stays in hospitals and nursing homes for chronic diseases—are not included in the above studies. If this data were included, the proportion of costs paid by health insurance would be considerably smaller than the data given above.

Types of Health Insurance. Health insurance is protection against hospital and medical costs or against loss of income resulting from illness or accident. Health insurance as a rule provides cash or service benefits. In a *cash benefit policy,* medical care costs are paid either to the insured or to the hospital or physician. In a *service benefit contract,* medical care services are provided according to the policy, and payment is made directly to the physician or hospital.

Health insurance protection may provide financial benefits for one or more of the following: hospitalization, surgery, general medical expenses, major medical costs including nursing care and prescribed drugs and medicines, and loss of income due to disability. You can buy these benefits separately or in combination.

There are now five types of health insurance policies: (1) hospitalization, (2) surgical, (3) general medical, (4) major medical expense, or comprehensive major medical expense, and (5) income protection. Trends indicate that medical expense plans will include more extensive coverage for the treatment of mental illness, fuller payments toward the cost of drugs and laboratory fees, additional provision for nonhospital and recovery care, and greater protection for the aged.

1. *Hospitalization insurance.* Hospital benefits can be provided to help meet part or all of hospital charges depending on the policy. A specific amount is allowed for each day in the hospital up to a limited number of days. A lump sum payment is made for laboratory, medicines, operating room, X ray, anesthesia, physical therapy, and other services relating to medical care and treatment of the patient while in the hospital.

2. *Surgical insurance.* Benefits for surgery provide payment according to a predetermined schedule of fees that states the maximum payment for each type of operation. Fees for office calls made before and after the operation may be included. Benefits vary with each policy.

3. *General medical insurance.* This protection provides for nonsurgical expenses, such as the physician's calls at home or hospital or the patient's visits to the physician's office. Benefits and coverage vary with the policy. The policy specifies the amount that is payable and limits the number of calls covered.

4. *Major medical expense insurance.* Benefits provide protection against the large costs of serious accident or prolonged illness. Insurance pays a share of the cost of treatment prescribed and performed by the physician, including hospital, surgical, and other medical treatment not covered by the basic (hospital, surgical, general medical) policies. Policies generally include a *deductible clause* varying from $50 to $500 and a *coinsurance provision,* which means that the insured pays a percentage of the total over and above the deductible portion of the expense. There is generally a maximum amount of benefit stated for each policy, which may range from $5,000 to $10,000.

Comprehensive major medical expense insurance is a combination plan that provides both basic and major medical protection. It generally has a coinsurance provision and a deductible clause (varying from $25 to $500), which may apply to some or all expenses depending on the individual policy. Like major medical expense insurance, the maximum benefits are usually quite high.

5. *Income protection insurance.* A loss-of-income policy (sometimes called accident and sickness indemnity or disability insurance) provides cash benefits according to the policy during the time the wage earner is out of work because of illness or accident. The type of policy issued determines (1) the length of waiting period before payment is made, (2) the amount of regular cash benefit, and (3) the length of time during which payments may be expected. Before buying such a policy, first consider how much protection you may already have through a company plan, a union plan, or workmen's compensation for accidents on the job.

Sources of Health Insurance. Health insurance benefits can be purchased through more than seven hundred commercial insurance companies, through more than seventy hospital and medical service plans like Blue Cross and Blue Shield, and through many independent group plans sponsored by consumer, community, fraternal, labor, industrial, or employer and employee groups. A brief summary follows:

1. *Insurance companies* issue policies for all types of health insurance on either an individual or group basis and pay benefits in cash.

Individual health insurance policies are purchased from a representative or agent and can be adapted to suit personal needs. A statement of health is usually all that is needed, although the insurance company may require a physical examination. There may be restrictions based on existing health conditions and age.

Group insurance may be available through a master policy issued to a business firm, labor union, professional or trade association, or other group of which you may be a member. Coverage varies with the group and the area. For the amount of protection provided, the cost of group coverage generally is lower than individual policies. If greater protection is desired, a group policy may be the base on which to build additional coverage through individual policies. Be sure to check the terms under which group coverage can be changed to an individual policy if you should leave the group.

2. *Hospital service plans* provide benefits for some or all of the costs of hospital services. These are available on an individual basis or through a group insurance plan. Benefits generally are available only in hospitals specified on the contract. Usually, payment is made directly to the hospital by the organization sponsoring the plan. If special accommodations or noncovered services are used, the patient is billed for the amount above the allowed coverage. Each contract states the coverage provided.

Blue Cross plans have contracts with local hospitals by which Blue Cross agrees to pay the hospital on behalf of its insured members for services specified, and the hospital in turn agrees to provide the services. Details of these plans vary with the areas or group being served. In some areas, the Blue Cross plan provides surgical benefits as well as hospital insurance.

Independent hospital service plans may be sponsored by industry, a trade union, a private group clinic, or other organized groups. Benefits differ with each plan.

3. *Medical benefit plans* provide benefits toward some or all of the costs of surgical and medical expenses. The amount of premium, benefits, and enrollment regulations vary according to the needs of the area and the scope of the plan. Medical benefit plans may be available on a group or on an individual basis. Benefits may be in the form of cash, service, or

a combination of cash and service depending on the plan. Each contract states the coverage provided.

Blue Shield plans are approved or sponsored by state or local medical societies. The provisions vary depending on the individual Blue Shield plan.

Independent medical benefit plans are sponsored by organized groups or by a group of physicians joined together in group practice. The plan may be affiliated with a health center, a clinic, or a group of clinics, or sometimes with a hospital where the patient receives service benefits from participating physicians.

Extent of Health Insurance Coverage. There has been ample indication of rapid growth in health insurance coverage, as shown in the accompanying table, Number of Primary Insureds and Dependents Protected by Health Insurance. By the end of 1961, 136,522,000 Americans were protected against some of the costs of hospital care. The number protected against some surgical costs reached 126,940,000. There were 94,209,000 persons who had regular medical protection (physicians' fees, laboratory expenses, and some X rays), and 34,138,000 were covered by major medical expense policies. A total of 43,055,000 wage earners were protected against a portion of loss of income during disability periods. Commercial insurance disability policies covered over 32 million of these wage earners.

From 1951 to 1961, the number of persons protected for hospital expense increased 60 per cent, the number under surgical expense protection increased 96 per cent, the number with regular medical expense insurance increased 240 per cent, those persons under major medical expense policies increased more than 300 per cent, and the number protected against loss of income showed a 13 per cent growth.

The American public continued to broaden its health insurance protection in 1961 to secure more adequate financing of health care costs. Of those persons insured against hospital expense, 93 per cent were also protected against surgical expense at the end of 1961, as compared to only 76 per cent ten years earlier. Those with hospital expense insurance and also regular medical expense protection at the end of 1961 were 69 per cent compared to only 32 per cent in 1951.

Distribution among Major Types of Insurers. The distribution of health protection among the major types of insurers is shown in three graphs on these pages. In 1961, insurance companies protected 55 per cent of those covered for hospital protection in contrast to 40 per cent by Blue Cross–Blue Shield organizations and 5 per cent by independent plans.

Insurance companies insured 57 per cent of those covered against surgical expenses in 1961, Blue Cross–Blue Shield organizations covered 37 per cent, and independent plans about 6 per cent.

NUMBER OF PRIMARY INSUREDS AND DEPENDENTS
PROTECTED BY HEALTH INSURANCE
in the United States, 1952–1961
(000 Omitted)

Type of protection	End of year	Number of people protected *		
		Total	Primary insureds	Dependents
Hospital expense	1952	90,965	40,114	50,851
	1953	97,303	43,166	54,137
	1954	101,493	44,053	57,440
	1955	107,662	46,826	60,836
	1956	115,949	49,253	66,696
	1957	121,432	51,158	70,274
	1958	123,038	51,593	71,445
	1959	127,896	53,569	74,327
	1960	131,962	55,283	76,679
	1961	136,522	56,801	79,721
Surgical expense	1952	72,459	31,856	40,603
	1953	80,982	35,372	45,610
	1954	85,890	36,462	49,428
	1955	91,927	39,023	52,904
	1956	101,325	41,937	59,388
	1957	108,931	44,603	64,328
	1958	111,435	45,078	66,357
	1959	116,944	47,487	69,457
	1960	121,045	49,306	71,739
	1961	126,940	51,169	75,771
Regular medical expense	1952	35,670	17,279	18,391
	1953	42,684	19,923	22,761
	1954	47,248	21,527	25,721
	1955	55,506	24,763	30,743
	1956	64,891	27,660	37,231
	1957	71,813	30,189	41,624
	1958	75,395	31,364	44,031
	1959	82,615	34,140	48,475
	1960	87,541	36,248	51,293
	1961	94,209	38,069	56,140
Major medical expense	1952	689	350	339
	1953	1,220	578	642
	1954	2,198	911	1,287
	1955	5,241	2,427	2,814
	1956	8,876	3,816	5,060
	1957	13,262	5,483	7,779
	1958	17,375	6,763	10,612
	1959	21,850	8,543	13,307
	1960	27,448	10,498	16,950
	1961	34,138	12,683	21,455

* Net total of people protected—eliminates duplication among persons protected by more than one kind of insuring organization or more than one insurance company policy providing the same type of coverage.

Courtesy of Health Insurance Council, Health Insurance Data, 1962, p. 22.

DISTRIBUTION OF HOSPITAL EXPENSE PROTECTION
In the United States, By Type of Insurer
1942, 1952, 1962

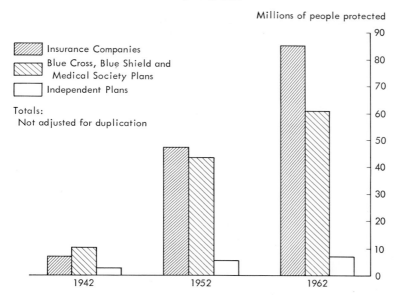

Millions of people protected

SOURCE: *Source Book of Health Insurance Data,* **Health Insurance Institute, New York,**
1963.

Blue Cross–Blue Shield insured about **47** per cent of those covered for
regular medical expenses, commercial insurance companies covered **45**
per cent, and independent organizations about **9** per cent.[7]

The rapid growth of major medical protection since **1952** is shown in
the graph, Growth in Primary and Dependent Coverage for Major
Medical Expense Protection. Over **34,138,000** persons were protected by
major medical plans by the end of **1961**, most of them under group plans.

Benefit Payments Raise Questions. A study of the accompanying chart,
Health Insurance Benefit Payments, indicates that the benefits paid by
all voluntary insuring organizations to insured persons showed nearly a
76 per cent increase from **1956** to **1961**. In **1961**, a new high of **$3.7**
billion was paid in hospital benefits; another **$1.8** billion in surgical-
medical benefits.

These are impressive growth figures for aggregate benefit payments.
But aggregate data do not tell the whole story. For example, how high is
the markup of insuring organizations? How much medical care insurance
can Americans afford as individuals or families? What per cent of income
is paid out in benefits by insuring companies?

[7] Will not add to 100 per cent due to rounding.

DISTRIBUTION OF SURGICAL EXPENSE PROTECTION
In the United States, by Type of Insurer
1942, 1952, 1962

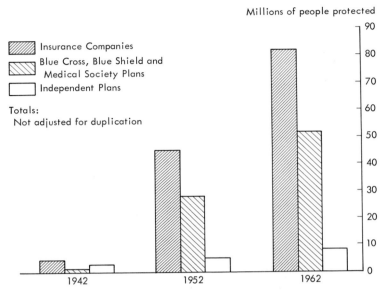

Millions of people protected

SOURCE: *Source Book of Health Insurance Data,* Health Insurance Institute, New York, 1963.

According to a Public Affairs Institute report,[8] the markup of commercial companies is "disturbingly high." Insurance companies selling to groups paid out 85 per cent in benefits, which was only 40.8 per cent of premium income on noncancelable individual cash-indemnity accident and health insurance. Blue Cross paid out 97 per cent of its income for benefits in 1958; Blue Shield paid under 90 per cent of its income in benefits in the same year. Insurance companies paid out about 85 per cent of income in benefits. In January, 1963, *Changing Times* reported that the operation expenses of all health insurance organizations ranged from 2 to over 12 per cent of their income.

Evaluation of Health Insurance Programs. Adequate medical care on the fee-for-service basis is too costly for most families. In the purchase of medical and hospital care, prepaid insurance is one practical solution for families of average income. Since sickness costs, including dental services, are unpredictable, unbudgetable, and often unbearable, prepaid insurance is a minimum essential for the physical and economic health of families with incomes under $15,000 a year.

[8] *Health Insurance for the Aged,* 1960, p. 30.

DISTRIBUTION OF REGULAR MEDICAL EXPENSE PROTECTION
In the United States, by Type of Insurer
1942, 1952, 1962

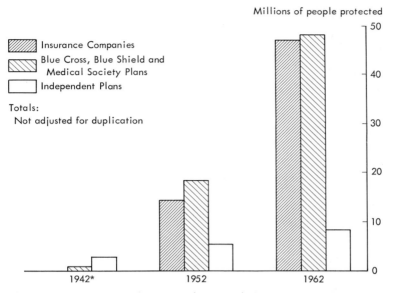

*Insurance companies did not cover regular medical expenses in 1942.

SOURCE: *Source Book of Health Insurance Data,* Health Insurance Institute, New York, 1963.

The choice of an insurance program that provides high-quality preventive diagnostic treatment and rehabilitation services by a personal physician at home, office, or hospital is one of the most urgent health problems that American families face. A realistic evaluation of the voluntary health insurance programs in the United States leaves no doubt that there are serious gaps, especially for the aged, for the unemployed, and only to a less degree for families with incomes under $10,000 a year.

Voluntary health insurance programs have many deficiencies. Blue Cross and commercial insurance plans do not encourage periodic examinations of well persons. In fact, diagnostic examinations even after illness are not generally provided for. Also, prepaid comprehensive service programs are only provided for about 3 per cent of those currently enrolled in prepaid health insurance plans. (Examples of such comprehensive plans are HIP of New York City, Group Health of Washington, D.C., and Kaiser-Permanente of the West Coast.) In effect, most health insurance plans emphasize hospital care for major illness, which discourages interest in preventive health examinations.

GROWTH IN PRIMARY AND DEPENDENT COVERAGE FOR
MAJOR MEDICAL EXPENSE PROTECTION
In the United States
1952-1962

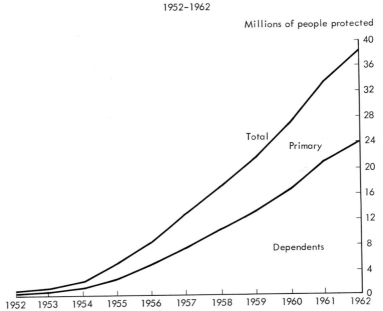

SOURCE: *Source Book of Health Insurance Data,* **Health Insurance Institute, New York,**
1963.

An unfortunate by-product of the increased use of hospital insurance
is the overutilization of hospital facilities. Patients insist on going to the
hospital, with little resistance from doctors, when their condition does
not warrant it. This is costly and increases the already high premium
rates of hospital insurance plans. There is also evidence of costly unnecessary surgery performed on insured patients because the basic fee
is assured. There is also mounting evidence that fees tend to increase
and surgery is more likely when paid for by insurance. In many insurance plans, the doctor takes the basic fee and bills the patient for an
extra fee.

A problem closely related to the unnecessary use of hospital facilities,
higher fees, and unnecessary surgery is the tendency to overstress curative care in the hospital at the expense of preventive care before the
possibility of hospitalization. There is need also to make more use of
less-costly outpatient care for convalescent patients rather than keeping
them in the hospital rooms that are needed for the acutely ill.

HEALTH INSURANCE BENEFIT PAYMENTS
In the United States, by Type of Insurer and by Type of Coverage
1957 and 1962

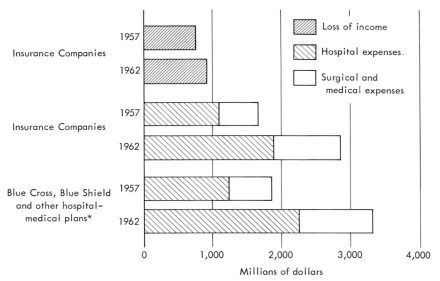

Millions of dollars

* Includes payments by independent and medical society–approved or–sponsored plans.

SOURCE: *Source Book of Health Insurance Data,* **Health Insurance Institute, New York, 1963.**

Delaware Combination Blue Cross–Blue Shield Plan.[9] The magazine *Changing Times* compared typical Blue Cross and Blue Shield plans with the Delaware combination Blue Cross–Blue Shield plan. This comparison study gives perspective on rates, doctors' fees, and coverage over age 65.

The Delaware Plan is a combined plan; that is, hospitalization and surgical plans are administered by one board. (Of 77 Blue Cross and 70 Blue Shield plans in the United States, only nine are thus combined.) The Delaware Plan is, like all plans, nonprofit and operated by a board of trustees on which are represented doctors, hospitals, employers, labor unions, and the public. Trustees receive no remuneration. Day-to-day operations are conducted by a professional, salaried administrator. Out of every dollar taken in by the Delaware Plan, 91 cents is paid out in benefits, 3 cents goes into a reserve, and 6 cents pays operation expenses. (Operation expenses nationally range from 2 to over 12 per cent.) Half a dozen different benefit programs are offered, both to groups and to those who belong to no group. (Almost every plan in the United States permits nongroup enrollment.) Enrollment is thrown open to nongroup applications for one week

[9] Courtesy of *Changing Times.*

twice a year with 30 days' advance notice. In this manner the plan hopes to bring in a representative group of people in good health as well as poor. If just anyone were allowed to join at any time he or she pleased, it is feared that many would join only when they felt a hospital stay or an operation coming on.

The standard Delaware program gives 70 days in the hospital in semiprivate room (in plans in other areas the coverage ranges from 21 to 365 days) plus 295 additional days at $10 a day. Monthly rates for this combined Blue Cross and Blue Shield benefit are:

	Individual	Husband and wife	Family
Group members	$4.84	$11.16	$12.28
Nongroup and all retired members	$6.49	$13.82	$15.07

(Nationally, the Blue Cross rate ranges from $1.58 to $10.03 for individuals and from $4.32 to $16.60 for families. Blue Shield rates go from $0.65 to $3.38 for individuals and from $2.15 to $9.31 for families.)

To the standard program may be added extended benefits, which resemble comprehensive or major medical coverage. These benefits cover part of most medical expenses for up to 730 consecutive days. Unless the value of services received during the 730 days exceeds $10,000, the member is eligible for additional services to bring the total value of care to $10,000. Extended benefits may be added to the standard program by group members for $1 a month for individuals, $2 for families. For nongroup members the additional monthly cost is $1.50 for individuals and $3 for families. (Nationally, 49 plans offer some kind of extended benefits.)

Once a person or family is enrolled in the Delaware Plan (and this is true of all other United States plans), coverage continues for life as long as payments are kept up and the member does not have duplicate coverage with another organization. Many members are in their 80's and one is 100. At age 65 or whenever separated from the group, a member begins paying at the nongroup rates.

65–National Senior Citizens Program. Since oldsters require, on the average, $2\frac{1}{2}$ to 3 times more care than younger people, they must be subsidized in some way. In the Delaware Plan, members pay what amounts to a 6 per cent premium during the years they are under 65 to take care of each other and themselves after they pass age 65.

The Delaware Plan does enroll people over 65 at a cost they can afford. (Nationally, around 70 Blue Cross and Blue Shield plans permit individual enrollment after age 65, and other plans have been preparing new programs for a first offering.) In Delaware, standard benefits for those enrolled over 65 consist of payments up to $16 a day toward hospital room and board for 30 days, plus $10 a day for another 30 days. Cost is $7.31 a month per person.

An extended benefit contract providing up to $16 a day for 180 days has been offered to those over 65. The cost is $10.33 per person per month.

Health requirements for applicants for these contracts consist of a waiting period for existing conditions. No one already in the hospital, of course, is accepted. In November, 1962, however, the Delaware Plan adopted what is known as the "65–National Senior Citizens Program" offered simultaneously by many state plans. There are no health requirements, and the plan provides up to $18 a day in the hospital and up to $4 a visit for visiting nurse service at home, the total period of payment not to exceed 70 days. Two days in a nursing home may be substituted for one day of hospital care.

Monthly cost of this program in Delaware is $12.75 for an individual, $24.50 for husband and wife. States offering this plan have been able to do so by cutting operating expenses to the bone and virtually eliminating reserves so far as such expenses and reserves would apply to this particular plan.

Blue Shield Payments for Operations. The surgical, or Blue Shield, part of the Delaware Plan is on an indemnity basis. This means that a fixed dollar amount is paid toward the cost of operation; for example, $100 toward an appendectomy, $75 toward a normal obstetrical delivery, and so on. This schedule of payments is included in all the Delaware programs described above. The actual fee charged for an operation may be more than the payments listed in the schedule.

Among plans nationally, this indemnity type is in the minority. In most Blue Shield plans, participating doctors accept the Blue Shield fee schedule as full payment for members with an annual income below a certain level.

Increased Use of Hospitals Raises Premiums. In 1946, the actual cost of keeping a person in the hospital averaged around $10 a day throughout the United States. In 1963, it was about $36. Estimates are that it will be around $52 by 1968, and it is already nearly $52 in California. Delaware is close to the national average at nearly $37. Doctors' fees are in a similar long-term upward trend.

One of the causes of this seemingly inexorable rise is the tendency for people, doctors as well as patients, to think of health insurance payments as "free" money furnished by "someone else." The less a person has to pay out-of-pocket toward his own hospital bill, the more he is likely to use the hospital's facilities.

There is evidence that this "disposition to use" is strongest where some agency such as the government is footing all or part of the bill. In Delaware, for example, and in the United States generally, each Blue Cross member spends an average of 1.1 days per year in the hospital. But in Saskatchewan, where the state actually subsidizes hospitalization to the extent of 60 per cent, leaving only 40 per cent to be paid by health insurance, utilization is almost twice as great at 1.9 days per member per year. This may mean that people in Saskatchewan spend too much time in the hospital or that people in the United States cannot spend as much time as they should. But whatever the explanation, one thing is sure: Increased use of hospital facilities, whether justified or unjustified, raises the premium cost to everyone covered by Blue Cross or any other kind of insurance.

Higher Fee Schedule for Service Contracts. There is a similar problem in relation to Blue Shield, especially under the "service contract." Under this arrangement, surgeons agree that for families making less than $7,500, let us say, they will accept as full payment the fees listed in the Blue Shield schedule, although such fees may be less than the going rate. Such an arrangement can help force premiums up, as the following example shows.

In some industrial states using the service contract, the dividing line used to be lower, for example $5,000. In other words, the surgeon agreed to accept the Blue Shield fee schedule as payment in full for patients with family incomes under $5,000. (For those with incomes above $5,000, the surgeon usually charged his regular fee, which might not be fully covered by the Blue Shield schedule of payment.)

But gradually the wage level rose so that more people were earning more than $5,000. The trade unions then appealed to Blue Shield to raise the ceiling to, say, $6,000. This proposal, in turn, was put up to the doctors, who naturally asked for a higher fee schedule. The higher fee schedule called for higher monthly rates for all members. The person who was hurt was the retired or fixed-salary person whose income had not gone up but whose cost of membership in Blue Shield was increased.

When the Patient Pays Part. One way to counteract these cost-increasing tendencies is for the insurance to pay most but not all of the hospital and surgical costs. The Delaware Plan, as now set up, pays on the average about 82 per cent of a member's total hospital cost. (Other plans pay for 66 to 100 per cent.) Mr. Maybee, the director of the Delaware Plan, is not concerned about the fact that members must pay on the average around 18 per cent of their hospital bill. He believes it demonstrates to members the real cost of hospital care and gives them an interest in keeping costs down and, in the long run, saves everybody money.

Similarly, he favors the indemnity plan for Blue Shield. In Delaware, the plan pays almost two-thirds to three-quarters of the fees commonly charged by surgeons. (Nationally, this percentage ranges from 64 to 85 per cent.)

The Delaware Plan is based on the belief that if the patient pays part of the fee he will take an interest in how much the surgeon charges. In actual practice, of course, some patients shy away from discussing fees with their doctors. Despite this tendency, Mr. Maybee still feels that the indemnity plan helps to keep costs down. He encourages Blue Shield members to discuss fees with their doctors.

Cost Analysis plus Members' Awareness of Costs. Another weapon employed by Mr. Maybee in the perpetual fight to keep costs reasonable is careful cost analysis, done with punched cards and computers. Here is an example of how such analysis can be used. Some years back, cost analysis showed that X-ray charges were using up 13 per cent of the Delaware Plan's total income. This seemed to be disproportionate. The plan allowed a flat $15 payment for X rays, and it was suspected that in some cases the high use of X ray stemmed from the activities of salesmen who were persuading doctors to buy small office X-ray machines that could be paid for out of the $15 fees.

At any rate, at Mr. Maybee's suggestion, the fee schedule was changed to 50 per cent of the actual cost with a limit of $25 to be paid per year. In other words, a patient could have up to $50 for X rays and be reimbursed for half. After this revision, the percentage of the plan's income paid out for X rays dropped from 13 to 7½ per cent.

Costs in Delaware are kept reasonable partly by alert administration and partly by members' awareness of the fact that in the long run, even on a group basis, they are paying for their own medical care. They realize that the money does not come from outer space.

Since Blue Shield and insurance company health care plans usually do not cover all medical care and surgery costs, the accompanying table, Private Practice Fees and Blue Shield Allowances, published in 1959 by the Medical Reference Bureau of Stanford, California, may be used as a guide in knowing what constitutes reasonable fees and Blue Shield allowances.

Commercial Insurance Medical Policies. There are about 839 insurance companies that have medical care plans on a profit basis. Many companies offer almost any kind of coverage from low-cost, inadequate plans to higher-cost comprehensive and major medical plans. Some are basic contracts designed to compete with the nonprofit Blue Cross contracts.

There are, however, three features in many commercial plans that distinguish them from most Blue Cross plans.

1. *Daily cash benefit.* The commercial company pays the subscriber in cash. Per day allowances, for example, may be from $10 to $20 or more. The higher the allowance, the higher the premium rate. If the allowance does not cover the daily room charge in the hospital, the subscriber pays the difference out-of-pocket. The commercial insurance company pays the policyholder; Blue Cross pays the hospital direct.

	Fees in private practice		Blue Shield allowances (range in various states)
	State A	State B	
Medical care, laboratory tests, X rays:			
First office visit	$ 8.00	$ 10.00	————
Subsequent office visits	$ 4.00	$ 5.00	————
First home visit	$ 8.00	$ 10.00	————
Subsequent home visits	$ 6.00	$ 8.00	————
First hospital visit	$ 5.00	$ 5.00	$ 3.00–$ 15.00
Subsequent hospital visits	$ 5.00	————	$ 3.00–$ 10.00
Night calls (11 P.M.–8 A.M.)	$ 10.00	$ 12.00	————
Consultation	$ 12.00	$ 20.00	$ 10.00–$ 15.00
Consultation with examination	$ 28.00	$ 25.00	$ 10.00–$ 35.00
Long stay with critically ill patient (per hour)	$ 16.00	$ 20.00	————
Hospital visit involving extraordinary procedures	$ 8.00	$ 20.00	$ 10.00–$ 35.00
Complete history and examination	$ 20.00	$ 25.00	————
ECG (electrocardiogram)	$ 15.00	$ 10.00	$ 12.50–$ 15.00
ECG with exercise test	$ 17.50	$ 15.00	$17.50
Basal metabolism test	$ 7.50	$ 6.00	$ 6.00–$ 10.00
Diabetes test	$ 2.00	————	$ 0.50–$ 1.50
Pregnancy test	$ 10.00	————	$ 5.00–$ 15.00
Blood cholesterol test	$ 5.00	$ 5.00	$ 4.00–$ 6.00
Red or white cell count	$ 1.50	————	$ 1.00–$ 2.00
"Pap" cervical smear	$ 15.00	$ 10.00	$ 5.00–$ 10.00
X ray, chest	$ 10.00	$ 10.00	$ 5.00–$ 15.00
X ray, upper gastrointestinal tract	$ 30.00	$ 25.00	$ 15.00–$ 35.00
Bone setting and casts:			
Compound fracture of collarbone	$ 85.00	$ 90.00	$ 35.00–$150.00
Simple fracture of upper leg	$150.00	$200.00	$ 70.00–$200.00
Ambulatory leg cast	$ 12.50	$ 15.00	$ 7.50–$ 45.00
Cast on forearm	$ 7.50	$ 5.00	$ 7.50–$ 18.00
Surgery:			
Tonsillectomy and adenoidectomy	$ 65.00	$ 75.00	$ 25.00–$ 75 00
Appendectomy	$150.00	$150.00	$ 75.00–$175.00
Removal of gall bladder	$237.50	$250.00	$125.00–$275.00
Surgery on inguinal hernias	$225.00	$225.00	$100.00–$200.00
Caesarean section delivery	$225.00	$250.00	$ 83.00–$250.00
Obstetrical delivery	$130.00	$150.00	$ 50.00–$150.00
Anesthesia:			
For first half hour or less	$ 17.50	$ 20.00	$ 5.00–$ 20.00
For second half hour	$ 7.50	$28.00 to $35.00	$ 5.00–$ 22.50
For each additional quarter hour	$ 5.00	$ 5.00	$ 4.50–$ 7.50

SOURCE: Reported in *Changing Times,* June, 1961.

2. *The deductible minimum.* Many companies, especially in major medical policies, begin payments only after a bill exceeds a substantial sum, such as $250 or $500. Some of the basic plans covering typical initial medical care costs have a small deductible minimum, such as $25 or $50. In fact, a small deductible discourages unnecessary hospitalization and cuts overhead expenses for the company. But it increases the policyholder's out-of-pocket cash cost.

3. *Coinsurance feature.* Commercial major medical policies, and some Blue Cross–Blue Shield plans provide that even after a medical care bill passes the deductible minimum, the company will pay only a portion, perhaps 75 per cent. This is called coinsurance, because the policyholder assumes part of the costs and the company a part. The accompanying chart shows A Major Medical Expense Plan.

A MAJOR MEDICAL EXPENSE PLAN

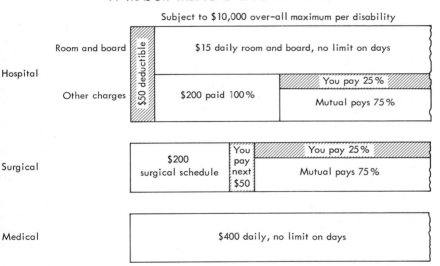

A few insurance companies have been experimenting with a *paid-up-at-65 policy,* which collects an extra premium through the years until age 65, and then provides some medical care for the remainder of life without further payments.

Another deviation in policy coverage is called *qualified impairment coverage,* which provides hospitalization at extra premium for persons with heart disease, diabetes, or other conditions that may make them ineligible for regular policies. In 1961, 67 companies wrote such contracts. In early 1962, 170 commercial companies were offering policies for "age 65 and over." This is a 57 per cent increase since 1958. The premium rates are considerably higher than for normal coverage.

Guides for a Commercial Insurance Policy: Some companies are reliable and experienced in the area of health insurance. But the same reliability does not characterize all of the 839 companies that have flashed into this field. Some have been cited by the Federal Trade Commission for inflated promises and misleading advertising; some have been called to account by state insurance commissioners.

1. *Know the company.* Before buying a policy, check with your state insurance commissioner, your Better Business Bureau, or buy through a local insurance agent you know and trust.

2. *Read the policy.* Study all the policy and ask questions. Weigh such features as daily cash benefit, deductible minimum, and coinsurance. If you can't get satisfactory answers to your questions, don't buy the policy.

3. *Compare both benefits and costs carefully.* It is easy for a company to advertise a policy offering "up to $10,000 protection," or "up to two years' hospital benefits." But the cost of these extreme offers has to be offset by excluding some other benefits.

4. *Do not take out two policies in the hope of reaping greater benefit.* The statistics of insurance and the legal qualifications for benefits make it unlikely that a subscriber will benefit from overlapping coverage in the long run. Furthermore, there are double premiums to pay. Some overlapping may be necessary if, for example, the employer's basic policy is too limited in coverage and a family needs additional coverage to plug the gaps. Most companies, and most nonprofit plans like Blue Cross–Blue Shield have major medical plans that fit their basic coverage plans.

5. *Cancellation by insurance companies.* When the National Opinion Research Center queried residents in New York State a few years ago, they learned that many of over 16,000 policies had been canceled by the companies while the policyholders were sick.

Independent Comprehensive Prepaid Medical Plans. There are outstanding clinics practicing group medicine on a fee-for-service basis, such as the Mayo Clinic, the Lahey Clinic, the Ochsner Clinic, and such famous hospital–medical school clinics as Johns Hopkins and Massachusetts General. None of these clinics and hospitals have prepaid insurance.

There were over eight hundred independent group plans issuing health insurance programs in 1961, according to the Health Insurance Institute. These plans were sponsored by industrial, community, private clinic, and college health groups. By the end of 1961, over 8 million persons were covered by prepaid independent comprehensive plans, out of a grand total of over 136 million persons covered by all health insurance plans in the United States. This figure compares favorably with the number of persons who have major medical coverage through commercial insurance companies (9,236,000 in 1961).

Most of the people who have prepaid comprehensive insurance plans belong to large group practice plans, such as Health Insurance Plan of Greater New York (HIP), with over 670,000 members; Kaiser Foundation Health Plans on the West Coast, with 675,000 members; the Ross-Loos Plan of the Los Angeles area, with 125,000 members; the Group Health Association of Washington, D.C., with 50,000 members; Group Health Insurance of New York City, with 575,000 members; Group Health Cooperative of Puget Sound, Seattle, with 51,000 members; and the Labor Health Institute of St. Louis, with 16,000 union members and their families. Most prepaid group plans, however, have fewer than five hundred subscribers.

Nearly a million members in about 18 independent plans are affiliated with the Cooperative Health Federation of America. Most of these plans provide for the use of Blue Cross for the hospitalization part of the benefits. Professional matters are controlled by medical men.

A study of the accompanying table, Comparison of Four Comprehensive Medical Care Plans, shows four different groups, comparing benefits, costs, membership, and exceptions. Generally, all four plans provide for prepaid comprehensive medical care at home, at the doctor's office, and at the group clinic or hospital. Regular medical examinations are not only provided for in the plans but all members are urged to have them. The emphasis is on preventive care. Statistics show that hospital confinement is less when preventive medicine is practiced.

Health Insurance Plan of Greater New York (HIP). By 1963, HIP had 670,000 members on its rolls. Groups of 10 or more may join if they represent 75 per cent of company employees and the employer agrees to pay half the premium cost.

Complete medical service is provided in office, hospital, or home. There are 1,000 doctors in 31 group practice centers in the Greater New York area and in an upstate clinic at Hudson, New York. Each group of physicians is an independent partnership owning and operating its own center. Total cost of these centers is estimated at more than $10 million.

The groups of doctors are paid a specified amount for each member each year regardless of the medical service provided. Few give full time to HIP subscribers, because the doctors carry on private practice as well. Although doctors' earnings vary with their group rules and the amount of practice, certified specialists in the busier centers are said to earn $25,000 to $30,000 annually.

HIP has no provision for hospital service and requires that subscribers belong to Blue Cross or have some other acceptable form of hospital insurance.

Certain standards, set up by a medical control board of 18 outstanding doctors, are required of all HIP groups. One requirement is that each group include family physicians, internists, or general practitioners, and

FOUR COMPREHENSIVE MEDICAL CARE PLANS—GROUP BENEFITS AND PREMIUMS [a]
July, 1963

	Health Insurance Plan of Greater New York (HIP)	Kaiser Foundation Health Plan (North California Region)	Labor Health Institute of St. Louis	Ross-Loos Medical Group of Los Angeles
Benefits [b]				
Hospital care: room and board	Covered under New York Blue Cross: 21 days per illness in semiprivate accommodations plus 180 days at half rate	111 days per illness per subscriber; 60 days, plus 51 at half rate for dependents	90 days at $15 per day plus half rate for additional 6 months	Covered by an associated insurance company: coverage in private or semiprivate accommodations plus other hospital charges, including blood and anesthesia to policy limit
Ancillary services [c]	Same as room and board	Full coverage for subscriber; generally half private rate for dependents	Included in room and board; operating room—$100 limit	Same as in room and board
Maternity	Same as above	Flat rates *	Included in above	Same as above
Surgical care	Covered	Covered *	Covered	Covered for subscriber; charges for dependents *
Normal delivery	Covered	Flat rates *	Covered	Same as above
General medical:				
Hospital	Covered	Covered	Covered	Same as above
Home	Covered	Covered *	Covered	Same as above
Office	Covered	Covered *	Covered	Same as above
Outpatient X ray and other diagnostic tests	Covered	Covered	Covered	Covered *

322

Home nursing	Visiting nurse service	Visiting nurse service	Visiting nurse service	No
Dental care	No	No	Covered except for orthodontics	No
Refractions [a]	Covered	Usual $1 office visit charge	Covered	Covered *
Prescribed drugs	No	Affiliated pharmacy discount	Affiliated pharmacy sells at discount	Affiliated pharmacies; no special discount
Ambulance	Covered from home to hospital	Covered	Covered	Covered up to $25
Other	Up to $350 for accidents or emergency illness when out of service area	Up to $500 per accident or emergency illness when out of service area	Dental plates and eyeglasses at nominal cost; chiropodists services; $25 emergency outpatient care; $100 special benefits	Amount varies with policy—accident or emergency in addition to hospitalization when out of service area
Preexisting conditions	No exclusions	Medical and surgical care ordered; hospital room and board, X-ray and diagnostic tests half private rate. Hospital drugs, etc., not covered	No exclusions	No exclusions
Mental illness	Not after diagnosis	No	Psychiatric diagnosis and 30-day hospitalization in a general hospital	Outpatient psychiatric care provided at clinic on fee basis
Other exclusions [e]	None	Now pay up to $300 for contagious diseases except polio and tuberculosis	Covers 14 days diagnostic care for TB, VD, drug and alcoholic diseases in a general hospital or up to $100 per year in a sanitarium	Contagious diseases when hospitalized

FOUR COMPREHENSIVE MEDICAL CARE PLANS—GROUP BENEFITS AND PREMIUMS [a] (continued)
July, 1963

	Health Insurance Plan of Greater New York (HIP)	Kaiser Foundation Health Plan (North California Region)	Labor Health Institute of St. Louis	Ross-Loos Medical Group of Los Angeles
Premiums monthly				
Single subscriber	$4.50 ($8.06 with Blue Cross)	$8.35	$12.80	*
Family	$13.50 ($22.52 with Blue Cross)	$19.85	$17.30	*
Special fees, etc.	$2, night calls	$1, all office visits; $3.50, home calls; $5, night calls. Maternity and obstetrics: $60, subscriber; $95, dependent after 10 months; $140, dependent before 10 months. Registration fee, $2; additional charge for subscriber over 65, $1.80; for dependent over 65, $1.20	Based on contributions by employers under "5 per cent of payroll plan"	Dependents fees: $1.25, office call; $5, home call; $0.75, ordinary lab tests; $20, minor operations; $25, major operations; $50, delivery; $1.25, refraction

[a] In case of multiple contracts, most prevalent group contract is cited.

[b] "Covered"—full coverage unless notation to the contrary.

[c] Unless noted, all plans exclude blood and blood plasma and administration of anesthesia.

[d] All plans exclude eyeglasses.

[e] Unless noted, all plans exclude VD; alcoholism; drug addiction; attempted suicide; cases covered by workmen's compensation, VA, or other public programs; cosmetic surgery; hospitalized care of TB; prosthetic appliances.

* Refers to special fees listed at end of table in each column.

specialists in each of the 12 basic fields. Continuing quality studies are conducted by HIP, assisted by the Commonwealth Fund, the Rockefeller Foundation, the United States Public Health Service, and the New York City Health Department.

Health education and preventive medicine made possible through HIP may have reduced the rate of hospital confinement of its members. The United States Public Health Service reported that the rate among 55,000 HIP subscribers in 1955 was 77.4 for each 1,000. In the case of a group of 53,000 New York residents, who, like HIP members, had Blue Cross hospital memberships but less comprehensive medical insurance, the hospital confinement rate was found to be 95.8 for each 1,000.

An infant death rate substantially lower than that of the city at large has been attributed to HIP emphasis on prenatal care and the fact that it has one qualified obstetrician for each 1,000 female patients of child-bearing age, whereas the over-all ratio for New York is one for 3,300.

In addition to undergoing close screening before being admitted to HIP practice, its doctors must meet performance standards. In a recent 10-year period, 27 were dropped from HIP practice for such reasons as refusal to make night calls or discrimination against HIP patients.

Five anti-HIP bills have been introduced in the New York State legislature at various times. HIP physicians have been ostracized by some hospitals and barred from one New York county medical society. But HIP continues to grow, operates in the black, and attracts new members.

Group Health Insurance of New York City. Also operating in New York City is Group Health Insurance (GHI), which is not to be confused with group practice, since it pays doctors on a fee-for-service basis and has no official concern with organization of medical facilities. The 575,000 members usually obtain their hospital insurance through Blue Cross.

In the 19 counties near metropolitan New York there are 11,000 participating doctors. Although nonparticipating doctors treat some members, they must accept the GHI fee schedule as full payment for their services. Under Blue Shield (The Doctors' Plan), the doctor is free to charge as much more than the schedule as he thinks the patient should pay, except when the scheduled fee must be accepted as full payment for families with incomes less than a specified amount.

The type of accommodation, instead of income, is the criterion for determining service benefits for hospital care. The plan has been under constant attack by organized medicine, including the New York State Medical Society, because of the fixed-fee feature and the fact that GHI control is divided equally between laymen and doctors.

In 1955, GHI started its "Family Doctor Plan," providing free choice of doctor for home and office visits, diagnostic examinations, and periodic checkups, with full service benefits. GHI paid out 79.2 per cent of its income for medical care costs of its subscribers in 1958, when its income was $9,700,000 and claims were $7,700,000. It had reserves of more than $2,000,000. GHI sponsored creation of the first community-wide dental insurance plan in the United States—Group Health Dental Insurance, Inc.

Kaiser Foundation Health Plan. The largest nonindustrial group started as an industrial plan for employees of the Henry J. Kaiser industrial and construction projects on the West Coast. Membership was opened to other persons in 1945, and industrial groups, cooperatives, and university faculties became affiliated. In 1963, more than 675,000 members were enrolled from Vancouver to Los Angeles and in Hawaii.

Although Kaiser employees represent only about 6 per cent of the present membership, Henry Kaiser, who successfully fought bitter attacks by organized medicine for years, retains control. Organized as a nonprofit corporation under California law, it is governed by a board of directors, which includes two members of the Kaiser family, two Kaiser lawyers, and four executives from Kaiser industries.

Hospital services are provided at 12 hospitals operated by Kaiser Foundation Hospitals, a separate nonprofit corporation. They are open to all. More than 40 outpatient medical centers are attended by nearly 700 physicians organized in autonomous medical partnerships.

Physicians connected with the Kaiser plan, with a few exceptions, have been barred from membership in local medical societies, and so from the American Medical Association, whose membership includes about 70 per cent of American doctors.

Ross-Loos Medical Group of Los Angeles. The Ross-Loos Medical Group in Los Angeles, controlled by participating doctors, is the largest of private group clinics among the nonindustrial plans. Its primary emphasis is on high-quality preventive medicine. It occupies a 13-story building in downtown Los Angeles as its principal clinic, with 12 branch offices and more than 130 full-time doctors.

In 1963, it had 125,000 members and cared for about 10,000 persons on a fee-for-service basis. About 38,000 members were in the nongroup classification.

When started in 1929, the purpose was to provide low-cost prepaid medical care for the 400 employees of the Los Angeles Water and Supply Department. The plan's organizers, Dr. Donald Ross and Dr. H. Clifford Loos, were promptly expelled from the Los Angeles County Medical Society. Later they were reinstated, after appeal to the American Medical Association's judicial council.

Group Health Association of Washington, D.C. Among the large urban cooperatives that have won determined legal battles waged against them by organized medicine is Group Health Association of Washington, D.C. It was organized in 1937, and after four years of litigation, the United

States Supreme Court upheld the verdict of two lower courts finding the American Medical Association and the Medical Society of the District of Columbia guilty of restraint of trade under the Sherman Antitrust Act.

A Labor-Management Health Center was built in a Washington suburb to accommodate the increasing enrollment in 1959 when the Transit Workers' Welfare Fund contracted with the Group Health Association to cover employees of transit systems and their families. The addition of about 10,000 persons brought the membership to 50,000.

Group Health Cooperative of Puget Sound. The Group Health Cooperative of Puget Sound, in Seattle, established in 1946, also won a hard battle with organized medicine. The Washington State Supreme Court ordered the King County Medical Society to cease its boycott of the cooperative. It has a membership of more than 51,000, operates an 83-bed hospital and is completing another $3,200,000 building with 172 beds, financed by bond sales to members. Most cooperatives enroll all persons in the community regardless of whether they are employed, and differences between the rates for group and nongroup members are slight.

Labor-Management Health and Welfare Funds. In 1913, the International Ladies Garment Workers Union established in New York the first union health center. When measures for compulsory health insurance administered by the Federal government were defeated after World War II, the AFL-CIO began active campaigns at the collective bargaining table to set up labor-management health and welfare funds.

In New York, the Union Health Center of the ILGWU employs 175 doctors, many part-time. Of 155,000 members in 1957, only one in four required medical attention. The pharmacy at the center supplies drugs at cost.

The United Mine Workers of America welfare and retirement fund, after years of opposition from organized medicine and overuse by miners and their families in the rural coal country, has greatly improved its operation. It has 10 hospitals in Kentucky, West Virginia, and Virginia.

In St. Louis, the Labor Health Institute, established by Teamsters' Local 688, covers about 16,000 persons—6,000 union members and their families, about 72 per cent of whom use the center annually. It employs 41 physicians and 14 dentists on a part-time basis.

Another St. Louis labor plan is that of the Medical Institute of Meat Cutters' Union, Local 88. It opened a $175,000 building with 22 physicians in 1958. Its services include dental care, and emphasis is placed on preventive medicine.

Quality Control and Choice in Prepaid Group Practice. Selecting a good doctor to begin with is no assurance that he will still be good ten years later. Medical science is developing so rapidly that a doctor has to take time off from serving his patients to keep abreast of his field. Some of the group plans provide for leaves of absence for study. This stimulates all doctors in the plan to improve their skills and knowledge. Prepaid plans, as a whole, have certain built-in quality controls: careful selection of doctors, the opportunity for doctors to keep up with medical developments, and the stimulation that comes from knowing that other good doctors are fellow workers.

Lack of freedom of choice by the doctor and the patient was a point that the AMA used for a long time in fighting prepaid group practice plans. But most group plans now provide for the patient's selection of the family doctor. This freedom of choice is important, but once a well-qualified doctor has been selected, it is also important that the family is able to pay him. Prepaid group practice plans with comprehensive benefits enable the average family to pay for the health services it needs on a budgeted basis.

These group plans are a voluntary way of helping many families meet their number-one financial problem—how to pay for modern medical care. No one has to join such a plan, and no one, having joined, has to remain in it. The existence of these plans broadens freedom of choice. This freedom will be restricted only if people are denied the opportunity to choose either an individual doctor or a group of doctors.

After a long and careful look at prepaid group practice plans that the American Medical Association opposed (107 plans were studied over a 3½-year period), an AMA commission reported in 1959 that these plans were doing their job well and had improved the quality and increased the quantity of medical care for moderate-income families.[10]

Dental Specialists. The high prevalence of dental neglect as a habit of the American people and the high cost of dental care for most families is a sad commentary on health and welfare in the United States. Perhaps the early beginnings of dental group care will eventually develop into more comprehensive plans at a reasonable cost to most American families, as they realize the great need for preventive dental care.

The general dentist is trained to provide dental care, including diagnostic, preventive, corrective, and reparative services. Dental specialists are trained in specific areas of dental care, such as:

1. Oral pathologist—diagnosis of mouth tissues, tumors, injuries
2. Oral surgeon—disease and injuries of the jaw and extraction of teeth
3. Orthodontist—irregularities of position of teeth
4. Pedodontist—dental care of children
5. Periodontist—diseases affecting the structure surrounding the teeth
6. Prosthodontist—dental appliances such as bridges and dentures

[10] Reported in *Public Affairs Pamphlet,* no. 283, 1959, p. 16.

Approaches to Dental Insurance. Dental care expenditures in 1956 accounted for 15 to 20 per cent of the total health care dollar.[11] The Health Insurance Institute reduced this figure to about 10 per cent of the medical care dollar in 1961. Dentists' fees have increased 30 per cent in the last decade. Americans pay about $1 billion annually for dental care.

Unfortunately, to save the cost, nearly 40 per cent of Americans receive no dental care during the course of a year, according to Dr. Aurelia Toyer in her report to the New York State Joint Legislative Committee on Health Plans. A Federal government study found that only 23 per cent of the families with incomes between $2,000 and $3,500 seek dental care, and only 45 per cent between $4,500 and $7,000 get adequate dental care. In addition, about 18 per cent of the population has never been to a dentist.

In general, there are three approaches to prepaid dental care: (1) indemnification against tooth problems by commercial insurance companies; (2) industry or union provision for dental care, either in dental clinics operated solely for workers or under contracts with dentists in group practice; and (3) dental service corporations set up to contract for the purchase of tooth care for groups.

Dental Insurance Plans. Two nonprofit companies—Group Health Dental Insurance, Inc., and Dental Insurance Plan, Inc.—have been operating quite successfully for some time. Groups of 25 and up subscribe through their places of employment or through unions. Members pay around $75 a year per family with children or $20 a year for an individual for basic tooth repair and preventive work, and they may use any of a large number of participating dentists.

For additional premiums, the companies will also pay for backlog work —the accumulated dental problems that most subscribers have when they enter the plan, and for such things as dentures.

Several commercial insurance companies have begun to sell dental policies, but many offer extremely limited benefits, and some are hardly worth even the low premiums.

A different approach is being taken by Continental Casualty Company, in a program for the employees of Dentists' Supply Company, in York, Pennsylvania. The program, which costs the company a half-million dollars yearly, covers 1,000 employees and 1,400 dependents. Comprehensive even to the point of including teeth straightening, it has a deductible feature, with the company paying 80 per cent and the patient 20 per cent of reasonable dental expenses above the deductible amount.

Union and Company Dental Insurance Plans. Union and company plans continue to increase in number in many industries. Some operate their

[11] O. W. Anderson and J. J. Feldman, *Family Medical Costs and Voluntary Health Insurance*. New York: McGraw-Hill Book Company, 1956.

own dental clinics (usually along with medical facilities). Others contract with specific dentists, often those in a large group practice setup, to have work done for members.

The International Longshoremen's and Warehousemen's Union–Pacific Maritime Association, which provides dental care for 13,400 children, uses three methods in various West Coast ports—insurance company indemnification, group practice clinics, and dental society service programs. Cost to the fund runs from $75 to $100 for first-year care down to $55 in later years.

Dental Service Corporations. The newest trend is for dentists, who are worried about unprofessional third parties coming between dentist and patient, to set up nonprofit corporations solely for the purpose of providing prepaid dental care to group purchasers. Similar to Blue Cross, the plans have the advantage of providing professional control of the quality of work done, of giving the patient unlimited choice in selecting a dentist, and of being able to return a slightly higher percentage of total premiums toward the care of patients.

In 1963, only four such corporations were actually operating—in California, Oregon, Washington state, and Rhode Island. Dentists in five other states (Arkansas, Colorado, Michigan, Missouri, and Pennsylvania) and in the District of Columbia had formed corporations but were not yet in business. Several states were snagged by the need for enabling legislation to make the corporations legal, while most of the others were still studying the question. (Meanwhile, some Blue Cross plans are expanding their dental benefits to a limited degree. And in Washington, D.C., a long-established consumer cooperative for prepayment of medical care has included dental work for an extra fee since 1956.)

The *New York Times* on June 7, 1963, reported an agreement to be signed between the Dental Society of the State of New York and Blue Cross for a new dental insurance plan in New York City and neighboring counties. More than 10,000 of the 12,500 practicing dentists in the state signed contracts to participate.

Disability Insurance. We have now studied the place and need for prepaid health insurance for medical care of individuals and families. These medical care plans provide the means to pay for most medical and hospital bills. But this coverage, under even the best of the medical care plans, is not enough for most Americans. Disability insurance is needed— protection against loss of income resulting from illness or accident. This kind of insurance pays cash benefits when the wage earner is unable to work.

Developed more than a half century ago, disability insurance was held by almost 50 million persons in early 1962. Over 226 insurance companies were actively writing this insurance in early 1962, compared to 205 companies in 1953. In 1961, these companies paid out a total of $855 million in benefit payments, excluding accidental death and dismemberment benefits. This sum was about 13 per cent of the over-all health insurance benefits.

Employees lost a total of 250.3 million workdays during 1960, according to data released by the United States National Health Survey.[12] On an average day during the year 1,050,000 workers were absent. This survey also revealed that the average worker had 16.2 days of restricted activity during the year due to some form of acute disability. Each person averaged 6 days of bed disability during this same period.

Many wage earners have made better provision against death—through life insurance—than against partial or total disablement during their earning period. The latter is the worst economically. The need for this kind of protection is apparent when the weekly or monthly paycheck stops because of disability. This insurance is designed to pinch-hit for the regular pay check.

How much does it pay? Ideally, disability income should fully replace regular income. Insurance companies learned, however, that this proved too tempting to workers who faked illness or planned accidents. So the policy now is to limit disability payments to about three-fourths of regular pay. Most wage earners carry only $100 to $150 per month. If income permits, the wage earner should take the maximum permitted by the insurance company.

Premiums vary greatly, as do provisions in the contract, and there are escape clauses, but some companies sell a $300 monthly benefit for total disability for about $190 annually. If the total disability occurs after age 60, only $150 per month is paid for life.

How soon does it pay? There is usually a 30-day waiting period before disability payments begin. Office sick leave can tide over a wage earner for up to two weeks. A month or more of absence may be taken care of through money due from the employing company's sickness-with-pay leave, the state disability law, personal savings, and union or fraternal organization funds.

How long does it pay? This is the heart of disability insurance, which most wage earners fail to consider. A wage earner should be self-insured for as long a period as possible to cut down the cost of the insurance and to improve the coverage. Perhaps the most coverage today is for $8\frac{1}{3}$ years. If the premium rate is too high, it is a good idea to settle for a longer waiting period before payments begin—60 days instead of 30 days.

Disability insurance is expensive and circumscribed by restrictions, but absolutely necessary. Almost half the number of disabled persons are disabled for six months or more. It is difficult to find the ideal contract; some

[12] Conducted by the U.S. Department of Health, Education, and Welfare, 1960.

are brazenly dishonest. To pick the best, ask many questions in addition to those above: How well does the insurance company pay? Is the contract cancelable by the company? Is there a waiver of premium? Is there full coverage for home confinement?

Limitations of Disability Insurance Contracts. It is important to examine a policy before buying and to know what to look for. For example, the most common limitations of disability contracts, according to some authorities, are these:

1. Certain kinds of disabilities are excluded. It is wise to read the exceptions or limitations that usually appear in small print. A remark credited to the radio and television artists Amos and Andy is apropos here. Oftentimes, insurance contracts "give it to you in big type and take it away in small type."

2. Too small disability payments or payments over a short period may be of little help.

3. A misstatement in the application form may take away certain kinds of protection.

4. Some contracts will pay little or nothing if confinement is not strictly within the home.

5. In many cases, the protection is removed in the event that the injured person can follow some other vocation.

6. Some contracts are cancelable by the company. This is sometimes the case in commercial group plans as well as in individual insurance.

7. There are contracts that limit payments to 12 months on any single claim or a total of 12 months on all claims. Obviously, such a contract does not give the kind of protection needed most.

8. Premium waiver may not begin on the first day of disability. In some cases, it begins after 6 months of permanent disability.

9. Sometimes, accidental injuries are inadequately covered by commercial contracts. The total amount to be paid may be limited in some manner.

These limitations should not be interpreted to mean that disability insurance is so inadequate that a family ought not to invest in this kind of security. On the contrary, every family needs protection against long-term disability, when income is likely to be cut off entirely.

Disability insurance is still the most certain method of family protection in the event of permanent disability. The problem, then, is to select wisely the policy that will protect the family best in terms of what the family income can afford.

Budgeting for Medical Bills. Medical costs are usually unpredictable, but health insurance makes these costs more bearable. In 1961, about 6.2 per cent of family income was used for medical care. This amounts to about $116 per capita, or about $406 for an average family. This statistic, which includes persons with no medical bill as well as those with many bills, cannot be used as a clear-cut guide on how a family should budget for health care, but it may be used as a guide in predicting possible expense.

If a family has extra heavy medical costs, the annual bills may be closer to $1,000. As a rough forecast, the Health Information Foundation suggests these figures:

Age	Annual bill
0–5	$ 48
6–17	49
18–34	98
35–54	108
55–64	129
65 and over	177

In the young family, each child runs up an average bill of nearly $300 just to be born. (Hospital bill, $130; doctor's fee, $120; drugs and medicines, $19; Laboratory fee, $3; other expenses, $10; total costs, about $282.) The payments from health insurance, perhaps $190, will take care of about 70 per cent of the bills. In this case, the family's additional cash payment would be about $85.

The U.S. Department of Labor has estimated the medical care of a family consisting of parents, a son age 13, a daughter age 8, in 20 different cities, to be $321 a year, or between 6 and 7 per cent of the family budget. This, according to the department, would provide for 17 visits to physicians, 3 tooth fillings, a couple of extractions, eye care, nonprescription medicines, and 10 prescriptions.

But one-third of American families pay a lot more for medical care than the average family; in fact, they pay three-fourths of all private bills for medical care. These were large families on the whole, according to the Health Information Foundation, with higher incomes and more formal education. They had better health insurance coverage than the average family. Of these families, 47 per cent spent between $300 and $499, 38 per cent spent $500 to $999, and the remaining 15 per cent spent $1,000 and over annually.

Studying these facts about family medical bills shows what factors to consider when estimating a medical care budget.

1. Number, age, and sex of family members
2. Family income
3. Cost of medical care in the community
4. Tax-supported health services available
5. Health insurance coverage already provided
6. Individual health problems in the family
7. Health standards wanted for the family

With these things in mind, fix a realistic monthly allowance for family health needs. It might be from 6 to 10 per cent of the family income or around $100 to $200 per person for a year. A reserve fund should be included in the budget. At the end of each year, evaluate the plan, make necessary changes for the next year, and let unused money accumulate for future emergencies. Even after a realistic health care budget is worked out, it is still, in part, unpredictable.

Setting up a Plan for Medical Expenses and Loss of Income. This is not such a difficult job if you keep in mind the basic principles. *First,* budget for the usual or routine expenses. Concentrate your insurance on the big, unpredictable costs. *Second,* buy a group policy, if possible. *Third,* get a blanket coverage. Avoid limited policies covering named diseases or accidents. *Fourth,* plan your basic protection around hospital and surgical costs. *Fifth,* select major medical insurance with deductible and coinsurance features. *Finally,* add income disability insurance with emphasis on long-term total disability.

If you can do all this, you can stop worrying about the blockbusters that may hit your family and begin worrying about the premiums—by far the lesser of two worries.

QUESTIONS FOR DISCUSSION

1. What are some of the simple health rules that most medical authorities would agree are good?

2. How does sane living lessen illness?

3. How do the claims of advertising copy for popular patent medicines square with scientific analysis?

4. What should you find out about a doctor before engaging his services?

5. Is medical care so expensive that it cannot be made available to all the people?

6. To what extent is health a national problem? A state problem? A local problem? A personal or family problem?

7. How would you decide whether to join a nonprofit voluntary prepaid health insurance group or buy a health policy from a commercial company?

8. Why are there so few cooperative health insurance plans in this country?

9. If you were selecting health insurance protection from a commercial company, what provisions in the contract would you consider important? Does your opinion agree with that of authorities?

10. What important questions must be answered when examining your own present and future health protection needs?

11. Why is it hard to find a good disability income insurance contract?

ACTIVITY PROBLEMS

1. Compare the claims made in the advertising of well-known patent medicines with scientific analyses.

2. Ask two or three doctors how they would go about selecting a dentist, a general physician, a psychiatrist, and an oculist. With this information in mind,

make a list of the questions you would want to ask a doctor before engaging his services.

3. Study a disability insurance contract, according to the following questions.

a. When does the policy go into force?

b. What are the benefits for loss of income?

c. Are there any other benefits, such as payment of hospital bills and so on?

d. Are diagnostic services included?

e. Under what conditions are benefit payments made? How much? For how long?

f. Are the first 5 to 10 days excluded in benefit payments?

g. Are the benefits reduced if you are not in continuous confinement?

h. Are both partial and total disability provided for?

i. Does the policy cover accidental death?

j. Are benefits reduced at certain ages?

k. Does the policy cover traveling outside the boundaries of the United States? Traveling in private or chartered planes?

l. Are there occupational and other restrictions and exceptions?

4. Investigate the medical care available for honorably discharged veterans. Consult the nearest Veterans Administration office or hospital or the local Red Cross chapter.

5. Compare a Blue Cross hospital insurance plan with similar protection offered by a commercial insurance company. How do premium rates and protection compare?

6. During the first 2 years of married life, a young couple recorded the following health and medical expenses.

Dental services	$164.00
Baby's birth:	
Hospital (six days)	61.00
Delivery	150.00
Anesthesiologist	25.00
Family doctor—home and office calls	47.00
Oculist:	
Examination	12.00
Glasses	22.50
Minor operation:	
Hospital (one day)	9.50
Doctor	35.00
Anesthesiologist	10.00
Prescriptions	32.00
Total	$568.00

They did not have hospital or medical insurance. Assuming that they had an annual family income of about $6,500 and lived in a large city, how could this family reduce these costs and still have as good or better health and medical service? Be specific. How much money could this family have saved during the 2-year period by using your suggestions?

SUGGESTED READINGS

American Journal of Public Health. "The 1959 Survey of Group Health," May, 1961.

Angel, Frank J. *Health Insurance.* New York: The Ronald Press Company, 1963.

California Medicine. "Solo Practice: Advantages and Disadvantages," October, 1960.

Changing Times. "Your Health, Your Doctor and Your Pocketbook," June, 1961; "New Dental Insurance, Too," June, 1957; "Blue Cross and Blue Shield—the Delaware Plan," January, 1963; "Medical Care Today—the Good and the Bad," "Budgeting for Medical Bills," "Be Smart about Health Insurance," "Finding a Family Doctor," June, 1961; "Health Insurance, in Force for Life," August, 1962.

Consumer Reports. "3 Questions to Ask before Choosing a Hospital," February, 1961, p. 84.

Council on Consumer Information. *Consumers Can Protect Their Own Health,* 1960; *How to Choose Your Doctor, Hospital, Health Insurance,* 1961.

Davis, Michael M. *Medical Care for Tomorrow.* New York: Harper & Row, Publishers, Incorporated, 1955.

Eilers, Robert. *Regulation of Blue Cross and Blue Shield Plans.* Homewood, Ill.: Richard D. Irwin, Inc., 1963.

Follman, J. F. *Medical Care and Health Insurance.* Homewood, Ill.: Richard D. Irwin, Inc., 1963.

Group Health Association of America. *Proceedings of the Annual Group Health Institute,* Washington, D.C. Also, *Annual Report.*

Group Health Cooperative of Puget Sound. *Annual Report,* Seattle, Wash.

Harris, Seymour E. *The Economics of American Medicine.* New York: The Macmillan Company, 1963.

Health Information Foundation. *Comprehensive Insurance for Physicians' Services,* New York, June, 1960; *The Level of Dental Health,* September, 1961.

Health Insurance Council. *The Extent of Voluntary Health Insurance,* New York, 1962.

Health Insurance Institute. *Source Book of Health Insurance Data, New York,* 1961, 1962; *Group Health Insurance Policies Issued in 1961; Report on Guaranteed Life Health Insurance for Persons over 65, for Persons under 65,* 1962.

Household Finance Corporation. *Money Management: Your Health and Recreation Dollar,* Chicago, 1961.

Journal of American Medical Association. "The Growth and Development of Medical Group Practice," Sept. 16, 1961.

Learner, Monroe, and Anderson, Odin W. *Health Progress in the United States.* Chicago: The University of Chicago Press, 1963.

Levy, Michael H. *Your Insurance and How to Profit by It.* New York: Harcourt, Brace & World, Inc., 1955.

New England Journal of Medicine. "The Next Ten Years in Medicine," Jan. 18, 1962.

Parents' Magazine. "How to Stretch Your Medical Dollar," October, 1961.

Pelton, Walter J., and Rowan, John C. *Digest of Prepaid Dental Care Plans.* Washington, D.C.: Government Printing Office, 1960.

Prepayment for Medical and Dental Care in New York, A report by the New York State Insurance Department, New York, 1962.

The Progressive. "The Medical Care Dollar," August, 1961.

Public Affairs Institute. *Health Insurance for the Aged,* Washington, D.C., 1960.

Public Affairs Pamphlet. *A Consumer's Guide to Health Insurance Plans,* 1962.

St. Louis Labor Health Institute. *Annual Report.*

Somers, Herman Miles, and Ramsay, Anne R. *Doctors, Patients, and Health Insurance.* Washington, D.C.: The Brookings Institution, 1961.

Surgeon General's Report on Smoking and Health. Health Service Publication no. 1103, Washington, D.C.: Government Printing Office, 1963.

U.S. Department of Health, Education, and Welfare, Social Security Administration. *Independent Health Insurance Plans, a List by States,* June, 1962.

The Wall Street Journal. "Dental Insurance," Jan. 13, 1960, p. 1; "AMA About Face," June 11, 1959, p. 1; "Health Insurance Plan for Aged in New York," May 10, 1963.

Weeks, H. Ashley. *Family Spending Patterns and Health Care.* Cambridge, Mass.: Harvard University Press, 1961.

12

SOCIAL SECURITY, LIFE INSURANCE, AND ANNUITIES

Every year in the United States, 200,000 more men die than women, and the ratio is increasing. In every adult age group, women already outnumber men. One reason is that medical science seems to have benefited women more than men. Deaths connected with childbearing, which used to help balance the hazards of being a man, have been reduced to near zero. More women are staying alive.

What about the men? Twenty per cent more men than women die of cancer. While this disease kills more women in their middle years, it strikes the men when they are under 30 and over 55. Still more important is heart disease, which is responsible for 40 per cent of all deaths. Between ages 40 and 75, nearly twice as many men as women die of heart disease.

Accidents account for more than three-fourths of the extra male deaths between ages 10 and 35. Between ages 20 and 24, more than six times as many men as women die in accidents—largely because of automobile accidents.

By 1975, at the present death rate, women will outnumber men in the United States by 3,600,000. Life insurance agents say that wives, generally, object to the purchase of life insurance because they do not want to think about the possible death of their husbands. But no widow objects to the life insurance payment when such death occurs. In a way, it is not life insurance that costs money; it is the things that the widow and children will need, and life insurance can provide that cost money.

But, some say, there is little or no need for personal life insurance because of pension plans, employee group life insurance, and social security. It is true that most families have one or more of these protections in the event of premature death of the major breadwinner. But the fact remains that these protections are only minimal.

Employee group insurance seldom reaches $5,000 in protection, and then only while the breadwinner is employed by the company. Retirement or a change in employment usually ends employee group insurance protection.

Present social security benefits will not meet the minimum needs of the average retired couple, and the cash grant of $255 for burial is hardly enough for this purpose. Social security is not enough insurance against death unless the covered breadwinner dies before the children are 18 years of age. The widow under 62 can then receive a maximum of $190.60 for herself and one child, and a maximum of $254 a month for two or more children under 18 years of age. When the children reach their eighteenth birthday, all payments in their behalf cease.

Social security, however, occupies a vital part in family financial planning. Modern insurance programming builds on a social security base and adds to meet needs according to the financial capacity of a family.

Defense against the Threat of Insecurity. Elmo Roper, a leading authority in measuring public opinion, concluded on the basis of twelve years of opinion polling that what the average American wants most in life is a sense of security.

No two families can successfully work out the same security program. But they can begin by noting the major hazards to security, and then find the best means for protection against them. The major hazards to financial security and the most common defenses employed are these.[1]

Unemployment: Unemployment compensation; a savings fund for contingencies

Illness: Health and medical insurance; a savings fund for emergencies

Accident: Accident insurance; in special cases, state workmen's compensation; a savings fund

Old age: Social security old-age insurance; retirement pensions; a savings fund; annuities

Premature death: Life insurance; survivors insurance under the Social Security Act

The particular needs of each family will be apparent to its members. For example, a government employee protected by civil service may not need unemployment insurance. A carpenter, on the other hand, is constantly faced with seasonal unemployment. Most professional people, such as teachers and doctors, usually have continuous work and should build their financial defenses around other insecurities than unemployment.

The needs of a family with several children are large compared with the needs of a childless couple. The latter could minimize its life insurance expenditures and build up larger emergency and retirement income funds.

[1] Adapted from E. Albert Gilbert, *Insurance and Your Security*. New York: Holt, Rinehart and Winston, Inc., 1948, p. 8.

The first important step, then, in planning a security program is to evaluate each hazard in terms of a family's particular needs. Then select the defenses that will best protect against the insecurities. This is, of course, easier said than done. But few informed persons would disagree with the following statements.

1. Protection of family dependents through insurance should be the first consideration. In purchasing insurance, the primary objective should be to get the most protection for the lowest cost that safety permits.

2. Investment for the education of children and for retirement should be a second but important consideration.

3. The financing to meet the minimum needs of a family should be the safest and best that is available—namely social security, United States savings bonds, and insurance.

Financial Security Goals. Every family has a level of basic living costs. How much it can save is determined by the difference that exists between this level and its income. The closer these two come together, the more difficult it is to save.

How much you can save is primarily controlled by how determined you are to save for future use. One thing is certain: unless you plan to save early and methodically, you are not likely to achieve your goals. There can be no evasion in setting aside the sum agreed on for savings.

No one is likely to argue that the savings pattern should be the same for all families having similar net incomes and spending units. For some families, it is important to concentrate on certain kinds of savings because they will sacrifice many things before touching these savings. Some families are unable to save at all, while some go to the other extreme and deny themselves daily "good living." It goes without saying that a happy medium between reckless extravagance and niggardliness makes for greater satisfaction and happiness.

1. *Insurance.* There should be life insurance and disability insurance on the breadwinner to protect the family from loss of income in case of death or of partial or permanent disability. Health and medical insurance is necessary to protect the family group against hospital and surgical-medical bills.

2. *Emergency fund.* A cash reserve fund should be built up to a minimum sum equal to 2 months' income.

3. *Educational fund.* Since most families hope to give their children a college education, the way to build such a fund is to begin as early as possible, but after goals 1 and 2 have been achieved.

4. *Retirement.* Old-age benefits under social security are a base for retirement, but not sufficient to maintain the standard of living to which most families are accustomed. Therefore, social security should be supple-

mented by investments and perhaps an annuity purchased just prior to retirement.

5. *A mortgage-free home.* Some families may aim to achieve this before adding to a retirement fund.

Social Security

The United States, in its early history, was a developing country with a vast frontier and a predominantly agricultural economy. One of the early forms of "social security" was the availability of up to 160 acres

HOW SOCIAL SECURITY WORKS

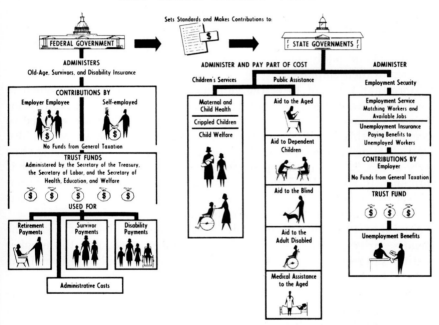

SOURCE: *Essentials of Social Security in the United States,* Social Security Administration, U.S. Department of Health, Education, and Welfare, 1962.

of free land, given by the government to any person who wished to be a farmer. American citizens have always been encouraged to provide their own security, to take advantage of the opportunities in a young nation, rich in natural resources, with a rapidly growing population.

That everyone should plan for his own security remains a cherished heritage of the American people. Essential to the purpose is an economy that provides full employment at a high wage level. Today, the great majority of Americans have savings, life insurance, a home, and other forms of personal property that contribute to security as well as to a high standard of living.

Individual effort by itself, however, is not sufficient protection against the insecurities of a society now highly industrialized and urbanized. Such a society, while increasing the productive capacity of the nation manyfold and providing the basis for an ever-increasing standard of living, has created a dependence on cash income that was unknown in the earlier history of the United States. Also, the small, mobile family of today, while well suited to an urban-industrial economy, is less able than the three- or four-generation family of the past to provide mutual care and support.

Therefore, the American people acted through their government to establish a social security system that protects against the risks common to all and against which citizens as individuals are unable to provide adequate safeguards. The system serves as a foundation on which individuals may build additional protection through their own efforts and with the help of their employers.

More than 9 out of 10 of the gainfully employed men and women in the United States are protected by old-age, survivors, and disability insurance (commonly referred to as social security). They are entitled to receive monthly benefits on retirement at age 65 or if they are disabled before that age and cannot work. Women may elect to receive benefits as early as age 62 but, by doing so, the amount of the monthly payment is permanently reduced. (Widows receiving survivor benefits at 62 are not subject to the reduction.) Of men and women 65 or older, more than 7 out of 10 were eligible in 1964 to receive benefits.

A total of 19 million people were drawing monthly benefits under the social security program at the end of December, 1963, and the number continues to rise. Payments in 1963 totaled about $15 billion. About four-fifths of the beneficiaries are aged persons.

Who Pays for Social Security? Under the social security program, workers contribute a small percentage of their earnings every payday to the social security system, and their employers put in a like sum. Most self-employed persons are also covered by the system and contribute at $1\frac{1}{2}$ times the rate of employees of business organizations.

Individual social security earning records of the millions of workers are kept up-to-date by the Social Security Administration's Bureau of Old-age and Survivors Insurance in Baltimore, Maryland, in one of the largest electronic machine operations in the world.

When any person begins to earn money through employment or self-employment that involves a social security tax, he applies for a social security account card. On this card is his name and his account number. This same account number is kept throughout the life of each card holder. If the person's name is changed, as in the case of marriage, application is made for a new card, showing the new name, but the account number remains the same.

The record of earnings is filed according to the account number. Social security account cards should be treated like an insurance policy. Keep the stub or lower half in a safe place. If the card is lost, take the stub to the nearest Social Security Administration office to obtain a new card.

If you are employed, your contribution is deducted from your wages each payday. The employer sends your contribution and his own matching contribution to the Internal Revenue Service at stated times. If you are self-employed, your contribution is payable when you file your Federal income tax return.

Military Service Credit. If a person performed active duty or active duty for training as a member of the uniformed services in 1957, or later, this service counts toward social security protection for himself and family. The base pay is credited to his social security record.

For active duty after September 15, 1940, and before 1957, social service credits of $160 a month may be given if this credit is needed when an application is filed. The social security office asks for proof of military service at the time of application.

Gradual Increases in Rates to 1968. To cover the cost of paying benefits to an increasing number of people, the law provides for gradual increases in social security tax rates—the last increase to go into effect in January, 1968.

Only the first $4,800 of a worker's annual earnings are taxable.

Calendar year	Employee per cent	Employer per cent	Self-employed per cent
1962	3⅛	3⅛	4.7
1963–1965	3⅝	3⅝	5.4
1966–1967	4⅛	4⅛	6.2
1968 and after	4⅝	4⅝	6.9

Tax contributions received under this schedule, along with the interest earned on invested assets of the funds, are expected on the basis of actuarial estimates to be enough now and in the future to pay all benefits in the present law.

A fixed percentage of one-quarter of 1 per cent of the tax rate on employees and on employers, and three-eighths of 1 per cent of the rate on self-employed persons, is credited to the Disability Insurance Trust Fund.

Old-age Retirement Benefits. Under the present law, benefits are payable to retired workers at age 65, or reduced-rate benefits may be paid as early as age 62. Benefits may also be paid to the following dependents: a wife or dependent husband age 62 or over, children under 18 or disabled before age 18, and a wife of any age caring for a child entitled to benefits.

The details for figuring benefits are complex. The social security office in your community gives exact information on benefits. The accompanying table, Examples of Monthly Payments, shows benefits, depending on age at the time the benefits start.

If a retired worker earns $1,200 in a year, $1 may be withheld for each $2 earned from $1,200 to $1,700. For every $1 earned over $1,700, $1 in benefits may be withheld.

For example, if the retired worker should earn a total of $1,750 a year, $300 (one-half of the first $500 over $1,200, plus the $50 over $1,700) in benefits would be withheld for that year. If the monthly benefit rate is $100, checks for the months of January, February, and March of that year would be held back to make up for the amount of benefits not due.

Regardless of the retired worker's total earnings for a year, benefits are payable for any month in which he neither earns wages of more than $100 nor performs substantial services in self-employment.

The decision as to whether a retired worker is performing substantial services in self-employment depends on the amount of time devoted to the business, the kind of services performed, how the services compare with the services performed in past years, and other circumstances of the particular case.

The earnings of a person who is receiving benefits as a dependent or as a survivor affect only his own benefits and do not stop payments to other members of the family.

Earnings from work of any kind, whether or not it is covered by the social security law, must be counted in figuring the amount of benefits due for a year. Total wages (not just take-home pay) and all net earnings from self-employment must be added together in figuring earnings for the year. However, income from savings, investments, pensions, and insurance does not affect old-age or survivors insurance benefits and should not be added to earnings.

In the year in which the retired worker first becomes entitled to benefits, he must count his total earnings for the entire year in determining the amount of benefits that can be paid to him.

After a retired worker is 72, he may earn any amount and still receive his full benefits each month. But for the year in which he becomes 72 his full earnings must be counted for the months before his seventy-second birthday to figure the amount of benefits due for the months previous to his becoming age 72.

Survivor Benefits. On the death of an insured worker, monthly benefits are payable to a surviving widow or dependent widower age 62 or over, children under age 18 or disabled before 18, a mother who has such a

Examples of Monthly Payments

Average yearly earnings after 1950	$800 or less	$1,800	$2,400	$3,000	$3,600	$4,200	$4,500	$4,800
Retirement at 65 or disability benefits before 65	$40.00	$73.00	$84.00	$95.00	$105.00	$116.00	$121.00	$127.00
Retirement at 64	37.40	68.20	78.40	88.70	98.00	108.30	113.00	118.60
Retirement at 63	34.70	63.30	72.80	82.40	91.00	100.60	104.90	110.10
Retirement at 62	32.00	58.40	67.20	76.00	84.00	92.80	96.80	101.60
Wife's benefit at 65 or with child in her care	20.00	36.50	42.00	47.50	52.50	58.00	60.50	63.50
Wife's benefit at 64	18.40	33.50	38.50	43.60	48.20	53.20	55.50	58.30
Wife's benefit at 63	16.70	30.50	35.00	39.60	43.80	48.40	50.50	53.00
Wife's benefit at 62	15.00	27.40	31.50	35.70	39.40	43.50	45.40	47.70
Widow 62 or over	40.00	60.30	69.30	78.40	86.70	95.70	99.90	104.80
Widow under 62 and 1 child	60.00	109.60	126.00	142.60	157.60	174.00	181.60	190.60
Widow under 62 and 2 children	60.00	120.00	161.60	202.40	236.40	254.00	254.00	254.00
One surviving child	40.00	54.80	63.00	71.30	78.80	87.00	90.80	95.30
Maximum family benefit	60.00	120.00	161.60	202.40	240.00	254.00	254.00	254.00

NOTE: Average yearly earnings of $4,800 are not generally possible for people now retiring since they must count some years in which less than $4,800 was creditable for social security purposes. However, beginning with 1963, women who are 65 or older and men who are 67 or older, and who have been regularly earning $4,800 a year since 1959, can have an average of $4,800 and qualify for maximum benefits.

SOURCE: "Your Social Security." U.S. Department of Health, Education, and Welfare, 1963, p. 9.

child in her care, and dependent parents. A lump sum of three times the monthly benefit, but not more than $255, is paid to the survivor if husband and wife were living together.

Disability Benefits. Monthly benefits are payable to workers who are totally and permanently disabled before age 65, and to their dependents who fall in the same categories as those of old-age beneficiaries. The law encourages rehabilitation of disabled workers under a Federal-state program of vocational rehabilitation.

Adequacy of Social Security. A family may receive benefits from social security that could otherwise be obtained only by having saved over $100,000 or by having insurance policies on which many thousands of dollars of premiums had been paid. Social security is the best investment a family is likely to have. For persons who cannot save, the forced savings of social security may prove to be the difference between receiving relief or not after retirement or disability. This is not to say that everyone escapes public relief who receives social security benefits.

The accompanying table, Current Payment Status, December, 1961, shows that the average monthly payment was about $73.

CURRENT PAYMENT STATUS, DECEMBER, 1961

Type of beneficiary	Number	Average monthly benefit
Retired workers	8,925,000	$75.65
Disabled workers	618,000	89.59
Wives	2,510,000	39.15
Aged widows	1,697,000	64.91
Children	2,279,000	45.98
Widowed mothers	428,000	59.38
Parents	37,000	67.15
Total	16,494,000	

A 1960 survey of the incomes of persons over age 65, by the Federal government, indicated that three-fifths had a total of less than $1,000; only one-fifth had over $2,000; and about half of the couples in which a husband was over 65, and who had their own household, had incomes of less than $2,600. About 15 per cent had incomes of over $5,000.[2]

A retired couple averaged about $125 a month benefit. Thirty per cent of the couples received less than $100 a month. Old-age assistance benefits to aged widows averaged about $65 a month benefit. Assuming that an

[2] *Health Insurance for the Aged,* Public Affairs Institute, 1960, p. 10.

aged couple needs $3,000 a year to live in reasonable, minimum comfort, present social security does not provide the necessary amount of money. Fortunately, social security income is not subject to the Federal income tax.

Any savings or additional insurance income would help this couple to live more comfortably. But even a maximum retirement income of $190 a month, fully insured, would not pay for all their needs without further aid of some kind. For example, social security is not likely to pay for the breadwinner's last illness and burial expenses; it will not pay off a mortgage or other debts; it will not pay income to a widow under 62 unless she has a child under 18; it will not provide college education funds; it will not allow invasion of principal in case of emergency; it will not allow income benefits to be taken in a lump sum.

Social security can do a great deal; it should not be underestimated, nor should it be overestimated. Social security is an excellent base on which to build more income protection within the limit of financial capacity. For the average middle-income family, it is now possible to build a life insurance program, coupled with social security, that will protect the family adequately when they need the greatest protection. In short, the average-income family is closer to financial security today than ever before.

Life Insurance

Social security provides a minimum subsistence for survivors. It is intended to keep them from actual minimal need, not to give them all the basic comforts of life. Life insurance will help complete a protection program. In evaluating family needs, these questions are pertinent:

1. Which family members should be insured?
2. How much insurance should be carried?
3. What kind of insurance is best?
4. What insurance companies should be selected?

But first, something about the nature of life insurance and the money value of the major breadwinner.

The Lengthening Life-span. Life insurance is a means of setting aside a portion of income during earning years to provide income for dependents when the major breadwinner dies. The premium rates are based on mortality tables, or life expectancy. A child born in the United States in 1959 had a life expectancy of 69.7 years, according to the accompanying table, Life Expectancy. A white male born in 1959 has a life expectancy of 67.3 years in contrast to a white female, who may live to be 73.9 years of age.

Since 1900, more than 22 years, or two-thirds of a generation, has been added to life expectancy at birth.

LIFE EXPECTANCY

Expectation of Life at Birth in the United States

(Years)

Year	White			Nonwhite			All races		
	Male	Female	Both sexes	Male	Female	Both sexes	Male	Female	Both sexes
1900	46.6	48.7	47.6	32.5	33.5	33.0	46.3	48.3	47.3
1910	48.6	52.0	50.3	33.8	37.5	35.6	48.4	51.8	50.0
1920	54.4	55.6	54.9	45.5	45.2	45.3	53.6	54.6	54.1
1930	59.7	63.5	61.4	47.3	49.2	48.1	58.1	61.6	59.7
1940	62.1	66.6	64.2	51.5	54.9	53.1	60.8	65.2	62.9
1950	66.5	72.2	69.1	59.1	62.9	60.8	65.6	71.1	68.2
1955	67.3	73.6	70.2	61.2	65.9	63.2	66.6	72.7	69.5
1958	67.2	73.7	70.3	60.6	65.5	63.0	66.4	72.7	69.4
1959	67.3	73.9	70.5	60.9	66.2	63.5	66.5	73.0	69.7

SOURCE: National Office of Vital Statistics, U.S. Department of Health, Education, and Welfare.

The gains have resulted mainly from reductions in mortality at the younger ages. More people are now living to an advanced age, but the increase in longevity in the older ages has been relatively small. Most of the improvement came during the first half of the century. There has been little significant gain in life expectancy since 1950.

The Money Value of Life. What is the present worth of a man's future earnings, in excess of expenditures on his own person, assuming the man is subject to existing mortality conditions? Dr. Louis I. Dublin, chief statistician for the Metropolitan Life Insurance Company, made an interesting study of this question and reported on it in his book, *The Money Value of Man.*

A less complicated version of this concept may be seen in the accompanying table, The Money Value of Life. A man, age 25, for example, will have normally about 40 years of earnings to age 65. If he averages $600 a month during this period, his money value would be about $280,000.

Not many breadwinners can afford enough life insurance to replace lifetime earnings in case of premature death, as the premiums would be over $4,000 a year, and not even the most avid life insurance salesman would urge it. Carrying five times a man's annual salary ($600 a month) in ordinary life insurance or $36,000 worth, would cost around $600 a year. This, too, would be too costly for a typical family man, earning

The Money Value of Life

Age	Years of earnings to 65	Average monthly earnings				
		$200	$300	$400	$500	$600
25	40	$96,000	$144,000	$192,000	$240,000	$280,000
30	35	84,000	126,000	168,000	210,000	252,000
35	30	72,000	108,000	144,000	180,000	216,000
40	25	60,000	90,000	120,000	150,000	180,000
45	20	48,000	72,000	96,000	120,000	144,000
50	15	36,000	54,000	72,000	90,000	108,000
55	10	24,000	36,000	48,000	60,000	72,000
60	5	0	0	0	0	0
65	0	0	0	0	0	0

SOURCE: Courtesy of United States Life Insurance Company, New York.

$7,200 a year, considering all his insurance needs. But there are better life insurance contracts than the ordinary life policy. It is a question of intelligent selection.

Sharing Risks by Life Insurance. Insurance is a plan by which large numbers of people, each in some danger of unforeseen loss, are brought together for mutual protection so that when one person suffers a loss, it can be made good by the premiums of all the others in the group. For example, term insurance is a year-to-year wager on survival. The insurance company statisticians, from a study of life expectancy tables and interest rates over the years, have figured out a system that works like this:

Of 1,000 men, age 30 and apparently healthy, two will die within the next year. If these men buy a $10,000 policy good for 5 years, insurance companies can sell it to each of them for about $55 a year. This will put enough money in the "kitty" to pay the salesmen's commissions, the in-insurance companies' overhead, and $10,000 to each of the 10 men who will die within the 5 years. The total five-year premiums of around $275, for those men who continue to live, remain in the "kitty."

The odds on the term insurance bet change each year as a man gets older, and the premiums have to go up at five-year intervals for a five-year term contract. At the age of 40, a $10,000 term contract costs about $85 a year; at age 50, about $160. Other kinds of life insurance, like ordinary life, have built-in savings in the policy, so the statisticians have to include interest in the cost calculations.

The principle of the law of probability, or the law of averages, is basic in figuring premium rates. Insurance companies have actuaries, skilled mathematicians, who study the proportion of people who die at certain ages. They figure rates of mortality based on hundreds of thousands of cases, and the results are compiled in mortality tables, which insurance companies use as the basis of figuring the rate to charge for a particular kind of insurance policy.[3]

Life Insurance Ownership. About 134 million Americans owned some form of life insurance protection by the end of 1963, according to the Institute of Life Insurance. Nearly three out of five adults had individually purchased life insurance, one out of four was protected by group life insur-

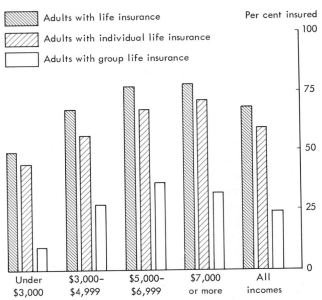

PER CENT OF ADULTS INSURED IN THE U.S.
BY FAMILY INCOME, 1960

SOURCE: *Life Insurance Fact Book,* Institute of Life Insurance, New York, 1962.

ance, and about 15 per cent owned both types, as shown in the accompanying chart, Adults Insured and Family Income.

About half the adults with family income of under $3,000 a year had life insurance, in contrast to over three-fourths with incomes of $5,000 a year and over. The average family having life insurance had about $15,300 of life insurance at the end of 1963, according to the Institute of Life Insurance.

How Much Life Insurance Should You Buy? Independent insurance advisors say that Americans lose millions of dollars annually because they do not

[3] For greater detail, see *The Life Insurance Public,* Institute of Life Insurance, New York. (Free copy)

know how to plan a protection program to fit their needs and pocketbook. Many families get a poor insurance deal because they (1) carry more insurance than they need, (2) carry a too expensive type of insurance, (3) carry too little insurance, (4) purchase too cheap insurance, (5) insure the wrong members of the family, (6) borrow on their insurance from the insurance company, (7) select poor companies and agents, (8) fail to relate life insurance to total family savings and protection needs.

If there is no financial risk involved in the premature death of members of the family who are not breadwinners, there is no urgent need for buying life insurance for those members. For example, it is questionable to buy a large amount of insurance for a wife when the husband is the bread-winner. It is preferable in such case to limit life insurance on a wife to a $1,000 burial policy. This reasoning is based on the assumption that a wife or mother cannot be called a substantial financial risk in most families.

Minor children, likewise, are not financial assets to most families. Burial insurance for children is a doubtful need for most families. Some insurance salesmen have been too enthusiastic in selling life insurance for unimportant or nonexistent needs. Most persons would never think about buying fire insurance on a house if they did not own a house. Why then buy life insurance on members of the family who do not have financial dependents?

Life insurance dollars should protect dependents. If there are no dependents, it is preferable to put the savings into good investments.

Practical life underwriters have worked out rough-and-ready rules for determining the amount of life insurance one should carry. These estimates are general enough to fit nearly everybody's case, but not particular enough to fit any case exactly. Though the most important reason for taking out life insurance is for protection of dependents, it is not necessary to provide income for dependents indefinitely. For many families, the monthly income need is around 50 to 65 per cent of present income.

The breadwinner may estimate the financial needs of his family at any particular time by preparing a table similar to the one shown here, Figure It Out for Yourself. Note that at the end of the first column the personal expenses of the breadwinner are estimated at 35 per cent. They are deducted because of the presumed death of the breadwinner.

The second column contains items B and C from which income may be derived during the family life cycle. Obviously, at the beginning of married life, the average young couple will not have income from all the named sources.

As there is likely to be a deficit in income on the death of the bread-winner, that is the important amount in deciding how much life insurance to carry at various periods of family life.

The advantage of using this table is that no two families are alike in

FIGURE IT OUT FOR YOURSELF

Just estimate the income your family would need EACH MONTH if you were not here to provide it

STEP ONE	EXPENSES PER MONTH
HOME	
Rent or mortgage...... $	
Upkeep	
Taxes and insurance...	
HOUSEHOLD	
Utilities	
Phone	
Laundry	
FOOD	
CLOTHING..........	
MEDICAL...........	
EDUCATION........	
RECREATION	
AUTOMOBILE	
Gas, oil, repairs.......	
Insurance	
TOTAL * $	

*Experience indicates that a family usually must reduce its present monthly budget when the head of the family dies. Of course, your portion of current overhead no longer would be necessary.

Deduction to be considered $
(about 35%)

MINIMUM INCOME REQUIRED MONTHLY $

And now, you are ready for Step Two.

STEP TWO

	FUTURE NEEDS

A As you have established in Step One to know that your family is provided for at least until your youngest child has completed high school (age 18), your wife would need for [   ] years a minimum monthly income of........................$

B Your Social Security would provide for this period (See Table I below) a minimum monthly income of ...$ [   ] *

*If you have more than one child, the amount will be larger for part of the period. See footnote below.

C Your present life insurance of $ [   ] would provide for this period of [   ] years (See Table II below) a monthly income of..........$ [   ]

indicating   **B + C** $
The additional monthly income required for this period of [   ] years ....   **Subtract** $
                                                 A−B+C

TABLE I	Average Monthly Wage	Widow and 1 Child	Widow and 2 Children	Widow and 3 Children
SOCIAL SECURITY SURVIVORSHIP MONTHLY BENEFIT PAYMENTS†	400	191	254	254
	350	174	232	254
	300	158	210	240
	250	143	190	202
	200	126	162	162

†Realize that as each child reaches age 18, his apportioned benefit payment ceases.

TABLE II	No. of Years	Monthly Income	No. of Years	Monthly Income
MONTHLY INCOME PRODUCED PER $1000 OF LIFE INSURANCE POLICY PROCEEDS	3	$28.79	11	$8.64
	4	21.86	12	8.02
	5	17.70	13	7.49
	6	14.93	14	7.03
	7	12.95	15	6.64
	8	11.47	16	6.30
	9	10.32	17	6.00
	10	9.39	18	5.73

(This table applies only to Equitable policies)

Since the minimum monthly income required is based on the number of years until the youngest child reaches 18, the additional social security income benefits for your other children are not included in the above calculations. Therefore, this extra or additional income might well be considered for emergency purposes.

SOURCE: Equitable Life Assurance Society of the United States, New York.

their financial needs. Most of the attempted formulas ignore individual financial differences.

Do not be surprised if you have to compromise. Most breadwinners cannot afford enough insurance to fill all family needs at one time. On the other hand, when dependents are on their own financial power life insurance needs decrease. To complete the picture, the final calculation, which is not shown here, is the cash or retirement income available at age 65 if the breadwinner lives.

To answer the question of how much life insurance a family needs (1) make a careful estimate of needs, (2) take into account present insurance and financial resources, (3) look at insurance policies in terms of the job they are intended to do rather than in terms of face value, and (4) include plans for the future in case the breadwinner lives after he retires.

When to Buy Life Insurance. If a man is single and has no dependents, the only life insurance needed is enough to cover debts and final expenses. It is true that the younger a man is when buying life insurance, the lower the annual premium for any policy. This argument has several weaknesses. In the first place, the final cost remains about the same because the younger a man is when buying insurance, the longer he pays. Buying early may mean several years of needless expense if there is no need for protection. The odds are almost 65 to 1 that a healthy man of 20 or 25 will live at least 5 years.

On the other hand, delay in buying life insurance risks the development of some health condition that may make it impossible to get insurance other than group insurance, or makes it necessary to pay a higher premium as a poor medical risk. From the standpoint of insurability, then, the sooner you buy, the better.

It might be better for a single person, in reasonably good health and with no dependents, to delay purchasing life insurance (except enough to cover debts and final expenses) unless he is eligible for one of the United States government life insurance programs for veterans.

For a newly married couple, with the wife working, about the same protection is needed as when single. If the wife is not working but could, some income should be provided for the readjustment period. In case there are sizable debts, it would be wise to cover them with reducing term insurance.

Here is one case. A young couple have been married a year or so. The wife is a college graduate but has never worked. They have purchased a home with a small down payment and a large, economy-size mortgage. A baby is on the way. Do they need life insurance? The question appears silly. A better question would be "How much life insurance?" Failure to insure the husband's life to a reasonable amount would be an unpardonable irresponsibility in this case, because there are dependents who need financial protection.

Consider another case. This young couple have been married a year. The wife taught high school before marriage. Her folks are moderately wealthy. They expect no child as yet; they rent an apartment, and have no big obligations. Do they need life insurance? There is probably no immediate need for life insurance unless each of them thinks it advisable to have a $1,000 ordinary life policy for funeral purposes. Conditions can change, of course. In the second example, if their present situation continued for many years, they might be considered irresponsible if they did not methodically and prudently invest each year to supplement their social security retirement or disability income.

Insurance Needs when Children Are Dependent. As a family increases in size, it may be necessary to add more insurance on the father to protect each new dependent. When the children are young, more life insurance may be needed on the father to protect the mother during the period before she can return to work.

Experts on family economics have found that the period when children are still dependents is a difficult one in which to protect a family adequately on a modest income. For such families, the following recommendations may be useful.

First, concentrate the insurance on the life of the breadwinner or breadwinners. Some insurance experts advise against insurance on the wife (if she is a full-time mother) and on the children. Others recommend a joint ordinary life policy of $1,000 for husband and wife to meet burial expenses or a separate $1,000 policy on the wife.

Second, many experts recommend, in addition to veterans' life insurance if available, the purchase of renewable term insurance during this period. A 20-year decreasing term insurance, for example, guaranteeing a stated income during the remainder of dependency in case of the breadwinner's death, would give dependents the most protection at the least cost.

Third, buy all the group life insurance and veterans' life insurance for which the breadwinner can qualify because it is the cheapest protection available.

Insurance Needs after Children Are Self-supporting. After the children are grown and self-supporting, insurance needs change. The reducing term insurance on the father for the protection of the children may be dropped because they are no longer dependents. Many mothers take a job during this period, and the extra income can be used for investment purposes to build up a larger retirement fund. Money that formerly went into added insurance for the children's protection can also be channeled into investments.

The closer both parents come to retirement age, the less need for life insurance, provided that an investment program has been growing steadily. Some savings might be used to purchase an annuity just before retirement. The point to be emphasized is that the problem of the economic future of the parents after the children are on their own financial power should be more a matter of savings and investments than of life insurance protection.

The Most Economical Use of Life Insurance. When buying a car, you have many models to choose from. Life insurance also comes in many models. Though the basic principles of life insurance are relatively simple, the many models offered may be confusing to the average consumer. This confusion often ends in the selection of the wrong kind of insurance for a good objective—either in increased cost of insurance without appreciable increase in protection, or in being underinsured by policies that are too expensive.

Fundamentally, life insurance is economic protection for dependents against the possibility of death of the breadwinner. This is the most economical use of life insurance. It is *not* a savings plan; it is *not* an investment plan. Savings can be built up faster, and with reasonable safety, through prudent investments. Also, life insurance is *not* a plan to send a child to college. True, it is sold for all these purposes, but there are better ways for knowledgeable couples to attain certain necessary objectives than through life insurance.

Here are the financial problems a family must face on the death of the breadwinner, arranged in order of importance: death expenses, dependency income for the children, temporary income for the wife, adjustment fund (1 to 3 years), paying up the house mortgage, college education fund, gifts and grants to charity. Wealthy families can afford to carry life insurance for all these objectives, but most families would not have sufficient money to live on if they tried to cover all of them.

Four Basic Types of Life Insurance Policies. Despite the many differing policies offered by life insurance companies, there are only four types of life insurance policies: (1) term, (2) straight life or ordinary life insurance, (3) limited-payment life insurance, and (4) endowment insurance. All these types have in their contracts one or two elements. Term insurance is pure protection in the event of death. The other three types have one additional feature—savings. It is the savings feature, primarily, that makes these other types more expensive. So forget about the advertising or selling gimmicks like "modified life," "whole life special," "special protection policy," "pure endowment," "joint life," "last survivor life," "family protector," "contingency life," "retirement income," "family income," "preferred risk," and many other catchy but confusing terms. Virtually, this whole mass of verbiage can be reduced to the four basic types: term, ordinary, limited-payment life, and endowment. In essence, all these types except term insurance (pure protection), have the term protection principle *plus* savings.

Remember the basic principle when planning a life insurance program for your family—to gain the most protection at the lowest cost. The accompanying table, What Various Policies Cost, shows that term insurance gives much more short-term protection per premium dollar.

WHAT VARIOUS POLICIES COST ($1,000 POLICY)
A Mutual Company

Type of policy	Age at issue		
	25	35	45
10-year renewable term	$ 4.93	$ 6.84	$12.89
Straight life (ordinary)	12.71	17.07	25.18
Payment to 65	14.37	20.79	35.30
20-payment life	23.33	27.97	35.30
Endowment at age 65	16.94	24.97	42.64
20-year endowment	39.35	39.73	42.64

Term Insurance—Maximum Protection at Low Cost. Term insurance is so named because it is sold for a term—usually for a period of 1, 5, 10, or 20 years, often with option to renew without another physical examination. Such policies are called "renewable term." The rate is increased at the beginning of each new term because the rates are based on the age of the insured, and because there are no extra premium charges for savings, as there are in all other contracts.

In term insurance, there are no savings or investment features. It cannot be used as loan collateral or be surrendered for cash. You pay premiums only as long as you keep the protection. But this kind of insurance gives the family the highest protection for a limited period for the least cost, and can be made the backbone of protection for dependents in event of premature death of the breadwinner. It provides almost twice as much protection per dollar cost as ordinary life—the next cheapest policy— during the early years of family life.

It is generally wise to purchase renewable term insurance rather than nonrenewable insurance because it is adaptable to situations where temporary or decreasing protection is needed. Term insurance is best planned on a reducing basis so that it may be reduced or terminated as dependents no longer require a large amount of protection. It should be increased to maximum protection as each child is born and decreased to the point of no insurance on the father for the children after they are economically independent, perhaps around the age of 22.

The maximum protection of the wife in the early years of marriage may be reduced gradually to zero when the husband reaches his retirement age at 65 or earlier. Then he could give up all life insurance with the possible exception of a $1,000 ordinary life policy (for last illness and burial) acquired shortly after marriage.

The accompanying chart, Life Insurance Program Using Reducing Renewable Term Insurance, shows how the purchase of renewable term insurance works out. It is further explained here.

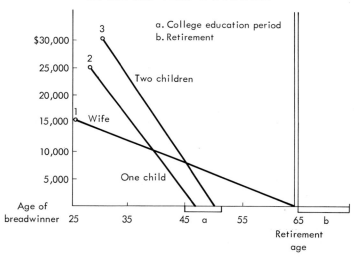

LIFE INSURANCE PROGRAM USING REDUCING RENEWABLE TERM INSURANCE

1. Purchase renewable term insurance in units of $1,000.

2. Calculate the protection needed by the family to maintain its present standard of living in case of the premature death of the breadwinner. Plan to protect the wife first if she is the first and only dependent. Add more protection for each child or other dependent.

3. Purchase maximum protection for the wife during the early years of marriage, and gradually reduce it to approximate zero when the breadwinner reaches age 65, or earlier.

4. The additional $10,000 insurance for the first child will be reduced annually until it reaches zero at about the time that the child is economically on his own, probably age 22 if he goes to college.

Before Buying Term Insurance. The breadwinner should fully understand a reducing term insurance program before embarking on it. It does not build up an educational fund for the children in the event that the insured person lives. Nor does it necessarily provide a retirement fund or funds for other purposes. Additional savings must be used to plug these gaps in family financial planning. But the savings in excess premiums that would otherwise go into more expensive life insurance can be placed in more productive kinds of investment.

The theory of term insurance is that the family would have insurance for less money plus a larger cash fund if needed. But there are these questions to consider. Will the family save and invest the difference between level premium insurance, such as ordinary life, and reducing term insurance premiums? Will they be able to save beyond social security benefits, which are inadequate for comfortable living during retirement years?

If the breadwinner is uncertain about carrying out the use of reducing renewable term insurance, it is better to pay a little more for combined term insurance and ordinary life and a savings plan, described later. However, the family would get about the same benefits by the purchase of renewable term insurance and separate ordinary life policies, or by purchasing all renewable term insurance with the privilege of converting to ordinary life insurance without a physical examination after the children are financially independent.

Buying Term Insurance. After considering the problems involved in a term insurance program, keep the following main points in mind when buying term insurance.

1. Purchase only renewable and convertible term insurance.

2. Buy several term policies rather than one or two large ones. This gives greater freedom in dropping policies that are no longer needed and allows more convenient distribution of premium due dates.

3. Be examined by your own doctor before applying for term insurance. The physical examinations are usually more severe than for other contracts. If possible, you want to avoid rejections by the company doctor. A good agent can be helpful in this matter. If you have once been rejected, other companies will know it because your record will be on file at the Medical Information Bureau, created by the insurance companies.

4. Since there are no loan values on term insurance, maintain an emergency fund to pay the premium in case you fall ill or lose your job.

5. Compare the net cost of policies sold by several companies, because the final cost varies considerably among a few companies.

6. Select agents who are trained to give honest, intelligent technical help in servicing your general plan.

7. Select insurance companies that are sound financially and have a record of efficiency in selling the kind of insurance contract you want. Some companies are very efficient in selling one kind of contract and less efficient in selling other kinds of insurance policies. Never accept the trite statement that all the good companies charge about the same premium rate.

8. Compare premium costs between stock and mutual companies. Do not

assume that a mutual company has lower-cost insurance because it has regularly returned a good dividend. Likewise, do not assume that a stock company policy is cheaper because the premium is lower. A stock company's premium is net and final—no dividends.

Investing the Savings Gained by Term Insurance. Is the family better off in protection of dependents and with more cash-in value at age 65 of the breadwinner? Yes, if the difference in the cost of straight life and a decreasing term policy is invested. Interesting details discovered by *Changing Times* magazine (October, 1962) are shown in the table on page 360, which compares Straight Life with 30-year Decreasing Term and Term-to-65 plus Mutual Fund Investment.

The buyer is age 35. In case A, he buys a $10,000 straight life policy for $237 a year and leaves the dividends to gather interest. In case B, he buys a $10,000, 30-year decreasing term, for $76 a year. In case C, he buys a term-to-65 policy for $120 a year. In both B and C, he invests the difference between the cost of the straight life policy and the two kinds of term insurance in a mutual investment fund that charges an 8 per cent sales commission. Dividends and capital gains are reinvested in the fund.

In case of death, the conclusions are: (1) death proceeds would be greater by a wide margin under the term-to-65 policy than under straight life; (2) straight life would yield a little higher death proceeds than decreasing term in the early years unless the mutual fund investment yielded more than 10 per cent interest compounded annually; (3) the term-to-65 is likely to produce more death benefits than the decreasing term.

If the breadwinner lives, the conclusions are: (1) both term programs will amass a nest egg much larger than the total value of the straight life (30-year term, $27,374; term-to-65, $19,542; straight life, $8,853). Warning: The difference in premiums must be invested each year without fail, and earnings and dividends must be plowed back.

Ordinary Life or Straight Life Insurance. Ordinary life or straight life insurance is payable at death of the insured, but one need not die to win on this contract. The same premium is paid as long as the insured lives. This is the most common kind of life insurance in the United States.

Since ordinary life is a combination of term plus savings, a reserve is accumulated, and in a few years, the policy has cash-surrender, loan, and other values. Consequently, the premium is about twice as expensive per $1,000 as term insurance, when first taken out.

Generally, the cash value at age 65 is ample to provide a paid-up policy equal to all the paid premiums. Many companies permit the cash value to be used to provide a guaranteed annuity, if by the age of, say, 70 to

A. STRAIGHT LIFE—IF BUYER DROPS POLICY AT END OF YEAR

Age at start of year	Premiums paid to date	This cash value	Plus these dividends
35	$ 237	0	0
50	3,792	$2,940	$ 923
64	7,110	5,600	3,253

Results at 65:
Total outlay $ 7,110
Insurance in force if premiums continued * $10,000
Insurance in force if premiums stopped $10,000 for 15 years, or
                                                 $ 7,330 for life
Cash if insurance surrendered $ 8,853

B. 30—YEAR DECREASING TERM PLUS MUTUAL FUND INVESTMENT

Age at start	Premiums paid to date	Amount invested to date	Insurance in force	Savings at 10 per cent
35	$ 76	$ 161	$10,000	$ 163
50	1,216	2,576	5,000	5,853
64	1,824	5,286	383	27,374

Results at 65:
Total outlay $ 7,110
Insurance in force if premiums continued   _____
Insurance in force if premiums stopped   _____
Cash value of mutual fund $27,374

C. TERM—TO—65 PLUS MUTUAL FUND INVESTMENT

Age at start of year	Premiums paid to date	Amount invested to date	Cash value of policy	Savings at 10 per cent
35	$ 120	$ 117	0	$ 119
50	1,920	1,872	$740	4,271
64	3,600	3,510	0	19,542

Results at 65:
Total outlay $ 7,110
Insurance in force if premiums continued   _____
Insurance in force if premiums stopped   _____
Cash in value of mutual fund $19,542

* Plus $3,253 in dividends.

75, there is no longer the need for protecting a dependent in event of the death of the insured.

A *family income policy* combines decreasing term with ordinary life insurance. It provides, in addition to the regular life insurance payment, income payment to the beneficiary if the insured dies within the stated period. The payments begin at death of the insured and extend to the end of the period. If the insured is living at the end of the period, the premiums usually decrease.

The advantage in this policy is that while the children are young there is greater protection than the family usually can afford on a permanent basis. The highest income is provided for the dependents during the first 20 years, when the need is greatest in case of premature death of the breadwinner. If the policyholder lives, the term insurance ends 20 years after purchase of the policy, and the premium is reduced accordingly. Only the ordinary life insurance remains permanently in this contract.

Limited-payment Life Insurance. Limited-payment life insurance is payable only at death of the insured. The premiums are payable only for a stated number of years or until the insured reaches a certain age, such as 60 or 65. Payments are usually limited, however, to 10, 20, or 30 years. Thirty-payment life, for example, provides for premiums to be paid for 30 years, after which the policy is paid up. The face value, however, is not paid until the insured dies. The premium rate must be considerably higher on this kind of policy than on ordinary life because it is fully paid up in a stated number of years.

Policies of this type are considered to be more appropriate for persons whose incomes may be expected to decrease appreciably in later life. It is not suitable for most young married couples, because the premium is so costly that they cannot afford to buy enough for adequate protection for dependents. Term insurance, in particular, and ordinary insurance will give a young family much more protection at lower cost at a time when the highest protection is most needed—the first 20 years of married life.

Endowment Insurance. Endowment insurance is a combination of temporary life insurance and periodic savings. If the insured dies, the beneficiary receives the face value of the policy. If the insured lives, however, the face value or amount is paid to him, or to some designated person, either in a lump sum or in the form of income. The protection offered not only is small compared to the cost but ceases when the policy matures.

This kind of policy should not be considered as permanent protection for dependents. It provides the least protection for a given premium, but includes the highest investment element of the above general types of policies.

Endowment policies can be purchased on a basis of 10, 15, 20, 25, or 30 years, or to mature in cash at specified ages. Since the company must have the stated amount (say $2,000, in a 20-year $2,000 endowment) available for payment at the end of 20 years, the premium rate must be higher than a 20-year family income policy.

In the latter case, the company might not have to pay the beneficiary for several years after the insured had stopped making premium payments, provided the insured continued to live. The company could use these funds to earn additional interest. The endowment policy, on the other hand, calls for payment at the expiration of a certain number of years. Consequently, higher premiums are necessary for endowment policies.

Settlement Terms of Life Insurance Policies. The method of payment of life insurance policies is important. There are several options, and choosing the right settlement option helps to accomplish the purpose of the insurance. Before purchasing an insurance policy, the settlement terms that are available should be discussed with a competent life insurance underwriter. Most policies have the following four optional settlement plans, which may be decided by the insured or by the beneficiary.

Option 1. The beneficiary may receive a lump sum. This may be a good option if the money must be used to pay expenses for sickness, taxes, and burial. On the other hand, a lump sum coming into the hands of a beneficiary who cannot manage it carefully may prove to be an unsatisfactory option. It is easy for the beneficiary to become a victim of poor investments suggested by well-meaning but uninformed friends or even by an investment counselor.

Option 2. The principal sum is retained by the company, and interest (about $2\frac{1}{2}$ per cent) is paid to the beneficiary for a certain number of years or for life. At the end of the period, the principal is paid to the children, or according to the terms of the contract—a good option, as it is not final, and allows time to consider.

Option 3. A third option provides for the payment of insurance in installments—annual, semiannual, quarterly, or monthly. Usually, the company will specify the minimum installment or the minimum number of payments it guarantees. It might be, for example, a guarantee of $100 a month for 30 years, or that principal and interest will be paid until exhausted. This option may fit nicely for the protection of children.

Option 4. The annuity or life-income settlement provides regular life income to the beneficiary. The company may guarantee either a specified number of payments or payments that will equal the principal. If the beneficiary dies before the guaranteed payments have been made, the remainder goes to the estate, or as directed. Guaranteed payments cost more, however, because the risk is greater to the company.

The accompanying table, Monthly Installment Payments for Each

$1,000 of Insurance, shows the amount due under options 3 and 4, as reported by an American life insurance company.

If option 3 is selected, the guaranteed income to a beneficiary will be $6.53 a month for 15 years for each $1,000 policy. A $15,000 policy would provide an income of $78.36 a month for 15 years.

MONTHLY INSTALLMENT PAYMENTS FOR EACH $1,000 OF INSURANCE

Option 3		Option 4		
Number of annual payments	Amount of payments	Attained age of payee		Monthly life annuity
		Male	Female	
1	$84.19	20	25	$2.69
3	28.69	25	30	2.89
5	17.59	30	35	2.96
7	12.84	35	40	3.13
9	10.21	40	45	3.34
11	8.53	45	50	3.59
13	7.38	50	55	3.88
15	6.53	55	60	4.24
17	5.88	60	65	4.67
20	5.16	65	70	5.20
25	4.34			
30	3.80			

If the widow is age 65 and is eligible for full social security coverage, she may wisely elect a monthly life annuity of $4.67 per $1,000 of insurance. A $15,000 policy would provide $70.05 a month for life, which would be in addition to her monthly social security benefit. The monthly life annuity would cease on her death.

There is no single option, of course, that will fit all needs. These four options, however, are planned to meet all possible choices.

Restrictions and Double-indemnity Clause. Before buying a particular policy, compare the contract with policies of other companies. Policies vary with regard to restrictions and advantages. Some companies, for example, will not accept the risk of death in air travel. Others will accept financial responsibility for travel on regularly scheduled commercial planes.

Some companies, for an extra premium, will include a double-indemnity clause that will pay double the face value of the contract in case of accidental death.

In case of total or permanent disability before age 60, some contracts provide for waiver of future premiums.

The disability income payment, not common any more, pays a stated income in case of total or permanent disability. This kind of contract is far more expensive.

Loan Value and Dividends. Most level premium policies have a loan value after the second year or so. The loan value and the rate of interest charged is stated in the policy. Sometimes, a loan can be obtained from a commercial bank at a lower rate of interest than most insurance companies charge. Consequently, it is a good idea to compare the total interest charges of a bank and of the insurance company before a decision is made for a loan on a life insurance policy.

If it is difficult to pay the premium, some policies contain an automatic premium-loan provision. If the policyholder takes advantage of this provision, the loan should be repaid as soon as possible; if long continued, the interest, usually 5 or 6 per cent, can destroy to a considerable extent the protection value of the policy. Consequently, borrowing on life insurance should be a last resort.

Dividends may be paid by mutual or participating companies. The policyholder may use them in any of four ways: (1) accept them in the form of cash, (2) allow the company to retain them at interest, (3) apply them to future premiums, or (4) use them to purchase more life insurance.

United States Government Insurance. Veterans of World War I, in good health, may still purchase a $10,000 United States Government Life Insurance policy in 5-year renewable term, 20- and 30-payment life, 20- and 30-year endowment, and endowment at 62.

National Service Life Insurance (NSLI) was issued to eligible persons who served in World War II and thereafter until April 25, 1951. Presently, term insurance up to $10,000 may be renewed every five years without a physical examination. It may also be converted into any one of the six permanent policies. NSLI was one of the best insurance buys ever offered, and it should be retained. The cost is low and the dividends, even on the term policies, have been generous. About 67 cents out of every premium dollar has been paid out in dividends. No commercial company can match it.

Korean War veterans called into service on and after June 27, 1950, and those who served after the war (until January 1, 1957), were automatically covered with a *free* $10,000 death policy, less any USGLI or NSLI in force at time of death. This free policy continued for 120 days after separation from service. Veterans could apply for a 5-year level-premium term policy before January 1, 1957, which could be renewed every 5 years at a premium rate for the then-attained age. This policy did not pay dividends and was not convertible to any other type of insurance.

Disabled veterans were allowed one year after the date that the Veterans Administration found them suffering from a service-connected disability to apply for insurance.

Generally speaking, new GI insurance can no longer be bought, with one exception. (Of course, Congress may change this policy when it pleases.) The one exception is for disabled veterans. For a small sum, a disabled veteran can add a rider to his old GI policy that would pay $10 a month for each $1,000 face value of his policy if he were totally disabled. If he had a $10,000 policy, this could add $100 a month to his income. He must be in good health to add the rider and collects only if disability occurs before age 60.

Under present policy provisions, a deceased veteran's wife might be wise to collect a life annuity. For example, if she is 55 years old, she can receive around $60 a month for life on a $10,000 GI policy in contrast to about $43 a month for life from a commercial insurance company. There is no special advantage to her if she collects the money for a fixed period.

It may be wise to hold on to the convertible term policy as long as possible and then convert to a level-premium straight life policy later. Even at age 40, a policyholder still pays only about $100 a year for a $10,000 term policy in contrast to $250 a year for straight life. However, term rates rise every five years. Premiums on permanent insurance remain the same. As a general rule, hold on to a term policy.

If a veteran becomes disabled, he should convert to permanent insurance because the law permits waiver of premiums for all types of policies. But in a permanent policy dividends are accumulating to build up cash values, something not true of term insurance. The veteran must be certain, however, that his disability will be permanent, because he cannot switch back to term insurance.

Group Life Insurance. The group plan of life insurance provides for insuring a large number of persons under a single policy, without medical examination and under a common employer or association. Usually, the firm pays half the premium, and the employee the other half. The premiums are considerably lower than individual term insurance because the overhead costs to the insurance company are lower.

Most group insurance is term insurance. Most contracts provide for conversion to a permanent plan of individual insurance, without medical examination, within 31 days after the employee terminates his employment.

Group insurance is not a substitute for other kinds of life insurance because, as a rule, the employee can buy only a limited amount, $1,000 to $5,000, depending on salary or wage income. The average amount of insurance per employee is around $3,500. About half of all the employees in the United States have group life insurance—50 million individuals in 1963.

Never turn down group life insurance. Take all the group insurance the firm or institution offers when you enter the busines world.

Industrial Life Insurance. Industrial life insurance is sold to individuals, usually in small policies of less than $1,000, and a weekly amount of 5 to 25 cents is collected by the insurance agent. This kind of life insurance is necessarily costly. A $250 policy costing about 25 cents a week adds up to $13 annually. This sum could purchase from $1,000 to $2,000 worth of term insurance for one year, depending on the age of the individual.

There seems to be little justification for industrial insurance in today's life insurance programs. Apparently, lower-income individuals are learning that industrial life insurance is expensive, because it represented only 6 per cent of all life insurance outstanding at the end of 1961. The average-size industrial policy in force is $400.

Savings Bank Life Insurance. Three states permit their savings banks to sell life insurance to people who live and work in the state. Usually, a single bank is permitted to issue a limited amount of life insurance—in New York State, $5,000 per policyholder; in Massachusetts, $10,000; and in Connecticut, $5,000. In New York State, however, an individual may purchase a maximum of $35,000 of life insurance by buying a $5,000 policy from seven savings banks.

Insurance is issued in all four of the major forms of life insurance. Savings bank life insurance in all three states is low in cost because there are no salesmen and no agents' commissions, lapses are low, and the mortality experience has been favorable. The issuance of policies is handled by the regular employees of each bank.

Other Organizations Issuing Life Insurance. The Wisconsin State Life Fund issues low-cost life insurance in amounts of $1,000 to $10,000 to residents of that state. The commissioner of insurance manages the business from his office.

The Presbyterian Ministers' Fund offers life insurance to all Protestant ministers, their wives, and students of the ministry. It is a mutual company, licensed to operate in only a few states, but can sell via mail to all persons who qualify in the United States and Canada. The net cost is very low.

The Teachers Insurance and Annuity Association of America sells life insurance and annuities to employees of colleges and similar institutions of education and research. The life insurance cost is low. Savings and profits are returned to policyholders.

Ratings of Commercial Life Insurance Companies. The American Institute for Economic Research has compared the net cost of life insurance issued by companies that are considered average, above average, or superior in financial standing.[4] The net costs of two types of life insurance—whole

---

[4] *Life Insurance and Annuities from the Buyer's Point of View,* Great Barrington, Mass., 1960. (The companies are rated in the order of the new cost per year over a 20-year period.)

life, and 5-year renewable term—were compared on original amounts of $25,000 at current premium rates and dividend scales. The whole life insurance policy of $25,000 is retained fully for 20 years, and the 5-year term is decreased by $5,000 at the end of each 5-year renewal period during the 20-year period.

The comparative net cost of the $25,000 whole life policy per year, for age 35 (for the 20-year period) ranged from a low net cost of $143.32 to a high of $197.18. The comparative net cost of the $25,000 5-year renewable term (reduced $5,000 at end of each 5-year period) during the 20-year period, for age 35, ranged from a low of $136.29 to a high of $207.58 premium rate annually. The conclusion is clear: it pays to compare rates even among the largest and strongest life insurance companies.

Suggestions for the Life Insurance Buyer. The major purpose of life insurance is protection of dependents, not savings. Term insurance gives much more protection for at least 20 to 30 years (up to about age 50 or more) per premium dollar. Savings and retirement income should be built through a prudent and regular investment program.

Buy all the group life insurance permitted by your firm or institution. Buy renewable convertible term insurance. Compare premium rates. Buy only from reputable, strong companies. Make term insurance the foundation of a life insurance program at least until all the children are no longer financial dependents. At that time, if the family investment program appears too modest, convert a part of the term insurance into straight life. The flexibility of renewable convertible term insurance and its low cost, when the most protection is needed, fully warrant its predominant use in a well-planned life insurance program under present economic conditions.

Purchase at least a $1,000 straight life policy early in married life on husband, wife, and each of the children, largely as a burial fund in case of premature death. Pay premium rates annually, if possible, because of reduced cost.

Annuities (Fixed and Variable)

Life insurance and annuities are exact opposites. Life insurance pays the beneficiary on the death of the policyholder. An annuity pays the policyholder for life. In life insurance, the company is betting that the policyholder will live. In an annuity, the company is betting that the annuitant will not live. Which means that if a family is young and growing up, life insurance protection for the family comes first.

The word *annuity* implies an annual payment. Today, however, any fixed periodic payment—yearly, monthly, weekly—for a given period of time or for life is an annuity. The essential feature of annuity payments is their payment as long as the annuitant lives. The annuitant pays a certain amount per month for a given number of years, or pays a lump sum just prior to retirement, and in return receives an income for life or variations of a deferred annuity.

No medical examination is required because the insurance company counts on the annuitant's death earlier than statistics indicate. The purchase price for women is higher than for men, because women usually live about five or six years longer than men.

The more frequent the payments to the annuitant (monthly, quarterly, yearly), the higher the purchase price. The annuity policy is primarily for the benefit of the annuitant and only secondarily of benefit to others. One can, however, select a "joint and survivorship" form that pays an income for life to two or more persons.

Kinds of Annuities. All annuities have three variables: how you pay for them, when you collect, and how you collect. Similarly, every annuity has a three-part name. A glance at the accompanying diagram, What Kind of Annuity? shows these three classifications and the various types of annuities available.

An *immediate annuity* is paid for in one lump sum, and annuity payments begin without delay. For example, to buy such an annuity for $100 a month at age 65, the annuitant would have to spend approximately $16,000. Generally, people buy an immediate annuity just prior to retirement, to continue as long as they live.

A *deferred life annuity* is one that begins to pay the annuitant at a later specified date, say at age 65. As in the immediate life annuity, it can be purchased in one lump sum years before benefits begin, or by installments covering perhaps many years.

Sometimes a deferred life annuity is paid to the annuitant until he dies, and then the remainder is paid to a named beneficiary until the entire cost of the annuity has been recovered. In other instances, if the annuitant dies, a lump sum is paid to a named beneficiary. The lump sum paid is the difference between the income payments received and the total premiums paid by the annuitant.

Both immediate life and deferred life annuities may be *joint and survivorship annuities*. Under this annuity policy, an income is guaranteed during the joint lifetime and is continued until the death of the survivor. This plan may fit a man and wife who have no other dependents, but may not be a good one for a husband with an invalid wife. It may not be a good policy if the annuitant had been rejected for life insurance, which might indicate that he may not need financial assistance after age 65 or so.

In any event, it is wise to have a thorough physical examination before taking out an annuity, especially if the annuity is to be taken out shortly before retirement or before the beginning of payments to the annuitant. For healthy persons reaching age 65 or older, it may be advisable to pur-

WHAT KIND OF ANNUITY?

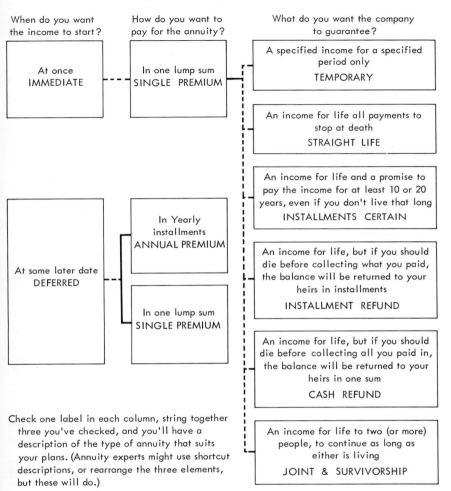

When do you want the income to start? / How do you want to pay for the annuity? / What do you want the company to guarantee?

At once IMMEDIATE --- In one lump sum SINGLE PREMIUM

A specified income for a specified period only
TEMPORARY

An income for life all payments to stop at death
STRAIGHT LIFE

An income for life and a promise to pay the income for at least 10 or 20 years, even if you don't live that long
INSTALLMENTS CERTAIN

At some later date DEFERRED --- In Yearly installments ANNUAL PREMIUM / In one lump sum SINGLE PREMIUM

An income for life, but if you should die before collecting what you paid, the balance will be returned to your heirs in installments
INSTALLMENT REFUND

An income for life, but if you should die before collecting all you paid in, the balance will be returned to your heirs in one sum
CASH REFUND

Check one label in each column, string together three you've checked, and you'll have a description of the type of annuity that suits your plans. (Annuity experts might use shortcut descriptions, or rearrange the three elements, but these will do.)

An income for life to two (or more) people, to continue as long as either is living
JOINT & SURVIVORSHIP

SOURCE: *Changing Times,* June, 1952.

chase an annuity just prior to retirement, because the older the annuitant, the higher the return.

One of the principal advantages of a joint life-and-survivorship annuity is that most of the need for life insurance (beyond the great need when children are still on the family payroll) is eliminated. For example, if husband and wife have an annuity or a combination of annuity, plus social security and some income from stocks, bonds, or real estate, which provide sufficient income, they need carry only permanent insurance (straight life) to cover funeral expenses, because the wife will be supported by the annuity income even after the husband's death. This arrangement eliminates paying heavy life insurance premiums during the retirement period when income is usually less than in the earning years.

Cost of Annuities. The cost of an annuity is based largely on the amount of income it will pay. Annuity rates are usually quoted in two ways: the amount of income the annuitant receives per unit of premium, or the amount the annuitant pays per unit. The accompanying table, The Cost of Annuities, gives some averages of costs from both points of view. The amount the annuitant pays for a given income depends on the income plan selected, on the age when payments begin, and on the sex of the annuitant.

THE COST OF ANNUITIES

Immediate Single-premium Annuities (Nonparticipating Rates)
(Income to Begin at Once)

Age at issue		Each $1,000 buys this monthly income—			Each $10 of monthly income costs—		
Male	Female	Life only	10 years certain	Refund	Life only	10 years certain	Refund
50	55	$4.20	$4.10	$3.70	$2,400	$2,450	$2,750
55	60	4.75	4.50	4.00	2,100	2,200	2,500
60	65	5.50	5.15	4.50	1,850	1,950	2,300
65	70	6.40	5.80	5.00	1,575	1,725	2,100
70	75	7.70	6.50	5.60	1,300	1,550	1,800

Deferred Annual-premium Annuities (Participating Rates)
(Assuming Income Starts at Age 60 for Men, Age 65 for Women)

Age at issue		Each $100 a year buys this monthly income—			Each $10 of monthly income costs this much a year—		
Male	Female	Life only	10 years	Refund	Life only	10 years	Refund
20	25	$35.00	$33.25	$30.75	$31.00	$33.00	$35.00
25	30	29.00	27.00	25.00	37.00	39.00	42.00
30	35	23.00	21.75	20.00	47.00	49.00	52.00
35	40	18.00	17.00	15.50	60.00	63.00	70.00
40	45	13.50	12.50	11.50	79.00	84.00	90.00

SOURCE: Copyright by *Changing Times,* The Kiplinger Magazine. The above figures are based on averages of several companies' rates.

It is well to remember these facts about costs: (1) a woman pays more than a man because she lives longer; (2) for each dollar of income, a cash-refund joint and survivorship plan costs most, and a straight life plan costs least; (3) the older the annuitant when the income begins, the less he will pay, as in the case of an immediate annuity; (4) with a deferred annuity, the younger the annuitant when he buys, the smaller the annual premiums will be.

Combination of Annuities and Investments. Should you put most or all of family savings into annuities? There are limitations to the judicial use of annuities. The major limitation is that they provide for a *fixed income* unprotected from inflation. For the same reason, placing all savings in investments might be too risky.

By judicious combination of annuities and investments, a greater fixed income could be obtained as well as a hedge against inflation. For example, if an elderly couple had $40,000 available at a retirement age of 65 (husband) and 64 (wife), they might invest all the money at 5 per cent, which would net an annual income of $2,000, hardly sufficient to live on. Their income could be divided as follows:

	Annual yield
$15,000 for straight life annuity for wife (at age 64)	$ 962
12,000 for straight life annuity for husband (at age 65)	975
13,000 in good common stock yielding 5 per cent	650
Total	$2,587

Thus, a greater income can be obtained by a combination of annuities and other investments.

Another way to achieve the same objective has been in operation since 1952. In that year, the Teachers Insurance and Annuity Association offered college teachers the opportunity to place from one-fourth to one-half of their pension contributions into selected common stocks through the College Retirement Equities Fund (CREF) and the remainder in regular annuities (TIAA).

This way to finance retirement has been called "inflation-proof annuities." The combined annuity (*fixed* dollar annuity plus the *variable* annuity based on the purchase of common stocks) has produced more income since its inception than the fixed income annuity. This was to be expected because stocks went up between 1952 and 1956. Between 1956 and 1964, the variable annuity continued to produce more income than the fixed dollar annuity.

Variable Annuities—Pro and Con. Despite the arguments, pro and con, over the variable annuity, offered by security dealers, investment bankers, mutual funds, and insurance companies, the two most important considerations from the buyer's point of view concern the tax angle and the final cost in making the investment.

When you buy a variable annuity, the dividends and capital gains are reinvested nearly tax-free by the insurance company. That makes the capital grow faster than is possible when you buy stocks or invest in mutual funds, because in these instances you pay taxes on capital gains and dividends in the year of purchase.

As for cost, variable annuities will probably carry a commission charge, or load, of around 12 per cent over a long period of time. This means that about 12 per cent of the premiums would go into commissions and expenses. For ordinary life insurance the figure is over 15 per cent. On most mutual funds, the load ranges between 4 and 9 per cent. On common stock purchased on a major stock exchange, the commission is much lower, running less than 2 per cent on purchases over $500.

By 1964, over 36,000 college teachers were contributing to the College Retirement Equities Fund. An ever-increasing number of large corporations is also providing variable pensions for their employees, including Warner-Lambert, Boeing Airplane, Pan American Airways, New Jersey Power and Light, to mention a few. Among the major life insurance companies, Prudential is offering variable annuities on an individual or a group basis.

The largest life insurance company, Metropolitan Life, was against the sale of either individual or group annuities by life insurance companies "under present conditions" (1959), which presumably meant that Metropolitan feared the possibility of a stock market crash and long-term inflation. In 1959, of the 257 life insurance companies that answered a mail poll conducted by Metropolitan Life, 210 opposed the sale of variable annuities. Of the rest, 26 voted in favor of selling such contracts, and 21 said they were undecided or had no opinion.[5]

How the Variable Annuity Works. If a buyer decides to set aside, say, $25 each month over a number of years for a variable annuity, the funds would be invested in common stocks. Each payment, after deduction of expenses, would be credited to the buyer's account units, determined by the current dollar value of a unit. The dollar value would go up or down depending on the market value of the stocks; the company makes no guarantees. When the buyer retires, all his variable contract account units would be converted into a fixed number of units. But instead of paying him each month in a *fixed* number of dollars, the variable contract provides for the *current* value of the units credited to him. Thus the dollar value of an annuity unit would change each month according to the investment results on the account.

The potential hazard of the variable annuity, then, is that stock prices may decline, and the investor may get back less than he put in. But in testimony before the Securities Exchange Commission in 1962, the Pru-

[5] *The Wall Street Journal,* June 18, 1959.

ANNUITIES: TO BUY OR NOT TO BUY

If you are	Start with you — Your life expectancy is	Suppose you buy an annuity of — $100 a month, guaranteed for life, but all payments stopping at death, it will cost	Suppose you invest the same amount and take $100 a month to live on—		
			You can live on interest only if your money earns about	With lower interest rates, you can top both interest and principal and your money will last	And if still living your life expectancy will then be
A woman age 65	17½ years (41% live at least 20 years)	$18,500	6½%	At 2%, 18 years; At 3%, 21 years; At 4%, 24 years	At age 83, 8 years; At age 86, 7 years; At age 89, 6 years
A man age 65	14½ years (27% live at least 20 years)	$17,750	7½%	At 2%, 15 years; At 3%, 17 years; At 4%, 18 years	At age 80, 7 years; At age 82, 6 years; At age 83, 6 years

SOURCE: Copyright by *Changing Times*, The Kiplinger Magazine.

dential Insurance Company argued that the danger is minimal; that the payments into a variable annuity over any modern 15-year period would have provided a greater return than fixed annuities. One reason for the delay in launching the variable annuity programs is that they have been ruled by the courts to be subject, not only to state insurance regulations, but to SEC regulations also.

The chief advantage of the variable annuity is that it serves as a hedge against diminished purchasing power due to inflation. The chief disadvantage is that income may be reduced during a period of stock market decline.

Should You Buy Annuities, Other Investments, or Both? Take a husband and wife needing at age 65 an income of $1,200 in addition to social security. They will have around $35,000 from life savings.

Using the accompanying table, Annuities: To Buy or Not to Buy, read across from left to right. Note first that there is a chance that the wife may live 17½ years beyond age 65 and the husband may live 14½ years beyond age 65, plus the chance of living at least 20 years. Then there is the cost of an annuity—guaranteeing an income but involving the risk of loss in case of early death. Then note the rate of interest that would allow the couple about $1,200 annually without using the principal. Next is shown the length of time their money would last if they put it in a bank or into savings and loan shares and withdrew about $1,200 a year, using up both interest and principal. Finally, note the average years of life remaining if they should outlive their capital.

From an investment point of view, the interest earned on the premiums is below that paid by most savings banks and savings and loan associations. Furthermore, if the policy is cashed within the first 10 years, the annuitant will receive less than he has paid into the account. However if the annuitant lives longer than the statisticians figure, the annuity may be a good bet. If there is continued inflation, and if the dollar should be devalued, deferred contracts, in particular, may not be valuable.

A variable contract would be better in case of inflation and devaluation of the dollar. In the long run, a prudent investor would purchase an immediate annuity (paying it in one lump sum just prior to retirement) combined with other sound investments, pension, and social security.

Returns to the investor differ greatly among companies and contracts. The American Institute for Economic Research, for example, made a study of the annual return for a $1,000 payment for several kinds of nonparticipating annuities available to a man age 65. The annual income that $1,000 would provide for a male, age 65, ranged from $76.86 to $58.69 in the case of immediate nonparticipating installment refund annuities.[6]

[6] *Life Insurance and Annuities from the Buyer's Point of View*, p. 84.

QUESTIONS FOR DISCUSSION

1. How do you account for the fact that many Americans do not plan an intelligent life insurance program for their dependents?

2. Does your state permit the sale of savings bank life insurance? Since only three states permit this kind of life insurance to be sold within their borders, inquire from your local banking and insurance sources why this kind of life insurance cannot be sold in your state, if that is the case.

3. Why do many life insurance agents recommend ordinary life insurance rather than term life insurance?

4. Why is an annuity, though sold by some life insurance companies, not life insurance?

5. How would you modify, if at all, the insurance program for this family?

The father is an engineer, 37 years old, and his wife is 35. They have two children: Jack is 8, and Peggy is 4. Their annual income is $10,000, but this may increase to a maximum of about $20,000. They own their home, but there is a $2,500 unpaid mortgage. The father's employer does not offer group life insurance and does not have a private pension plan. The father is fully covered by social security.

This family owns, at present, $28,000 in life insurance. All the policies are on the life of the father, the only breadwinner in the family. His insurance program is as follows.

Date purchased	Age	Amount and kind	Annual premium
1951	21	$ 5,000 whole life	$ 72
1955	25	10,000 whole life	158
1959	29	7,500 family income	202
1963	33	1,000 whole life	21
1963	33	4,500 20-year term	46

6. What are the fallacies in the statement that "all standard contracts cost the same"?

7. Determine the benefits you might receive from the present social security law by creating your own hypothetical case.

8. Under what conditions might it be wise to purchase an annuity as part of a retirement program? What kind of annuity?

ACTIVITY PROBLEMS

1. A young married couple has an income of $4,500 for their first year. He will be fully covered by social security. For the next 10 years, their certain income will increase each year until it reaches about $9,000 at the end of the decade. They have no other income. They had an emergency fund of $500 when married.

Mary Ann was born on their third anniversary, and John was born during their sixth year of married life. They are planning to send both children to college. The questions are these.

a. How can this family plan a life insurance program during the first 10 years that will give the dependents the most protection at the lowest cost?

b. In the event that the breadwinner lives, how can this family save money for the college education of the two children?

c. What changes, if any, would you suggest for this family after the children are through college and are financially independent?

d. Together with social security, full coverage, what additional insurance and investments would you suggest for this family?

e. What will the total security program cost this family at various stages of their family life?

2. Obtain the rates of a typical life insurance company for renewable term insurance, ordinary life insurance, 20-payment life insurance, 20-year endowment insurance, and an annuity purchased just prior to retirement at age 65, for a man at ages 25, 35, and 65. On the basis of the information obtained, which type of insurance would you recommend in each of the following cases?

a. A man, recently married, age 25, whose dependent wife will need about $200 a month for life in the event of the death of her husband during the first 5 years of married life.

b. A man 35, with dependent wife and two children, ages 8 and 12.

3. Ask a life insurance agent how he would answer these questions and statements.

a. "All my savings are going into investments. Why bother about life insurance?"

b. "I have no dependents. Why should I buy life insurance?"

c. "I don't believe in buying life insurance on my children."

4. Suppose a widow is left with $35,000 from life insurance. She is debating whether to take it in a lump sum and invest it or to take a definite amount each month for as long as she lives. What are your arguments for and against each course?

SUGGESTED READINGS

American Institute for Economic Research. *Life Insurance and Annuities from the Buyer's Point of View,* Great Barrington, Mass., 1960.

Barron's Financial Weekly. "Met vs. Pru: The Variable Annuity Touches Off a Financial Free-for-all," Jan. 23, 1956.

Carson, John J., and McConnell, John W. *Economic Needs of Older People.* New York: Twentieth Century Fund, 1956.

Changing Times. "Inflation-proof Annuities," December, 1955; "What You Should Know about Annuities," June, 1952; "Put It in the Child's Name," April, 1963; "Straight Life: Best All-around Policy," July, 1963; "Money Talk for Newlyweds," June, 1963; "Life Insurance for Kids," December, 1959; "Your GI Insurance Today," June, 1963; "Buy Term Insurance and Invest the Difference," October, 1962.

Cohen, Jerome B., and Hanson, Arthur W. *Personal Finance: Principles and Case Methods.* Homewood, Ill.: Richard D. Irwin, Inc., 1964, chaps. 7, 8.

Consumers Union Report on Life Insurance Policies and Costs, Mount Vernon, N.Y., 1965.

Council on Consumer Information. *Helping You Plan Your Life Insurance Program,* Greeley, Colo., 1956.

Dublin, Louis I., and Lotka, Alfred J. *The Money Value of Man.* New York: The Ronald Press Company, rev. ed., 1946.

Flitcraft, Inc. *Flitcraft Compend,* New York, latest edition.

Hathaway, Barbara H. *Your Life Insurance.* Garden City, N.Y.: Doubleday & Company, Inc., 1962.

Hendershot, Ralph. *The Grim Truth about Life Insurance.* New York: G. P. Putnam's Sons, 1957.

Household Finance Corporation. *Your Savings and Investment Dollar,* Chicago, 1963.

Institute of Life Insurance. *Life Insurance Fact Book, 1964* (annual); *Handbook of Life Insurance,* latest edition, New York.

Johnson, George E. *Variable Annuities.* Washington, D.C.: The Reprint Company, 1961.

Levy, Michael H. *Your Insurance and How to Profit by It.* New York: Harcourt, Brace & World, Inc., 1955.

Lovelace, Griffin M. *Life and Life Insurance.* New York: Life Insurance Agency Management Association, 1962.

Miller, Jerome S. *Your Personal Insurance Guide.* New York: Simon and Schuster, Inc., 1955, chaps. 4, 5.

National Underwriter Company. *Little Gem Life Chart,* Cincinnati, latest edition.

Prudential Insurance Company of America. *The Aims, Background and Case for a Variable Annuity Contract,* New York.

Rogers, Donald I. *Teach Your Wife to Be a Widow.* New York: Holt, Rinehart and Winston, Inc., 1953.

Soule, George. *Longer Life.* New York: The Viking Press, Inc., 1958.

Teachers Insurance and Annuity Association, College Retirement Equities Fund. *TIAA CREF 1963 Annual Report,* New York.

U.S. Department of Health, Education, and Welfare, Social Security Administration. *Your Social Security* (annual leaflet); *The Social Security Disability Insurance Program,* 1962; *Social Security Benefits,* latest issue; *Financing Your Social Security Benefits,* latest issue.

Veterans Administration. *National Service Life Insurance and Serviceman's Indemnity,* Washington, D.C., latest edition.

13

THE FEDERAL INCOME TAX

We are all familiar with Benjamin Franklin's remark: "In this world nothing is certain but death and taxes." And the older one grows, the more certain he feels that old Ben was so right. The tax burden on the family increases yearly despite efforts on the part of the taxpayer to take advantage of every legal deduction. It is said that one newlywed, filling out his income tax return, listed a deduction for his wife, and in the section "Exemptions for children" penciled the notation, "Watch this space." He should meet the man with six "little deductions" who said, "It's got to be sort of a game with us. Every time the government raises taxes, we counter with another exemption."

Taxes in the United States are levied by three forms of government—the Federal government, the states, and local governments. All three governments have been collecting more and more taxes as the years have passed. In this chapter, we shall be concerned only with the Federal income tax because this is the one that hits the hardest.

The Federal Budget. In the fiscal year 1963, Federal budget expenditures were $92.6 billion. Budget receipts were $86.4 billion, leaving a budget deficit of $6.2 billion. The budget deficit was financed by borrowing, with a resulting increase in the public debt. Although increasing in amount, the trend of the outstanding public debt relative to the total output of goods and services in the nation—gross national product—has been declining since the end of World War II. The debt was about 54 per cent of gross national product at the end of fiscal year 1963, compared to a peak of 133 per cent at the end of fiscal 1946, and 58 per cent at the end of fiscal 1960. This is shown in the accompanying chart, Public Debt as a Per Cent of Gross National Product.

Federal budget expenditures have been increasing in amount since 1955, but have remained a relatively stable proportion of the total output of goods and services in the nation. In fiscal 1963, as in fiscal 1952, expenditures were about 20 per cent of the gross national product, as shown in the accompanying chart, Budget Expenditures as a Per Cent of Gross National Product.

More than $58 billion, about three-fifths of total budget expenditures during fiscal 1963, were for national defense and for international and

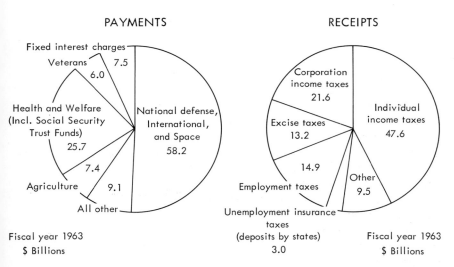

PAYMENTS

Fixed interest charges — 7.5
Veterans 6.0
Health and Welfare (Incl. Social Security Trust Funds) 25.7
National defense, International, and Space 58.2
7.4
Agriculture 9.1
All other

Fiscal year 1963
$ Billions

RECEIPTS

Corporation income taxes 21.6
Individual income taxes 47.6
Excise taxes 13.2
14.9
Other 9.5
Employment taxes
Unemployment insurance taxes (deposits by states) 3.0

Fiscal year 1963
$ Billions

SOURCE: *Your Federal Income Tax*, Internal Revenue Service, Treasury Department, 1964.

space programs—activities necessary for national security and for maintaining our international position. In addition, two other categories of Federal budget expenditures are related to the cost of the nation's past wars—those for veterans' benefits and for interest on the public debt, largely incurred during periods of war.

Expenditures in fiscal 1963 for veterans' benefits and services were $6 billion, and expenditures for interest on the public debt were $7.5 billion, as shown in the accompanying charts, Income and Expenditures. These two categories accounted for 12 per cent of total 1963 budget expenditures. Thus, almost 65 per cent of the budget reflects the combined cost of past wars and of meeting current national defense and international and space objectives.

Relationship between Taxes and Family Welfare. Most families are only vaguely aware of the benefits they receive from local, state, and Federal

PUBLIC DEBT AS A PER CENT OF GROSS NATIONAL PRODUCT

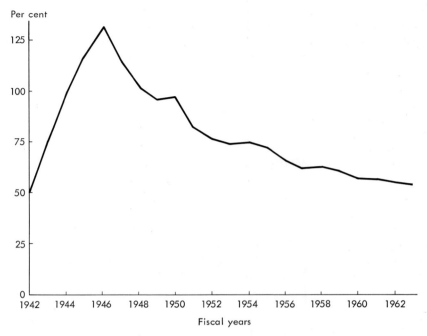

FEDERAL PAYMENTS AS A PER CENT OF
GROSS NATIONAL PRODUCT

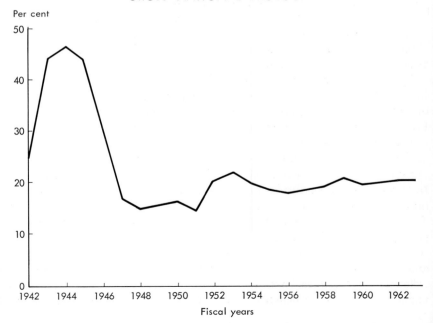

SOURCE: *Your Federal Income Tax,* Internal Revenue Service, Treasury Department,
1964.

governments. But they are increasingly aware of the higher taxes they must pay. It is a good idea to be conscious of the reasons for the tax burden as well as conscious of income tax deducted from the pay check, local property taxes, consumption taxes, such as entertainment, communications, sales, and excise taxes, and many others that could be named.

Too many families are as unaware of the relationship between their taxes and their personal and family welfare as was the father of five children of school age who complained about his property tax of $185. A more thoughtful neighbor asked him where he could obtain schooling for his five children for less money.

There is a difference between tax expenditures that improve our standard of living and maintain our freedom and taxes that are wasteful and unproductive. It is up to the consumer-citizen to eliminate the latter and cheerfully provide for the former in his financial planning.

All the tax problems that the head of a family may face obviously cannot be included in this chapter. Tax rates that are mentioned will become outdated. Tax laws are changed, revised, and amended annually. But the general tax principles may remain the same for many years. Therefore, the explanations that are given here are intended to make the breadwinner (1) evaluate and appreciate the necessity for taxes, (2) establish and keep adequate tax records to simplify preparing his tax reports and to prove his deductions, (3) take full advantage of reducing his taxes honestly, and (4) seek expert counsel when needed.

A family with ordinary sources of income and modest property usually can handle its tax problems without too much difficulty. There are times, however, when it is wise to seek the advice of a tax expert. It is the essence of good consumer procedure to know when to go to the expert. This is especially true in certain matters that pertain to Federal income tax and to gift, estate, and inheritance taxes.

Securing Information about Your Income Tax. Almost all individuals and families have to pay a Federal income tax, which has become a major individual and family expense. The tax law is so complex that one out of every four or five tax returns includes errors. Most persons pay too little; only a few pay too much.

The Internal Revenue Service has a budget that permits the staff to examine only a modest percentage of the returns. The larger the return, however, the more likely that it will be checked. More than half of the returns checked are found to be inaccurate, most of the errors being in the arithmetic, number of exemptions, allowable personal deductions, and reporting of complete income.

Many persons could probably save some money by consulting a tax expert. There are, however, free and inexpensive sources of income tax information besides the instruction pages that accompany the income tax form mailed to each taxpayer on record. Also in the offices of the Internal

Revenue Service in the various cities, there are experts who help taxpayers without charge.

There are two inexpensive informative pamphlets, *Your Federal Income Tax* [1] and J. K. Lasser's *Your Income Tax*,[2] which are revised annually. Property owners, or anyone buying or selling property, or anyone with unusual expenses and income would probably save money by consulting these sources.

Who Must File Tax Returns. Every citizen or resident of the United States, whether an adult (under 65) or a minor, who had a gross income of $600 or more in the previous taxable year must file a return in order to claim the withholding tax. Persons over 65 are not required to file a return unless their gross income is $1,200 or more for the year.

The return must be filed in one of 64 collective districts, usually the one closest to the taxpayer's legal address, not later than April 15 of each year.

Tax Forms. The Federal government provides four main tax forms to cover the sources of income of 55 million people who file each year: Form 1040A, Form 1040 (with use of tax table), Form 1040 (with computation of taxes), and Form 1040W.

Form 1040A. This form may be used if the total income is less than $10,000 for the year and consists of income from which taxes have been withheld (shown on Form W-2), and not more than $200 in dividends, interest, and other wages from which there has been no withholding of tax.

The special card form (1040A) is for persons making less than $5,000 annually, consisting only of wages reported on W-2, and not over $100 in wages, interest, and dividends from which no tax was withheld. You may either figure your own tax or ask the Internal Revenue Service to help you. This is the easiest form to use. If, however, your deductions exceed 10 per cent of income, you would probably want to use Form 1040W or Form 1040.

Form 1040 with use of Tax Table. This form can be used in two different ways. It may be used by persons with income less than $5,000. If the income consists of only wages or salary, use only the first two pages of the form. The Tax Table (given in the instructions pamphlet) has already allowed 10 per cent for deductions. If that amount would cover your possible deductions, simply ascertain your tax from the table, after reading the instructions at the top.

Form 1040 with computation of taxes. You must use Form 1040 (unless you use Form 1040W) if your income is $10,000 or more. Either of these forms must be used if you itemize your deductions, but you may take the standard deduction, which is generally wise when deductions are less than 10 per cent of income.

Form 1040W. This form, used first in 1959, contains two pages stream-

[1] Washington, D.C.: Government Printing Office.
[2] New York: Simon and Schuster, Inc.

lined from Form 1040. You may use this form if (1) Your income consists of salary and wages to any amount, (2) You have no more than $200 in dividends and interest, and (3) You have no other income. You can itemize your deductions or take the standard deduction. Form 1040W is easier to fill in than Form 1040.

Declaration of Estimated Tax. For persons whose incomes are derived from other sources than salary and wages (professional and business services, investments, farmers), there is no withholding of taxes. Such persons report (on Form 1040-ES) an estimate of their income for the year to come, the amount expected to be withheld, and the amount in excess of estimated taxes over estimated withholding. Payments are due on April 15, June 15, September 15, and January 15.

You are required to file a Declaration of Estimated Tax if (1) expected income not subject to withholding tax is more than $200; or (2) expected income exceeds your withholding tax (if any) by $40 or more, and you can reasonably expect gross income exceeding:

Single	$ 5,000
Married (but not entitled to file a joint return)	5,000
Married (entitled to file a joint return)	10,000
Surviving spouse	10,000
Head of household	10,000

Joint or Separate Returns for Married Persons. Most married persons have a choice of filling either a joint or a separate return. Usually, the tax on a joint return is lower than on a separate return. To be certain about this, compute the tax liability both ways and select the return with the lower total tax. Only a husband and wife can file a joint return. If a spouse dies during the year, the surviving spouse can still file a joint return. In case of a divorce on or before December 31, a joint return cannot be filed. A wife does not need to have a separate income when a joint return is used.

Under Age 21. A minor must file a tax return if he has income of $600 or over. He is entitled to a personal exemption of $600 on his own return.

If the minor is under 19 or a student, the parents may also claim the child as a dependent if they finance over half of his support, and even if the child earns more than $600.

A minor whose total income is less than $600, and subject to withholding tax, should file Form 1040A, accompanied by the withholding Form W-2, as he is entitled to a refund.

Unmarried Head of Household. An unmarried person required to maintain a home for himself and others may have expenses comparable to a family. To file as a head of household, the person must have paid for over half of the cost of maintaining the home, and lived there himself along with related persons, unmarried children or grandchildren, or married child.

If a father and mother qualify as dependents, a son or daughter can file as head of household even if the parents live in another home (not in a nursing home).

Claiming Exemptions. You are permitted to subtract $600 from your income for each exemption. Don't forget to count yourself as one exemption. A person who is blind or over age 65 is entitled to two exemptions.

You are entitled to one exemption for each child if, during the taxable year, the child

1. Received less than $600 gross annual income (unless under 19 or a student, in which case the limitation does not apply); and

2. Received more than half of his support from his parents (or from husband or wife if a joint return); and

3. Did not file a joint return with her husband (or his wife); and

4. Was either a citizen or resident of the United States, or a resident of Canada, Mexico, the Republic of Panama, or the Canal Zone; or was an alien child adopted by and living with a United States citizen abroad; and

5. Either had your home as his principal place of abode and was a member of your household for your entire taxable year, or was related to you in one of the following ways:

Mother	Stepbrother	Father-in-law	Blood relatives:
Father	Stepsister	Brother-in-law	Aunt
Grandparent	Stepmother	Sister-in-law	Uncle
Brother	Stepfather	Son-in-law	Nephew
Sister	Mother-in-law	Daughter-in-law	Niece
Grandchild			

Taxable Income. All income that is not specifically exempt is subject to tax. Examples of income that must be reported:

Wages, salaries, bonuses, commissions
Dividends, interest, tips, gratuities
Pensions, annuities, and endowments
Rents, royalties, patents, copyrights
Business and professional profits
Profits from sale of cars, real estate, securities
Estate and trust income, contest prizes
Military pay, gambling winnings

The following are examples of income that are tax-exempt and should not be reported.

Scholarship and fellowship grants
Interest from state and municipal bonds
Federal and state social security income

Workmen's compensation and damages
Gifts and inheritances
Income from health and accident insurance policies
Casualty insurance income
Disability and death benefits
Life insurance paid in a lump sum
Railroad Retirement Act benefits
Government benefits to veterans and their families
Dividends from veterans' insurance

You must report your gross income regardless of the deductions through withholdings on the part of your employer.

Adjusted Gross Income. Adjusted gross income is the balance remaining after deducting from gross income the following:

Expenses of business or profession
Expenses of rental property
Transportation expenses in connection with your work
Travel expenses in connection with your work away from home
Losses incurred in the sale of securities, real estate, and other types of property
Sick pay (if included in gross income)
Fifty per cent of capital gains

Dividend Income. Previously, a taxpayer could exclude from his taxable income the first $50 of dividends received from domestic corporations— $100 for a husband and wife if each received at least $50 of dividend income. In addition, a taxpayer was allowed a credit against his tax equal to 4 per cent of his dividend income in excess of the exclusion.

The Revenue Act of 1964 doubles the exclusion from $50 to $100—from $100 to $200 for married couples—and repeals the 4 per cent dividend credit. The increase in the exclusion takes effect in 1964, while the credit is reduced to 2 per cent in 1964 and repealed in 1965.

At present, 6.2 million taxpayers receive dividend income. The combined effect of these two changes will be to reduce taxes for the two million investors with moderate stockholdings because the increase in the dividend exclusion more than offsets the loss of the dividend credit. The changes will not affect the 1.7 million small investors whose dividends do not exceed $50—or $100 if married. In other words, 60 per cent of all dividend recipients will come out as well, or ahead, just from the dividend provisions in the Act.

The 2.5 million large investors might find that the loss of the dividend credit is not fully offset by the increase in the dividend exclusion. However, the disadvantages to all these large investors will be more than offset by the new lower rates—both individual and corporate.

To retain the dividend credit along with the other provisions benefiting shareholders would give them a disproportionate share of the benefits of tax reduction and revision as compared with nonshareholders. The act lowers individual income tax rates and thus reduces taxes on dividends and salaries; it lowers the corporate tax rate, making more dividends possible and adding value to shares; and it doubles the exclusion of dividend income from taxable income.

Moreover, the 4 per cent dividend credit discriminates in favor of shareholders with large dividend income—principally those in the high income brackets—as compared with the largely middle- and lower-income shareholders with more modest amounts of dividends. This discrimination results because the 4 per cent credit provides a larger and larger amount of tax credit as dividend income increases.

The 4 per cent dividend credit is the equivalent of a four-point reduction in the tax rates applied to those dividends for which the credit is received. The reduction in most income brackets of four points or more means that, with respect to dividends taxed in these brackets, the reduction completely offsets the elimination of the dividend credit. With respect to dividends taxed in those brackets where only a three-point reduction is provided, the remaining point of the dividend credit is, in almost every case, completely offset by the combination of (1) the greater-than-four-point reductions in the first two brackets (and, where applicable, in the higher brackets), (2) the doubling of the dividend exclusion, and (3) the rate reduction on nondividend income.

Thus, the effect of the dividend provisions and individual rate reductions alone is such that almost all taxpayers will pay lower taxes.

Rents, Royalties, and Other Income. Rent includes income from real estate and any other form of property. In rented property, ordinary expenses and repairs are deductible expenses. Capital expenditures or improvements must be added to the cost of rented property and depreciated over its remaining life.

Royalties and rental income are reported in the space indicated on the tax return. But the details on depreciation are listed in a separate schedule.

Any other source on income, as from estates and trusts, prizes, alimony, recovery of bad debts, losses, and so on, must be reported where indicated on the tax return.

Reporting Deductions. Prior to the Revenue Act of 1964, single persons with incomes as low as $667 and married couples with incomes as low as $1,333 paid individual income taxes. In our society it is difficult to provide even minimum levels of subsistence on incomes such as these. This is poverty in every sense of the word.

To help these millions of Americans who are not sharing fully in the nation's prosperity, a minimum standard deduction is included in the 1964 Revenue Act.

The minimum standard deduction means that everyone will be allowed to deduct at least this minimum amount—in addition to his personal exemption—from his income before computing his taxes. The minimum is $200 for a single individual, $400 for a married couple, and an additional $100 for each dependent up to a ceiling of $1,000. Taxpayers who are 65 and over, or who are blind (and also their spouses if 65 or over, or blind), are allowed an additional $100 on their minimum standard deduction. This does not interfere with the additional $600 personal exemption such taxpayers now receive.

A taxpayer may choose to take a standard deduction, which cannot exceed 10 per cent of the taxpayer's income, or $1,000, whichever is less. The minimum standard deduction will be available as an alternative to the standard deduction or to itemizing deductions. The new minimum standard deduction means a higher deduction, and a lower tax bill, for all those who have used the standard deduction and have:

No dependents and income of less than $3,000
One dependent (a wife or any other dependent) and income of less than $4,000
Two dependents (a wife and child or any other two dependents) and income of less than $5,000
Three dependents and income of less than $6,000
Four dependents and income of less than $7,000
Five dependents and income of less than $8,000
Six dependents and income of less than $9,000
Seven dependents and income of less than $10,000

Additional benefits, of course, will go to low-income taxpayers 65 or over or blind.

Persons with the lowest incomes will benefit the most from the minimum standard deduction. The total tax loss to the government from the provision is estimated at $320 million.

Of this amount, $170 million, or 53.1 per cent, will go to an estimated 8.3 million taxpayers with incomes of less than $3,000 a year. Another $100 million will go to taxpayers with incomes between $3,000 and $5,000 —nearly 3 million taxpayers. This means that 84.4 per cent of the benefits will go to taxpayers with incomes under $5,000 a year. The remaining $50 million of tax relief will go to 2.1 million taxpayers with incomes of more than $5,000 but less than $10,000.

Some taxpayers who itemize their deductions may find it simpler and more advantageous to switch to the new minimum standard deductions. Those who can claim deductions larger than the new minimum through itemizing will, of course, continue to itemize their deductions. And those taxpayers for whom the standard deduction exceeds the minimum standard deduction will continue to take the standard deduction.

This provision means that single individuals will remain free of income tax liability until their incomes exceed $800 ($600 personal exemption plus $200 standard deduction) rather than the previous $667. A married couple (with no dependents, filing a joint return), once subject to tax on that part of their income in excess of $1,333, will be taxed only on income in excess of $1,600. A married couple with two children will be subject to tax on income in excess of $3,000, rather than on the excess of $2,666. The minimum standard deduction grants tax relief to 13.4 million taxpayers with incomes under $10,000 and takes a total of about 1.5 million low-income returns off the tax rolls entirely. It is the most effective way to make sure that the low-income people who need it most get their fair share of the benefits of the tax reduction.

Contributions. The Revenue Act of 1964 contains five provisions affecting the tax treatment of charitable contributions. These provisions will:

1. Increase the allowable tax deduction for certain contributions made by individuals
2. Permit the "carryover" of certain excess contributions by individuals
3. Delay the deduction for contributions of future interests in tangible personal property until the donor's rights to the property expire or are relinquished
4. Limit the organizations to which an individual may make deductible contributions and claim an unlimited charitable deduction
5. Extend the period of "carryover" of excess charitable contributions made by corporations.

Increased Deduction for Contributions by Individuals. Under the old law, individual taxpayers were allowed a deduction of up to 20 per cent of their adjusted gross income for contributions to specified categories of philanthropic organizations. An additional deduction, amounting to another 10 per cent of a taxpayer's adjusted gross income, was permitted for contributions to churches, schools, hospitals, and certain medical research organizations. This resulted in a maximum 30 per cent deduction where such charitable contributions were involved.

The 1964 act extends the additional 10 per cent deduction to include contributions to any organization to which the basic 20 per cent limitation applies if the organization is publicly supported. This allows an individual to deduct annually up to 30 per cent of his adjusted gross income for contributions to most types of charitable organizations.

This provision will provide uniform tax treatment of gifts to organizations which are supported by the general public. It will aid in the advancement of activities such as symphony orchestras, museums, libraries, and the work of community chests and cultural centers. Organizations such as the American National Red Cross and the American Cancer Society, which receive nationwide public support, will also become eligible for larger tax-deductible contributions.

The additional 10 per cent deduction will not be extended to organizations such as fraternal societies, war veterans posts, trusts, and private foundations. However, the basic 20 per cent deduction will still apply to them.

Carryover of Excess Contributions by Individuals. Under previous law, contributions in excess of the 20 per cent and 30 per cent limitations were generally not deductible, neither in the year of the contributions nor in subsequent years. The act permits a taxpayer to carry over for five years certain charitable contributions which are greater than the allowable amount deductible in the year paid. This means that the "unused" contributions to publicly supported organizations may be deducted from income earned in the next five years, subject to the 30 per cent limitation. The carryover provision generally applies only to gifts to publicly supported organizations and does not apply to contributions to private foundations.

Gifts of Future Interest. Prior law allowed a taxpayer to deduct a donation to a charitable organization and still retain possession of his donation. For example, a person could stipulate that at some future date a certain painting would be transferred to a specified art gallery. Until that time he would retain the painting for his own enjoyment. Previously, he was permitted to treat this donation as a charitable contribution at the time he made the gift of future interest, to the extent of the value of that interest. This gave rise to considerable abuse.

Under the 1964 act, a taxpayer will be permitted a charitable deduction only when the property is actually transferred. That is, a contribution of future interest in tangible personal property will be an allowable deduction only when all the donor's interests in and rights to the possession of the property have expired or are relinquished.

Unlimited Deduction. In certain instances, taxpayers are permitted an unlimited deduction for contributions to charitable organizations. Under prior law, taxpayers could deduct charitable contributions without regard to the 20 or 30 per cent limitation if the sum of all contributions plus income tax liability was greater than 90 per cent of their taxable income in the current year and eight of the last ten taxable years.

The 1964 act provides that this unlimited deduction will be available only where the charitable contributions are made to organizations to which the 30 per cent limitation would apply or to privately supported foundations which actually conduct active charitable programs or which expend all of their income and 50 per cent of the gift in question for specified purposes within three years after they receive the contribution. Thus, only contributions to such organizations may be included in satisfying the 90 per cent test. The unlimited deduction will not be available with respect to gifts to private foundations which do not meet the foregoing requirements.

Interest Charges. If you itemize deductions, you can deduct interest paid on your personal debts, such as bank loans or home mortgages. Interest paid on business debts should be reported in the separate schedule in which business income is reported.

Do not deduct interest paid on money borrowed to buy tax-exempt securities or single-premium life insurance.

In figuring the interest paid on a mortgage on your home or on an installment contract for goods for your personal use, eliminate such items as carrying charges and insurance, which are not deductible, and taxes that may be deductible but should be itemized separately.

If interest charges are not stated separately on installment purchases of personal property (such as automobiles, television sets, and the like), you may deduct an amount equal to 6 per cent of the average unpaid monthly balance.

You *can* deduct interest on:

Your personal note to a bank or an individual
A mortgage on your home
A life insurance loan, if you pay the interest in cash
Delinquent taxes

You *cannot* deduct interest on:

Indebtedness of another person, when you are not legally liable for payment of the interest
A gambling debt or other nonenforceable obligation
A life insurance loan, if interest is added to the loan and you report on the cash basis.

Nondeductibility of Certain Taxes. The Revenue Act eliminates the deductibility from personal income of certain state and local taxes. The provision does *not* affect real estate taxes, general sales and use taxes, personal property taxes, state and local income taxes, and gasoline taxes, all of which remain completely deductible. Nor does it affect taxes which are paid in connection with the operation of a business or with investment property; these, too, remain allowable deductions.

The provision affects only a small part of the deductions formerly claimed by the average taxpayer. It affects only about 12 per cent of the amount previously deducted by individuals for payment of taxes which were not business expenses. The provision will increase Federal tax revenues by an estimated $300 million per year. In addition, it will eliminate the discrimination resulting from the fact that certain of the taxes could previously be deducted by taxpayers in some states but not in others.

The following are the principal state and local taxes which will no longer be allowable deductions:

Taxes on cigarettes and tobacco
Taxes on alcoholic beverages
Poll taxes
Miscellaneous selective sales taxes (such as admissions taxes, occupancy or transfer taxes)
Automobile license plates
Drivers' permits

In addition, foreign taxes (other than real property and income taxes) will similarly not be deductible.

Under the old law, the special excise taxes of many states were not deductible by the consumer because they are imposed on the manufacturer, wholesaler, or retailer—not on the consumer. In other states the same taxes are imposed on the consumer or are imposed on the seller but are separately stated and collected from the consumer and were, therefore deductible by the consumer. For example, 47 states impose a tax on alcoholic beverages, but those of only 16 states were deductible by the consumer. Cigarette taxes of only 25 states of the 47 which impose them were deductible by the consumer.

The consumer generally bears the ultimate burden of a special excise tax, whether it is imposed directly on him or on the seller and whether or not it is separately stated. But deductibility depended on only one distinction—the legal wording of the state statute. Therefore, the criterion for deductibility discriminated against those persons in states which, in legal form, impose their taxes on the seller, rather than the consumer, without stating the taxes separately.

This provision in the new tax law will simplify the task of preparing a tax return for the average taxpayer who itemizes. The taxes for which no deductions are allowed are among those for which it is most difficult to keep accurate records.

Most taxpayers who once itemized these taxes as deductions resorted to rough estimates of the amount of cigarette and alcohol taxes paid, and this often resulted in controversy with the Internal Revenue Service. Moreover, it was often difficult for the average taxpayer to distinguish between taxes which were deductible and those which were not. For example, the cigarette tax of one state may have been deductible while the tax of the neighboring state was not deductible. As a result, some taxpayers did not take full advantage of all available deductions, while others did—especially those who could afford tax advice.

This provision will end the discrimination between taxpayers of different states and between the average taxpayer and the taxpayer with professional tax advice. It will simplify preparation of tax returns and eliminate many potential controversies with the IRS.

It will not deprive taxpayers of any essential deduction, nor will it adversely affect homeownership, since property taxes and interest payments continue to be fully allowable deductions.

Medical and Dental Expenses. If you itemize deductions, you can deduct, within the limits described below, the amount you paid during the year (not compensated by hospital, health, or accident insurance) for medical or dental expenses for yourself, your wife, or any dependent who received over half of his support from you whether or not the dependent had $600 or more income. List on an attachment sheet the name and amount paid to each person or institution.

You can deduct amounts paid for the prevention, cure, correction, or treatment of a physical or mental defect or illness. If you pay someone for both nursing and domestic duties, you can deduct only the nursing cost.

You can deduct amounts paid for transportation primarily for and essential to medical care, but not for any other travel expense even if it benefits your health. Meals and lodging while you are away from home receiving medical treatment may not be treated as medical expense unless they are part of a hospital bill or are included in the cost of care in a similar institution.

Subject to the limitations set forth below, you *can* deduct as medical expenses payments to or for:

Physicians, dentists, nurses, and hospitals
Drugs or medicines
Transportation necessary to get medical care
Eyeglasses, artificial teeth, medical or surgical appliances, braces, etc.
X-ray examinations or treatment
Premiums on hospital or medical insurance

You *cannot* deduct payments for:

Funeral expenses and cemetery plot
Illegal operations or drugs
Travel ordered or suggested by your doctor for rest or change
Premiums on life insurance
Cosmetics

Under prior law, all medicine and drug expenses of taxpayers over 65 were subject to a 1 per cent floor. This meant that payments for medicines and drugs were deductible only to the extent that they exceeded 1 per cent of adjusted gross income (which is total income for most wage and salary earners).

The 1964 Revenue Act removes this 1 per cent floor and makes payments for medicines and drugs for persons 65 and over *fully* deductible from their income for tax purposes. Elimination of the 1 per cent floor applies to medicine and drug expenses of a taxpayer 65 or over and those of his or her spouse. It also applies to expenses paid on behalf of dependent parents age 65 or over.

The medical expenses of most taxpayers are subject to a floor of 3 per cent of adjusted gross income. However, the 3 per cent floor does not apply to medical expenses of taxpayers or dependent parents over age 65. The new provision will *not* change these rules.

Elimination of the 1 per cent floor will help to further ease the burden of medicine and drug expenses for persons 65 and over. It is only a small step toward solving the problem of medical care for the elderly. But it will provide an annual tax saving of $10 million for the 3.4 million elderly taxpayers.

Expenses for Care of Children and Other Dependents. The cost of caring for children and disabled dependents may be deducted, with certain limitations, from an individual's income for tax purposes if the care involved permits the individual to be gainfully employed.

Under former law, a maximum deduction of $600 was available to all employed women, whether single or married, and also to widowers and divorced or legally separated men for expenses for the care of children under 12 and disabled dependents of any age. A married woman, however, could not claim the deduction if she and her husband together earned over $5,100, and for every dollar they earned over $4,500, they had to subtract a dollar from the maximum $600 allowable.

In recognition of the fact that the cost of care increases when there are more children or dependents, the new tax law allows additional deductions of $300 for two or more children or dependents. Thus, the maximum deduction would be $600 for one child or dependent and $900 for two or more children or dependents. The deduction cannot exceed the actual cost of care for dependents in any case.

The 1964 act also raises to $6,000 the income limitation which applies to married women. For every dollar she and her husband earn over $6,000 they must subtract a dollar from the maximum allowable deduction. This means that if they have one child or dependent they cannot claim the deduction if they together earn over $6,600. With two or more children or dependents the deduction vanishes at $6,900.

The provision also allows a married man to deduct the cost of child care if his wife is in an institution for at least 90 days. If his wife is at home but unable to care for herself, a married man is also eligible for the deduction, subject to the $6,000 income limitation applicable to married women.

The act also raises the age of children covered by this deduction to include those under 13. The present provision which allows disabled dependents of any age to be included will remain unchanged.

This provision will result in an annual tax saving of $15 million for those who are eligible for the child care deduction.

Casualty Losses and Thefts. The 1964 Revenue Act changes provisions covering the deduction of personal casualty or theft losses for income tax purposes by allowing deductions only to the extent that the loss resulting from each casualty or theft exceeds $100. This limitation is similar to $100 deductible feature of an auto insurance policy: The policyholder absorbs the first $100 of any loss. In the case of a husband and wife who file a joint return, only one $100 floor applies to each casualty or theft even if property of both is involved. For example, if a thief stole the husband's watch and the wife's ring at the same time, the total value (not exceeding cost) of both watch and ring is deductible except for $100.

Taxpayers may deduct losses of property not connected with business or investment if such losses arise from fire, storm, shipwreck, or other casualty or from theft. This deduction was previously available without limitation to all taxpayers who itemized personal deductions rather than using the standard deduction.

The old law allowed minor personal casualty or theft losses to reduce a person's gross income and thus reduced his taxes. Minor losses of this type are normal occurrences for many taxpayers and, as such, should be treated as ordinary living expenses.

It is only where large or extraordinary personal casualty or theft losses occur that tax relief is warranted. This is the reason for the $100 "floor" which the act places under each casualty or theft loss: It eliminates the minor deductions. No upper limit is placed on the amount that can be deducted.

This provision does not affect losses incurred in a taxpayer's trade or business or losses incurred in connection with any transaction entered into for profit. Such losses will continue to be fully deductible.

The provision will increase Federal revenues by $50 million a year.

Expenses for Education. Expenses for education may be deducted if the education was undertaken primarily for the purpose of maintaining or improving skills required in your employment or other trade or business, or meeting the express requirements of your employer, or the requirements of applicable law or regulations, imposed as a condition to the retention of your salary, status, or employment.

Expenses incurred for the purpose of obtaining a new position, a substantial advancement in position, or for personal purposes are not deductible. The expenses incurred in preparing for a trade or a business or a specialty are personal expenses and are not deductible.

The rules for reporting deductible education expenses are the same as those for the reporting of "Employee Business Expenses." If you are required therein to attach a statement to your return explaining the nature of the expenses, also include a description of the relation of the education to your employment or trade or business. If the education was required by your employer, a statement from him would be helpful.

Miscellaneous Deductions. If you are divorced or legally separated and are making periodic payments of alimony or separate maintenance under a court decree, you can deduct these amounts.

You may deduct gambling losses only to the extent of gambling winnings.

You *can* deduct cost of:

Safety equipment
Dues to unions or professional societies
Entertaining customers
Tools and supplies
Fees to employment agencies

You *cannot* deduct cost of:

Travel to and from work
Entertaining friends
Bribes and illegal payments

Capital Gains and Losses. Capital gains or losses are those that arise from selling or exchanging any kind of property. Capital assets are of two different types (excluding sale of assets in a business): non-income-producing assets and income-producing assets. Your home or car are examples of non-income-producing assets. If you sell either one for more than you paid for it, the profit is considered a capital gain. If a loss is sustained, the loss cannot be deducted.

Profits made in the sale of income-producing assets, such as stocks, bonds, and rental property, must be reported as capital gains, and any losses from sale are reported as capital losses.

Capital gains and losses may be either short term or long term. A short-term capital gain or loss is on capital assets held for 6 months or less. A long-term gain or loss is on capital assets held for more than 6 months.

If you sell your home at a gain and buy within one year another house that you use as your residence, the gain is not taxable if the cost of the new house equals or exceeds the sale price of the old one. You are allowed additional time in case of military service or construction of a new home.

Assume that you bought a house several years ago for $8,000 and sold it for $15,000. If you purchased a new house for $15,000 within the time limit, the profit of $7,000 need not be reported. If the new house is later sold for $18,000 and the sum not invested in another home, a capital gain of $10,000 must be reported.

Securities and Capital Gain. The tax advantage is considerable if you hold on to your securities to establish a long-term gain. Only half of your long-term gains (held for 6 months or more) need to be added to ordinary income for tax purposes. A person taxed at 50 or 60 per cent on the income tax scale will probably aim his investments at capital gains rather than recurrent income because the latter is taxed at 50 or 60 per cent, but the long-term gains will be taxed at a maximum of 25 per cent.

Informed investors sell some securities toward the end of the year to establish capital losses to offset earlier capital gains. After 30 days have elapsed, they buy back the securities at about the same prices. They have thus minimized their tax. The tax law does not recognize losses if the same stock is bought within either 30 days before or 30 days after the tax-loss sale—a total of 61 days.

What the Tax Cut Means to You. The following table, Comparison of Income Taxes under the Revenue Act of 1964, indicates the Federal income tax cuts provided in the new tax legislation upon which the Congress finally agreed on February 26, 1964. About two-thirds of the reductions take effect this year with the full cuts to be effective in 1965. The tables are based on taxable income; that is, your gross income minus the various deductions and exemptions to which you are entitled. In order to figure out what the tax cut will mean to you personally you must figure your "taxable income" and then refer to the closest figure to that amount in the tables.

Examination of Returns and Penalties. Sample checking is employed for the bulk of the tax returns. The higher the income, the greater the chance for an audit. When deductions are itemized, the probability of checking is greater. Professional and self-employed persons are likely to be checked.

If the Internal Revenue Service indicates that you have not paid all your taxes, it is up to you to prove otherwise. You can, of course, appeal to a tax court or a Federal court in case you are unable to convince the examining official in your district office.

As a general rule, the Internal Revenue Service has three years, dating from the day of filing, to examine returns and to collect additional taxes. This three-year period is *not* applicable if (1) you filed no return at all (indefinite liability); (2) you filed a proved fraudulent return (indefinite liability); or (3) more than 25 per cent of your total gross income is not

COMPARISON OF INCOME TAXES UNDER THE REVENUE ACT OF 1964

Taxable income after deductions and exemptions	1963 tax	1964		1965	
		Tax (under bill)	Amount saved	Tax (under bill)	Amount saved

Married couples filing jointly

Taxable income after deductions and exemptions	1963 tax	Tax (under bill)	Amount saved	Tax (under bill)	Amount saved
$ 2,000	$ 400	$ 325	$ 75	$ 290	$ 110
3,000	600	500	100	450	150
4,000	800	680	120	620	180
6,000	1,240	1,080	160	1,000	240
8,000	1,680	1,480	200	1,380	300
10,000	2,200	1,950	250	1,820	380
12,000	2,720	2,420	300	2,260	460
16,000	3,920	3,500	420	3,260	660
20,000	5,280	4,720	560	4,380	900
28,000	8,520	7,580	940	7,100	1,420
40,000	14,520	12,900	1,620	12,140	2,380
52,000	21,480	19,200	2,280	18,060	3,420
76,000	36,720	32,940	3,780	31,020	5,700
100,000	53,640	47,880	5,760	45,180	8,460
200,000	134,640	118,680	15,960	110,980	23,660
400,000	313,640	271,680	41,960	250,980	62,660

Single persons

Taxable income after deductions and exemptions	1963 tax	Tax (under bill)	Amount saved	Tax (under bill)	Amount saved
$ 2,000	$ 400	$ 340	$ 60	$ 310	$ 90
4,000	840	740	100	690	150
6,000	1,360	1,210	150	1,130	230
8,000	1,960	1,750	210	1,630	330
10,000	2,640	2,360	280	2,190	450
12,000	3,400	3,040	360	2,830	570
16,000	5,200	4,610	590	4,330	870
20,000	7,260	6,450	810	6,070	1,190
32,000	14,460	12,960	1,500	12,210	2,250
50,000	26,820	23,940	2,880	22,590	4,230
70,000	42,120	37,390	4,730	35,190	6,930
100,000	67,320	59,340	7,980	55,490	11,830
200,000	156,820	135,840	20,980	125,490	31,330

listed on the return (the Federal government has five years to collect the tax or to start court proceedings).

Penalties may be inflicted for failure to file a return, and failure to pay your tax on time. Six per cent interest is charged on unpaid taxes. Both fines and jail sentences are provided for fraudulent returns. There are other penalties, too.

Suggestions for Legitimate Savings in Taxes. You are expected to use all legal means to keep your taxes as low as possible. A tax saving is equivalent to an increase in income. If you do not take full advantage of the law, you will be paying more taxes than the government expects of you.

A good tax lawyer is likely to protect the tax interests of a wealthy person. But most people have income from wages and salary. How can they take full advantage of the law? The following ideas are worth investigating.

1. Most married couples can save in taxes by filing a joint return.

2. Many people overlook legitimate deductions.

3. If you are reporting on a cash basis, it may be possible to defer payment of part of your salary to the following year when your income may be lower. (Some corporate executives have a deferred-compensation plan with their companies.)

4. People in the high income tax brackets may find it profitable to invest in tax-exempt bonds.

5. Retain stocks at least 6 months before selling them.

6. When purchasing old rental property, depreciation can be charged off against the rent before reporting the net rent for tax purposes. A larger percentage of the rent is currently tax-free than in the case of new houses.

7. People who have their own businesses can charge off a great deal to legitimate operating expense and entertainment and travel expenses.

8. Transferring income-producing property to children's names can effect considerable tax savings.

9. If you eventually reach the $25,000 and over bracket, taxes can be reduced considerably via gifts, family trust funds, and family corporations.

10. Moderate-income families can bunch their deductions in alternate years. Take the standard $1,000 deduction one year; then bunch into one year contributions, doctor bills, property taxes, etc., that you normally pay each year.

11. Corporate executives prefer stock-option plans to a raise in salary.

12. A joint return provides for a $100 dividend exclusion, in contrast to $50 in separate returns.

13. A joint return is advantageous if an uncle, aunt, or niece receives chief support from a married couple.

14. Alimony to a previous wife under a court decree can be deducted on a joint return with a present wife.

15. A joint return may not be as good as separate returns when you have (1) capital losses, (2) net capital losses from an earlier year, and (3) medical expenses paid by each spouse and each has income.

16. Have your company carry insurance on you if you are an executive. Savings could be 10 times the insurance premium.

There are many other legal ways to reduce taxes. On the other hand, what was a legal device or technique to reduce taxes at one time may later be declared illegal by court decision or revision by Congress. If in doubt, get expert advice. The Internal Revenue Service will be helpful on many questions. On others you may need a lawyer who specializes in tax problems.

QUESTIONS FOR DISCUSSION

1. When a person does not pay a Federal income tax, does it mean that he pays no Federal taxes?

2. How is our standard of living improved through the use of tax money?

3. What present limitation is there on medical and dental expenses for income tax deduction purposes?

4. Is it necessary that you prove all your income tax deductions?

5. In what way does a homeowner have an advantage over a renter when paying the Federal income tax?

6. Can food baskets donated to charity be used as a basis for income tax deductions?

7. Why is there a limit to Federal income tax deductions for contributions?

8. If you identify a tune on radio or television and win $15,000 in prizes, why must you pay a Federal income tax on your winnings?

9. Under what conditions is income splitting advisable when making out a Federal income tax return?

10. From suggestions in this chapter, make a list of deductible expenditures of which you should keep a daily record to help you when making out your Federal income tax and for proof, if needed.

11. Who must file a Federal income tax return?

12. Who must file a declaration of estimated tax?

13. Where can you get reliable free advice regarding income taxes?

14. When would you recommend that a person use Form 1040A? 1040W? 1040?

15. What is the difference between "gross income" and "adjusted gross income"?

16. What is meant by a capital gain or loss?

17. How are profits and losses incurred on the sale of a home treated for tax purposes?

18. How can people with average incomes save on income taxes?

ACTIVITY PROBLEMS

1. Will Rogers once said: "Income tax has made more liars out of the American people than golf has." This may be true for some taxpaying citizens, but others become tax liars only through ignorance, fear, or laziness. It might be enlightening to check Will Rogers' statement with as many income taxpaying persons as you can. Try to categorize the opinions. Present a summary of the interviews to the class for discussion.

2. Some persons know when they make income tax "boners." Others never realize the mistakes they have made until the Internal Revenue Service notifies them. Using J. K. Lasser and Sylvia F. Porter's *Managing Your Money* (New York: Holt, Rinehart, and Winston, Inc., 1961, pp. 379–413), prepare a list of

possible boners that might be made in income tax returns and check their frequency by interviewing several taxpaying individuals. Which boners are made most frequently? Do not omit "overpayment" as one kind of boner.

3. Talk to a representative of the Internal Revenue Service about the taxes due the Federal government if a person wins a jackpot on a radio or television show or wins in the Irish sweepstakes, in bingo, or a raffle. How can these taxes be reduced to a minimum? Would the person be better off by refusing to accept a jackpot?

4. What percentage of the total income of your family was paid out in taxes in a recent year? You cannot get a completely accurate answer to this question, but you can secure tax facts with regard to (a) personal income taxes; (b) taxes on real and personal property; (c) sales taxes on such items as tobacco, gasoline, clothing, and food; and (d) Federal excise taxes.

5. Those who read this chapter are likely to be students in college. Make a list of the taxes that you pay. How much do you pay each month? What percentage of your monthly income is paid out in taxes?

6. In September, 1956, Mr. Hale bought a house as a residence for his family at a cost of $14,000. In 1964, he sold it for $18,000, after spending $1,200 for major improvements on the house. One month later, he purchased a home for $24,000. What are his income tax problems?

7. A person may exclude from his income tax the first $50 of stock dividends, and a couple owning stock jointly can exclude $100. How do you figure the amount that is taxable if the husband owns some of the stocks and a part of the stocks is jointly owned?

SUGGESTED READINGS

Changing Times. "Your Income Tax," April, 1963; "Tax Help for Single People," March, 1963.

Cohen, Jerome B., and Hanson, Arthur W. *Personal Finance Principles and Case Problems.* Homewood, Ill.: Richard D. Irwin, Inc., 1964, chap. 11.

Dickerson, William E., and Stone, Leo D. *Federal Income Tax Fundamentals.* Belmont, Calif.: Wadsworth Publishing Company, Inc., 1961.

Federal Tax Course. Englewood Cliffs, N.J.: Prentice-Hall, Inc., latest year.

Holzman, Robert S. *Federal Income Taxation.* New York: The Ronald Press Company, 1960.

Individual Federal Income Tax Specimen Returns, Completely Worked Out for Filling in. Englewood Cliffs, N.J.: Prentice-Hall, Inc., latest year.

Investor's Tax Guide. New York: Merrill Lynch, Pierce, Fenner & Smith, Inc. (free).

Lasser, J. K. *Your Income Tax.* New York: Simon and Schuster, Inc., published annually.

U.S. Treasury Department, Internal Revenue Service. *Farmer's Tax Guide,* Publication no. 225 (free); *Your Federal Income Tax,* published annually; *U.S. Income Tax Form 1040 and Instructions,* latest year (free); *Tax Guide for Small Business,* Publication no. 334, latest edition; *Teaching Federal Income Taxes,* Publication no. 19, latest year (free).

14

SAVINGS, INVESTMENTS, ESTATE PLANNING, AND WILLS

We might as well admit, at the start, that saving money is not easy. So many people feel like the wife who said: "But why should we save for the future, Roscoe? If there is anything we want in the future, it'll be available on the credit plan."

Saving money takes discipline, planning, cooperation, and plain hard work. But it is so important to family security and happiness that it is worth this effort. Savings based on a well-planned and purposeful program, balanced with present needs, can be an exciting experience when a family has agreed on its financial security goals.

Every family needs to accumulate funds for use during the more expensive stages of the family life cycle—especially the high school and college period—and for recreation, pleasure, rewards, vacation, household furnishings and equipment, or new furniture. In addition, every family needs to build a reserve fund for the expenses of illness, death, loss of income, and other unforeseen emergencies. It needs savings to ensure financial security in old age or for protection should the breadwinner become incapable of further earning. The payment of life insurance and disability insurance premiums and payments toward the purchase of a home are usually classified as protection for the family.

Putting the American Way of Life into Action. The major goal of family savings is to achieve family happiness through protection. There is, however, another desirable reason why a family should plan its own financial security above the minimum social security benefits. A family that plans its own financial security program—insurance, emergency fund, educational fund, retirement, and possibly its own home—and begins to accumulate its own wealth is not likely to fall for the philosophy of "let the government take care of us."

A family that has planned and saved, sometimes even at the expense of better current living, has too much at stake to support legislation that may substitute government funds for family funds. In other words, family planned and earned financial security is one of the concrete ways by which we can put into action our belief in the American way of life.

What Are Savings? An economist might describe saving as "accumulating wealth through the postponement of consumption." He looks at savings as the first step in creating wealth—that is, the first step in increasing the economy's ability to produce more and better things.

If you decide to bank some of your money for later spending, the bank will lend a part of it to a manufacturer who needs more capital to install new machinery. This is a form of savings that diverts your present spending to new machinery to produce more goods for everyone. This is one function of savings.

What if you, and most Americans, decide to spend all your income in buying things? This would result in less money for producers who want money to expand, and the demand for savings would exceed the supply. This, in combination with other factors, can produce inflationary pressure.

What if you, and most other Americans, decide to double your savings at a time when business does not want to expand? The supply of savings exceeds demand. This, in combination with other factors, can produce a recession.

This is an oversimplified description of the role you play when you drop coins in a piggy bank or put dollars in your bank account. We can draw several useful conclusions from all this.

1. Saving as an operation has an overriding public significance as well as a personal and private one.

2. Savings are not "money not spent." They are money spent at one time instead of another time.

3. The important idea is that savings are money that is not spent for "current consumption."

What has this to do with you and your spending patterns? For one thing, it leads to the idea of what savings are: the difference between your current consumption expenses and your current income. Thus, money you spend for food, clothes, and taxes is not savings. Money you put into bank accounts, stocks, bonds, or real estate is savings. Another lesson to learn from the economist's approach is that of choosing how to spend. When most people choose to save, it actually means choosing to spend more on capital goods, as when you buy a house or stocks, or on future enjoyments, such as college education for your children, retirement, or a trip around the world later on. When you save, you deny yourself something you could have now in order to have something later.

Why Families Save. The greatest incentive to save is provided when savings have a purpose, such as for an emergency fund, an education, homeownership, or a new car—those objectives in life for which money is necessary. Families with the foresight to establish both short-range and long-range goals for the use of money are the ones who seem to get ahead most rapidly. They find that planning helps them place the proper emphasis on the desired goals.

According to researches, three main brackets include the purposes for which families save.

1. Short-term spending plans—saving for something wanted badly in the near future, a car, a home, a vacation
2. Long-term spending plans—college education for children, retirement, buying into a business
3. Financial security—a rainy-day fund, investments, an estate for children or grandchildren, retirement

According to research in the behavioral sciences, a family's major future obligations for retirement and for the education of children may lead to concern but not always to saving.[1] Families may have some long-range concerns, but except for the major contractual commitments in insurance, mortgage, and retirement programs, many appear to be operating on a relatively short-run strategy. According to the researchers, a substantial number of persons are unable to plan. Those who say they are unable to plan are less likely to have hospitalization insurance or liquid assets. They also have less education.

Families with higher incomes do most of the saving and hold most of the assets. Families in the middle range of incomes, $5,000 to $7,500, do less saving, apparently because they prefer to have a higher standard of living immediately—a new car every other year, shrubbery for the yard, a bedroom for the new baby, a long vacation trip, and so on. Often the choices are not this clear-cut.

Who Are the Savers? Families that have received a substantial increase in income are likely to be savers. Their living has been adjusted to a certain standard, and it takes time before they move up to a higher standard of living.

There are other factors that influence a family's ability or desire to save.

1. Occupation. More lower-income wage earners and clerical workers on steady jobs eke out savings than professional and salaried people—perhaps because of the fear of losing their jobs. High-income salaried people often save quite a bit.

[1] James N. Morgan, "Planning for the Future and Living with Risk," *The American Behavioral Scientist*, May, 1963, p. 40.

2. Medical expense. Families having constant large medical bills are not savers. The fewer medical bills, the higher the savings.

3. Age and family cycle. Generally, young single persons and people past 65 produce relatively few savers. The heaviest proportion of families with savings comes from the 35 to 64 age bracket. Couples under 45 with young children and persons over 45, with or without children, are those who seem best able to save.

4. Once a person gets into the habit of saving money, he tends to retain the habit. Conversely, a person who is used to satisfying impulses of the moment and to avoiding choices and decisions finds it hard to save.

5. Contractual savings is the easiest way to save for many people. Commitments to mortgage payments, insurance premiums, pension contributions, and regular monthly investment plans almost always produce continued savings.

6. The big influence on the nature of savings is the great change in the financial tools that families have to work with. Two or three decades ago, the family that didn't save might find itself on charity and in the county poorhouse. But private pension plans, social security, and other government financial aid programs have reduced the need for saving to prevent poverty. Families now plan protection largely by investing in life insurance, disability income insurance, and medical aid insurance. In a strict sense, social security taxes and health insurance premiums are not savings, but the benefits from these affect retirement and emergency fund requirements and savings.

Increase in Personal Savings. In the years from 1951 to 1963, the total amount of personal savings, according to *Economic Indicators*, increased from $17.7 billion to $26.2 billion. During this 12-year period, personal savings as per cent of disposable personal income (personal income less personal taxes equals disposable income) remained quite constant. This is shown in the accompanying table, Distribution of Total Personal Income.

The savings during the 12-year period ranged from 6 to 7.9 per cent of disposable income. At the end of 1961, the total amount of personal savings (not including securities and bonds valued at about $300 billion) in selected savings institutions was as follows:

	Billions of dollars
Commercial banks	$75.9
Savings and loan associations	70.8
Mutual savings banks	38.3
Mutual funds	24.9
U.S. savings bonds (current redemption value of bonds held)	46.5
Credit unions	5.7
Postal savings	0.7

SOURCE: Federal Home Loan Bank Board; National Association of Investment Companies.

DISTRIBUTION OF TOTAL PERSONAL INCOME
(In Billions of Dollars)

Period	Personal income	Personal taxes	Disposable personal income	Consumption expenditures	Personal saving	Savings as a per cent of disposable income
1951	$256.7	$29.2	$227.5	$209.8	$17.7	7.8
1952	273.1	34.4	238.7	219.8	18.9	7.9
1953	288.3	35.8	252.5	232.6	19.8	7.8
1954	289.8	32.9	256.9	238.0	18.9	7.4
1955	310.2	35.7	274.4	256.9	17.5	6.4
1956	332.9	40.0	292.9	269.9	23.0	7.9
1957	351.4	42.6	308.8	285.2	23.6	7.6
1958	360.3	42.3	317.9	293.2	24.7	7.8
1959	383.9	46.8	337.1	313.5	23.6	7.0
1960	400.8	51.4	349.4	328.5	20.9	6.0
1961	416.4	52.8	363.6	338.1	25.6	7.0
1962	440.5	57.6	382.9	356.7	26.2	6.8

SOURCE: *Economic Indicators*, February, 1963.

So it's a fact. Families are saving about the same per cent of their disposable income as they saved twelve years ago. This fact surprises many persons who thought it was no longer necessary to save money, or at least not necessary to save as much.

There is no set pattern of saving and investing for a family with a specified income. Needs and wants are different among individuals and families during the various stages of the family life cycle.

The median amount of liquid assets (accounts in savings institutions, checking accounts, United States savings bonds, and so on) and securities that could be sold on short notice held by households in January, 1963, was about $900.[2]

What to Do with Your Savings. People use various savings instruments to meet different objectives. Usually, the higher the return on savings, the less safety of the principal. If you want liquidity (getting cash quickly), do not expect long-term growth. If you want certainty of income, do not expect a high yield.

A study of the accompanying table, Comparative Savings Instruments, can help you to decide on what to do with your savings. Surveys of consumer finances by the University of Michigan, Ann Arbor, indicate that people generally buy government bonds for safety of principal and a fair

[2] *Economic Indicators.* Washington, D.C.: Government Printing Office, February, 1963.

Savings investment	Principal	Inflation	Rate of return, %	Certainty of continued return	Smallness or lack of selling charge or other fees	Liquidity under all conditions	Chance for long-term growth
Cash	Exc.	Poor	0	.....	.....	Exc.	None
Life insurance	Exc.	Poor	3⅓	Exc.	Fair	Exc.	Poor
United States savings bonds	Exc.	Poor	3¼	Exc.	Exc.	Exc.	Poor
Savings account in commercial bank *	Exc.	Poor	1-3	Exc.	Exc.	Exc.	Poor
Postal savings	Exc.	Poor	2	Exc.	Exc.	Exc.	Poor
Mutual savings bank *	Exc.	Poor	2-3½	Exc.	Exc.	Exc.	Poor
Federal savings and loan association *	Exc.	Poor	3-4½	Exc.	Exc.	Exc.	Poor
Credit union	Exc.	Poor	3½-4½	Good	Fair	Good	Poor
Corporate bonds	Good	Poor	4-4½	Good	Fair	Good	Poor
Corporate stock	Fair	Exc.	3-5	Poor	Fair	Fair	Good
Growth common stocks	Good	Exc.	2-3½	Fair	Fair	Fair	Exc.
High-grade preferred stocks	Good	Poor	4½-5	Good	Fair	Fair	Poor
High-grade convertible preferreds	Good	Good	4-4½	Good	Fair	Fair	Good
Convertible bonds	Good	Good	3-4½	Good	Fair	Good	Good
Investment companies (mutual funds)	Poor	Good	3½-5	Poor	Poor	Fair	Good
Common trust funds	Fair	Fair	2-3	Fair	Fair	Good	Fair
Real estate mortgages (as investments)	Fair	Poor	5½-6	Poor	Poor	Poor	Fair
Unimproved real estate	Fair	Good	......	Poor	Poor	Poor	Exc.
Your own home	Fair	Good	0	.....	Poor	Poor	Good

* Insured up to $10,000.

SOURCE: Adapted from "What to Do with Your Savings," *Changing Times*.

return on their investment, growth common stocks as a hedge on inflation and a chance for long-time growth, and real estate mortgages for a reasonably high rate of return. As might be expected, people with fairly low incomes and small assets selected savings bonds and savings accounts, while the proportion who preferred common stocks was largest among the spending units with large incomes and considerable assets.

Savings Institutions

Only those savings media which are generally known as savings institutions—savings and loan associations, commercial banks, mutual savings banks, credit unions, and postal savings—are considered in this section of the chapter. These savings institutions are differentiated from other kinds of investment by their relative liquidity and safety, and by the fact that they are under state or Federal control. These institutions have as their major purpose the safekeeping of savings of individuals and institutions. Savings in these institutions, as a group, are not well protected against inflation because they provide for a return of a fixed number of dollars of principal plus interest regardless of the value of the dollar.

Savings and Loan Associations. The savings and loan associations had their origin in 1831, in a suburb of Philadelphia, in the form of a home-building society. In this society each of six members would give a certain sum each month until there was enough to build a home. The house was built and auctioned off to one of the members. Later, one could become a member by simply opening a savings account or by borrowing to finance a home.

At the end of 1963, there were 6,300 savings and loan associations in the United States with assets of more than $91 billion, representing the savings of over 37 million shareholders. Among savings institutions, only commercial banks have more total savings on deposit—$100 billion at the end of 1963.

The whole purpose of savings and loan associations is to assemble loan capital for homeownership. Over 80 per cent of their assets are invested in first mortgages on real estate—mostly one- to four-family homes. The balance in assets, not in cash, is invested in government bonds. Every third home in this country is financed through a savings and loan institution.

Operation of Savings and Loan Associations. Since 1933, when Congress enacted legislation providing for Federal savings and loan associations, federally chartered associations have grown until there are presently over 1,900. There are over 2,300 with state charters. Most savings and loan associations are mutual organizations. The saving members of the association are the owners. Borrowers also may become owners.

A small number of associations (about 7 per cent) have organized as stock corporations. No permanent stock is issued except in sixteen states, including California, Ohio, and Illinois. In the case of all federally chartered associations, and some organized in several states, each member is entitled to one vote for each $100 in his savings account, with a maximum of 50 votes. In Federal associations, each borrower has one vote.

There are two major types of accounts. The "savings account" may be opened with any amount of money. All transactions are, recorded in the account holder's passbook. Additions and withdrawals can be made. Dividends are credited either quarterly or semiannually. "Investment accounts" can be opened and added to with $100 or in even multiples of $100. Dividends are generally paid quarterly.

Except for checking accounts, many savings and loan associations offer regular banking services such as Christmas savings accounts, renting safe-deposit boxes, cashing bank checks, selling money orders, redeeming Series E savings bonds, and advising on investments.

How Safe Are Savings and Loan Associations? Because these associations specialize in a high-return type of investment—first mortgages on homes currently bearing interest at 6 to 7 per cent—and enjoy some tax advantages, they usually pay dividends that are higher than the interest on bank savings accounts. In 1964, the associations were paying from 4 to 4.8 per cent per year, compounded quarterly. How safe are the savings in the savings and loan associations that pay high dividends?

All federally chartered associations are members of the Federal Home Loan Bank System, a chain of eleven district banks that provide some of the funds to member associations. Accounts are insured in all 1,900 federally chartered associations up to $10,000 per account in any one institution by the Federal Savings Loan Insurance Corporation (FSLIC). State-chartered institutions may belong to the Federal Home Loan Bank System (2,300 in 1964). Being members, they have to operate under the same regulations as Federal associations, thus savings are just as safe as in Federal associations.

A few state associations belong to the bank system without carrying the insurance coverage, and some are neither system members nor insured. A few state systems have accounts insured by private insurers. Unfortunately, a few of these uninsured or poorly insured associations, notably a small group of organizations in Maryland in the guise of savings and loan associations, mulcted several thousand people of their savings in 1961–1962. All these organizations were state-chartered in Maryland; none held a Federal charter; none was insured by the FSLIC, the Federal government agency that underwrites accounts up to $10,000 in 4,200 federally and state-chartered units.

But what of the savers in other savings and loan associations? Are they running the risks that occurred in these few Maryland units? A review of the record of the FSLIC, created in 1934, can provide reassurance. In all its history, only 40 associations out of 4,200 needed financial assistance in 29 years. In 29 of these cases, the FSLIC made direct contributions to the distressed unit. In 3 cases, purchase of all or part of the assets provided a solution. In only 7 cases was it necessary to go into receivership, and in those cases, insurance was paid to the savers.

On the basis of this fine record, it might be reassuring to put your savings in an association protected by the FSLIC. At present, over 60 per cent of the 6,300 savings and loan associations are federally insured, covering about 95 per cent of all assets in all savings and loan associations.

Liquidity. Although insured savings and loan accounts compare favorably with savings in banks for safety, there is a difference in liquidity (right to get your money when you want it). In a bank you can withdraw your savings when you want them on short notice. When you withdraw savings from a savings and loan association, you are really selling shares to the association.

A savings and loan association has the bulk of its money tied up in long-term mortgages. An association could be perfectly sound yet be unable to meet all withdrawal requests if presented at one time. So it must reserve the right to go on a "notice basis." Under normal conditions, you would have no trouble getting your money. Enough money keeps coming in daily to take care of normal dividends. The association can call on the Federal Home Loan Bank System for aid in a pinch. It would take an emergency affecting all associations at the same time to bring about the "notice basis"—a delayed payment program. The typical notice that could be required is 30 days.

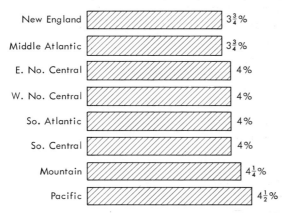

MEDIAN DIVIDEND RATE
(Paid by Associations, by Regions)
(December 31, 1961)

New England	$3\frac{3}{4}\%$
Middle Atlantic	$3\frac{3}{4}\%$
E. No. Central	4%
W. No. Central	4%
So. Atlantic	4%
So. Central	4%
Mountain	$4\frac{1}{4}\%$
Pacific	$4\frac{1}{2}\%$

SOURCE: *Savings and Loan Fact Book,* United States Savings and Loan League, Chicago, 1962.

Dividends. Savings and loan associations receive income from interest on mortgage loans—about 6 per cent—interest on Federal government securities, and from certain fees and rentals. Interest on first mortgages accounts for about 80 per cent of the total income. Expenses ordinarily run about 1 per cent. Reserves take about ½ of 1 per cent. This leaves about 4½ per cent—sometimes more—available for dividends to shareholders, as shown in the accompanying chart, Median Dividend Rate.

In 1964, most California-based associations paid 4.8 per cent dividends quarterly. The mountain and Pacific coast areas have usually paid the highest dividends. Dividends are ordinarily credited to the account, so the saver gets the benefit of compound interest. This is extremely important, because without compounding annually, it would take longer to double the amount of investment by leaving in the accumulated dividend. This is shown in the accompanying table, Doubling Your Capital.

DOUBLING YOUR CAPITAL
(At Different Rates of Interest, Compounded Annually)

Rate of return, %	Approximate number of years	Rate of return, %	Approximate number of years
1	70	6	12
2	35	6½	11
2½	28	7	10¼
3	23½	7½	9½
3½	20½	8	9
4	17½	9	8
4½	15¾	10	7¼
5	14¼	11	6⅔

If You Decide on a Savings and Loan Association. You can help protect your savings in a savings and loan association by following these suggestions.

1. Find out whether the association is operating under a Federal or state charter. In most cases, either form of organization is safe.
2. Be sure that the accounts are insured, preferably by the FSLIC.
3. Find out the current dividend rate, how long the present rate has been in effect, when it is paid. Beware of too high a dividend rate.
4. Investigate the management.
5. Look over several recent financial statements. (A good association will be from 13 to 15 per cent liquid; about 80 per cent of assets in first mortgages; not over 5 per cent of assets in borrowed money.)

Commercial Banks. We are primarily concerned here with savings accounts in commercial banks. Banks perform so many services that they are known as "department stores of finance." Most of these services are known to undergraduates—loans, checking accounts, safe-deposit boxes, investment services, collection services, issuing travelers' checks and letters of credit, selling and redeeming United States savings bonds, performing trust functions and so on.

There are more than 13,000 commercial banks in this country having various kinds of savings accounts. Over 45 million depositors have over $53 billion in these banks. The average savings account in commercial banks is $858. On these savings accounts (called time deposits), commercial banks currently pay from 2 to 4 per cent interest. On these time deposits or savings accounts, banks may require a waiting period of 30 to 60 days for withdrawal of money, but this is seldom carried out.

Safety and liquidity. No saver of an insured account has lost his money since 1935. In the event there are heavy withdrawal demands and the insured bank's cash and liquid securities are used up, the bank can borrow from the Federal Reserve Bank to pay depositors. If the bank is still unable to pay all depositors, the bank goes into receivership, and the Federal Deposit Insurance Corporation (FDIC) makes funds available to the depositors.

Over 90 per cent of commercial banks are insured. The law limits insurance to $10,000 per depositor in any one bank, but does not prohibit a person from having several deposits of $10,000 in several insured banks.

Interest on Savings in Commercial Banks. Commercial banks are not as generous as savings institutions in their interest returns, largely because they have more expenses, not the least of which is expected profits for their stockholders. Thus, most commercial banks pay from 2 to 3½ per cent interest currently.

The interest is usually credited to the account every 6 months and is compounded, as in the savings and loan associations. There are several ways of determining interest. It is possible for six different banks to state that they pay interest at the rate of 1 per cent per annum, but the variations in returns to the depositor may be as extreme as $3.96 to $7.88 for a 6-month period.

It pays to select a bank that uses the best interest method.[3] If there is a choice, select the plan that provides for interest to be paid semiannually, computed on the lowest monthly balance for each month. By this method, interest can be earned on sums withdrawn between the semiannual payment dates.

Mutual Savings Banks. Mutual savings banks are defined as banks of deposit, without stockholders, having as their basic mission the continuous promotion of true thrift at the local or community level. The first savings

[3] *Methods and Procedures in Computing Interest on Savings Deposits.* New York: Savings and Mortgage Division, American Bankers Association.

bank was established nearly 150 years ago. In 1963, there were 522 such banks located in 17 states, with over $40 billion of deposits and over 21 million depositors.[4] They have successfully weathered wars, panics, and depressions. No new institutions have been chartered since 1934, owing largely to the rapid development of savings and loan associations and to certain changes in commercial banking.

These banks are termed mutuals because they are owned and operated for the benefit of their depositors. None of these banks is chartered by the Federal government. The depositors do not have any rights in management. Most state charters invest management in a self-perpetuating board of trustees. Most members of these boards are civic-minded persons with no financial interest in the institution, and they serve without salary.

Safety of Deposits in Mutual Savings Banks. All mutual savings banks are regulated by state banking departments. Most of them are permitted to purchase farm mortgages, real estate mortgages, railroad and public utility bonds, state and municipal bonds, and Federal government bonds. A few states permit them to invest in industrial bonds, consumer loans, bank stocks, and FHA Title I loans. Mortgage loans, however, account for about 60 per cent of the assets; then, in order, come Federal government securities and private corporation securities. Such a variety of investment opportunities gives these banks more flexibility in their investments than most savings institutions are allowed.

Deposits in a savings bank are recorded in a passbook. The depositor can withdraw sums at any time, although the bank has the right to require a notice of from 30 to 90 days of intention to withdraw. In practice, savings banks pay immediately.

Many kinds of accounts can be opened in savings banks, such as "individual account," "joint account," "organization account," "school savings account," "payroll deduction account," "special account," "Christmas club account," and "vacation club account." The average regular account in a mutual savings bank was about $2,000 in 1963. Fewer than 30 of the 522 banks have service charges.

Most of these banks have been very prudent in their investment policies. They are also carefully supervised by state banking departments. Furthermore, 234 of the 522 mutual banks are members of the FDIC, with deposits insured up to $10,000 per deposit. No depositor has suffered a loss in an insured bank since the FDIC was established.

Comparison of Dividend Return. Since these banks are mutuals, they pay dividends, not interest. Dividends accrue on deposits. Since most of their investments are long-term, like mortgages, the returns are relatively high

[4] Connecticut, Delaware, Indiana, Maine, Maryland, Massachusetts, Minnesota, New Hampshire, New Jersey, New York, Ohio, Oregon, Pennsylvania, Rhode Island, Vermont, Washington, and Wisconsin.

—generally higher than savings in commercial banks, and usually slightly lower than savings in savings and loan associations and in credit unions. Most mutual savings banks have paid between 2 and 4 per cent annually on savings.

Credit Unions. A credit union is a cooperative association organized to promote savings among its members and to provide for them short-term consumer loans at relatively low interest rates. At the close of 1962, 13,795,906 people had joined 21,032 active credit unions in this country.[5] Credit unions have actually doubled their membership since 1950.

The average credit union in the United States has an average membership of 650. Most credit unions are small in terms of total assets. At the end of 1962, 53.1 per cent of all credit unions held assets of $100,000 or less. Only 14.1 per cent had assets worth $500,000 or more. Most of these assets are in the form of loans to members.

Credit union membership is predicated on a common bond. People who are united by employment, by membership in church or association, or by living in the same well-defined neighborhood can easily operate a credit union because they are usually well acquainted with each other. Employee groups account for 85 per cent of credit union accounts. In the United States, over 32 per cent of all credit unions serve employees in manufacturing industry alone, with government employees accounting for over 13 per cent of the total.

Compared to savings already listed for competing savings institutions (commercial bank savings of about $88 billion, savings and loan of about $84.4 billion, mutual savings of about $41.3 billion) credit unions held only about 2.9 per cent (over $6.2 billion) of the personal savings in all savings institutions in the United States at the end of 1962. Credit unions have actually grown faster since World War II than other financial institutions, but they still own only a small portion of personal savings. We have already discussed credit unions as lending institutions in Chapter 4.

Federal and State Supervision of Credit Unions. The credit union movement in this country began in 1909, when Massachusetts passed the first credit union law. Today, most states and the District of Columbia permit credit unions. The Federal Credit Union Act was passed in 1934, permitting the chartering and supervision of Federal credit unions.

There are now over 21,000 active credit unions, with 14 million members, and about half of the credit unions elect Federal government supervision. In most states, the state banking commission supervises state-chartered credit unions. All laws treat credit union operations in substantially the same way. Under them, credit unions are strictly regulated, and each one is examined regularly by the government.

[5] *The 1963 International Credit Union Yearbook.* Madison, Wis.: Credit Union National Association, 1963.

Government examination is backed by auditing by an elected committee composed of credit union members. This committee must examine the books, verify member accounts, and check the cash and investments at frequent intervals. Larger credit unions employ public accountants for this auditing.

In many states, credit unions are required to buy surety bond coverage, which protects the credit union against dishonesty and robbery. In many areas, credit unions have banded together to set up a stabilization fund, which is available when needed. Credit unions, unlike some of the other savings institutions, do not have the safety feature of federally sponsored insurance of accounts. Despite this, the safety record has been good.

Bad debt losses have been low and almost always adequately covered by reserves. Credit unions are required to set aside a reserve against losses. Federal credit unions must transfer to the legal reserve 20 per cent of each year's net earnings until the the reserve equals or exceeds 10 per cent of the amount paid in on shares. Furthermore, the treasurer must be bonded. Adequate security is required on all loans over $400.

Surplus funds of the Federal credit unions are invested in government securities, in loans to other credit unions, or in shares in federally chartered savings and loan associations. Furthermore, all Federal credit unions are examined and supervised by the Bureau of Federal Credit Unions. Funds of a Federal credit union must be deposited promptly in a bank insured by the FDIC.

Membership in a credit union is usually obtained by purchasing at least one share, normally for $5. In many instances, employers have a payroll deduction plan for the purchase of shares. Shares of credit unions are not transferable, but they may be repurchased by the credit union. The major use of funds is in consumer lending to their own members. The low true interest rate for twelve months is usually stated as 12 per cent for twelve months. In actual practice, the true annual interest rate is slightly under 10 per cent.

Comparison of Dividends and Safety. Generally, credit unions pay members the highest returns on their savings when compared with the other institutions mentioned in this chapter. Because almost all loans are consumer loans returning up to 12 per cent annual true interest, and operating costs are low, some credit unions pay dividends as high as 6 per cent. Those that charge less than 12 per cent interest are able to pay dividends of 4 to 5 per cent. A very small percentage of credit unions pays no dividends.[6]

Despite the good record of credit unions, the safety of savings may not be quite as good as in some other savings institutions. But investment

[6] See Bureau of Federal Credit Unions' latest report on operations of Federal credit unions. Washington, D.C.: Department of Health, Education, and Welfare.

in a credit union with a fairly long history of prompt payment may be desirable for a part of one's savings.

Postal Savings. In 1910, Congress established the postal savings system, primarily to provide immigrants with an absolutely safe place for their savings. Since then, people in the lower economic levels have used the postal savings system more than other individuals. At present, less than 2½ million people have accounts totaling less than $2 billion—much less than the peak of $3.4 billion of deposits in 1947. There has been a steady decline in the use of the system; at the end of 1961 there was less than $0.7 billion in postal savings.

Any person age 10 or over can open one account in his or her name. No joint accounts are permitted. No account may be opened for less than one dollar, nor can any fractions of a dollar be deposited at any time. There is no passbook. Deposits are evidenced by certificates in various denominations of from $1 to $500, inclusive. These certificates are not negotiable or transferable.

There is a limit of $2,500 per depositor. The certificates can be cashed in any post office at any time. If a depositor dies, the account is payable to the legal representative of his estate.

Postal deposits earn interest at the rate of 2 per cent compounded annually (except in Mississippi, where the rate is 1½ per cent). To earn interest, the money must be left in for at least 3 months. Savings and interest are completely guaranteed by the Federal government.

The interest rate of 2 per cent compounded annually is well below the other savings rates studied in this chapter. Since the other savings institutions are relatively safe and pay considerably higher returns, the postal savings system is becoming an increasingly unimportant savings institution.

Investments

In the first section of this chapter, you have seen how savings can achieve financial security for the family. In the opinion of experienced financial advisers this means, first, adequate insurance protection for dependents; second, a cash reserve in a savings account or in United States savings bonds; and, third, for some families, a mortgage-free home. Following these, there should be an educational fund for the children and a basic retirement plan through United States savings bonds, annuities, insurance, social security, and private pension plans, if any.

You are now in a position to consider investment in other kinds of securities in the hope of getting larger returns on savings. If you have some success in a carefully planned investment program, the time will come when you get the urge to consolidate and conserve what you possess. In that event, you will want to become informed on trust plans and estate planning in general. As your estate grows, it will become increasingly important to make adequate changes in your will. Aside from providing adequate insurance protection for your dependents, making a proper will is perhaps the next most important financial duty a person has to those dependent on him.

Caution—Investment Entails Risk. All investment entails risk. People are not infallible. Various degrees of quality determine whether one is investing, speculating, or gambling. It is difficult, of course, to draw a line separating each from the other because they are bound to overlap. A bond, for instance, is not always an investment. A stock is not necessarily a speculation. Nor can we trust all investment trusts.

Mark Twain's Pudd'nhead Wilson may have had something for the amateur in the security markets when he said: "April is a particularly risky month in which to speculate in the stock market. The other months are February, December, March, November, May, October, June, August, July, September, and January."

America's favorite, Will Rogers, said: "I'm not so much worried about the return *on* my money . . . what bothers me is the return *of* my money."

An internationally known banker said it this way: "After a lifetime of earning, the man who still has his savings intact, *without any interest*, is indeed a rare and fortunate person."

The following advertisement by the New York Stock Exchange represents an enlightened point of view, coming from within the professional circle.[7]

"I TRIED TO GET RICH QUICK!"

"In my own business, I base my judgment *only on facts*—all the facts I can get. Tips, rumors, and hunches are *out*.

"I don't know why I thought the stock market would be *different*. It's *business*, too—a cross section of *all* business. But, in my dealings there, I tried to take an easy short cut on facts. . . .

"I listened to tips . . . took rumors at face value . . . relied on intuition rather than on information. *I tried to get rich quick.*

"See this headgear I'm wearing now? I put it there . . . no one else is to blame. It's to remind me—'get-rich-quick' promises are *no* substitute for *facts*."

The man's right!

Precisely the same principles that apply to *any* successful business activity apply to dealings in securities.

There is no short cut to wealth . . . no sure, easy way to make money quickly . . . either on this Exchange or anywhere else.

Tips and rumors—promising great rewards without effort or thought—are merely traps for the unwary, the ill-informed, the heedless.

[7] In *Chicago Sun,* February, 1946.

In investment, there is *always* a degree of risk, whether in stocks, bonds, or *any other* form of property.

RISK—GAIN

Experienced investors *know* this. Before they act, they *get the facts* . . . not to eliminate risk (for it can never be done away with entirely) but to avoid *needless risk*.

Facts *can* be had. Every company whose securities are listed on this Exchange has agreed to disclose essential facts needed to form reasoned investment decisions.

True, it takes seeking to get this information. Facts aren't handy as gossip, on every street corner, but they *are* available . . . in the reports of listed companies . . . on the market pages of your newspaper . . . at the offices of member firms of this Exchange.

Considerations before Investing in Securities. If you contemplate entering the securities field, it is important to discover whether you should be in the investment market at all. Ask yourself the following questions, and give yourself honest answers.

1. Do I have the emotional stability and temperament that is needed when investing in securities, particularly if the value of my securities slides downward?
2. Is the basic financial protection of my family adequately planned?
3. Is there a chance that some of the cash invested in securities may be required for current family needs?
4. Do I need the income from the securities to live on in part or in full?
5. Am I in an unfavorable position in the income tax bracket so that taking additional profits would add too much to my net income?
6. Have I paid in full for the automobile, home, furniture, and so on?
7. Will I have to pay for advice in my investing program, or can I rely on my own information and judgment?

The answers to these questions will help you to make an intelligent decision in regard to whether you should invest in conservative bonds, real estate, or carefully selected stocks, or perhaps establish a trust.

After facing the facts regarding your present status and probable future abilities to maintain the family financial responsibilities through the retirement period, the second consideration is the purpose of your investments. Do you want your investments (1) to yield high income or a steady income, (2) to be sold again to make a profit, or (3) to have a cash or liquid characteristic?

In any purposeful investment program, the aims or objectives should harmonize with individual or family needs and plans. Select securities that will best fit the family objectives.

Basic Investment Principles. The purpose or objective of the investment program can be further clarified by pointing out a few basic investment principles that wise financial counselors have successfully used. In purchasing any stock or bond, *security of principal*, or *safety*, is the most important factor for sound investing. Such a plan as setting up an educational fund for the children, for instance, demands a high degree of safety.

Next in order is *stability of income*. Usually, when security of principal prevails, you will also find little extreme variation from year to year in yield or income. After the children are through school, and when a man feels more inclined to reach for an easy chair than the lawn mower, he becomes more interested in stability than in growth.

The third principle is *growth, or appreciation, of capital*. You should not jeopardize security and stability of income for growth unless you can afford the luxury of a speculative or semispeculative program. Investment for growth of capital is generally not advised for the small investor who is dependent on the income from his securities, except perhaps as a hedge on inflationary prices.

Generally, it is desirable to have a high degree of *marketability* in an investment. This quality, however, is of less importance for personal investments than for the investments of a bank or an insurance company, which may be called on to meet large cash demands. A speculator also must have a high degree of marketability in his investments so that he can sell immediately if necessary. Bonds, as a rule, suffer from fewer marketability opportunities. Real estate may likewise be difficult to sell at the right price during certain periods in the business cycle.

In these days of high income surtax rates, *tax exemption* of securities is important. Some securities, such as state and local bonds and certain kinds of Federal bonds are tax-exempt. Consequently, a person in the higher income bracket should be more interested in tax-exempt securities. There is, however, no magic in a poor security, no matter how tax-exempt.

Freedom from care is a desirable characteristic in an investment, especially if a person is emotionally affected by personal attendance to his investments. By the time a man has accumulated retirement capital, he may want to be free from investment worries.

Diversification is an important principle in any investment program. It is the key to balancing the other investment principles. You must realize that you cannot have income, safety, and growth all at the same time. In investment planning, that old bromide, "You can't have your cake and eat it too," is very applicable. Any plan will be a compromise in which you must weigh appreciation of capital against security, and yield today against yield tomorrow.

Diversification should be carefully planned. The best financial brains cannot accurately predict the performance of any single investment five or ten years hence. Consequently, no one should place all or most of his investment resources in one or two securities. Diversification can be accomplished by thoughtful selection of industry, company, and type of security. The law of averages can be applied so that a loss or decline in one security or industry is not likely to follow in all the other securities and industries.

Some financial advisers use *geographic diversification*. The theory is that investing in securities of companies in different geographic areas, including foreign countries, serves as a hedge on possible adverse experiences of companies in certain sections. Some large corporations operate all over the world and therefore partially qualify in meeting geographic diversification.

Besides following the above principles of diversification, many financial counselors recommend *limitation of investment*—that is, that not more than 10 per cent of the fund be placed in any one industry, and that the amount invested in one security be limited to 5 per cent of the fund.

Another way of securing diversification is to invest in the common stock of a well-known sound *investment trust*. Such organizations are established to buy and sell securities of other companies. When purchasing common stock in an investment trust, you share in the profits of a diversified list of companies and obtain the advantage of expert and experienced management. There is a risk, as in all investments in common stock. It is important, therefore, to select the investment trust only after careful investigation. No investment trust is any better than its management.

Get the Facts, Know the Risks. After the major objectives or purposes have been decided, you are in the best position to select securities—some for safety, others for income stability, profit, and liquidity.

Few persons appreciate the difficult problems involved in selecting securities. The following advice is given by Bernard Baruch, one of the most successful stock speculators.

If you are ready to give up everything else—to study the whole history and background of the market and all the principal companies on the board as carefully as a medical student studies anatomy—if you can do all that, and, in addition, you have the cool nerves of a gambler, the sixth sense of a kind of clairvoyant, and the courage of a lion, you have a ghost of a chance in Wall Street.

Emil Schram, former president of the New York Stock Exchange, once said for newspaper publication:

People who are unable to judge values or have a competent adviser judge for them have no business in buying securities. Those who scorn factual information and who conduct their operations on the basis of tips, rumors, hunches, and impulses are misusing our facilities. They contribute to market instability and render an absolute disservice to our general economy.

Both these leaders in the investment field emphasize two things: *get the facts, know the risks.* The Securities and Exchange Commission (SEC), the Federal body that regulates the stock exchange business, frequently receives complaints from people who, without the facts and without knowing the risks, have purchased certain securities and lost money. Their common complaint is, "Why weren't we protected?"

Facts on securities are available. Much material is on file with the SEC, and information may be obtained from other reliable sources.

A good general knowledge of the nature and performance records of securities and real estate can be obtained from professional people— bankers, brokers, trust company experts, and experienced real estate dealers. These experts, spending full time on this job, are in the best position to keep you informed about possible changes in your investment portfolio due to changes in the business cycle, changing industrial trends, price levels, and many other causes. This is necessary if you are to keep your money in investments.

The average person should complete a savings plan and financial independence plan before he speculates. Do not speculate with these savings. In fact, do not speculate unless you can afford to lose.

The important point is to get the facts, know the risks, about the two major classes of securities: bonds and stocks.

Facts about Bonds. When you buy bonds of a corporation, a state, or a city, you are lending money to that institution or organization. You are the creditor, and in return for the loan, the institution pledges to pay you a specified amount of interest on specified dates.

Many books have been written about bonds, and the ordinary investor can only hope to acquire a reasonable understanding of principles and various grades of bonds.

There are so-called *gilt-edge bonds,* those usually regarded as the highest grade. The organizations behind them have had a long record of paying interest and principal on time and of earning more than they spend. Such bonds have price stability and are easily marketable. There are also low-grade bonds, those usually issued by organizations that have spotty financial records. Often, the latter grade of bond is issued by comparatively new concerns.

Bonds have various maturity due dates. Those that mature within a few months or years are known as *short-term issues. Long-term issues* will mature late in this century.

Moreover, bonds have a stated rate and an effective rate of return. The *stated rate* is printed on the bond. The *effective rate* is the real return on the bond, and it depends on what is paid for the bond. If the coupon on the bond is 5 per cent, and par ($1,000) is paid for the bond, the return will be 5 per cent. If a person pays above par, the effective return will be less; if below par, the effective return will be above 5 per cent. Thus, a 5 per cent $1,000 bond, maturing in 10 years, purchased at 110, would be figured as follows.

$50 minus $10 (premium of $100 divided by 10) equals $40.
$40 divided by 1,050 (1,100 plus 1,000, divided by 2) equals 0.00381, or 3.81 per cent.

Consequently, the real or effective return in the above instance would be 3.81 per cent and not 5 per cent. To compute the exact yield to maturity of bonds purchased below or above par, it is necessary to use a complicated formula. Security dealers use bond tables that have been worked out from the formula. Ordinary citizens should do likewise.

The fundamental principle to remember about bonds is that their income is fixed. The owner of the bond is a creditor who receives interest on his loan to the borrower. Therefore, he cannot share further if the borrower prospers. On the other hand, he does not share fully in the misfortunes of the borrower, because bonds generally have first claim on the assets of the company.

Facts about Stocks. When you buy stock in a company, you become a part owner of the concern. If the business succeeds, it will pay dividends. If dividends are high, you may also profit by an increase in case you sell the stock. On the other hand, if the business fails or does not pay dividends for a considerable length of time, you may lose your entire investment or a part of it.

There are two kinds of stock. The *common stock* does not carry a fixed dividend. In fact, the board of directors need not declare dividends even if a large profit is made, although that is unlikely. This fact adds to the risk. Usually, if profits are large, holders of common stock get higher dividend rates. Likewise, when profits are small, dividend rates decline or are nonexistent. If a company goes bankrupt, its common stock may plunge to zero—no value. The bondholders' claims on the company's earnings and assets come first, then the preferred stockholders' claims. The common stockholders get what is left, if anything.

On *preferred stock,* the return on investment, if one gets it, is fixed and limited. For the last 30 years, preferred stocks of high grade have yielded about 1 per cent more income than high-grade bonds. Dividends on preferred stock may be cumulative or noncumulative. Cumulative dividends that are not paid when they should be paid (usually quarterly) accumulate and must be paid, if earnings permit, before dividends can be paid on the common stock. Since the stockholder has no claim for dividends on preferred noncumulative stock, cumulative stock is generally a better buy.

Generally, the return on preferred stock is definite, a stated 4 or 5 per cent. In some cases, such as in *participating preferred stock,* the stock is permitted to share in the earnings in excess of the stated rate of dividend. Participating preferred stock is generally a better investment than nonparticipating preferred stock.

Sometimes preferred stock is issued with a conversion feature that permits it to be exchanged for common stock at a given ratio. These are rather popular stocks during an inflation period, when conversion into common stock is possible. *Convertible preferred stock* is generally a better investment than *nonconvertible preferred stock.* Ideally, the best preferred stock to purchase would be a cumulative, participating, convertible stock, but these stocks are rare because of the demand for this type of stock by pension funds, savings banks, and corporate investors. As a result, the price for this stock has increased to a point where the yield is too low for an individual investor. It would be better for the individual to buy "blue chip" common stock instead.

Here is a summary of bonds and stocks evaluated in terms of the three major principles of sound investing.

	Safety	Income	Growth
Common stock	Least	Variable	Best
Preferred stock	Good	Steady	Variable
Bonds	Best	Very steady	Generally steady

Analyzing Industries and Securities. Industries and companies have important characteristics that make for strength or weakness for investing purposes. These qualities, as a rule, are not so important as the quality of management. Nevertheless, the characteristics of industry and of the companies within each industry should not be overlooked.[8]

Read the best and latest information available. Begin by reading reports and annual guides published by the leading financial services.[9] A weekly publication presents current statistics and market data on leading companies and their securities.[10] The financial sections of newspapers, especially the large metropolitan press, have articles by financial specialists, and of course, there are financial newspapers and weeklies.[11]

[8] There is valuable reading in the pamphlet *The Background of Investment,* published by the American Institute for Economic Research.

[9] Moody's Investors Service, Fitch Investors Service, and Standard & Poor's Corporation.

[10] *The Outlook.*

[11] *The Wall Street Journal* (New York, San Francisco, and Dallas editions), *Journal of Commerce* (New York and Chicago editions), *Barron's,* and the *Commercial & Financial Chronicle* are among the best current newspapers offering information about securities.

If you live in a large city, consult a reputable brokerage firm, which will have analytical guides for investors that present important, timely, and interpreted information on industries, companies, and securities. If your community does not support a brokerage firm, consult the officers of your bank.

Investment advisory and counseling firms are located in the larger cities. Trust companies, especially in the large cities, have experts available for investment counseling. There are also statistical organizations that analyze general business trends and recommend the purchase and sale of specific securities.

Since the final responsibility for investing your funds rests with you, no matter how much paid or unpaid advice you receive, the kind of information you get and analyze yourself is considerably important.

Some of the important questions to be answered about an industry, such as petroleum, railroads, public utilities, and so on, are these.

1. Who are its customers?
2. What basic factor determines demand of the product or service?
3. Who are its competitors?
4. What threat do they offer?
5. How is the raw material supplied?
6. What is the labor situation?
7. How is the industry likely to be affected by world events?

When you are satisfied that the industry is a good one, the job of selecting a company within that industry begins.

Selecting a Company for Investment. At least four important factors should be investigated before selecting a company for investment: its economic position, its management, its financial condition, and the price of its securities.

To analyze the *economic position,* you will need the same kind of information about a company that you would obtain when selecting a good industry. Particular attention should be given to the standing of the company within its industry and to the competition it faces from similar companies.

Management is most important because you are relying on the managerial skill of others to run the business in which you are investing. This is a hard thing to judge. Generally, you must rely on the published financial reports of the position of the company, its earnings, and so on to size up the reputation and imagination of the officers and directors.

Financial condition, like management, is different for each company. Once you are satisfied that the industry is sound and the company's standing within the industry is good, your next job is akin to dissection. Take the company apart, and see what makes it tick, according to its financial reports.[12] It is well to keep in mind that the earnings of a company over a period of several years are more significant than the figures for any one year. Moreover, the total figures are of little importance; it is the relationship of the figures that is important. Not total net income, but net income per share; not total current assets, but current assets in relation to current liabilities.

Usually, *price* is the crucial factor in selecting a security, especially common stock. Common stock prices not only vary with the ups and downs of general business conditions but also vary irrespective of earnings. The problem is to discover whether the current price is reasonable in terms of prospective earnings. In deciding the question of price, the answers to the following questions are considered important by financial experts.

1. What are the prospects of the company in terms of competition and growth?
2. How does the current price-earnings ratio compare with ratios of typical past years? With that of similar companies?

Buying and Selling Securities. If you buy securities, you must be prepared to watch them and know when to sell. It is not wise to go into the security-buying game with the intention of putting the securities in a safe-deposit box and forgetting about them. Securities must be watched and worked continuously. There are times when you should unload—sell.

The key to successful investment requires keen judgment in *timing purchases and sales.* Consequently, you must either do your own research and play a lone game or find someone to advise you continuously. Admittedly, the job of individual research is almost impossible, but you can study the important sources of financial information and consult with competent, informed persons.

All kinds of people sell investment advice. The professionals range from the honest, studious, objective, and well informed to the tip-sheet operators. Before selecting an adviser, investigate him just as if you were hiring him to operate your business. The Better Business Bureau in your community will at least steer you away from the dangerous financial operators. Your banker or attorney is usually helpful.

The absolute minimum requirement for a securities adviser is that he have a clean bill of health from the Securities and Exchange Commission and from the state department of securities. A good adviser will not be embarrassed if you ask him these questions.

---

[12] One of the best sources that the author knows on this problem is the booklet *How to Read a Financial Report,* published by Merrill Lynch, Pierce, Fenner & Smith, Inc., available from the firm's New York office or its offices in over one hundred other cities.

1. How long have you been in business?
2. What are your financial sources?
3. What outside agencies investigate your business?
4. Do you belong to any professional organizations?
5. What are your fees?
6. Have you an interest in the securities that you are advising me to buy?
7. Can you name any local business leaders as references?

Where Securities Are Bought and Sold. There are thousands of different stocks and bonds—all are called "securities"—but the ones that are bought and sold most frequently are those that are traded on the floor of the New York Stock Exchange. The securities of more than 1,100 major companies are listed on that exchange, which means that they have been accepted for trading there. All buying and selling is done between the hours of 10 A.M. and 3:30 P.M., New York time, Monday through Friday. The exchange is closed on Saturday the year round.

The New York Stock Exchange is a voluntary association, established in 1792, and it functions as an open auction market in the Stock Exchange Building in New York City. Functionally, it is an organization consisting of 1,366 members who have bought memberships (commonly called "seats") on the exchange.

Many of these members represent brokerage firms whose primary business is carrying out the orders of other people, the public generally, for the purchase or sale of securities. They are paid commissions for executing these orders for their customers. To provide service for investors throughout the country, these firms maintain many branch offices. All told, there are 661 member firms of the New York Stock Exchange that operate 935 branch offices in 379 cities.

Before the exchange agrees to list the securities of any company, it must be assured that the company is a substantial concern, that its securities are legally issued and widely owned, and that the company agrees to issue adequate public statements of its financial condition regularly.

Only member brokers can execute orders to buy or sell listed securities on the exchange. If an order is given to a brokerage firm that is not a member, it is turned over to a member broker. In such a circumstance, a small commission or service fee in addition to the commission of the member broker may be charged.

How Unlisted Securities Are Bought and Sold. The New York Stock Exchange, or "Big Board," is the largest formal market for stocks and bonds, but there are thousands of security issues that are not traded on that exchange. Many are traded on twenty-four other exchanges, such as the American Stock Exchange (New York City), the Chicago Stock Exchange, the Los Angeles Stock Exchange, and so on.

Still other stocks and bonds are not listed on any exchange. These securities are called unlisted, or off-board, securities; they are traded in what is popularly called the "over-the-counter" market. Government and municipal bonds are mainly traded in that market. So are the stocks of most banks and insurance companies, as well as the securities of many big corporations.

By and large, however, unlisted securities are those of small companies that are likely to be better known locally than nationally. They are bought and sold not only by many brokers who are members of the New York Stock Exchange but also by thousands of local security dealers.

Suppose a man in New York owns some stock in an Ohio machinery company, and he wants to sell it. He does not know what it is worth because there is no regular market for that stock, and its price is not published in the newspapers, as the New York Stock Exchange prices are in many papers.

He goes to his broker, and the broker may ask for a price quotation by phone or wire from other brokers or security dealers who trade entirely in unlisted securities. He may find that the best bid for the stock is $23, while the lowest that anybody else is willing to sell it for is $25. If the stock is traded frequently, the difference between bid and offer prices may be less. If it is almost unknown, the broker may have a hard time finding a market at any price.

In many over-the-counter transactions, the broker or dealer will buy the security himself, or he will sell such a security out of the supply of such stocks that he owns. In such trades, the dealer acts as a principal instead of as an agent, and the customer and the dealer agree on what is a fair *net price,* which includes a return to the dealer in place of a commission. In the end, the dealer may gain or lose on such transactions.

Brokers will handle over-the-counter transactions either as a principal or an agent (on either a net price or commission basis) as the customer chooses.

How to Do Business with a Broker. Here is what actually happens when a customer—let us call him Kenneth Smith—enters a broker's office to place an order for 100 shares of Typical Manufacturing Company.

Mr. Smith goes directly to the desk of the man who regularly handles his business (we shall call him John Ross). Ross is registered with the New York Stock Exchange, which means that he is qualified as a man of good character and has passed an examination on the operation of the securities business. He is an employee with the title of "account executive." He is a man who thoroughly knows his business.

Smith might ask Ross for information about Typical Manufacturing and discuss the findings with him. But in this instance, Smith has already checked on the company and knows that he wants to buy 100 shares of common stock. So he gets right down to business.

"What's Typical selling at now?" he asks.

If Typical Manufacturing were one of the major companies, Smith would not have to ask, for he could look at the big electric quotation board that automatically shows the price at which the last previous sale was made. It also shows the high and low prices for the day and the closing price on the preceding day. The quote board provides that information on 209 leading stocks, but Typical is not among them.

"Sorry, I don't know the quote," says Ross, "but I'll let you know in a minute." Ross knows he can get the quote by a quick phone call.

While Smith waits, he looks at the screen on which the ticker tape is projected to see if any sales of Typical are being reported then. When a stock is sold on the exchange floor, that transaction is reported on the tape. The price is shown and the number of shares involved in the sale. Because there are so many transactions, it is necessary to use a kind of shorthand, and the various stocks are referred to by initials or combinations of letters, such as C for Chrysler Corporation, CP for Canadian Pacific, and CGW for Chicago Great Western.

"Typical is quoted at 25 bid, 25¼ asked," says Ross in a minute or so. By that, he means that $25 a share is the highest price that anyone is then willing to pay for it and that $25.25 is the lowest at which anyone is willing to sell it.

"Shall I place your order at the market?" he asks. A *market order* is one for immediate execution at the best price that prevails when the order reaches the floor of the exchange, regardless of how the price may have changed—up or down a fraction of a point, sometimes more—in the interval between the time the order is placed and the time it can be filled.

Smith agrees. His order is immediately phoned to one of the booths on the floor of the exchange. There one of the floor brokers goes to the trading post at which Typical is bought or sold. There are 18 such posts on the floor of the exchange, and at each of them a certain number of stocks are regularly traded.

At the trading post, the broker asks what the market is. Other brokers with orders to buy or sell Typical Manufacturing make their bids or offers in an audible voice. Secret transactions are not permitted on the exchange floor.

The broker immediately fills Smith's order at the lowest price at which the stock is offered, and Ross is advised by phone that the order has been filled.

The whole operation may have taken only two or three minutes. Smith may still be in the office. If he is, Ross will tell him that the purchase has been completed. If he is gone, Ross will telephone him.

As a matter of fact, most customers are likely to place their orders and handle all their business by telephone. Others do it wholly by mail. It is not necessary for a customer to go to a brokerage office to place an order.

A customer, if he wants, can set the price that he is willing to pay. This is called a *limit order*. Smith might tell his broker, for instance, to buy Typical only if it could be bought at 24½. Further, he might say that any such order is good for a day, a week, a month, or indefinitely. Then if Typical is offered at 24½ within the time that Smith has set, his order to buy is executed, unless there are other similar orders on file that have precedence. Of course, the price of Typical might move up to 26 or 27. In such case, Smith would have lost his chance to buy at 25 or thereabouts. That is why any decision to buy that turns exclusively on the probable gain of a fraction of a point is likely not to be a good decision for most investors.

Limit orders can also be used in reverse—in selling stock. Thus, if Smith owned Typical, he might tell his broker to sell the stock, if he can, at 26.

Round Lots and Odd Lots. One hundred shares—a *round lot*—is the usual unit of trading on the New York Stock Exchange. But that does not mean that a customer can only buy or sell 100 shares at a time. Many people want to buy only 5, 10, or 25 shares at a time. These are called *odd lots*.

Suppose Smith wanted to buy only 10 shares of Typical. When the broker gets that order it is filled through an odd-lot dealer whose business it is to buy or sell in less than 100-share units. Such odd-lot dealers do business only with other brokers on the stock exchange floor, not with the public. For rendering their service they charge 12½ cents per share on stocks selling below $40, 25 cents per share on stocks above $40.

Apart from that extra service charge, the 10-share order does not cost any more per share than a 100-share order. On a 10-share order for Typical, Smith would pay the price that prevailed on the next round-lot sale after the broker gives Smith's order to the odd-lot dealer. Suppose the next sale was at $25. Smith would pay $25 per share, plus the service charge for the odd-lot dealer. If Smith were selling the stock, he would sell at $25, less the service charge.

When Smith gets the bill the next day, it will state exactly what he bought, the price, the commission, postage or tax, if any, and total amount due. Brokers do not make a charge for special services, such as research or information, carrying an inactive account, or safekeeping of securities.

After Smith pays his bill—probably by check—he can obtain his stock certificate, which shows that so many shares of Typical Manufacturing Company have been registered in his name and that he is entitled to all rights, privileges, and dividends due the stockholders in that company. But Smith, like an increasing number of customers, may find it more convenient to leave the certificate in safekeeping with his broker. That way he has protection against losing the certificate, and it is there when he wants to sell the stock.

Brokers' Commissions. The New York Stock Exchange sets minimum commission charges that brokers must use for the purchase and sale of stocks for customers. The following rates prevail for stocks selling for $1 per share and above.

Money value of 100-share unit	Commission charge for 100-share unit
If less than $100	As mutually agreed, about 6%
$100–$399.99	2% of money value + $3
$400–$2,399.99	1% of money value + $7
$2,400–$4,999.99	½% of money value + $19
$5,000 and above	1/10% of money value + $39

Most people purchase stocks in odd lots (less than 100 shares). The commission rates on odd-lot sales are the same as above, less $2, but in any event not less than $6 per single transaction. These rates are applicable both when you sell and when you buy. Commission rates on the American Stock Exchange are similar to those for the New York Stock Exchange.

The Federal government also levies a tax on all sales of stock. The Federal stock transfer tax is 4 cents on each $100 (or fraction thereof in excess of $50) of the actual value of the total shares sold, but in no case will the tax be more than 8 cents on each share. The minimum on any transaction is 4 cents.

The New York State stock transfer tax is on all stocks sold on the New York Stock Exchange regardless of where the seller lives. The New York State tax is as follows:

Per share selling price of stock	Tax per share
Less than $5	$0.01
$5–$10	0.02
$10–$20	0.03
$20 or more	0.04

There is also a small Securities and Exchange Commission fee of 1 cent for each $500 or fraction thereof of money value involved.

The table on page 430 shows the total costs in buying and selling 10 shares when 100 shares (a round lot) sold at $29⅞. The odd-lot buyer actually paid $30 per share, and later sold the stock when round lots were selling at $29⅞, so the odd-lot seller received $29.75 a share.

Thus, the total cost of buying and selling 10 shares would add up to $16.70, or $1.67 a share.

Monthly Investment Plans. You do not have to be rich to own stocks. If

	Total	Per share
Buying costs for:		
Odd-lot differentials	$1.25	$0.125
Commission	7.00	0.700
Total cost	$8.25	$0.825
Selling costs for:		
Odd-lot differentials	$1.25	$0.125
Commission	6.95	0.695
Federal tax	0.12	0.012
New York State tax	0.12	0.012
SEC fee	0.01	0.001
Total cost	$8.45	$0.845

you are budget-minded, you can buy stocks for as little as $40 each quarter or as much as $1,000 a month on a monthly investment plan.

Most brokerage firms that are members of the New York Stock Exchange offer a monthly investment plan. You simply sign an agreement to invest regularly over a specified period and give your choice of stock. You may withdraw at any time. Each time you make a payment, your broker buys full or fractional shares, depending on the cost of the stock and your payment plan. You pay the regular charges for this service. The exact number of shares or fractions thereof will be credited to your account. Dividends are mailed to you or are reinvested automatically if you desire.

One of the advantages of a monthly investment plan is that it offers the opportunity of *dollar averaging,* as illustrated below.

How Dollar Averaging Works

	First quarter	Second quarter	Third quarter	Fourth quarter
Amount invested	$100.00	$100.00	$100.00	$100.00
Price per share	$20.00	$25.00	$12.50	$20.00
Number of shares purchased	5	4	8	5
Total number of shares owned	5	9	17	22
Total invested	$100.00	$200.00	$300.00	$400.00
Average cost per share	$20.00	$22.22	$17.65	$18.18

In dollar averaging, you invest the same fixed sum regularly into the same stock or stocks regardless of current price. Your fixed amount of money buys more shares when the stock is low, fewer shares when the stock is high. Dollar averaging over several years results in the average cost of all shares purchased being lower than the average price at which shares were bought. In other words, your cost per share will be below the average of the prices at the separate times you made your purchases.

According to the National Association of Investment Companies, over 15 million common stocks have been purchased through over 200,000 accounts since monthly investment plans were introduced in 1954. Over 55 per cent of the plans in force are quarterly, and most individuals automatically reinvest dividends. The most popular issues subscribed to under these plans are "blue chips" (good-quality common stocks) like General Motors, American Telephone and Telegraph, Phillips Petroleum, and others. This is a plan for steady investors, not for those interested primarily in day-to-day fluctuations of the market.

Investment Clubs.[13] The National Association of Investment Clubs says there were at least 8,170 local investment clubs (over 100,000 members) in 1962. An investment club is a group of people (usually from 8 to 20) who band together to contribute to a central fund that is invested in securities. Investment decisions are generally made by the members, but many clubs get such guidance from investment specialists. These groups look upon their clubs as a source of profit, but just as importantly as a source of education through the pooling of investment knowledge.

To give an idea of how one club works, here is a good example from the Midwest. The club is chartered to take in 25 members. All members serve on the board of directors, which annually elects officers. Each person owns one share of the 25 shares authorized. Each member puts $25 per month in a pool.

The group meets monthly, receives a monthly progress report, and listens to reports on present stocks held and on proposed purchases. Discussion follows these reports. Decisions are made by a democratic vote— one vote per member. The treasurer carries out the wishes of the group. Usually, each monthly report is made by a new team of three members. An executive committee is empowered to act on emergency investment decisions that may come up between the monthly meetings.

Caution: It takes expert advice to organize a club. There are state and SEC rules to contend with. A lawyer club member and a connection with a good brokerage firm are recommended.

Figuring Profit on a Monthly Investment Plan. Investing small sums regularly in good-quality common stocks has great advantages, but there is one hitch. You should know the true annual growth rate, and this is not too easy to measure. As an example, suppose you had invested $10 a month for 52 months, and your holdings are worth $650. Are you better off than if you had put $10 per month for 52 months in a savings and loan association

[13] *Investor.* New York: Dealers Digest Publishing Company. (Good ideas on organizing a club.)

PROGRESS CHART FOR MONTHLY INVESTMENT PROGRAMS

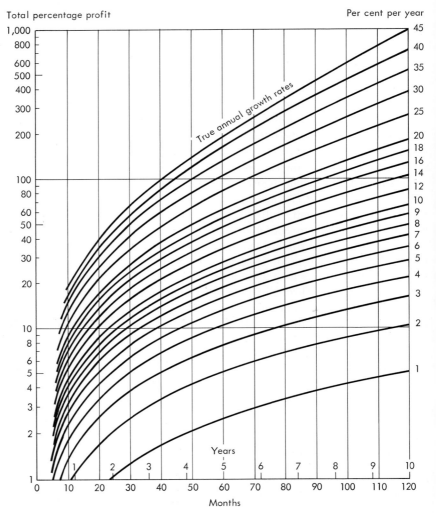

SOURCE: Prepared by Carleton Financial Computation, South Bend, Ind.

paying 4½ per cent? The accompanying chart, Progress Chart for Monthly Investment Programs, will give you the answer.

You will need to know your gross profit and the number of months you have been investing. In this example, you invested $520 for 52 months, and your stocks are presently worth $650, so the gross profit is

$$\frac{\$650 - \$520}{\$520} \text{ or } 25\%$$

Now find this figure on the left side of the chart, and pencil a horizontal line through it. Then, on the bottom line of the chart locate 52 months. Draw a vertical line through this figure. These two lines will cross on, or close to, one of the curves labeled "True annual growth rates." In this case, the lines cross above the 10 per cent curve. So the true annual rate of growth is slightly over 10 per cent, more than double the 4½ per cent you could receive from a savings and loan association.

Commenting on the plan in his book *Wall Street: Men and Money*, Martin Mayer observes that if a small investor put $100 a month for 12 months into the Monthly Investment Plan, he would pay a broker's commission of $67.92. If he had bought the stock in one lump, he would have paid only $14.85 in broker's commissions. If the purchase had been made on the Monthly Payment Plan and the stock had increased in value 15 per cent at the end of the first year, the investor would still own stock that was worth less than the cash he had put in. Even if the investor had hit on a stock that paid a dividend of 6 per cent, it would take two and a half years for the dividends to catch up with the commissions. For these reasons many brokers are cautious about pushing the Monthly Investment Plan. They will often counsel their customers to save until they have enough money to buy in larger amounts. This is almost certainly sound advice.

Securities and Exchange Commission Study. In mid-1963, the first two of a series of reports (2,100 pages) on the study of securities markets was made public by the Securities and Exchange Commission. This study is important to the investor because it points up some of the questionable practices in the securities markets. The special study (in the first two reports) made these specific recommendations.

1. The two firms handling nearly all of the odd-lot buying (less than 100 shares) should be more closely regulated by the New York Stock Exchange—abuses in commission charges.
2. The "specialists" are not performing effectively their major objective—stabilizing the market by maintaining a fair and orderly continuity in the prices of the stocks assigned them. During the severe May, 1962, price break, these specialists "did not have a significant stabilizing effect."
3. During crises like the May, 1962, break, all short selling should be banned.
4. A vast overhaul of the whole over-the-counter mechanism is needed. (There is no centralized place to buy and sell these stocks.)

One of the outcomes of the study is likely to be closer policing on the trading floor, thus marking the end of the present era of mild regulation. The report should not impair public confidence in the securities markets, but should strengthen it as the suggestions for raising the standards are put into practice.

Why Common Stocks? Common stocks have proved superior to other forms of investment because they have delivered the three objectives of a good investment to more people, in greater measure, than any other method of investing capital. These three objectives are: (1) original capital value keeping ahead of the purchasing power of money; (2) reasonable and continuous income; and (3) a display of long-term growth of capital value and income. The preservation of capital can be seen in the accompanying chart, Industrial Stock Prices versus Cost of Living. Over this 61-year period, the cost of living increased by 278 per cent, while stock prices advanced over twelve times. Thus the increase in stock prices was 4.6 times that of the cost of living.

INDUSTRIAL STOCK PRICES VS. COST OF LIVING

SOURCES: *Consumers' Price Index,* Dow-Jones Industrial Stock Average, compiled by Bureau of Labor Statistics, U.S. Department of Labor.

The annual record of industrial share dividends from 1901 to 1961, compared with the cost of living, is shown in the chart, Industrial Stock Dividends versus Cost of Living. In this 61-year period, industrial dividends increased over eight times, or at an annually compounded rate of 3.7 per cent. This contrasts with comparable figures for the cost of living, which increased 2.8 times—a rate of 2.2 per cent.

Common stocks, furthermore, have a built-in growth feature. The tendency is for corporations to grow and for their stocks to acquire increasing value as the population increases and standards of living rise.

What about Bonds? Just as well-selected common stocks are good investments from the long-term point of view, bonds tend to be relatively assured investments from the short-term point of view; but they carry long-time risks. The chart, Corporate Bond Prices and Loss in Purchasing Power, graphically illustrates the long-term risks inherent in bond invest-

INDUSTRIAL STOCK DIVIDENDS VS. COST OF LIVING

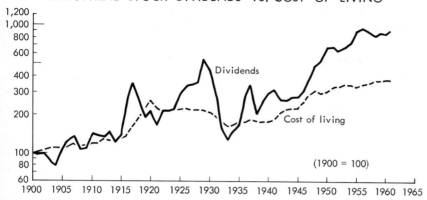

SOURCES: *Consumers' Price Index,* **Dow-Jones Industrial Stock Average, compiled by Bureau of Labor Statistics, U.S. Department of Labor.**

CORPORATE BOND PRICES* AND LOSS IN PURCHASING POWER

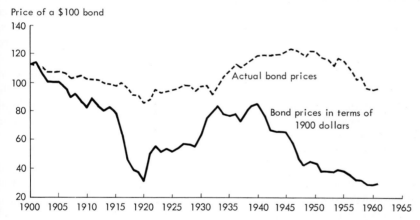

*Price of a 4% bond with a term of 20 years, computed from average annual bond yields.

SOURCES: Macauley's Bond Yield Index, 1900–1935; Moody's Aaa Corporate Bond Average, 1936–1961.

ments. Between 1900 and 1920, the dollar lost more than 60 per cent of its purchasing power. If a bond investor bought at the highs in 1900 and was compelled to sell in 1920, he would have lost about 75 per cent of his original investment, in terms of purchasing power.

After 1920, interest rates declined and bond prices moved up until, by 1946, bonds had achieved record highs, with yields around 2½ per cent. Thereafter, bond prices turned down again. This does not mean that you should avoid buying bonds. Their relative dollar stability and assured near-term prospects mean they can be used as insurance of investment funds against the short-term risks of common stocks.

Why Investment Companies? Technology, expanding social concepts, and exploding political boundaries have brought rapid and far-reaching changes in many kinds of common stocks and in certain kinds of bonds. Some old industries have their backs to the wall and have to fight for their lives, while new industries spring up almost full-grown.

In short, the essence of life is change; the essence of investment success lies in capitalizing on change. Detecting change and then deciding what course of action to pursue requires considerable research if successful investment is to be maintained. Fortunately for a growing number of investors, such services are offered by modern investment companies.

An investment company or trust is a means of acquiring an interest in a diversified list of stocks. If, as a whole, the stocks go up, you make money. But if they go down, you suffer a paper loss, or a real loss if you sell. Buying shares in an investment company, therefore, does not remove the risk. It just transfers the job of selection to someone else—management. The advantage is that you spread a relatively few dollars over a number of different stocks and bonds and thus diversify your risks. Furthermore, if the company is well managed, these stocks and bonds are selected on the basis of careful research by professional analysts.

How do you select a good investment company or trust? There were over 400 such institutions in the United States with total assets of approximately $28 billion in 1963.[14] There are aggressive salesmen in this field today, so beware. To select the company or trust most suitable to your needs, use this three-step process.

1. Make up your mind what you want your investment to do for you. Do you want a safe investment that will pay a low but regular return? Or would you rather take more risk in the hope of getting a larger return?
2. Study the performance records and see which trusts have shown the best management. Some of these trusts have had only average management.
3. Check the commissions (called "loading") and other charges to make sure that you are not paying too much for this service. Bear in mind, however, that good management is worth a reasonable brokerage commission and other charges.

Two Kinds of Investment Companies. There are two kinds of investment companies—open-end and closed-end. *Open-end trusts* (called "mutual funds") are those whose shares are redeemable at any time at approximate asset value. (Mutuals had about $22.6 billion in assets and over 2.1 million shareholders in 1962.) These trusts will also sell new shares at any time.

---

[14] *Investment Companies.* New York: Wiesenberger & Company, 1964, p. 18.

Thus, the number of outstanding shares is always changing. There is generally a loading charge of 6 to 9 per cent when you buy this type of share; when you sell, you usually receive the net asset value of the shares without deduction or charge. In purchasing mutual shares, the loading charge of 6 to 9 per cent can wipe out earnings of 3 to 4½ per cent a year for a couple of years. Therefore, never buy mutual shares unless you can afford to keep them for several years. There are a few funds, such as Scudder, Stevens and Clark and Loomis Sayles, both of Boston, the De Vegh Fund of New York, and the Haydock Fund of Cincinnati, that do not have a loading charge at all. As a result, these funds are not popular with brokerage houses.

Closed-end trusts, on the other hand, have a fixed number of shares outstanding. Since these trusts do not issue new shares or redeem old ones, you acquire shares by buying from someone who wants to sell. This is why closed-end shares are sold on stock exchanges or over the counter just as industrial stocks are traded. You pay a regular broker's commission when you buy or sell these shares.

Closed-end shares are affected by the law of supply and demand. They may sell for more than net asset value or for less depending on demand or popularity. At times, closed-end trusts invest heavily in one company and get involved in its management. So if you want diversification, investigate before you invest.

Both kinds of investment trusts are in the business of investing money entrusted to them by their shareholders. It is difficult to say that one type is better for all investors than the other. There are differences, however, that are worth investigating.

Major Objectives of Investment Trusts. Answers to this question are given in the latest edition of Arthur Wiesenberger's book *Investment Companies.* This comprehensive volume covers both open-end and closed-end trusts. Here are some of the major objectives of investment trusts.

1. Long-term growth of capital and income.
2. Long-term growth of capital only.
3. High current income.
4. Stability and dependable income.
5. Concentration of a particular industry, such as Chemical Fund, Inc., Atomic Development Mutual Fund, and the Axe Science and Electronics Corporation.
6. Concentration on a particular type of security, such as bonds or preferred stocks. There are very few such funds. Examples are the Bond Fund of Boston and the Franklin Custodian Funds—Preferred Stock Services.
7. Heavy investment in special situations thought to be undervalued.

So-called *common stock funds and trusts* keep most of their capital invested in common stocks. A *balanced fund* generally keeps about a quarter of its capital in cash, bonds, or preferred stocks. The balanced fund gives more protection against declining prices in return for less profit in a rising market. It is well to remember that when you buy stability or high income, you lose much of your chance for growth of capital. Also a trust that limits itself to one industry or security sacrifices flexibility. In trusts that invest heavily in special situations, you lose diversification and accept greater risks.

Selecting an Investment Trust. It is important to select a trust with your own investment objectives in mind and one that has a good record. The largest and best-known trusts are not necessarily the best. Some trusts appear to be more interested in commissions than in good management and performance. Usually those that do best are the ones in which management has its own money at stake. No one man could own a substantial interest in a trust with a half billion dollars in assets, but some trusts have substantial sums invested by the managers and their families.

An investor buying shares after a long rise in stock prices will probably be paying for past large gains. He himself, therefore, is liable to a capital gains tax without realizing capital gains. The purchase of *closed-end shares at a discount* can partially offset this tax.

If you want the best that investment companies or trusts have to offer, be prepared to study the field. Also, do not use money you will be needing soon. Plan to invest a fixed sum each month. If possible, select a company or trust that has as many of the following characteristics as possible.

1. Investment objectives that fit your own
2. Reasonable acquisition costs and management fees
3. Alert, experienced, intelligent, successful managers
4. An outstanding record in the last 15 years
5. An opportunity to reinvest capital gains and some dividends without payment of commission
6. For most investors, diversification of the investment

Performance of Mutual Funds. In the year June, 1962, to June, 1963, only 7 of the 20 largest funds were able to increase their assets values per share (prices) more than the 25.94 per cent rise in the Dow-Jones industrial average.[15] The Dow-Jones average is derived from the stock prices of 30 large "blue-chip" industrial concerns traded on the New York Stock Exchange. The Dow-Jones composite average includes a composite of 65 common stocks (35 railroad and utility stocks and 30 industrial stocks).

How did mutual funds perform from June, 1962, to June, 1963? Not very well. Investing in a mutual fund, however, should not be placed on a one-year comparative basis with individual performance of common stocks. A performance comparison over a 5- or 10-year period makes more

[15] *The Wall Street Journal,* July, 1963.

sense, because capital gain distributions and total reinvested dividends build up the total value of the original investment.

The Wharton School of Finance and Commerce, University of Pennsylvania, made such a study, covering the operation of 152 funds for nearly six years, from the end of 1952 to the fall of 1958. One conclusion was that "the average performance by the funds did not differ appreciably from what would have been achieved by an unmanaged portfolio with the same division among asset types."

In other words, if you had been able to buy an average of all 152 funds, you would have nearly doubled your money (96.7 per cent). But had you been able to buy an average of the 500 stocks in Standard and Poor's composite stock index, you would have gained more (139.5 per cent). But half of the funds did better than the composite stock average. A few performed a great deal better—one specialty fund gained 257.3 per cent. At the other extreme, one fund (only bonds in its portfolio) increased only 6.4 per cent. The common stock funds with growth objective did the best, showing an average gain of 134.3 per cent.

The moral to this is that you should not buy shares in just any mutual fund. Selectivity is absolutely essential. Management can be good, poor, or indifferent. For performance records in the last 10 years, read *Investment Companies, Johnson's Investment Company Charts,* or *Investment Trusts and Funds from the Investor's Point of View,* all listed in the Suggested Readings at the end of this chapter.

Bonds—Federal, State, and Municipal. United States government bonds are regarded as the safest investment in the world. They are payable from tax revenues of the Federal government. Federal government bonds have always been paid in full on maturity date. There are only two Federal savings bonds now—E and H bonds. The *Series E savings bond* is known as an appreciation bond rather than an income bond. That is, you purchase them at 75 per cent of the maturity (par) value, and if you hold them to maturity, the dollar value reaches 100 per cent. For example, the Series E savings bond (purchased for $18.75), if held for 7 years and 9 months, will pay $25. This is a 3¾ per cent rate of return, compounded semiannually. This bond, sold before maturity date, will yield a correspondingly lower rate of return.

The *Series H savings bond* is a current income bond, for individuals only, bearing an investment yield approximately equal to the Series E bond. It is issued in denominations of $500, $1,000, $5,000, and $10,000, and these are the amounts you pay when buying the bonds. The interest is paid by check semiannually beginning 6 months following issue date. The checks vary in amount over the 10-year life of the bond. (If any of your bonds are lost, write the Bureau of Public Debt, Division of Loans and Currency, Chicago, Illinois.)

State bonds. The debts of the states rest on the ability of the state governments to meet their obligations when due. They cannot be compelled to pay their debts. On the other hand, state governments are desirous of maintaining sound credit rating with investors, and therefore defaults need not be anticipated. The major advantages of state bonds are safety, liquidity, and exemption from Federal income tax. These bonds are hard to obtain, since they are held largely by savings banks and insurance companies. The rate of interest, too, is low—around 2 per cent per annum.

Municipal bonds. Local governments do not have the status of sovereign powers in law. This makes the position of the investor in their securities similar to that of investors in private corporations. However, local governments are subject to state regulation. Therefore, the legality of municipal issues is determined by the state governments. Unlike most state governments, local governments may be used to enforce payment of bonds in default.

The major advantage of municipal bonds is exemption from Federal income tax. There are several possible disadvantages. The yield is low, under 2 per cent per annum. During depressions, many local governments have been in default on their bonds. The complex legal aspects involved in determining the investor's position with respect to individual issues make them less attractive to ordinary investors.

Foreign public bonds. Selection of public bonds in the foreign field is not advisable for most investors. For the last quarter of a century, thousands of ordinary American investors have had little or nothing to show for their gambles in foreign securities. Canada is one of the few countries having a good record on bonds.

People are tempted to purchase foreign bonds because the stated yield is usually high. It is well to recall that the higher the anticipated yield, the greater the risks. Financial experts are still of the opinion that foreign securities are too much of a gamble for most Americans. Until foreign bonds are safe, it is wise to select United States government bonds.

Bank Stocks and Real Estate Mortgages. *Bank stocks.* Most bank stocks represent liabilities of small banks. Measured in dollars, however, the largest banks have over half the total par value of bank capital stocks. Market analysts sometimes argue that New York City banks offer safer bank stocks than those of smaller communities. This is based, in part, on the unique position of the New York banks in the center of the investment world. This point of view is not accepted by those who claim that the New York banks must keep larger reserves on hand (which have no earning power) than are necessary for banks in smaller cities.

Banks, generally, are unsatisfactory media for investment purposes. This is especially true for the small investor because the amount of published information on the bank is inadequate for a good analysis. The ordinary person would not know the actual values of the figures given nor the adequacy of the reserves.

Real estate mortgages. Real estate loans occupy an important place in the investments of many people. The small investor, however, finds that real estate mortgages are difficult to purchase. For many years, these long-term investments were so good in terms of net yield that only persons in favored positions or with the right contacts were able to make real estate loans. Life insurance companies and large trust funds have accumulated a high percentage of the best real estate mortgages. Savings banks likewise have invested perhaps as much as one-half of their deposits in mortgages.

Mortgage loans are among the most desirable kinds of investment for persons equipped to appraise them accurately and to manage them economically. Few persons can qualify for the purchase of a mortgage, but more could do so if they would learn how to appraise real estate or take advantage of professional aid. Appraisal of real estate considers such factors as probable change in the neighborhood, possible increase in taxes, increase in labor costs and in the price of building materials, the possibility of reduced rents, title to the property, insurance costs, and the constant cost of upkeep. These facts are difficult for the average investor to secure.

Men in the mortgage business recommend that the average person should limit his loans to first mortgages on fully developed residential property in good shape, in a favorable neighborhood, and in amounts not exceeding 60 per cent of the current value of the property. Such loans would qualify for safety and income. Mortgages do not qualify in terms of liquidity in case you need cash during the period of the mortgage.

Taxes Affect Financial Planning. Taxes are necessary to manage our freedom and general welfare, but they make it difficult for many persons to provide adequately for the future. Therefore, the effect of taxes on financial planning needs more and more attention from investors. Because taxes change, usually increase rather than decrease, no specific examples are given here. We can only point up the nature of the problem.

For example, with the prospect that taxes will remain high for an indefinite period, interest in tax-exempt securities has grown, particularly on the part of commercial banks, casualty and fire insurance companies, and individuals in the middle and higher income brackets.

It is important to examine, under the guidance of financial experts and advisers, the tax laws that exist when you are setting up a family financial plan. Being aware of tax effects on financial planning is the important thing to learn. The following illustrations touch only a few of the many complex tax effects that give additional savings at the present time.

1. Certain kinds of quasi-Federal government securities issued between September 1, 1917, and February 28, 1941, are fully exempt from Federal income taxes.

2. Interest on bonds of a state or political subdivision is also exempt from Federal taxes and from income tax levied by the state from which the bond was issued.

3. Bond income may be reported on an accrual and amortizing basis. This procedure is useful only to wealthy persons.

4. If a security is held for less than 6 months, the entire profit or loss must be included in the income figure; if it is held 6 months or more, only half the gain or loss is computed. Therefore, avoid selling securities held less than 6 months unless establishing a loss turns out advantageously.

Estate Planning and Wills

Long-term financial planning for your family involves the coordination of insurance protection, social security, cash, stocks, bonds, and real estate. *Estate planning*, essentially, involves the total program for the use, conservation, and disposal of all properties either before or after death. The core of all estate planning is provision for adequate care of dependents and consequently the maintenance of the bulk of an estate for use by the dependents.

Too often, people have the idea that estate planning is only for persons in the upper 10 per cent income classification. Nothing could be further from the truth. Some families of moderate income need it the most. A couple just starting a home may not have need for long-term planning in the sense that it is used here. Such persons will begin with plans suggested in Chapters 2 and 10 to 12 with the emphasis on a small savings account, life and disability insurance, educational funds for the children, and a retirement plan.

But all these financial assets are the beginnings of an evolving long-term plan. The earlier you know your security goals in life, the sooner you can establish an over-all estate plan. Early planning has the advantage of permitting you to work toward the known and accepted goals.

A trust is an obligation through a contract whereby the *trustor* (one who establishes a trust) places his property in the hands of a trustee for the use of beneficiaries. A *trustee* is a person or company named to hold title to property and to manage it. Although a trustee may be an individual, it is wiser to select a good trust company. A trust company will negotiate a *trust agreement*, which states the terms under which the trust is to be administered.

There are three kinds of trusts: testamentary trusts, life insurance trusts, and living or voluntary trusts. (More recently, "common trust funds" have become legal in a few states.)

Testamentary Trusts. A testamentary trust is created by a will and does not take effect until the person dies. In many cases, a man would be wise to leave his property in trust for his wife rather than to will it to her directly. This is especially appropriate if there is danger of the widow's dissipating the estate through personal incompetency or poor advice from well-meaning friends.

A testamentary trust generally instructs the trustee to distribute to the widow a life income from the estate. If the income is inadequate, the trustee can be instructed to use a part or all of the principal. After the death of the widow, the remainder of the trust would be paid to the children, or the property can be held in trust for the children until they are of legal age.

Experts generally agree that the trustee should be given some discretion, consistent with safety of the principal. This is especially important when a trustee is working under a will, because investment conditions may change. He should be permitted to adapt the trust to the new conditions.

A testamentary trust may serve the purpose, too, of reducing estate, legal, and administration expenses. For instance, if a man leaves a sizable estate to his wife, half of the estate is subject to the Federal estate tax to the extent that it is greater than the exemption, the other half being allowed as a marital deduction. In case the wife dies without remarrying, the entire estate, minus exemptions, becomes taxable. On the other hand, if the estate had been left in trust for the wife's lifetime, with the principal payable to the children after she dies, the entire estate would have been taxed only on the death of the husband. There would not be a tax on the death of the wife.

Life Insurance Trusts. A life insurance trust is created during the lifetime of the insured through a written agreement with a trustee, usually a bank or trust company, to handle the proceeds of life insurance. Most insurance trusts do not become active until after the death of the insured, whereupon the trustee collects the proceeds of the insurance policies that have been made payable to it. The trustee then administers and distributes such proceeds in accordance with the terms of the agreement.

An insurance company can and does distribute the proceeds of life insurance according to agreement, but it cannot serve as a legal trustee. For instance, an insurance company cannot enforce "discretionary" requests; the funds are not segregated as in the other trusts; and it has less flexibility. Consequently, if flexibility is desirable and investing is essential, it will not do to select an insurance company as trustee. On the other hand, if installment distribution is all that is desired, an insurance company can do the job cheaper, because there is no charge for this service.

In addition to the above advantage, there are two outstanding uses for a life insurance trust. First, and most important, is the case where insurance is required to furnish funds not otherwise available to take care of death taxes and other estate shrinkage items and to prevent enforced liquidation of a business interest. To illustrate it simply, the trustee is authorized to buy the stock from the executor of the estate, thus placing cash funds in the hands of the executor and retaining the investment, which may be valuable but does not have a ready market. Second, an insurance trust is about the only means of providing complete discretion in the administration of insurance proceeds for the support of beneficiaries whose needs cannot be served through fixed installment payments.

Once a life insurance trust is decided on, the procedure is to consult a competent life insurance agent. A lawyer can then draft the agreement according to the wishes of the insured. The insurance policies are then assigned to the trustee, or the latter may be named beneficiary. If the insured wants a more flexible plan, such as changing of beneficiaries or receiving cash surrender value, the trustee should be named as beneficiary.

Persons with only a $5,000 or $10,000 insurance policy should not use an insurance trust plan. In such cases, the proceeds should be paid to the beneficiary directly in a single cash payment or by settlement option agreed on.

Living, or Voluntary, Trusts. A living, or voluntary, trust is one that is set up and operating during the lifetime of the trustor, and is governed by the terms of a written agreement between the trustor and a trustee. It has three primary purposes: (1) to help create an estate, (2) to help take care of an estate already created, and (3) to help administer the estate both during lifetime and after death.

This trust is essentially a management trust designed to transfer supervision of investments, real estate, stocks and bonds, and anything of sufficient value to a qualified trustee engaged in the business of trust management. This kind of trust is becoming more and more popular with moderately wealthy to wealthy people.

There are two kinds of living trusts—revocable and irrevocable. A *revocable living trust* gives the trustor the opportunity to see how his properties are managed during his lifetime, and he can make adjustments as he sees fit. The trust continues after death, which makes it unnecessary to establish a testamentary trust. It is free from accounting and inventory from the probate court, and thus affords privacy. It can care for any future situation, such as cases of physical or mental incapacity of the trustor.

An *irrevocable living trust* cannot be changed or canceled. It has some of the advantages of a revocable trust, but must give up forever the properties assigned to the trust. Only an extremely wealthy person could afford this kind of trust because the major advantage pertains to some tax saving. Gift taxes may have to be paid at the time that the trust is established. However, no estate or inheritance taxes need to be paid on the property at the time the trustor dies.

Trust Management. There are hundreds of individual trust accounts, each with its particular reason for being. The major responsibility of all trusts is to keep funds invested and provide a constant flow of income for the persons named in the trust.

Investment decisions, although conveyed over the signature of a trust officer, are the product of group analysis—the joint efforts of the top investment brains within the trust company. There is a trust investment committee containing respresentation from the board of directors, the senior executives from the bank, and, of course, the trust department. This committee makes direct use of the bank's credit division and its research group. The policies and decisions of this committee, such as (1) whether to buy common stocks or preferred stocks, (2) in what companies and what proportions, (3) whether to buy industrial or railroad bonds, and the like, are reviewed by the bank's board of directors.

Within the limits established by the board of directors, the policy committee decides what to buy, what to sell, when, and at what price. In each case, the committee has before it full information about the requirements of the account—its present holdings, which include a schedule of principal maturities and diversification as between preferred and common stocks; government, municipal, industrial, utility, and railroad bonds; mortgages and real estate; oil interests; and so on. The trustee cannot sell anything from its own holdings to trusts of which it has charge. All purchases must be with or through independent brokers or dealers.

Each account is reviewed by the committee at regular intervals. Meanwhile, the research and analysis group is constantly studying new information about individual companies whose investments are held in the trust department, and reports these facts to the committee. Any changes that are made are conveyed to the trustor over the signature of the administrative officer of the account.

Qualifications of a Trust Company. A trust company is a permanent organization and is accessible every business day. There is no death inconvenience in a trust company, in contrast to the possible death of an individual executor. The financial responsibility of the bank is back of the trust account.

Trust companies are organized under state laws and are supervised and examined by proper state officers. They also have their own internal audit and dual control. Each trust account is segregated from the other accounts. Every transaction is posted on the day it occurs, and every account must be in balance at the close of business every day.

Trust officers must be impartial. Their responsibility is to carry out the trust agreement and the will with sympathetic consideration for the needs and rights of the beneficiaries. A trust officer is skilled in determining and settling tax liabilities, thus protecting estates from needless shrinkage.

Administrative Costs. Trusts have a considerable volume of estate business over which to spread the costs of trust business. Individuals cannot hire bookkeeping, clerical, and stenographic services for a given estate at so low a cost, to say nothing about the cost and value of the investment services. The total fees paid to the bank and to the attorney for the estate are no greater than the aggregate fees that would be approved by the court for payment to an individual executor and attorney.

There is no uniformity of administration charges. The American Bankers Association has recommended the following fees on a trust estate of $100,000 that yields 6 per cent for 20 years.

Acceptance fee	**$2,500**
Annual fee on income	600
Termination fee	2,500

Spread over a 20-year period, the total annual charges would average $850, or less than 1 per cent of the estate.

An examination of the cost of administering living trusts reveals that costs are likely to be higher than those recommended by the American Bankers Association. In one large city, the costs of administering a living trust were found to be as follows.

No initial fee.

Five per cent on the gross annual income of the trust estate ($50 minimum).

Five per cent on the market value of the principal of the trust estate whenever it is disbursed or distributed by the trustee.

Where there are cotrustees acting with the trust company, commissions are divided on the basis of three-fifths to the corporate trustee and two-fifths to all other trustees.

Most trust companies hesitate to accept an estate under $50,000. In the larger cities, a common minimum value of an estate that would be accepted is $100,000.

Common trust funds are operated by trust companies for the benefit of small estates. Small estate funds (at present restricted by Federal Reserve regulations to a maximum of $25,000 per estate) are pooled so as to broaden the diversification. Only a few states have made common trust funds legal—notably New York and Pennsylvania. Such pooling gives promise of sound management of small estates.

Powers Included in a Trust. The powers included in a trust generally should be as extensive as possible. The trust company must have power to sell, to purchase, to invest, to repair, to pay taxes, to sue and defend in court, to mortgage property, and so on. Certain discretionary powers given to a trustee are known as the "prudent man rule" in some states. In such a case, the creator of a trust puts it squarely up to the trust company to act honestly, reasonably, and with prudence.

This broad power to act—of course within the rules set up by state legislation and in some cases by the Federal Reserve System—is considered necessary for the best interests of the beneficiaries. The trustee is liable if he does not use "prudence, discretion, and intelligence." Leaving a trust fund idle would constitute negligence in the eyes of the law. In general, the trustee must live up to management characterized by prudence, discretion, and intelligence.

Should You Create a Trust Fund? The idea behind a trust fund is sound. But as your estate increases, you should be sure that you want to create a trust fund. It should not be done hastily, because it involves a lifetime plan for establishing, conserving, and distributing an estate. If, for instance, you expect your assets to net 12 per cent income, you would not set up a trust because most trustees will not take that kind of risk. And rightly so, because they have a conservative function as well as an income function. Certain risks cannot be reconciled with safety. Also, if a father has a son who is an excellent businessman and usually doubles his money annually, he may prefer to will his portion outright and not bother with a trustee.

Locating a good trustee is difficult, especially if an active business is left. Trusts are reluctant to run businesses. If you can find an experienced person to continue the business, it may be a wise move, but an individual trustee may die, which complicates matters.

In case you consider creating a trust, discuss the matter with the family attorney, a trust officer, and a good life insurance agent. Give them all the facts and family objectives to think over for a while. Out of the joint thinking, the advantages and disadvantages of your particular case will come to light. From such an analysis, you will be in a better position to make up your mind.

If you are not completely satisfied with the idea of a trust fund, the best advice is to leave it alone. It is fundamentally important that you be entirely satisfied before entering into such a plan. On the other hand, for a family inexperienced in business and desiring enjoyment out of life, but wanting fair returns on their investments, a living trust should be considered.

The Necessity for Making a Will. A will is the means by which you can definitely and positively direct the economical and orderly disposal of your estate to persons of your own selection. You should make a will as soon as you are married or whenever you have dependents. Furthermore, your will should be kept up to date.

Do not be among the 70 per cent of those who die in this country without a will. Modern young people should face the necessity of making a will as part of their family objectives and financial security goals. Replace any unpleasant thought of death of the testator by the happier thought of providing for those you love who will go on living.

When a person fails to make a will—that is, dies *intestate*—an administrator is appointed by the probate court to distribute the estate to the heirs of the *decedent*—the person who has died. Usually, problems of heirship arise to plague everyone. Jerome K. Jerome has said that if a person dies leaving a will, then all his property goes to whoever can get possession of the will; but if a man dies without a will, then all his property goes to the nearest villain. Jerome was exaggerating somewhat. Each state, however, has a different law of descent. If a person dies without a will, his real estate in one state will go to one set of heirs, and to another set in another state.

If a man fails to leave a will in Illinois, for instance, the law will divide his estate. If he leaves a wife and children, the wife will get only one-third of the estate; the other two-thirds will go to the children. If the children are minors, their inheritance becomes involved in guardianship proceedings. If he leaves a wife and no children, the wife gets all the personal estate, but only half of the real estate. The balance of the real estate will be divided among the wife's parents, brothers, and sisters. If he leaves no wife or children, the entire estate goes to the parents, brothers, and sisters. If no survivors exist, the estate will go to the county, nothing to charities.

Legality of Wills. Most states will give some protection to a man's wife against his creditors and the handing over of certain properties to other people. Certain kinds of property, usually the home, are exempt from creditors forever or for several years, depending on the state law.

Each state determines the qualifications of a person eligible to make a will. In the first place, each state requires that the person reach a minimum age. In some states, such as Massachusetts, the minimum age for either sex is 21. In a few states, the minimum age for the male may be 21 years, and only 18 years for the female. In addition, some states prescribe a lower age for personal property and a higher age for real property.

Another requirement provided for in the laws of the various states pertains to having a sound mind and to acting on one's own volition, free from undue influence. The question is a technical one. Wills have been contested successfully and unsuccessfully on the basis of competence to make a will. The courts have usually held that a testator is of sound mind if he is capable of understanding what he has written into the will. If he fails to provide for near relatives without any rational explanation, the will may be inoperative. In cases of disinheritance, it is therefore important to name names and give reasons.

Wills made on deathbeds or when the testator is very ill are vulnerable to attack. No one should take this chance. Make a will when you are in good health.

Writing your own will. The greatest creator of litigation is the man who believes he has sufficiently mastered the technicalities of drafting a will and writes his own will. It is said that St. Ives, the patron saint of lawyers, extends to none a heartier welcome in the life beyond than to the so-called "lawyer's best friend," the Jolly Testator Who Makes His Own Will!

Contests over wills may go on for years. You remember the famous will contest of *Jarndyce v. Jarndyce,* recounted by Charles Dickens in *Bleak House.* It will bear rereading. We are told, incidentally, that Dickens himself was a little bitter over the time consumed by some necessary litigation in his own life.

Essentially, a will is a legal document. It is advisable, therefore, that a good attorney be hired to draw it. A will need not be long. Lawyers have sample forms available. Many good wills do not use the standard forms provided for such purposes. Well-known Americans have drawn wills in only one or two sentences.

Formalities of Making a Valid Will. Certain formalities are to be observed in making a valid will. In the first place, hire a good lawyer who is capable of advising you properly. He will draw up a will that will do exactly what you—the testator—intend. In most states, the following factors are necessary in making a valid will.

Signature. The will must be signed by the maker or testator. If the will covers more than one page, the testator usually signs each of the pages. It must be signed in the presence of the witnesses. The signature should be exactly as written in the body of the will. Wills have been thrown out of probate courts because the name was incorrectly spelled in the signature of the maker of the will.

Witnesses. Most states require two or three witnesses. It is wise to have younger persons, but of legal age, act as witnesses. If the wife or the beneficiary of the will or the spouse of a beneficiary acts as a witness, such persons may be disinherited. The will should state that all witnesses signed in the presence of each other. The addresses of all witnesses should be included in the document. Even if the state requires only two witnesses, it is generally wise to have three witnesses in the event that one dies before the will is probated.

Alterations. Do not take a chance on a will being voided because of alterations or erasures. It pays to have the entire will redrafted. As a rule, witnesses do not read the will. They usually are present only at the signing of the document. If called to testify later on with regard to alterations or erasures in the will, most witnesses would be unable to state whether the erasures existed at the time of the signing.

Terms. In addition to making the will legal, care should be taken so that the will distributes the properties in the way desired by the testator. This is not difficult in a simple case, but becomes technical in the event of an involved will. The first step in making a will is an appraisal of the properties or the entire estate. Careful estimates of estate shrinkage from taxes, administrative costs, and immediate expenses should be made. Provision for meeting such expenses by the use of life insurance is an excellent idea. After expenses have been cared for, the disposal of the estate is next on the agenda.

Disposal of an Estate. If a will is to do exactly what the maker wants it to do, expert advice is necessary. For example, if the testator has contacts in two states, perhaps an apartment in New York, though his principal business is in another state, it is possible that both states will want inheritance taxes after his death. Such double taxation has been upheld. The heirs to the Campbell Soup fortune could tell you that Pennsylvania and New Jersey each took 15 million dollars—just out of one little can of soup!

Also, out-of-state real property needs to be handled carefully. Usually, it is wise to get rid of such real property or place it in a revocable trust. In this way, the property will be taxable to the estate, but will not be a part of it, thereby eliminating a substantial estate expense.

Some lawyers include in wills a direction to pay debts. This has little meaning, since all debts must be paid anyhow. And it may be harmful because the direction to "pay all my just debts," means all debts, moral and legal. There is no point in inviting a lawsuit.

In making gifts, use fractional parts of the estate rather then fixed amounts or particular items. If a son is willed $25,000 and the rest (say, $100,000) is willed to the wife at the time an estate is worth $200,000, and death occurs without changing the will, the estate may have shrunk to $35,000. The son, in most states, will still get $25,000 and the wife the remainder—$10,000. Worse yet, the tax comes out of the residue.

Joint wills between spouses, as a rule, are undesirable, because they have the effect of preventing revocation without notice during the life of both parties and any revocation of the survivor.

Another important factor in drawing up the terms of a will is the determination of the portion of the estate that will bear the taxes. In some states, the taxes are paid out of the residue of the estate, which is the portion remaining after special gifts. Gifts in contemplation of death are taxable, but are never a part of the estate itself. The point is to be careful so that the residue, which is so often left to the wife, is adequate. One method for accomplishing this purpose is to require the insurance beneficiaries to pay their share of the taxes and that each devisee or legatee bear his pro rata part. Exactly what should be done depends on the particular estate and the law pertaining to these matters.

If the testator, for instance, has provided $500 a month for his wife by certain insurance options, Federal laws require such insurance to pay its pro rata share of the estate tax, unless the will provides otherwise. The effect of this may be to reduce the widow's income to $375 a month, which is less than the husband considered adequate. Consequently, the tax apportionment clause should be drafted as a part of the estate plan so that the benefits of the legacies will be carried out as intended.

Duties of the Executor of a Will. An independent executor should be designated and given as broad powers as the trustee. If the testator, for example, got a loan commitment from the bank so that ready money would be available for taxes, which must be paid in cash, then the executor should be given the power to draw on this money. It may be wise to require the beneficiaries to join in the execution of the notes, at least to the extent of the properties they will receive from the estate. This power makes borrowing much simpler.

Another requirement is early distribution of the estate. Income taxes can be saved in this way. The executor should also be under no duty to post bond—it saves expense. He should be given discretion about whether or not the estate income should be paid during the executorship. This power will mean substantial income tax savings for the family.

Whether the executor is a person or a corporation, the major qualifications are (1) ability and experience in business; (2) financial responsibility; (3) some knowledge of accounting; (4) experience in administering estates; (5) adequate facilities for safekeeping of securities, correspondence, and the like; and (6) time to do a good job.

It is customary to name a member of the family or a close friend of the family as the executor. Under certain conditions, such persons may be satisfactory. The fee of an executor or trustee is fixed by law or by court and is the same for individuals as for corporations, though the individual may waive the fee. Therefore, it is generally wise to select the best person or corporation.

The administration of an estate is a highly specialized business. An inexperienced person must hire a lawyer to do the work for him. These are some of the things that an executor must do.

1. File the will in the probate court.
2. Select and retain legal counsel. It is usually customary to name as counsel for an estate the lawyer who drew the will.
3. Aid the attorney in presenting to the court an application for letters testamentary, the oath of the executor, and proof of the legal heirs.
4. Assemble, take possession of, and safely hold all personal assets.
5. Withdraw bank deposits; locate and assemble securities; arrange for collection of interest and dividends.
6. Collect all debts due to the estate—through litigation, if necessary.

7. Take charge of real estate, if the will so provides; ascertain status of taxes and mortgages against the property; inspect the condition of the property; provide for management and collection of rents.

8. If life insurance is payable to the estate, file the necessary papers, collect on all policies, and determine what to do with the proceeds.

A Common Disaster Clause. Simultaneous death (such as the death of a husband and wife in one accident) are not uncommon. In the event there is no will, all the property would pass to the children, if any. If there were no children, there may be a legal battle over which person died first. If the court had evidence that the husband died first, and if the wife had a will, this property would be disposed of according to her will. In the absence of a will, any property she left would go to *her* relatives.

Many inequities result from simultaneous deaths. Therefore, a will should provide for the disposal of the property if both husband and wife die in the same accident. A common disaster clause may read: "Any person who shall have died at the same time as I, or in a common disaster with me, or under such circumstances that it is difficult to determine which died first, shall be deemed to have predeceased me." In case there is only one bequest, to the wife perhaps, and in case she does not survive the testator, the property may be left in the will to a daughter or son or to both of them. This is a useful clause in cases of common disaster.

Letter of Last Instruction. Your executor or lawyer should have a letter of last instruction that is not a part of your will. This letter is usually opened at death and contains the following information.

1. Exact location of will.

2. Instructions about funeral and burial. Veterans should remember that they may request burial in a national cemetery and save their estate some expense.

3. Location of all documents, such as birth certificate, social security card, marriage certificate, discharge papers, and the like.

4. Lodge or fraternal membership certificates.

5. Location of all safe-deposit boxes.

6. List of insurance policies and where deposited.

7. Pension statements and records.

8. List of all bank accounts, stocks and bonds, real and other property, and their locations.

9. Instructions concerning a business, if any.

10. Statement of reasons for disinheritances, if any.

Wills Should Be Reviewed. Many persons hesitate to draw a will, feeling that such a document, once executed, exists for all time. Nothing is further from the truth. A will is operative and binding only at the date of the maker's death. Before death, you can make any number of wills, each of which in succession should include terms that revoke and cancel all prior wills. Or you may supplement or modify an existing will by the addition of a *codicil,* which is an amendment to a will. Whenever your family or financial conditions change, a new will should be made to meet the new conditions.

You should reread and reconsider your will each year, or oftener, if necessary. A will that may be just at the time of its making may be very unjust a few years later. Take the case of a single man, the sole support of an aged and widowed mother. He marries, dies by an accident, and his wife survives. His estate consists solely of personal property of a substantial sum. When he executed his will, he was engaged to marry the woman he later did marry, but no mention was made of her in his will.

Unfortunately for the mother in such a case, the law in Illinois provides that a will executed prior to the testator's marriage is revoked by the marriage. The decedent's mother would not receive any of the estate, since it consists solely of personal property and belongs to the widow in its entirety under the law.

The moral is obvious. Review your will at least once a year in the presence of your attorney. If you are married, both husband and wife should review their wills together. There may have been changes since a year ago in the size of the family, in residence, or in tax laws. The kindest thing to do for dependents and loved ones is to be sure that your will follows your intentions.

Where to deposit a will. After you have executed a will, the safest place for deposit is with the trust company you may have named as executor or in a safe-deposit box. As a safe-deposit box may be sealed for a while after death, it is preferable to place the original will with the trust company and to place the receipt for the original will and a copy of the will in the safe-deposit box. Most banks make no charge for the safekeeping of wills in which they are named as executor or trustee.

QUESTIONS FOR DISCUSSION

1. Why should some persons stay out of the stock market and invest only in high-grade United States government bonds?

2. Why is it important for your investment objectives to harmonize with family needs?

3. How would you apply the three major principles for investing in securities?

4. What is your personal reaction to the statements of Bernard Baruch and Emil Schram quoted in this chapter?

5. When selecting a company for possible investment, why is it important to examine carefully its economic position, management, financial condition, and the price of its securities?

6. Explain how you would do business with a stockbroker.

7. What are the advantages and disadvantages in investing in (*a*) United

States government bonds, (b) state and municipal bonds, (c) foreign public bonds, (d) bank stock, and (e) real estate mortgages?

8. When planning an investment program, why is it important to give close attention to taxes?

9. Why should a family complete its savings, educational, insurance, and basic retirement program before entering the security market?

10. What is the meaning of estate planning?

11. Under what circumstances would you select a (a) living trust, (b) testamentary trust, and (c) life insurance trust?

12. Under what conditions should one select a good trust company as executor of a will?

13. How do you account for the fact that so many persons die without leaving a will?

14. Under what conditions might it be satisfactory to write your own will? Why is it dangerous to prepare your own will?

15. Why is it important to review a will at least once annually?

ACTIVITY PROBLEMS

1. You have $5,000 in cash to invest. Compare the advantages and disadvantages of investing this money in (a) a local savings and loan association, (b) United States savings bonds Series E, (c) a savings account in a local bank, (d) a good industrial bond, (e) common stock in a well-known and successful corporation, (f) high-grade preferred stocks, and (g) a mortgage on a new home in an urban community.

2. Interview a judge of the probate court in your county. Find out (a) how many family heads die without leaving a will, (b) what the disadvantages are to the family when there is no will, (c) how many wills are contested and the chief reasons for contesting them, (d) what happens in your state if a husband or wife dies without leaving a will, and (e) who can make a will in your state.

3. The Federation of Women Shareholders in American Business, Inc., New York City, is interested in providing women with an economic education. Among other objectives, the Federation works toward (a) appointment of women on boards of directors of major corporations, (b) increased attendance of women at stockholders meetings, (c) organization of regional stockholders meetings, and (d) increased distribution of information concerning the rights and responsibilities of women as owners. What reactions do you have to these objectives? Perhaps you would like to get more information from the Federation office.

4. A large title and trust company advertised the following message: "If your will was written before April, 1948, it is probably out of date." This advertisement refers to the provision for "marital deductions," effective April, 1948. In what way does the above provision affect a will written before April, 1948?

5. Select five stocks on the New York Stock Exchange. Keep a daily record of their performance for about two weeks. Read all the factual material that you can find about the stocks you selected. Some reliable sources of information are the security and industry surveys published by brokerage firms; analytical guides for investors; special up-to-date booklets on such industries as the petroleum,

utilities, steel, chain stores, air lines, and so on; *Standard and Poor's Stock Guide.* After securing all the information possible on the five stocks, would you retain all the stocks at this time? Support your decisions by facts.

6. Comment on these wills.

a. "I have no available property; I owe a great deal; the rest I give to the poor."

b. "All my worldly goods, now or to be in store, I give them to my beloved wife, and hers forevermore. I give all freely, I no limit fix. This is my will, and she's executrix."

7. A study of surveys conducted by trust companies indicates that administration expenses seldom will be less than 10 per cent on an estate. On estates of less than $20,000, the cost may run from 15 to over 25 per cent. Ask a probate judge about probate costs in your county. Can probate costs be reduced? If so, how?

SUGGESTED READINGS

Armbruster, Dorothy M. *Pennies and Millions.* Garden City, N.Y.: Doubleday & Company, Inc., 1962. (A Woman's Guide to Saving and Investing)

Barnes, Leo. *Your Investments.* Larchment, N.Y.: American Research Council, published annually.

Callahan, Parnell. *How to Make a Will.* New York: Oceana Publications, latest edition.

Changing Times. "Savings & Loan Associations," January, 1961, and March, 1962; "Your Investments: How Fast Are They Really Growing?" July, 1963; "Mutual Funds: Pick with Care," February, 1963; "Mutual Funds and How to Pick Them," March, 1962; "Investments: Is the 'Front-end Load' Fair?" April, 1960; "Invest in Foreign Stocks?" June, 1963.

Clendenin, John C. *Introduction to Investments.* New York: McGraw-Hill Book Company, 3d. ed., 1960.

Cohen, Jerome B., and Hanson, Arthur W. *Personal Finance: Principles and Case Problems.* Homewood, Ill.: Richard D. Irwin, Inc., 1964, chaps. 12–15, 17.

Crane, Burton. *The Sophisticated Investor.* New York: Simon and Schuster, Inc., 1959.

Credit Union Yearbook. Madison, Wis.: Credit Union National Association, published annually.

Donaldson, Elvin F., and Pfahl, John K. *Personal Finance.* New York: The Ronald Press Company, 3d. ed. 1961, chaps. 7, 8, 14–18, 22.

Engle, Louis. *How to Buy Stocks.* New York: Bantam Books, Inc., latest edition.

Estate Planning for the Young Professional Man. Indianapolis: Research & Review Service of America, 1959.

Forbes. "1962 Mutual Funds Ratings," New York (special).

Forecast for the Home Economist. "Investing for the Budget-minded," June, 1959.

Fortune. "Personal Investing Portfolio," 1962 (reprints); "Estate Planning: New Growth Industry," March, 1956.

Goldberg, Philip J. *Estate Planning.* New York: Oceana Publications, 1960.

Handbook of Savings and Loan. Chicago: American Savings and Loan Institute, latest edition (free).

Household Finance Corporation. *Your Savings and Investment Dollars*, Chicago, 1963.

How to Invest. New York: Merrill Lynch, Pierce, Fenner & Smith, Inc., latest edition; *How to Read a Financial Report*, latest edition.

Investment Trusts from the Investor's Point of View. Great Barrington, Mass.: American Institute for Economic Research, latest edition.

Johnson, Hugh A. *Johnson's Investment Company Charts.* Buffalo: Hugh A. Johnson, latest edition.

Leffler, George L. *The Stock Market.* New York: The Ronald Press Company, 2d ed., 1957.

McClanahan, W. S. *Estate Planning for Physicians.* Indianapolis: Research & Review Service of America, Inc., 1959.

MacNeill, Earl S. *What Women Want to Know about Wills.* New York: Harper & Row, Publishers, Incorporated, 1959.

Masteller, Kenneth C. *How to Avoid Financial Tangles.* Great Barrington, Mass.: American Institute for Economic Research, latest edition.

Merrill Lynch, Pierce, Fenner & Smith, Inc. *Security and Industry Survey*, quarterly, New York; *The Investor's Reader*, bimonthly (free); *Over-the-Counter Securities.*

Moral, Herbert R. *Buying Country Property.* New York: The Macmillan Company, 1947. (Excellent and nontechnical)

Morgan, James M. "Planning for the Future and Living with Risk," *The American Behavioral Scientist*, May, 1963.

New York Stock Exchange Fact Book. New York: New York Stock Exchange, latest edition; also *The Exchange*, monthly.

Plum, Lester V., Humphrey, Joseph H., and Bowyer, John W. *Investment Analysis and Management.* Homewood, Ill.: Richard D. Irwin, Inc., 1961.

The Retirement Council. *Retirement Money Guidebook.* New York: Harper & Row, Publishers, Incorporated, 1963.

Rogers, Donald E. *Teach Your Wife to Be a Widow.* New York: Holt, Rinehart and Winston, Inc., 1953.

Savings and Home Financing Source Book. Washington, D.C.: American Home Loan Bank Board, latest edition.

Savings and Loan Fact Book. Chicago: United States Savings and Loan League, latest edition.

Securities of the United States Government. Boston: The First Boston Corporation, annual.

Security Owner's Stock Guide. New York: Standard & Poor's Corp., monthly.

Smith, Ralph Lee. *The Grim Truth about Mutual Funds.* New York: G. P. Putnam's Sons, 1963.

Stephenson, Gilbert Thomas. *Estates and Trusts.* New York: Appleton-Century-Crofts, Inc., 1960.

Trigger, Raymond. *How to Run a Successful Investment Club.* New York: Harper & Row, Publishers, Incorporated, 1958.

The Wall Street Journal. "Investment Clubs," October, 1962; "Excerpts from

SEC Letter and Second Part of Report on Stock Markets," July 18, 1963. (Daily financial newspaper, special educational rates. New York: Educational Service Bureau, Dow-Jones & Co.)

Wiesenberger, Arthur. *Investment Companies.* New York: Arthur Wiesenberger & Company, annual.

Wise, T. A., and editors of *Fortune. The Insiders.* Chicago: Scott, Foresman and Company, 1963.

Wormser, Rene A. *The Story of Family Estate Planning and How to Apply It to Your Own Personal Problems,* 1956. (Free copy: City Bank Farmers Trust Co., New York.)

Wormser's Guide to Estate Planning. Englewood Cliffs, N.J.: Prentice-Hall, Inc., 1958.

15

CONSUMER PROTECTION: PRIVATE AIDS

Primitive man did not need standards other than his taste, his needs, and the limitations of his stomach. But as soon as he became a trader, standards for measurement (quantity and quality) came into existence. Only a few generations ago, the woman who managed a household made most of the clothes worn by the family members. She canned much of the food. She baked bread. Today, these functions, as well as a host of others, for the most part are done outside the home.

The household manager and other members of the family now buy consumer goods in the market. Consequently, the homemaker's role as a purchasing agent is very important. It is not too much to say that, for many families, the intelligence with which the homemaker plans and buys is a prime factor in determining the standard of living of the family.

Problems of Informing Consumers.[1] Today, our system of consumer protection is a three-way partnership involving the consumer's prudent management of purchases, the efforts of producers and retailers to serve the consumer, and government regulation of marketing. Most of this text, so far, has been concerned with the consumer's self-improvement and management of his buying decisions. There are problems connected with providing information for the intelligent consumer, however, and in this chapter we will consider the nature of standards for consumer goods, the present role of business in establishing standards, and the efforts of privately financed, nonprofit consumer testing agencies to test consumer goods.

One of the major consumer challenges is the need for better information

[1] Based in part on Samuel L. Myers's article, "An Economist Considers the Problems of Informing Consumers," Council on Consumer Information, Selected Proceedings, 1961, p. 95.

about the product or service for which consumers spend their money. The statement of Senator Philip H. Hart, quoted in the first chapter, is worth repeating here: "Consumer intelligence is not at stake in this inquiry. The right to information is." This is the heart of effective consumer education. Without adequate information on a product or service, the consumer cannot hope to make intelligent choices in the market place. Unintelligent choices in the market place lead inevitably to dissatisfactions on the part of consumers and to much waste of human and natural resources. If consumers are to perform their role effectively, they must be adequately informed.

Business Discovers Consumers Want to Know. At the turn of the century and for many years—until recently—the major efforts of consumer legislation were basically primitive. Then an effort was made to enlist the cooperation of reputable businesses in providing truthful and factual information to consumers. And business discovered through consumer surveys that "consumers want to know." The result was a kind of alliance between business and consumers.

Within a five-year period (1927 to 1931), as Dr. Myers points out, a number of testing laboratories were established by major department stores, mail-order firms, laundries, and dry cleaners, as well as one by consumers themselves. During the decades that followed, large numbers of certification and labeling programs sponsored by trade associations were launched. Lumber, leather-glove, mirror, broom, hosiery, and other manufacturers developed such programs. In addition, citrus fruit and apple producers, soap guilds, textile fabric finishers, and manufacturers of boys' apparel, all entered the act to label and certify their products for "consumer guidance."

The National Bureau of Standards, in conducting investigations for the Temporary National Economic Committee, compiled data indicating that by the late 1930s, fully 700 of the 1,300 trade associations were conducting some kind of labeling or consumer standards program.

Then, advertising media prepared to enter this alliance of consumers and business. Radio stations and periodicals such as *McCall's Magazine* were about to launch consumer information seals of approval when, quite abruptly, the whole movement collapsed. The long-drawn-out hearings of the Federal Trade Commission, directed against the old, established *Good Housekeeping* Seal of Approval, merely lent drama to the culmination of a movement that would inevitably have collapsed of its own weight. In having business interests provide them with information, consumers were faced with such an amazing conglomeration of symbols, seals, and labels— many of which were meaningless—that they were more bewildered and confused than ever.

Consumer Cooperation but Not Alliance with Business. It should be stressed that consumers must work with, reason with, and cooperate with business interests to some degree. Long ago, the American Standards Association attempted through consumer-business negotiations to correct deceptive certification by developing a valid certification procedure. The National Retail Merchants Association developed, with consumer representation, the washability symbols that were released in 1961.

The National Institute of Dry Cleaners, in drawing up its Life Expectancy Table for textiles in 1961, worked under the guidance of a distinguished consumer leader. Consumers cannot fully isolate themselves from business. Nevertheless, to go to the other extreme and ally themselves with business is to establish a questionable alliance.

Alliance of Government with Consumers. The third concept underlying programs for providing information to consumers is that the Federal government should ally itself with consumers to get quality and performance facts from business. A reader of the historic 1926 *New Republic* articles by Stuart Chase and Frederick Schlink, in which they pleaded for the development of a "science of buying and consuming," is struck by the fact that, from its inception, the consumer testing movement aspired for a consumer-government alliance against business.

The National Bureau of Standards conducted tests for Consumers' Research, Inc., before 1930, but this activity was short-lived, because Congress would not permit it. A bitter struggle between consumer and business groups, as a result of the innocent and routine proposal of the Office of Price Administration during World War II to require the grade labeling of canned goods during the first half of 1943, culminated in another setback for consumers.

There is already a trend toward increasing representation in state governments. California has a consumer representative in the governor's cabinet. Likewise, it appears certain that some type of consumer representation in the executive branch of the Federal government is imminent. In March, 1962, President John F. Kennedy created a Consumer Advisory Committee to advise the Council of Economic Advisers, which is another advisory committee. In 1964, President Johnson appointed a consumer representative to his White House staff. This is progress on the national level—a candle lighted in consumer darkness.

Many consumer leaders are of the opinion that what is needed is a Department of the Consumer in the president's cabinet. Such a department could then function directly for the consumer interest much like the Departments of Agriculture, Labor, and Commerce, which attempt to protect the interest of the farmer, the worker, and the businessman.

A fourth concept concerning getting information to consumers came at the behest of commercial interests. The Textile Labeling Act, for example, fits the Du Pont competitive problems more snugly than it does the consumer's need for more fabric information. The FHA Title I program is more successful as protection for the loan portfolios of commercial banks than it is as succor to the homeowner with repair and maintenance problems.

Can Consumers Do It Themselves? This brings us to the fifth concept concerning getting information to consumers: Consumers should do it themselves. It would be trite to recite all the arguments purporting to prove that consumers are not a unified, cohesive vocal group. The fact is that consumers have failed to organize effectively in the United States.

The most successful attempt to inform consumers on goods and services must be credited to Consumers Union, and in a less degree to Consumers' Research. But most of the problems connected with securing important information about products and services cannot be solved by these two consumer testing organizations.

Need for Adequate Standards for Consumer Goods. A standard is defined as "a physical, written, graphic, or other representation of a product or a procedure established by authority, custom, or general consent with which other products or procedures of a like nature are compared for identification or measurement or to which they are made to conform." [2] The basic role of standards and specifications is to supply a common language understood and respected by seller and buyer. In the production and exchange of goods, standards function in somewhat the same way as mathematics function in the language of the sciences. Unfortunately, when it comes to consumer goods, the ultimate consumer is caught in a social lag.

The development of a common language between buyer and seller of goods is long overdue. To realize the lack of, and need for, adequate and meaningful standards, review your own experience with commonly used consumer goods, such as fresh fruits, frozen foods, prepackaged foods, or household appliances, automobiles, tires, and drugs, just to mention a few consumer products. Although the details vary from product to product, in broad outline the problem of costly confusion, meaningless product differentiation, and few standards available to consumers is duplicated in most lines of consumer goods.

Accompanying the lack of adequate standards and the poor communication of existing standards are the complex elements of planned and unplanned obsolescence of consumer products (especially appliances, cars, and household furniture) and design that is tied to sales rather than to product function. When marketing strategy is based on frequent style changes, certain inevitable results follow—the tendency to use inferior

[2] Jessie V. Coles, *Standards and Labels for Consumer Goods.* New York: The Ronald Press Company, 1949, p. 107.

materials, to short-cut the time necessary for sound product development, and to display a basic neglect of quality and adequate factory inspection of the product.

To say that there is a dearth of information on the quality of consumer goods is revealing only one aspect of the problem. In fairness to a processor or manufacturer, most consumer goods do not have generally acceptable standards, and many goods have no standards at all. This is to say that the marriage of science and producer is far from realization. This is a problem that consumers can do little about except appeal to business to tell, in understandable language, the product's ability to perform satisfactorily the functions for which it was purchased.

What Are Quality Standards? Quality standards are descriptions (preferably printed) of commodities in terms of net weight, accurate size dimensions, content, and other important characteristics, according to the product. They should be written in clear, simple words and phrases that the average consumer will understand. They should answer the following questions about the quality of a product.

1. What is it made of?
2. How is it made?
3. How will it perform?
4. How should it be used?
5. How should it be cared for?

In thinking about standards, the consumer must be careful not to confuse standards with standardization. Producers sometimes use standardization and simplification interchangeably, generally meaning agreement in standard sizes, as in the case of containers, or limiting the variety of a product. The major objective of standardization, or simplification, is to minimize waste in industry. The major objective of quality standards is to answer the question: "How good?" or "How poor?"

Business and Government Have Quality Standards. A smart businessman buys on the basis of quality and price information. Government also buys according to the specifications of technical experts. In general, business and government have long insisted on dealing with known quality factors. In fact, industrialization has literally forced standards into the trade channels. For example, recognition of the need for interchangeable parts is characteristic of modern industry. Complexity of materials requires more and more standardization. When a lumberman orders a certain quantity of No. 1 white pine 2 by 4-16s, he knows what he wants and will receive without advance inspection. In fact, it is difficult to imagine business going on today without a common medium of standards and measurements.

The Federal government can buy paint or anything else according to detailed specifications. It tests the product after it is delivered to see that the specifications were met. Consumers cannot possibly specify exactly what they require in a paint formula, nor can they check its specifications after purchase. Yet it is not practical to insist on transferring all industrial and government practice across the retail counter.

Quality standards among businessmen have aided consumers indirectly. The research necessary to set up acceptable quality standards often has resulted in improved products for consumers. Sometimes, such research results in greater safety, as in the case of many electrical appliances, and in less cost because of simplification through standardization.

Consider the convenience in purchasing a man's shirt. You ask for a Sanforized white cotton shirt, size 15½, 35-inch sleeve, and do not have to worry about the fit and shrinkage. Such standards make shopping more accurate and satisfying.

Quality Standards Should Cross the Retail Counter. Businessmen—producer, wholesaler, and retailer—are specialists. They have quality information, and they can buy and sell informatively among themselves. Why should this information end on the retailer side of the counter?

Consumers know that standardization and simplification have made considerable progress within industry. Retailers have been aided by such industrial research. It seems logical to conclude that the same commodity information that is valuable to industry is also important to the consumer. If an automobile accessories shop can buy tires from a manufacturer on the basis of quality standards, for example, why not pass the same information on to the ultimate consumer of the product?

The buyer for a luggage department uses his knowledge, based on years of experience, to set up specifications for the manufacture of the kind of luggage he wants to sell in his department, or he uses it to select styles from available wholesale stock. At any rate, he is a retailer specialist bargaining with a wholesale specialist on more or less even terms. But consumers are generalists in buying. They purchase hundreds of items and cannot be expert on luggage. They need simple informative labels to compare the goods on the basis of quality and price relationship.

Some quality-rated products can be purchased today in retail stores— but not many. Consumers and retailers should work together for a good informative program in selling and advertising all consumer goods and services.

Style Appeal versus Durability. There are some products on which the consumer places a higher premium for individuality than for quality. Industrial buyers, on the other hand, will insist on quality standards as well as on individuality appeal. This should not mean, however, that a man buys a hat with no reference to quality. Though decision for its purchase may be based on what it does for his appearance, such factors

as shrinkage after cleaning, colorfastness, and retaining of shape should
enter into the transaction. When they do not, the person is a poor consumer.

Such poor consumers do exist—apparently in considerable number. In
fact, some manufacturers and retailers insist that consumers are not
interested in selecting products on the basis of quality characteristics.
These persons say, for example, that people do not want style goods to be
durable. "Distinction is to be found," they contend, "not in the quality
of one's purchase, but in their multiplicity and frequency."

This point of view may be temporarily advantageous to sellers because
of possible increased sales. But in the long run, minimizing quality, even
in clothing, can have only adverse effects on the standard of living of a
majority of families, who as yet have inadequate incomes. These families
cannot afford a buying principle that places emphasis on poor quality and
frequent replacement.

Do Consumers Know What They Want? As a matter of fact, the theory
that consumers are more interested in "distinction" at the expense of
"quality," even with regard to clothing, has been challenged many times,
and the contention does not always hold up. In the case of dresses, the
reasons for discarding them are more likely to be splitting, fading, or
shrinking of the fabric.

Even though a certain segment of business believes in the theory that
most consumers are not interested in selecting commodities on the basis of
quality characteristics, nearly all producers and merchants agree that
consumers are entitled to know precisely what they are paying for. But
there is wide disagreement among businessmen about the proper ways for
keeping consumers informed. There is also disagreement on how standards
and labels should be developed.

Consumers should take advantage of this disagreement by letting
businessmen know what they want in the way of standards and informative labels. But first: Do consumers know what they want? Do they know
the consumer aids that are available at present? Do they know how to
improve consumer protection and services?

Arguments of Business against Grade Labeling. When consumer goods are
described in generally recognized standards, buyers can identify and compare goods. And when consumers can do this, their satisfaction with
purchases is increased. This satisfaction is enhanced especially when information on goods is provided in terms of function or performance in use.

Only a small beginning has been made to date in the use of meaningful
standards for consumers' products in retail stores. Standards that adequately describe quality and performance are seldom used in advertising
and on labels (as we learned in the chapters on food and clothing). Why?

The arguments of business against a simple, understandable plan of grade labeling, as an example of quality standards, are these.

1. The measure of quality on the product may not stand up in a court test if it does not meet the specified grade on the label.
2. Some competitors may not live up to the standards established.
3. Consumers may think that grades below A or 1 are not desirable.
4. In the case of foods, quality would deteriorate because processors would only meet the minimum of each grade.
5. Consumers would continue to buy by brand names, anyway.
6. Large sums of money spent on promoting brand names and a good company image might be lost if brand names became meaningless.
7. Prices might settle at one grade level for each of the grades.
8. Advertising agencies, newspapers, and magazines fear a loss in their income.
9. The cost of testing, labeling, and enforcement would be added to the retail price of the goods.
10. Some fear the unknown and the untried.
11. Others object because selling by brand permits retailers to sell at higher prices than the quality warrants.

Answers to Objections to Grade Labeling. Proponents of quality grade labeling have answers to these fears and objections. Fear of expensive court cases is dispelled after examining the Canadian experience, where compulsory grade labeling has been in existence for years. Federal grades on fresh meat have not ended in costly court fights.

In answer to the contention that it is impractical to test quality objectively, the facts are that most food products are presently purchased by retailers according to standard grades. It is only when foods are sold to the consumer that brands replace objective grade designations.

Whether consumers would buy on the basis of brand names rather than by grades is a matter of educating the consumer. Canadians, and many people in Western European countries, do not appear to ignore grade letters.

The real fear of business is that consumers would base their selections on objective grades if given this opportunity. To argue that business would not abide by the grades is a sad commentary on the personal morals of American businessmen.

Regardless of how the pros and cons of quality standards may be argued at the consumer level, the fact is that consumers are still amateurs (not by choice) in a complex market such as Wesley C. Mitchell never dreamed of when he wrote, in 1912, his now famous essay, *The Backward Art of Spending Money.* "Surely," he wrote, "no one can be expected to possess the expert knowledge of the qualities and prices of such varied wares." [3] This was written before cars achieved a mass market; before electric refrigeration, automatic washing machines, air conditioning, radio, and television; before frozen foods, dried milk, powdered coffee, prepared baby foods, and cake mixes; before synthetic fibers; before detergents and wash-and-wear fabrics; before plastics, synthetic rubber, and countless current consumer goods. In this vast vacuum, consumers are forced to depend almost entirely on brands and trade-marks and at best on minimum standards as in the case of canned foods.

Are Brands and Trade-marks Quality Certification? Are brands and trade-marks helpful to consumers? Marketing experts never intended to promote brands and trade-marks to give consumers objective quality information, except incidentally. These experts in merchandising know that the Trade Mark Act does not permit the registering of a word or symbol that seeks to indicate the quality of a product. Most producers, nevertheless, make the claim of quality in their advertising.

The real purpose of brands and trade-marks is to lift these goods out of price competition and to extol the virtues of a particular product via a brand name. The hope is that consumers will be educated to buy by brand name rather than by precise quality. And it works. When a manufacturer is able to sell a product by brand name, he may safely spend big sums for advertising to assure continued patronage.

Trade-marks and brand names are not evidence of high quality. The trade-mark is merely a letter, word, or symbol to identify the manufacturer, just as brand names identify the manufacturer. In today's complex market there are scores of different brands, sometimes over a hundred, of the same product. How is the consumer to know which one is best for what purpose? Some consumers assume that certain companies can do no wrong, that the seller must tell the truth, and if he does not, some private or public agency will somehow bring him to account.

Alert consumers, and they are increasing in number, who read *Consumer Reports* or *Consumers' Research Bulletin,* have begun to doubt their faith in brand names only. In fact, consumer confidence in advertising and selling has been badly shaken. This situation has brought forth much soul searching on the part of businessmen, advertising executives, media owners, regulatory agencies, and political leaders.

What else could be expected when we witness true wood names being placed on fabricated materials in furniture; misleading quality designations in first, second, and third lines of brand-named car tires; degrading of car models, as in the case of some models put out by the "big three"

---

[3] Wesley C. Mitchell, *The Backward Art of Spending Money.* New York: McGraw-Hill Book Co., 1937, p. 7.

automobile manufacturers. And this is typical in present-day marketing methods.

In an effort to offset the need for reliable, factual information on consumer products, as found in *Consumer Reports* and in *Consumers' Research Bulletin,* some national advertisers of branded products organized the Brand Names Foundation, Inc., which stresses the idea of "buying by brand" alone.

How Reliable Are Labels? Labels come in many forms. They may be stamped on fruit and on unpackaged fresh meat; sewn on clothing; pasted on containers and wrappers of canned and frozen foods, bottles, candy, and so on. But they have one thing in common. The label is the "window" of the can, package, or product.

The information on a label varies considerably. In general, however, labels contain:

1. Name and address of producer or distributor
2. Name and picture of the product
3. Contents
4. Brand name and trade-mark
5. Maturity of product
6. Size and style of product
7. Directives for use
8. Claims for what the product will do
9. Weight, measure, or count

Experienced consumers disregard the information on labels if it is too technical or the print is too small. There are such special labels as the "Consumers League" label (no children employed and conditions of work good), and the "Union" label (only union labor employed). The *Good Housekeeping* Seal of Approval, the *Parents' Magazine* Seal of Commendation, and the American Dental Association endorsement are regarded as stamps of approval of safety and satisfactory quality.

With the notable exception of labels on foods, drugs, cosmetics, furs, and textiles entering interstate commerce, labels on merchandise are of little value. They are not a reliable guide to quality or even a guarantee of uniformity. Often, there is much confusion and misunderstanding— even mislabeling of products. A good illustration of this confusion is in the variety of labels on smoked ham—"uncooked ham," "smoked," "tendered," "fully cooked," to name only a few.

When labels contain factual information that consumers can rely on (usually based on good standards), as in the case of the textile standard L22, they benefit both consumers and the producers who use them.

FTC Principles for Guarantees. Historically, guarantees and warranties have been used by business to cause disadvantage to competitors. These claims were usually regarded as mere trade puffing. Who could believe in guarantees filled with so many "hidden limitations"? Furthermore, legal action against a guarantor was useless, ending with the buyer "holding the bag." A common expression was this: "A guarantee is as good as the retail store desires to make it"—meaning that the manufacturer's responsibility ended when the retailer sold the product.

In 1960, the Federal Trade Commission issued *Guides Against Deceptive Advertising of Guarantees* to make guarantee claims more meaningful. The guide lists seven principles to be followed *voluntarily* by business or risk being ordered to do so by the FTC. Following is a summary of these principles.

1. In general, an advertised guarantee shall clearly and conspicuously disclose three things:

(*a*) The nature and extent of the guarantee, including what product or part is guaranteed, all characteristics or properties covered by or excluded from the guarantee, its duration, and what must be done by a claimant before the guarantor will fulfill his obligation, such as return of the product and paying service or labor charges.

(*b*) The manner in which the guarantor will perform. The guarantee must state exactly what the guarantor will do under the guarantee, such as repair, replacement, or refund. If the guarantor or recipient of the guarantee has an option as to what may satisfy the guarantee, this should be set out.

(*c*) The guarantor's identity. This also shall be clearly revealed in any documents evidencing the guarantee. Purchasers often are confused when it is not clear whether the manufacturer or the retailer is a guarantor.

2. When guarantees are adjusted on a pro rata basis, the advertising should clearly disclose this fact and the basis on which they will be prorated.

3. Claims such as "Satisfaction or your money back" and "Ten-day free trial" will be construed as a guarantee that full refund will be made at the purchaser's option. Any conditions or limitations on this guarantee shall be conspicuously revealed.

4. If "life," "lifetime," or similar guarantees relate to any life other than that of the purchaser or original user, the life referred to must be clearly disclosed.

5. Advertising containing savings guarantees ("Guaranteed to save you 50 per cent," "Guaranteed lowest price in town") must clearly state what the guarantor will do if the savings are not realized, together with any limitations that he may impose.

6. A seller or manufacturer must not advertise or represent that a product is guaranteed when he cannot or does not properly and scrupulously fulfill his obligations under the guarantee.

7. The manner in which a guarantee is used frequently constitutes representations of material facts. (For example, "Guaranteed for 36 months" applied to a battery implies that it can normally be expected to last 36 months and should

not be used in connection with a battery that can normally be expected to last for only 18 months.)

Warranties as a Marketing Device. Since the guides against meaningless guarantees were issued, new and longer warranties as a marketing device are the trend among manufacturers, according to a study by Lippincott & Margulies, Inc.[4] The report, based on a study of 50 major companies, notes that in most cases warranties have doubled or tripled in the length of time for which products are guaranteed. And bonuses, such as services, are becoming a part of the warranties.

Service groups (repairing services) have been fighting longer warranty plans. For example, the Federation of Television & Radio Service Associations sounded a "call to arms" to fight against extended warranties and called the extended warranty a "monster created by the manufacturers." Such guarantees "tend to be misleading, in that they convey the impression that appliances are relatively free of the need of services." Such warranties also represent "an additional drain on the dealers," since there is "little opportunity for him to recoup labor charges." [5]

What have consumers gained? Read a "service free" car sales brochure: "Built to take care of itself—30,000 miles or more between major chassis lubrication—go 6,000 miles between oil changes—take your car in for service only twice a year—new, longer 24,000-mile warranty."

Now look closely at the manuals for the owner that come with the car, and note these facts.

1. Those long stretches between oil changes and grease jobs are hedged with qualifications. Intervals of 30,000 miles between grease jobs apply only to certain parts, usually the front suspension.

2. Many other parts require routine attention more frequently than twice a year.

3. The longer gaps apply only to late-model cars.

4. They "chain you" to the dealer where you purchased the car by requiring that the car be serviced there at stated intervals.

How Good Is a Guarantee, Warranty, or Service Contract? Since many people are confused by what is covered in guarantees, a national appliance dealers' association has defined terms that it hopes dealers will agree to use: *guarantee* to mean coverage of parts and labor; *warranty* to cover parts only; and *service contract* to mean a continuation of protection, regardless of type, for which the customer pays a flat fee.

[4] "The Manager's Letter," *Appliance Manufacturer*, Nov. 20, 1961, p. 4.

[5] *Air Conditioning, Heating & Refrigeration News*, Nov. 12, 1962, p. 11; Oct. 29, 1962, p. 1.

The fine print can be confusing. In many cases, even during the first year, the consumer pays for service calls and labor costs to put "free" parts in the washer, for example. (Parts are covered by the manufacturer; the dealer decides whether or not to add free labor.) It can be worse still to find that defective parts (such as the whole tank of a water heater) must be returned, prepaid, to the manufacturer. If the refrigerator breaks down when the dealer is closed, the consumer is lucky to obtain service elsewhere at any price, because some servicemen will not touch an appliance from another dealer while it is in the warranty period.

A few manufacturers have extended warranties to five years, but the trend is to sell more service contracts at the time the appliance is purchased. How good is the "second-year service contract"? It usually costs $18 to $25 on a washer, or $10 to $15 on a refrigerator. Is it a good buy?

It depends on the price, the appliance, and the coverage spelled out in that fine print. New parts are a minor item in the second year of most appliances, according to *Home Furnishings Daily*, which reminds dealers of the profit in service contracts, especially in "chaining the customer to the store."

Here are questions to ask about guarantee, warranty, or service contract.

1. Who pays for parts? For labor costs? Are service calls included? What are time limits on each of these?

2. Can repairs be made without returning product or parts to the factory and, if not, who pays for shipping and delivery?

3. Will the dealer make arrangements elsewhere for service if you move before your service contract expires? What coverage applies if an authorized dealer is not available?

4. What parts, precisely, are covered? In a service contract, are you paying for protection already provided for five years by the manufacturer, such as the sealed unit of a refrigerator?

Caveat Emptor versus Caveat Venditor. Should *caveat emptor* (let the buyer beware) be replaced by *caveat venditor* (let the seller beware)? Law and public opinion alike recognize that the buyer should be able to accept the merchandise as it is represented. Perhaps what is required is a more positive approach in the form of a legally enforced responsibility. This could mean not only that all information about the prices and qualities of goods offered by sellers would have the status of a warranty, but also that such information would have to rest on the seller who chooses to identify the goods with his trade-mark. On nonbranded goods, the responsibility would be that of the final seller.

This principle is not an innovation. The principle of full disclosure, for example, has been accepted in the food and drug industries. Declarations of ingredients in food and warnings against possible damage in proprietary medicines are label requirements under present law. In 1960, Congress passed the Federal Hazardous Substances Labeling Act which requires full warning on the labels of potentially poisonous products, such as insecticides, pesticides, cleaning agents.

As early as 1916, the New York Circuit Court of Appeals, in the famous product liability case, *MacPherson v. Buick*, proclaimed the principle of seller liability when Judge Benjamin N. Cardozo said that a manufacturer by placing a car on the market assumed a responsibility to the consumer that rested not on a contract but on his (the consumer's) relation to the seller, which arose out of the transaction itself.

In 1960, the Supreme Court of New Jersey, in another automobile product liability case, reinforced this earlier decision. A study by Cornelius W. Gillam, "Products Liability in the Automobile Industry," makes this statement: *"Caveat emptor* has become *caveat venditor,* and no one supposes that the change is not appropriate and essential under conditions of modern industrial economy, with its impersonal markets and highly developed division of labor among the multitude of specialists."

An interesting aspect of the 1960 New Jersey suit against both the dealer and the Chrysler Corporation was that the courts held there was no proof that either company had been negligent in making or servicing the car, but awarded the $30,000 anyway. The court's reasoning? Despite the lack of evidence of negligence, something obviously went wrong with the car's steering gear (after 10 days and 468 miles of driving). Therefore, the car had not lived up to Chrysler's "implied warranty" that its products are fit for use, and the corporation and its dealer must pay for damages that the car caused.[6]

Guarantees Depend on Reliability of Guarantor. "Implied warranty" does not necessarily alter the nature of guarantees to consumers when the consumer does not suffer physical injury. A typical guarantee still depends on the reliability of the guarantor. A guarantee is usually valid only between the retail seller and the consumer buyer. Even so, the buyer is not likely to sue for damages unless the amount involved is large. Such a case may be rare because the courts may allow as damages the difference between the value of the item and what its value should have been as warranted. The buyer is likely to lose in dollars even if he wins the case.

No doubt the seven-point guide for sellers to use voluntarily in advertising guarantees or risk action by the FTC will tend to curtail the irresponsible seller. The National Better Business Bureau's support of these guides should help in clarifying the advertising of guarantees, but there will always be the need for effective policing.

Consumers can do their part (1) by demanding money back or correc-

6 *The Wall Street Journal,* Aug. 31, 1960.

tive action by the seller, (2) by writing to the nearest Better Business Bureau and to the advertising media in which the guarantee appeared, (3) by writing to the president of the manufacturing concern, and (4) by sending copies of the letters to the FTC in Washington, D.C. Only in this way can consumers hope to get effective enforcement of guarantees or warranties.

Business-sponsored Consumer Aids

Trade associations are conscious of consumer relations, realizing that consumers often have unsatisfactory experiences with the goods they purchase. One of the chief reasons for this dissatisfaction seems to be the lack of useful information concerning the character and performance value of merchandise. Therefore, it is easy to understand the consumer's request for some assurance of the quality of the products he buys, and the manufacturer's efforts to devise some means by which to gain the consumer's confidence in his product or service.

This has led to the adoption by various trade associations of methods of certification or guarantee of commodities. Some of the trade associations' certification and labeling methods have been based on superficial inspection and testing. Others have granted approval based on scientifically conducted tests made in conformity with nationally recognized methods.

Private Testing Agencies. The *American Standards Association* is regarded as one of the top private agencies dealing with standardization and testing methods. The ASA (formerly known as the American Engineering Standards Committee) was organized by five leading technical societies in 1918 for the purpose of developing a plan for cooperation in standardization work. The ultimate hope was to evolve voluntary standards that would serve a relatively wide market.

The membership of the ASA is made up of many technical societies, trade associations, and governmental agencies, as well as over 2,300 industrial concerns. The association is supported by membership dues and by subscriptions. Before a standard can be approved, it must have the general acceptance of all groups concerned with the particular product. So far, several hundred standards have been approved.

Ever since 1932, the American Standards Association has had a Committee on Ultimate Consumer Goods to promote the development of standards for certain consumer commodities sold on the retail level. Much investigation has gone on, but progress has been slow, owing in a large degree to a lack of funds and disagreement about the use of quality terminology. This confusion points up the difficulty that industry continues to have when it comes to the problem of how quality identifications are to be presented to the consumer.

The *American Society for Testing Materials* is regarded by some authorities as the second most important private testing agency in the United States. It is an independent association working on standardization of specifications and methods of testing. It has a membership of over 4,200, made up of individuals, companies, laboratories, universities, governmental agencies, libraries, and technical schools.

The ASTM was one of the founding societies of the ASA and is affiliated with the *International Association for Testing Materials*. It has been chiefly instrumental in developing most of the test methods for textiles that are in use today. Like the ASA, this society concentrates on standardizing aids to industry directly.

Agencies Serving Consumers More Directly. The *American Gas Association* is financed by gas companies and businesses engaged in the manufacture of gas appliances. Gas appliances carelessly made and installed could be a source of much danger. The AGA Laboratory Seal of Approval is available to a manufacturer who has met certain standards. A manufacturer may also qualify for a "Certified Performance" marker if he can prove that his gas appliance has met additional specifications in efficiency, convenience, and performance.

Today, it is claimed that more than 90 per cent of all gas appliances sold in the United States carry the AGA Laboratory Seal of Approval. Some cities require compliance with its standards. To insure reasonable honesty on the part of manufacturers using its seal, the American Gas Association carries on a continuous inspection system in the factories.

Underwriters Laboratories Seal of Approval is insurance to the consumer that an electrical appliance has passed its safety tests.

Electrical Testing Laboratories, with the aid of the Illuminating Engineering Society, worked out standards for an IES seal on the ETL Certificate of Compliance shield. This certificate can be placed on any lamp that has met the required standards. Perhaps as many as fifty different lamp manufacturers use this certificatee. ETL maintains a continuous checking service in the factories. The manufacturer pays about 3 cents a lamp for the testing service and around 10 cents a lamp to an advertising agency hired to promote the use of IES lamps.

ETL will test any product in its line for a manufacturer for a fee, but permits use of its seal only on products whose standards are printed on the label where the consumer can read them. These standards are based on performance requirements, not on construction specifications. The ETL has the final word when granting its seal of approval.

Consumer Services of Individual Stores. A few large retailers have developed rather extensive programs of merchandise testing and of informative labeling. Among them are Macy's of New York, Gimbel's of Philadelphia, Marshall Field of Chicago, Lit Brothers of Philadelphia, Kaufmann's of

Pittsburgh, and various mail-order houses, such as Sears, Roebuck and Company and Montgomery Ward. Moreover, certain large chain stores—notably the A & P, Safeway, and J. C. Penney—test, grade, and label some of their products.

Sears, Roebuck and Company has maintained its own laboratories and staff of technicians since 1911. This is reportedly the largest privately owned merchandise testing laboratory in the world. The company sets up minimum standards arrived at through agreement among the general merchandise office, the buyers, the merchandise comparison office, and the technical laboratories.

The primary function of the testing is to aid buyers in the selection of merchandise. The company gives special attention to its own trade-marked goods. A close analysis of the descriptions in its catalogues indicates the influence of the laboratory technicians over the advertising department.

J. C. Penney Research and Testing Laboratory in New York City was established in 1930. Most of the merchandise handled by the J. C. Penney stores is tested. The laboratory is equipped to do physical, chemical, and some types of biological testing. Besides setting up standards and testing the products, the laboratory also checks all returned goods to discover whether the article had some inherent fault that did not show up in previous tests. Staff members also spend time in the various mills and factories that produce merchandise for the J. C. Penney stores.

Macy's Bureau of Standards, established in 1927, is primarily interested in the adaptability, performance, durability, and care of merchandise sold by Macy stores. It is concerned largely with these factors from the consumer's point of view. The bureau has also established many standards for goods sold under Macy's brand names. It studies and recommends more effective garment, rug, and fur cleaning, waterproofing, mothproofing, and so on; prepares informative labels for the merchandise; assists in the training of buying and selling management personnel; and is continually working on adequate but easy-to-understand terminology for informing the buying public.

Macy's service supplements the store's guarantee policy, making it more reliable and less costly to both consumer and owner, and more enforceable than most so-called product guarantees.

Some of the large food chains, like A & P and Safeway Stores, grade certain foods according to U.S. Department of Agriculture standards—the most acceptable grades for food products. The A & P, in particular, also has developed its own grades for its store brands. As a rule, U.S. Department of Agriculture graded goods are more reliable.

Seals—How Reliable Are They? Seals or certifications of approval of products as "guaranteed," "certified," "approved," or "tested" are promoted by business to put a quality ceiling on certain kinds of services for consumers

EXAMPLES OF SEALS

The Seal	*Where it is found*	*What it means*
American Gas Association	on gas appliances—ranges, refrigerators, heaters, clothes dryers.	Products have been tested by AGA and are certified for conformity to requirements of the American Standards Association, and are factory tested at least annually to insure continued conformity.
American Institute of Laundering	on labels attached to fabrics and ready made merchandise—clothing, bedding, draperies.	Products have passed ALL tests for shrinkage, color and sunfastness, fiber strength, resistance to perspiration, launderability of zippers, buttons and snaps and general appearance after laundering.
Canadian Standard Association	on electrical, gas or oil equipment and plumbing brass; on general products certified to show conformity with quality and performance standards.	Products are certified by the manufacturers to conform to CSA Standards of safety and performance.
Underwriters' Laboratories, Inc.	on all appliances, equipment and materials which could possibly be fire or accident hazards or used to stop the spread of fire.	Products have passed original and periodical factory tests and examination in accordance with standards for safety.
United States Testing Company	on products continually tested and certified by the U.S. Testing Company.	Products have been tested and meet the requirements of the U.S. Testing Company and are qualified for materials, construction, use and performance. They are factory re-inspected to insure continued quality.
CONSUMER MAGAZINES Parents Magazine Good Housekeeping Chatelaine McCalls	on any article or appliance tested and approved in the laboratories of one of these magazines.	Products have been tested and have met specific requirements set up by each magazine before receiving the *guaranteed, commended, investigated and approved, laboratory use-tested, or certified* seal. Refer to the magazine for an explanation of the policy and meaning behind statements made.

SOURCE: *Money Management: Your Shopping Dollar*, Household Finance Corporation, Chicago, 1963.

and are issued to manufacturers for products that meet the requirements of a testing organization. The accompanying illustration, Examples of Seals, provides information about a few of the many seals currently used.

In most cases, it is difficult to know whether consumers benefit from these seals. The American Institute of Laundering tests for colorfastness in fabrics. Its seal of approval tells consumers that the material withstands laundering. It is an aid to know that a garment can be laundered rather than requiring dry cleaning.

The magazine seals of approval are probably more valuable to the magazines than to the public. A seal, for example, that promises "replacement or refund of money for any product advertised in the magazine whose performance proves to be defective" has little significance or meaning when selecting garments or fabrics. It does not carry the authority of the American Standards Association L22, which is a collection of standards for textile fabrics for 75 end uses in the areas of garments for men, women, and children, and of household furnishings. Approval of American Standard L22, in 1960, was the culmination of the cooperative efforts of more than 40 organizations, representing 10 years of work by a group of highly trained people in textiles.

This points up the fact that a healthy skepticism should prevail on seals that are not directly related to known tests, as they are in American Standard L22. In short, to make intelligent use of seals, consumers must know (1) who approves the product, (2) what tests were made, (3) what the test results were, (4) what the certification includes, and (5) what the specific terms of the guarantee are and how long they are effective. Present seals of approval on consumer products fail to give answers to all these requirements.

Better Business Bureaus. The United States Supreme Court has declared that "voluntary action to end abuses and to foster fair competitive opportunities in the public interest may be more effective than legal processes." This point of view was central in the thinking of a group of businessmen who organized the National Vigilance Committee in 1911. In 1916, this group adopted the name of *National Better Business Bureau.*

Since 1916, this central organization and some local but independent bureaus in many cities in the United States have worked hard to protect decent business and consumer interest. The local Better Business Bureaus are maintained by business itself for the purposes of (1) promoting and maintaining advertising and selling practices that are fair to business and to consumers; (2) protecting business and the consumer from frauds, misrepresentations, and chicanery in business transactions; and (3) providing certain aids for consumers in their quest for full value for their money. Millions of "facts" booklets—*Cosmetics, Health Cures, Legal*

Problems, Used Cars, Home Building and Buying, Investments, Color Television, and others—are distributed free.

The annual report of the Association of Better Business Bureaus for 1962 gives an impressive list of requests for information and services rendered. More than 2½ million requests for information from business and the public were recorded in 128 separate bureaus. This represents a 6 per cent increase over 1961 totals. These 128 bureaus investigated more than 40,000 advertisements, and 570 trade practice conferences were held in 60 different classifications of business, resulting in the adoption of voluntary restraints against advertising abuses.

The work of the bureaus on checking advertising is especially noteworthy. Complaints come usually from business competitors and consumers. However, the major approach is the daily job of "shopping the ads." Trained persons study the local advertising, then check the advertised articles in the stores.

In the event that slight misrepresentations are found, the merchant is shown just how the advertising misrepresents the merchandise. If the merchant refuses to correct or improve the advertising, more drastic action is generally used. As a last resort, the bureau will turn the case over to the proper governmental agency, usually the Federal Trade Commission.

There are certain services that the bureaus do not give to consumers. If anyone calls the bureau by telephone and asks for the name of a reliable laundry, the answer is something like this: "I'm sorry, but we can't do that. We cannot tell people where to go or where not to go. We simply give the facts, if there are any in our records, and let people make up their own minds."

Professional Associations Aiding Consumers

Professional associations and organizations are another source of consumer protection, and they have done outstanding work in promoting consumer education. The effective programs of some of these associations will give an idea of what they are accomplishing.

American Home Economics Association. The AHEA is primarily an educational organization with about 30,000 members engaged in the fields of family economics, home management, family relations and child development, foods and nutrition, textiles and clothing, housing and household equipment, and art. The organization is active in extension service and in college clubs with over 20,000 students majoring in home economics. Through its publication, the *Journal of Home Economics,* and joint projects with trade associations, the American Standards Association, and legislative activities, the AHEA has been an important information center.

The Consumer Interests Committee promotes important consumer programs and serves as a clearinghouse for all consumer activities. The textile section was a prime mover in seeking a way to set standards for consumer goods. Today, the efforts of the AHEA revolve around consumer legislation, consumer education, and promotion of standards of quality for consumer goods. It strongly supports the broadening of the L22 standards until they cover performance qualities of all textiles.

Some of the most outstanding work of the AHEA has been in the field of food facts and fallacies. This is in keeping with one of its major contributions—giving information to consumers. The AHEA has supported programs for consumer protection against misrepresentation and misleading advertising. Work in the areas of trading stamps, credit charges, fictitious pricing, good labeling, and bait advertising has received a large share of attention.

The AHEA is preparing to take even greater interest in improving the position of the consumer. To commemorate its golden anniversary (in 1959), the committee on philosophy and objectives set forth the new direction for home economics. Among the 12 objectives, three were specifically related to the consumer. This organization of over 30,000 members in almost every county or small political unit in 50 states could become the most effective consumer educational force in the United States.

American Medical Association. There are several medical, surgical, and dental associations that have established standards of materials and practices. These standards are of direct value to consumers.

The American Medical Association, an organization of physicians, is active in the improvement of quality and standardization of medical products. Most of the testing and education is done by five committees. Some of the findings are reported in its publication, *Journal of the American Medical Association.*

The Council on Pharmacy and Chemistry, one of the five AMA committees, judges products claimed to have therapeutic values. The accepted and unaccepted products are described in the *Journal* and published annually in a separate brochure.

The Council on Physical Therapy investigates and reports on the merits of nonmedical apparatus and devices offered for sale to consumers as well as to physicians and hospitals.

The Council on Foods and Nutrition checks the health claims made by producers for their manufactured foods. It concerns itself only with foods sold for dietary purposes. It merely "accepts" foods that offer truthful advertising and labels. The use of the seal is granted to products that are accepted. It definitely does not "approve," "recommend," or "grade" food products. Foods submitted for analysis are accepted or rejected, and are so published in the *Journal.* No attempt is made to equate quality and price relationships.

The Committee on Advertising of Cosmetics and Soaps was formed to advise the manager of the *Journal* on advertisements of cosmetics and soaps that are submitted to him.

The Bureau of Investigation has for its primary purpose the investigation and dissemination of information on "patent medicines," quacks, medical fads, and other aspects of pseudo medicine.

The American College of Surgeons is actively engaged in standardization of surgical dressings on the basis of use and characteristics. The college also develops standards for hospitals with respect to services, treatments, and records.

The American Institute of Homeopathy published the first *Homeopathic Pharmacopeia* in 1897. The standards set up by this organization are for the use of the pharmacist as well as the physician. The Federal Food, Drug, and Cosmetic Act recognized these standards as well as those found in the *United States Pharmacopeia* and in the *National Formulary*. These are not government publications. They are published by scientists, doctors, and pharmaceutical manufacturers.

These standards are reviewed periodically to incorporate the latest scientific information. When new drugs are discovered, the experts study the evidence of their effectiveness, the right dosages, and the best processes for their manufacture, packaging, and labeling. This information is made available to doctors and pharmacists.

In general, a drug or standard preparation with the letters U.S.P., H.P., or N.F. on its label has been processed, packed, and labeled according to standard specifications.

American Dental Association. The American Dental Association is a professional association with a membership of a high percentage of the more than 100,000 dentists in the United States. Its Council on Dental Therapeutics evaluates dental therapeutic agents and dental cosmetic agents sold by companies directly to the public or to the profession. In the council's *Accepted Dental Remedies* are up-to-date descriptions of basic drugs used in dentistry. The council does not evaluate medicated mouthwashes sold to the public, because it feels that they are useless when used without professional supervision. Toothbrushes and cleansers for dentures are also not considered for acceptance. The council, however, continues to give consideration to dentifrices that claim to have evidence against tooth decay or any other mouth disorder.

Until 1960, the best the council had to say about dentifrices was summed up in the terse statement: "The function of a dentifrice . . . is to aid the brush in cleaning the teeth."

In 1960, there was one exception, when the official *Journal of the American Dental Association* published a report that began, "After careful consideration of the results of clinical studies conducted on Crest toothpaste, manufactured by the Procter & Gamble Company, the Council on Dental Therapeutics has recognized the usefulness of the dentifrice as a caries (decay) preventive agent. . . .'"

There were resentful reactions on the part of toothpaste manufacturers because ADA allowed its name to be used. Many dentists also resented such commercialization of their professional organization.

Actually, the ADA recognition of Crest, according to a report in 1961, *The Medicine Show*, by Consumers Union was "hedged and tentative." In view of ADA's long-standing invitation to dentifrice manufacturers to seek the kind of recognition given to Crest, it would seem to be a fair conclusion that no such evidence exists up to now. The patent on Crest formulation is held by the Indiana University Foundation, where the experiments were conducted at a cost of over $3 million financed by Procter & Gamble, who have an exclusive license to produce and market the toothpaste.

The Procter & Gamble promotion and advertising of Crest was objected to by the ADA as "gross exaggeration and a misleading distortion." Then why was nothing done about these claims? The two Federal agencies that have some control over dentifrices, the Food and Drug Administration and the Federal Trade Commission, did not have enough power. Until Congress changed the law, in 1962, the FDA could only review the "safety" of the product, not its efficacy. Now that the FDA has the efficacy power, it can seize a product if its label is false or misleading. And the burden of proof is the company's headache.

The curbing of misleading advertising is the responsibiilty of the FTC. To prove the claims as false in regard to Crest is almost an impossibility because hearing examiners and judges (not ordinarily trained in scientific disciplines) have usually considered laboratory evidence, even if inadequate, more convincing than testimony by experts. The American Dental Association has complained about the ineffectiveness of the FTC under present rules. The remedy, said ADA, is an amendment that would shift the burden of proof to the advertiser, and until this happens, consumers must be wary of claims for dentifrices. Incidentally, the ADA does recognize the suitability of baking soda mixed with powdered salt as a cleansing agent.

The contributions of the AMA and ADA could be much greater. At the present time, the chief weakness is their inability to reach the consumer. Modern advertising reaches millions, whereas statements by medical associations may reach only a few thousand. Perhaps the greatest benefit is in the professional use of the standards set up, rather than in giving direct information to the consumer. A good consumer-education program in the schools could inform families of the importance of this kind of information and on how to get up-to-date consumer information.

Other Consumer Protection Associations. There are other consumer protection movements and associations of considerable importance in the United States on the local, state, and Federal levels. They are described in Chapters 16 and 17. Some of these are centered in state colleges; others are local consumer associations. Labor, too, has set up a consumer organization with headquarters in New York City.

Such organizations as the National Young Women's Christian Association (YWCA) and the American Association of University Women have active consumer-education programs. Credit unions, cooperatives, women's clubs, parents' organizations, local labor unions, and religious groups have some consumer-protection activities.

The extension services of many universities are extending consumer education to the urban centers where 90 per cent of the population lives. This particular service has tremendous possibilities because university extension services have the largest adult education programs in the United States.

Consumer-financed Nonprofit Testing and Rating Agencies

For any desired product, the consumer encounters a multiplicity of brands and models. Is there some rational basis for choosing one over the other? Not the wild, unsupported (and often unsupportable) advertising claims, hundreds of which impinge on the consumer's senses every day. Not the kind of judgment a consumer can make from even a careful examination at the point of sale. Not the sweet purrings of an attractive salesperson, often less informed about product differences than the customer, and possibly biased by "push money" (money paid for urging a certain brand on customers). Not even your own experience, or your neighbor's, can be a rational basis for selecting many products that are bought infrequently, such as refrigerators and automobiles, which are changed radically from year to year.

Suppose a conscientious consumer decides, for some major purchase, that he is going to try to determine which of a number of products or models of products is best. In a simpler society, he might have a chance. But in countries with complicated technologies, he is stymied by the complexities and properties of new materials—plastics, synthetic fibers, urethane foams, transistors, new insecticides, and drugs—about which he is given little information and has had no previous experience. He is perplexed by the various ways these materials are used in finished products—the virtues of one kind of weave over another, or of one construction technique over another (for example, printed versus wired circuits). No sooner did the conscientious consumer learn how to distinguish a better from a poorer carpet sweeper than the vacuum cleaner faced him. As he mastered the qualities of the upright vacuum cleaner, there came the tank and canister cleaner to consider. When he caught up with these, they sprouted revolving brushes and created a whole new set of problems requiring knowledge before decision.

With the development of still newer products—automatic clothes washing machines; automatic moisture-sensing clothes dryers; dishwashers; floor scrubbers; air conditioners; sudsing, nonsudsing, and controlled-sudsing detergents; wash-and-wear, drip-dry, and easy-care clothing; and on and on—the poor consumer might have given up a long time ago. (Indeed, even the manufacturers find it difficult to keep up with the rapidly changing scene.)

Why Consumer Testing Is Necessary. Why should the consumer be concerned about making a rational choice? There are wide differences in over-all quality between competing models of most products, and it follows that the individual consumer who buys an inferior product wastes his money and lowers his standard of living.

Professor Arthur R. Oxenfeldt, in a study published in 1950 in the *Review of Economics and Statistics*, has estimated, using *Consumer Report* ratings as a basis, that the consumer could increase his standard of living by $1\frac{1}{2}$ to 2 times if he bought the products rated best rather than those rated average. In a broader sense, economic resources are wasted when they are used to make inferior products. The same metal, the same plastic, the same labor can be used to make a product that lasts longer and provides more satisfaction than a poorer product.

It is of interest to the individual consumer and to the country as a whole that rational choices be made. But how? If the consumer cannot have all the necessary technical disciplines himself, he can join with other consumers, and together the group can employ them. This is the essence of a consumer testing organization: the application of technical knowledge to consumer problems, particularly to the problem of product purchasing but more broadly to the problem of consumer welfare.

With such a tool, a consumer organization can concern itself more knowledgeably and therefore more effectively with general problems that have their solution in legislation or industry-wide action such as health, safety, allocation of radio and TV frequencies, watering of ham, standards of identity and grades for foods and other products, labeling, weights and measures, and many similar matters.

Consumers' Research, Inc. (CR). In the early 1920s there was an outburst of inaccurate and misleading advertising. The prosperity following World War I brought forth a tremendous flow of consumer goods on the market, aided by mass production techniques worked out by Henry Ford and others after him. This flow of products was pushed by new methods of advertising and by what Thorstein Veblen called the "higher salesmanship." Many of the new products were shoddy and poorly designed, calling for critical examination. In a way, the testing of consumer goods at this time was an inevitable response to confused disappointment in the mass-produced outflow of products. Consumers began to ask: Is there "soapier soap," "coffier coffee"?

This confusion set the scene for what became a best-seller—*Your Money's Worth*, by Stuart Chase and F. J. Schlink, in 1927. The book revealed the multiple methods used by business to deceive consumers, and shortly after it appeared, thousands of letters flooded the offices of the publishing company. People were concerned. Primarily, they wanted to know, "How can I select the best product?" To the authors and a small group of their friends, these letters expressed the development of a new attitude—a consumer-minded attitude—on the part of the American people. Out of Mr. Schlink's attempt to answer the queries, the Consumers' Club was organized in White Plains, New York. In 1929, the club became Consumers' Research, Inc., and in 1933 it moved to Washington, New Jersey, its present home.

This testing agency publishes twelve monthly issues of *Consumers' Research Bulletin* and its *Annual Bulletin*. The subscription cost of the former is $5, and of the latter, $7. Consumers' Research claims around 100,000 mail subscribers and is bought on newsstands by an additional 10,000 readers. Its financial resources are about $750,000 annually. Besides product ratings, the *Bulletin* carries ratings of motion pictures and phonograph records, short editorials, and the Consumers Observation Post. CR does not have an aggressive sales promotion department. Sales are largely dependent on recommendations by subscribers.

Most of the testing is hired out to well-known testing laboratories and to specialized consultants. Listings in the *Bulletin* are usually arranged in alphabetical order: A, recommended on the basis of quality; A-A, highest recommendation; B, intermediate with respect to quality; and C, not recommended. Price ratings, 1, 2, or 3, are given in some ratings, 1 being low and 3 high price. Quality judgments are wholly independent of price with one exception—automobiles.

Evaluation of Consumers' Research. 1. The control of CR limits its potential effectiveness. Although nonprofit, the board of trustees is limited to 5 persons including the president and his wife. It is a self-perpetuating organization, which excludes fresh ideas that might come from a board elected from among its subscribers. CR's full-time staff comprises approximately 80 persons, including about 15 technical experts. The board does not permit the employees to belong to any other organization without written permission. Consequently, there is no labor union in the plant.

2. Some people question the reliability of the test reports in the *Bulletin* by arguing that large corporations pay fees to secure the highest ratings. There has never been proof of these accusations, and their reliability can

be questioned for at least two reasons. First, a successful court suit on this count would be the easiest method to destroy the testing organization, and there are plenty of businessmen who would jump at this opportunity. Second, over a period of years, the products of large corporations receive about the same percentage of "not recommended" and "recommended" ratings as other producers.

3. The financial resources of CR are limited to the sales of its publication (no advertising income is permitted). Testing of consumer products is expensive, and consequently, CR is not able to test as many products as the subscribers might like. To rate more consumer goods, CR frequently borrows test samples of large, expensive items from manufacturers who sign affidavits that the goods were typical and selected at random. Typewriters, for example, were rented.[7] Consumers would feel more assured if all the products tested had been purchased in retail stores by persons unknown to the stores, rather than using samples that may not be selected at random. As a matter of policy, consumer products to be tested should be purchased in different sections of the country to protect against the possibility of a better or poorer quality shipment to other sections.

4. Branded products available in one section of the United States are not available in other sections. California and the West Coast in general have many branded products not available elsewhere. Subscribers in some sections are unhappy because their needs are not served.

5. Consumer testing agencies restrict most of their tests to branded goods nationally distributed. This policy, a practical one to testers, excludes the testing of local unbranded products.

6. Some subscribers would prefer to have CR test most of the products by its own staff in its own laboratories. When representatives from industry want to discuss and examine the data on the testing of their products, it is more satisfactory to talk with the scientists and experts who did the testing. When tests are farmed out to many different laboratories, adequate discussion by fellow testers and experts is usually impossible.

7. A certain number of social-minded subscribers do not want to purchase products from businesses that have poor working conditions and low wages for their employees. CR insists that this social concern should have no place in reporting the results of testing. This decision is more reasonable today than it was when CR was established in 1929, because the Federal government has set up minimum wages for goods sold interstate. Furthermore, unionization of plants and the nature of competition makes this limitation appear less important even to social-minded people.

When the Technical, Editorial, and Office Assistants Union attempted

[7] Sylvia Lane, "A Study of Selected Agencies That Evaluate Consumer Goods Qualitatively in the United States," unpublished doctoral dissertation. Los Angeles: University of Southern California, 1957, p. 106.

to unionize the CR plant, and agreement seemed unlikely, a strike was called in September, 1935, which lasted four months. The National Labor Relations Board ordered CR to bargain with the employees and to reinstate three discharged employees. CR refused to comply with the order. A group of CR's suberibers, organized to aid in settling the strike, decided to set up a new consumer testing agency.[8]

Consumers Union of U.S., Inc. (CU). Arthur Kallet, former secretary of Consumers' Research, and ten former CR staff workers set up the new testing agency, Consumers Union, in New York City. Mr. Kallet was director of CU until his retirement in 1957. He remained on the board of directors for a few years following retirement. In 1955, CU moved to spacious new quarters in Mount Vernon, New York.

Consumers Union is a nonprofit organization established in 1936. It is chartered under the Membership Corporations Law of the State of New York and derives its income solely from the sale of its publications (800,000 subscribers and 150,000 newsstand buyers.) In addition, the expenses of occasional research projects of a public service nature may be met in part by nonrestrictive, noncommercial grants.

Consumers Union has no connection with any commercial interest and accepts no advertising. Its ratings and reports on products are solely for the information and use of the readers of *Consumer Reports* and may not be used in advertising or for any commercial purpose. The pocket-size *Buying Guide* is issued in December. It condenses articles in previous issues of *Consumers Reports* and includes some new material and buying advice.

The purposes of Consumers Union, as stated in its charter, are "to provide for consumer information and counsel on consumer goods and services . . . to give information and assistance on all matters relating to expenditure of family income—to initiate and cooperate with individual and group efforts seeking to create and maintain decent living standards."

Any subscriber may become a member of Consumers Union by so requesting at the time he subscribes to *Consumer Reports* or by written application at any time. Any subscriber becomes a member also by voting in the annual election of directors; ballots are mailed to all subscribers. Membership entails no financial or other obligation, except that members are expected to exercise their right to vote in the annual election of the board of directors.

The subscription rates are $6 for one year, $10 for two years, $14 for three years. A special reduced rate of $4 is available for group members, this rate applying to each order when five or more are entered together.

CU is served by its board of directors, numbering 17 in 1964, which

[8] Helen Sorenson, *The Consumer Movement.* New York: Harper and Row, Publishers, Incorporated, 1941, p. 47.

functions through five committees. The board deals with broad policy considerations. The operation of CU, which includes testing, publishing, and servicing of the readership, is supervised by the director and a management staff of 23, including the heads of 13 departments. The total staff numbers more than two hundred persons, as shown in the accompanying chart, Consumers Union Staff Functions and Organizations. All except the management staff work under a contract between CU and the American Newspaper Guild, AFL-CIO.

CU publishes information on more than 200 different consumer products each year. In deciding what products to test, CU polls its readers with questionnaires. If sizable numbers reply that they want reports on hi-fi equipment or clothes dryers, the staff gives full consideration to these products in preparing a list of upcoming test projects. After the staff has approved a project, a market survey is made to find out trends and pricing practices in the industry involved and to determine which brands and models—in terms of availability and consumer interest—are to be tested.

To obtain samples of products for testing, CU has a "ready reserve" of some 85 shoppers located in some 60 cities scattered throughout the United States. On orders from CU, these typical buyers go to the regular retail stores, and without revealing CU connection to the seller, buy the specified brands at the merchant's regular price. The products are picked up immediately and shipped to CU headquarters.

CU tests over 90 per cent of all the products in its own laboratories. To conduct its complex testing and rating work, CU now has seven technical divisions—appliance, audio, automotive, chemistry, electronics, textiles, and special projects. In tests of boys' clothing—polo shirts, blue jeans, and shoes—CU's engineers used 96 boys, ages 6 to 12. As many as seven hundred women volunteers participated in comparison tests of 44 brands of nylon hosiery. A panel of 56 men use-tested eight widely sold brands of electric shavers.

Consumer Reports has a reputation among publishers second to none in being the most carefully prepared and edited magazine in the United States. Only the best professional writers are employed. The articles must not only be interesting, readable, and not too long, but must be accurate in reporting the data derived from scientific testing. The testers have the final word on the technical accuracy of the articles. The introductory paragraphs in each article tell what was tested and why, pointing out the limitations of the test, if any, and giving advice on how to use the test results for maximum satisfaction.

The reports present ratings of the brands in order of their estimated over-all quality and performance. In the range of ratings, the highest is rated by a check mark for an Acceptable brand that is also outstanding in quality and performance. The lowest rating, Not Acceptable, is for a

CONSUMERS UNION STAFF FUNCTIONS AND ORGANIZATION
January 1962

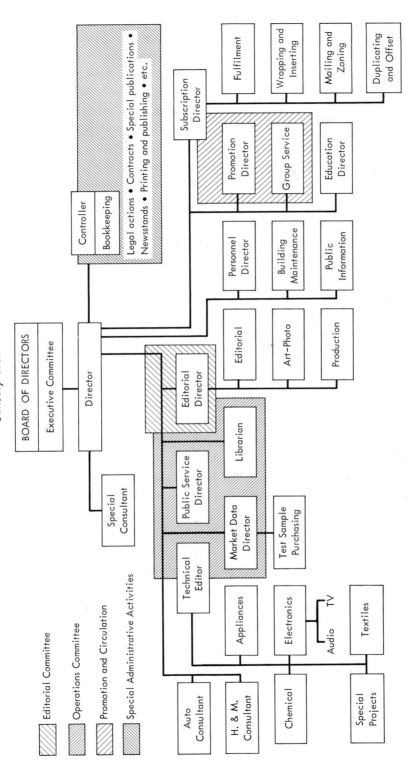

SOURCE: Consumers Union of U.S., Inc., Mount Vernon, N.Y., 1962.

brand that was particularly poor in performance or displayed a safety hazard during the testing of the sample. If an Acceptable brand is sufficiently low in price to represent an outstanding value, it may be designated as a Best Buy. Thus, the consumer gets comparative information that cannot be obtained from the advertising or labeling of products, no matter how truthful, or from over-the-counter inspection, no matter how careful.

A public service department investigates broad areas of public concern, among them radiation hazards, air and water pollution, and car accidents. The staff gathers information, working with scientific and technical consultants and with government agencies. Its recommendations and findings are presented for remedial action by consumers and by appropriate departments or agencies of government. By initiating investigations early— before public agencies begin investigation—the public is made aware of the dangers. Usually, the public agencies take over from that point and carry on the needed investigations.

The monthly publication also carries regular reports on health and on economics. The health reports cover such vital subjects as cancer research, new drugs, food fads, and alleged weight reducers. They also point out the real or potential dangers of certain chemical additives and pesticide residues in foods and are widely recognized and commended by many authorities.

Regular articles on economics relate the product on the market to the broad marketing realities that consumers face. Typical subjects include the consumer's need for standard grades and labels in meats and other foods; packaging practices that mislead shoppers; pros and cons on installment buying and credit cards; the costs of price-fixing ("fair trade") laws to consumers; and government actions affecting consumer welfare.

In addition to these services, CU rates movies, represents consumer interest in hearings of Congressional committees (usually invited), and often confers with Federal agencies (FDA, FTC, and National Bureau of Standards) on problems of common concern.

In another service, CU sponsors conferences at universities and colleges to help them conduct a workshop on consumer welfare problems. CU has also made modest grants to universities for special research on matters of interest to consumers.

CU has issued special publications on consumer problems. Examples are *The Medicine Show,* 250 pages, over 165,000 copies sold; *Health Guide for Travelers; The Consumers Union Report on Family Planning,* 146 pages, over 88,000 sold; *Passenger Car Design and Highway Safety; Silent Spring,* special edition, over 38,000 sold; *The Consumers Report on Wines & Spirits,* over 36,000 sold; and in 1963, an important book, *Smoking and the Public Interest,* over 136,000 sold. Other consumer-oriented books will be forthcoming.

Evaluation of Consumers Union. In general, the comments in the numbered paragraphs 2 to 5 concerning Consumers' Research may be applied also to Consumers Union.

1. In the beginning, Consumers Union hoped to help the lower-income and middle-income groups to get "more for their money." In 1963, despite the expenditure of much money and effort to be read by the lower-income group, which could profit the most from the reports, the median income of CU subscribers was in the $10,000 to $15,000 bracket.

2. To rank products in the order of best over-all quality is difficult. If one brand had all the virtues or defects, the problem would be simple. Normally, a large variety of factors must be weighed and scored by some kind of weighting system. The end decision, then, depends on the nature of the scoring system. Despite this difficulty, and because great care is exercised in deciding on a scoring system for particular products, the results in ranking products are useful in making consumer decisions.

3. Consumers Union purchases directly from retailers all the products to be tested, and they are removed from the store immediately. Many consumer testing organizations in various countries received their testing samples as gifts from manufacturers and distributors. Even under the best precautions, subscribers would have the right to question such a method of securing samples.

4. Consumers Union has been taken to task for not being as experimental as it was during its early years. This criticism is less true since 1957, when a new director was appointed. In March, 1961, the new director advised the board: "An experimental approach is an inevitable part of any growth program, and indeed some degree of experimentalism—with all its implied risks—seems to me a precondition to a viable organization. . . ." It would, no doubt, be easy for the board to "settle down into comfortable and prosperous middle age," as economist John Kenneth Galbraith pointed out in a letter to CU, which was printed in the Anniversary Issue of 1961. Indications of the experimental attitude that now exists are the publications listed above, the funds given for specialized study in major universities on consumer problems, and the financing of part of the important college and university consumer education workshops. More is in the works for future development. For example, hardly any use is made of hundreds of thousands of unsolicited letters from subscribers, which are filled with potentially useful information to consumers.

5. Some kind of regional activity may be necessary because of the increasing use of local and regional brands. CU used to have a Western Consumers Union, but it was 20 years ahead of its time. Perhaps the time has come to think seriously about regional Consumers Unions.

How Useful Is Comparative Testing and Rating? The accompanying questionnaire, How Useful Is Comparative Testing and Rating? gives answers derived from various studies and articles. The best all-round answer was given by Dr. Arthur Kallet, when he was director of Consumers Union.

Suppose a buyer were in the market for an automatic washing machine and suppose that the buyer knew an intelligent housewife who had actually used in her own kitchen, each with several loads of clothes, the twelve leading washing machines on the market. Which would the buyer find more useful, the hyperbole of the advertisements and sales claims for the different washers? Or the housewife's off-the-cuff reactions as to ease of loading and unloading, ease of setting controls, ease of adding detergent, cleanness of the clothes, effectiveness of dryer, noisiness, etc.? Substitute for the housewife engineers able to examine and test all of the machines side by side under simulated home-use conditions, keeping accurate records of the behavior and operation of each machine, scoring each factor studied in terms of its effect on the utility and desirability of each machine. There is, of course, room for error, but even in the absence of standards and of a multiplicity of test samples of each model, there are enough differences in design and construction affecting performance and convenience to make purchase decisions based on such tests far more reliable than decisions based on brand names, price, advertising, or the chance recommendation of a neighbor or a salesman.[9]

How Useful Is Private Laboratory Testing? The consumer should be aware of the basic differences in objectives of private testing laboratories of business and of independent nonprofit testing agencies, such as Consumers Union; Consumers' Research; and the National Bureau of Standards of the Federal government.

The testing laboratory of a large mail-order house like Sears, Roebuck & Company, or a manufacturer like General Motors and General Electric, is just as capable of good testing as Consumers Union or the National Bureau of Standards. The point is that Sears, for example, does not test for the same reason as Consumers Union. The philosophies of both testing agencies are different.

The private testing laboratories do not score one brand against other brands of the same product as CU and CR do. For example, the aim of Sears is "Product improvement and product development." Its merchandise is appraised for (1) performance, (2) design, (3) quality from the customer's viewpoint, (4) dollar value and correctness of manufacturing cost, and (5) appearance and aesthetic value.

As a private retail chain store system, Sears is primarily interested in setting up standards based on what the consumer says he wants in a given

---

[9] Dickson Reck (ed.), *National Standards in a Modern Economy.* New York: Harper and Row, Publishers, Incorporated, 1956, p. 279.

HOW USEFUL IS COMPARATIVE TESTING AND RATING?

Question	Answer
Do brand ratings influence buying patterns of households that refer to them?	Yes. (Sargent study,[a] Lane study,[b] Dear CU letters [e])
Do households that consult consumer publications do more shopping around than nonconsulting households?	Yes. (Sargent study [a])
Do people who consult consumer publications have higher formal education than nonconsulting persons?	Yes. (Sargent study [a])
Is CU rendering a valuable social service in helping some 4 million readers to stimulate quality improvement?	Yes. (Sargent,[a] Lane,[b] Beem [c])
Do CU ratings encourage product improvement?	Yes. (Werner,[d] Dear CU letters [e])
Do CU ratings influence consumer purchases? (Asked of retailers.)	Yes. (Home Furnishings Daily, Oct. 7, 1959, p. 30; Dear CU letters; [e] Nelson Foote [f])
Do CU ratings save readers money?	Yes. (CU returns of 40,000 readers: [g] 32.6 per cent saved $50 to $100 a year; 37.7 per cent saved $10 to $50 a year; 29.7 per cent saved less than $10 a year.)

[a] Hugh W. Sargent, Consumer Product Rating Publications and Buying Patterns. Urbana, Ill.: University of Illinois Bulletin, December, 1959.

[b] Sylvia Lane, "A Study of Selected Agencies That Evaluate Consumer Goods Qualitatively in the United States," unpublished doctoral dissertation. Los Angeles: University of Southern California, 1957, pp. 491, 535.

[c] Eugene R. Beem and John S. Ewing, "Business Appaises Consumer Testing Agencies," Harvard Business Review, vol. 32, no. 2, pp. 113–126.

[d] M. R. Werner, "A Detective Agency for Wary Buyers," The Reporter, reprint, 1958

[e] Consumers Union, Mount Vernon, N.Y., 1961.

[f] Lincoln Clark (ed.), Consumer Behavior.

[g] The Wall Street Journal, Mar. 15, 1962, p. 1.

product. But the consumer cannot ask for standards that he does not know should be in the product he wants to purchase. The real question is: Would the consumer be influenced in his purchase of what he says he wants if he knew important facts that he is not aware of about the product? There is so much about consumer goods that does not meet the eye—much that a customer would see and should see if he could—much that might decisively influence his purchase.

Private laboratory testing is commendable and tends to give customers a better break in product satisfaction than no testing. The limitations are that the customer does not know (1) what tests were made, (2) results of the test, and (3) how the product compares with competitors' products. So if a consumer wants more significant product information, he must go elsewhere—to *Consumer Reports* or *Consumers' Research Bulletin*.

Changing Times, The Kiplinger Magazine. *Changing Times* was first issued in January, 1947. During the first year and a half, this monthly magazine seemed to be designed primarily for businessmen. Gradually the magazine broadened its content until today it can be described as a magazine for consumers. Most of the articles concern such subjects as budgeting, investing, saving, buying insurance, borrowing money, buying or building a home, running a car, and protecting health. Some of the articles have excellent charts and tables useful to a consumer. On the whole, the articles are objective, readable, and to the point.

Occasionally, an article appears that omits important information for the consumer. When this occurs, one is tempted to say that the magazine has forsaken the consumer interest; but perhaps it would be more accurate to say that the magazine was not designed to be a 100 per cent consumer magazine. At $6 a year, consumer-minded citizens can get their money's worth. At least, its subscribers, mostly nonbusiness people, think it is worth the price. Like *Consumer Reports* and *Consumers' Research Bulletin, Changing Times* accepts no advertising.

New subscribers receive an up-to-date 96-page book, *99 New Ideas on Your Money, Job and Living*. This volume is a collection of consumer articles and ideas from recent issues of the magazine.

QUESTIONS FOR DISCUSSION

1. What is the basic difference between a "standard" and "standardization"?

2. Why is quality information on consumer goods a necessity today?

3. There are many private aids and services available to consumers who may be looking for information on merchandise. Recall the last time that you made use of one or more of such private aids or services. Was the information satisfactory?

4. What help can you obtain from the American Medical Association and the American Dental Association?

5. Can you depend on the information on labels that a consumer cooperative places on its products? Why do cooperatives use the U.S. Department of Agriculture standards whenever possible?

6. How do the Better Business Bureaus serve consumers? What are the limitations of their service?

7. Can you name any private organizations whose seals of approval or guarantees are practically worthless to consumers?

8. How would you evaluate the gaurantees of *Good Housekeeping* and *Parents' Magazine?*

9. Examine a recent catalogue of Sears, Roebuck and Company. Can you see any evidence of the Sears testing laboratories in the descriptions of the merchandise?

10. Consult *Consumer Reports* and *Consumers' Research Bulletin* for some merchandise that you expect to purchase in the near future. Did you find the information that you need to make an intelligent selection?

11. What are some of the limitations of consumer-owned testing services?

12. What is the consumer's stake in standards?

13. Do labels include information concerning "invisible qualities" in the product?

14. What are the limitations of brand names and trade-marks?

15. How valuable is a "guarantee" or "warranty" to consumers?

16. What are the limitations of private-store testing of consumer products?

17. Why is it important to read the introductory material in CU and CR publications before reading the ratings of the products?

ACTIVITY PROBLEMS

1. The point is raised from time to time that consumers do not want grade labeling. (See Jessie V. Coles, *Standards and Labels for Consumers' Goods,* pp. 328–330.) Why not take a poll of as many housewives as possible? Ask them whether or not they prefer grade labels. Be sure that each housewife understands the meaning of grade labels.

2. Make a table or chart of all the private organizations that help consumers to select goods more intelligently. Indicate for each organization: (*a*) nature of membership, (*b*) kind of products tested, (*c*) who pays for the service, (*d*) interest of agency in sales, (*e*) to whom it is of value, and (*f*) limitations.

3. Secure materials from as many private organizations that test consumer goods as possible. Arrange an exhibition of the material secured. Make a placard for each agency, and include an evaluation of the service on each placard.

4. If possible, visit a good private testing laboratory or secure detailed information from such an agency or institution. Report all essential facts to the class. No doubt you will receive considerable material that can be displayed. Keep in mind, particularly, the reliability of the testing information that is made available to consumers.

5. Test the buying habits of students. Select such merchandise as food brands, electrical appliances, and antiseptics. List the brands in the order of frequency of purchase. How do these purchases compare with the information given by private consumer rating agencies?

6. Arrange a panel discussion on grade labeling. Invite a housewife who is known for her interest in consumer welfare, a national chain food store manager, a cooperative food store manager, and the owner of a privately owned food store. After the panel discussion, compare the conclusions with those offered by other sources, such as Jessie V. Coles, *Standards and Labels for Consumers' Goods,* pp. 323–384.

7. Set up criteria for the selection of commercial teaching materials. How do the commercial materials used in this course rate according to your criteria? You may want to check a selected list of commercial aids rather than all materials used. See such sources as Consumer Education Study, *Catalog of Free and Inexpensive Teaching Aids for High Schools,* Washington: National Association of

Secondary-school Principals; and an unusual document listed as "Chapter 5, Conclusions and Recommendations," prepared by Hill & Knowlton, Inc., a New York public relations firm.

8. Arrange with Consumers Union, Inc., Mount Vernon, New York for a showing of the new film "Consumers Want to Know." Prepare a paper on your reactions and evaluate the film.

9. Compare *Consumer Reports* or *Consumers' Research Bulletin* with *Changing Times*.

SUGGESTED READINGS

Association of Better Business Bureaus. *Facts You Should Know about Your Better Business Bureaus*, New York.

Beem, Eugene R. "Consumer-financed Testing and Rating Agencies," *Journal of Marketing*, January, 1952. (Excellent)

———— and Ewing, John S. "Business Appraises Consumer Testing Agencies," *Harvard Business Review*, March–April, 1954. (Excellent)

Changing Times. "Miracle Cosmetics: How Safe? How Good?" April, 1962; "Those Service-free Cars," May, 1963.

Coles, Jessie V. *Standards and Labels for Consumers' Goods.* New York: The Ronald Press Company, 1949.

Consumer Reports. "How CU Works," May, 1956, pp. 257–270; "This is Consumers Union," May, 1961; "Annual Survey," latest edition.

Consumers' Research Bulletin. "Chemicals in Your Food," September, 1961; "A Study of Some Food Labels," June, 1961; "Read the Label," February, 1960.

Council on Consumer Information. Selected Proceedings, Annual Meeting, 1961, pp. 81–100; Selected Proceedings, "The American Home Economics Association and the Consumer" by Dorothy M. Sherrill, 1961, pp. 68–76; "Consumers Look at Labels" by Jessie V. Coles, 1964.

Cunningham, Ross M. "Brand Loyalty." *Harvard Business Review*, vol. 34, no. 1, p. 117.

Federal Trade Commission. *Guides against Deceptive Advertising of Guarantees*, 1960; *Guides against Deceptive Pricing*, 1964.

Food and Drug Administration. *Read the Label*, Washington, D.C.

Fortune. "U.S. Business' Most Skeptical Customer," September, 1960.

Gilbert, Eugene. "How to Win Tomorrow's Top Consumer," *Printers' Ink*, vol. 259, no. 12, p. 63.

Harris, Richard. *The Real Voice.* New York: The Macmillan Company, 1964.

Home Furnishings Daily. "Magazine Wields Big Stick," October, 1959.

Journal of Home Economics. (Annual report published in each September issue.)

Kaplan, Morris. "Make Your Product Tests User Tests," *Product Engineering*, Feb. 6, 1961, p. 56.

National Better Business Bureau. *Guarantees*, New York, June, 1960.

Oxenfeldt, Alfred R. "Consumer Knowledge: Its Measurement and Extent," *Review of Economic Statistics*, vol. 32, no. 4, p. 306.

Reck, Dickson (ed.). *National Standards in a Modern Economy.* New York: Harper & Row, Publishers, Incorporated, 1956.

Sargent, Hugh W. *Consumer Product Rating Publications and Buying Behavior.* Urbana, Ill.: University of Illinois, December, 1959.

Sorenson, Helen. *The Consumer Movement.* New York: Harper & Row, Publishers, Incorporated, 1941.

Taylor, Donald A. "Certification Marks—Success or Failure?" *Journal of Marketing,* vol. 23, no. 1, p. 46.

Tyler, William D. "The Image, the Brand, and the Consumer." *Journal of Marketing,* vol. 22, no. 2, p. 163.

The Wall Street Journal. "Guiding Buyers," Mar. 15, 1962, p. 1; "General Motors Warranty" ad, Sept. 27, 1962; "Ford Warranty" ad, Sept. 28, 1962; "Products on Trial," Aug. 3, 1960.

Werner, M. R. "Detective Agency for Wary Buyers." *The Reporter,* Apr. 17, 1958.

16

CONSUMER PROTECTION: THE FEDERAL
GOVERNMENT AND THE CONSUMER

A deputy commissioner of the Food and Drug Administration, John L. Harvey, said in 1955: "It is abundantly evident that the complexities of modern civilization require a greater degree of protection to the consumer than is now available. Obviously, he is largely beyond self-protection." [1] Seven years later, in 1962, the late Senator Estes Kefauver told a group of consumer leaders in Washington, D.C., that "the consumer is the forgotten man in our governmental structure."

Protection of the consumer interest, in an era of technological revolution, cold war, strontium 90, subsidies, and recessions, continues to languish as a do-it-yourself program in many respects. In our democratic society, government at all levels inevitably succumbs to powerful lobbies seeking special privileges. Consequently, if consumers are to receive any protection, they must organize and become articulate in making their demands known. Unity of consumers, however, seems unlikely in the foreseeable future.

The main reason for this lack of unity is that consumption is a function common to all and peculiar to none. We are all consumers, but we think of ourselves first as workers, teachers, retailers, farmers, manufacturers, doctors, lawyers, and so on, and only secondarily and incidentally as consumers. Psychologically, community of interest with these primary income groups far overshadows the broader interests of being consumers. The primary group interest comprises a vertical division of our economy. All members can unite to promote the interests of the group. On the other hand, since consumption is a function rather than a group, and comprises a horizontal division across an entire population, there are no group members to promote the interests of all concerned. It becomes apparent, then,

[1] *Food Drug Consumption,* March, 1955.

that in our democratic society, where government responds to pressure groups, inarticulate consumers are at a distinct disadvantage. And lacking organization, consumers are largely at the mercy of effectively organized groups.

The Need to Protect Consumers. Democratic government is powerless to act, for the most part, in the absence of expressed need. The consequence for consumers is that government action is inevitably tardy, sporadic, and ineffective.

Interest groups are organized primarily to improve the relative position of their members; they are not organized to improve the position of all members of society. The interest groups attempt to present their own special intents as being identical with the interests of the general public, but their behavior frequently indicates a pathetic ignorance of consumer welfare.

This is not entirely a criticism; freedom to organize and speak are guaranteed by the United States Constitution. Prevalence of active groups is a barometer of social action. Recognition of antisocial behavior, however, is important to an understanding of consumer problems. It is also important to recognize this aspect of the problem if the unrepresented consumer is to survive the fierce conflict of interests.

As long as the market place was an adequate regulator and coordinator of economic activity, admittedly in the distant past, less need existed for government to act as protector of consumer interests against exploitation by producer interests. But as industrialization developed with its urbanization, consumer dependence on sources of supply beyond their own control continued to increase rapidly. This increasing consumer dependence, in turn, has been responsible for partial public realization that the health of each individual is becoming inseparably bound up with the health of the entire community.

As merchandising and marketing practices grow progressively more complex, the unassisted consumer becomes progressively more defenseless. Consumer education is not even in the race with technological and marketing advancement. In fact, it appears that the consumer is becoming more confused and illiterate as a buyer in an increased ratio with modern business and marketing advancement.

Failure of Education to Help Consumers. A traditional national respect for the "acquisitive spirit" has relegated intelligent consumption to a position of relative unimportance. In fact, there is much evidence to support the contention that extravagant spending is a badge of honor; conspicuous consumption—emulation of people of great wealth—is an indication of financial power and success. As a result, certain types of wastefulness have received social approval.

The attitude of consumers regarding intelligent consumption is, to a large extent, the product of our educational system, which, in turn, is largely a product of the traditional American pursuit for the highest material standard of living. Much of the responsibility for the retarded development of intelligent consumption must rest on our educational system, which is weighted in favor of the producer interest as against the consumer interest. In short, our system does a good job of teaching how to make money, not how to spend it intelligently.

The solutions to improving the consumption habits of people are not simple at all. The late President John F. Kennedy emphasized this in his special "consumer message" to Congress in 1962.

The march of technology has increased the difficulties of the consumer along with his opportunities. . . . Rational choice between and among [products] would require the skills of the amateur electrician, mechanic, chemist, toxicologist, dietician, and mathematician. . . . Marketing is increasingly impersonal. Consumer choice is influenced by mass advertising utilizing highly developed arts of persuasion. The consumer typically cannot know whether drug preparations meet minimum standards of safety, quality, and efficacy. He usually does not know how much he pays for credit; whether one prepared food has more nutritional value than another; whether the performance of a product will in fact meet his needs; or whether the "large economy size" is really a bargain. Additional legislative and administrative action is required, however, if the Federal government is to meet its responsibility to consumers in the exercise of their rights. These rights include—

1. The right to safety . . .
2. The right to be informed . . .
3. The right to choose . . .
4. The right to be heard—to be assured that consumer interests will receive full and sympathetic consideration in the formulation of Government policy, and fair and expeditious treatment in its administrative tribunals.[2]

The Problem of Government Regulatory Agencies. Back in 1872, Congress evidenced its first interest in consumer problems when it enacted a law to protect consumers from frauds involving the use of the United States mails. Since then, legislation and executive action in the name of consumer protection has produced a sprawling, uncoordinated maze of laws and agencies, frequently working at cross purposes, and usually cursed by a too-little-too-late timidity. Thus, consumer interests have not been served.

The regulatory agencies were set up by Congress under its power to regulate commerce in the public interest. But though many of their de-

---

[2] Message from the President of the United States Relative to Consumers' Protection and Interest Program, 87th Congress, 2d Session, House of Representatives, Doc. no. 364, Washington, D.C., Mar. 15, 1962.

cisions (as for instance those of the Interstate Commerce Commission affecting railroad rates, the Federal Power Commission in setting gas rates, the Federal Trade Commission in its decisions with respect to unfair business practices) are of direct concern to consumers, they are not regarded as an interested party. Even if consumers were allowed to appear in these cases, under existing circumstances they would not be in a position, generally speaking, to prepare and present significant data.

In actual practice, the regulatory agencies are preoccupied with settling conflicting claims among rival groups of producers. Thus, the Interstate Commerce Commission is caught in disputes between railroads and trucks, the Civil Aeronautics Board between large certificated carriers and the smaller air lines, the Federal Communications Commission between rival applicants for television and radio licenses, the Federal Power Commission between gas producers and public utility companies, and the Tariff Commission between companies that want tariff protection and those that do not.

One can go on almost indefinitely with such a roster of conflicting producer groups that are fighting to make their views prevail with the agencies of regulation. Is it surprising then that, amid this constant tug of war between contesting private interests, there is little room for the consumer to be heard? And, unlike these private pressure groups, which are well organized, highly disciplined in the art of exerting influence, and omnipresent when decisions are to be made, consumers are scattered, unorganized, and often unaware that decisions of vital import to their standard of life are being made. The initiative for action has been left increasingly to the companies that are being regulated. As the late Dr. Walton Hamilton, after a lifetime of study of these agencies, said in his last book:

> The result is that the commission on all its levels becomes busy, in fact over-busy, but largely with detailed problems of the moment, problems which have been raised by complaining parties. It has adequate legal authority to raise questions on its own motion, but amid all the bustle of everyday activity there is very little leisure in which to do it. The larger questions of holding the regulated industry to its function, of improving its capacity to serve the public, of looking to the hazards ahead and guarding against them, and of making of it a more effective instrument of the general welfare are neglected. Matters of policy get immersed in the quagmire of detail. The agency fails to direct the activities of the industry to public objectives, and the industry is left to effect for itself such structure and practices as serve its purposes.[3]

Although charged to act in the public interest, regulatory commissions can

[3] Walton Hamilton, *The Politics of Industry.* New York: Alfred A. Knopf, Inc., 1957, p. 155.

fulfill that obligation only if the public interest is defined with respect to each issue. But there are few opportunities and few effective spokesmen to define the public interest, and in the heat of controversy, the general welfare is all too often overlooked. The major issue, then, is how to place the public welfare in the forefront of governmental regulatory activities. Without the balance wheel of concern for the general welfare, government by regulatory agencies tends to solve only short-term, shortsighted, private struggles for privilege.

In most of the issues raised before government regulatory agencies, the interests of the ultimate consumer have been those most consistent with the general welfare. In many countries, notably Great Britain and Sweden, where governmental regulatory agencies have been subject to detailed investigations (the Final Report of the Committee on Consumer Protection, 1962, and Sweden's Cartel law), the public interest is specifically defined as the interest of the ultimate consumer.

As government by regulatory agencies has expanded, the necessity for an increasing emphasis, within government, on the interests of the ultimate consumer has become urgent. The effective expression of the ultimate consumer's interest is now essential to the very functioning of government and to the economy.

Extent of Federal Consumer Protection Activities. There are at least thirty-three Federal departments, agencies, or commissions that claim to have "direct consumer activities" in their programs. In 1961, the Committee on Government Operations made its 338-page report on *Consumer Protection Activities of Federal Departments and Agencies.* Only two departments and agencies stated that they perform no activities of this nature. In a total of 296 activities listed by 33 Federal departments and agencies, only 103 activities dealt directly with protection of the consumer.

For direct consumer activities, the estimated cost totaled $272 million, and the number of full-time Federal employees was almost twenty-two thousand. The cost of total direct consumer-advancement activities was $681 million, and the number of full-time employees was nearly forty-three thousand.

Among the many agencies to regulate or strongly influence the market behavior of private business—the Federal Power Commission, the Federal Communications Commission, the Interstate Commerce Commission, the Maritime Commission, the Civil Aeronautics Board, the United States Tariff Commission, the Packers and Stockyards Administration, the National Bureau of Standards, the several marketing agencies of the Department of Agriculture, the several commissions in the Department of the Interior handling natural resources and public lands, the Federal Reserve Board, and so on—there are a number whose operations are more directly consumer-oriented.

The two most important agencies, the Food and Drug Administration and the Federal Trade Commission, are given a detailed analysis here. The other more directly consumer-oriented agencies include (1) the Bureau of Home Economics of the Department of Agriculture; (2) the Antitrust Division of the Department of Justice, whose legislative mandate to preserve a competitive market place is an important objective to ultimate consumers; (3) the Bureau of Labor Statistics, whose Consumer Price Indexes are, or could be, an important guide to consumers; and (4) the Federal Housing Administration and Veterans Housing Administration, because these agencies have become so influential in setting the prices of homes and in providing the basis and promotion of widespread consumer credit. The operation of all these agencies provides a test as to whether policies now in effect have enhanced consumer welfare.

Early Attempts to Supervise Food and Drugs. The protection of the ultimate consumer from the questionable and rapacious practices of producers is not a modern invention. In the precapitalistic feudal economy, the consumer was protected by guild regulations covering the size, weight, and quality of products.

During the era when the United States economy was largely agricultural, most consumers were fairly well protected by common law—recourse to the courts. But in the last quarter century or more, the legal protection provided by common law has been entirely inadequate. To try to meet these new conditions, due to the mass production and mass distribution revolution, a few states attempted to protect consumers in the latter part of the nineteenth century against abuses in the sale of food and drugs. In 1848, the first Federal inspection action was taken on imported drugs, medicines, and related products. Later, importation of impure tea and adulterated food was stopped.

In the 1890s, attempts were made to authorize limited supervision by Federal regulation of interstate sales of foods and drugs. This campaign was led by Dr. Harvey W. Wiley of the Bureau of Chemistry in the Department of Agriculture in 1890.

Pure Food and Drug Act of 1906. In 1906, the Pure Food and Drug Act was passed by Congress. It took Upton Sinclair's *The Jungle* (a novel on the unsanitary conditions in the Chicago meat-packing plants) and the exposé of political and economic corruption by the muckrakers in the family magazines, notably *McClure's*, to get the average citizen stirred up sufficiently to overcome the influence of business in Congress against food and drug regulations.

The Pure Food and Drug Act of 1906 had several weaknesses that began to appear as time went on. For one thing, women began to use cosmetics in the "roaring twenties." The cosmetic trade, quite untouched by moral and safety principles, had scores of cases of poisoning in the 1920s, caused by hair dyes, face bleaches, face creams, rouges, powder, and hair tonics.[4] In 1937, in *The American Chamber of Horrors*, Ruth de Forest Lamb described the cosmetic industry in detail. Thus the public was made aware of the need to have Federal regulation of the cosmetic industry.

Another weakness in the original act was its failure to regulate advertising as well as labeling. The truth, even if presented on labels, could be and was misrepresented in false and misleading advertising. With the advent of radio and television, this problem became acute.

Federal Food, Drug, and Cosmetics Act. A third weakness in the 1906 act was the failure to provide for the safety of drugs and medical preparations for human use before making them available to the public. In 1936, the public became aware of this weakness when 73 persons died from the use of a patent medicine, Elixir Sulfanilamide. So in 1938, the 1906 act was amended to include the Federal regulation of cosmetics and to prohibit the sale of drugs and medicines until they had been proved safe for human consumption. The effort to include the regulation of false and misleading advertising under the Food and Drug Administration was defeated, but the Wheeler Tea Act provided for regulation of untruthful advertising in another Federal regulatory agency, the Federal Trade Commission.

By the early 1940s, the great increase in the use of chemical food additives led to the demand for protection from dangerous chemicals in food. The FDA did not have authority to prevent their use unless it was first demonstrated beyond a reasonable doubt that the chemical additives were dangerous to human beings. Finally, in 1958, this was corrected. Chemicals in the form of food additives must now be proved harmless to human beings before they can be used in food as preservatives or emulsifiers.

Drug Amendments of 1962. On October 10, 1962, the Drug Amendments of 1962, overhauling and strengthening the drug provisions of the Federal Food, Drug, and Cosmetics Act, became law. The amendments deal mainly with drugs sold only on prescription and with "new drugs." A new drug is one that is not generally recognized by qualified experts as safe and effective for the uses recommended in its labeling.

Here are some of the major changes in the law.

1. Before the new amendments, only safety clearance of new drugs was required. Now there must be substantial evidence that any new drug is effective as well as safe before it can be approved for marketing.

2. All manufacturers must now have adequate controls—test procedures and checks—with trained personnel and proper facilities, to assure the reliability of drugs. Absence of such controls will of itself violate the law, without the necessity for proving that a particular shipment of the drug was defective.

[4] Stuart Chase and F. J. Schlink, *Your Money's Worth*. New York: The Macmillan Company, 1927, p. 22.

3. Previously cleared drugs may be ordered off the market immediately if new information indicates an imminent hazard to health. And any prior approval may be withdrawn, after a hearing accorded to the manufacturer, in any case where tests or experience show that the drug is not safe or will not be effective for its intended uses.

4. The FDA is given 180 days instead of 60 days to consider a request for a safety clearance of a new drug, and the new drug cannot be marketed without FDA approval.

5. Manufacturers are required to report promptly to the FDA on experience with new drugs, including any adverse effects they learn about after the new drug goes on the market. This also applies to previously cleared new drugs and antibiotics.

6. A firm legal basis is provided for regulations to prevent testing of drugs on humans unless and until specified safety conditions, including thorough animal testing, are met.

7. Manufacturers are required to get assurance that the patient's consent will be obtained if experimental drugs are to be used, unless this is not feasible or unless the investigator believes that obtaining such consent would be contrary to the patient's best interest.

8. All drug producers must register annually with the FDA, even if their output does not actually move in interstate commerce.

9. The FDA is directed to inspect each registered establishment at least once every two years.

10. The scope of authority for inspection of manufacturers of prescription drugs is broadened to include legal access to pertinent records, files, papers, processes, controls, and facilities.

11. Authority is provided for the Federal government to establish an official name for a drug when this is desirable in the interest of usefulness and simplicity. Drug labels must bear the established name of the drug and, for prescription drugs, the quantity of each active ingredient.

12. Prescription drug advertisements must include a brief summary of side effects, contraindications, and effectiveness, as well as the established name for the drug and the quantitative formula.

13. The FDA batch testing and certification of safety and effectiveness is extended to all antibiotic drugs for humans. This adds some thirty groups of antibiotic drugs and their derivatives to the five previously subject to this requirement. Manufacturers pay fees to cover the costs of the FDA tests.

Consumers have every reason to hail the Drug Amendments of 1962 as a major advance in the cause of safe, effective, and honestly promoted drugs.

A final set of drug control rules by the FDA included these requirements for drug manufacturers.

1. Prove to the satisfaction of the FDA that new drug products are effective as well as safe.

2. Adopt the "good manufacturing practice" guidelines of the FDA at all drug-production and drug-testing facilities.

3. Include in all advertising of branded drug products the drug's technical, or generic, name as well as brand name, and list any side effects it may have had on previous users.

The last requirement was hotly opposed by many drug firms. The FDA's purpose is to acquaint consumers with the generic term so that they can shop for drugs and get the lowest price possible.

In recognition of the protests of drug companies, the final set of rules omits an earlier proposal that would have permitted the FDA to pass on certain advertising before it is used. Another change gives drug producers the right to demand a prompt ruling on the safety and effectiveness of a new drug if the FDA fails to clear it for use within the specified 180 days.

Federal Hazardous Substances Labeling Act. This act went into effect on February 1, 1962. It is enforced by the FDA. Accidental poisoning from hazardous household substances accounted for 40 per cent of fatal poisoning of children under 5 years of age, according to statistics. In one year, 1959, doctors reported over 90,000 fatal and nonfatal poisonings in this age group.[5]

This act is a lifesaving measure, aimed at alerting parents and others to the potential dangers in common articles stored and used around the home. But the law can fulfill its job only if consumers read and heed the labels on such articles.

All household products that are toxic; corrosive; irritant to skin or eye; strong sensitizers; flammable or extremely flammable; or generate pressure, which presents a special hazard, are required to bear warning statements on their labels. Some such products have carried warnings for years. All must now do so.

The law and regulations reserve the skull and crossbones and the word "POISON" for highly toxic substances to mark their extreme hazard. Highly toxic products must also bear the word "DANGER." Many products are extremely flammable or corrosive or have some other special hazard such as danger of inhalation. All other products that can cause illness or injury must be marked "CAUTION" or "WARNING."

Instructions for safe use and storage must also appear on the labels of all substances covered under the Federal Hazardous Substances Labeling Act. The statement "Keep out of the reach of children" must also appear on such labels.

FDA Consumer Consultant Program. It is claimed that the Food and Drug Administration regulates consumer products that consume about one-

[5] *FDA Memo for Consumers.* Washington, D.C.: Food and Drug Administration, U.S. Department of Health, Education, and Welfare, Nov. 26, 1962.

fourth of a typical family's income.[6] Perhaps this is one reason for "consumer interest being at its highest peak in years," according to George P. Larrick, Commissioner of the FDA. Mrs. Carla Williams, First Director of Consumer Programming for the FDA, believes that her group of dedicated consumer consultants in 18 districts in the United States can reduce the $1 billion annual loss due to the purchase of worthless or dangerous foods, drugs, and cosmetics. In addition, she points out that "over $500 million is wasted each year on falsely promoted vitamin products and so-called health foods."

The consumer consultants act as "liaison" between the FDA and the consumer. Through speaking before community groups, appearing on radio and television interview shows, creating and manning FDA exhibits and consumer survey work, these women are creating a two-way flow of information. They explain, on one hand, the FDA's regulatory programs, its laws, and its jurisdictions. On the other hand, by tapping consumer opinion, they determine the reactions and attitudes of the American public toward the food, drug, and cosmetic products that come under the FDA's jurisdiction.

In this way, consumers may have a better understanding and appreciation of the protection offered their health and pocketbook and, at the same time, their comments and criticisms are helpful to the FDA in conducting its programs and policies.

Inspection Work of the FDA. The Food and Drug Administration had 771 inspectors in the field in the 1963 fiscal year, visiting factories and processing plants and looking for samples of products that may violate the law. Eighteen district offices are equipped with laboratories where analysts test the samples.

The inspectors stationed throughout the United States are the eyes and ears of the FDA. It is their job to cover the broad span from raw materials of the farm and sea to the market basket of the American housewife.

In a typical day in one district, inspectors might carry on sanitary inspections of food factories and warehouses; make a "control" inspection of a drug factory to determine whether its processing has built-in safeguards to assure potency and purity; investigate an injury complaint associated with a food, drug, or cosmetic; collect samples of regulated products for laboratory analysis; attempt to purchase a prescription drug from a drugstore (without a prescription) because of reports that the store was selling dangerous drugs without physicians' authorizations; supervise the reconditioning of seized goods under terms of a court order; and testify in Federal court as witnesses in a contested case.

[6] Richard D. Morse, "The Significance of the Food and Drug Laws to the Consumer," *Food Drug Cosmetic Law Journal*, July, 1956, p. 346.

Together, the inspectors and analysts get the evidence that is presented to the Federal courts for action. Preparation of the cases for the U.S. district attorneys throughout the country is handled by a small legal staff in the general counsel's office of the U.S. Department of Health, Education, and Welfare, after the FDA's administrative officers have reviewed the evidence. This assures uniform enforcement throughout the United States. In the fiscal year 1962, 1,612 actions were brought in Federal court. The great majority of these were seizure cases, in which the purpose is to take filthy, spoiled, or harmful products off the market. Over 15 million pounds of unfit or contaminated foods were seized—144 tons a week.

If the goods are in very bad condition, the court may order them destroyed. If they can be made to comply with the law, the court may order them released for sorting, cleaning, relabeling, and so on, with the owner paying for supervision by FDA inspectors. Occasionally, the owner protests the charges of violation and the case goes to trial in a Federal court. However, since the FDA requests seizure only when it has scientific evidence to support its charges, it wins a large majority of the cases contested.

Other types of Federal court actions are criminal prosecutions of firms or individuals alleged to be responsible for violations, and injunction suits to prevent further traffic in violative goods. Of the 314 criminal prosecutions instituted in 1962, 150 involved 235 individuals or firms selling prescription drugs without authorization. In many of the cases, the defendants were persons with no professional training who sold the drugs at truck stops, in general stores, or through peddling. Ninety-six prosecutions were based on the shipment of filthy or decomposed food or insanitary operations. Other violations were shipment of substandard foods and drugs, and false and misleading claims for drugs and dietary supplements.

About 15 cents per person, or a total of $28,280,000, was appropriated for this work for the year beginning July 1, 1962, not counting income from services for which the manufacturers pay the costs. The FDA had 3,012 budgeted positions for this period for employees to administer the law covering products that had a sales value of more than $110 billion.

Inspection covers about 100,000 factories and public warehouses, in addition to about 700,000 retail establishments subject to the act. Enforcement must be selective—in the fiscal year 1962, a total of 55,000 establishment inspections were made, and 62,712 domestic samples were collected for analysis, plus 14,541 import samples. Thus, only a fraction of the foods and drugs bought by the American public can receive attention.

Strengthening the FDA. Consumer leaders generally agree that the FDA, over the years, has been the most consumer-minded agency or commission in the Federal government. Consequently, the report on the Food and

Drug Administration by the Citizens Advisory Committee, October, 1962, under the chairmanship of Dr. George Y. Harvey of the University of Missouri, should be studied carefully. This hard-hitting and industry-oriented committee report evoked reaction among agency officials ranging from a "wait and see" attitude to frank statements that the report was "naïve and unrealistic," according to the *Drug Trade News*, November 12, 1962. The committee believes that the FDA will be strengthened by carrying out the following recommendations.

1. Substitute "preventive policy" in place of "after-the-fact" enforcement.
2. A change in the role of the commissioner of the FDA with a major change toward decentralization of decision making.
3. Upgrading of the scientific program by setting up a Food and Drug Institute headed by a scientific director to attract better scientists and result in improvement of analytical methods.
4. Improve FDA-industry relationships.
5. A National Advisory Council to the commissioner, appointed by the Secretary of Health, Education, and Welfare, authorized to make annual reports to the Secretary.
6. Upgrade personnel and provide better training opportunities for the staff.
7. Provide more effective program planning.
8. Educational program should emphasize education of the consumer, of industry, and of the state food and drug agencies rather than publicize the FDA.
9. Closer cooperation between the FDA and the public health service and other governmental agencies.
10. Development of FDA programs to strengthen the state laws and administrative agencies and to maximize consumer protection by coordinated harnessing of Federal, state, and local regulatory programs.

Implementation of these recommendations could lead to improvement in the effectiveness of the FDA. It is possible, however, that the drug industry, with profit motives in mind, might acquire too much influence over FDA policies. Politicians, too, might acquire unhealthy influence over the organization. Many consumer leaders are much concerned about producer-oriented and politically administered Federal agencies that have been organized, theoretically, to protect the public.

There are two basic reasons for keeping the FDA independent of political and industrial pressures. (1) The FDA is basically concerned with protecting consumer health and safety. (2) To the extent that the FDA—through its declarations of standards of quality, standards for fill-of-containers, and its prohibition of mislabeling and misrepresentation—enables the consumer to become a better-informed buyer in the market, it meets one of the basic prerequisites of a free-enterprise competitive economy and thus is of basic significance to all consumer citizens.

Federal Trade Commission. At the present time, the Food and Drug Administration and the Federal Trade Commission are more concerned with consumer interest than are the other Federal agencies. The FDA is almost wholly oriented to consumer protection, but the FTC has been mostly producer-oriented until recent years. The FTC, however, does have important consumer protection authority, its use depending largely on the economic philosophy of the five commissioners who are presidential appointees.

The primary objective of the Federal Trade Commission is the maintenance of free and fair competition in the economy (1914 act). In 1938, the FTC was given authority to control false advertising of foods, drugs, cosmetics, and curative or corrective devices, which actually gave the commission broad authority to protect consumers. Until 1958, the producer-oriented FTC was not active in the consumer interest. Under new leadership in 1958, and later, the FTC has become a more effective consumer watchdog.

The major work of the FTC is law enforcement relating to false advertising and other unfair and deceptive acts in commerce. From the standpoint of case volume, fictitious pricing is still the chief evil in the field of false advertising.[7] Closely related to fictitious pricing is bait advertising (to attract customers for higher priced goods). This is especially true in the case of household appliances and home improvements.

A short listing of other deceptive acts against which the FTC has taken action includes the trickery of advance-fee real estate advertising, lotteries, phony correspondence schools, false investing opportunities, and a legion of other deceits and frauds, embracing health shoes, trusses, dietary foods, weight reducing, hair restoring, contact lenses, hearing aids, car products, TV parts, and many others. The target for all this deception and fraud is the consumer.

In 1960, the FTC devoted about two-fifths of its budget to fraud and deceptive practices (abuses against consumers) and three-fifths to anti-monopoly practices (mostly interbusiness problems with consequent price effects on consumers).[8] One of the most dramatic activities was the investigation of payola and television advertising in 1959–1960. In less than four months, the FTC made 155 investigations, 60 complaints were issued, and 16 consent decrees were accepted. This was action with dispatch, and not typical of the FTC until this period.

The FTC has issued *Cigarette Advertising Guides* (1955), *Tire Advertising Guides* (1958), and *Bait Advertising* (1959) ; has called its first con-

[7] *Consumer Protection Activities of Federal Departments and Agencies,* 8th Report of the Committee on Government Operations, Washington, D.C., 1961, p. 198.

[8] Daniel J. McCauley, "The Federal Trade Commission, the Consumer and the Public," Selected Proceedings of the Council on Consumer Information, 1960, p. 49.

sumer conference on public deception (1959) ; and issued *Guides Against Deceptive Advertising of Guarantees* (1960 and 1963).

More recently, the FTC has cooperated more effectively, and liaison has been established, with several Federal departments and agencies: the Post Office Department (use of mails in matters dealing with lotteries and frauds) ; the Food and Drug Administration (labeling and misbranding) ; and the Department of Justice (sharing responsibilities in antitrust cases). The FTC works fairly closely with state and local authorities and with the Better Business Bureaus in the larger cities.

In addition to regulating unfair advertising, the FTC administers the Wool Products Act of 1940 (labeling of fiber content), the Fur Products Labeling Act of 1951 (prohibits use of false names of furs), the Flammable Fabrics Act of 1953 (forbids highly flammable fabrics), and the Textile Fiber Products Identification Act of 1959 (which became effective on March 3, 1960, and goes beyond the Wool Products Act in identifying fabric content). In the Textile Fiber Products Act, the value to consumers is limited, because the act did not specify the particular quality and grade of each fiber.

How Effective Is FTC Protection of Consumers? The FTC is as effective in protecting consumers as its administration. The annual budget since 1960 of $2 million to $3 million for investigations, travel, testing, court costs, and so on, is a pitifully small sum. Business offenders are subject to fine or imprisonment or both (very few, since FTC prefers not to be punitive). The usual punishment is a small fine (looked on by offenders as a cost of doing business), and imprisonment is difficult because the offender is a corporation. What is needed can be summarized:

1. A change in attitude on the part of the public and the government toward economic cheats and frauds. These cheats are no less crooks simply because they are businessmen. Some of them not only take consumers' money but endanger consumer safety at times.

2. Dedicated commissioners, who will carry out their responsibilities as good public servants.

3. Power to issue temporary cease-and-desist orders whenever the FTC can show that irreparable harm would result if challenged practices were not stopped immediately. FTC Chairman Paul Rand Dixon said in 1963: "Any unprincipled advertiser can delay justice long enough to make a killing. He can steal the business of the competitors. . . . He can defraud the public; and all it will cost him are the fees for a smart lawyer and an argument with St. Peter." [9]

4. The Carl A. Auerbach study of the FTC in 1962 called for a reorganization of the commission to cut down the influence of lawyers and to put nonlawyers in more influential positions. In the advertising field, it suggests that the FTC con-

[9] Quoted in *Changing Times*, May, 1963, p. 13.

centrate on the big national ads and turn the smaller problems over to the individual states.[10]

There are, no doubt, many other suggestions to improve the effectiveness of the FTC in protecting the consumer interest. There are no easy solutions. But the difficulties involved—internal reform, overlapping jurisdiction with other agencies, more power to act—should not delay a rebuilding program to fit present-day conditions.

The FTC has so many laws to enforce, backed by a history of so many contradictory decisions, and characterized by inconsistent policing and enforcement procedure, that its program appears to depend almost entirely on the policy decisions of the five commissioners. A marked change in direction and a greater clarification of top policies could provide better consumer protection even without an increased appropriation.

Bureau of Home Economics. This is probably the oldest consumer agency in the Federal government, originally launched after the Spanish-American War as a kind of early point 4 program to aid in the promotion of higher living standards in the Philippine Islands. Early in the twentieth century, its activities were expanded for the benefit of Southern farm families.

Then, through a tie-in with the Extension Division of the U.S. Department of Agriculture, it became an integral part of the department's program, known as the Home Demonstration Agent's Program. Its objective as defined in a 1951 pamphlet was primarily "to help rural families obtain and manage an income—both money and nonmoney—that will contribute to better living for the family."

To that end, over the years, the Bureau of Home Economics conducted research and tests on the basis of which a series of pamphlets were issued —"how to" booklets on a great variety of home activities, which became the basic consumer information source for not only the Department of Agriculture but also for the entire Federal government. Editors of women's magazines, "household hints" newspaper columnists, and home service radio commentators have leaned heavily on this material for years, and accordingly, urban families as well as rural have benefited from it.

The testing, research, and publication program of the Bureau of Home Economics has been markedly curtailed, and its emphasis has been altered. As it is now slanted, policywise, the Home Advisers Service (the current name for the program) is so limited in scope as to bring forth justified protests from American home economists. The question of appropriateness is, here, of less significance than the emphasis of the agency.

While home service and market news broadcasts have a place, they are no substitute for home equipment testing. To trade the research and test-

[10] *Advertising Age,* Dec. 10, 1962, p. 1.

ing program of the Bureau of Home Economics for an effort to promote farm produce is to trade a hard-won heritage for unsubstantial pottage.

Should Conferences Replace Research and Testing? Instead of testing textiles and issuing pamphlets on how to buy, use, and care for them, the home demonstration agent in the field today has only a conference on textile problems to offer to rural or urban consumers—a conference attended by textile manufacturers, department store representatives, and uninformed consumers. Instead of testing various cooking utensil materials and publishing results on how to buy, use, and care for them, this problem is also handled in a conference that may be dominated by the local representative of the manufacturer or store with the most time and personnel to spend at an all-day conference.

The Bureau of Home Economics has discontinued its entire major appliance-testing program so that, in the future, advice on how to buy, use, and care for home freezers, refrigerators, washing machines, and other household appliances will likewise be handled on the local conference basis.

So far as consumer welfare is concerned, there has probably never been a less auspicious time for dropping the appliance-testing program. To benefit from the FHA Title I guarantee of installment debt, appliance manufacturers have launched an industry-wide major change in appliance construction. Instead of the familiar plug-in, free-standing units, the new style of refrigerators, stoves, freezers, washing machines, room air conditioners, and the like, are so designed that they are built-in—that is, attached to the structure of the house. In the trade press there is frank discussion about the potential problems of such appliances: the lack of standards in size, color, and shape and the unknowns about maintenance and repair costs and performance.

But not only for appliances is this the worst possible time to drop this limited program of government research and testing of consumer goods. On today's market are miracle fibers, new dyes, new insecticides, plastics, new drugs, new chemical additives for food, new packaging materials, new surfacing materials. The electronic industry promises new devices and appliances far beyond television. In all foods, the trend is toward more and more processing. And what is needed is more and more aid to the consumer.

Antitrust Division of the Department of Justice. The Antitrust Division has had far better leadership than the Federal Trade Commission. Indeed, some of its actions have been vigorous and forthright. The work of the Antitrust Division involves more than mergers. These are a factor, but in some industries the merger movement seems to have gone about as far as it can go.

Besides mergers, the years following World War II have seen the rapid growth of vertical monopolies in a number of agricultural processing industries—especially in milk distribution, in shoes, and in credit jewelry; franchise selling in liquor, food, cosmetics, appliances, rugs, furniture, building materials, automobile supplies, and brand clothing; rigidly controlled retail prices in drugs, all hospital, medical, and dental supplies, books, jewelry; in such services as funerals, barbering, insurance and real estate selling, and dry cleaning; and, finally, a great increase in price leadership practices made effective through the mushroom growth of trade association activities. Even such details as trade discounts for cash or early payment of bills, or amounts acceptable as advertising allowances, are not infrequently dictated through trade association insistence on a "follow the leader" policy.

The appropriation of the Antitrust Division should be considerably enlarged to give the Federal antitrust laws a chance to maintain or restore a freely competitive market for those remaining consumer goods and services not already exempted from antitrust laws either by state or Federal legislation.

It may well be that the Europeans are right—that our antimonopoly laws have simply driven cartels underground via trade associations or have raised them into the never-never land of boards and commissions where state police power enforces cartel policies in the name of consumer protection. But until it has been demonstrated and documented that our economic system cannot function competitively, the consumer will continue to be vitally interested in a strong, well-supported, active Antitrust Division of the Department of Justice.

Bureau of Labor Statistics. Fluctuations in the Consumer Price Index have been the basis for more policy decisions, both in business and government, than almost any other collection of data. So far as the ultimate consumer is concerned, these apparently dry figures have a quite bouncy quality when it comes to interpretation.

If the index goes up a point, spokesmen note that it was only one up—simply a sign of continued stability. If it goes down a point, consumer prices are coming down and no bones about it—inflation has been defeated. To the ultimate consumer, the index always seems in some way or another to be behind what it really costs to live. And it may well be that this worm's-eye view has some significant reality behind it.

For example, although the budget for this statistical program has not been cut, no appropriations have been made for continuing the City Worker's Family Budget investigation. The last such survey was made in 1950. Since that date, there has been a sizable change in at least one aspect of family spending—a great increase in consumption credit. According to the overly cautious estimate of the Federal Reserve Board, better than a third of the nation's families have almost one-third of their disposable income committed to fixed payments for mortgage debt, insurance, and installment debt.

When goods are bought on time payment plans, the carrying charges for those goods vary on a true-annual-interest basis from a low of about 16 per cent (the revolving credit charges of most department stores) to as high as 150 per cent for some soft goods. The greater part of this debt is concentrated on particular lines of goods, such as automobiles and consumer durables, and in many instances, installment sales account for 60 to 80 per cent of the sales. If carrying charges were added to the cash price of the goods, the index for these items would be pushed up. And if, on top of those carrying charges, the index also reflected late-payment charges, credit insurance charges, collection agency fees, court costs, and attorneys' fees—all of which are paid by the defaulting installment purchasers—the index might be pushed up still more.

In the light of the role played by consumer credit, added funds should be allocated for a detailed and up-to-date investigation of urban family budgets by the Bureau of Labor Statistics.

Federal Housing Administration and the VA Program. The significance of the programs of these agencies as they affect the total economy has been repeatedly stressed, especially in the early 1960s. In spite of the vast influence already credited to them, however, their effects have been understated. The present vast expansion in short-term consumption debt depends almost directly on the widely promoted homeownership program of these two agencies. Easy installment terms, the greater selling emphasis on credit terms as opposed to cash, the use of goods to disguise a loan as a sale—all these practices are based on the assumption of most sellers that, small though it may be, equity in a home can be tapped to create other consumption debts. Thus, these two housing programs have, in an almost literal sense, put a new type of currency—credit—into the hands of a great number of consumers. The consumer's name on a piece of paper buys either money or goods.

The cost of consumption credit, a cost borne by the low-income and middle-income groups, has not been calculated. Under the FHA's Title I program and under the similar program in the VA, all too many families got $500 worth of asbestos siding at a cost of $2,500. Meantime, however, their slender equity, already overburdened by a second government guaranteed debt, has continued to function as a credit basis for debts to commercial lenders and sellers.

Ordinary installment debts are burdened with costly interest, service, and collection charges. Even government-promoted and guaranteed installment debt under Title I carries an interest charge of 9.7 per cent, though this is only about half, or even less than half, the average interest charge on the bulk of nonguaranteed installment debt. Experience with

Title I guaranteed debt (see Senate Hearings on the FHA scandals), however, indicates that unless and until the FHA takes definite steps to protect homeowners, the current drive of the "glamour kitchen salesman" may well turn existing home equity into Title I open-end mortgage debt for built-in appliances. This will cost an unknown sum for repair and maintenance as well as a greater unknown sum for the price of the goods. Title I "dynamiter" salesmen have proved their competence in selling home improvements on a so-much-a-month basis without much clarity about the total of the debt incurred. And large appliance manufacturers have cooperated with this practice by an announced policy of not advertising, nor even suggesting, retail list prices on built-ins.

FHA Guarantees Influence Costs. In the primary aspects of these housing programs—the guarantee of home mortgages amortized over 20- to 30-year periods—the lenders and the builders have held an almost unchecked sway over both lending policies and building prices. Through their appraisals of the value of a house to determine how much of the debt the Federal government will guarantee, these two agencies are, of course, influencing prices.

Neither the veteran nor the average home buyer is usually aware of either his rights, his obligations, or his risks as a homeowner under a government guaranteed program. Veteran privileges are sold. The apparent health of the soundly amortized, government guaranteed mortgage is, at present, no more reliable than the individual homeowner's understanding of this privilege rooted in his homeownership—consumer credit.

There is not, of course, any essential or necessary conflict between government guarantee of consumption debt and the general welfare. Under circumstances, however, where the agency that is promoting consumption debt views the issues through lenders' spectacles and draws up rules and regulations from that outlook, a distorted policy is almost certain to result.

Bankers are in a competitive market, and there is a scramble for consumer paper. Therefore, a new service business has developed—debt poolers, or debt advisers, private agencies that for a fee of 12 per cent of the debt advise burdened families on how to manage their incomes to clear up present debts and to prevent future debt. Since 1960, some three hundred to four hundred such businesses have started anew in major cities of the United States, and legislation to set up a regulatory agency to control them has been introduced in several states.

Here again the problem (costly consumption credit) is one of informed choice. But information about the actual cost of consumption credit is hard to come by. And the legal status of the signer of a conditional sales contract or a Title I contract is far from enviable. Small claims courts have been rendered functionless in this field through price inflation. Their limits are too low. Higher courts are expensive luxuries. Wage garnishments and liens on homes have been increasing substantially.

Perhaps a continually rising disposable income can cushion the impact and continue to nourish this expansion of consumption debt, provided, of course, that debt and income distribution are in some reasonable balance. But from the consumer's point of view, income, savings, and debt data, as now cast up in government reports, leave much to be desired. In this area —governmental economic investigation and reporting—a number of significant questions are unasked or unanswered, because the pressure of minority groups for other answers to other questions is continuous and persistent.

Consumer Advisory Council. The Council of Economic Advisors established the Consumer Advisory Council by direction of President John F. Kennedy in his special message to Congress on March 15, 1962. This newly formed council consists of twelve members—six men and six women with long-time interests in consumer programs and representing all parts of the country. Various other interests are represented—business, law, the press, women's organizations, educational institutions, and consumer organizations. A modest budget and a small staff were provided for the first year of operation.

In addition, one representative from each of 22 government departments and agencies, whose activities bear significantly on consumer welfare, was designated as the contact for the council for such information and consultation as may be needed. Each representative has the responsibility of advising and assisting the head of his agency to assure "adequate and effective attention to consumer interests in the work of the agency, to act as liaison with the consumer and related organizations, and to place increased emphasis on preparing and making available pertinent research findings for consumers in clear and usable form."

On January 3, 1964, President Lyndon B. Johnson announced the continuation of the Consumer Advisory Council by Executive Order.

This is not the first consumers' advisory group established by the Federal government. During the early 1930s, a consumer-oriented group was appointed to work with labor and business advisory boards on acceptable levels for prices and wages. A similar council was appointed to work with the Agricultural Adjustment Administration, and during World War II, the price control and rationing agencies had advisory groups.

Program and Accomplishments of the CAC. The Consumer Advisory Council (CAC) planned a somewhat broader program when it met in September, 1962. It was concerned with protecting consumer interests, but has devoted considerable effort to other areas as well. For example, of special interest in the 1962 program relating to acceleration of economic growth were the forces determining consumer decisions to save or to consume.

Five committees have worked on half a dozen selected topics related to the following areas.[11]

First, advise on issues of broad policy (a committee on consumer credit and economic welfare, another on consumer standards, grades, and labels).

Second, provide advice on governmental programs protecting consumer needs (committee on interrelations among Federal agencies and between Federal and state agencies).

Third, provide advice on needed improvements in the flow of consumer research material to the public (committee on two-way flow of information between government and consumer).

Fourth, give interested citizens and organizations a voice in these matters (committee on effective representation in government).

What was accomplished by the CAC during its first year? Helen Canoyer, chairman of the council, reported its activities in this manner.

The Consumer Advisory Council has issued statements favoring "truth-in-packaging" and "truth-in-lending," and they have urged the administration to take additional steps to combat the denial of consumers' rights on the grounds of race. The Council has expressed its opposition to the principles and purposes of the "Quality Stabilization" bills. These statements in whole or in part have been officially released to the press. The Council has endorsed proposals to assure the safety, effectiveness, and reliability of therapeutic, diagnostic, and prosthetic devices, and to extend to cosmetics the premarketing testing for safety that is in effect in the fields of drugs and food additives. They have also urged new requirements for cautionary labeling of hazardous substances and containers regulated under the Food, Drug, and Cosmetics Act. The Council has set out a list of principles which they would like to see used as guides in housing policy, including a massive education program for prospective home buyers. They have called for more funds for consumer research and information work by the several departments and agencies. This Council has also evaluated and made recommendations to Federal departments on the basis of the pilot project carried out by the Government Printing Office and the Post Office, whereby over a quarter of a million special order blanks for consumer publications were distributed through a sample of 100 out of the nation's 35,000 post offices.

The Consumer Advisory Council has urged that certain studies or investigations be undertaken on a number of topics. Among these are the following, some of which, it is gratifying to note, are now the subject of active inquiry: the nature of guarantees and warranties within major areas of consumer expenditure; the establishment of standards for sizes of clothing and knit garments; the possible adoption of Federal safety standards for electrical equipment; the possibilities

[11] Helen Canoyer, "The Consumer Advisory Council: Its Origin, Purpose and Problems," Address before the Annual Meeting of the American Home Economics Association, June 27, 1963.

for more intensive and extensive work by private and governmental agencies in strengthening and unifying standards and simplified practices programs; the promotion of national standards in the field of highway safety; and the development of uniform warning labels in the form of pictorial symbols on toxic substances.

To sum up our accomplishments to this date: We have set our sights on a limited number of long-range study topics on which we have made interim recommendations; we have responded to specific requests for advice from the Administration; we have learned at least how much there is to know about government activity in the consumer field; and we have established working relations with consumer assistants in several Federal departments and agencies. After a certain amount of spinning of wheels, some of which is bound to happen by the very nature of a pioneer effort, we have the show on the road. I am confident that we have ended our first year with a record of accomplishment, and I hope it will be a sufficiently strong record to warrant the continuance of consumer representation of some *permanent* kind at a high level in the Federal government.[12]

Problems of the Consumer Advisory Council. The Consumer Advisory Council has been working under a tremendous handicap from the beginning, because business in general did not welcome this organization. As a matter of record, the National Association of Manufacturers considered such a consumer council "unnecessary and undesirable." The Chamber of Commerce told the President that such an organization would be most "ill-advised." Organized retailers opposed the CAC. The trade association press editorialized against it. The only friendly note that Consumers Union found came from *Advertising Age*.[13] This was anything but a friendly atmosphere in which to be born, kept alive, and, hopefully, to be effective in strengthening and restoring the power of the consumer as a rationally motivated, well-informed arbiter in the market place.

The difficulties foreseen for CAC are obvious even to its best friends, and its members are aware of many problems. An advisory committee to another advisory committee is too far from the seat of power. The budget is so small that only one of the five committees could function in early 1963.

The council is supposedly an orphan in the inhospitable bureaucratic world. Some members of the council, and other consumer leaders, feel that it should be given a home where it is really wanted, and where it will have direct contact with the persons who make policy decisions.

The CAC has an important job to perform, the need for which, difficult though it may be to fulfill, is pressing. The United States has suffered

[12] Canoyer, *op. cit.*
[13] *Consumer Reports,* September, 1962, p. 464.

because the voice of the consumer has been absent from Federal government deliberations. The existence of the CAC is a long overdue recognition of this fact, and it could be a step toward remedial action.

More than thirty years of interrupted consumer representation at the Federal level has made one lesson clear. To be effective, consumer representation must be permanent, continuous, and at a high level. Furthermore, the leadership in particular, as well as the other consumer members, must be consumer-minded in addition to having a good understanding of the economy of the United States.

President Johnson's Committee on Consumer Interests. On January 3, 1964, President Johnson created, by Executive Order, the President's Committee on Consumer Interests and continued the Consumer Advisory Council. Mrs. Esther Peterson was appointed Special Assistant to the President on Consumer Affairs. Mrs. Peterson was also appointed Chairman of the Committee on Consumer Interests.

The Committee on Consumer Interests is composed of representatives of the Departments of Justice; Interior; Agriculture; Commerce; Labor; and Health, Education, and Welfare; the Housing and Home Agency; the Federal Trade Commission; and the Council of Economic Advisors. It is possible that the President may appoint other government employees and private citizens to represent consumer interests.

The functions of the committee shall be to "consider the Federal policies and improve the Federal programs of primary importance to consumers. It will focus on consumer needs which can appropriately be met through Federal action, whether under existing laws or new legislation."

President Johnson said the action he was taking would "assure that the voice of the consumer will be loud, clear, uncompromising, and effective in the highest councils of the Federal government." The President said further: "This committee will be vigilant to keep consumers informed so they are not completely at the mercy of those who exact unfair prices or levy unfair charges."

The effectiveness of the committee is untried at this writing. We can be sure only of one thing. For the first time in our history, the consumer interest will be directly represented in the White House. This is a step in the right direction. Perhaps someday consumers can be represented on the President's Cabinet.

A Bill to Establish a Department of Consumers. In 1961, a bill to establish a Department of Consumers was sponsored by Senator Estes Kefauver and 23 cosponsors. Its principal task was "to present the viewpoint of consumers of goods and services within the United States in the formulation of policies of the Government." Though this 1961 bill was not passed, it is of interest to consumers to examine its provisions.

1. The department would have the responsibility of presenting the consumer viewpoint when economic policies were being developed at the highest levels of government.

2. As part of its principal function, the department would "represent the economic interests of consumers of the United States in proceedings before courts and regulatory agencies of the United States."

3. The department would be empowered to intervene in matters vitally affecting consumers before the regulatory bodies by presenting information showing the consequences of the proposed action on consumers. In no way was it proposed that the power of the regulatory agencies be reduced or abridged. The purpose of intervention was merely to insure that, so far as the consumer interest is concerned, action would not be taken without some foreknowledge of its effects on consumers.

4. Similarly, in matters involving the judicial branch of government, the department would have the right to certify information to the proper official for presentation before the district courts and to secure leave to present the consumer point of view before appellate courts.

5. The department would also have certain operating responsibilities resulting from the transfer to it of a list of units and functions already set up or carried on by other departments or agencies. Transfer would be made where consolidation in a consumer-oriented department would lead to more efficient operation, higher morale, and a general strengthening of the over-all program through the new focus and unity of purpose.

6. The proposed transfers included the Food and Drug Administration, the Division of Prices and Cost of Living of the Bureau of Labor Statistics, the Institute of Home Economics and Human Nutrition, and certain elements of the National Bureau of Standards engaged in research with respect to, or testing of, consumer goods. In other cases, the department would be authorized to establish cooperative relationships with existing consumer services for more effective coordination of programs and policies.

7. The department would serve as a central clearinghouse for complaints from consumers who do not know where to turn for help. If the matter involved was within the jurisdiction of another department or agency, the complaint would be forwarded for its attention and appropriate action. If the matter involved a violation of law or of a judicial decision, it would be transmitted promptly to the appropriate officer or agency together with evidence and information concerning the probable violation, and the department would ascertain "the nature and extent of action taken with regard to probable violations so reported."

8. The department would set up advisory committees and hold an annual consumers conference "for the purpose of obtaining information, recommendations, and suggestions necessary or desirable for the effective performance of other functions of the department."

9. The department was authorized to "receive, assemble, evaluate, act upon and disseminate information helpful to consumers of the United States in performing their economic function more efficiently, including information concerning commercial and trade practices adversely affecting their economic interests."

Congress, itself, would be among the chief beneficiaries of a Department of Consumers. Time and again, in considering legislation, Congress needs an evaluation of its likely effect on consumers. And after the legislation has been passed, Congress needs to know whether the ends sought for in the legislation have been achieved or if further action is necessary. At the present time, it is difficult and often impossible for Congress to secure this kind of information. There is need for an agency that can collect such information, interpret it with intelligence and skill, and present it with courage and honesty.

Kefauver Bill for a Consumer Office. A new Kefauver bill was introduced in 1963, to set up a Consumer Office with the following functions.

To represent the viewpoint of consumers in the formulation of government policies;

To represent the economic interest of consumers before regulatory agencies and courts (including the right to intervene as a party in proceedings);

To conduct annually a National Consumers Conference; and

To gather and disseminate information helpful to consumers, "including information concerning commercial and trade practices adversely affecting their economic interests."

The office would be required to conduct surveys of production, systems of distribution, price levels and their reasonableness, the quality and suitability of goods affecting consumers, and the degree to which trade and commerce succeeds in satisfying consumer needs for goods and services.

The bill differs from prior ones in making no provision for bringing together in the new agency many consumer-oriented activities in various Federal government agencies. Senator Estes Kefauver said that "this was the one provision of the previous bills to which there was considerable objection."

When introducing the bill, Senator Kefauver called attention to the atrophy of competitive forces in many industries, to the "serious hazards" that have come with the great variety of goods and services now available, and to the fact that in the day-to-day operations of many regulatory agencies "the public interest has been all but obliterated. More often than not the issue of whether a decision accords with the interests of the public is never even raised."

He called for an office of consumers "daily to be a burr in the hides of government officialdom, to get important consumer issues raised, and to aid in their settlement in such a fashion that consumer interests will be heard and taken account of."

Senator Kefauver emphasized that creation of the new office was essential despite the existence of the Consumer Advisory Council. He referred to this council as "an advisory group to an advisory group," meeting infrequently, composed of busy people with other professional interests and lacking "an adequate staff working consistently day in and day out on consumer problems." And he added that "in its present environment," the Consumer Advisory Council "also lacks the independence to speak out on issues important to the consumer."

Need for Federal Concern for Consumer Protection. The desirability of consumer representation in the Federal government has been the basis for increased public discussion and some Federal government action. This concern with consumer problems is directed at violations of law and questionable business practices that may violate no present law. This growing consumer interest may also be explained as a social reaction to diminishing price competition in the market place. Other consumer proponents are concerned about the waste, fraud, and inefficiency that result from various schemes directed against the consumer.

Some economists stress the need to bring back into the market place a rational umpire—the consumer. Their argument is that "consumer sovereignty is the keystone of our economic system"; that the "weakening of the power of the consumer as a rationally motivated, well-informed arbiter in the market place threatens us with the loss of a balance wheel for the whole economic system." [14]

The urgency of this movement to establish consumer offices in both the Federal government and in state governments is not felt by all. Many elements of the business world object to unnecessary interference by government. The United States Chamber of Commerce and the National Association of Manufacturers challenge the need for more consumer representation in government. [15]

There was a time, 150 years ago, when people gathered in small halls across the United States to discuss major problems affecting the nation's economy. These people, mostly farmers, talked about the lack of information, the lack of educational programs, the lack of quality standards, the lack of credit at nonusurious rates, the lack of labeling and resources to enforce standards. These meetings were called "Agricultural Societies." The United States was then a nation of farmers whose knowledge of credit, sales, seeds, and so on, was limited.

Out of these meetings developed the United States Department of Agriculture, whose far-flung activities eventually influenced the life of nearly every farmer. But it was not until the USDA was established as a branch of the Federal government that our nation was able to make the collective

[14] From an unpublished paper, "The Consumer and Government," read by Dexter Masters, then Director of Consumers Union, at the consumer conference called by The Consumer Research Institute, San Francisco State College, August 28–30, 1962.

[15] *Business Week,* "Special Voice for Consumers?" Apr. 8, 1961, p. 70; *The Wall Street Journal,* Nov. 11, 1960.

effort in the production of farm goods that has been, and still is, the envy of the world.

Today, only 10 per cent of our population lives on farms. Families now function as spending units, and increasingly their standards of living are determined by their ability to spend wisely. Their needs for guidance as spending units is reminiscent of the pioneer farmers' needs. The problems of consumers today, like the problems of the pioneer farmers, cannot be solved until the resources of the Federal government are fully directed to the consumer interest.

The Consumer Advisory Council is only a beginning. What is needed is a Department of Consumers that will come close to doing for the nation's families as spending units the kind of educational and service job that the Department of Agriculture achieved when most families lived on farms.

Perhaps it is along such basic and meaningful lines as the USDA's program—county agents, home demonstration agencies, rural electrification program, farm financing agencies, standards of labeling for feed and seed, farm experimental stations, to name only a few—that a new Department of Consumers should be planned, if the United States economy is to be guided wisely in the future—which means to be guided by informed consumer choice. In this way, a rational umpire—the consumer—may be brought into the market place.

QUESTIONS FOR DISCUSSION

1. What are the most significant gains for consumers in the Food, Drug, and Cosmetics Act of 1938?

2. What recommendations would you support in improving the present food, drug, and cosmetic legislation?

3. In what ways does the Federal Trade Commission protect the ultimate consumer?

4. Which of the three methods used by the Federal Trade Commission for the prevention of unfair competition and unfair or deceptive acts or practices is most effective from the consumer point of view?

5. Should consumers depend on the states to pass satisfactory legislation affecting labels?

6. Should consumers work for a Federal Department of Consumers or for a privately controlled consumer standards agency?

7. Is "consumer sovereignty" the keystone to our economic system?

8. What did the late President Kennedy mean when he said, "The march of technology has increased the difficulties of the consumer along with his opportunities"?

9. What were the important changes in the Drug Amendments of 1962?

10. Why did Congress pass the Federal Hazardous Substances Labeling Act?

11. Do you agree with the statement that the Food and Drug Administration has been more consumer-oriented than any other Federal agency?

12. How would you modify the Consumer Advisory Council?

13. Compare the merits of the Kefauver Consumer Office Bill and the Department of Consumers Bill of 1961.

ACTIVITY PROBLEMS

1. Three major divisions of the National Bureau of Standards—Simplified Practice, Trade Standards, and Codes and Specifications—are especially concerned with buyer-seller relationships. Find as many useful illustrations as possible for each of these areas of buyer-seller relationships.

2. Consult city authorities to see what standards are set up locally with regard to the slaughtering, processing, and selling of meat. Try to discover the effectiveness of these regulations and how enforcement is managed.

3. Collect many labels from canned goods. Analyze each label according to exactly what it tells you. Are some kinds of information legally required on the label? Do U.S. Department of Agriculture grading labels carry more accurate and important information for the consumer than private grades and descriptions?

4. Study two of the recent *News Summary* reports of the Federal Trade Commission. Make a report to the class on the nature of the FTC activities as seen through these reports.

5. Summarize a recent annual report of the Food and Drug Administration.

6. Show the film entitled "Your Meat Inspection Service." Plan a discussion around this film.

7. Write to the Chairman of the Consumer Advisory Council, Executive Office of the President, Council of Economic Advisors, Washington, D.C., for the latest annual report of the CAC. Prepare a report to the class emphasizing the effectiveness of this advisory organization to consumers.

8. Should consumers press for a Department of Consumers or settle for a Consumer Office as outlined in the Kefauver bill in 1963? Why is it so difficult to get consumers effectively represented at the Federal level?

9. Do you think that the consumer activities of the Federal agencies need to be coordinated? How about a permanent 10-man council with authority to probe any phase of any agency's procedures and make recommendations for changes?

10. What is the extent of Federal participation in direct consumer activities? Write to your Congressman for the 8th Report by the Committee on Government Operations on Consumer Protection Activities of Federal Departments and Agencies, 1961.

SUGGESTED READINGS

Annual Report of the Consumer Advisory Council, Executive Office of the President, Council of Economic Advisors, Washington, D.C.

Brady, Mildred Edie. *Testimony at FCC Hearings.* Mount Vernon, N.Y.: Consumers Union, Inc., Dec. 8, 1959.

Business Week. "Special Voice for Consumers," Apr. 8, 1961, p. 70.

Christian Science Monitor. Mar. 27, 1961, p. 2; Apr. 6, 1961, p. 5.

Consumer Reports. "An Official Consumer Voice in Washington," September, 1962, p. 463; "Where . . . Was the FCC?" January, 1960, p. 9; "A Department of Consumers in Washington, D.C.," June, 1959, p. 276; "Key to the Economy: Restoring Consumer Confidence," January, 1961, pp. 38–40; "Drug Safety," March, 1963, p. 134; "50 Years of the Food and Drug Act," July, 1956; "Toward Safer Drugs," October, 1962, p. 509.

Council on Consumer Information. "The Federal Trade Commission, the Consumer and the Public Interest," by Daniel J. McCauley, Jr., *Selected Proceedings of Sixth Annual Conference,* 1960; *Selected Proceedings of Fifth Annual Conference,* 1959 (whole issue); *Selected Proceedings of Ninth Annual Conference,* 1963 (whole issue); "Consumers Look at Federal Protective Services," by Monroe W. Karmin, 1959. Greeley, Colo.: Colorado State College.

Family Economic Review. "Highlights of 1962 Drug Amendments," March, 1963.

Fortune. "The Root of the FTC's Confusion," August, 1963, p. 114.

Galbraith, J. K. *American Capitalism: The Concept of Countervailing Power.* Boston: Houghton Mifflin Company, 1952.

Hannah, Harvey H. *Consumer Statutes Administered by the Federal Trade Commission.* Washington, D.C.: Federal Trade Commission, Dec. 21, 1959.

Harris, Richard. *The Real Voice.* New York: The Macmillan Company, 1964.

Harvey, George Y. Report to the Secretary of Health, Education, and Welfare on the Food and Drug Administration by Citizens Advisory Committee. Washington, D.C.: Food and Drug Administration, Oct. 2, 1962.

Harvey, John L. *The Federal Hazardous Substances Labeling Act.* Washington, D.C.: Food and Drug Administration, 1961.

House Document no. 364. *Consumers Protection and Interest Program,* Message from the President of the United States. Washington, D.C.: Superintendent of Documents, Mar. 15, 1962.

Kintner, Earl W. "Advertising at the Crossroads," speech on Dec. 4, 1959; "The Role of the Federal Trade Commission in Consumer Protection." Washington, D.C.: Federal Trade Commission, Sept. 23, 1960.

The Progressive. "A Voice for Consumers," January, 1959, p. 41.

Senate Bill 1688. *To Establish a Department of Consumers,* 87th Congress, 1st Session. Washington, D.C.: Superintendent of Documents, Apr. 20, 1961.

Sinclair, Upton. *The Jungle.* New York: Harper & Row, Publishers, Incorporated, 1951.

U.S. Congress. *Federal Hazardous Substances Labeling Act,* Public Law 86-613, 86th Congress, S. 1283. Washington, D.C.: Government Printing Office, July 12, 1960.

U.S. Congress, House Subcommittee on the Committee on Government Operations. "Consumer Protection Activities of Federal Departments and Agencies," 87th Congress, 1st Session, H. Rept. 1241. Washington, D.C.: Government Printing Office, 1961.

U.S. Congress, Senate Subcommittee on Administrative Practice and Procedure to the Committee on the Judiciary. "Report on Regulatory Agencies to the President Elect," 86th Congress, 2d Session. Washington, D.C.: Government Printing Office, December, 1960.

U.S. Department of Health, Education, and Welfare, Food and Drug Administration. *Federal Food, Drug, and Cosmetic Act, as Amended,* 1958 revision; *Annual Report; Weekly Releases; FDA 1963; Food Additives, 1962; Food Facts vs. Food Fallacies, 1963; Drug Amendments of 1962; Your Money and Your Life, 1963.*

The Wall Street Journal. "FDA Posts Stiffer Drug Control Rules," June 20, 1963, p. 1.

Warne, Colston. *Fictitious Pricing and Bait Advertising.* Mount Vernon, N.Y.: Consumers Union, Inc., Dec. 21, 1959.

Williams, Carla S. "FDA's Consumer Consultant Program," Selected Proceedings of the 7th Annual Conference of the Council on Consumer Information. Greeley, Colo.: Colorado State College, 1961.

17

CONSUMER PROTECTION ON THE STATE
AND LOCAL LEVELS

In the United States, the Federal government possesses constitutional authority to regulate products that cross state boundaries. This leaves a large area of consumer products to state and local regulations. It is estimated, for example, that about 40 per cent of all food, drugs, and cosmetics move in intrastate commerce.

There is little Federal protection of housing with the exception of some supervision by the Federal Housing Administration and the Veterans Administration on less than 50 per cent of home loans. The consumer is, therefore, dependent on local and state standards and supervision in housing.

On the whole, there is little Federal regulation of utilities (water, gas, electricity, and telephone services) except for long-distance telephoning and interstate pipe lines. This, too, is left to state and local regulation.

Medical standards and practices are dependent almost entirely on state and local regulation and licensing to minimize quackery and malpractice.

The important area of weights and measures depends on local and state laws and inspection. The Federal government has the authority to establish standards for weights and measures, but it is up to each state to supervise the standards set up by the Legislature. As a result, the quality of state legislation and the effectiveness of enforcement vary widely among the states. There are still three states—Hawaii, Mississippi, and Arkansas —with little or no weights-and-measures controls as of June, 1964, according to Malcolm Jensen, chief of the Office of Weights and Measures.[1]

The general lack of effective state and local regulations and inspection systems is illustrated in a story told by Upton Sinclair to Mrs. Helen E.

[1] Hearings, House, Consumer Protection Activities. Washington, D.C.: Government Printing Office, 1962, p. 8.

Nelson, consumer counsel of California. Mr. Sinclair commented that, after the Federal Meat Inspection Act was passed by Congress, when Federal inspectors in the Chicago packing plants refused to pass a carcass, it was dropped through a hole cut in the floor and sold on the local market. While this is not done today, the story points up the fact that there can be that "hole in the floor" through which consumer goods may enter the state market unless state and local laws exist and are enforced. As a matter of fact, some 20 per cent of our fresh meat is sold intrastate.

The problem of local protection in intrastate consumer products and services is complicated by overlapping of local and state authority in regulating some goods—notably, trade in foods and drugs—primarily to assure their purity. A similar duality occurs in the efforts to control advertising so as to reduce misrepresentation.

The greater amount of attention has centered on Federal protection for the consumer interest, but the states have been giving more attention to this problem.

State Government Consumer Programs

At the beginning of 1963, at least fourteen states had either organized special consumer offices, or they were in the planning and discussion stages.[2] This field is vast, complex, and changing almost from month to month. Yet there is merit in assembling the information as of a given year. Any given description will always be a part of the history of the consumer movement and will be the basis for understanding any changes that occur from year to year. As a matter of fact, few adults are aware of the changes that have occurred up to 1965 throughout the United States.

A brief history of consumer protective activities will be useful in understanding the gaps that presently exist at this level and the efforts that a few states are making to close some of the consumer protection gaps.

The states have different patterns of consumer protective services, which vary greatly in the nature and effectiveness of the work done on behalf of the consumer. Some states have made modest to substantial progress in this area; on the other hand, most of the states have made few gains. Nevertheless, the trend is toward more and better protection for consumers at the state level.

The states where consumers have formed their own voluntary associations—California, Massachusetts, Michigan, and Maryland—have the best opportunities to advance consumer protective laws and to encourage effective enforcement of these laws. Each of these state consumer associations is sparked by people who are members of college and university faculties, labor unions, consumer cooperatives, credit unions, women's clubs, professional organizations, and parents' associations. Each of these

[2] Dr. Colston Warne, unpublished survey. Amherst, Mass.: Amherst College, 1963.

state consumer associations still faces the problem of inadequate memberships and financing. Nevertheless, each of these organizations has made progress in advancing consumer welfare.

Office of Consumer Counsel in California. California and Massachusetts were the only states in 1964 with active state-sponsored consumer counsels. In 1959, Governor Edmund G. Brown called for the establishment of the Office of Consumer Counsel, and the attorney general established a unit within the Department of Justice to deal with consumer frauds. An economist, Mrs. Helen E. Nelson, became the first consumer counsel on October 2, 1959.

The function of the Office of Consumer Counsel is to represent the consumer before the Legislature and before state agencies and administrative bodies and to advise the Governor on consumer problems. California is unique among the 50 states in that the governor can evaluate all legislation in the light of its effect on the people as consumers.

The legislation creating the office states its functions as follows:

1. To advise the governor on matters affecting the interests of the people as consumers.
2. To recommend to the governor and to the Legislature legislation to protect and promote the interest of the people as consumers.
3. To study consumer problems and report on them to the people.
4. To appear before governmental commissions, departments, and agencies to represent and be heard on behalf of consumers' interests.

The consumer counsel and the consumer frauds unit of the attorney general's office have worked together closely in stimulating and assisting local law enforcement agencies; in drafting and working for needed legislation to secure consumer rights; and in investigating such problems as health and dance studio rackets, trade school buncos, and abuses in appliance repairs.

Legislation was enacted bringing under strict regulation private institutions issuing diplomas. Preventive action was taken in one major case of abuse in the sale of trade school training courses.

In his first message to the Legislature, Governor Brown called for the enactment of legislation to establish the consumer's legal rights in paying on installment contracts, conditional sales contracts, and revolving charge accounts.

The consumer counsel's office published and distributed a booklet, *Credit Costs Money,* which translates some commonly quoted credit charges into true annual interest rates and cites some examples of the cost of credit.

The administration, initially under the leadership of the consumer counsel, waged a vigorous campaign against referral selling rackets.

Credit buyers were protected by the following legislation.

1. The Unruh Retail Credit Sales Act set the maximum service charge on revolving charge accounts at 1½ per cent a month, or at a rate of 18 per cent simple annual interest. The attorney general's office published and distributed a booklet, *Know Your Rights When You Buy on Time,* to inform consumers of their new rights under this act.

2. Legislation to prohibit the misuse of prepaid service contracts by health and dance studios was enacted.

3. The consumer counsel vigorously opposed a bill to increase substantially the maximum legal charges that industrial loan companies may exact of borrowers. As a result of this opposition, the bill was returned to committee, and the increases were revised downward.

Further legislation represents advances in protection of home buyers and investors.

1. Laws governing second trust deed financing were strengthened. And a program of aid to investors was set up to assist consumers who had invested in bankrupt 10 per cent trust deed companies.

2. To keep more home buyers from resorting to second mortgages, a law was passed raising ceilings on the amount that may be lent on a home by state chartered savings and loan associations.

3. Legislation was enacted authorizing the creation of private mortgage insurance corporations in California to guarantee loans for new homes.

Automobile warranty frauds were curbed by putting automobile warrants under the regulation of the insurance commissioner. The following legislation was enacted to protect automobile buyers.

1. A law was passed requiring all automatic transmission fluids sold in California to be registered with the state Bureau of Weights and Measures.

2. A law was passed governing the advertising of gasoline octane ratings.

3. The Rees-Levering Automobile Buyers Bill was passed, improving the automobile buyer's legal rights when contracting to purchase an automobile on credit.

Early in his administration, Governor Brown appointed a commission to study and report on medical care and health needs in California. Provision was made for regional advisory committees to the Hospital Advisory Council in its responsibility of bestowing Federal and state tax money for private hospital construction. Regional committees for southern California and for northern California were appointed by the director of the Department of Public Health. Representatives of consumer organizations were included.

The following legislation involved medical care costs and insurance.

1. A law was passed to exempt prescription drugs from the state sales tax.

2. A law was passed providing a ten-day free look at any individual health insurance policy.

3. A recommendation by the commission on medical care costs that individual health insurance policies be grade-labeled was introduced in the Legislature.

4. A law was passed giving the insurance commission authority to adopt regulations for removing from the market policies whose benefits· are inadequate in relation to their premiums.

New, improved standards for poultry inspection were set by the state Department of Agriculture. A bill that would have lowered the grade standards for eggs by increasing the proportion that might have more blood spots, cracked or leaky shells, and the like, was vetoed by the governor.

1. A law was passed requiring poultry meat sold in whole carcasses to be labeled with the name of any spoilage retardant added.

2. Deceptive labeling of out-of-state poultry as local or home-grown was prevented by a law requiring all chicken sold for food in California to bear the name and address of the packing plant where the chickens were processed.

3. A law was enacted prohibiting anyone but the consumer from removing from poultry the official inspection mark for wholesomeness, and prohibiting marking "inspected for wholesomeness" on any poultry meat that had not been inspected.

At the 1961 session of the Legislature, a law was passed permitting the state Department of Public Health to pick up where the Federal Food and Drug Administration leaves off in safeguarding users of cosmetics in California against adulterated or misbranded cosmetics. Food additives and adulterated food were redefined by law to correspond to the latest Federal definition. California laws regarding color additives in foods and drugs were put on a par with Federal regulations. The spray-residue enforcement program in the state Department of Agriculture was stepped up.

There was other legislation involving health and safety.

1. The governor called on the state Legislature in 1961 to pass a Hazardous Household Substances Act comparable to the Federal law.

2. A law was enacted setting up clear and specific sanitation requirements for restaurants and food-vending machines.

3. Protection of children was enhanced by a law requiring plastic bags used in retail sales to be clearly labeled that they are dangerous to children.

4. A law enabling the state Department of Public Health to undertake a campaign against cancer quackery was enacted.

There were substantial additions to the staff and budget of the state Bureau of Weights and Measures. A new state weights-and-measures laboratory was equipped.

Rules and regulations were adopted to enable the counties to institute uniform package-checking procedures for policing the weight of package contents. Some proposals were defeated that would have further weakened the weights and measures laws.

An official sales tax collection schedule was established. Legislation was passed to guarantee that all the money paid as sales tax reaches the state.

Legislation was also passed requiring all taxable items sold in one transaction to be totaled, and the sale tax applied to the total, except where taxable and nontaxable items are sold in the same transaction; then the sales tax has to be applied to the total price of the taxable items only if the customer so requests.

A law was enacted to require trading stamp companies to let stamp savers choose between cash and merchandise when they redeem their stamp books and to protect consumers from fly-by-night trading stamp companies.

Connecticut Department of Consumer Protection. Public Act Number 412 of the 1959 general assembly of Connecticut created the Department of Consumer Protection, which administers a wide variety of legislation designed for the protection of Connecticut consumers. The department enforces the laws pertaining to the manufacture and sale of foods, drugs, and cosmetics to insure that they are manufactured and sold under sanitary conditions, properly packaged, labeled, honestly advertised, and of proper quality.

The testing of scales, weights, and measuring devices and enforcement of the Unfair Sales Practices Act also come within the jurisdiction of the department. In addition, the department is responsible for the inspection and licensing of slaughterhouses, inspection of meat and meat products, of eggs, potatoes, and apples, of kosher products, and of pharmacies and pharmacists. And, curiously, the department also supervises boxing and wrestling.

The department also cooperates with the state's advertising media to help clean up misleading "gimmick" advertising, designed to lure the public into business establishments.

A Law for Licensing and Regulating of Food Vending Operators and Their Machines was enacted with jurisdiction for enforcement in the Department of Consumer Protection. The act protects consumers by insuring that the machines contain only foods that are edible and wholesome, free from pathogenic microorganisms, unadulterated, and, if in package form, labeled truthfully and in compliance with the Connecticut Uniform Food, Drug, and Cosmetic Act. The act also provides that all foods, beverages, and ingredients sold in vending machines shall be obtained from sources that comply with state and Federal laws and regulations.

Connecticut also has an Itinerant Vendor Law, which provides that any person conducting a sale under the designation of "Going Out of Business," "Selling Out," "Liquidation," "Loss of Lease," "Forced to Vacate," or any other statement of like meaning must file an application with the Department of Consumer Protection including a complete, accurate inventory of goods, wares, and merchandise on hand at the place where the sale is to be conducted, with the inventory sworn to, and a $500 special deposit submitted. This deposit is returned 60 days subsequent to the surrender and cancellation of the license, provided that all claims authorized by statute have been satisfied.

The Department of Consumer Protection presented a bill before the general assembly that authorized the commissioner to promulgate regulations dealing with the manufacture, storing, transportation, and sale of frozen foods, including sanitary control measures and temperature controls. Shortly after the passage of this act, Connecticut was besieged from all sides by industry. They asked that Connecticut not hastily write regulations, as it was obvious that, should one state start writing regulations, many other states would copy the same type of regulations. Connecticut took the matter up with the Association of Food and Drug Officials of the United States, which participated in this national project. Subsequently, many meetings were held, and the many ideas were consolidated into what is known as the AFDOUS Frozen Food Code. Connecticut was the first state to adopt this code.

On September 27, 1961, a public hearing was held in Connecticut for the purpose of presenting tentative standards and regulations for frozen desserts and frozen dessert mixes. Under date of October 17, 1961, these standards were presented to the attorney general, who officially passed on them. Regulations on frozen desserts were amended to bring them more closely in line with present-day needs.

Since October, 1961, Connecticut has had a sixteen-point law concerning a pharmacy code of ethics. This code of ethics details the professional conduct of both the licensed pharmacist and the licensed pharmacy as far as the health and safety of the consuming public is concerned. The state also has a pharmacy regulation law concerning the sale of patent medicines and drugs in vending machines.

The Department of Consumer Protection helped to prepare material used for an exhibit by Professor Ruby Morris of Connecticut College when she appeared before Senator Philip H. Hart's committee in Washington to testify on deceptive packaging. Many more areas of consumer protection have been discussed for this department. One of these is the field of hearing aids.

The Connecticut State Labor Council has passed a resolution encouraging its members to participate actively by making recommendations that will assist the department in more effectively meeting consumer needs.

Massachusetts Advisory Consumer Council. An Advisory Consumer Council was established as early as 1958 in the office of the attorney general. An early accomplishment of the council was its publicizing of truth in lending on November 21, 1959, when the New England Consumer Conference at Boston College included a session on Cost of Credit.

The Massachusetts Consumer Conference held on April 14, 1962, at Boston College included a session on Consumer Credit. At the request of the council, the attorney general filed bills in both the 1961 and 1962 sessions of the Legislature requiring full disclosure of credit costs. Both bills received state-wide support and publicity, although neither became law.

The Advisory Consumer Council also gave its support to the Federal Truth-in-lending Bill (H 1740). Two of its representatives appeared before the Production and Stabilization Subcommittee of the Senate Committee on Banking and Currency on July 24, 1961. The attorney general of Massachusetts appeared before the Douglas Committee on May 15, 1962, and summed up its activities in the field of consumer credit in Massachusetts and the work of the Advisory Consumer Council in this area.

A number of bills to establish a usury law in Massachusetts were introduced in the 1961–1962 legislative session. One was submitted by the Commissioner of Banks. A strong resolution was prepared stating that this bill would "legalize usury rather than prevent it" and was adopted by the Massachusetts Consumer Conference. The bill went through nine successive redrafts.

The Usury Law Committee of the council and the conference mailed a statement to all legislative members with a copy of a bill prepared by the committee, which in effect would amend the most objectionable sections of the bill, but it did not become law.

The Advisory Consumer Council participated with the Massachusetts Home Economics Association; the Better Business Bureau of Metropolitan Boston; the Consumers Union of the U.S.; the Massachusetts Teachers' Association; and the Massachusetts State Labor Council, AFL-CIO, in sponsoring several state-wide conferences on consumer problems at which food and drug problems received prominent attention.

The council was also active in the area of nutritional quackery. For example, it investigated complaints dealing with daily broadcasts over a local radio station. The broadcaster and representatives of the radio station were invited to appear at a meeting along with various nutrition authorities who had been critical of the broadcasts. Thereafter, the council recommended the matter to the attorney general. The Federal Communications Commission and the Food and Drug Administration took action.

The council has studied the standardizing of weights on canned and packaged goods, the clear marking of net contents of canned and packaged foods, the dating of frozen foods sold in Massachusetts, misleading advertising by home freezer supply firms, and numerous individual complaints from irate citizens who felt that they were cheated in some business transaction.

The attorney general and the Advisory Consumer Council combated a patently illegal method of regulating milk prices, which led to the ultimate rescission of an order setting minimum resale prices for milk in the greater Boston area.

In the field of commuter transportation, the council and the attorney general cooperated in attempting to show the fallacy of continued cuts in commuter transportation and rises in passenger fares, and the failure to provide alternative transportation when services were terminated.

The Advisory Consumer Council encouraged the Insurance Department of the state to use its price-fixing power in the field of compulsory automobile insurance. The number of classifications of drivers was expanded, and prices were revised to reflect more closely the costs of each group. The council refused to endorse a bill written by insurance companies who wanted to be released from the price control provisions of the existing "compulsory" auto insurance law.

The council aided assistant attorneys general in investigating the many complaints concerning consumers' relationships with the accident and health divisions of the insurance industry. The major purveyor of this insurance in Massachusetts sent their vice president from Washington, D.C., to confer with the council, after which he ordered a wholesale cleanup of practices in the state.

Since the inception of the Advisory Consumer Council, various members have taken active personal roles in the movement to amend and/or repeal both state and Federal statutes on so-called fair trade practices.

The great bulk of consumer inquiries and requests for assistance have concerned or involved complaints about false advertising, bait advertising, and the various consumer frauds. Many of the requests for help have been referred to the attorney general's office by the Better Business Bureaus and other interested groups.

The Consumer Council in the Governor's Office in Massachusetts. On October 31, 1963, the Commonwealth of Massachusetts adopted an act establishing a consumer council. This law was effective at the end of January, 1964. This council is in the office of the Governor. It consists of eight persons to be appointed by the Governor for terms concurrent with that of the Governor. One of these members will be a member of the Massachusetts State Labor Council, AFL-CIO. No more than five shall be members of the same political party. Five members, serving ex officio, will be the attorney general, the chairman of the Public Utilities Commission, the commissioner of banks, the commissioner of insurance, and the commissioner of labor and industries. The chairman of the council will be designated by the Governor.

The duties of the council will be to conduct studies, investigations, and research; to advise the executive and legislative branches in matters affecting consumer interests; to coordinate consumers' services carried on by departments and agencies; to further consumer education; to inform the public, through appearances before Federal and state committee, commission, or department hearings, or otherwise, of such policies, decisions, or legislation as are beneficial or detrimental to consumers; to inform the Governor, the attorney general, and other law-enforcement agents of such violations of laws or regulations affecting consumers as its investigations or studies may reveal; and to study and report all matters referred to it by the general court or the Governor.

The council may appear, through its chairman or a member or person designated by him, or through the attorney general, in behalf of the people of the commonwealth before boards, commissioners, commissions, departments, or agencies of the commonwealth in any hearing or matter affecting the rights of the consuming public or in any proceeding seeking the curtailment of railroad services or an increase of rates or costs of services or commodities, and shall be deemed an aggrieved party for the purpose of judicial or administrative review of any decision or ruling in any such proceedings in which it has so appeared, any other provision of law to the contrary notwithstanding.

Department of Consumer Protection in Kansas. In Kansas, a Department of Consumer Protection was established in the office of the attorney general in 1962. The head of this office indicates that "the primary function of this department will be to collect and disseminate as widely as possible information concerning questionable merchandising schemes which may be employed in this state. The department will, in addition, cooperate with various law enforcement agencies, prosecutors, business and consumer groups, both in Kansas and elsewhere."

In announcing establishment of this department, he said that "an ever-growing army of hucksters, pitchmen, and con artists have been preying on an uninformed public through the use of fraudulent and deceptive selling and advertising practices."

Maryland Consumer Protection Program. In 1961, Attorney General Thomas B. Finan ordered an examination and study of the laws of Maryland to determine whether the maximum protection for its citizens was being provided against the various types of frauds and swindles. Personal contact was made with all prosecuting attorneys, police chiefs, and Better Business Bureaus in the state to ascertain what they believed to be the most prevalent types of fraudulent activity in their areas.

The survey revealed that approximately 75 per cent of the complaints received from the public concerned home improvement and repair frauds. As a result of the complaints and of convictions for fraud against several owners of home improvement businesses whose operations had been scandalous, the Governor of Maryland appointed a commission to investigate the home improvement industry. This commission recommended legislation regulating the home improvement and construction industries in Maryland.

An examination of the state laws also revealed that the food and drug laws had not been rewritten since first enacted in 1910. The attorney general, with the cooperation of the state health and agricultural agencies, caused a joint resolution to be introduced in the Legislature calling on the Governor to appoint a commission consisting of the heads of all agencies involved and representatives of the pharmaceutical industry and the medical profession to study the Maryland law and undertake a major revision of its provisions. This resolution specifically directed the commission to determine whether or not uniform food and drug laws should be enacted in the state. It was passed unanimously by both Houses and signed by the Governor.

Another commission is currently studying the problem of interest rates on loans and purchases in Maryland. The attorney general's office is also moving to enforce a law regulating the savings and loan industry.

Consumer Protection Division in Michigan. The Consumer Protection Division in the office of the attorney general of Michigan was established in January, 1961. The immediate impetus for this project was a steady increase in requests for intervention by state law enforcement personnel from Michigan consumers who felt themselves cheated or unfairly treated in the market place.

During the year, the attorney general issued a series of biweekly newsletters to more than five hundred newspapers, radio stations, and TV stations in the state, describing cheats and frauds currently producing numerous complaints.

A related effort, resulting from cooperation with local prosecutors, sheriffs, and other local law enforcement personnel, was a series of consumer protection bulletins issued from time to time on specific cases, describing in detail the methods, probable route, and legal status of suspect activities known to be circulating in the state.

At the end of its first year, the Consumer Protection Division had accepted approximately 356 complaints. Of this number, 106 were closed after successful adjustment or reference to prosecutor or private counsel. More than a dozen intensive investigations were conducted by the division.

The Second Annual Attorney General's Conference on Consumer Protection was held in Detroit on November 2, 1961, with the theme of

"Everyday Household Buying." Speakers were Mrs. Helen Ewing Nelson, consumer counsel of California, Dr. Kenneth L. Milstead of the Food and Drug Administration, and Senator Philip A. Hart, who conducted the hearings on packaging and labeling practices held by the Antitrust and Monopoly Subcommittee of the Committee of the Judiciary of the United States Senate.

Consumer Protection Advisory Council in Minnesota. In November, 1960, Attorney General Walter F. Mondale established a Consumer Protection Unit in his office, and in the fall of 1961, he appointed a 16-member Consumer Protection Advisory Council. This council is composed of leaders in business and labor. Its members serve without pay.

During the first year, the council considered the following proposals for bills that were forwarded to the attorney general for his referral to the 1963 session of the Minnesota Legislature.

1. An act relating to debt prorating and financial planning services
2. An act relating to private schools maintaining or conducting courses for profit or for tuition
3. An act relating to instruction in social training
4. An act relating to the prohibition of referral selling
5. An act relating to the prevention of consumer fraud
6. An act relating to the registration of offerings of subdivided real estate

In addition, it was recommended that legislation be passed creating a formal consumer's council to be appointed by the Governor or the attorney general, which would continue to examine problems of the consumer and recommend legislative solutions.

New Jersey Consumer Frauds Bureau. The Consumer Frauds Bureau of the state of New Jersey issues a *Buyers' Guide* and urges consumers to bring their problems to this bureau, organized under the supervision of the attorney general. In June, 1961, an act was approved which tightened the provisions shielding consumers against fraud.

Consumer Protection in New York State. In January, 1955, Governor Averell Harriman of New York created the Office of Consumer Counsel—the first such office in any state. He appointed Dr. Persia Campbell, a foremost consumer economist, to the head post, gave her cabinet status, and assigned broad responsibilities to the office. She was to "understand the problems of the consumer" and "defend and advance the interests of consumers on every front and at every level." Thus, her field of interest seemingly was almost as broad as government itself.

But the newly formed office was eliminated by the next governor of the state, Nelson A. Rockefeller, who turned its functions over to the Bureau of Consumer Frauds, under the control of the attorney general. Nevertheless, the experience of this short-lived office contributed heavily to the current movement by other states to take governmental action on behalf of the consumer.[3]

One of the major functions of the Office of Consumer Counsel when it was in operation was to promote favorable legislation in the interest of the consuming public of New York State, and it undertook a watchdog role toward all legislation, to the end that the public welfare aspects of any proposed bill would be called to the attention of both the Legislature and the Governor. Sometimes this meant opposing, in whole or in part, legislation backed by the lobbies of special interest groups.

To cite one example, in 1957, the Office of Consumer Counsel succeeded in having the Legislature enact an "all goods bill." This new law for the first time systematically established many types of protection for the consumer. It makes mandatory a full disclosure, not only of the cost of the item that is being purchased, but also of all additional charges.[4]

In addition to promoting legislative measures, Dr. Campbell accepted the responsibility of assisting other departments in the development or amendment of programs that had special consumer significance.

The forum method was employed to get the facts and opinions of both the consumer and the expert. Three different conference levels were established: (1) a state Consumer Advisory Committee, (2) a governor's conference to which representatives of various economic groups (producers, distributors, merchants, advertising and media representatives, as well as consumers) were invited, and (3) community conferences in different localities throughout the state. The information obtained in these ways was not only used in the Office of Consumer Counsel but was passed on to other state regulatory agencies.

Soon after the new office had become established, it became apparent that an active research program was needed. Besides guiding the formulation of legislative proposals and compiling new statistical information, research efforts provided material for a large consumer education program. When Dr. Campbell's progress report was published in 1958, nearly a million pieces of literature had been distributed. Dramatic skits had been made available to schools and clubs. Radio and television broadcasts were conducted, and some two hundred speaking engagements had been fulfilled.

Dr. Campbell also emphasized that one of the principal responsibilities of her office was to coordinate and strengthen the consumer services already being performed by existing agencies and departments of the New York State government. Even though the scope was broad, and many other state agencies had already been assigned to areas of consumer interest, she

[3] *Christian Science Monitor,* Boston, Jan. 9, 1961, p. 3.

[4] Senate Subcommittee of the Committee on Banking and Currency, *Consumer Credit Labeling Hearings,* 1960, pp. 104, 113.

felt that the Office of Consumer Counsel in no sense competed with, or infringed on, these other jurisdictions.[5] Instead, she stressed that it was the function of the consumer office to broaden existing consumer welfare programs and to provide the meeting ground for interagency cooperation on problems of mutual concern.

Several lessons were learned by New York State in this experience. It was found that consumer representation in government would not work if delegated to any agency concerned with the problems of any particular segment of the population. Another point was that consumer representation is not effective unless it is given rank in the governmental hierarchy and support from the executive office. Still another, and even more important one, is that no consumer spokesman can long speak effectively without advice from and contact with consumers themselves.[6]

Many of the responsibilities previously assigned to the Office of Consumer Counsel were transferred to the Bureau of Consumer Frauds, whose membership includes various assistants, investigators, and statisticians. The Bureau of Consumer Frauds has been granted the power to issue subpoenas and investigate, to issue injunctions in "bait advertising" cases, to issue injunctions in persistent business fraud cases, and to obtain a temporary injunction pending decisions in quo warranto matters.[7]

Fraudulent selling practices have been the chief target of the bureau's activities. And the promulgation of codes for specialized groups has been the corrective measure most frequently attempted—codes of ethics plus court cases. Attorney General Louis J. Lefkowitz had, as an aid to his consumer program, an organized committee of one hundred housewives serving as a voluntary advisory group.

Consumer Advisory Council in Washington State. The state of Washington has a Consumer Advisory Council attached to the office of the attorney general. Bills embodying the legislative program of the council were passed during the 1961 legislative session.

The program included a bill dealing with monopolies and restraints of trade in intrastate commerce, also a bill tightening the regulations relating to false and deceptive advertising. A division of the attorney general's office was set up in Seattle to enforce the new Consumer Protection Act.

Observations on State Consumer Programs. When observing state governmental programs to advance the position of the consumer, it is apparent that pattern conformity has not been the rule. California has experienced a degree of success with its Office of Consumer Counsel, directly under the Governor. Other states have had some success in establishing a Bureau

[5] *Consumer Reports,* November, 1958.
[6] *Ibid.*
[7] Paul L. Adams, *Report of Attorney General's Conference on Consumer Frauds,* State of Michigan, Sept. 23, 1960, p. 9.

of Consumer Frauds. Still others have developed effective forms of consumer councils.

Fundamental to any consideration of consumer legislation would be clarification of objectives and functions of a state consumer program. The following ideas should be considered.

First, the gaps that exist in the way the state serves the consumer interest should be identified, and a suitable specialist representing the consumer should be available to challenge special-interest groups. The fact that producers are also consumers does not guarantee that the consumer side will be considered in legislation.

There is need to coordinate the existing agencies or responsibilities already assigned to numerous state departments or offices. This will promote efficiency and effectiveness in protecting the consumer interest.

Education of the consumer should be one feature of any state-sponsored program. An active research program on behalf of consumers is necessary, along with regular reports to the public, the Governor, and the Legislature.

No spokesman for the consumer can be effective without regular contact with the consumers he represents. Therefore, conferences and workshops and the use of advisory consumer councils are indispensable.

The organizational model for state consumer protection might have one of the following patterns established by statute, executive order, or legislative resolution.

1. Consumer counsel in the office of the Governor, as in California
2. Consumer protection counsel, bureau, or section in the office of the state attorney general as in California, Massachusetts, Michigan, and New York
3. Consumer advisory council, an appointed group of consumer-minded citizens representing various organizations and educational institutions in the state, as in Massachusetts
4. Interdepartmental consumer interest committee, under the chairmanship of a consumer counsel and made up of representatives of consumer interest agencies, commissions, departments, and authorities of the state
5. Joint select consumer interest committee, made up of members of similarly named committees of the two Houses of the state Legislature

States might also try the technique of conferences. In July, 1960, to illustrate, the state attorneys general met to discuss the consumer protection activities of their offices. Individual states can profit by following the example of Michigan, where the state attorney general has held annual conferences on consumer protection, attended by government officials and by representatives of the public, including such consumer interest groups as credit unions, cooperatives, consumer associations, labor unions, and consumer-minded housewives.

In California, Maryland, Massachusetts, Minnesota, and New York, an assistant attorney general has been assigned to head a consumer division in that office. In some states, this unit is called the Bureau of Consumer Frauds and Protection. In New York State, for example, this bureau has been successful in investigating and prosecuting frauds against consumers, many of which were brought to the attention of the bureau by consumer complaints.

For the states, there are already such Federal models as the Food, Drug, and Cosmetic Act, and the Food and Drug Administration. Another prototype is the Model Weights and Measures Law, prepared by the National Conference of Weights and Measures. Three published surveys, however, throw light on what the states are doing to protect consumers in the fields of food and drugs and of weights and measures.

1. Consumer Protection Activities (Part I—Regulation of Weights and Measures by State and Local Governments). U.S. Congress, House Subcommittee of the Committee on Government Operations, 87th Congress, 2d Session. Washington, D.C.: Government Printing Office, 1962.

2. Consumer Protection Activities of State Governments (Part I—The Regulation of Drugs and Related Products). U.S. Congress, House Committee on Government Operations, 88th Congress, 1st Session. Washington, D.C.: Government Printing Office, 1963.

3. A private study, *Second National Survey of Weights and Measures Legislation, Administration, and Enforcement*, 1963, by Dr. Leland J. Gordon of Denison University, Granville, Ohio.

Handicaps of State Consumer Agencies. Persons closely connected with state consumer offices, agencies, and departments generally agree on the following handicaps. The two most severe handicaps are inadequate appropriations and personnel. There are other limitations of consumer protection, such as intense political opposition from organized business interests at times, and a lack of active interest on the part of citizens in general. It takes a dramatic consumer case or incident to stir the public into action. Despite these and other handicaps, progress is being made in better consumer protection at the state level.

Private, State, and Local Consumer Associations

The state and local private consumer associations and councils are still relatively small in terms of potential membership and always short of needed financing. Yet they have demonstrated the power of active, informed, and dedicated groups in protecting and advancing consumer welfare. Currently, there are active consumer associations in four states —California, Maryland, Massachusetts, and Michigan. There are four fairly active local associations—Chicago, Cincinnati, New York City, and St. Louis.

It is not impossible to report all the consumer protection services provided by villages, cities, townships, and counties through their local governments. Local executive offices are usually responsible for law enforcement, public health, weights and measures, and low-cost public housing, to mention only four areas. The organizational model for state governments, listed in the previous section, might have ideas for city governments that are planning additional consumer protection.

Association of California Consumers. The Association of California Consumers was formed in 1959 as an independent consumer organization, its membership being concentrated principally in the San Francisco Bay area and, to a lesser extent, in the Los Angeles area. But members are spread from San Diego to Humboldt County—a distance of well over 700 miles. Plans for the association include:

1. Surveying packaging and weights and measures as the principal area of concern in 1963
2. Developing exhibits and a program kit for use in speaking to groups
3. Publishing a bulletin dealing with consumer problems and association activities
4. Developing area chairmen, responsible for organization in their region, together with materials to assist them and targets to aim for (One possible avenue of approach is the development of local consumer associations to be affiliated with the state-wide organization. This has already taken place in San Diego and Sacramento. The state-wide organization might ultimately be a federation rendering educational, news, and legislative services.)
5. Exhibiting at the California State Fair in Sacramento

On December 1 and 2, 1962, the third annual convention of the Association of California Consumers was held in San Francisco. The focus of the convention was on the growth and effectiveness of the organization as an advocate of consumer protection at both the state and national levels.

Maryland Consumers Council. The Maryland Consumers Council was organized at Rockville, Maryland, in May, 1961. The spark came from the Co-op Congress, an elected body representing 23,000 members of Greenbelt Consumer Services—the largest consumer cooperative in the United States. As stated in its articles of incorporation, the purpose of the council is to provide information and educational services to consumers, to develop areas of agreement, to offer assistance and consultation, to promote and perform research, and to encourage improvement and enforcement of pertinent laws for the benefit of consumers. A distinguished technical advisory committee has been recruited from the large number of well-qualified technical people in the Baltimore-Washington area.

In 1962, the council had a successful consumer workshop attended by 72 representatives from 20 organizations, including the Maryland Farm

Bureau, AFL-CIO, the Grange, several cooperatives including a rural electric cooperative, Group Health, Greenbelt Consumer Services, Maryland Home Economics Association, women's clubs, and the Weights and Measures Association.

The council has been active on only one legislative issue—the Truth-in-lending Bill—but it has begun to have some influence on the thinking of the state government on consumers' problems, according to a report issued by the council.

Massachusetts Consumer Association. The Advisory Consumer Council sponsored a 1962 summer conference, at which the Massachusetts Consumer Association was organized. This association provides research information and educational services to consumers and encourages sound legislation in the interest of the consumer.

In February, 1963, the legislative committee of the association held an open meeting of the members to discuss legislation filed in the 1963 session of the general court, specifically, An Act Establishing a Consumer Council. On October 31, 1963, the Governor of Massachusetts signed a bill establishing a Consumer Council in the Office of the Governor. This legislative victory climaxed a ten-year effort of the Massachusetts Consumer Association to establish a consumer council in the Governor's office.

Michigan Consumer Association. On January 21, 1960, the Michigan Consumer Association was incorporated. Active in initiating the organization were members of the faculties of five universities and members of the League of Women Voters, of the AFL-CIO, of the Detroit Better Business Bureau, and of the Michigan Credit Union League. The purpose of the association is to provide research information and educational services to consumers, to develop areas of agreement, to offer assistance and consultation, and to encourage sound legislation in the interest of the consumer.

Dr. Milton J. Huber, then executive secretary of the association, has reported the following activities.

1. Sponsoring consumer workshops throughout the state
2. Preparing a series of articles for mass distribution entitled *Our Daily Bread*
3. Promoting better consumer education in colleges and universities in the state
4. Consulting with the Governor on legislation vital to consumers
5. Testifying before legislative committees
6. Researching commercial debt-pooling businesses (consumer debt counseling for a fee)
7. Promoting a consumer counsel to the Governor's office

Chicago: Advisory Committee on Consumer Education. The Mayor's Advisory Committee on Consumer Education had its initial meeting on November 20, 1958. This committee is an outgrowth of a consumer education program carried on by the Chicago Department of Weights and Measures for more than eight years. Once confined chiefly to PTA groups and women's clubs, the program has been progressively broadened to include member organizations of the Chicago Federation of Settlement Houses, the Association of Community Councils, newcomer groups organized under the auspices of the Mayor's Commission on Human Relations, Chicago Housing Authority community organizations, Americanization classes for non-English-speaking residents of Chicago, and similar groups.

The object of the committee is to study consumer problems and to bring these problems and their solutions to as wide a Chicago audience as possible. The public information subcommittee planned a series of TV shows on various aspects of the consumer problem: housing, food buying, installment plans, money management.

Consumer Conference of Greater Cincinnati. The Consumer Conference of Greater Cincinnati began modestly in depression days (1934) and has grown to a membership of approximately six hundred. Until 1958, it was under the leadership of Maude Jackson. Though it is an independent consumer organization, it has close links with the School of Home Economics of the University of Cincinnati and meets on the campus of that institution. Each month the conference publishes a news bulletin containing items of consumer interest and help. Monthly industrial visits are made to business firms in and near Cincinnati.

Each year the organization has at least one consumer program on the local educational TV and radio stations. It works closely with the Better Business Bureau, the Retail Merchants Association, the Food and Drug Administration, and many local business firms. Eight or nine monthly meetings are held each year at the University of Cincinnati. For a number of years the conference had weekly radio programs with timely information for the consumer. Joint retailer-consumer committees discuss common consumer problems, such as advertising, labeling, warranties, and credit charges.

Metropolitan New York Consumer Council. In June, 1959, the Metropolitan New York Consumer Council held its organizational meeting. Present were representatives from some 36 organizations, such as credit unions, labor organizations, church groups, consumer cooperatives, and family service agencies. Since then, the council has worked on an informal basis under the direction of a steering committee.

The purposes of the council are:

1. To bring together organizations and individuals who have an interest in the advancement of consumer knowledge and welfare.
2. To stimulate and aid consumer information and education programs that assist families with money management and buying problems.

3. To express the consumer point of view to the executives and legislators of the city, state, and Federal governments.

Since the council was formed, it has carried on a number of important educational programs—for example, it has conducted a nine-week consumer information course for educational directors and financial counselors of union locals, credit unions, churches, settlement houses, and housing cooperatives. Among the subjects covered were housing, family money management, shopping for food, health care, and family insurance protection. Working in cooperation with the New York City Housing Authority, council members offered 12 consumer courses in the city's low-income public housing units.

The council has requested action against consumer frauds in short-weighting of meat, gasoline, oil fuel, and in improper labeling, and has advocated a consumer counsel in the mayor's office and reinstatement of the Office of Consumer Counsel at the state level.

St. Louis Consumer Federation. The St. Louis Consumer Federation was originally set up early in 1933 by Prof. Paul H. Douglas when he was an official of the NRA, long before he became United States Senator from Illinois. This organization has continued to aid consumers to become more intelligent buyers and to promote social action in the consumer's interest. It publishes a newsletter on consumer concerns, holds public meetings and consumer conferences, has taken a stand on state and Federal issues, and is vigorous in promoting consumer education. The federation protested the introduction of a bill in St. Louis that would permit removal of the pasteurization date from milk containers.

The purposes of this federation are:

1. To keep consumers well informed on subjects that concern their expenses and therefore their standard of living
2. To keep consumer interest organized
3. To make consumers politically effective
4. To secure representation at the Federal, state, and local levels

Most of the federation's activities have been concerned with standard milk ordinances, a milk strike to reduce prices, nutrition courses, informative labeling and grading of canned goods, unsanitary bakeries, rodent control, inflation, credit and installment buying, and the high price of drugs.

Voluntary Consumer Organizations

There are voluntary professional consumer organizations of considerable importance in the United States. Five professional consumer associations are functioning at the present time—The Council on Consumer Information, The Center for Consumer Affairs, The Consumer Research Institute, the AFL-CIO Community Service Activities consumer program, and The Centre Consumers Association.

It is of historical interest that the efforts in 1948 to establish the Consumer Education Association (which published the *Journal of Consumer Education*), The Institute for Consumer Education at Stephens College (1937 to 1942), and the National Association of Consumers all came to an end within a few years following their first birthday.

The Council on Consumer Information. The Council on Consumer Information (CCI) was born at a conference of 21 educators in the consumer field on the University of Minnesota campus in April, 1953. The Preamble of the Constitution of the CCI reads: "This organization is concerned with problems of our economy considered from the point of view of the ultimate consumer of goods and services. . . . People, as consumers, need information to use the economic resources available to them in a way to secure maximum satisfaction. . . ."

The need for the council grew out of the fact that teachers and research workers interested in consumption specialize in many fields, including economics, sociology, psychology, education, natural sciences, home economics, business administration, and public welfare. Publications on consumer problems come not only from educational institutions but also from business, consumer, labor, farm, and government groups. It is difficult to keep abreast of the contributions from all these sources.

The CCI is politically nonpartisan and takes no stand on any issue of public policy. It brings together significant contributions from many consumer areas by the following activities.

1. Publishing a newsletter
2. Publishing a discussion pamphlet series with the pros and cons of issues vital to consumers
3. Acting as a clearinghouse in distributing consumer materials and publications
4. Sponsoring an annual conference for informal exchange of consumer information and ideas

Typical council pamphlets are:

Consumers Look at Farm Price Policies
Consumers Look at Fair Trade
What You Should Know about the Law of Estates
Helping You Plan Your Life Insurance Program
Consumers Look at Burial Practices
The Consumer and Antitrust

Watch Your Weights and Measures
Bringing the Consumer Point of View into Government
Consumers Look at Discount Houses
Consumers Look at Federal Protective Services
Consumers Can Protect Their Own Health
How to Choose Your Doctor, Hospital, and Health Insurance
Consumers Look at Deceptive Packaging

The council completed its tenth annual conference in 1964. Selected proceedings are published for each annual conference. Some of the most significant thinking in the field of consumer welfare is included in the official papers presented at these conferences.

Among the council's 1,200 members from every section of the United States are leaders in college and university teaching and research in consumption; leaders in local, state, and Federal consumer protective agencies; many representatives of business firms vitally interested in the consumer; representatives of consumer associations, credit unions, cooperatives, labor unions, women's clubs; also housewives and college students.

The CCI is, in fact, the only nationwide professional consumer educational organization in the United States. Unfortunately, its financing is inadequate, with a $10,000 annual budget. Consequently, the council depends on a part-time paid executive secretary, with headquarters at Colorado State College, Greeley, Colorado. Despite its limited financial resources and modest paid memberships, the CCI, next to Consumers Union, is the most influential consumer organization in this country.

The Center for Consumer Affairs. The Center for Consumer Affairs was established in March, 1963, by the University of Wisconsin Extension Division. Dr. Gordon E. Bivens of the economics department is the present director of the center. Its objectives are:

1. To identify and analyze problems of concern to consumers
2. To develop among consumers an understanding of the economic system of the United States
3. To foster appreciation of the consumer's responsibilities and opportunities in the economy

The Center for Consumer Affairs plans the following activities.

1. Sponsoring workshops, clinics, and institutes on consumer affairs
2. Offering credit and noncredit courses on consumer financing, consumer marketing, and family finance
3. Sponsoring action-oriented research on topics like consumer credit, burial costs, trading stamps, family financial counseling, and legal protection for consumers

4. Developing the usual aids for use in consumer education

5. Conducting experimental work in family financial counseling and training of counselors

Since consumer affairs have many dimensions, the center plans to use people trained in economics, law, social work, psychology, home economics, communications, sociology, political science, and possibly others.

The Consumer Research Institute. The Consumer Research Institute was established in 1961 with headquarters at San Francisco State College and with Dr. Roy C. Cave as the director. This nonprofit consumer research organization has held consumer conferences and has an ambitious program. The institute expects to carry on research in the following areas of major consumer problems.

1. Investigating the buying and saving habits of the middle-income group

2. Determining through the use of tests, questionnaires, interviews, and observations how consumers behave in the market place

3. Determining how consumers plan their income before buying expensive consumer goods (a car, air conditioning)

4. Preparing annotated sources of consumer information

5. Developing programs for training consumer teachers or counselors

6. Setting up a consumer information center or library

7. Establishing an adult consumer education program

8. Developing interesting and effective teaching standards and materials in the field of consumer education

At the 1962 conference, nationally known experts read papers on such topics as advertising, consumer sovereignty, credit unions, installment credit, food and drug protection, regulation of insecticides, weights and measures, deceptive packaging, cooperatives, antitrust legislation, frauds and misrepresentation, small loans, and private aids to consumers. All the papers dealt with these problems as they related to the state of California.

Following the conference, the board of directors of the institute prepared a summary and recommendation paper that was to be used to "stimulate subsequent steps in the direction of improvements in existing legislation and its enforcement and also new legislation where needed." [8]

In 1961, the institute published *Cooperative Development and Outlook in East and Central Africa* (56 pages) and has also issued a reprint of *Comparison of Consumer Credit Costs*, originally published by the California Credit Union League. *The California Consumer* is published quarterly.

AFL-CIO Community Service Activities. The Community Service Activities

[8] *Proceedings of the Conference on Consumer Protection in California*, Aug. 28–30, 1962, p. i; Jan., 1963.

has existed for many years. The consumer program, however, was officially opened in 1959 when the AFL-CIO executive council adopted the following resolutions.

The AFL-CIO Community Service Activities recognized the importance of meeting the personal and family needs of union members as consumers of goods and services. . . . A more concentrated effort is needed to provide esssential information to both union members and their spouses on the general subjects of how to stretch the dollar. . . . It is recommended that . . . counseling be extended to include counseling in these consumer problems. . . .[9]

The consumer program of the Community Service Activities has three important parts, according to Julius F. Rothman, staff representative of the AFL-CIO: (1) consumer information courses, (2) consumer conferences, and (3) consumer clinics.[10]

The consumer information courses generally consist of about eight weekly sessions, each lasting from two to three hours and open to husbands and wives. The courses vary depending on the needs of the group, but most families want instruction on spending plans, buying techniques in general, specific buying skills in clothing and appliances, food marketing and nutrition, credit and installment buying, legal consumer protection, health care, and insurance.

Consumer conferences are set up for the purpose of discussing an immediate pressing consumer problem—cost of credit, garnishments, cost of drugs—and taking a position in regard to the problem.

The consumer clinics are direct services to persons who are in trouble and in need of legal or other expert guidance on garnishment and wage assignments, home repairs, health care debts, correspondence school contracts, frauds, or credit problems. A panel of experts is present to advise. Any interested person can attend these clinics.

With nearly 13 million union members, an effective consumer education program could be of inestimable value in promoting consumer welfare and in conserving family resources. But there are many problems to overcome —problems that have plagued the consumer movement in general—such as inertia, inadequate formal education, years of poor consumption habits, and failure to recognize that dollars won in collective bargaining can be lost in unwise consumer decisions, or that money saved in the market place can increase the family's standard of living. One of the major difficulties was the recruiting of well-informed instructors and clinicians.

The Centre Consumers Association. In June, 1963, the Board of Directors

[9] *AFL-CIO Federationist,* January, 1959.
[10] *Selected Proceedings of Sixth Annual Conference of the Council on Consumer Information,* 1960, pp. 86–91.

of Consumers Union decided to encourage the development of a local consumer group as an experiment to create and encourage consumer consciousness. It was decided to try an area where there was a large potential group of the educated middle class of people. State College, Pennsylvania, was selected and a small sum of money was made available.

One year later, June 3, 1964, The Centre Consumers Association was an operating group with elected officers, a constitution, regular dues, 127 members, and an official organ, *High Times*.

There are four active committees. (1) The Survey Committee designs questionnaires to secure information for committees. (2) The Product Pricing Committee checks and reports to the membership the availability and prices on selected products sold in the community. (3) The Health, Education, and Welfare Committee had two projects going in 1964–1965 —the content labeling on prescription drugs and the sanitary status of local restaurants. (4) The Services Committee for its first project made a comparison of the services and cost available through each of the four local banks. A survey on home repair services and costs was also reported to the membership via *High Times*.

The idea of local consumer groups is not a new one. There are several very active and successful local consumer organizations in Great Britain. There is no good reason why they should not be successful in the United States. After all, most of us would not object to receiving information on prices and quality on consumer goods and services in the local community.

Consumer Protection a Three-way Partnership. In this country, consumer protection is a three-way proposition, involving the consumer's wise management, producer efforts to serve the consumer efficiently and ethically, and effective government consumer protection and regulation in the market place. As the first requirement, all consumers should become better informed and serious about their own responsibilities as consumers.

Some consumer problems can be resolved by improved individual consumer skills, information, and attitudes. Other consumer problems can be resolved only by group or social action. In some consumer matters, action is needed on both individual and group levels.

On the individual level, consumers can improve their economic competence and satisfaction by:

1. Carefully considering what they want out of life
2. Knowing what is available to meet their needs and desires
3. Learning how to select the most suitable quality at the best price
4. Consciously supporting economic distribution channels that are efficient and are working for the best interest of consumers as well as producers
5. Acquiring the ability to use and care for goods to the best advantage

6. Improving their skill in dealing with salespersons and service store personnel
7. Using advertising intelligently to prevent being exploited
8. Insisting on adequate information concerning all products and services

All this is important. But many of these goals can be achieved best by working through properly qualified private and public organizations and agencies. It is apparent that the role of government in economic affairs is bound to assume increased importance. Consumers must make up their minds about the issues and then do something about promoting them.

Some of the keenest consumer observers have said that the United States has glorified production and disparaged the activity of intelligent consumption. We ignore the fact that the national welfare is determined ultimately by how well money is spent rather than by how much is produced. As the marketing system becomes more complex, the most sophisticated consumers still remain amateurs in the art of spending money. It is at this point that more effective consumer protection is needed on all levels of government, so that consumers can make intelligent decisions in the market place.

Consumers must also be concerned about a desirable balance between consumer protection and producer interest. The nation can consume only what is produced. Consumers, as well as producers, gain when investors, workers, farmers, retailers, and business in general discover new ways to increase production and to introduce new products and services. Consumers have a common interest with ethical businessmen and should work with them to improve standards in the market place.

A three-way partnership of prudent consumers, ethical producers, and effective government protection of consumer welfare is a goal worth striving for.

QUESTIONS FOR DISCUSSION

1. What are the advantages of having an Office of Consumer Counsel in the states of California and Massachusetts?

2. If you live in New York State, try to find out why Governor Nelson Rockefeller eliminated the Office of Consumer Counsel established by Governor Averell Harriman.

3. What has the Department of Consumer Protection done for consumers in Connecticut?

4. What are the accomplishments of the Advisory Consumer Council in Massachusetts?

5. What has the Consumer Protection Division in Michigan accomplished since it was established in 1961?

6. What has the Consumer Protection Advisory Council in Minnesota accomplished to date? (Minnesota students may like to follow through on the six

consumer bills that were proposed for the 1963 session of the Minnesota Legislature.)

7. Which state has the best consumer protection organization? Why?

8. Why is it difficult to organize consumer protection in a state?

9. Would you join a consumer association if you had one in your state? Give your reasons for joining or not joining.

10. How do you account for the fact that there are only about four active local consumer organizations?

11. After reading some of the publications of the Council on Consumer Information, what are your conclusions about the organization's efforts to aid the consumer? Would you join the CCI?

12. If you live in California, are you a member of the California Consumer Association or the Consumer Research Institute? Why or why not?

13. Why is consumer sovereignty important in our economy?

ACTIVITY PROBLEMS

1. If you have a consumer organization in your community, invite its president and other enthusiastic members to attend a class discussion of its purposes and activities and the results of its combined efforts. Possibly the class might attend one or more of its general and committee meetings. That is where you will see the best in organized consumer education functioning on the local level.

2. Think of all the ways in which people might learn how to develop pride in being intelligent and skilled consumers. Does this pride tend to decrease as the family income increases? If a manufacturer takes pride in his products and an athlete takes pride in excellent performance, why should not an individual take pride in being a good consumer?

3. It is said that producers voluntarily change their conduct to the advantage of consumers only when such changes further their private ends. Discuss this assumption with several businessmen. Report their reactions to the class, and open a class discussion of the issue.

4. In this century, the idea of the "welfare state" has become fairly popular throughout the world. Even England, long a stronghold of individual liberty, has gone far in the use of collective action in economic affairs. Some people in our country believe that government should protect the welfare of all the people. Others are more friendly to the idea of individual responsibility for one's own welfare. There are, of course, several economic roads before us. How to choose among the major lines of political-economic policy is one problem of major importance facing consumer citizens in our country. How would you cast your vote? It might be wise to do some reading before making a decision. (See William Van Til, *Economic Roads for American Democracy*. New York: McGraw-Hill Book Company, 1947; Harold G. Moulton, *The Dynamic Economy*. Washington, D.C.: The Brookings Institution, 1950.)

5. The statement is made that the foundation of consumer education is to (a) help each of us to develop a sense of values, (b) determine what we most want out of life, (c) set our goals and see them in proper balance, then (d) act

according to our developed principles. What are your reactions to the above point of view? Support your views in an objective manner.

6. After examining the organizational models of consumer protection in California, Massachusetts, Connecticut, and Michigan, which one do you think protects the consumer best?

7. Prepare a paper on consumer protection legislation and enforcement in your state.

SUGGESTED READINGS

AFL-CIO Community Service Activities (in consumer programs). *Safeguarding* and *Five Objectives* (and other pamphlets), New York.

Association of California Consumers. *The California Consumer* (official organ), San Francisco.

Brecher, Ruth, and Brecher, Edward. "How to Avoid Being Cheated by the Pound, Gallon, or Yard," *Redbook*, August, 1960.

Brown, Edmund G. *A Consumer Policy for California*. Sacramento: State Printing Office, 1963.

Brunn, George. "Problems of Organizing Consumers," Selected Proceedings of Eighth Annual Conference of the Council on Consumer Information. Greeley, Colo.: Colorado State College, 1962.

Campbell, Persia. "Consumer Representation in State Government," Selected Proceedings of Fifth Annual Conference of Council on Consumer Information. Greeley, Colo.: Colorado State College, 1959.

Chicago, The Mayor's Advisory Committee on Consumer Education. "Betty Budget Series" (and other material for radio and TV).

Consumer Conference of Greater Cincinnati. *Consumer Conference News*. Cincinnati: School of Home Economics, University of Cincinnati.

Consumer Reports. "Consumer Representation in Government," November, 1958.

Consumer Research Institute. *Proceedings of the Conference on Consumer Protection in California*. San Francisco: San Francisco State College, 1962.

Council on Consumer Information. *Newsletter*, "Bringing the Consumer Point of View into Government," 1958; "Watch Your Weights and Measures," 1957; "Selected Proceedings of Annual Conferences," especially 1960, 1961, 1962, 1963. Greeley, Colo.: Colorado State College.

Gordon, Leland J. *Second National Survey of State Weights and Measures Legislation, Administration, and Enforcement*. Granville, Ohio: Denison University, 1964.

Hamilton, David. *Consumer Protection in New Mexico*, Publication 54. Albuquerque: Division of Government Research, University of New Mexico, 1958.

Hayhurst, Donald E. *Protection of Consumers in West Virginia*. Morgantown, W.Va.: Bureau of Government Research, 1959.

Lampman, Robert J. "An Appraisal of Consumer Protection," *Journal of Home Economics*, September, 1962, pp. 555–563.

Nelson, Helen E. *Consumer Council News Exchange*, Office of Consumer Council.

Sacramento, Calif.: Governor's Office, State Capitol. Also, *Consumer Council*, report of the first two years; "The Consumer Looks at Basic Issues," address before the Association of California Consumers, Nov. 4, 1961.

New York Metropolitan Consumer Council, New York.

St. Louis Consumer Federation. *Newsletter*, St. Louis.

U.S. Congress. *Consumer Protection Activities of State Governments: Part 1. The Regulation of Drugs and Related Products. Part 2. The Regulation of Foods and Related Products.* House Committee on Government Operations, 88th Congress, 1st Session, H. Rept. no. 445. Washington, D.C.: Government Printing Office, 1963.

U.S. Congress. *Consumer Protection Activities: Part I. Regulation of Weights and Measures by State and Local Governments.* Hearings before a Subcommittee on Government Operations, House, 87th Congress, 2d Session. Washington, D.C.: Government Printing Office, 1962.

18

THE INTERNATIONAL CONSUMER MOVEMENT[1]

Intelligent American consumers should be interested in and knowledgeable about the consumer movement in the rest of the world. There is a rapidly developing European consumer movement. An unprecedented number of consumer protection organizations has emerged in Europe, some stimulated by the cooperative movement, some given governmental assistance, and some arising from independent efforts. The same forces that have brought into existence consumer organizations in Europe have spread to Canada where the Consumers Association of Canada has embarked on a consumer testing movement. The consumer movement has likewise spread to the Near East, Iceland, Australia, New Zealand, and Japan.

Although the structures of the consumer organizations of the world vary, all have one central element in common—to furnish impartial advice and recommendations concerning trade-marked consumer goods. Consumers in all countries are increasingly angered at being misled as to product claims and are bewildered by competing advertising slogans. The spectacular advance of new technologies has created a vacuum in product information which has not been filled by producers. The consumer movement forms a practical answer that can improve living standards by directing consumers toward meritorious products and away from those that contain virtues which exist only in the promoter's imagination.

[1] The sources of information on the consumer movements in the world are many. The author's visit to countries in Western Europe and to Japan in 1962 and 1963 gave him valuable information and insight. Much information comes from unpublished sources. Notable among the unpublished sources is the material collected by Dr. Colston E. Warne, who is of Amherst College and president of Consumers Union of U.S., Inc. Dr. Warne has been most generous in permitting the author to use his excellent material on the consumer movements of the world. The consumer organizations in various countries have also been generous in their efforts to be informative and to discuss common problems.

The heart of the modern consumer movement lies in accurate testing and more testing, and in the issuing of reports on testing that will guide consumers to a higher standard of living.

The consumer movement, however, is more than a testing organization. It is also an educational organization—a new and significant phase of adult education. It punctures false claims, it spreads knowledge of new quality products, it harnesses science for the service of the buyer. The consumer movement also helps restore the capacity of the competitive system to reward those companies that are producing better products. The central aim of the consumer movement is to help organize the economy in ways that will best serve the consumer interest.

Another purpose of the consumer movement is that of becoming a countervailing power in legislation that will afford better protection to all consumers against the more common hazards of the market place, such as elaborate packaging, extravagantly promoted brand names, deceptive weights, improper measurements, restraints on retail competition, fictitious prices, unknown credit terms, restrictive patenting and licensing arrangements, tariff barriers and many other impediments to competition.

Just as the International Labor Office for more than forty years has been championing the development of international labor standards, the international consumer movement has an obligation to insist that a parallel international organization be developed to promote international consumer standards. Just as the earlier legislation insisted that water supplies be sanitary and that food be unadulterated, so in this period of chemical revolution, new social safeguards on the social front must be developed.

Types of Consumer Movements. Consumer movements throughout the world are of three different types.

In the United Kingdom, Australia, The Netherlands, Belgium, Canada, and France, as in the United States, consumer testing is undertaken without government support. The private consumer testing agencies in these countries have been most careful to steer clear of business entanglements. They have recruited technical personnel to give impartial assessments of products bought on the open market. The most rapidly growing testing agency among these newer movements, Consumers' Association, Ltd., in the United Kingdom, had a membership of over 400,000 at the end of its seventh year, 1964.

The second type of consumer organization undertakes consumer testing through government subsidy. The two most vigorous examples of this type are Norway and New Zealand. Both of these product-testing groups have been in a position to publish comparative product ratings as well as to handle consumer complaints. In New Zealand, the government has linked the testing facilities of its Bureau of Standards and of its universities with the consumer testing movement and hopes to develop a quasi-autonomous consumer testing movement supported by voluntary subscriptions. This effort, like the Norwegian, has as its basic objective the governmental establishment of a nonpartisan consumer movement.

The third type of consumer agency that has emerged in the international picture is the extension of the work of standards associations into the field of comparative product reporting. Notable examples in this field are in England and in Japan. In Japan, until 1963, the newly formed Japan Consumers' Association used a combination of government subsidy, subscriptions to its magazine, donations by manufacturers of products to be tested, and government testing agencies. In 1963, the JCA made a serious effort to reduce possible outside influences when it decided to purchase in the open market the products to be tested. It remains to be seen whether this association can demonstrate complete independence and objectivity and yet become self-sustaining.

Most of the organizations in the nearly two dozen countries described in this chapter deserve more attention than space permits, but the brief summaries will give a picture of the great progress made on behalf of consumers in these countries. There is ample reason to believe that other countries, notably many of the newly formed nations in Africa, will also be active in promoting the consumer interest.

International Organization of Consumers Unions (IOCU)

Dr. Colston Warne, President of Consumers Union of the United States, was largely responsible for promoting the creation of an International Organization of Consumers Unions. After many preliminary discussions with consumer leaders in Europe and elsewhere, the Consumers Union of the United States appropriated funds for an organizing meeting of consumer union officials at The Hague, Netherlands. On April 1, 1960, the International Organization of Consumers Unions was made a *stichting* (foundation) under Dutch Law, and it functions in accordance with legal regulations. The registered office is at The Hague, Netherlands. The financial resources consist of the *Stichting* Fund, contributions from members, and the sale of its publications.

The IOCU is affiliated with the United Nations as a Non-Governmental Organization (NGO). Applications are pending for liaison or advisory status with special organizations of the United Nations, including United Nations Educational, Scientific and Cultural Organization (UNESCO), Food and Agriculture Organization of the United Nations (FAO), and World Health Organization (WHO). The IOCU had consultative status with the Economic and Social Council and UNESCO in 1964.

The IOCU has an authorized observer at all meetings of the Bureau Européen des Unions Consommateurs. The BEUC is composed of the

IOCU member organizations and other consumer groups in the European Economic Community (EEC—Common Market). The EEC authorities have agreed to give special consideration to consumer problems presented by a committee composed of authorized representatives of four groups of organizations: consumers unions, trade unions, family organizations, and consumer cooperatives.

The nature of the activities that are to receive the attention of the IOCU can be seen from the agenda of its Second Biennial Conference at Brussels, in March, 1962. The conference included sessions on ways to set up a consumers' union; on international collaboration; on how to compile a brand list; on setting up testing laboratories; on consumer education and cooperation with schools and other organizations; on relations with the communications media; on subscription administration; on printing, editing, artwork; on ways to handle complaints; and on copyrights, translations, and legal responsibility.

Efforts have been made to select a list of branded products that are generally sold in all or most of the countries represented in the IOCU. The first major international test project was to be on watches.[2] Eight IOCU member organizations, including Consumers Union of U.S., Inc., were involved in this project. International testing of consumer products used extensively in many countries could be a unique contribution to the improvement of products as well as an aid to consumer buying in the markets of the world.

Consumers Union of U.S., Inc., Consumers' Declaration. On June 30, 1962, the board of directors of Consumers Union of U.S., Inc., suggested the following Consumers' Declaration for adoption by the International Organization of Consumers Unions (IOCU):

It is fitting that delegates to the Brussels Conference of the International Organization of Consumers Unions should speak for a voice which has so far been largely silent—the consumer interest.

The organizations we represent in 16 countries are already supplying some information to consumers about the merits of consumer goods. But there is more to be done. The purpose of an economy is to produce goods and services, large in quantity, high in quality, reasonable in price for maximum satisfaction in consumer use.

Provide Information. Consumers cannot do their job of spending individual and family income efficiently, unless they can exercise intelligent choice among the goods and services available on the market. For intelligent choice, they must be better informed not only about the goods and services but also about the terms and conditions under which they are promoted and made available. That the consumer be better informed is a chosen task of the consumers' organizations gathered at Brussels. The task is tremendous and much more must be done in

_____
[2] "Product Testing Catches on Abroad," *Business Week,* July 28, 1962.

the schools and through the mass media (press, radio, and TV), so that our societies will have a firmer foundation under their chosen way of life. We recognize, at the same time, that this foundation must also be strengthened by a system of law and regulation which sets and enforces rules of proper economic conduct in the public interest.

Provide protection. So far as possible, standards of quality for consumer goods and services should be developed and publicized, valid methods for testing individual items against the standards made available, and the results communicated in a meaningful way, so that more efficient use can be made of our economic resources and also of time, energy, and patience. This will help protect the responsible businessman as well as the consumer from misleading and deceptive practices at the market, though it is recognized that certain harmful practices can only be regulated and controlled by force of law.

Remove restraints and rigidities. Restraints and rigidities that continue to exist in our economic and legal systems impose an improper burden on useful economic activity. These vary from the price fixing imposed by private monopoly to outmoded licensing laws imposed by public authority, and further, to restrictive tariffs and other obstacles to the free flow not only of goods but also of research, of initiative and of those energizing individual capacities on which progress depends.

Among our major objectives, therefore, are more information for the consumer, more effective methods of quality identification and measurement with a view to increasing performance value, and also continuous improvement in our economic and legal systems to ensure the most efficient use of resources for our individual and collective satisfaction.

In this connection, the world consumer movement must not only accent the standards appropriate to advanced countries; it must also devote energy to the development of consumer educational and protective programs in the developing countries through the specialized agencies of the United Nations.

Brussels Consumers' Declaration of 1964. In January, 1964, the Council of the International Organization of Consumers Unions recommended to the IOCU a Consumers' Declaration that is short, clear, and can be readily translated into other languages. It is written in such a way as to be applicable to all countries irrespective of their social, economic and political condition. The following declaration was drafted, expressing further the sound reasons for an International Organization of Consumers Unions.

The purpose of an economy is to produce, for the maximum satisfaction of consumers, goods and services which are: good in quality; sufficient in quantity; safe; reasonable in price.

In practice, consumers frequently find goods of shoddy quality; insufficient legal control to guarantee safety; gluts or scarcities; prices having no relation to quality; confusing advertising; insufficient information; poor retail service.

Consumers should not acquiesce in this state of affairs, but are urged to act, individually and via their consumers' organizations, to get improvement.

To do so, consumers are urged to organize themselves to: fight ignorance with reports and labels based on comparative tests on consumer goods and services; with accurate, unbiased advice on buying consumer goods and services; with the information necessary to assess the validity of advertising claims and the value of the goods inside the packaging; make themselves heard in every section of the government or economy where the consumers' interest is, or may be, involved. This is particularly important where the quality and price of goods or services are involved and essential where there is any question of safety.

To achieve this, the consumer organizations are urged to enrol, wherever possible, the help of governments, educators, the press, radio and television.

They are urged to work not only for well-educated, conscientious consumers, but for those who are uninterested and hard to reach: not only for the consumers in advanced countries, but for those in the underdeveloped areas as well.

Consumers everywhere should be able, if they so choose, to buy goods and obtain services whose essential qualities they can discover without great effort on their part, and which are safe, of good quality and reasonable in price.

Objectives of the IOCU. As a result of the conferences and manifestos of the International Organization of Consumers Unions, the objectives of the organization can be summed up as follows.

1. To promote international cooperation in the field of comparative testing of consumer goods
2. To act as a clearinghouse for test methods, plans, and publications
3. To promote international cooperation among organizations supplying information to help families with the wise expenditure of family income
4. To regulate the use of consumer product ratings, reprints, and published material subject to such rules as may be promulgated by the organizations concerned
5. To give grants to noncommercial organizations concerned with consumers' interests
6. To publish information on subjects related to consumers' interests and welfare
7. To take such actions as may further the objects of the International Organization of Consumers Unions and its member organizations.

Rules, Services, Responsibilities of the IOCU. The IOCU is a noncommercial organization. Its members agree to refrain from any use of their membership for advertising purposes, for promoting the sale of any product, or for any commercial purpose whatsoever. The name of IOCU or references to IOCU publications and other materials may not be used for advertising or for any commercial purpose.

The following publications, available at first only in the English language, are for the use of members of the IOCU.

1. IOCU Bulletin. A bimonthly report on joint test projects, news from consumer organizations, details of published test results, consumer test equipment,

operational methods of different consumers' associations, the juridical position of the consumer, and other matters of interest about consumers. Subscription rate: Dutch florins 25 per year. No reduction allowed to agencies, etc.

2. Circular Letter. A monthly review of the future testing plans of IOCU members, news from the headquarters office, financial reports, and other confidential items. The Circular Letter is sent to members of the Clearinghouse Committee only.

3. Yearbook. Information about all IOCU members and other consumers' organizations.

4. *International Consumer*. Published six times a year.

The membership of the IOCU consists of four categories: the Council (the governing body), the Executive Committee of the Council, the Clearinghouse Committee, and the Consumer Education and Welfare Committee. For each category, the Council has prepared specific rules to cover requirements for eligibility; the IOCU has pledged specific services; and each member organization, in turn, agrees to specific responsibilities.

Eligible to nominate a member into the Council are organizations that:

1. Are active on behalf of consumers
2. Are nonprofit-making and independent of industry and business support or influence
3. Regularly undertake comparative testing according to rulings laid down by the Council and publish the results of such tests, including brand names and prices
4. Do not accept advertisements in their publications
5. Do not allow commercial exploitation of their test results in any way whatsoever
6. Comply with such requirements as may be laid down by the Council

Eligible to the Clearinghouse Committee are organizations that:

1. Are active on behalf of the consumer
2. Are nonprofit-making and independent of industry and business support or influence
3. Do not accept advertisements in their publications
4. Do not allow commercial exploitation of their test results in any way whatsoever
5. Undertake to abide by the rules laid down by the Council

Eligible to the Consumer Education and Welfare Committee are organizations that:

1. Are active on behalf of the consumer
2. Are nonprofit-making and independent of industry and business support or influence

Each Clearinghouse Committee member is entitled to these services:

1. Five copies of the IOCU Bulletin
2. Five copies of the Circular Letter
3. Two invitations for guest delegates to the biennial conference
4. Application for participation in joint test projects
5. Suggestions to the Council how existing services may be improved and others developed
6. To request a copy—in the original language—of the full articles mentioned in the IOCU Bulletin
7. To request copies of other members' test methods
8. Permission to quote free of charge full reports or specified extracts, whether in the original language or in translation, of other members' test reports
9. To request drawings and specifications of other members' special testing equipment

Each Clearinghouse Committee member organization pledges itself to these responsibilities:

1. To contribute to the IOCU a sum equal to $\frac{1}{2}$ per cent of its gross annual revenue or such sum as the Council may determine
2. To complete such questionnaires as the Council may instruct the Administrator to dispatch
3. To obtain permission in writing before publishing full reprints or extracts or summaries of other members' test reports
4. To reimburse other members for expenses incurred when applying for test methods, specifications, or other materials
5. To keep strictly confidential and not pass on to others outside the IOCU other members' test methods or specifications of testing equipment except where cooperation with an outside laboratory makes this necessary (In such cases, instructions to such laboratories should not mention the name of the IOCU member whose test methods are used.)
6. To provide the editors of the IOCU Bulletin with bimonthly English summaries of published test reports
7. To provide the IOCU with five copies of all its publications free of charge
8. To treat all information contained in the Circular Letter as strictly confidential
9. To appoint a staff member to handle the IOCU correspondence and send news of special activities to the IOCU office and to the editor of the IOCU Bulletin

Each Consumer Education and Welfare Committee member organization is entitled to these services:

1. Two copies of the IOCU Bulletin
2. One invitation for a guest delegate to the biennial conference

3. To suggest to the Council how existing services may be improved and others developed

4. To request a copy—in the original language—of the full articles mentioned in the IOCU Bulletin

5. Access to the IOCU files on promotion and educational materials

Each Consumer Education and Welfare Committee member pledges itself to:

1. Contribute to the IOCU annually the sum of Dutch florin 530 or such sum as the Council may determine

2. Provide the editors of the IOCU Bulletin with bimonthly English summaries of its publications

3. Complete such questionnaires as the Council may instruct the administrator to dispatch

4. Provide the IOCU with five copies of all its publications free of charge

5. Report to the IOCU annually on its consumer education work and plans

6. Appoint a staff member to handle the IOCU correspondence and send news of special activities to the IOCU office and to the IOCU Bulletin editor

The following nonprofit testing organizations were members of the IOCU Clearinghouse Committee in 1963.

Founding date	Country	Organization
1959	Australia	Australasian Consumers' Association, Ltd.
1957	Belgium	Association des Consommateurs
1947	Canada	Consumers' Association of Canada
1935	Denmark	Statens Husholdningsrad
1951	France	Union Fédérale de la Consommation
1953	Iceland	Neytendasamtokin
1955	Israel	Israel Consumers' Association
1960	Japan	Japan Consumers' Association
1953	Netherlands	Nederlandse Consumenten Bond
1950	Netherlands	Nederlandse Huishoudraad
1959	New Zealand	Consumer Service of New Zealand
1953	Norway	Forbrukerradet
1956	Sweden	Statens Konsumentrad
1955	United Kingdom	Consumer Advisory Council
1957	United Kingdom	Consumers' Association, Ltd.
1936	United States	Consumers Union of U.S., Inc.

In 1963, the IOCU was under the following management.

President: Dr. Colston E. Warne, president of the Consumers Union of U.S., Inc., United States.

Secretary: Mrs. E. A. Schadee-Hartree, of the Nederlandse Consumenten Bond, The Netherlands.

Treasurer: Mr. Caspar Brook, director of the Consumers' Association, Ltd., United Kingdom.

The members of the Council were:

Mr. L. Darms, president of the Association des Consommateurs, Belgium.

Dr. H. Epstein, council member of the Australasian Consumers' Association, Ltd., Australia.

Mr. B. Gulbrandsen, president of Forbrukerradet, Norway.

All inquiries for applications for membership, subscriptions to the IOCU Bulletin, and related information should be addressed to:

J. H. van Veen, Administrator of IOCU
36, Surinamestratt,
The Hague (Den Haag), Netherlands
Telephone: 11.04.48
Cables: INTEROCU–HAAG

Consumer Organizations from Canada to the Near East

The world-wide enthusiasm for consumer testing is illustrated by the experiences of the president of the IOCU, Dr. Colston Warne. On a trip around the world, whether in Australia, New Zealand, Japan, Pakistan, or Tel Aviv, he was greeted by a delegation at the airport, flanked by newspaper and radio reporters. Everywhere the influence of Consumers Union of U.S., Inc., and the International Organization of Consumers Unions was felt. Even where no independent consumer movement existed, such as in Pakistan, Dr. Warne's visit caused newspaper editorials requesting consumer protective measures and the formation of an independent consumer agency.

The problems of consumers in all countries of the world are similar, and cooperation to solve them was expressed by the formation of the International Organization of Consumers Unions in 1960. As another example, the possible techniques of joint cooperation have been explored by the Consumers Union of U.S., Inc., and the Consumers' Association of Canada. The Consumers Union of U.S., Inc., already had a circulation of fifty-three thousand in Canada, but the Consumers' Association of Canada decided to enter the field of consumer testing of Canada-made products and to publish its test results.

Australia. The Australasian Consumers' Association, Ltd., founded in 1959, is a wholly independent, nonprofit organization whose principal object is to help its members to get the best possible value for their money.

It does this by testing consumer goods and services, and publishes the results in *Choice*, which is available only to members.

Canada. The Consumers' Association of Canada started as a women's organization for consumer education and consumer protection but included men in 1961. Observing the marked success of testing groups in other countries, the fourteenth annual meeting held in Toronto, September 12 to 14, 1961, adopted the recommendation of a special committee to include testing of products on the Canadian market. Any person living in Canada may become a member of the association on payment of an annual fee to be prescribed from time to time by the Delegate body.

In 1961, the meeting also passed resolutions dealing with the labeling of textiles, meat inspection, chemical sprays, grade standards for canned fish products, aspirin, trading stamps, labeling of soap, ground beef, a food and drug directorate, standards of inflammability for fabrics, serial numbers on household equipment and appliances, and the metric system of measurement.

The first issue of a new testing magazine, *Canadian Consumer*, published six times a year with an annual subscription rate of $3, appeared in English and French in mid-1963.

India. The Consumers' Association of India was established in April, 1959, as a nonprofit consumer organization. It plans to publish a journal, books, pamphlets, and reports. The affairs of the association are managed by a governing council. Income is obtained from membership subscriptions of four classes: student members, ordinary members, corporate members, and sustaining members. It has no testing facilities as yet.

Japan. The Japan Consumers Association was established on September 6, 1961. It is composed of women's organizations, including the Housewives Association, educational and professional organizations, some trade unions, the Japan Chamber of Commerce and Industry, and the Japan Productivity Center. Its plans are as follows.

1. To conduct laboratory tests and research on quality and the efficiency of consumer products and services
2. To publish the results of the tests through its own publications
3. To conduct investigations and surveys concerning living conditions, standards, advertising, trends in prices, credit and taxation, and other economic factors affecting consumer interests
4. To investigate consumer complaints
5. To coordinate and exchange information with consumer education organizations in foreign countries
6. To conduct consumer education seminars, lectures, and other courses

The plans also include a publication, *Better Buying*, and textbooks to be published regularly.

The Consumer Product Testing Laboratory, Housewives Association (Shyfu Rengokai, Nichiyohin Shikenshitsu) was founded in 1956 by the Housewives Association to conduct tests on consumer products on request. Test results are published in a monthly bulletin, but no ratings are given for the products tested. The laboratory also handles consumer complaints on a limited basis.

It is planned to establish a research institute to be financed by the association through subscriptions and the sale of publications. Consumer products will be tested on a larger scale. No advertising will be accepted, and commercial use of test results will not be allowed.

The Testing Laboratory, "Living Journal," Ltd. (Kurashinotecho-Sha, Jikkenshitsu), publishes a magazine on home economics and science and devotes part of its space to laboratory tests on consumer products. Some of the tests are conducted by the company itself; others are subcontracted to outside laboratories on a contract basis because of insufficient testing facilities on the part of the publishing company. The company accepts no advertising, gives no seals of approval, and allows no commercial use of its test results. Occasionally, it publishes brand ratings on the basis of a test.

New Zealand. The Consumer Council was established on September 23, 1959. There are four district committees covering Auckland, Wellington, Christchurch, and Dunedin. The council deals with all matters of concern to consumers: shortages of goods and services, inferior quality, adulteration, health and safety measures, lack of desirable standards, excessive prices, legal inequalities, and loan and credit malpractices. The council and district committees investigate suggestions and complaints from consumers and propose remedies. Results of quality testing of products are published periodically. Two publications, available only to members, are issued: *Consumer,* a quarterly, and *Consumer Newsletter,* at irregular intervals.

The council's source of income is from members' subscriptions. The secretarial and administrative facilities, however, are provided by the New Zealand Department of Industries and Commerce. The council meets regularly and provides direction to the permanent secretariat. The members of the council are appointed by the government, but policy is determined by the council, which is financially self-supporting, and thus able to operate as an entirely independent body.

The council does not have any testing facilities of its own, but uses the laboratories of the Department of Scientific and Industrial Research and also has private laboratories under contract.

The Philippines. Government and commercial sources report that there is no consumer protection association in the Philippines, although the Philippine Standards Association may eventually develop along those lines.

The work of this association has been limited to standardization and quality certification of finished products.

This nonprofit association was established in 1955 in Manila. It does not issue a regular publication, but announces test results to newspapers, trade associations, and business firms. Members of the association are professional engineers, chemists, and businessmen. Its income is derived from voluntary contributions of local industry and from annual fees for its certifying and grading services. It does not have any laboratory facilities and, therefore, must refer all cases to government testing bureaus, the National Science Development Board, or one of the local universities.

Taiwan. There is no private organization in Taiwan devoted to testing on a broad scale in behalf of consumers, but there are three governmental agencies concerned with the quality and testing of commercial products.

The National Bureau of Standards describes the standards for a limited number of products. Its central purpose is to protect public health and safety. The bureau publishes *Standard,* a Chinese-language monthly.

The Provincial Department of Health assists the National Bureau of Standards by licensing medicines and canned foods and by making spot checks of these items at consumer outlets.

The Provincial Bureau of Commodity Inspection and Quarantine inspects the quality of export products in an attempt to impose some standardization.

Consumer Organizations in Western Europe and Israel

Consumer testing in advanced technological countries is moving forward more rapidly than in the United States, though, of course, the independent testing movement and the level of government protection of the consumer had an earlier beginning in the United States. Nevertheless, with the rapid extension of brand-name advertising and the rise of living standards in many other countries, the consumer protection and testing movement has made rapid progress.

Austria. At the end of 1960, the Verein für Konsumenteninformation (Society for Consumer Information) was founded with its main office in Vienna. As of the same date, two previously existing societies were disbanded, but their functions were taken over by the new society, which is sponsored by four member organizations.

1. Der oesterreichische Arbeiterkammertag (Austrian Chamber of Labor Diet) (With the exception of public employees and farm workers, all Austrian employees are obligatory members of the Chamber of Labor. Each of the nine Austrian federal provinces has a separate chamber.)
2. The Austrian Trade Union Federation
3. The Austrian Federal Chamber of Commerce (of which any Austrian firm is an obligatory member)

4. Die Praesidentenkonferenz der oesterreichischen Landwirtschaftskammern (The president's conference of the Austrian Chambers of Agriculture of the nine Austrian federal provinces)

The four member organizations finance the new society and name representative members to the supervisory board which decides on the budget and the general work program. Apart from these principal matters, the executive secretary (a nominee of the Vienna Chamber of Labor approved by the other members) directs the operations of the society with relatively little overseeing.

The chief emphasis of the society is on quality tests, using its own testing facilities as well as outside testing laboratories, and on publishing results periodically in the form of a list detailing the advantages and disadvantages of products deemed recommendable to the public. Products found inferior are excluded from the list. In this indirect way, manufacturers of low-quality goods are given the opportunity and incentive to improve their products. The society does not issue seals of approval. However, it may recommend seals of other organizations. For example, it has recommended the placing of orders only with those sales agents using special-seal order forms issued by a certain agents' association.

The society planned to issue three different types of publications: an informative periodical bulletin distributed to member organizations and to subscribers, occasional brochures devoted to lengthy studies and investigations, and press releases. No advertisements will be accepted.

Attempts to establish a consumer protective organization in Austria date back many years and were initiated by Austrian labor organizations. In 1955, the Vienna Chamber of Labor established the Society for Purchasing Counsel. In 1958, the Austrian Trade Union of Building and Wood Workers, backed by the Austrian Trade Union Federation, established a similar society. The functions of these earlier societies are now carried on by Verein für Konsumenteninformation.

Belgium. The Association des Consommateurs (formerly Union Belge des Consommateurs) was founded in 1957 as a nonprofit independent association of private consumers. Its activities cover educational work, including shopping-club meetings and general information published in *Test Achats* (both in French and in Flemish), and information on the comparative value (price quality) of products available on the market.

Tests have been carried out on ball-point pens, corned beef, pressure cookers, electric irons, new floor coverings, plastics, table syrups, yogurt, edible oils, liquid bleaches, canned pineapple. Under agreements concluded with other consumer associations, the results of tests carried out in other countries have been published by the association.

Another consumer association, the Union Féminine pour l'Information et la Défense du Consommateur (UFIDEC), was founded in 1959, as a nonprofit association. Its associate members include Femmes Prévoyantes Socialistes (Socialist Women's Provident Association) and Ligue Nationale des Coopératrices (National Women's Cooperative League). There are also six affiliated member organizations.

UFIDEC is active in these fields.

1. Encouragement toward better household management, primarily through research, experiments, and information on domestic science
2. Protection of the consumer against all forms of abuse or fraud in the matter of quality or price
3. Representation of the consumer on all bodies dealing with questions that affect his interest, whether or not in conjunction with other economic or social bodies
4. Education of the consumer on as wide a range of consumer problems as possible, particularly through publications, courses, lectures, seminars

The association does not automatically publish results of comparative analyses. It uses laboratory tests to determine the composition or properties of certain products, particularly food and cleaning products. The results of this research educate the consumer by showing where fraud is possible, by checking the good faith of trade classifications, by exposing practices designed to deceive the consumer, and by backing appeals to government departments when necessary.

France. The Union Fédérale de la Consommation issues a monthly mimeographed informational bulletin and a series of buying pamphlets. The UFC has a program of testing in the fields of textiles and foods as well as consumer information and education. It launches consumer programs on radio and television and represents consumers for other private and public groups.

The UFC has also cooperated with other groups in setting up a model house and in a program for quality marking. Committees have been established as liaison between consumer and distributive groups in a number of cities.

Some 35 women's, family, and trade union groups are active members of the association. As a result of the numerous meetings, which its representatives have attended, the UFC has spread the idea of consumer conscientiousness in France. It has also helped to develop the idea of international association through publicizing the work of other movements.

Qualité-France (National Association for the Defense of French Quality) is a nonprofit association founded in 1948. The members of the board of directors represent the government, production, trade, and consumption. Until 1957, the Commissariat Général à la Productivité bore an annually decreasing proportion of the total expenditure, and the remainder was covered by fees paid by the firms inspected. The association is now financed entirely by the firms that are inspected.

Qualité-France lays down minimum acceptance standards for products in the specifications that are published by the association after consultation with technical committees. These specifications are public documents and may include prescriptions affecting the producing form, its premises and equipment, and its resources and methods of inspection. If products submitted by manufacturers for examination meet the required standards, they are awarded a Certificate of Quality, which gives the consumer clear, impartial information and serves as a guarantee, the association being responsible. The association makes frequent use of external laboratories and testing centers. All approved products are subject to inspection, which is repeated several times a year.

Qualité-France is clarifying its relationship with production, distribution, and consumption sectors by agreements already concluded or under discussion, and has sought to have its functions defined in an agreement with the state.

The Association Française pour l'Information en Économie Ménagère (French Association for Home Economics Information) was formed in 1955 under the patronage of the Ministries of Agriculture and National Education and began to operate at the end of 1957. It is a nonprofit association and is controlled by a board on which at least two-thirds of the seats are reserved for users' representatives drawn from other home economics associations, both public and private. The remaining seats are filled by representatives of bodies specializing in consumer protection and information.

The board is assisted by a technical committee on which are represented the more important research and documentation centers. There are three main departments—documentation, information service, and liaison—which will no doubt assume further responsibilities as a result of the interest that the Institut Pédagogique National (National Educational Institute) is showing in the work of the association. The association is to take over the institute's information service so far as home economics is concerned. The 54 regional centers under this authoritative body offer an immense scope for action.

The Association Française de Normalisation (French Standardization Association) is a private organization founded in 1926. The board of directors consists of representatives of industry, commerce, consumers, public authorities, and technical centers. Their fields of activity include:

1. Definition of French standards for all categories of products, particularly household appliances

2. Verification of products conforming to these standards and the issue of quality stamps attesting to conformity

3. Publication of a buyers' guide to household equipment

4. International research under the International Organization for Standardization (ISO) to fix the principles underlying the certification of products, standard quality marks, and information labels

The Association pour la Diffusion des Techniques Ménagères (ADTM) (Association for Dissemination of Home Economics Techniques) is a private, nonprofit association founded in 1952 by persons concerned with consumer education and by consumers who elect among themselves a board of 33 members representing Paris and the provinces. There are 1,800 establishments, home economics centers, individuals, and miscellaneous bodies throughout the country in touch with the association.

A technical committee prepares and directs all the work concerned with tests that the ADTM arranges in home economics centers and also publishes papers connected therewith. A consultative committee of manufacturers has been formed alongside the association, which links producers, consumers, and education in home economics by:

1. Testing articles and products used in the home
2. Disseminating home economics information and documentation
3. Organizing study days, demonstrations, and instruction
4. Helping to equip home economics centers
5. Taking part in activities designed to bring together or promote joint action by individuals or bodies interested in the development and wide-scale application of *modern* methods for the housewife

The Laboratoire Coopératif d'Analyses et de Recherches (Cooperative Analytical and Research Laboratory), affiliated with the cooperative movement, was established in the form of a nonprofit association at the disposal of consumer groups for analyses and tests of consumer goods, including food and beverages in particular. Its fields of activity include analytical control and technical advice, research work, and consumer education and protection.

In December, 1960, a National Committee on Consumer Problems was set up under the Ministry of Commerce to ensure permanent consultation between representatives of the public authorities and of consumer organizations on everything concerned with consumer problems, and to study the proper methods of developing information and education for consumers. It will take part, as and when needed, in defining the quality of products and, each time it is consulted by the ministry concerned, it will supply information on draft laws and regulations that may impinge on consumer problems and on the methods of dealing with them.

Ireland. The Irish Housewives Association is a voluntary organization, nonpolitical and nonsectarian, its object being to unite housewives so that they may realize and win recognition of their right to plan an active part in all spheres of planning for the community. The organization is the only voluntary one in Ireland concerned with the protection of the rights of the consumer. It was founded in 1942 by a group of housewives who were anxious that commodities should be evenly distributed at fair prices during World War II. Its income is derived from annual subscriptions of members, proceeds from social functions, and the sale of a yearbook published by a subcommittee.

The association's program includes the following activities.

To further cooperation between producer and consumer and manufacturer and consumer, while watching the difference between producer and consumer prices

To agitate for legislation requiring the weight and nature of contents to be clearly marked on all packaged goods

To further the work of the Institute of Irish Industrial Standards through members appointed to sit on advisory committees

To investigate any rise in consumer prices and to protest when these are excessive

To encourage sales resistance by consumers when prices are excessively high or quality below standard

To press the need for the registration of all nursing homes

To help with the care of the aged

To raise funds for world refugees

To continue work with the International Alliance of Women, with which the association is affiliated

Israel. The Israel Consumers Association was founded in 1955 on the initiative of the International Women's Zionist Organization. It maintains offices in Tel Aviv, with branch offices in Haifa, Jerusalem, and Rehovot.

The purposes of the association are to protect the rights of consumers; to represent consumers in Israel in industrial, commercial, and other bodies; to improve the standard of production and services; and to raise hygienic conditions in production and marketing. The association publishes at regular intervals a periodical, *Consumers' Tribune,* in English and Hebrew.

The association is an independent and unaffiliated body. It accepts only individuals, not institutions or organized groups, as members. The sources of income are annual membership fees fixed at an amount that includes subscription to the association publications. During the years 1958 through 1960, it received an annual grant from joint funds of USOM, Tel Aviv, and from the Israel government.

The association has no facilities for comparative testing and therefore has not published brand names and test results. Its cooperation with other organizations is limited to casual activities. The Better Business Association, promoted by the Rotary Club of Tel Aviv–Jaffa, generally refers complaints of consumer goods or services to the association.

Italy. The Unione Nazionale Consumatori was formed in Rome in 1955 for the representation and protection of consumers. A monthly magazine, *Comprare,* for educating and orienting the consumer, was published for the first time in December, 1960. The union has also published several reports and studies.

The union is open to individual consumers as well as to trade unions and consumers' cooperatives, but membership is reported to be small. It receives income from membership fees and the sale of publications and from government subsidies if and when obtainable. It has no facilities for comparative testing and does not publish brand names and test results.

The Istituto Qualità Italia (National Association for Maintaining and Controlling Quality and Awarding the Quality Seal) was founded in January, 1959, as a result of numerous exchanges of views between manufacturers and traders, consumers, university teachers, market research specialists, and others, following the Journées d'Études Qualité-Europe held in Brussels. It is an independent and entirely objective association, directed by a board with up to 30 members.

The institute has adopted a set of rules that clearly define the objectives and principles that will serve as guides for future activities, for example, the objective certification of quality of products by means of a seal. Though the intention is to adapt these rules to Italy's specific requirements, the institute has based them on those already followed by similar bodies, such as Qualité-Belgique and Qualité-France. Numerous Italian firms have applied for permission to display the seal.

The Netherlands. The Nederlandse Consumenten Bond (NCB) (Netherlands Consumers Union) was formed in January, 1953, and continues to register steady growth. There are 24,000 subscribers to its bulletin. Sources of income are subscription fees from private memberships and contributions received from participating organizations.

The NCB was established as a consumer counterweight against the increasing number of agreements and mergers in industry and commerce. Any consumer whose interests are not dominated by any other economic interest may become a member. Participating organizations may in no way be related with trade or industry. It is a nonprofit organization that accepts no advertising, allows no commercial use of its test results, and receives no subsidies. Brand names and test results are both published. The NCB has selected dramatic items to arouse public interest. It has developed use tests and is eager to cooperate with other organizations.

The Stichting Consumenten Contact Orgaan (CCO) was founded in

August, 1957, for the general protection of consumer interests. Its members include the NCB, cooperatives, and three labor unions. The CCO has a government grant up to 50,000 guilders for comparative testing. It has tested large, expensive items, such as vacuum cleaners and spin dryers, and has plans for other testing. The CCO works with the national standardizing body on methods of test. Tests are made in a private laboratory.

The Nederlandse Huishoudraad (NHR) (Household Council of the Netherlands), formed in 1950, is a council through which 16 women's organizations, three national advisory services, and seven specialist organizations cooperate. These organizations have approximately 380,000 members, who are asked to contribute information on household problems.

The council has an interest in the home as a whole, and presents the case for housewives to private organizations, such as designers, architects, and government authorities. For tests, which are made on receipt of complaints, the NHR uses scientific institutes and laboratories. It often cooperates with the government-sponsored National Organization for Applied Scientific Research.

Switzerland. In Zurich is the Suisse Institut für Hauswirtschaft (Swiss Institute for Household Economics), which was founded in 1948 by the Women's Third National Congress. Its fields of activity include:

1. Textiles. Testing and comparison of automatic washing machines and study of the many problems involved, such as effects of bleaching. Research is being carried on. Comparisons of automatic clothes dryers and of washing of wool, silk, and man-made fibers with special products are planned or under way.

2. Home. Comparison of floor waxes, polishes, electric irons, ironing equipment, knitting machines, vacuum cleaners. Comparison of lacquers is planned.

3. Kitchen. Comparison of electrical kitchen equipment, dishwashing machines, coffee percolators, pans for electric stoves, cleaning of heating units; comparison of refrigerators, freezers, ovens, and grills; research on pan handles, heights of working areas, time and energy management in households.

4. Money management.

The institute is responsible not only for testing and research work, but also for information. To spread knowledge, it has prepared a collection of general information for rural extension work and for home economics teachers. The institute has received a small subsidy from a governmental agricultural fund, but more aid is expected to be included in a new professional law that is being revised. In such case, the institute would be under the control of the Federal Trade and Labor Office Industry, Vocational Training Section.

United Kingdom. The Consumers' Association, Ltd. (CA) was incorporated in March, 1957, and published the first issue of *Which?* on October 7, 1957. This monthly magazine had about 400,000 subscribers in 1964.

A council of eleven is elected annually. The members are unpaid and may not be directly engaged as principal in the manufacture, distribution, or sale of goods or commodities; in the rendering of services to the public; or as a servant or agent in promoting the sale or use of such goods, commodities, or services.

While its constitution permits the association to undertake any work on behalf of the consumer, its policy is to concentrate on comparative product and service testing and publishing of the results. About 150 test projects a year are undertaken. A cumulative index in each issue of the magazine lists reports published to date. CA is nonprofit-making and completely independent financially.

The Consumer Advisory Council of the British Standards Institution was established in 1955 to assist in developing a system of standards and a certification mark for consumer products. From January, 1957, to May, 1963, the council issued a bimonthly publication, *Shopper's Guide,* which published test reports on named products and gave general information of value to a shopper. Its discontinuance leaves *Which?* alone in the field of nonprofit, independent testing and reporting of comparative price and quality of consumer products in England.

The Federation of Consumer Groups was formed on March 16, 1963, by virtually all the local consumer groups. The federation now publishes the fortnightly digest, *Consumer News,* which was formerly published by the Consumers' Association, Ltd. Presumably, the bulletin will continue to publish consumer news of interest to all the local consumer organizations in Oxford, Nottingham, Cambridge, Manchester, and many other cities in England, Wales, and Northern Ireland.

For some time, consumer-minded leaders in England urged the government to establish a Consumer Council. In the early summer of 1963, the Board of Trade appropriated $148,000 for the first year's operation.

The council has a full-time director and a part-time chairman. It will do no comparative testing, and complaints will be handled by the Citizen's Advice Bureau. As the council does not have any powers, *Which?* magazine, May, 1963, commented: "Consumers can do one of two things. Either they can sit down and moan because the Consumer Council has no teeth. Or they can get up and give it some."

In June, 1963, the Research Institute of Consumer Affairs (RICA) was established in London by the Consumers' Association, Ltd. It exists to undertake research on behalf of consumers. It collects information about services of all kinds, investigates experiences with consumer goods, and reports on monopolies. The research is publicized in books and pamphlets, and in *Consumer News.* The institute will also organize consumer conferences and manage a lecture service.

RICA has a small research staff financed by subscriptions, but this independent research organization hopes to secure some financing from foundations and other nongovernment- and nonbusiness-controlled sources.

West Germany. The Arbeitsgemeinschaft der Verbraucherverbaende E.V. (Working Group of Consumer Organizations) is located in Bonn-Beuel. Founded in 1953, it consisted of 7 member organizations; ten years later there were 20, representing about seven million persons, and covering a wide variety of German consumer groups.

The statutes of the organization provide that it must be independent and have purely nonprofit and common-interest aims. Its purposes are to represent the interests of consumers in relation to legislation, administration, and business, and to provide accurate and independent information and counsel relating to consumer goods and to the expenditure of family income. The organization's income is derived from membership dues and the sale of publications.

For comparative tests of consumer goods, the Institut für Warenpruefung (Institute for Commodity Tests) is connected with the Arbeitsgemeinschaft, but it has no testing facilities of its own. It collaborates with independent German testing institutes, laboratories, and research institutes of various German universities.

The results of comparative testing are published monthly in *Verbraucher-Rundschau*. Additional informative publications are also issued from time to time. They are available in eight major German cities for the information and guidance of consumers.

Over the years, a number of other groups have been moving closer to the idea of consumer testing. In Stuttgart-Hohenheim is the Bundesforschungsanstalt für Hauswirtschaft (Institute of Home Economics), which does excellent work in basic studies of foodstuffs and home equipment. It publishes a considerable number of bulletins of high quality and has cooperated in a home economics demonstration located in the center of Stuttgart. The institute tries to carry out fundamental research only, which means developing of test methods and testing of types only, not single products.

Consumer Organizations in Scandinavia and Finland

Informative labeling in Scandanavia as pioneered in Sweden gives consumers the information they need to spend money wisely and to get the best value for their money. In Sweden, the labels remain on exported products and may be printed in the language of the country importing the goods.

Finland is particularly interested in care labeling, and has developed a series of symbols now generally referred to as the International Care Labeling Code for Textiles. As in Norway and Sweden, care labeling in

Finland gives honest information to consumers. It is financed by fees for the labels and by government grants. All interested parties are represented in the preparation of the labels, and national standards are used when these exist. Swedish standards are used when available if Finnish standards have not been developed.

The system of care labeling used in Denmark is the same as that used in Finland, and is considered the international system with some minor changes.

The Danish Standards Association is a member of the International Organization for Standardization (ISO) and participates in the work of the various ISO technical committees, among these the ISO/TC 73, which concerns marks indicating conformity with standards.

Consumer cooperatives in Finland work together for quality and are keenly interested in consumer education as well as in manufacturing, distribution, and retailing. Only Iceland has a higher percentage of cooperative business. Finland leads Norway, Sweden, and Denmark in the percentage of total cooperative business.

Finland has two members on the Northern Committee, as do Norway, Sweden, and Denmark. This committee, representing these four countries and appointed by their respective governments, is coordinating consumer activities in Scandinavia.

Denmark. Consumer activity in Denmark is channeled mainly through two organizations, the Statens Husholdningsrad (Danish Government Home Economics Council) and the Danish Housewives' Consumer Council, which jointly share the same building in Copenhagen. Both these organizations are governed in such a way as to elicit the cooperation of a wide variety of participating groups, although the former is supported through governmental funds, the latter through grants from constituent organizations. While there are a number of overlapping areas between the two, the former is dedicated centrally to research and testing problems, and the latter centrally to consumer representation and consumer informational problems.

Statens Husholdningsrad devotes its central effort to the quality testing of products in a wide variety of fields, including foods, textiles, and household equipment. It employs films, exhibitions, and radio programs, and handles the complaints of consumers. The laboratories of the council are engaged in the testing of brands of equipment available on the Danish market.

The test reports, published in monthly bulletins, give comparative brand performances, together with other useful consumer information, particularly concerning the product use and product attributes. Coupled with this product research is an interest in such problems as heat conductivity of materials and construction characteristics of equipment. The agency also cooperates with a quality declaration program, sponsored by producers and consumer groups in Denmark, by checking on colorfastness and wearing characteristics.

Special studies were made in the field of nutrition to assess varying techniques of food preservation. Research of a practical character, such as the best type of covering for preserves, is undertaken at the request of household and governmental organizations.

The council has been concentrating on raising quality standards of consumer goods and propagating objective consumer information. It will continue to influence public opinion, to further the consumer's sense of quality and price, and, for this purpose, be guided by objective research of consumers' habits and needs.

The Danish Housewives' Consumer Council is made up of representatives of 12 important women's organizations in Denmark. Work of the council includes consumer education, the representation of consumers on government boards and committees, handling of complaints, work with quality marks and seals, and publicity about its work in the press, on radio and TV, and by meetings. The council also cooperates with consumer organizations in other countries.

The council has published a series of booklets on such subjects as clothes for infants and necessary layette garments, what to look for when buying bedding, the fit and construction of shoes, the urgent need for wider adoption of national standard sizes for labeling garments, the reading and use of the DVN Informative Label, and on many other subjects of interest to the housewife and home economist. There are kits for use in schools to teach garment-size designations.

An investigation resulted in the use of new weights on nearly all food packages. A committee is at work on improved legal protection for consumers in the field of packaging. The council is making excellent use of its limited income to protect consumers.

Consumers in Denmark may fill in complaint forms and send defective merchandise to the council if it is a small thing that can be easily shipped, such as a pair of shoes, a blouse, or hose. About 1,000 complaints a year are investigated, and in many cases (about 60 per cent) the consumer has a proper complaint, and he is given repair without charge, money back, or a replacement. There is a special complaint board for shoes, and consumers are represented in retailing, manufacturing, and importing firms, and in the shoe repair industry.

A textile engineer handles textile complaints that come to the council. These are processed either by direct reply or by referring the complaint to a laboratory for investigation. Consumers do not pay for this work. The council sends the bill to the textile industry organization, which pays without a report or a discussion. The industry is responsible and prefers to pay and assume that the charges are correct, justified, and have been competently handled. The council has planned a similar arrangement with the furniture industry.

The Dansk Varedeklarations-Naevin (DVN) (Danish Institution for Informative Labeling) is a private institution established in 1957 by organizations of commerce, industry, and consumers, from which it receives contributions. Firms that want their goods provided with declarations and the mark of DVN pay a yearly fee, a contribution to administrative expenses, and the expenses for approval and testing.

The institution works for voluntary use of instructive marking of consumer goods sold in the retail trade. Each declaration gives instructive facts about the goods; therefore all declarations are named "Varefakta." The purpose of declaration of consumer goods is to help consumers to judge the contents and quality of the goods in question. The institution must see that the declarations are uniform and correct, and the registered mark DVN on products indicates that the information given on the label is correct.

The Danish Housewives' Consumer Council assists the DVN in helping consumers to understand labels and look for them when shopping. There is also a program for care labeling of garments and textiles. Small tapes sewn into a garment show with line drawings and a few numbers whether washing or dry cleaning is permissible, water and ironing temperatures, and the kind of bleach that may be used. A large X indicates any process that is not to be used.

About 150 of the more than 500 laundries have been granted a seal. These laundries do more than 50 per cent of all laundry work in Denmark. All military laundering is sent to approved laundries. The council suggested this. The system of checking involves visits to laundries and examination of garments that have been through ten to fifty washings. The checking is carried out in a thorough manner by the Technological Institute. A similar system was started in 1961 for dry-cleaning establishments.

In textile labeling (the four "F" seal), there is a special mark for imports. Standards are developed by committees that include representatives from consumers, traders, manufacturers, and research institutions. The Danish Housewives' Consumer Council works with the textile testing organization in the development of standards. The manufacturers must agree to have their products checked by random sampling. Legal action can be taken by the Board for Textile Testing if there is a violation of the contract.

The Danish Standards Association is an independent, nongovernmental organization, consisting of a council of 29 members appointed by the Ministry of Commerce, representing several governmental departments, trade organizations, and technical high schools. The budget of the association is based on a yearly contribution from the government and contributions to a similar amount from private sources, such as industrial organizations, trade organizations, and larger firms outside these organizations. Smaller contributions are also received from various societies and institutions. The association has registered the mark DS to be used on products to indicate conformity with Danish standards. The use of the mark without license is not permitted. The licensee must certify that he is able and willing to manufacture the products in question according to Danish standards.

Finland. The Finnish Institute for Informative Labeling consists of 23 associations and firms representing manufacturers, consumers, trade, and research. Branch committees, which prepare the labeling specifications and corresponding test and measurement standards, have been formed within the institute.

Informative labeling is voluntary, covering at first a fairly limited number of commodities and manufacturers. Public reaction toward the system has been favorable, and the Finnish government is participating in its financing. A manufacturer is free to decide which of the standardized labeling statements he wants to use concerning the characteristics of his product.

The institute examines the product concerned and is allowed to buy samples for examination from any retail outlet. If the product does not correspond with the standardized statement, the manufacturer can be refused the right to use labels approved by the institute. The labels bear a four-pointed "compass rose" sign.

The care symbols are line drawings on tape that can be sewn into garments in the factory. A line drawing of a pan of water with recommended temperature in numbers shows whether the garment can be washed in very hot water or must be washed in lukewarm water. There is a large X if not washable at all.

A line drawing of a hand iron with temperatures indicates regular ironing and the equivalent of a cool iron. For dry cleaning, there are easy-to-understand symbols, and if a garment is not suitable for dry cleaning, a large X is used. The space for bleach also uses a symbol, and if no bleach may be used an X appears in the space. The line drawings and numbers make the message completely clear, and no language is needed.

In Finland there are detergents with the informative label and the care symbols to indicate the proper temperature of water for different kinds of fabrics.

Kotitalouskeskus (Centralen for Huslig Ekonomi) is an independent organization supported by housewives' societies. It is engaged in testing appliances and equipment and has published the results of investigations on floor care; tea kettles and coffee makers; cooking pots, pans, and frying pans; kitchen planning and arrangement of cupboards; and size and arrangement of clothes closets.

SOK and OTK cooperatives use the best available test methods and are concerned with the quality of their own products and of the goods they buy from independent manufacturers and importers to stock their thousands of retail stores. OTK maintains a generous supply of complaint forms in retail stores and shops. Any consumer may send one to the complaint department, with or without the merchandise, and the complaint will be investigated and an adjustment made.

An education arm of these cooperatives issues magazines, film strips, and press releases, and sponsors meetings, study groups, and courses. All possible methods are used to reach consumers.

Tyotehoseura (TEHO) (Work Efficiency Association) works with the building industry, forestry, agriculture, and domestic economy to plan good buildings and model kitchens on farms and to study work processes on farms and in the forestry industries so that all tasks may be performed in the most efficient manner. They have an excellent display of model houses for farms, model barns, and a model kitchen.

Iceland. Neytendasamtokin (The Consumers' Union) is a wholly independent association, and no other association or institution appoints any representatives to its management. It was founded in 1953 on the initiative of a number of interested persons who called a public meeting for its establishment. The management of the union consists of a chief executive board of five, but a representative council of twenty-seven is also elected at the general meeting. There are about 4,300 members.

The position of the union has been strengthened since 1957, but before that was recognized officially and received a grant. Earlier the union had been sued for publishing the findings of quality control in the form of a warning. Proceedings lasted for five years and the union lost before the lower court, but was completely acquitted by the Supreme Court of Iceland in February, 1960.

This verdict recognized the Consumers' Union as a qualified party in law to safeguard consumers' interests. The acquittal meant that the union was authorized to tell the truth officially about consumer goods if this was in the interests of consumers as a whole. The Minister of Commerce agreed to appoint a committee, to include a representative of the union, that would deal with the marking of goods relating to regulations, as this was lacking in the country. The union wanted information concerning net weight and ingredients to be given on packages and fixed by law.

Since its inception, the union has granted legal aid and information to the public and runs an office for this purpose. The publication of guides continues (at one time there were 14 publications and 8 booklets). These are supplied free to members on payment of a small annual subscription, but their cost is defrayed mostly by advertising, which must be unostentatious. The union has concentrated on the publication of news items in the press, and there has been less need for the regular issue of the publications, which are first and foremost documentary. To introduce consumers' views, the union cooperates with various official institutions, including the price control authority, the electricity board, and ministries.

A committee for the assessment of dry cleaners and laundries has been reorganized on the basis of experience gained. Cleaners and laundries can now display placards on their premises and are free to participate through their trade organizations. Most of these firms near and in Reykjavik are members of the committee and pay a fee on receipt of placards.

Norway. Forbrukerradet (Consumers' Council) is an independent institution having its own secretary. The statutes of the council were formulated by royal resolution of September 11, 1953. The council consists of a chairman and seven members who are appointed by the crown on the recommendation of seven cooperative and consumer organizations.

The main object of the council is the testing of consumer goods. It receives 95 per cent of its income from government appropriations and 5 per cent from the sale of publications. A magazine, *Forbruker rapporten*, first published as a quarterly, gives results of testing and advice on purchasing. The total circulation of the fourth issue in 1961 was 50,000 copies. When an increase in price is possible, there may be ten issues annually.

Forbrukerradet handles complaints, which total more than 2,000 a year. There are consumer days in different areas, which members of the council staff attend on a rotating basis, make speeches, and answer questions. In addition to the magazine, there are special publications, including a *Family Account Book* and books on buying. Consumers are kept informed through press releases, radio, lectures, courses, conferences—in fact, in every possible way.

The council is financed by the state. There is, however, no further contact between the council and the ministries other than assurance that the work is carried out according to the statutes and that the accounts are properly kept. The Norwegian government has increased the budget of the council every year, and it is now approximately ten times the amount set aside for the work in 1953.

On the initiative of the council, the Central Committee for Informative Labeling and Quality Marking was founded in 1954. The committee consists of 24 members representing the consumers' industry and research. Its purpose is the promotion and coordination of informative commodity labeling and quality marking. Informative labeling is used on the commodities of 80 producers, and the number is increasing rapidly.

Norway is unique in having a consumer cabinet post, the Royal Ministry for Consumer and Family Affairs, which is filled by a woman. She works in close cooperation with the Forbrukerradet through its household research division and its information services.

Other active groups in Norway include the government Research Department for Home Economics, the National Standardizing Organization, and the Informative Labeling Organization.

Sweden. The Swedish consumer movement is divided into a number of cooperating agencies. At the peak is the Statens Konsumentrad (National Council for Consumer Goods Research and Information), a governmental agency that supplies money to various consumer institutions and serves as a coordinating agency. It also engages in statistical investigations.

Money has been granted for research concerning creaseproof textiles, floor materials, and indoor lighting; investigation into the good fit of shoes; functional studies and testing methods for furniture; films concerning kitchen planning and informative labeling; and courses for group-study leaders on consumer questions.

The council consists of a chairman and 14 members appointed by the king for two years. Seven persons are chosen from consumer and wage-earning interests, four from scientific and other expert groups, and three represent business interests.

The Kooperativa Forbundet (KF) (Cooperative Union and Wholesale Society) is the central organization for the local consumer societies in Sweden and has its own factories in many branches. For example, in the food business, it has flour mills; macaroni factories; bread mills; oil mills; margarine and chocolate factories; and canning factories for meat, fish, vegetables, and fruit. It also has factories for chinaware, shoes, rubber tires, detergents, textiles, furniture, and so on. The union also serves as a wholesale society for the local consumer societies buying goods from the private trade in Sweden and from abroad.

In the laboratories of the factories, the goods manufactured are tested continuously and are compared with corresponding items on the open market. The union has a central food laboratory, a test kitchen, and a textile laboratory, all of which work in close collaboration with the factories and the different departments of KF, where, among other things, the informative labeling of the foods is made up. The union also takes part in the work of international organizations that include the standardization of testing methods in their programs.

Informative labeling in Sweden is the work of the Varudeklarationsnamnden (VDN) (Institute for Informative Labeling). It is one of several independent organizations affiliated with the Swedish Standards Association. The activities of the VDN are financed partly by the government, with contributions from various national organizations, and partly by the fees paid by business enterprises using the institute's design.

When a manufacturer or producer requests a label, the VDN organizes a committee to work on the test methods, specifications, and the list of items that must be included in the label. This working group includes consumers, producers, and technical experts. When the test methods have been prepared, the specifications are worked out for the content of the label. The draft VDN sheet is circulated to all interested organizations— including the industry, retailers, importers, wholesalers, and distributors— and to consumer organizations and technical specialists. The items on the label must be accurately worded, must refer to test methods, and must give bad features as well as good features.

Each VDN sheet includes an example of a correct label for the product. The manufacturer must prepare the label, must make sure that all products labeled meet the standards, and must agree to have random samples checked. Each manufacturer must check-test his own products to determine the grade and regularly recheck to make sure standards are maintained. In Sweden some competitors are interested enough to do check testing.

The VDN is concerned with consumer education. It issues booklets and uses press releases and leaflets, radio, and TV to help people understand the meaning of the labels. The first print order for a booklet is usually about 150,000 copies, and these are supplied to schools, libraries, organizations, and other groups. The manufacturer also promotes the label. About 30 committees have beeen working on projects, and about 75 specifications have been completed.

The Statens Institut for Konsumenfragor (National Institute for Consumer Information) was established in 1945 by home economists and housewives and by other organizations and was drawn into the government group in 1957. The institute works with a testing laboratory. Results of tests are published by brand name and in three forms: the magazine *Rad och Ron* (Advice and Discovery), popular bulletins, and technical bulletins.

There are about 18,000 subscribers to the magazine, but testing information reaches a much wider audience through libraries, newspapers, and other magazines. The best-selling popular bulletin is on infant care which sold 120,000 copies in 4½ years. The bulletin on cleaning methods has sold 28,000 copies since 1958; advice on laundering has sold 13,000 copies since 1959. The sale, plus free distribution, amounts to more than 100,000 copies of popular bulletins a year. The institute also sells about 30,000 garment patterns a year. A bulletin on kitchen planning sold 8,000 copies in 7 months. Technical bulletins for industry give full and complete information about the tests.

The Svenska Slojdforeningen (Swedish Society for Industrial Design) has a membership of designers, manufacturers, and consumers. The work of the institute is 116 years old. There are about 16,000 subscribers to *Form* and *Kontur*. About 400 designers have applied for membership and been accepted. Manufacturers must apply for membership. All applicants must meet the standards of the institute. The consumer section includes housewives' organizations, cooperatives, and other groups working with consumers. The general members section has about 20,000 members.

Sweden also has the Svenska Standardiserings Kommission (Swedish Standards Association) and the Statens Provningsangstalt (State Research Laboratory).

SUGGESTED READINGS

Atkinson, Isobel. "The Voice of the Consumer in Canada," Selected Proceedings of the Fifth Annual Conference of the Council on Consumer Information. Greeley, Colo.: Colorado State College.

"Canadian Consumer Problems," Proceedings of National Conference of the Consumers' Association of Canada, June 20, 21, 1962.

Consumer Affairs Bulletin. London: International Cooperative Alliance.

Consumer News. London: Federation of Consumer Groups.

Consumers on the March, Proceedings of the Third Biennial Conference of the International Organization of Consumers' Unions. The Hague, Netherlands.

Final Report of the Committee on Consumer Protection. London: Her Majesty's Stationery Office, July, 1962.

Forbruker rapporten. Forbrukerradet, Oslo, Norway.

Harvey, Mrs. W. B. "The Consumer Looks at Protection in Canada," Selected Proceedings of Third Annual Conference of the Council on Consumer Information, St. Louis, April, 1957, pp. 7–10.

International Consumer, Journal of the International Organization of Consumers' Unions. The Hague, Netherlands.

Meynaud, Jean. *Better Buying through Consumers Information.* Paris: Organization for European Economic Cooperation, European Productivity Agency, 1961.

Warne, Colston E. "The Consumer Looks at Foreign Consumer Programs," Selected Proceedings of Third Annual Conference of the Council on Consumer Information, St. Louis, April, 1957, pp. 3–6.

———. "A Digest of the Leading Consumer Movements of the World, 1962" (unpublished).

Which? London: Consumers' Association, Ltd.

NATIONAL CONSUMER ORGANIZATIONS

Austria

Association of Austrian Consumers' Organizations. Vienna XVI, Austria: Thaliastrasse 2.

Consumer Information Service of the Chamber of Labor for Upper Austria. Austria: Arbeiterkammer, Linz, Volksgartenstrasse 40.

Verein für Konsumenteninformation. Vienna VI, Austria: Mariahferstrasse 81.

Belgium

Association des Consommateurs. Brussels, Belgium: 23 rue Royale.

K.A.V. Housewives' Council. Brussels 3, Belgium: 111 rue de la Poste.

Quality Control Bureau. Brussels, Belgium: 25 Square de Meeus.

Union Féminine pour l'Information et la Défense du Consommateur. Brussels: 21 Boulevard de l'Empereur.

Canada

Consumers' Association of Canada. Ottawa 3, Ontario, Canada: 1245 Wellington Street.

Denmark

Danish Housewives' Consumer Council. Copenhagen 5, Denmark: Amager Faelledve 56.

Danish Standards Association. Copenhagen 5, Denmark: Vesterbrogade, 12.

Statens Husholdningsrad. Copenhagen 5, Denmark: Amager Faelledve 56.

England (See United Kingdom)

France

Association pour la Diffusion des Techniques Ménagères. Paris 16e, France: 163bis, avenue Victor-Hugo.

Association Française pour l'Information en Économie Ménagère. Paris 6e, France: 13, rue Ferou.

Association Française de Normalisation. Paris 2e, France: 23, rue Notre-Dame des Victoires.

Laboratoire Coopératif d'Analyses et de Recherches. Gennevilliers (Seine), France: 10, avenue Louis Roche.

Qualité-France. Paris 2e, France: 18, rue Volney.

Union Fédérale de la Consommation. Paris 8, France: 21, Rue Clement Marot.

Iceland

Consumers Union. Reykjavik, Iceland: Austurstraet 14.

Ireland

Irish Housewives Association. Dublin, Ireland: 19, Ely Place.

Israel

Israel Consumers Association. Tel Aviv, Israel: 8 Beth Hashoeva Lane.

Italy

Istituto Qualità Italia. Milan, Italy: 3, Piazza Meda.

Japan

Housewives Association. Tokyo, Japan: No. 15, 6-Bancho, Chiyoda-ku.
Industrial Arts Institute. Tokyo, Japan: 313 Shumomaruko-machi, Ota-ku.
Japan Consumers' Association. Tokyo, Japan: No. 5-2-Chome Kanda Ogawa-
    machi, Chiyoda-ku.
Japan Industrial Standards Committee. Tokyo, Japan: 3-1, Kasumigaseki,
    Chiyoda-ku.
Japan Productivity Center. Tokyo, Japan: No. 3-5-Chome Ginza, Chuc-ku.
Japan Textile Color Design Center. Osaka, Japan: 8, Bingomachi 3-Chome,
    Higashi-ku.

Netherlands

Nederlandse Consumenten Bond. Huygenstraat 2-'s-Gravenhage.
Nederlandse Huishoudraad. Annapaulownaplein 7-'s-Gravenhage.

Norway

Forbrukerradet. Oslo, Norway: Fr. Nanseus plass 2.
Government Research Department for Home Economics. Oslo, Norway: Stabekk.
Royal Ministry for Consumer and Family Affairs. Oslo, Norway: Akersgatan 42.

Sweden

Kooperativa Forbundet. Stockholm Sö, Sweden.
Statens Institut for Konsumenfragor. Stockholm, Sweden: Ralambsvagen 8.
Svenska Slojdforeningen. Stockholm, Sweden: Nybrogatan 7.
Svenska Standardiserings Kommission. Stockholm, Sweden: Tegnergatan 11.
Varudeklarationsnamnden. Stockholm 3, Sweden: Box 3295.

Switzerland

Suisse Institut für Hauswirtschaft. Zurich 6, Switzerland: Nordstrasse 31.

United Kingdom

British Standards Institution. London W1, England: 2, Park Street.
Consumers' Association, Ltd. London WC2, England: 14 Buckingham Street.
The Research Institute of Consumer Affairs. London WC2, England: 27 John
    Adam Street.

West Germany

Arbeitsgemeinschaft der Verbraucherverbaende, E.V. Bonn-Beuel/Rhein, Ger-
    many: Friedrichstrasse 23.
Bundesforschungsanstalt für Hauswirtschaft. Stuttgart-Hohenheim, Germany:
    Garbenstrasse 13.

INTERNATIONAL CONSUMER ORGANIZATIONS

European Organization for Quality Control. Rotterdam, Netherlands: Weena
    700.

International Cooperative Alliance. London W1, England: 11 Upper Grosvenor Street.

International Office of Consumers Unions. The Hague, Netherlands: 189 Harstenhoekweg.

International Organization for Standardization. Geneva, Switzerland: 1-3, rue de Varembe.

19

AUTOMOBILE INSURANCE, FAIR TRADE
LAWS, AND FUNERAL COSTS

Automobile Insurance

Automobile insurance is becoming increasingly important as registrations soar toward 100 million from fewer than 90 cars in 1896. This vast increase in number, and expansion in the use, of motor vehicles has been accompanied by a widespread need for insurance protection. In fact, Americans are spending more than $6 billion a year to keep their cars insured. Yet this figure is less than is needed.

Some cars are uninsured; many cars are covered only for liability and only for minimum amounts. At a rough estimate, it would cost about $200 a year to keep the average American car reasonably insured. Actually, the cost of keeping the average car reasonably well insured throughout its useful life is almost as great as the original cost of the car.

Books and pamphlets on life insurance and on health insurance are readily available, but automobile insurance has almost completely escaped critical study. There has never been a large-scale investigation of car insurance. When state insurance commissioners take action on rate increase applications, complaints pour in, and public protest is usually loud, but nobody has known what to do about the constant increase in rates.

Consumers Union Study of Rates. Fortunately, in 1962, Consumers Union, Inc., publisher of *Consumer Reports*, made the first comprehensive study in the United States of automobile insurance rates and related matters.[1]

More than eight hundred firms sell automobile insurance in the United States. Some are stock companies, which are owned by stockholders. Many are mutuals, which are owned by the policyholders. Some sell through independent agents, others directly to the insured. A detailed account of the advantages and disadvantages of "independents" and "bureau com-

[1] See *Consumer Reports*, March–July, 1962.

panies" is given in the Consumers Union study. And the experience of 6,620 members of Consumers Union in regard to claim handling, policy cancellations, and refusals to renew car insurance should be useful, because the major companies are evaluated in terms of satisfaction and dissatisfaction with the quality of company service.

Premium Rates versus Good Service. A few dollars saved on premium rates may mean little if an insurance company gives poor service on its claim adjustments, or if it cancels the policy because of a few minor claims in one year.

Car owners see advertisements for "new low rates," "overnight service," and "noncancellable automobile policies." They hear stories of claims paid in full immediately or cases in which companies refuse even to discuss a claim settlement until suit is threatened. They hear of cancellation of policy because the driver is "getting too old," or because a son has reached driving age.

Many persons suspect that "low-cost" insurance must be inferior insurance. How can the consumer compare the rates of some eight hundred companies writing automobile insurance in the United States? How can he thread his way through the many uncertainties in selecting automobile insurance? Shop around and compare rates and reputation for service. Ask your friends for their experiences.

Kinds of Insurance Coverage. There are five kinds of insurance coverage that a prudent person should weigh carefully: liability, medical payments, uninsured motorist, collision, and comprehensive. Liability and collision insurance are the most expensive.

Liability insurance. Liability insurance covers bodily injury liability and property-damage liability. Bodily injury liability coverage pays the sum for which the car owner becomes legally liable if his car injures someone. Property-damage liability pays the amount for which the car owner becomes legally liable for damage to property—another car, a telephone pole, a building. Liability insurance is the heart of an automobile insurance policy. No prudent person would drive even temporarily without liability insurance, and in some states, it is compulsory. Liability insurance also pays the cost of legal defense. The practical question is what liability limits to carry.

The insurance company pays no more than the amounts specified in a policy. Liability limits are usually described by a series of three numbers separated by diagonal lines—for example, 10/20/5. This set of numbers describes a policy that pays a maximum of $10,000 for bodily injury to one person, a maximum of $20,000 for bodily injury to more than one person, and a maximum of $5,000 for property damage in one occurrence.

Insurance companies offer liability up to 300/500/100 and even higher. The difference in the cost of liability of 10/20/5 (around $100) and liability of 50/100/5 coverage is usually small. No matter where you live, be sure to meet the requirements of the financial-responsibility laws of the states in which you drive.

Medical payments insurance. This insurance ($2,000 coverage may cost around $10) pays medical and hospital bills, and funeral expenses if there is a death in an automobile accident, regardless of fault. This is good insurance since it protects all passengers in the car. It is not a duplication of your medical and hospital insurance.

Comprehensive physical damage insurance. This insurance pays for loss if your car is stolen, damaged, or destroyed by fire, hail, hurricane, and most other causes, and also pays for losses due to vandalism. This policy does not pay for collisions, mechanical breakdown, wear and tear, or freezing.

Driving without comprehensive insurance is a gamble, but full comprehensive coverage is quite expensive. A $50 deductible provision (the car owner pays the first $50 loss) may be available at about 45 per cent of the full coverage rate. The cost of such a policy depends on where the car owner lives and on the age of the car.

Collision insurance. This insurance covers damages to a car if it is upset or hit by another car or fixed object. Collision coverage is primarily valuable for losses due to an upset that is not the fault of someone else or where the question of fault is debatable.

Full coverage on collision is expensive. Collision rates vary with the age of the car. The rate for new models is based on the original factory price of the car. Last year's models may pay off at only 87.5 per cent of the original factory price. The premium remains the same. A point is eventually reached where the premium is out of all proportion to the coverage. Consequently, a car more than four years old may have too little coverage compared to the premium paid.

Uninsured motorist insurance. This more recent form of coverage insures the driver and passengers against injury by a driver who carries no insurance or by a hit-and-run driver. It is automatically included in some policies. The premium is small because the risk is small.

Premiums Based on Classes of Drivers. Insurance companies set up classes of drivers and assign each class a rate based on its own accident and claims record. The class depends on the use made of the car and on the age of the male driver. Premiums vary also according to the place of residence, and for comprehensive and collision coverage, they vary with the value of the car.

Premiums are generally lowest if the car is driven only for pleasure, with no male driver under 25 years of age. A single male driver under the age of 25 will pay about two or three times as much as a single male driver over 25.

Preferred risks. For years many insurance companies have cut rates for drivers who passed stiff eligibility tests. The criteria among companies varies, but these are the most common: (1) driving record, (2) occupation, (3) driver under 25 years or over 65, (4) alcoholism or physical handicap, (5) condition of car, and (6) merit rating if the insured has avoided traffic trouble. Discounts in premium, if a driver qualifies, generally range from 10 to 25 per cent below the company standard rates.

Special or Package Policies. Some insurance companies offer a package of various kinds of insurance, which usually costs less than if selected separately. Strictly speaking, however, the differences in premiums on standard policies and on the special or package deals are not comparable because of the differences in coverage. Then, too, maybe a car owner wants only liability coverage. The premium for a standard liability policy would be less than the package would cost. On the other hand, if a car owner wants to combine comprehensive and collision insurance, the package savings may run to around 15 per cent.

Some companies combine the special or package deal and the merit-rating plan. In 1962, one large automobile insurance company announced that good school grades would get California students and their parents a 20 per cent discount in auto insurance. California was selected as the first state for the program because state laws there permitted immediate introduction of the new plan.

What Insurance Coverage Do You Need? If insurance is purchased through the dealer who sells the car, you will usually get only collision and comprehensive coverage. If the car is a late model, buy liability insurance before driving it off the lot. Here is the order in which some automobile experts rate the need for various kinds of coverage.

1. *Liability.* A must for all drivers. Awards of $50,000 are common, and verdicts run much higher at times. Buy 50/100/5 if you can afford it.

2. *Comprehensive physical damage.* A must on a new car. You might omit comprehensive on an old car if you can absorb the loss. Repair costs are usually higher than the value of an old car.

3. *Collision.* A good idea for a late-model car that you own outright. Repair costs run high. If you need to economize, you might omit it for an older car. If you need this insurance, buy a $50 or $100 deductible policy.

4. *Medical payments.* Some motorists can do without this protection. It may be worth the premium if the family is large or in case of car-pool driving.

5. *Uninsured motorists.* Inexpensive but the risk is very small.

Shopping for Insurance Rates. To aid you in comparing automobile insurance rates, make out a chart (similar to the accompanying Policy Specifications Chart) for each company you select for bids. Then select the coverages you want. When asking for and comparing rates, be sure that they are for the same coverage.

POLICY SPECIFICATIONS CHART

Type of coverage	Family or independent policies	Special or package policies
Liability	Limits:_____ / _____ / _____	$_____,000
Medical	$500	$_____,000
Uninsured motorist	Yes	Yes
Collision	$_____-deductible	$_____-deductible
Comprehensive	Full coverage	Full coverage
Towing	Yes	Included with collision or comprehensive
Other	None	None

SOURCE: *Consumer Reports,* June, 1962.

After receiving the bids, record them on a blank similar to the accompanying Rate Comparison Blank. The lowest rate quoted is not necessarily the best buy. Give some consideration to membership fees, service, discount for two or more cars, premium rates, cancellation and renewal record. Also check on the financial stability record of each company in *Best's Insurance Guide.* The Consumers Union recommended list of automobile insurance companies will be useful (*Consumer Reports,* June, 1962).

"Fair Trade" and the Consumer

"Fair trade" is the attempt to maintain retail prices at a fixed level. Since the first so-called fair trade law was passed in California in 1931, in the depth of the depression, some 41 states have passed similar price control legislation. Fair trade pricing is considered to be effective in 23 states. In these 23 states (New York, Illinois, and California are among them), a fair trade agreement is binding on all dealers selling a product if at least one dealer agrees to the minimum resale price. A violator may be sued and prevented from selling the product on the ground that he is guilty of "unfair" competition.

Fair trade is less effective in 18 other states because it is enforceable only among the dealers who sign an agreement. Nine states and the District of Columbia have no fair trade laws.

Support seems to be growing in Congress for a Federal fair trade law. In 1964, for example, a fair trade bill called the Quality Stabilization Act, which would give manufacturers the right to establish minimum retail prices, was proposed in both houses of Congress, but was defeated.

The Quality Stabilization Act. The proposed Federal legislation would for the first time make price fixing by manufacturers nationwide and enforceable by Federal law. It would impose restraints of trade on the nine states

RATE COMPARISON BLANK

Name of company					
Safe-driver or merit rating (yes or no)					
Liability	$	$	$	$	$
Medical	$	$	$	$	$
Uninsured motorist	$	$	$	$	$
Collision	$	$	$	$	$
Comprehensive	$	$	$	$	$
Towing	$	$	$	$	$
Total	$	$	$	$	$
Membership fees	$	$	$	$	$

SOURCE: Consumer Reports, June, 1962.

(and the District of Columbia) that have steadfastly rejected price control laws. Their only recourse would be action by their legislatures to make the Federal measure inoperable in their states.

If the Federal Quality Stabilization Act were passed, manufacturers could refuse to sell their goods to retailers who sold to customers at less than the fixed prices. The effect would be to permit some manufacturers to do what other manufacturers under the antitrust laws have been heavily penalized for doing. The aim of the act is to choke off the competition with small businesses of price-cutting discount stores and supermarkets. Though the bill is called the Quality Stabilization Act, it does nothing to stabilize quality. It would only stabilize prices.

Events Leading to Federal Legislation. In 14 states, state supreme court decisions have ruled the nonsigner clause unconstitutional under state constitutions. In four other states, lower courts have ruled the nonsigner clause unconstitutional. In nine more states, the courts have not tested the law.

In 1937, fair trade agreements under state fair trade laws were exempt from prosecution under the Sherman Antitrust Act. This exemption was secured by passage of the Miller-Tydings Act, which was a rider to a necessary District of Columbia revenue bill.

In 1951, the United States Supreme Court dealt fair trade a blow when it ruled that price maintenance agreements were not binding on retailers who did not sign them. Congress then passed the McGuire Act in 1952, allowing states to pass laws binding signers and nonsigners alike if one retailer in the state signed a fair trade agreement.

In 1958, another United States Supreme Court decision had a telling impact on fair trade. The Court ruled that a retailer doing business in a fair trade state could set up an office in a non–fair trade jurisidiction, and from that office offer for sale, by mail, merchandise in the fair trade state below the price set for it there. Largely as a result of this decision, several large appliance manufacturing companies discontinued fair trade prices on houseware items.

With state fair trade laws being torn apart by state courts and by the United States Supreme Court, the fair trade lobby turned to the United States Congress for enactment of a national fair trade law. They were given sympathetic hearings by Senator Humphrey's Senate Subcommittee on Small Business. The House Rules Committee also appeared sympathetic to the act.

Arguments for the Quality Stabilization Act. Pressure for the act has been intense. Lined up behind it are about seventy trade associations, led by the American Pharmaceutical Association and many brand-name manufacturers. Among those testifying for the act were representatives from the National Wholesale Druggists' Association, the National Association of Retail Clothiers, the American Fair Trade Council, Inc., the General Electric Company, the Sunbeam Corporation, the Esso Standard Oil Company, the Atlantic Refining Company, the National Retail Hardware Association, the National Association of Retail Druggists, and others.

Most of the arguments for the Quality Stabilization Act are based on two assumptions. The first assumption is that fair trade protects the small retailer from the big national chains, discount houses, mail-order companies, and large retailers. The chains and large retailers by loss-leader price cutting drive out the small competitor and tend to become monopolistic. After becoming monopolistic, they raise the price of products, with no competition from small retailers, who have been driven out of business.

The second major assumption is that fair trade legislation is necessary to protect the property right of a manufacturer in his brand name and good will. A manufacturer has built up good will for his product, it is argued, by establishing a good trade name through advertising. The retailer buys the product for which the trade name is a symbol. The manufacturer retains the symbol of the product as his property. When a retailer sells the product below the minimum established price, the product is damaged in the eyes of the consumer. This damage, in turn, injures the property right of the manufacturer in his brand name and good will.

It is also argued that high profit margins improve the quality of the product, and higher prices and profit margins protect jobs.

Arguments against the Quality Stabilization Act. In reply to the danger that small business may be driven out by big business through lower prices on national trade-marked goods, several observations can be made. There is presently adequate legislation to protect the small retailer and the consumer from monopoly practices. Safeway Stores, for example, a national chain of food supermarkets, was once charged with price discrimination by the Antitrust Division of the Department of Justice and enjoined from further actions of this type.

Second, loss-leader selling is merely price cutting. Some retailers, too often, have called any kind of price reduction "loss-leader selling." As a matter of fact, there is little evidence to indicate that price reduction, or so-called loss-leader selling, has been responsible for small-business failures. A Department of Justice study has shown that these failures are more prevalent among small businesses in states with fair trade laws than in those where the free market prevails.

The claim that a fair trade law is essential to the property right and good name of a manufacturer was challenged by Dr. Fritz Machlup, in testimony before Senator Humprey's Subcommittee on Small Business, in 1958. He found it difficult to understand why a customer should lose confidence in the quality of a product when a retailer sells it below the price charged by another retailer. He quoted a study of the Canadian

Restrictive Trade Practices Commission, which found no evidence to support the contention that a consumer's favorable attitude toward a product had been lessened by a lower retail price.

Dr. Machlup argued that a serious loss of value of trade-mark property as a result of price competition is of no public concern and would not need remedial measures in the public interest. The purpose of the trade-mark law is to protect the consumer against deception.

Proponents have argued that high profit margins resulting from fair trade legislation would improve quality. Actually, there is good reason to believe that without the spur of competition, quality tends to deteriorate. If the Quality Stabilization Act becomes law, retailers will depend on high prices for profits rather than on competition and volume turnover.

It is also difficult to see how higher prices will protect jobs, as argued by the proponents of this act. The evidence points in the other direction. Higher prices mean smaller sales, and these in turn mean less production and fewer jobs. Higher prices are also likely to wipe out wage increases. The worker suffers on both counts.

Opponents of fair trade argue that big business has everything to gain from fair trade. Producers can set prices to assure a maximum profit on branded merchandise. They can then produce goods for the big outlets under private-store brand names. The big outlets will be able to compete better than ever against small retailers, in whose name fair trade is invoked. Big outlets can carry both fair trade nationally branded goods and their private brands. Since there will be no competition from the national brand names, private brand products will also rise in price.

Government Agencies Opposed to a Federal Act. There is little doubt that fair trade laws increase the price of the goods that are fair traded. The U.S. Department of Justice, through an extensive study in states having fair trade laws, found that consumers paid from 19 to 27 per cent more for 132 items in those states.[2] Fair trade laws reduce the standard of living of the consumer by raising the price of most fair trade items.

Finally, fair trade items with higher price tags make it more difficult to compete with foreign goods in the domestic market. There is no better way to step up imports at the expense of jobs than through so-called fair trade. The higher prices of American fair trade goods allow goods from abroad to compete more successfully in the American market.

The Bureau of the Budget reported the following agencies as opposed to the Quality Stabilization Act: Departments of Commerce; Justice; Labor; Agriculture; State; Defense; Health, Education, and Welfare; and Treasury; Federal Trade Commission; Small Business Administration; General Services Administration; Council of Economic Advisers; Board

[2] *U.S. Senate, Hearings before a Subcommittee of the Select Committee on Small Business.* Washington, D.C.: Government Printing Office, 1958, pp. 277–279.

of Governors of the Federal Reserve System; Veterans Administration; and the Consumer Advisory Council.

The Consumer Is the Victim. Fair trade laws under any name mean higher prices for consumers. The Department of Justice estimated that a Federal fair trade law could increase prices about 20 per cent on sales covered.[3] The Consumer Advisory Council reported on June 4, 1963, that the Quality Stabilization Act would limit the freedom of retailers to sell goods at their own prices, would work against "free enterprise and the best interests of consumers," and would hold back progress by denying consumers the benefits of increased efficiency and improved production.

The terms "fair trade" and "quality stabilization" have the sound of "fair plan" and "getting your money's worth," but they are deceitful labels. Since, under fair trade, retailers cannot sell any product below the minimum price set by the manufacturer, fair trade amounts to legalized price fixing. In effect, the manufacturer and the dealer are conspiring to deprive the consumer of the opportunity of shopping around for the best quality at the best price.

High Funeral Costs

The high funeral costs in the United States account for an expenditure of more than $2 billion a year—a figure determined by adding the Department of Commerce estimate of personal spending as a result of death in 1962 to what florists say was spent on funeral flowers. Another expensive item, not included in the $2 billion, is the cost of shipping bodies by train or plane. One in ten of all the dead are shipped elsewhere for burial. The cost of transporting a body by rail is twice the cost of a first-class ticket, and air charges are higher than rail charges.

The Department of Commerce figures for the cost of a "regular adult funeral" average out at $1,160. A more realistic figure would be about $1,500 for the disposition of the mortal remains of an adult American. A little less than thirty years ago, the figure was only $350. The National Funeral Directors Association (NFDA) likes to quote $755 for the funeral itself, but admits that this does not include extras like clothing, vault, obituaries, flowers, transportation, and clergy. The *Exchange,* a florist trade journal, puts the total average floral bill at $275. James Worley, executive vice president of the American Cemetery Association, estimates conservatively that cemetery expenses are around $300. Add all these items and the figure of $1,500 may be a bit too low.

The Consumer versus the Funeral Director. The average consumer averages only one funeral in about fifteen years. In the throes of grief and shock, he is a poor match for the funeral director. Uppermost in his mind are questions like these: Where do I begin? What should be done? What will peo-

[3] *The Wall Street Journal,* July 3, 1963, p. 1.

ple expect me to do? He has no accurate knowledge of costs and standards, and no knowledge of the laws regarding disposal of the dead. He also must make decisions on the spot, influenced in most cases by a little ready insurance money. There can be no thought of shopping around.

The funeral director takes control and suggests a burial according to the presumed financial status of the deceased or family. From the "arrangement conference" to the "last resting place," the funeral director is likely to take the lead. In the end, the average funeral may cost up to $1,500. Need a dignified funeral cost that much?

A peculiar factor in the funeral industry is that generally the same services are rendered for funerals of varying price ranges, with no ceiling other than what the traffic will bear. Usually the cost of the funeral is a considerable markup on the wholesale price of the coffin.

Jessica Mitford, in her book *The American Way of Death*, advances the thesis that the American funeral is an extravagant affair "methodically designed to extract maximum profit for the trade." The Mitford book, only one in a series of books and articles in the same vein, has caused the industry to state its case.

The Funeral Industry and Its Problems. *The National Funeral Service Journal*, a trade journal, stated that a funeral director "must condition the public mind to associate established funeral customs with all that is desirable in the American way of life." The basis for doing this, the writer said, lies in "cultivating certain subconscious opinions regarding the funeral service." And he added that "chief of these is the acceptance of the funeral as a valid status symbol—which in fact it is." In short, it is argued, with some justification, give the public what it wants.

There seems to be little doubt that the funeral industry as a whole has some special difficulties. The death rate, for example, is going down, and the funeral market is limited by the death rate. Meanwhile the number of funeral homes grows. Some 25,000 funeral homes share 1,750,000 deaths annually, for an average of 70 funerals each. In fact, 60 per cent of the funeral homes average one funeral a week while the famous Forest Lawn Memorial-Park in Los Angeles has about 6,000 funerals a year.

There is no doubt, too, that the funeral industry faces increasing costs. Chapels are luxuries with wall-to-wall carpeting, expensive organs, "slumber rooms," and the "selection room" where coffins and burial garments are displayed. A hearse costs about $15,000. Labor costs have increased. Furthermore, calls have to be answered around the clock. According to NFDA, the average funeral home represents an investment of $116,459 for land, buildings, equipment, cars, inventory, and service charges outstanding. The total annual pretax income for the owner of an average funeral home comes to $20,671, says the NFDA.

Public Protests against High Costs. With all the built-in extravagance attached to the rites of death, is it possible for a prudent person to have a dignified and inexpensive funeral? Many people think it is possible. Doctors, lawyers, clergymen of all faiths, union officials, cooperative organizations, and consumer groups are protesting against funeral practices that are needlessly costly and often relegate spiritual values to a place of minor importance.

In 1962, *Medical Economics*, a national physicians' journal, carried an article entitled "Fighting Fancy Funerals." In May, 1963, the *Stanford Law Journal* featured an article, "Funeral Prearrangement: Mitigating the Undertaker's Bargaining Advantage." The National Council of the Churches of Christ in the U.S.A. has a report on burial costs. Booklets have been issued by the Union of Orthodox Jewish Congregations of America, the Protestant Episcopal National Council, The United Presbyterian Church in the U.S.A., the Unitarian and Congregational churches, and the Quakers—all of them giving aid and direction in dignified and inexpensive funerals.

Reducing Funeral Costs. Here are suggestions for the average consumer confronted with arranging for a funeral.

1. Discuss the funeral arrangements with your minister, rabbi, or priest. It is generally wise for the clergyman to accompany a member of the family to the funeral parlor to help resist any pressure toward overspending.

2. Arrange for the service to be held at your church.

3. Select an inexpensive casket and consider limiting or omitting flower displays.

4. Omit embalming and hold the service as soon as possible.

5. Arrange for cremation or for delivery of the body if it has been willed to a medical or scientific society. These methods of disposition appeal to many public-minded and sophisticated persons today.

6. Permit the funeral to center around the spirit rather than the body by having the casket closed during the service. Many families prefer to have the casket removed from the actual service.

7. Keep the graveside service, if any, private—only for the family and close friends.

8. Request the funeral director, in advance, to provide a detailed, itemized estimate of the funeral costs.

9. Join a memorial association if possible.

Most families who have given thought to the subject agree with the Jewish decree that the funeral should be conducted with "dignity, sanctity, and modesty."

Memorial Associations. Membership in a memorial or funeral society can be a solution if there is such a society in your community. In 1950, there were about eight societies, and in 1963 there were more than ninety in the

United States and Canada, with a membership approaching fifty thousand families.

All memorial societies are nonprofit, and membership fees are nominal. A few societies are merely educational, acting as sources of information; others contract with funeral homes to provide a dignified, simple, and modest burial.

The major objective of all memorial societies is to smooth the path for the family and guarantee that the family will not have to deal with the funeral director personally. Some arrange for adequate services for as little as $150. Others advocate a private funeral or cremation plus a simple memorial service later.

The Chico Christian Burial Society (Chico, California) with a membership of three thousand, has its own cemetery and complete facilities for preparation, care, and disposal of the body. The cost of a funeral is $200, which covers casket, grave, cement grave liner, digging and filling the grave, and complete service.

Labor unions have been increasingly active in burial benefit programs. One union plan, for example, made arrangements in advance with reputable funeral homes to provide a simple but dignified funeral service at a cost of $175. This cost includes removal and preparation of the remains, a simple casket, and the use of the chapel, hearse, and one limousine. Some unions also own their own burial grounds, in which the average cost of the graves is $30. The cemetery service of its crew costs about $75. The total cost for all funeral and burial facilities and services is about $280.[4]

SUGGESTED READINGS

Advertising Age. "Price Bill That Hurts Retailers as Well as Consumers," Nov. 18, 1963, p. 113.

The Atlantic Monthly. "Undertaker's Racket," June, 1963, p. 56.

Backman, Allen E. "Consumers Look at Burial Practices," Greeley, Colo.: Colorado State College, Council on Consumer Information, 1956.

Bowman, LeRoy. *The American Funeral.* Washington, D.C.: Public Affairs Press, 1959.

Casualty Insurance Handbook. New York: Insurance Information Institute, 1963.

Changing Times. "What's New in Auto Insurance," July, 1960, pp. 41–44; "Furor on Funerals," November, 1963, p. 7.

Consumer Reports. "Consumers Union Auto Insurance Project," March–June, 1962; "Ways of Death" and "The Funeral Industry," January, 1964, pp. 40–43.

[4] See Jessica Mitford, *The American Way of Death,* pp. 297ff. for a directory of memorial societies and related organizations.

Cooperative League of the U.S.A. *Memorial Associations, What They Are—How They Are Organized*, Chicago.

Cummings, Parke. *American Death*. New York: Little, Brown and Company, 1959.

Daley, Arthur. *The Funeral*. New York: E. P. Dutton & Co., Inc., 1961.

Driver, Helen Irene. *Life and Death*. Philadelphia: W. B. Saunders Company, 1960.

Good Housekeeping. "Memorial Societies," August, 1962, p. 133; Mitford, Jessica. "The American Way of Death" (condensation of the book), February, 1964.

Habenstein, Robert W. *Funeral Customs*. Milwaukee: Bulfin Printers, 1960.

Haller, William. *Consumers Look at Fair Trade*. Greeley, Colo.: Colorado State College, Council on Consumer Information, 1955.

Harmer, Ruth Mulvey. *The High Cost of Dying*. New York: Crowell-Collier Publishing Co., 1963.

Lee, Stewart M. *Consumers Look at Discount Houses*. Greeley, Colo.: Colorado State College, Council on Consumer Information, 1958.

Levy, Michael H. *Your Insurance and How to Profit by It*. New York: Harcourt, Brace & World, Inc., 1955, chap. 11.

Life. "Outrage over Death," Sept. 20, 1963, p. 98.

Mitford, Jessica. *The American Way of Death*. New York: Simon and Schuster, Inc., 1963.

Saturday Evening Post. "Can You Afford to Die?" June 17, 1961, p. 24.

U.S. Senate, *Hearings before a Subcommittee of the Select Committee on Small Business*. Washington, D.C.: Government Printing Office, 1958.

U.S. Senate, *Hearings before a Subcommittee on Antitrust and Monopoly*. Part 1. "Funeral Directors." Washington, D.C.: Government Printing Office, 1964.

The Wall Street Journal. "Fair Trade Opponents Fear Bill in Congress," July 3, 1963; "Fair Trade Revival," Mar. 21, 1963, p. 1.

Wrightman, Hazel H. *The Funeral Industry*. Boston: Houghton Mifflin Company, 1962.

INDEX